TRIADS AND TRINITY

One of the triads of Mycerinus. From the left: the Goddess Hathor, King Mycerinus, and the Nome-goddess of Diospolis Parva. A group in schist, Cairo Museum.

TRIADS AND TRINITY

J. Gwyn Griffiths

CARDIFF
UNIVERSITY OF WALES PRESS
1996

© J. Gwyn Griffiths, 1996

All rights reserved. No part of this book may be reproduced, stored in a retrieval system, or transmitted, in any form or by any means, electronic, mechanical, photocopying, recording or otherwise, without clearance from the University of Wales Press, 6 Gwennyth Street, Cardiff CF2 4YD.

British Library Cataloguing in Publication Data

A catalogue record for this book is available from the British Library.

ISBN 0-7083-1281-0

Typeset by Action Typesetting Limited, Gloucester
Printed in England by Bookcraft, Midsomer Norton, Avon

CONTENTS

Preface	ix
Abbreviations	xiii
Introduction	1

Part I. EGYPT

1 Egypt's Early Tradition	11
1 A Possible Triad in Prehistoric Egypt	11
2 Egyptian Views of Three	16
3 Human and Divine Groupings of Two and Three	19
4 The Triads of Mycerinus	21
5 Old-Kingdom Triadic Groups in Statuary	26
6 Early Religious Texts	29
2 The Developed Egyptian System	44
1 The Book of the Dead	44
2 The Baw as Divine Triads	45
3 Osirian Triads	46
4 Conceptual Triads	50
3 Amarna Triadic Doctrine	56
1 A Triad of God, King, and Queen	57
2 A Shared Priestly and Prophetic Role	59
3 The Triad of the Early Doctrinal Name	61
4 Relation to the Basic Aims	70
4 Triadic Topography	80
1 The Dyad and Triad at Elephantine	81
2 Triads of One Sex	83
3 The Principal Theban Triad	86
4 The Theban State Triadic Doctrine	89
Appendix: A Conspectus	91

Part II: MESOPOTAMIA AND ADJACENT AREAS

5 Mesopotamia Types and Regions	117
1 Cosmic Groups	117
2 An Astral Triad	118

3	City Groupings	119
4	Hittites, Hurrians, Ugarites	121
5	Heliopolis-Baalbek	122
6	Palmyra	126

Part III: THE INDO-EUROPEAN TRADITION

6 Early Indian Religion — 129
1. A Pre-Aryan Culture — 129
2. Divine Groupings and Functional Divisions in the *Rig-Veda* — 130
3. Impersonal Triadic Groupings — 134
4. The Three-headed Gods — 137
5. Groups of Three Deities — 138
6. The Role of the Three Social Classes — 141

7 Iran — 151
1. A Variety of Groupings — 151
2. Three Divine Judges — 151
3. Zervanism and the Tetrad — 152
4. Mithraism — 152

8 Greece — 156
1. Accepted Triads — 156
2. Divine Children in Triads — 157
3. Triple Features and the Triune Concept — 158
4. The Philosophical Tradition — 161
5. Three Gods in Unity — 162
6. The Twelve Gods — 164

9 Rome and Etruria — 166
1. The Capitoline Triad — 166
2. The Etruscan Triads — 169

10 The Celtic and Germanic Peoples — 174
1. The Celtic Three Brothers — 174
2. The Female Triad: Matres, Matronae, Matrae — 177
3. Male Triads — 178
4. The Tricephaloi — 180
5. Aphoristic Triads — 182
6. Triads of Northern Europe — 183

Part IV: THE MATRIX OF THE CHRISTIAN DOCTRINE

11 Possible Hebraic Antecedents — 193
1. Divine Pluralism in the Old Testament — 193
2. Abraham and the Three Visitors — 194
3. The Extension of Divine Personality and the Creative Word — 196

4	Wisdom	198
5	The Role of Rûach as Spirit	200
6	Philo on Pneuma	202
7	The Function of Angels	203

12 The Evolved Christian Creed   207
1	The New Testament	207
2	The Process of Definition	208
3	Individual Contributors	209
	(i) Tertullian	209
	(ii) Clement of Alexandria	211
	(iii) Origen	213
	(iv) Athanasius	215
	(v) Philo's Trinity	217
	(vi) Plotinus	218

13 The Likely Sources   223
1	Abstractions and Divine Beings	223
2	The Ubiquitous Divine Triads	226
3	Gnosticism and the Female Element	231
4	The Missionary Motive	236
5	Alexandrian Christians and Egyptian Religion	248
6	The Triune Emphasis in the Graeco-Egyptian Milieu	251
7	A Confluence of Two Traditions	262
8	Relationships in the Interior Structure	265

14 Concluding Remarks   280
1	The Heritage of Israel and Judaism	281
2	Phases of Greek Philosophy	282
3	Egyptian and Graeco-Egyptian Theological Systems	284
4	Unity and Equality	287
5	A Christian Innovation	290

Appendix: The Pallid Pantheon of Ancient China	314
Sectional Bibliography	318
Notes to the Illustrations	350
Index	355

KATINKAE

UXORI

CARISSIMAE

DOCTISSIMAE

Preface

The subject of this book was offered by me as a research project by the Warden and Fellows of All Souls College, Oxford, when I took up a Visiting Fellowship there in 1976-7. I need hardly say that my time there proved stimulating and helpful. My wife and I received many kindnesses and I renewed these contacts in later visits. I am especially indebted to Mr Peter M. Fraser for sponsorship and constant advice; his own scholarly standards always proved a spur. I am indebted also to the late Professor B. K. Matilal, Professor Rodney Needham, Mr John G. Simmonds and Professor Bryan Wilson for their generous encouragement. Then and during the intervening years my studies have embraced other areas too. In 1980 Brill of Leiden published my *Origins of Osiris and his Cult*, an enlarged and revised version of an earlier work. In January of 1991, as the fruit of my now wider interests, Brill produced my study of divine judgement in the ancient religions (*The Divine Verdict*. Supplements to *Numen*, 52: Studies in the History of Religion).

My interest in the present theme derives initially from the work and influence of Siegfried Morenz, who held a Chair of Egyptology in Basle and Leipzig. I had the pleasure of his company in a symposium arranged at Strasbourg by Professor Philippe Derchain in 1969, and after that we often corresponded. Of course it is in his books and articles that Morenz published his investigations of the theme. At a later stage Professor Wolfhart Westendorf of Göttingen showed a lively interest in the same subject, and my contact with him, ever since we first met in Cairo, has been equally helpful. Two other German scholars, Professors Hellmut and Emma Brunner, of Tübingen, also merit my warmest gratitude. My wife and I spent a happy semester with them at Tübingen University's Egyptological Institute, and their expertise in the fields of Egyptian religion, literature and art has been a constantly deployed boon.

At the University of Wales College of Swansea I have received every encouragement, especially from the Department of Classics and Ancient History, which now flourishes in spite of a generally adverse climate; much of the praise for this is due to the enlightened leadership of Professor Christopher Collard. Egyptology has a due place in the Ancient History course under the guidance of Professor Alan B. Lloyd, author of the acclaimed three-volume Commentary on the Second Book of Herodotus. He is now the Head of our Department. Our Wellcome Museum of Egyptian and Graeco-Roman Antiquities has been under the tutelage of my wife, Dr Kate Bosse-Griffiths. From these colleagues I have received every kind of aid, both practical and intellectual. The same is true of my wife's successor in the Museum, Dr David Gill.

In this kind of work one regards librarians almost as mystagogues. My debt concerns in particular the library of the University of Wales College at Swansea and its sister library in Cardiff; the library of the Ashmolean Museum in Oxford and of the adjacent Griffith Institute as well as of the Oriental Institute; in Oxford again, the Bodleian Library, the Peet Memorial Library in The Queen's College, the Codrington Library of All Souls College, the Indian Institute, the Theology Faculty Library, Rhodes House, Pusey House, and the Radcliffe Science Library; in London the British Library and that of the Department of Egyptian Antiquities in the British Museum; also the Warburg Institute. In Cairo my wife and I have been favoured by the Library of the Cairo Museum and that of the German Archaeological Institute in Zamalek. Two seminar libraries in Bonn were helpful during one semester: those of the Classics and Egyptology departments. A semester in Tübingen brought similar aid from as many as four academic institutes. Librarians have always been kind to me, and for my part I have zealously tried to keep their rules.

In this work I have given a good deal of attention to aspects of Judaism and Christianity. My early studies in the University of Wales included eager attendance at a class conducted by Theodore H. Robinson; it was devoted to the Gospel of Mark and included much discussion of the Semitic background – a field later to be ably examined and admirably expounded, especially with reference to Paul and Matthew, by my fellow-student W. D. Davies, now Professor Emeritus at Duke University, Durham, North Carolina. My continued contact with him has proved most helpful. So has my friendship with Dr Pennar Davies, formerly Professor of Church History and Principal at the Memorial College, Swansea. My brother, the late Revd D. R. Griffiths, who lectured on New Testament studies at the Cardiff University College, was naturally often consulted. I have benefited, too, from converse over many years with Professor B. R. Rees, who formerly held the Chair of Greek in the same college; his two recent authoritative volumes on Pelagius are, of course, relevant to the theme of the present work.

I owe a special debt to the late Revd Professor Cecil J. Mullo Weir, of Edinburgh, who was my first tutor in Hebrew when he was a Lecturer in the School of Oriental Studies at the University of Liverpool. There, too, I was taught Egyptian by the late Professor A. M. Blackman, who was intensely interested in religious themes. My contact with his successors, Professors H. W. Fairman, A. F. Shore and Kenneth Kitchen also proved stimulating. It was Blackman and Fairman who introduced me to the monuments of Egypt and Nubia when I acted with them as archaeological assistant to the Egypt Exploration Society. Later visits to Egypt included an academic session in the University of Cairo as Guest Professor in Egyptology and Classics; in these departments I was much indebted respectively to Professors A. M. Bakir and M. M. Salamouni. In Cairo my wife and I also received constant and kind aid from Professors Hanns Stock, Dieter Arnold and W. Müller-Wiener at the German Archaeological Institute; and in the Library of the Cairo Museum Dr Dia Abou-Ghazi patiently dealt with our enquiries.

I have mentioned the primary stimulus which I received from Siegfried Morenz. Yet my approach differs from his in several respects. Unlike him I have attempted a detailed analysis of the Patristic sources which reveal the evolution of the Christian doctrine with the possible impact of other traditions. These include the Hebraic and Greek ideologies. The former of these had a vital impact on the doctrine of the Holy Spirit, although not on structural triadism, which was much indebted to Neoplatonism. It was Egypt, however, that produced the earliest emphasis on triunity or trinity, and eventually this idea was wedded to a similar trend in Greek thought. The resulting amalgam, in my view, was the decisive influence on Christian Trinitarianism.

While my survey of comparable religious ideas includes a worldwide spectrum, following the plan adopted in my recent book *The Divine Verdict* (Leiden, 1991), the basic importance of Egypt in the Christian context has demanded, it seems to me, special attention to the evolution of both triads and trinities in that area. The theme has often been handled, but mine is the first exposition to attempt detailed documentation. Naturally I have not neglected previous discussions, and I am indebted in particular to the work of Jan Assmann, Hellmut and Emma Brunner, Peter M. Fraser, M. Heerma van Voss, Erik Hornung, L. Kákosy, Hermann Kees, Theodor Kraus, Jean Leclant, Siegfried Morenz, Herman te Velde, W. Westendorf, and Jan Zandee. Throughout, at the same time, I have worked from the original sources in both literature and iconography, and have offered several new interpretations, as with the Theban state triad and the Graeco-Egyptian amalgam. If the length of my part I (on Egypt) might suggest an imbalance, its content relates to one of the main issues raised; indeed, it is essentially integrated into the substantive argument.

I have also worked from the original sources in Coptic, Latin, Greek, Hebrew and Welsh. On the early Celtic material I have benefited from the work of Professor D. Ellis Evans, of Jesus College, Oxford, a former pupil of mine in Classics. For the Indian material I received valuable guidance from the late Professor B. K. Matilal, and for the Avestan literature from Dr M. E. Tucker. Professor David Hawkes has again aided me on the Chinese traditions. In these and other areas I have tried to use authoritative translations. Errors or infelicities that remain should, of course, be assigned to me.

Iconography is an important part of the material adduced, and it would have been possible to deploy numerous illustrations. Instead I have been content to select a comparatively small number, aiming at representative types and at examples which are discussed in detail (as with the Egyptian prehistoric triad).

As for doctrinal issues, the Christian Trinity is still the subject of debate, though no longer, happily, with the virulent acerbity which sometimes marred the earlier controversies. Their sinister echoes resonated in the burning of Servetus in 1553, his denial of the Trinity having been condemned by Roman Catholics and Calvinists alike. The present study is not intended to demean the still widely accepted doctrine, and even less the recent innovative interpretations concerning the inner converse and parity of the Persons. It aims rather at a historical account of comparative theology in this area, pointing to clear changes in the Christian concepts and to some extraneous influences which cannot well be denied. A marked feature of the early Christian ideology was its subordinationist approach, which was later abandoned; it was prominent, however, in the contemporary Egyptian and Greek theologies.

'To cover the whole spectrum of the ancient religions may seem a bold venture.' After this statement in the Preface of my book *The Divine Verdict* (1991), I attempted a vindication of the principles behind the venture. The same arguments apply to the present work, even if the theme is now still more restricted. Indeed its detailed exposition often demands rigorous analysis. But religious doctrines do not suddenly appear in a vacuum, and a study of their historical context is bound to be worthwhile.

In conclusion I am much indebted to the University of Wales Press Board for undertaking the exacting and expensive task of publication. In particular I am grateful to the Director, Mr Ned Thomas and to Ms Liz Powell of the editorial staff; also to the press reader and to the copy editor, Mr Henry Maas. Ms Susanne Atkin has kindly compiled the Index. Care, courtesy and patience have marked all their dealings.

JOHN GWYN GRIFFITHS

Department of Classics and Ancient History,
University of Wales, Swansea

Abbreviations

See also *Annual Egyptological Bibliography* (Leiden); *Lexikon der Ägyptologie* (Wiesbaden); *Peake's Commentary on the Bible* (ed. M. Black and H. H. Rowley, 1962); *The Oxford Classical Dictionary* (2nd edn., 1970); and *The Cambridge History of Judaism* (1984ff.).

Abh.	Abhandlungen
ADAIK	Abhandlungen des Deutschen Archäologischen Instituts Kairo
Arch. Camb.	*Archaeologia Cambrensis.*
BD	Book of the Dead: Edouard H. Naville (ed.), *Das Aegyptische Todtenbuch der XVIII bis XX.* Berlin, 1886; repr. Graz, 1971.
Bertholet, *Wb. Rel.*	A. Bertholet and H. F. von Campenhausen, *Wörterbuch der Religionen*, 3rd edn., rev. Kurt Goldammer. Stuttgart, 1976
BIFAO	*Bulletin de l'Institut Français d'Archéologie Orientale*
H. Brunner, 'Egyptian Texts'	*Near Eastern Religious Texts relating to the Old Testament*, ed. W. Beyerlin (tr. J. Bowden). London, 1978, 1–67
CAH	*Cambridge Ancient History*
CT	*The Coffin Texts*, ed. A. de Buck, 6 vols. Chicago, 1935–56
CHJ	*Cambridge History of Judaism*
Fs.	Festschrift
Gardiner, *Egn. Gr.*	Sir Alan H. Gardiner, *Egyptian Grammar.* 3rd edn. Oxford, 1957
Hastings, *ERE.*	*Encyclopaedia of Religion and Ethics.* Edinburgh, 1908ff.
Helck, *Beziehungen*	*Die Beziehungen Ägyptens zu Vorderasien im 3. und 2. Jahrtausend v. Chr.* 2nd edn. Wiesbaden, 1971
Junker and Winter, *Geburtshaus*	H. Junker and E. Winter, *Das Geburtshaus des Tempels der Isis in Philä.* Vienna, 1965

LÄ	*Lexikon der Ägyptologie*, ed. Wolfgang Helck, Eberhard Otto and Wolfhart Westendorf, 6 vols. Wiesbaden, 1975–86
Leclant and Clerc, *IBIS*	Jean Leclant and Gisèle Clerc, *Inventaire Bibliographique des Isiaca*, 4 vols. 1972–91
Leclant, *Mons. thébains*	*Recherches sur les monuments thébains de la XXVe Dynastie*. Cairo, 1965
LSJ	Liddell and Scott, *Greek–English Lexicon*, 9th edn, rev. H. Stuart Jones. Oxford, 1925–40
MÄS	Münchner Ägyptologische Studien
MDAIK	*Mitteilungen des Deutschen Archäologischen Instituts, Kairo*
MIO	*Mitteilungen des Instituts für Orientforschung* (Berlin)
OBO	*Orbis Biblicus et Orientalis*
OCD²	*Oxford Classical Dictionary*, 2nd edn., ed. N. G. L. Hammond and H. H. Scullard, 1970
ODCC	*Oxford Dictionary of the Christian Church*, ed. F. L. Cross and E. A. Livingstone, 2nd edn. 1974
Posener, *Dict.*	Georges Posener (ed.), *A Dictionary of Egyptian Civilization* (tr.)
Pyr.	*Pyramid Texts*: Kurt Sethe, *Die altägyptischen Pyramidentexte*, 4 vols. 1908–22
RÄRG	Hans Bonnet, *Reallexikon der ägyptischen Religionsgeschichte*, 1952
Rel.	Religion
RGG	*Die Religion in Geschichte und Gegenwart*, Tübingen, 1909ff.
RVV	*Religionsgeschichtliche Versuche und Vorarbeiten*
Sandman	M. Sandman, *Texts from the Time of Akhenaten*, Brussels, 1938
Sauneron, *Esna*	Serge Sauneron, *Le Temple d'Esna*, Vols. I–V, Cairo, 1959–62
TDNT	*Theological Dictionary of the New Testament*, ed. G. Kittel, tr. and ed. G. W. Bromiley
Urk.	*Urkunden des aegyptischen Altertums*, 8 vols. Leipzig, 1904–16

Wb.	*Wörterbuch* (with various works)
Wb.	*Wörterbuch der ägyptischen Sprache*, ed. A. Erman and H. Grapow, 7 vols. Berlin, 1926–63; repr. 1982
ZÄS	*Zeitschrift für ägyptische Sprache und Altertumskunde*
ZDMG	*Zeitschrift der deutschen morgenländischen Gesellschaft*

Introduction

'Triad' is a word of Greek origin, and the Greeks used τριάς in the first place of the number three. In the *Phaedo*, 104 A ff. Plato discusses its role as an odd or uneven number. Aristotle[1] remarks that before three can exist there will be a third unit in two. Elsewhere[2] he states that three signifies 'all', and that 'in three ways' is the same as 'in all ways'; and he proceeds to connect the idea with the Pythagoreans. Theophrastus, *De ventis*, 49, uses the form of a group of three days, while the metrist Hephaistion, writing probably in the second century AD, uses it of a system of three strophes (ed. M. Consbruch, 1906, p.61, 16f.). It is noteworthy that it was not, apparently, applied by the Greeks to a group of three deities. In Christian usage, however, the word is applied in Greek to the Holy Trinity, ἡ ἁγία Τριάς,[3] although the term is noticeably absent from the New Testament. At the same time early Christian authors use it of various entities and abstractions. Clement of Alexandria in his 'Miscellanies' speaks of a triad consisting of 'flesh, soul, and spirit'[4] and of 'the holy Triad, faith, hope, and love'.[5] Groupings of three show a similar variety of application in many areas and cultures, but in this study we are concerned with triads of divine persons. There may, of course, sometimes be a connection between the divine triad and a triad of other entities, in which case it will be our obvious duty to explore the connection. Groupings of three abstractions tend to come later than divine triads, but they are not necessarily engendered by them. Three deities are sometimes grouped in prehistoric representations. In this study such evidence is considered at the beginning of the discussion relevant to each area.

The term 'trinity' is derived from the Latin *trinitas*, which was first used by early Christian writers. Tertullian[6] uses the term of abstractions and also of the divine Trinity.[7] In one place he uses it of man's triple nature according to the Valentinian concept (*trinitas hominis apud Valentinum*).[8] In medieval Latin an adjective *trinitarius* (or *trinitarus*) was evolved to mean 'ternary' or 'threefold', and the phrase *trinitarus et unus*, which occurs first in the eleventh century, had the theological sense of 'triune'.[9] This last word, meaning 'three in one', appeared first in English in the seventeenth century, being used of the Godhead in the

Trinity.[10] The *Oxford English Dictionary*, s.v., quotes an instance of its application to a non-Christian religion: Budge, *A Guide to the 3rd and 4th Egyptian Rooms of the British Museum* (1904), 82, no.129, speaks of a figure of a woman 'adoring the triune form of the sun-god', though he does not specify the three forms. Latin usage thus follows that of the Greek τριάς. Although *trinitas* does not primarily mean anything beyond 'a group of three', the use of the term, as well as of its modern derivatives, has been inevitably coloured by the doctrine of the Trinity, which the *Oxford Dictionary of the Christian Church*[11] defines as 'the central dogma of Christian theology, viz. that the One God exists in Three Persons and One Substance'. In the present study we shall use the term 'Trinity' to refer to the Christian doctrine, but we shall have occasion to notice that doctrinal parallels occur in a number of pre-Christian theologies which will therefore attract the adjective 'trinitarian' in the sense referred to in spite of the anachronism involved. The Christian terminology will be hard to avoid in other ways too, although a projection of Christian ideas into earlier religions must obviously be eschewed. Religious ideas, however, do not arise *in vacuo*, and one of the aims of this book is to examine the possibile antecedents of Trinitarianism.

A feature of the developed Christian doctrine has been a stress on the co-equality of the Three Persons of the Trinity, in spite of, or because of, the tendency of the early centuries to ascribe degrees of subordination to the Son and the Holy Ghost, the Father being regarded as possessing absolute unity and transcendence. In AD 381 the Council of Constantinople expressly condemned Subordinationism. The deities comprising the non-Christian triads are naturally presented in varying relationships, and their explication invites our attention. So does the rich symbolism which often enters into their significance, just as the roles of the Three Persons of the Trinity are associated with lofty spiritual ideas.

A word which has proved troublesome in tracing the relationships of deities is 'hypostasis'. The Greek ὑπόστασις means primarily 'standing under'; various meanings ensue, including 'sediment', 'duration', 'foundation', 'substructure', 'substance', and 'reality'; and in philosophical writings the last two meanings can refer to the contrast between substances and the reflections of them in a mirror.[12] That there is some divergence (and confusion) in the modern use of the term is shown by Helmer Ringgren in the Introduction to his book *Word and Wisdom*, which bears the subtitle 'Studies in the hypostatization of divine qualities and functions in the Ancient Near East'. He points out (p.8) that the personified Wisdom of the Old Testament is regarded by some as a 'hypostasis', but not by others. Scholars who have denied it, he says, have used the term in its later theological sense of 'person in the Trinity' or the like. Ringgren himself uses a wider meaning, following Oesterley,

Box and Mowinckel, and he quotes a definition from Oesterley and Box: a hypostasis is a 'quasi-personification of certain attributes proper to God, occupying an intermediate position between personalities and abstract beings'.

In Greek philosophical writings, as we have seen, the term came to be used for 'objective reality' in contrast to 'illusion'; but in Christian discussions from about AD 350 it came to mean 'individual reality' and 'person'. When the term was translated by *substantia* in the West, an unfortunate confusion resulted, since it led to the interpretation that the three 'Hypostaseis' in the Godhead were three 'Substances', thus denying the doctrine of the unity of substance in the Three Divine Persons,[13] a heresy usually referred to as that of 'tritheism'. The sense which has been established in English usage derives from the meaning in Christian theology; it is 'personality, personal existence, person', distinguished from both 'nature' and 'substance'; and the verb 'hypostasize' or 'hypostatize' means 'make into or regard as a self-existent substance or person; embody, impersonate'.[14] Clearly this is also the meaning followed up to a point (it is modified in 'quasi-personification') by Ringgren and others; it comes from early Christology rather than from Aristotle and the Neoplatonists, but is now given a wider application. This is the sense which it will be given in this study.

In particular contexts where the Greek word is used, the meaning will nevertheless demand on occasion a degree of special attention. Thus one of the Coptic texts from Nag Hammâdi (II, 4) is entitled *The Hypostasis of the Archons*.[15] Roger A. Bullard, who has published the text with a translation and commentary, shows that, whereas 'nature' or 'essence' is here a possible translation, 'origin' is also a legitimate meaning.[16] He cites valuable studies of the word's development in Greek by H. Dörrie[17] and R. E. Witt;[18] and the work in question may belong to the third century of our era. Peter Nagel preferred to translate the title (which occurs at the end) as *Das Wesen der Archonten*.[19]

Such semantic problems do not, happily, arise often in the approach to a study of divine triads, provided one does not attach to the word 'triad' itself any circumscribed definition. When three deities are grouped together in art or in literature frequently enough to suggest that they are regarded as forming an established group, for our purposes they constitute a triad. The character of the iconography or the textual material may vary a great deal, as in social origin or status; its motivation and genesis may vary; the grouping will remain valid if it occurs frequently, as an attestation of religious experience. Clearly its significance will be easier to grasp in cases where artistic representation is accompanied by textual material.

A temptation which might well arise from the wide-ranging nature of the sources would be to generalize about the potency of the number three. From this danger we are guarded to some extent by the restricted nature of our theme. We are dealing not with all manifestations of the significance of three, but only with its import in the world of the gods. Previous writers, notably Hermann Usener in his *Dreiheit* and Willibald Kirfel in his *Die dreiköpfige Gottheit*, especially the former, tackled the much wider question of the role of three in the culture of various societies. They were, therefore, tempted, perhaps legitimately, to generalize in the manner I have mentioned. Thus Kirfel begins his discussion with a consideration of quite vast issues. It is not only objects, pictures, actions and words, he urges, that can have a symbolical sense; numbers, too, often possess it in association with objects, forms, and colours. Following Leo Frobenius, he sees the numbers three and four playing a leading role in the cultures of the ancient world, the former being associated with a lunar, the latter with a solar, viewpoint. With the dominance of three he links the concept of time which especially presents itself under the aspect of past, present and future. Presumably he derives the division from the tripartition of the lunar month. A culture dominated by the number three, he avers further, fulfils itself in movement and activity.[20] It is refreshing, in view of the wide scope of these statements, to find him adding that the four-based and three-based cultures are not sharply distinguished from one another, and originally, perhaps, not at all. It is indeed doubtful whether any culture can be properly described as dominated by ideas relating to one number. We shall have occasion to observe that several numbers have special potency within a culture. While it would be a hopeless task to essay the comparative significance in any area of the various potent numbers, from time to time it will be salutary to glance at the numerical potencies that exist side by side. It does not follow, of course, that a society that gives prominence to three will for this reason produce a great number of divine triads in its religious system; or that a society devoted to nine will produce many enneads. The converse might indeed apply to divine triads: where they are prominent, the popularity of impersonal triads might well follow. Kirfel's book is a fine study of three-headed deities, and, in so far as it deals with the same theme as Usener's, it fully bears out his claim to present areas neglected by Usener, in particular Hinduism and Buddhism, on which Kirfel was an expert. But two-headed deities are also known, and a brief consideration of these would have improved the perspective.[21]

Caution is similarly desirable in dealing with claims relating to the universal and fundamental potency of a number such as three. Thus the view that the importance of three derives from its position as 'the original final number of primitive man' ('die ursprüngliche Endzahl der primitiven Menschheit', in the sense that primitive man could not count beyond three), which was put forward by H. Diels[22] and H. Usener, is one which awaits confirmation from anthropologists and ethnographists. Certainly, examples of the prevalence of the idea have been cited. Yet theoretically a total of three mastered numbers leaves open the possibility that any one of the three will be dominant. G. E. R. Lloyd has shown that 'pairs of opposites' appealed very much to early Greek thinkers, and he has discovered in the process that such an approach can be paralleled in prehistory.[23] There are clear examples in some modern primitive societies of 'dualist classifications of reality', such as those collected by Rodney Needham;[24] they include day and night, hot and cold, right and left. He has shown, in an analysis of the clasifications of Purum society (a tribe of Manipur on the Indo-Burman border who speak a Tibeto-Burman language), that they use a dualistic approach, as in the terms left, right; strangers, family; inferior, superior; female, male; mortals, gods (or ancestral spirits); death, life. Here is a 'system of categories, which orders both social life and the cosmos'.[24] If classifications of this kind could be shown to be universal, one might argue that two and not three is the basically important number of primitive man. One wonders whether any society exists to which such antitheses are unknown.

An interesting feature of the Purum society, according to Rodney Needham,[25] is that the dyadic classifications exist side by side with a social structure that is inherently triadic. This is a relationship which we shall have constantly to examine in relation to the gods. The ambitious scheme evolved by Georges Dumézil for Indo-European religion and society will demand special attention.

Apart from the books by Usener and Kirfel, there have been few studies of divine triads, although several scholars who have discussed the Christian Trinity have been tempted to deal with possible antecedents. In some ways the most comprehensive treatment has been that by the Danish scholar Ditlef Nielsen, *Der dreieinige Gott in religionshistorischer Beleuchtung* (2 Vols.). The first volume is entitled *Die drei göttlichen Personen*, the second *Die drei Naturgottheiten*. Nielsen had previously published a book called *Die altarabische Mondreligion und die mosaische Ueberlieferung*, and his main interest was in the Semitic and Arabic areas, as shown too in his *Ras šamra Mythologie und Biblische Theologie*. Comprehensive though it is, his study of 'The Triune God' contains little about the religions of Egypt and India – two spheres where the theme is abundantly attested. Nielsen's view is that the Christian Trinity derives ultimately from the ancient religion of the Arabs and that primitive Semitic ideas persisted in Syria, where the Christian Church imbibed them and afterwards gave them new applications. In a review of the first volume, Theophile James Meek[26] says of the Trinity that 'this has been such a universal idea the world over that one wonders whether in many instances it has not sprung up independently'; he adds, 'Resemblance of ideas does not necessarily presuppose connection.' In the present study I hope to give some detailed attention to the immediate intellectual background from which the doctrine of the Trinity emerged; but a descriptive account of the ancient triadic systems will not be too closely geared to the Christian phenomenon. In 1963 Peter Gerlitz published his investigation of the external influences on the development of the Christian doctrine; this will be discussed in some detail (see below chapter 14).

NOTES

[1] *Metaph.* 1081ª34.

[2] *De caelo*, 268ª10. Cf. below p. 135.

[3] See LSJ s.v.; E. A. Sophocles, *Greek Lexicon of the Roman and Byzantine Periods,* s.v.; G. W. H. Lampe, *A Patristic Greek Lexicon*, s.v., where the earliest authors quoted are Theophilus of Antioch, Clement of Alexandria and Hippolytus of Rome.

[4] *Str.* 3. 10 (ed. O. Stählin, p.227, 10).

[5] Ibid. 4. 7 (ed. O. Stählin, p.273, 6).

[6] *Adv. Val.* 17. 2 (ed. A. Kroymann, p.767, 22).

[7] *Adv. Prax.* 3. 1 (ed. Kroymann and Ern. Evans, p.1161, 6).

[8] *De praescr. haer.* 7 (ed. R. F. Refoulé, p.192, 8). On *trinitas*, see further A. Souter, *A Glossary of Later Latin to 600 AD* (Oxford, 1949), 430.

[9] R.E. Latham, *Revised Mediaeval Latin Word-List*, 494.

[10] *OED*, XVIII (1989), 568, a.

[11] *ODCC*[2,] 1394.

[12] See LSJ s.v., p.1895, III.2.

[13] For brief discussions of these trends, see *ODCC*[2] s.vv. Hypostasis and Tritheism.

[14] *OED*, VII, 579, 5.

[15] For a translation, see Roger A. Bullard and Bentley Layton in *The Nag Hammadi Library in English*, ed. James M. Robinson, 152–60. The title is translated 'Reality of the Rulers' (p.152).

[16] *The Hypostasis of the Archons*, 42–3.

[17] Nachr. Göttingen (1955), 35–92.

[18] In *Amicitiae Corolla, (Fs. J. Rendel Harris*, ed. H. G. Wood, London, 1933), 319–43.

[19] *Das Wesen der Archonten aus Codex II der gnostischen Bibliothek von Nag Hammadi*. Convinced as he is that the Coptic derives from a Greek original, Nagel also supplies a reconstructed Greek text.

[20] W. Kirfel, *Die dreiköpfige Gottheit* (Bonn, 1948), 7.

[21] Some attention is given to both groups in R. Pettazzoni (tr. H. J. Rose), *The All-knowing God* (London, 1956), ch. 4.

[22] *Festschrift Theodor Gomperz* (Vienna, 1902), 8 n.3. He also states that the sacredness of 'dreimal Drei' is characteristic of Aryan religious usage in its entirety.

[23] *Polarity and Analogy: Two Types of Argumentation in Early Greek Thought* (Cambridge, 1966).

[24] *Structure and Sentiment* (Chicago, 1962), 95–6. For right and left, see also the book edited by him, *Right and Left*; cf. too his *Belief, Language, and Experience,* 156.

[25] *Structure and Sentiment*, 95–6.

[26] *American Journal of Semitic Languages and Literatures* 40 (1924), 146.

Part I
EGYPT

1

Egypt's Early Tradition

The triadic grouping of gods was an early and persistent tradition in the religion of Ancient Egypt. The best-known example is perhaps that of Osiris, Isis, and Horus, and the relationship within the triad is often on a family basis of father, mother, and child, although there are triads with three gods or three goddesses,[1] the leading deities of one locality being sometimes thus combined. A result of the prominence of this structural element in Egyptian religion has been the suggestion of some scholars, notably the late Siegfried Morenz, that Egypt may well have influenced, in this matter, the formulation of the Christian doctrine of the Trinity. Conversely, Serge Sauneron[2] has asked 'whether the idea of a triad is not a modern creation'; perhaps he is suggesting that a Christian concept has coloured our interpretation of Ancient Egyptian data. Certainly the Egyptians produced more systematic doctrine about the Ennead of Heliopolis (which really comprises four pairs of deities with Atum at the head), or the Ogdoad of Hermopolis. Yet the triadic groups are so conspicuous at all times in dynastic Egypt that they must be faced, as H. te Velde rightly avers, as an inescapable fact of the situation. A celebrated instance from the Old Kingdom is the series from the Pyramid Temple of Mycerinus, in which the Pharaoh is shown between the goddess Hathor and a nome-goddess. This dates to a little before 2500 BC.

1. A Possible Triad in Prehistoric Egypt

In her study of *The Cultures of Prehistoric Egypt*, Dr Elise J. Baumgartel ventured to locate the first instance of an Egyptian triad in prehistoric times. The evidence is found on a decorated vase whose provenance is unknown, but whose origin in prehistoric Egypt is beyond question. At present it is in the Metropolitan Museum of Art, New York, and, apart from its religious interest, it is an impressive work of prehistoric art.[3]

The vase has lug handles, and around these there are wavy lines arranged like a necklace. Above are depicted the hills, which presumably overlook a river valley. Below are plants, trees and birds (flamingos); and a group of ibexes are depicted in the middle register. The only human element in these surrounding decorations is contributed by a group of

A. Shrine with Two Figures    B. Divine Female with upraised hands   C. Vase from El-Amrah near Abydos

Figure 1. A possible prehistoric triad

four women, the first of whom is clearly more important than the others, since she is larger and has an elaborate hair-do. If they are connected with the central religious scenes, it is perhaps as worshippers or attendants.

There are three main scenes in the middle, and in each a boat is portrayed (Fig.1A). Each is equipped with numerous oars, and at the stern or prow a large branch arises. In the centre of the boat are two objects that look like cabins, save that one is fitted with a tall canopy that perhaps converts it into a shrine, while the smaller cabin seems to act as an antechamber. The use of shrines in boats, whether for funerary or processional purposes, became very common in Egypt, and Early Dynastic evidence supports it.[4] A tall shrine, rather similar to ours, appears in the Old-Kingdom tomb of Ptah-hetep.[5] An emblem is displayed on top of a pole which rises from the ancillary cabin. It consists of two concentric curves which almost form circles. The same symbol is repeated fourteen times in the space above.

The two figures within the shrine, if shrine it is, are presumably deities. The larger of the two is a goddess. Although the form is stylized, she is clearly meant to have generous and voluptuous proportions – a predilection often evident in the physical standards of the ancient world, from the Venus of Willendorf to the Aphrodite of Cnidos and of Melos. Beside her there is a male form who is possibly ithyphallic. The fact that his body is shown as very thin in comparison with hers may simply imply a distinction of sex. Dr Baumgartel rightly notes that the size of his head is only 'a fraction of that of the woman's'. It is not quite true to say that he is a 'little man', since he is almost equal in height to his partner. Doubtless she is the dominating figure, and Dr Baumgartel's interpretation that a 'sacred marriage' is being depicted here is not unreasonable. A possible objection is the doubtful extent to which the male figure is shown as ithyphallic. As compared with the later figures of Min or Osiris, the emphasis is not very clear. Can it be that male sex alone is indicated?

In the next scene (Fig.1B) the tall canopy of the shrine has disappeared. Standing on one cabin is probably the same divine female; this time her hands are held upwards over her head. Beside the second cabin stand three females, and this group of four seems to correspond in some way to the group shown below the boat. But, if they represent the same group, then the figure throwing up her hands will not be the goddess herself; she may be only her high priestess. On the middle level there is a fifth female figure in the same posture. This time there is an additional emblem above one of the cabins – the two-barbed emblem which Wainwright called the 'Z' sign which seems to be paralleled in early Iran and Iraq.

Another enigmatic sign, or group of signs, here is that below the middle of the boat. The lower one looks like the hieroglyph for *p*, which Gardiner[6] interprets as a 'stool of reed matting'. Dr Baumgartel[7] compares a shape on a vase now in Brussels (see her Vol. I, 64, Fig.14), but there is no detailed resemblance beyond the rectangular form; nor is the sign above it easy to parallel.[8] Probably it is unwise to look for a hieroglyphic explanation. A reed mat under a tent may be indicated.[9]

However, the deities are our main interest, and a vase from El-Amrah near Abydos is relevant (Fig.1C). This site, incidentally, has given its name to the Amratian prehistoric culture, which probably belongs to the early part of the fourth millennium BC. Here again there are figures on a boat, but the first boat in this case carries a standard denoting hill country. A conspicuous female figure has her hands raised above her head, perhaps in an ecstatic dance; it is, at any rate, the very same posture as we saw on the other vase. On the second boat shown on the El-Amrah vase the same standard is depicted as on the other vase. It is the double concentric circle, rather like a penannular ring, but recalling, too, the posture of raised arms displayed by the female figures. The standard seems, however, to suggest horns rather than arms. Clearly the identification of the goddess depends a good deal on how these forms are explained. A similar posture is shown by some female figurines, and Westendorf[10] has put the problem succinctly as follows:

> Its interpretation as a 'dance' is not wholly satisfactory but rather raises the question of what this dance attitude is supposed to express. Is it an act of human homage to a divinity? Or is it the goddess herself, a 'Great Mother', lifting her arms to heaven? Or are the arms supposed to imitate the cow's horns of the sky-goddess ...

The figurines have been elaborately studied by Peter J. Ucko,[11] who stresses the variety of posture revealed when all the types are analysed; there are many figures, for instance, with arm-stumps and others with arms protruding downwards. All this, in Ucko's opinion, 'makes it unlikely that their significance should be sought in symbolic terms'. Dr Baumgartel, who interprets the dance (if it is a dance) as a 'cow-dance' (Vol. II, 145), a phrase which is itself not easy to interpret (does it mean 'a dance like that of a cow'? Has any one seen cows dancing?), wants to explain the concentric curved circles of the boat-standards as 'the horns and arms of the cow-goddess'. This double interpretation seems to impose too great subtlety on a simple design.

We come now to the scene where it is claimed that there is a triad (Fig.1C, left). Here on one of the boat cabins appears a group of three figures, and of these the central figure can be recognized as the goddess of the first scene. She is accompanied by a male figure, who may well be the same person as the one who is with her in the first scene. She is placing her left hand on the head of another female, who is smaller. The male figure on her right is placing his left hand behind the waist of the goddess in the centre, while in his right hand he is holding a crook. On the second cabin stands another male figure, who is holding something in his left hand; from his cabin emerges a standard consisting of horns with what looks like a falcon in between.

Of the group of three, Dr Baumgartel says (II, 146): 'This, to my mind, is the first divine triad so far known in Egypt, and it consists of mother, father and daughter.' The centrality and importance of the goddess must certainly be recognized. It is also possible that a triad is being represented, unless one wishes to argue that the grouping is fortuitous, or that the fourth figure, who stands apart, should be taken into account. Both the male figures are in fact provided with phallic indications, but there seems to be no reason for the ithyphallic interpretation. The crook in the left hand of the male in the triad is undoubtedly significant. It occurs with the sign of Min on a palette from El-Amrah, as Dr Baumgartel shows (II, 89); it is also, of course, one of the eventual insignia of the dynastic Pharaoh and of Osiris.

The goddess in the triad is probably an early form of Hathor, and the boat standards depict the horns of Hathor as a cow-goddess. The horns with a falcon in between suggest the relationship between Hathor and Horus, and the Narmer palette brings this out at the dawn of the dynastic era. Hathor is the original mother of Horus, and her son is identified with the living Pharaoh. A similar relationship is indicated in the triads of Mycerinus, which Dr Baumgartel rightly invokes. Where one must disagree with her is in the invocation of a Great Mother goddess of fertility. Peter Ucko's criticisms of this theory are, for the most part, well founded. One vital objection is that, if fertility is taken in its widest sense to include the products of the earth, then one has to face the fact that in Egypt the god of the earth is Geb, a male deity; other deities connected with fertility, especially Osiris and Neper, are also male, although the serpent-deity of the harvest, Renenwetet, is female. Another objection is that early Egyptian society shows little sign of having evolved from a matriarchy. It is strongly patriarchal.

Yet the role of the cow-goddess Hathor as mother of the Pharaoh is prominent from the very dawn of the dynastic era, as witnessed by the Narmer palette. If Hathor is the goddess in the New York vase, and if the leading male figure is the Horus chieftain – and this will certainly follow if my explanation of the bird in the standard as a falcon is accepted – then the relationship depicted will be that of mother and son. The first scene will involve not a sacred marriage, but a ritual grouping of mother and son. This will agree with the fact that the male figure is slightly shorter than that of the female. It will also imply that the phallic indications throughout do not adumbrate anything more than male sex. As for the triad, this will include mother and son again, with the addition, perhaps, of the son's spouse or of a related goddess. A difficulty in the interpretation hitherto accepted is that, if a sacred marriage occurs in the first scene, then the ruler eventually acts as both son and lover of the principal goddess. It is true that there may be a suggestion of this in the later Egyptian concept of the *Ka-mwt.f* ('the bull of his mother'), but this is not attested until the New Kingdom. The original idea seems to be simpler: the ruler is the son of the cow-goddess Hathor, who is a goddess of sexual fertility and also of the heaven. At the same time the ruler is the falcon-god Horus, himself a sky-god, and their relationship is graphically figured, if my interpretation is right, by the symbol of the falcon within the cow-horns.[12]

A final point may be made concerning methodology. In the case of Egypt, prehistorians have long since realized that the evidence reveals a number of symbols which reappear in the dynastic era. These are often associated with religion, and it is obviously a wise plan to exploit the interdependence of the historic and the prehistoric.

2. *Egyptian Views of Three*

Since all our subsequent evidence derives from the historical era, the dawn of which is accompanied by the ability to write, record and calculate, it is proper to ask whether the Egyptians attached any special significance to the number three. We are confronted at once by the important fact that the Egyptians, in their system of writing, expressed plurality by repeating three times one or more of the signs with which the singular was written; later a determinative of plurality was used – three strokes or small circles (grains of sand). In addition, it is true, distinctive phonetic endings for the plural (and dual) were often expressed. Why they should have used a triple and not a double repetition is explained by the fact that they thought of two as expressing a separate category.[13]

In this way three becomes an indication of plurality as far as the writing system is concerned. It is a meaning attaching also to the repetition of words: thus *nfr nfr* is used in a comparative sense, 'of better quality', but *nfr nfr nfr* of the superlative, 'excellent' (see *Wb.* II, 253, 17–18). The question arises whether it assumes this meaning elsewhere too. In Egyptian the word for 'three' is ⸗, *ḫmtw*, the Coptic derivatives being s. ϣomñт b. ϣomт a. ϩaмт .[14] The use of the phallus in the writing has no significance other than its phonetic indication of *mt*.[15] When used independently of persons, the number is sometimes written as three seated men, 𓀀𓀀𓀀, and when the noun is used with the number, it generally follows it, as in 'three people', *ḫmtw rmt̠*.[16] However, the noun may also come first, while the number is written as a cipher after it, as in *wsḫt* 3, 'three freight ships' (*Urk.* 1, 108, 14),[17] though the numeral is still read first. Here, if confusion with the plural sign were possible, the following phrase, which uses the numeral 4, is decisive.

A striking fact about *ḫmtw*. 'three', is that it is not elaborated into a collective abstract **ḫmtt*, 'triad', although the process occurs with several other numerals, as with *fdw*, 'four', *ifdt*, 'quartet'; *ḫmnw*, 'eight', *ḫmnt*, 'ogdoad'; *psḏ*, 'nine', *psḏt*, 'ennead'.[18] Gardiner[19] states that 'there existed also a set of collectives corresponding to the English "triad", "trio", "quartet", etc.', but it is not clear that he means that there were equivalents specifically for the terms mentioned by him. The collective abstracts are written similarly to the feminine of the cardinals, but probably differed in stress and vocalization.[20] Rather different is the independent use of the cardinal number substantivally.[21] Occasionally, however, there may be doubt as to whether such a use occurs or the employment of an abstract. Thus in Utterance 205 of the *Pyramid Texts* the King is assured of supplies of food and drink and we are told

> for it is the King who is at the five portions of meals in the Mansion, the three (*ḫmtt*) being in heaven with Rê, and two (*snty*) being on earth with the Two Enneads.
>
> (Pyr. 121c–d W)

Faulkner[22] appears to take all three numerals here as collective abstracts, 'because the King is he who is at the quintet of meals in the Mansion. The trio (of meals) is in the sky, with Rēʿ and the pair is on earth with the Two Enneads.' In the case of *ḫmtt* either interpretation is possible.[23]

Although *ifdt*, 'quartet', is apparently not used of gods, it can refer to the four corners or the four supports of heaven.[24] The word *ḫmnt*, 'ogdoad', also occurs as a collective abstract;[25] it is used of a group of eight days;[26] and sometimes it may have been used of the Eight Gods of Hermopolis,[27] although they are more commonly referred to as 'The Eight',[28] and are also alluded to in the place-name. *Ḫmnw*, 'The Eight' (Hermopolis, el-Ashmunein).[29] It is clear, however, that even if *ḫmnt* was used occasionally as a collective abstract with reference to the group of eight gods who were regarded as primal creator-gods, yet this use, as Sethe admits, was only in imitation of the long-established position of the *psḏt*, 'the Ennead'. This is the collective abstract which is doctrinally basic in early Egyptian religion.

Was three regarded by the Egyptians as a magic number? In support of this, Sethe[30] adduces instances from the Demotic Magical Papyrus of London and Leiden (of the third century AD). In one case the following instruction is given concerning the recitation of a spell:

> [Say it] opposite (17) the Shoulder constellation on the third day of the month, there being a clove of three-lobed white garlic and there being three needles (18) of iron piercing it, and recite this to it seven times; and put it at thy head.
>
> (P. Mag. Lond. Leid. 8, 16–18)[31]

Here there is a triple use of three, followed by one use of the magic number seven. In the much earlier medical texts allusion is sometimes made to three vessels, or days, or pills;[32] but the number four is much more frequently thus used,[33] and in any case it might be argued that applying a medicament in such quantities or for three or four days was based on reason rather than magic. Rather different is the question of how many times a medico-magical spell is to be recited; 'four times' is predominant here again.[34] In a wider context we find allusions to images of the gods being worshipped in temples three times a day, and similar instructions for the ablutions of priests and for the making of offerings to the gods, but Sethe[35] rightly concedes that these arrangements derive merely from the division of the day into morning, afternoon and evening. Even so all his examples are from the Graeco-Roman era, and Bonnet,[36] emphasizing this, raises the question of the possibility of foreign influence. Nor does Kees[37] include three among the sacred numbers; to him its importance is rather in its connotation of plurality and its relation to the Ennead.

Sethe[38] in his discussion uses 'Runde oder heilige Zahlen' as a heading, and states that in general only those numbers can be considered sacred or round whose choice seems to be arbitrary, such as the division of the day into twelve or of the hour into sixty parts, but not such cases as those where an inner basis for the choice was present, as in the number of the months (balance between the orbit-time of sun and moon) and the division of the month into decans (regard for the decimal system). Clearly the concept of a round number differs from that of a sacred number. Sethe cites the thirty years of the King's Jubilee festival as a round number, suggesting that a convenient or approximate number is aimed at.[39] Both round and sacred numbers have an element of the irrational about them, and even if a rational explanation may elucidate the origin of their importance, it does not follow at all that it applies to the conscious or unconscious extension of their influence. Thus, if the phases of the moon lie behind the significance of the numbers seven and nine, yet it is clear that the significance extends far beyond any such associations.

Concepts of space and its division are shown by Sethe[40] to lie behind the prominence of four in Egypt. He cites the four quarters of heaven and corners of the world (North, South, East, West), and the application of the same number to the supports of heaven, the winds, the races of mankind, the barbarian peoples, the feet of animals and of furniture, the faces of certain gods or demons[41] and the horns of certain fantastic animals. He refers also to the frequency with which the *Pyramid Texts* mention four gods, goddesses or spirits without reference to the four quarters of heaven; there are likewise four sons of Horus, and four jackals draw the barque of the sun, while the ceremony of 'Opening the Mouth' lasts for four days. Many other such groups are cited, and the list clearly includes items which are not in the 'sacred' or 'round' category. Four feet are ascribed to certain animals because that is a perceptible fact; similarly the four feet of a chair.

Sethe sees the prominence of four in Egypt gradually yielding to that of seven. Certainly there are plenty of irrational sevens. Sethe[42] cites the seven cows of the underworld; the seven gods and serpents with which the dead must associate; the seven scorpions which accompany Isis in the Delta in the Metternich Stela; the seven Hathors who help with childbirth, and several medical groups of seven. Many examples apply to ritual procedures. Multiples of seven (14, 21, 42, 70, 77, 770, 7,000) have a certain importance;[43] also 75, although not strictly a multiple.

By comparison, the prominence of three is negligible, and, as we have seen, a rational explanation of its use is often possible. Even the related number nine, in spite of the illustrious light shed on it by the Ennead of Heliopolis, does not achieve widespread currency in a special sense. Sethe[44] cites the Nine Bows, a nocturnal journey of heaven made nine times, the complaint of the 'Peasant' made nine times, and the nine friends accompanying the dead; only the first of these expressions seems significant. In the late magical papyri nine competes with seven for favour. Kees[45] refers to the 'nine children of Rê' in the Edfu texts.

We must conclude that in Egyptian tradition the number three lacks any inherent claim to be considered a sacred or magic number. A significance it does have is that of plurality.

3. Human and Divine Groupings of Two and Three

There are many natural groupings of animals, men, and gods, and the dyad is common in many contexts. In the art of the ancient Near East, an antithetic grouping of two animals occurs often. Among the earliest examples in Egypt are sets of two dogs (or jackals or hybrids) facing each other on the obverse of a slate palette of the Late Predynastic era; they are also shown on the reverse, in this case guarding a palm-tree and a group of confronting giraffes.[46] A well-known instance is seen on the slightly later Narmer palette, on the obverse of which are two fantastic lion-like or panther-like creatures facing each other; here an antithetic group of men is added, and they are holding ropes round the necks of the animals.[47] Here too a deity enters into a dyadic arrangement, for two Hathor-heads are figured on the top of both sides of the Narmer palette. Since the Hathor-head in this case is partly a cow-head, the animal antithetic group is really present. It was the view of Dr Elise J. Baumgartel[48] that the antithetic group 'seems influenced by Sumerian art, which likes antithetical groups, whilst they are rare in Egypt.' The latter statement is scarcely acceptable, although the Mesopotamian occurrences are common.[49] In Egypt the dual group is common with the gods Horus and Seth, sometimes on the *serekh*-sign,[50] and often in depictions of 'Uniting the Two Lands',[51] and of 'the Purification of the Pharaoh or the deceased';[52] and there are many other contexts where the concept of Egypt as a union of 'Two Lands' has produced an artistic dualism.[53] Thus there is a doubling in the case of Wepwawet, although the figures are shown standing one behind the other;[54] the vulture-goddess Nekhbet of El-Kâb is juxtaposed with the cobra-goddess Wadjet of Buto, as, for instance, on the gold mask of Tutankhamûn; the uraeus itself is often produced in a double form.[55] Whereas the doubling of the eye of the sun-god is a natural result of a person being regarded as having two eyes, the other dualities have another explanation. The unity of Egypt under Narmer was preceded by a condition when the country was divided into two; before that there may well have been a predynastic union.[56] A political and historical reason therefore emerges for the dualism described; and this is more satisfactory than the assumption of a philosophical polarity in the manner of Frankfort,[57] who spoke of the 'embodiment of the two gods (Horus and Seth) in the person of the Pharaoh' as 'another instance of the peculiar dualism that expresses a totality as an equilibrium of opposites'.

At the same time, since the antithetic group normally entails two figures facing a central figure, it may be regarded as a triadic grouping. The dyad proper seems to arise when a man is represented with his wife. While the male deceased is sometimes figured in splendid isolation in tombs of the Old Kingdom, as in the tombs and stelae of Sabu (also called Ibebi) of the Fifth Dynasty and Ihynes of the Sixth,[58] his wife is represented with him on the stelae of the courtier Sethu (Fifth Dynasty, Gîza), of the priest Nekheftka (Fifth Dynasty, Saqqâra), and in the tomb of Iasen (Fifth or Sixth Dynasty, Gîza); children and domestic servants may also appear in such a grouping. There are many instances in the Cairo Museum of the same grouping in statuary,[59] a celebrated example being the painted statues of a royal pair, Rahotep and Nofert.[60]

When a man and his wife are represented in statuary, the forms are broadly similar in size, but usually there are indications that the wife is regarded as slightly less important.[61] When a child is present, or more than one, they are shown so small that the impression of a dyadic grouping is scarcely impaired.[62] On occasion, a son is shown not so much smaller than his father and mother, and in such a case a triadic effect is achieved.[63] Sometimes the dyad consists of a group other than a man and his wife. Groups of two men occur in statuary, without an indication of their relationship;[64] or a man may be represented with his son,[65] on a roughly similar scale. What seems more remarkable is the double representation of the same man, Nedjem-yeb (Sixth Dynasty, Abydos), a notion confirmed by the hieroglyphs.[66]

The question naturally arises whether the representation of gods in the Old Kingdom follows a similar pattern, the truism being accepted that the divine world is in some ways a reflex of the human world. Representations of the King being suckled by a goddess clearly belong to the family grouping, and in the Fifth Dynasty tomb of Sahurê it is the vulture-goddess Nekhbet of El-Kâb who gives her breast to the young King; the creator-god Khnum stands behind her accompanied by the inscription *he who ensures that he may live healthily for ever*.[67] The hand of a fragmentary fourth figure is shown clasping the body of the young King, so that this figure, presumably regarded as the King's father, Nekhbet being his mother or foster-mother, completes the family triad. Borchardt believed that the father may be Rê;[68] and he pointed out that other goddesses, including Hathor, Bastet, Selqet, and Satet, are sometimes given this suckling role.[69]

4. The Triads of Mycerinus

In this triadic grouping the role of Khnum, although conceptually vital, is outside the triad proper, which really follows the family unit. Such a unit is rarely shown with gods during the Old Kingdom, unless the celebrated triads of Mycerinus be regarded as following such a pattern. The divinity of the Pharaoh certainly permits the idea. These triads derive from the valley temple of Mycerinus at Gîza, which was excavated by Reisner[70] from 1908 to 1910. Five triads were recovered, four of them in excellent condition; fragments of others were also found. Artistically they are among the treasures of Ancient Egyptian sculpture, and a study by Wendy Wood[71] presents effective reproductions as well as a fresh assessment of their significance. In each group the Pharaoh Mycerinus is accompanied by two other figures, those of Hathor and of a nome-goddess. Structural as well as religious questions arise in the study of these groups, but the two are naturally connected.

The nome-goddesses figured on the four complete pieces relate to the nomes of Thebes, Diospolis Parva, Hermopolis and Cynopolis; these are respectively the fourth, seventh, fifteenth and eighteenth of Upper Egypt.

They are shown with the nome-symbols on their heads. Under them are inscriptions such as:

> I give to you every good thing and all offerings which are in Upper Egypt, for you have appeared in glory as the King of Upper and Lower Egypt for ever.

This concerns the nome-goddess of Diospolis Parva.[72] The other corresponding inscriptions also refer to Upper Egypt. With the figure of the King are the words

> Horus Ka-Khet,[73] King of Upper and Lower Egypt, Men-kau-rê, beloved of Hathor, mistress of the sycamore tree, in all her seats.[74]

The other inscriptions relating to the King are similar. Skilfully carved in dark grey wacke, the figures are only about two-fifths life size, and the presumption is that there must have been many others in addition to those extant. In fact the import of the inscriptions with the nome-goddesses demands the representation of both Upper and Lower Egypt, since the goddesses are bestowing gifts and offerings on the King and greet him with veneration at the same time. Clearly this must be seen to be happening throughout Egypt. 'There can be no doubt', says Edwards,[75] 'that Mycerinus intended to have forty-two of these triads, each showing him in company with a different *nome*-god or goddess'; but he adds that 'possibly the remainder were never carved'. Apart from their divine attributes, the goddesses are human in form; they constitute the earliest sculptured figures of deities in the Old Kingdom,[76] and are among the most impressive achieved in Egyptian art at any time.

The representation of Upper and Lower Egypt in a royal religious context is not without parallel. In the architectural complex which was adjacent to the Step Pyramid of the Third-Dynasty King Djoser there were Upper and Lower Egyptian dummy chapels which were probably connected with the deities of the nomes of Upper and Lower Egypt and also with the idea, prominent in the King's *Heb-sed* or Jubilee Festival, that those deities sanctioned the re-enactment of his coronation. In a funerary context this would naturally refer to his repetition of it in life after death.[77] Forty alcoves flanking a colonnade linked to Djoser's *Heb-sed* court may also have been connected with the deities of the nomes.[78] Like these deities, the 'Nile-gods' too were associated with localities, evolving later into representatives of Upper and Lower Egypt.[79]

Wendy Wood[80] argues that thirty triads[81] could not have been meaningfully disposed under cover in the Valley Temple of Mycerinus, and that only in one area of the temple, the eight portico chapels, can the triads 'be placed in harmony with the architecture'. Her argument leads her to assume that only eight triads were made, and that these represent only the nomes 'in which the cult of Hathor had been established with the support of royal patronage'. She justly emphasizes the prominence of Hathor in the extant triads, and her suggested structure of disposition has some support in the Valley Temple of Sneferu. A weakness in her theory is that in it the pan-Egyptian stress of similar patterns gets lost in the restriction to nomes where Hathor was prominent; it is also strange to find a suggestion that 'range in quality' – that is, artistic quality – was a factor in deciding the location of the triads. If the reconstruction suggested has several attractive points, especially in relation to the known plan of the building, it gives Upper Egypt a disproportionate emphasis[82] and limits unduly the significance of Hathor in the whole scheme.

In the five extant triads Mycerinus himself is four times the central figure; in one Hathor occupies the centre. The inscription under the King expresses his special relationship to Hathor, and so does, in two cases, the posture of the figures. While it may be true that as *Mistress of Dendera* Hathor exerted influence throughout Upper Egypt during the Old Kingdom, as is indicated by inscriptions ranging from Thebes to Memphis,[83] her position theologically transcends this evidence. In the earliest theology Hathor is the mother of Horus, and so of the Horus-King, and on the Narmer palette her position in his role is strongly suggested. In the *Pyramid Texts* the relationships of Horus and the King are proclaimed to merge:

> Art thou Horus, the son of Osiris? Art thou, O King, the oldest god, the son of Hathor? Art thou the seed of Geb? Osiris has ordered that the King should appear as the double of Horus.
>
> (*Pyr.* 466a–467a)

The gods have been demanding the King's credentials,[84] and Osiris announces the identification which favours him. In his official titulary Pepy I calls himself *Son of Hathor, Mistress of Dendera*, a phrase which apparently replaces the more usual *Son of Rê*. The numerous occurrences have been ably studied by Fischer;[85] the less frequently attested type describes Pepy as *Son of Atum, Lord of Heliopolis, and of Hathor, Mistress of Dendera*. Later texts also describe Horus as the son of Hathor,[86] and the suckling of the Horus-King by Hathor in the form of a cow clearly expresses the same idea. On the two sides of the Narmer palette the King is shown with Upper and Lower Egyptian crowns respectively, suggesting his unification of the 'Two Lands'; on top of each side are two large figures of Hathor's cow-head with human face, and these figures flank in each case the palace façade which bears the name of Narmer. If Hathor's motherhood is not unequivocally thus expressed, at least a close association is suggested; also there is the idea that the victories of Narmer depicted below have been achieved under her aegis. The four Hathor-heads on the apron worn by Narmer on the side of the palette where his figure dominates[87] are indicative of a personal relationship, and the identification of Narmer with Horus is suggested by the human arm of the falcon. That the Hathor-figure is really the goddess of heaven is assumed by Schott[88] without discussion. He refers to Quibell, *Hierakonpolis*, I (1900), Pl.XV, 7, where he sees the hieroglyph for 'Narmer' protected by the 'Upper Egyptian goddess of heaven'; above the name is certainly a vulture with outstretched wings.[89] This must be Nekhbet, the vulture-goddess of El-Kâb, and there is no similarity to the bovine head which appears eight times in all on the Narmer palette.

Hathor as the mother of Horus is a concept indicated by her very name, which means 'House of Horus'; and although the representations of her giving suck, as a cow-goddess, to the Horus–King, begin only in the New Kingdom, there is enough early evidence to enable such representations to be given an ancient origin. Amenophis II is shown as a child on his knees taking suck from a Hathor who is wholly animal in form; in the same sculptured group the King appears standing beneath her head. See Bonnet, *Bilderatlas*, 30 (= S. Allam, *Beiträge zum Hathorkult*, Pl.8), and the photographs from the Hathor-shrine in Deir el-Bahari in Naville, *The XIth Dynasty Temple*, I, Pls.27, 30, 31; the same theme occurs in a painting in the shrine, see Naville, ibid., Pl.28c. The birth scene which illustrates the divine origin of the King also shows Hathor giving suck to the infant: see Al. Gayet, *Le Temple de Louxor* (Paris, 1894), Pl.66, Fig.192, where the goddess is shown twice as a cow, and a better publication and discussion in H. Brunner, *Die Geburt des Gottkönigs* (1964), Pl.12; also Naville, *The Temple of Deir El Bahari*, II (1896), Pl.53 with p.17, where the two cows are figured as well as two nursing and suckling goddesses with the Hathor-crown and double feather on the sun-disc. In the case of the nursing goddesses Hathor is indubitably meant; cf. Frankfort, *Kingship and the Gods*, 172 and 385. The two cow-figures are explained by Brunner as Wadjet and Nekhbet,[90] but in the reliefs at Deir el-Bahari and Luxor it would seem likely that the two groups have a similar reference. Certainly we must bear in mind that in the tradition several deities are ascribed this function, and that it may apply to one of three phases in the King's life – his natural birth, his birth to life as a King (coronation) and his birth to life after death.[91]

It is, of course, possible and indeed feasible to combine the idea of Hathor's relationship to Horus with her role as a goddess of heaven. There may be affinities with the Hesat-cow and with Mehet-Weret, the heavenly cow that personifies the primal waters of the sky from which the sun is born. The difficulty is that no early association of these deities with Hathor seems to influence her iconography, although the sun-disc between Hathor's horns connects her clearly enough with the heaven.

The Hathor-heads on the apron worn by Narmer have been well dealt with by Allam,[92] who shows that a festal garment is indicated in which the Hathor-heads adorn the top of pearl-pendants attached to a leather girdle. He also shows that a similar garment is worn by King Scorpion on his mace-head and by Djoser on a fragment of a statue; the latter instance is especially relevant as many Hathor-head pendants are there shown.[93] A passage adduced by Allam from the *Pyramid Texts* seems likewise to bear on this garment:

> How beautiful is the sight of the King! His head-band is that of Rê's brow, the apron upon him is that of Hathor, his feather is the feather of the falcon, when he ascends to heaven among his brothers the gods.
>
> (*Pyr.* 546a–b)

A slight difficulty here is that the determinative of šnḏwt suggests not an apron, but the kilt with the penis-bag; perhaps more than one type of garment could be indicated by the word. Certainly the regal and divine importance of the garment is signified. Allam rightly rejects Sethe's suggestion that a sexual meaning is present, and he propounds the view that the 'feather' (šwt) mentioned refers to a Lower Egyptian crown.[94] Since this is a Horus-crown, what is significant is that Hathor and Horus are again associated – and even apart from the possible mention of a crown. Wearing the clothes and attributes of deities clearly confers their power and protection, or even identity with them. In one of the spells of the *Coffin Texts* the deceased says: *I have clothed myself with the garment of this great one (Hathor); I am the great one* (*CT* VI, 62i–k).[95] In the case of the Horus-King it is the protection of his mother Hathor that will be signified.

So, then, the relationship of Mycerinus and Hathor in the triads is that of a Horus-King with his mother,[96] and it is a relationship that has found several other modes of expression. If a family group is suggested, then it is mother, son and daughter (or son); there is no indication of an exact relationship for the nome-deity, but this figure is subordinate to some extent, suggesting the younger daughter or son.[97] Conceptually the protection of Hathor as a cosmic deity of heaven and of fertility (she is 'Mistress of the Sycamore') is the important element;[98] both she and the nome-deity are contributing to the King's well-being in the afterlife. That the whole of Egypt is thus contributing is probably the function of the nome-deities in this series of triads.[99] Bernard V. Bothmer[100] has pointed out that although a sculptured group appears at Saqqâra from the Third Dynasty, it is in a very fragmentary state.[101] The triads of Mycerinus are the first instance of an extant group, and they are impressive in the sense of unity achieved from diverse figures. One element in this unity is what Bothmer calls 'the striking resemblance of the three faces'; he finds that it indicates 'the identity of man with god, the presence of the deity in man, and the divine sanction of Egyptian kingship'.[102] The sanction, it may be added, is now directed to the realm of sovereignty in the afterlife, and Hathor, from this viewpoint, may represent the celestial world,[103] while the nome-deity represents the terrestrial world. Unity in the triad is a theme to which we shall be returning. In this early instance it is both conceptual and artistic; and the King is the focus.

The mother here is a divine mother, but it is worth noting that Old-Kingdom funerary art is not averse to the representation of human mothers. Thus in the Fourth-Dynasty tomb of Ka-nofer in Gîza the doorjambs are decorated with coloured reliefs showing Ka-nofer with his mother on one side with his wife on the other.[104] In the Fifth-Dynasty tomb of Rê-wer a finely sculptured relief shows the deceased seated before a standing figure of his mother Hetep-heres.[105]

5. Old-Kingdom Triadic Groups in Statuary

As far as statuary is concerned, the valuable study by Bodil Hornemann, *Types of Ancient Egyptian Statuary* (Copenhagen, 1951–69) enables one to follow the evolution of the triadic group. It is in the Fifth Dynasty that the first instances occur which relate to human families. A group of three boys is figured in limestone in a piece now at Boston (06. 1882);[106] it derives from Gîza, as does a group (Cairo J. 66616) described by Selim Hassan as the 'Triple Statuette of a Man' from the tomb of Rê-wer, though he also refers to it as 'three male figures standing side by side',[107] and, as one figure is shown clasping the other above the waist, it is tempting to interpret them as three separate persons, especially as there is no inscription to indicate otherwise. But there are instances with inscriptions which prove that a triple representation of the same man was practised. From the tomb of the same Rê-wer[108] comes a triple statue of the deceased (Cairo J.66615) in which the three forms are very similar, and two inscriptions give the same name and titles.[109] There are two triads also in the tomb of Pen-meru from the same dynasty. One (Boston. 12. 1484) shows two standing male figures with one standing female figure; two figures of children appear as well, but they are very small, reaching only to below the knees of the adult persons. Hornemann classifies this as a group of five figures,[110] and W. S. Smith describes it rightly as a triad which is 'really a family group with two small children'.[111] What is noteworthy, however, is that the two adult male figures are both called *Pn-mrw*, although their faces are by no means similar: the deceased is represented twice. In the other triad (Boston. 12. 1504) from the same tomb, three standing males are figured,[112] and W. S. Smith[113] hails this, with the other group, as the first occurrence of the triad in large private statues. But again the name *Pn-mrw* is inscribed with each of the figures, who here show considerable similarity, although their head-dress varies. The triad is really a triple statue of the deceased.[114]

A problem is manifestly posed by these and other instances of duplication and triplication. In the case of Pen-meru the triple statue bears inscriptions which refer to his offices or attributes: from left to right the inscriptions[115] are: (1) *revered by the Great God*; (2) *controller of the offering kiosk*; (3) *transactor of the King's business*.[116] It might be argued, therefore, that in this case the triple representation reflects three different aspects. One might also invoke the principle of more powerful perpetuation of the person, in line with the concept of three as indicating pluralism. Again, a possible idea is a reference to different periods of a person's life, an idea borne out by cases where the representations diverge a good deal. Duplication can, of course, be more easily disposed of, by recalling the principle of the *ka*; or by invoking the constant duality which marked the Egyptian concept of kingship. If it was objected that this would imply an unseemly arrogation of royal attributes, one might reply that even in the process of funerary identity with Osiris the privilege was eventually passed from the Pharaoh to his people. A more valid objection to this idea[117] is that the Pharaoh himself did not often indulge in a duplication of statues in this manner, although the Fourth-Dynasty Queen Mertitefes appears twice in a group at Leiden (D. 125).[118]

Jean Capart once referred to these groups as 'pseudo-groupes'.[119] Perhaps 'tautological groups' would be a better term, since there is no conscious or unconscious denial of reality. In a valuable study devoted to this theme, Charles Boreux[120] includes triadic instances. Analogous to the group at Leiden[121] in which Queen Mertitefes, a spouse successively of Snefru and Kheops, appears twice side by side with a naked young male called Khenu, is the group at Copenhagen,[122] in which two seated male figures represent the same person, called Ieti-sen. The name Khenu[123] seems to mean 'porter' or the like, and one wonders whether a personal valet is figured in each group. In the case of Mertitefes, Capart suggested tentatively that the duality arose from the fact that she was the spouse of two Pharaohs.[124] Since such a reason is absent in other cases of duality, it is hardly acceptable in this case. Furthermore, the whole question of her identity in this group has been raised by W. S. Smith, who states that 'there has never been any reason to assign it to the famous Queen Merytyetes, the wife of Sneferuw', his strongest argument being that her titles are unsuitable for a queen.[125]

A distinction of youth and age is well urged by Boreux[126] in the case of Seden-maat, a Fifth-Dynasty group of two in which Borchardt wanted to see two different persons.[127] Yet the matter here must remain in doubt because of the likelihood that an inscription below the figure on the right has disappeared. Boreux finds the same principle operating in a triple statue from Sedment discovered by Petrie. Certainly these three Sixth-Dynasty statues in ebony form a clear instance of three stages of life being indicated, the youth, middle age, and the elderly state of Meryrê-hashetef being purposively portrayed.[128] A rare feature of these figures is their nudity. The advance in age is expressed facially rather than elsewhere, although the figures relating to the older phases are a little stouter and are shown carrying suitable attributes; also height increases with importance. Petrie advances two different explanations for the triple appearance.[129] He states that 'the figures are modelled of different ages, and this gave the choice of enjoying the freshness of youth, the vigour of maturity, or the dignity of age'. But he also states before this that 'the motive of having several statues of the deceased, as found in Old Kingdom tombs (for instance *Deshasheh*, xxx, xxxi)[130] was to ensure that there should be a dwelling for the *ka* in case one figure was injured'. It is the former explanation that is the more acceptable in the matter of triple representation; and it is not so much a choice of one life-phase that is implied so much as the reliving of the phases of the life that has just ended.[131] A possibility that complicates the idea a little is that the three statues may have been made by different sculptors and were therefore contemporary with the three ages.[132] Yet there must have been a planned purpose of portraying successive phases. A similar group was made for Mersuankh at Gîza;[133] in this case the figure representing youth is shown standing beside two seated figures who portray more mature stages; and three lines of inscriptions name Mersuankh. Here the standing youth reaches only the level of the two seated figures, the difference in age being expressed by a difference in size as well as in other ways.[134] A relation is also discernible between the real triads and those which are tautologous. The figure of a man accompanied by his wife and son will show them clasping each other as a token of affection. When two members of a tautologous triad do this, as in the case of Rê-wer (Cairo J. 66616, discussed above), this may seem highly illogical, but it clearly shows the influence of the family groups, however unthinkingly this pattern may be followed.[135]

In the Old Kingdom this idea was not applied to the King, only to private persons, and the reason for this distinction may be that the Pharaoh was represented in the sculpture of that age as in a state of ideal maturity, but with no suggestion of old age.[136] His identification with Osiris after death, as well as his divinity in life, were clearly inhibiting factors. Since private persons before long shared the privilege of the Pharaoh in being identified with Osiris, this may explain why they are no longer shown after the Old Kingdom in repetitive groups reflecting different ages. A paradox, however, then emerges. Occasionally the Pharaoh, after the Old Kingdom, is figured in such groups. Neferhotpe I of the Thirteenth Dynasty, in a group in a naos from Karnak, is shown twice.[137] Boreux[138] refers to the ten statues of Lisht[139] where the Pharaoh Sesostris I is shown with different facial expressions which may be due to the varying interpretations of different artists. From the reliefs which adorn the thrones of these statues it is clear that they have geographical affiliations – to Upper and Lower Egypt and to cities in these regions. Associations with the regions and the cities are assigned also to the gods represented, especially to Horus and Seth.[140] Probably five of the statues faced the south, and five the north. There seems to be no connection, therefore, with the triadic principle.

Gods do not appear to be treated in a comparable tautologous fashion as far as statuary is concerned, but the use of three Horuses in the royal titulary of Pepy I in the Old Kingdom may be a parallel.[141] The normal form of the titulary names one Horus only: the King in fact is called Horus. Sometimes two Horuses appear, and probably they refer to the theology of the 'Two Lands', Buto and Hieraconpolis being perhaps the Horus-centres implicated.[142] The three Horuses seem to imply plurality; there were many falcon-gods in Egypt, and with the supremacy of Horus they tended to be identified with him. A pan-Egyptian meaning accordingly emerges – 'all the Horus-gods throughout Egypt'.[143] One may compare the later use of the title 'Horus of Horuses' – applied, for example, to Horus of Edfu[144] and to Osiris.[145] In Spell 198 of the *Coffin Texts* (III, 119c–d) the deceased envisages himself as one of three falcon-gods who ascend to the sky.

An instance in sculpture where three probably denotes plurality is the group of three heads in red granite from Tanis; the group derives from the Middle Kingdom, and the assumption of plurality comes from the theme: they are the heads of Asiatic prisoners.[146]

6. Early Religious Texts

A triadic structure can be found in the Ennead of Heliopolis, which is described in the *Pyramid Texts* (1655a–b, *the Great Ennead of Gods which is in Heliopolis*) only by superficially explaining the nine as a multiple of three and ignoring the natural structure of four marital pairs headed by Atum. Whereas it can be shown that the Ennead sometimes exceeds the original nine, it by no means follows that this is because of a basic concept of plurality.[147] In the case of the 'Nine Bows' (*psdt pdwt*), which represent peoples or areas ruled by the Pharaoh,[148] the constituent units are often named, and sometimes they include Upper and Lower Egypt. Many specific lists of these people appear in the New Kingdom, and although their identity is much debated, especially in the case of the Hau-nebut, it is clear that a defined number of peoples is intended, referring usually to foreign enemies at a particular time.[149]

An allusion to the creative activity of Atum in Heliopolis occurs in Spell 80 of the *Coffin Texts*, and there is one strange expression in it which has been interpreted to refer to the change from monism to triadism. The deceased is speaking and he identifies himself with the principle of never-ending life:

> I am one who lives, lord of years, living for ever, lord of eternity, whom Atum, the eldest one, created in his glorious power when he engendered Shu and Tefenet in Heliopolis, when he was one and when he became three.
>
> (*CT* II, 39b–e)

For the last two clauses I have followed the interpretation which has won general acceptance. Černý, for instance (*Ancient Egyptian Religion*, 43), paraphrases the clauses thus: 'With Show and Tfenet, Atum becomes all three, all being of one substance, a transcendental conception which reminds one very much of the controversy among Christians of the fourth and fifth centuries concerning the relation and precedence of the three Persons of the Trinity.' It is not often that Černý gave himself to flights of fancy, but he did so on this occasion, for there is nothing in the Egyptian about 'all being of one substance';[150] perhaps Černý was pursuing the doctrine that Atum had created Shu and Tefenet by the process of masturbation, an episode which is described simply and plainly in the *Pyramid Texts* (1248a–d).

The last two of the clauses are rather difficult, for ⟨hieroglyphs⟩ has been rendered by Faulkner[151] very differently: *when he was alone in his existence, without me*. He takes *m-ḥmt-i* as the prepositional phrase meaning 'in the absence of, without',[152] and the spellings sometimes converge with that of *ḥmt*, 'three'.[153] The pronoun in *without me* will refer to the deceased. Of the three readings recorded by De Buck two (B1C and B2L) support this rendering, but the third (B1P) gives a plural sign which supports the meaning 'three'.[154] Perhaps the latter meaning is favoured by taking the two clauses *m wn.f* and *m ḫpr.f* as balancing one another, 'when he was...' and 'when he became...'; certainly a comparable antithesis arises from 'alone' and 'three'. The context portrays Atum as the original being who is self-begotten and creates the other gods; and in the reading of B1P the meaning presented is that in creating Shu and Tefenet he has produced a divine triad which is a family unit, but one of a very rare kind, consisting of father, son and daughter. More precisely, the father is regarded as a bisexual being, as the reference of the double pronoun 'He-She' shows (*CT* II, 161a); and it is noteworthy that the triad consists of a monad conjoined to a dyad, the latter consisting of a marital pair.[155] It is doubtless the triad of Atum, Shu, and Tefenet that is referred to in the *Coffin Texts* (II, 146b, P. Gard. II), where the deceased says that he has come *among the three of Shu*; or perhaps it is *as the third of Shu*, in which case Shu and Tefenet are the other two. Other texts state that his *fourth is Shu*, the deceased being presumably added to the triad.[156]

A description of the birth of Horus-Sopd in the *Pyramid Texts* depicts the more normal way in which a family of three is achieved, even when it is divine. Osiris is probably being addressed:

> Thy sister Isis has come to thee, joyous through love of thee. Thou hast placed her upon thy phallus. Thy seed comes forth into her, so that she is equipped as Sothis. It is Horus-Sopd who comes forth from thee as Horus who is in Sothis.
> (*Pyr.* 632a–d, TPMN; cf. 1635a–1636b, MN)[157]

If Osiris is addressed in the *Pyramid Texts* 965a, PMN, then Sothis is his *beloved daughter*, who is given the name of Year; but her relationship to both Osiris and the King is not consistently presented.[158] Sometimes the King, Orion and Sothis are regarded as forming a triad, as when it is said of the King and Orion, *Your third is Sothis, pure of thrones* (*Pyr.* 822a, PMN);[159] the King is also grouped with Nut and Sothis (*Pyr.* 1082a–d, PMN). Their exact relationship is not, however, clear. Sometimes they appear as two brothers with Sothis as sister, but at other times Sothis has the King as her son.[160]

A triadic schema emerges in parts of the *Pyramid Texts* where Horus and Seth are said to co-operate for the benefit of the King or of Osiris–King. A few instances may be selected:[161]

> Horus and Seth take hold of the King's arm, they conduct him to Dat.
> (*Pyr.* 390b, WN)
> Stand, O King, says Horus. Sit, O King, says Seth. Take his arm, says Rê.
> (*Pyr.* 473b–c, WN)

In the latter instances Rê may be regarded as addressing the two other gods, so that the triad in which the King or Osiris–King is flanked by Horus and Seth is again present. One naturally recalls the representations in which these two gods, as well as others, are shown purifying the King.[162] Their representation in reliefs showing the union of the Two Lands also completes a triadic schema, since the King is symbolized in the centre by his cartouche.[163]

According to a statement at the end of an utterance the King belongs to a group of three:

> The King is the third when he appears in glory.
> (*Pyr.* 514e, W)

Before this we are told that the King *has built the city of the god as it should be built* (d) and that he *has united the heavens and has power over the southern and northern lands and over the gods of the primal age* (b–c). By the expression *the third* is meant the idea that the King completes a group of three.[164] Sethe takes the verb ḫʿi (514e) as referring to the King's accession to the throne as King of Heaven, and he compares *the King appears in glory as Sobek son of Neïth* (510a, W) – a wider sense in fact.[165] The context, however, seems to include the sovereignty of Egypt with that of the heavens (see especially b–c). In his earthly sovereignty Horus and Seth or Horus and Thoth are sometimes ritual companions of the King; and Faulkner (p.101) believes that these gods make up the triad; and he refers to Gardiner's article on the 'Baptism of Pharaoh' (*JEA* 36, 1950, 3ff,). But, if the emphasis is on the King's heavenly sovereignty, then Orion and Sothis will qualify as well, as Sethe remarks.

Sometimes the support envisaged for the deceased King is bestowed by deities who are related through Osiris, but without any triadic suggestion, unless the King is excluded from the group:

> Isis nurses him (the King), Nephthys gives him suck, Horus receives him beside him.
> (*Pyr.* 371c–372a, WN: N has *Horus receives him, may he live for ever*)

In another utterance Atum joins the helping group as the father who guides:

> The King goes up on the thighs of Isis, this King ascends on the thighs of Nephthys, his father Atum grasps the King's hand for him.
> (*Pyr.* 379c–380a, WPM; P adds *n ʿnḫ, of life* or *for life*)

These words accompany the ascent of incense.

Other gods may accompany the King in such a group, as when his ascent to heaven is thus described:

> This King goes to the heaven, this King goes to the heaven with Shu and Rê.
> (*Pyr.* 313c, T)

When the King is said to be on the throne of Geb, his father Geb is pleased with him according to a recitation assigned to Nut, who is the wife of Geb (*Pyr.* 2a–3a, T). Here the triad is therefore a family group. Geb is the father of Osiris in the Heliopolitan Ennead, and so can be the father of Osiris-King. If Atum is named as the King's father, that implies an extended use of the term; indeed the extended family may also be implicated, for which Detlef Franke has found ample evidence in the Middle Kingdom: see his *Altägyptische Verwandtschaftsbezeichnungen im Mittleren Reich* (1983), 204ff.

A triple grouping of gods occurs in allusions to the mounds or villages of Horus, Seth, and Osiris (*Pyr.* 218d–f, WTMN; 222b–c, N); here the first two gods probably cover the land of Egypt, whereas Osiris has reference to the realm of the dead, a distinction borne out once by the inclusion of Iaru instead of Osiris (*Pyr.* 487a–c, WN), the Field of Rushes assigned to Iaru being envisaged as a celestial region. Another triad of divine beings who are regarded as being helped by the deceased King are the messengers of Horus, Seth and Thoth; the King is said to bring to Horus his eye, to Seth his testicles, and to Thoth his arm (*Pyr.* 535a–c, TN),[166] the reference being to the parts of these gods' bodies which were mutilated in the conflict of Horus and Seth. Doubtless the idea is that the King will similarly benefit, if necessary, on the principle of reciprocity. The King is once apparently presented to a triad of goddesses (*Pyr.* 556a, TMN) called Isis, Asbet, and Nephthys; the second of these is not of frequent occurrence: in P. Bremner-Rhind 22, 22 (ed. Faulkner) there is mention of the flame of Asbyt who has power over fire;[167] while in P. Salt, 10, 1 (ed. Derchain) her name follows that of *Rekḥet*, 'Flame', treated as a goddess. Derchain[168] describes Asbyt as an epithet of Isis, but in the Pyramid locus she is clearly an independent goddess. Here follows, after *This is the King, O Isis, this is the King, O Asbet, this is the King, O Nephthys*, an injunction in the feminine singular:

> Come thou, that thou mayest see thy son.
>
> (*Pyr.* 556b, TMN)

Faulkner[169] suggests that 'the three goddesses are regarded as one', in which case it would be the first instance in Egyptian literature of the triune concept. It is more likely, however, that Isis, the first-named of the group, is meant here, since the living King, as Horus, is her son.[170]

When we are told that the King traverses the heaven with Orion and the underworld with Osiris (*Pyr.* 882c, PM), the spatial division prevents a grouping of three; what is envisaged is a pair in heaven and a pair in the underworld. But a clear pictorial image of a triad emerges in another utterance:

> Isis has thine arm, O Osiris, Nephthys has thine hand.
> Go thou between them.
>
> (*Pyr.* 960c, PMN; cf. 1004d, PMN)

It is remarkable that the picture corresponds to triads in statuary that was evolved much later. Isis, Osiris, and Nephthys appear in a group sculptured in black granite during the Thirtieth Dynasty;[171] and in a similar group of the Saïte era, but in bronze, Isis and Nephthys are shown placing their hands on the shoulders of Osiris.[172] In relation to Osiris the two sisters Isis and Nephthys are, of course, the weeping mourners or kites, and their function is described in the *Pyramid Texts* (1280a ff., P).[173]

An allusion to the birth of Horus in Khemmis foreshadows the foremost of the Osirian triads: it refers to *Isis the Great* and to *Horus the young child*, who is to go to see *his father Osiris* (*Pyr.* 1214b–1215b, PMN). On the whole, however, the group is not given prominence in the *Pyramid Texts*.[174]

A triad headed by Thoth is apparently mentioned in Spell 277 of the *Coffin Texts*:

> Becoming Thoth. I have sat with (*m*; var. *ḥr*, 'on', perhaps in a judicial sense) the Eye of Horus as head of the Three Gods who give commands among the gods in the affairs of Thoth.
>
> (*CT* IV, 18a–c)

Faulkner[175] compares the epithet used of the sun-god, *Soul (ba) of the Three*, citing *Wb.* III, 283, 12 (= Naville, *BD* 64, 11).[176] A tetrad of judging deities might consist of Thoth, Khons, Rê, and Iesdes; they are mentioned as such in *Lebensmüde*, 23ff.[177] This would suggest that the allusion in the *Coffin Texts* concerns also a triad presided over by Thoth. One might compare a passage in the *Book of the Dead*, 18 (ed. Naville, 23–4), where Thoth, Osiris, Anubis and Iesdes are named as members of the *Djadjat* or tribunal which judges the dead. However, other passages of the spell name other deities, and their number also varies. Nor do the gods associated with Thoth enable us to establish clearly who constituted a triad including him or supervised by him.[178] In one sense he belongs mythically to the group of fighting gods, Horus and Seth, since he judges between them and reconciles them.[179]

A spell in the *Coffin Texts* (160) contains an interesting application of the triadic concept to the world of the dead. Among the aims of the spell is *knowing the souls of the West* (var. *of the Westerners*) and it concludes with an allusion to the triad which constitutes this group:

> I know the souls of the West (*var.* Westerners). They are Rê (*var.* Atum), Sobek, Lord of Bakhu, Hathor, Mistress of the Evening.
>
> (*CT* II, 386d–387a. S2P ends with *Seth, Lord of Life*. Cf. *BD* ed. Naville, 108, 15)

In the later versions found in the *Book of the Dead* there are also vignettes showing these deities, but it is noteworthy that Hathor and not Seth is represented as the third.[180] Here is, of course, a good instance of Seth in a beneficent role; far from being here a 'god of confusion' he is a protagonist of Rê in the fight against the forces of confusion as embodied in Apopis, and in fact is mentioned previously in the spell as carrying out this action on behalf of the sun-god.[181] The triad does not appear to have established itself outside this funerary context, and its main emphasis is clearly on Rê, his victory over Apopis becoming symbolical of the triumph of life over death as it does in such works as the *Book of Amduat*.

A parallel group is mentioned in connection with the 'Souls of the Easterners':

> I know the souls of the Easterners (*var.* of the East). They are Harakhty, the calf of Khwrer, and the Morning Star.
>
> (*CT* II, 371b–372a, cf. *BD*, ed. Naville, 109, 10–11)

The identity of the second god named is not clear, nor do the vignettes help very much, although a calf is depicted as one of the group. It is a celestial region that is implied by the East here, and, in view of the parallelism with the spell previously cited, it is likely that the West also, though more frequently used of the earthly realm of the dead, here refers to a region of heaven.[182]

Since the *Coffin Texts* do not relate to Kings or Queens, they do not contain the triadic groupings in which the King is in the company of two deities, such as the *Pyramid Texts* often portray. They share, none the less, with those texts the basic funerary belief that the deceased is associated or identified with Osiris and that his son plays the dutiful part of Horus, who is also the *pillar of his mother*. This relationship is a part of the strong emphasis on the family which finds expression in the *Coffin Texts* and which was evidently potent in the development of the triad as a family grouping. Two groups of spells (II, 131–46) seek to ensure the reunion of a family in the afterworld: one (II, 131–5) proclaims that the reunion is effected by divine decree, as in Spell 131:

> Geb, foremost of the gods, has decreed that there be given back to me my family and my children, my brothers and sisters, my father, my mother, and all my servants and my dependants.
>
> (*CT* II, 151c–d)

A good early definition, incidentally, of the Egyptian extended family.[183] In the second group of spells (II, 136–46) the gods are threatened if they do not secure this reunion with the family. Spell 146 is particularly expansive, for a man's family (*3bt*) is here said to include his father and mother, children, brothers and sisters, loved ones, friends, associates and servants who worked for him on earth, and also the concubines whom he has known. If there be delay in allowing the reunion of these with the deceased, Rê shall be impeded and sumptuous offerings taken away from the altars of the gods; but, if the request is granted, Rê's barque shall be facilitated and all offerings abundantly resumed.

Close relatives, at the same time, are given priority, and that is true also of the triads based on the family. We have seen that a fondness for triadic groupings often appears in early statuary, although the constituent elements vary considerably. In the literature such groupings may derive from a background in myth or cult, and they rarely adumbrate, with the exception of the Osirian groups, a triad that eventually becomes frequent and established. Nor does the funerary literature outside the *Pyramid Texts* and *Coffin Texts* provide clear preferences of this kind, as is apparent from a valuable survey of the private tombs of the Fourth and Fifth Dynasties.[184] In the offering formula Anubis is the only god who appears in the Fourth Dynasty, but afterwards he is joined by Osiris and Khentamenthes as well as other gods;[185] no fixed triad, however, emerges.

NOTES

[1] Cf. H. te Velde, 'The Structure of Egyptian Divine Triads', *JEA* 57 (1971), 80–6. On the present prehistoric theme, cf. J. Gwyn Griffiths in *Actes du Symposium International sur les Religions de la Préhistoire* (Capo di Ponte, 1975), 317–22.

[2] In. G. Posener, *Dict. of Egyptian Civilization* (London, 1962), 290.

[3] See E. J. Baumgartel, *Cultures of Prehistoric Egypt*, II (London, 1960), 145ff. with Pl.13.

[4] Cf. ibid. I, 13, and Petrie, *Royal Tombs*, I, Pl.17, 26 (ivory tablet of Semerkhet of the First Dynasty) (= W. B. Emery, *Archaic Egypt* (Harmondsworth, 1961), 86, Fig. 49).

[5] Cf. J. Settgast, *Untersuchungen zu altägyptischen Bestattungsdarstellungen* (Glückstadt, 1963), Pl.6.

[6] *Egyptian Grammar* (3rd edn., Oxford, 1957), 500, Q3.

[7] Op. cit. II, 146.

[8] It ends in small rings, which Dr Baumgartel compares with a sign in Quibell, *Hierakonpolis*, I (London, 1900), Pl.38 (granite vase). It occurs also below in a simpler form (alabaster vase). Cf. Emery, *Archaic Egypt*, 100, Fig.63.

[9] I owe this suggestion to my wife, Dr Kate Bosse-Griffiths.

[10] W. Westendorf, *Painting, Sculpture and Architecture of Ancient Egypt* (New York, 1968), 13. See also the vase reproduced by him on p.14.

[11] *Anthropomorphic Figurines*, Royal Anthropological Institute Occasional Paper No.24 (London, 1968). See esp. p.428.

[12] For other predynastic occurrences of falcons see J. Gwyn Griffiths, *The Conflict of Horus and Seth* (Liverpool, 1960), 132–3; J. Vandier, *Manuel d'archéologie égyptienne*, I, 1. *La préhistoire* (Paris, 1952), 340ff.

[13] R. O. Faulkner, *The Plural and Dual in Old Egyptian* (Brussels, 1929), 8; E. Edel, *Altägyptische Grammatik* (Rome, 1955–64), 115ff. For a case of 'three' being replaced by ʿš3, 'many', see P. Kaplony, *MIO* 11 (1966), 161 n.91; cf. E. Hornung (tr. Baines), *Conceptions of God in Ancient Egypt* (London, 1983), 218–19.

[14] *Wb.* III, 283; Edel, *Altägyptische Gr.*, 168–9, § 392.

[15] Gardiner, *Egn. Gr.*, 456, D 52.

[16] *Wb.* ibid.

[17] Edel, op. cit., 170, § 394.

[18] Sethe, *Von Zahlen und Zahlworten bei den alten Ägyptern* (Strasbourg, 1916), 18–19. He remarks on p.19 that the feminine form of the cardinal may have been thought of as a collective.

[19] *Egn. Gr.*, 192, § 260. Cf. G. Lefebvre, *Grammaire de l'égyptien classique*

(Cairo, 1940), 108, § 204 (including other formations).

[20] Edel, op. cit., 176, § 404.

[21] Cf. C. E. Sander-Hansen, *Studien zur Grammatik der Pyramidentexte* (Copenhagen, 1956), 34, § 103.

[22] *The Ancient Egyptian Pyramid Texts*, 37-8.

[23] In his *Ägyptische Grammatik* (Wiesbaden, 1963), 65, Sander-Hansen treats the collective abstracts as extended usages of the independent numeral.

[24] Sethe, *ZÄS* 47 (1910), 9-10. Cf. D. Kurth, *Den Himmel stützen* (Brussels, 1975).

[25] *Wb.* III, 282, 13.

[26] *Pyr.* 746c; cf. Sethe, *Von Zahlen*, 9, § 17.

[27] Sethe, *Amun und die acht Urgötter von Hermopolis* (Abh. Berlin, 1929), 43, § 83, a postulated form; cf. p.44, § 86 (a writing in the Twenty-fifth Dynasty).

[28] *Wb.* III, 283, 3.

[29] Sethe, *Amun*, 36ff. §§ 65ff.

[30] *Von Zahlen*, 37f.

[31] Tr. by F. Ll. Griffith and Herbert Thompson (London, 1904), 67.

[32] See H. von Deines and Westendorf, *Wb. der medizinischen Texte* (1962), s.v. ḥmt, p.658. Cf. p.569 s.v. hrw.

[33] Cf. P. Ebers, 248; 249, 250, 314; 449; 777, all ending with *on four days*; and 384, where one is told to wash the two eyes with *this milk four times every day*. See further *Wb. der med. Texte*, s.v. *fdw*, pp.309-10 and also s.v. *hrw*, pp.569-70, where 'four' far exceeds the other numbers in use.

[34] Ibid. 739.

[35] *Von Zahlen*, 37-8.

[36] *RÄRG*, 873.

[37] *Götterglaube*², 158.

[38] Op. cit., 31.

[39] See E. Hornung and E. Staehelin, *Studien zum Sedfest* (Aegyptiaca Helvetica, 1, Geneva, 1974), 51ff.

[40] *Von Zahlen*, 31f.

[41] Cf. Ph. Derchain, *Hathor Quadrifrons* (Istanbul, 1972).

[42] *Von Zahlen*, 33-7.

[43] Cf. Kees, *Götterglaube*², 158f.

[44] *Von Zahlen*, 38-9.

[45] Op. cit., 158. Cf. J. Gwyn Griffiths, *Orientalia* 28 (1959), 38.

[46] Petrie, *Ceremonial Slate Palettes* (London, 1953), 13 and Pls.B 8, C 9. Cf. 'The Two Dog Palette', ibid., 13 and Pl.F 15-16; Vandier, *Manuel*, I (1952), 579ff.

[47] Petrie, op. cit. 17 and Pl.K 26; Vandier, *Manuel*, I, 595ff.

[48] *The Cultures of Prehistoric Egypt*, II, 95; 104 (quoted).

[49] H. Frankfort, *Cylinder Seals* (London, 1939; repr. 1965), 205: 'Throughout Palestine, Syria, Mesopotamia and Persia, and at all times, a simple antithetical group of animals flanking a plant is known...' Cf. Anton Moortgat, *Die Kunst des alten Mesopotamien* (Cologne, 1967), 50, Fig.34.

[50] J. Gwyn Griffiths, *The Conflict of Horus and Seth*, 138.

[51] Ibid. 69ff.; J.-E. Gautier and G. Jéquier, *Fouilles de Licht* (MIFAO 6; Cairo, 1902), 35-7; cf. W. Wolf, *Die Kunst Aegyptens* (Stuttgart, 1957), 367, Fig.312.

[52] Gardiner, *JEA* 36 (1950), 3-12; Gwyn Griffiths, op. cit., 123ff. The protagonists vary. For the deceased being purified see F. Daumas, *La Civilisation de l'Égypte pharaonique* (Paris, 1965), Pl.107 (a chantress of Amûn).

[53] Eberhard Otto, 'Die Lehre von den beiden Ländern Ägyptens in der ägyptischen Religionsgeschichte', *An. Or.* 17 (1938), 10–35.

[54] Bonnet, *RÄRG.* 755, Fig.179; E. Otto, op. cit., 12.

[55] Gwyn Griffiths, *JEA* 47 (1961), 116ff.; Ebba Kern Lillesø, ibid., 61 (1975), 137ff.

[56] Cf. Werner Kaiser, *ZÄS* 91 (1964), 117ff.

[57] *Kingship and the Gods* (Chicago, 1948), 21.

[58] Both from Saqqâra and in the Cairo Museum. Other subsidiary figures, such as bearers of offerings, appear with them. Cf. too the Old-Kingdom stela of Nykawrê, also from Saqqâra.

[59] In one case (the group which bears the number 48076) the man's wife places her right hand on his right shoulder.

[60] Though separate, they form a group. Cf. W. S. Smith, *A History of Egyptian Sculpture and Painting in the Old Kingdom* (Oxford, 1946), 21; idem, *The Art and Architecture of Ancient Egypt* (Harmondsworth, 1958), 47; Vandier, *Manuel*, III, 42f.

[61] See Borchardt, *Statuen*, I, nos.6, 89, 95, 107, 123, 158.

[62] Ibid. I, nos. 22, 55, 100, 105, 125, 151.

[63] A good example ibid. I, no. 101 (Fifth Dynasty, from Saqqâra), where the mother occupies the central position.

[64] Ibid. I, nos. 133, 165, 168.

[65] Ibid. I, 150.

[66] Ibid. I, 219. The phenomenon occurs, of course, elsewhere. Cf. Dows Dunham and William Kelly Simpson, *The Mastaba of Queen Mersyankh III* (Boston, 1974), 20; also Selim Hassan, *Excavations at Gîza 1929–30* (Oxford, 1932), 115 and Pl.72.

[67] Borchardt, *Das Grabdenkmal des Königs S3ḥu-reʿ*, II (Leipzig, 1913), 35f. and Pl.18.

[68] Ibid., 36.

[69] In his *Das Grabdenkmal des Königs Ne-user-reʿ* (Leipzig, 1907), 40f. Borchardt reproduces a relief of Sakhmet in this activity.

[70] See his *Mycerinus: The Temples of the Third Pyramid at Giza* (Cambridge, Mass., 1931), 34–54 and 108–15 with Pls.36–46.

[71] *JEA* 60 (1974), 82–93 with Pls.23–5.

[72] For the inscription see Reisner, *Mycerinus*, Pl.46b and p.110. There are only minor differences from his translation.

[73] 'Bull of the Ennead'. See Drioton, *ASAE* 45 (1945), 53–4.

[74] Reisner, op. cit., Pl.46a and p.109.

[75] *The Pyramids of Egypt* (rev. edn., London, 1961), 123f.

[76] Cf. W. Wolf, *Die Kunst Aegyptens*, 148.

[77] See H. Ricke, *Beiträge zur ägyptischen Bauforschung und Altertumskunde*, 4 (Zurich, 1944), 84ff. Cf. Edwards, op. cit., 41ff.; Jean-Philippe Lauer, *Saqqara* (London, 1976), 133ff.

[78] Edwards, op. cit., 45. That the origins of the *Heb-sed* Festival predate Mycerinus is shown by E. Hornung and E. Staehelin, *Studien zum Sedfest* (1974), 16ff.; cf. A. M. Blackman, *Studia Aegyptiaca*, I (1938), 4–9.

[79] E. Otto, *Studia Aegyptiaca*, I (1938), 27f. Nile-gods (or fertility gods, as they can more properly be termed) are shown with nome-deities in the sun-sanctuary of Ne-user-rê: see E. Edel and S. Wenig, *Die Jahreszeiten reliefs aus dem Sonnenheiligtum des Königs Ne-user-re* (Berlin, 1974), Pls. 4–7. See further John Baines, *Fecundity Figures* (Warminster, 1985), 97–8.

[80] Op. cit., 83-5.

[81] With the suggestion that this was then the number of nomes. The exact number at the time of Mycerinus is not known, but even by the time of Sesostris I there were apparently not more than thirty-six. See W. Helck, *Die altägyptischen Gaue* (Wiesbaden, 1974), 11f. and 199f.

[82] Admitted by the author on p.93 and not effectively condoned by the remarks on the geographical affinities of the materials used.

[83] Wendy Wood, op. cit., 87, following evidence adduced by H. G. Fischer in his *Dendera in the Third Millennium BC* (New York, 1968).

[84] Cf. Faulkner, *Pyramid Texts*, 93.

[85] *Dendera in the Third Millennium BC.*, 37ff. On p.38 he talks of 'the types that claim descent from Hathor of Dendera', thereby opting for the vaguer kind of relationship.

[86] In my *Conflict of Horus and Seth*, 13, I expressed a degree of doubt, querying whether 'son' in the *Pyr.* passage might mean 'descendant'. I now consider that the supporting evidence removes this doubt, including the texts there cited.

[87] Petrie, *Ceremonial Slate Palettes*, Pl.J 25; more clearly in Schafik Allam, *Beiträge zum Hathorkult (bis zum Ende des Mittleren Reiches)*, MÄS 4 (Berlin, 1963), Pl.II.

[88] *Hieroglyphen* (Abh. Mainz, 1950; Wiesbaden, 1951), 23 n.2. In his *Mythe und Mythenbildung im alten Ägypten* (Unters. 15, Leipzig, 1945), 16, Schott refers to early attempts to associate Hathor as a goddess of heaven with the sun-god Rê; this, he says, did not occur in Heliopolis, where the goddess of heaven was Nut, but elsewhere Hathor becomes the partner of Atum, and Schott finds in this association with the sun-cult the main factor which impelled Mycerinus to portray Hathor, in his triads, as his protecting goddess. Schott also notes that in the Fifth Dynasty Rê and Hathor are associated in a general way, without reference to particular cult-centres.

[89] Thus too Petrie in his note on this ivory cylinder, op. cit., 7; also Quibell on p.37 of Vol.II (London, 1902), who notes that the 'protecting vulture' is faced by the 'hawk deity of Nekhen' – the Horus-falcon.

[90] Cf. H. Altenmüller, *Die Apotropaia und die Götter Mittelägyptens* (Diss., Munich, 1965), 82ff.

[91] Cf. C. J. Bleeker, *Hathor and Thoth* (Leiden, 1973), 32f.

[92] *Beiträge zum Hathorkult*, 129f.

[93] See Firth and Quibell, *The Step Pyramid*, II (Cairo, 1935), Pl.59; cf. I, 66.

[94] One of the less prominent crowns, consisting of a double feather (*Šwty*) with cow and ram horns; see Abubakr, *Untersuchungen über die ägyptischen Kronen* (Glückstadt, 1937), 40-3.

[95] See Drioton in *Mélanges Mariette* (1961), 173-5; cf. my *Plutarch's De Iside et Osiride*, 267-8.

[96] Cf. Allam, op. cit., 11-12, though he does not stress the relationship. Bernard V. Bothmer, in a fine study of the Boston triad, 'Notes on the Mycerinus Triad', *BMFA* 48 (1950), 10-17, remarks on the gesture of Hathor towards the King, that it was common in the Old Kingdom, to show the relationship between wife and husband and between parent and child; cf. his phrase on p.15, 'her motherly gesture'.

[97] Cf. the remarks of Bothmer, ibid., 10, on this goddess in the Boston triad: 'the beautiful figure of a fully developed girl ...'

[98] Cf. E. L. B. Terrace in Terrace and Fischer, *Treasures of the Cairo Museum* (London, 1970), 45-6.

[99] Cf. my remarks above and Vandier, *Manuel*, III, 22; Terrace, op. cit., 48; Cyril Aldred, *Egypt to the End of the Old Kingdom* (London, 1965), 113. Allam thinks that only the nomes with a cult of Hathor are intended; cf. the view of Wendy Wood, cited above.

[100] Op. cit., 16.

[101] Four figures were there sculptured. See Firth and Quibell, *The Step Pyramid*, II, Pl.63 ('Feet of Four Statues').

[102] Bothmer op. cit., 17. Aldred, loc. cit. finds a resemblance only in the goddesses: 'The goddesses have the features of the queen as is usual in Egypt.'

[103] Cf. Hans-Wolfgang Müller, *Ägyptische Kunst* (Frankfurt am Main, 1970), xv, no.29, of Hathor: 'Als mütterliche Göttin geleitet sie den wieder Erstandenen in das himmlische Reich.'

[104] See C. S. Fisher in *BMFA* 11 (1913), 21.

[105] Selim Hassan, *Excavations at Gîza 1929–30* (Oxford, 1932), 7f. with Fig.5 and Pl.4. A man's wife can of course be shown as the mother of his child or children as in the triad from Saqqâra (Fifth Dynasty) representing a man with his wife and son, the wife-mother being in the centre: see Borchardt, *Statuen*, I, 79–80, no.101, with Pl.23; Hornemann, *Types*, V, 1376. There is an example from the Middle Kingdom (University College London, 16650) of a woman, Iaket, figured as the dominant central person of a triad, with her husband, Khentekhtaihotpe, on her left, and their son, Kashu, on her right: see Hornemann, *Types*, V, 1373, and Anthea Page, *Egyptian Sculpture, Archaic to Saite, from the Petrie Collection* (Warminster, 1976), 21–2, no. 23. Other triadic groups of the MK are given by Steindorff, *Cat. of the Egyptian Sculpture in the Walters Art Gallery* (Baltimore, 1946), Pl.12, but he questions the genuineness of no.52. Family groupings naturally vary; thus whereas Mersuankh in one group is with his wife, in another he is with his two daughters: see S. Hassan, op. cit., Pls.73 and 74.

[106] Hornemann, *Types*, V, 1360; cf. *BMFA* 5 (1907), 21.

[107] Op. cit., 21 with Pl.22; Hornemann, *Types*, V, 1361; Porter-Moss-Málek, *Top. Bibl.* III², i, 268.

[108] Several others of this name are known: see Porter-Moss-Málek, *Top. bibl.* III², i, Index of Private Names.

[109] S. Hassan, op. cit., 12–13 with Pls.8, 1 and 9; Hornemann, *Types*, V, 1364.

[110] *Types*, VI, 1476; cf. Porter-Moss-Málek, *Top. Bibl.* III², i, 83; C. S. Fisher, *BMFA* 11 (1913), 20.

[111] *A Hist. of Egyptian Sculpture and Painting in the Old Kingdom*, 53 with Pl.21d.

[112] Hornemann, *Types*, V, 1363; W. S. Smith, op. cit., Pl.21c.

[113] Ibid.

[114] Cf. Porter-Moss-Málek, ibid.

[115] The readings are taken from W. S. Smith, op. cit.

[116] On this title (*irì-ḥt-nswt*) see B. Gunn in *Teti Pyramid Cemeteries* (Cairo, 1926), 157 ('Concerned with the King's Affairs'); W. Helck, *Beamtentitel* (1954), 26–8; Klaus Baer, *Rank and Title in the Old Kingdom* (Chicago, 1960), 164. Fischer, *Dendera*, 10, translates tentatively 'concerned with the king's property'; cf. his discussion on pp.69–71.

[117] Cf. Charles Boreux, *Guide-Catalogue Sommaire* (Louvre, Paris, 1932), 240. The examples he cites are of the duplication of royal objects or attributes.

[118] Jean Capart, *Recueil de monuments égyptiens* (Brussels, 1902), Pl.4.

[119] *L'Art égyptien. Études et Histoire*, I (Brussels, 1924), 221–2. Cf. the definition

of research ascribed to a character in *Lucky Jim* by Kingsley Amis: 'the shedding of pseudo-light on non-problems'.

[120] 'Quelques remarques sur les "pseudo-groupes" égyptiens', *Mélanges Maspero* (Cairo, 1935-8), I, ii, 805-15.

[121] D 125, from Gîza. See Capart, *Recueil de monuments égyptiens*, Pl.4 and description; cf. Petrie, *A Hist. of Egypt*, I[10] (London, 1923), 50 with Fig. 35; Boreux, op. cit., Pl.I, 2.

[122] A.a.b. 27. From Saqqâra, Old Kingdom. See Maria Mogensen, *Inscriptions hiéroglyphiques du musée national de Copenhague* (Copenhagen, 1918), 1 with Pl.I.

[123] *Wb.* III, 286, 17 ('Sackträger'); Ranke, *PN* I, 270, 4, 'der Opferträger(?)', but a religious connotation seems unnecessary.

[124] Loc. cit.

[125] *Hist. of Egyptian Sculpture and Painting*, 79. Cf. his remarks on Queen Meritites in *The Old Kingdom in Egypt* (*CAH*, 1965), 28-9.

[126] Op. cit., 807-8.

[127] *Statuen*, I, 99 (no.133) with Pl.30.

[128] See Petrie and Brunton, *Sedment*, I (London, 1924), 2-3 (Petrie) with Pls.7-10; further lit. in Porter-Moss, *Top. Bibl.* IV (1934), 115. The statue portraying the youth is in the BM: see *Introd. Guide* (1964), 216 with Fig.80 (p.217).

[129] Op. cit., 3.

[130] Petrie, *Deshasheh* (London, 1898), 14, says that there were seven stone statues of Nenkheftka (Fifth Dynasty) in his *serdab*, also two of his wife, and six of his son. Cf. S. Hassan, op. cit., 1, of the tomb of Rê-wer ('it may be inferred that there were once more than a hundred statues and statuettes of Rê-wer contained in the tomb').

[131] Cf. Boreux, *Mélanges Maspero*, I, ii, 809f.

[132] This was Petrie's view in *Sedment*, I, 2-3.

[133] Fifth Dynasty (Cairo J. 66618). See S. Hassan, op. cit., 114 with Pl.70; Boreux, op. cit., 811 n.5 with Pls.3, 5; Hornemann, *Types*, V, 1366; further lit. in Porter-Moss-Málek, *Top. Bibl.* III[2] (1974), 270.

[134] H. G. Evers, *Staat aus dem Stein*, II (Munich, 1929), 124 n.756, avers that this was not done in the Old and Middle Kingdoms; cf. W. Wolf, *Die Kunst Aegyptens*, 681 n.3 to section 59; both are discussing the triple statue from Sedment.

[135] Cf. Boreaux, op. cit., 811-13.

[136] Thus Boreux, ibid.

[137] Cairo Cat. 42022. See G. Legrain, *Statues et statuettes* (Cairo, 1906), 13 with Pl.13. The figures closely resemble one another, but Legrain, p. 14, wonders whether one is the son or brother of Neferhotpe. Statues and reliefs of Sesostris III often portray the King at a different age-phase: see Boreux, *Mons. Piot* 32 (1932), 3-20.

[138] Op. cit., 814.

[139] J.-E. Gautier and G. Jéquier, *Fouilles de Licht* (Cairo, 1902), 30-8 with Pls.9-14.

[140] Cf. Alan H. Gardiner, *JEA* 30 (1944), 25ff.; J. Gwyn Griffiths, *The Conflict of Horus and Seth* (1960), 69-70; cf. Wolf, *Kunst Aegyptens* (1957), 317f.

[141] H. Gauthier, *Livre des rois*, I, 146, no.V; 151, no.II; *Pyr.* 7a (P) and 786c (P); other instances in H. Müller, *Die formale Entwicklung der Titulatur der ägyptischen Könige* (Glückstadt, 1938), 60-1. Cf. J. von Beckerath, *Hdb. der ägyptischen Königsnamen*, 56.

[142] J. Gwyn Griffiths, 'Remarks on the Horian Elements in the Royal Titulary',

ASAE 56 (1959), 63-86, this point on pp. 83-4; other views are given by H. Müller, op. cit., 58.

[143] My remarks, ibid., 85. Cf. the use of three Horus-falcons in early forms of the funerary offering-lists: see Petrie, *Medum* (London, 1892), 24 with Pl.13 (= T. G. H. James, *British Museum: Hieroglyphic Texts from Egyptian Stelae*, I (2nd edn., London, 1961), 1, no.2 (1242) with Pl.1 (the tomb of Rê-hotep, Fourth Dynasty)); also W. Barta, *Die altägyptische Opferliste* (Berlin, 1963), 42 with Fig.3 (the tomb of Nefert-iabet, Fourth Dynasty). In other instances, however, there are more than three: see Barta, op. cit., Figs.1 and 2, and this Horus on a standard is often associated with the words *idmyt* and *idmy*, meaning types of linen of superior quality, perhaps, in origin, of sacral significance: see *Wb*. I, 153, 15-18; Junker, *Gîza*, I (1929), 177-8; W. S. Smith, *ZÄS* 71 (1935), 136-42. It follows that there is no triadic significance.

[144] Cf. Gerd Schäfer, 'König der Könige' – 'Lied der Lieder' (Abh. Heidelberg, 1974), 20.

[145] J. Gwyn Griffiths, *Class. Phil.* 48 (1953), 151, citing *BD* 36 (Ani), where Osiris is called *Lord of Lords, King of Kings, Horus of Horuses*.

[146] Borchardt, *Statuen*, II, 14, no.396 with Pl.65; Hornemann, *Types*, V, 1368a.

[147] *Pace* Barta, op. cit., 48-50.

[148] *Pyr.* 202b, WN; cf. J. Gwyn Griffiths, *Orientalia* 28 (1959), 37.

[149] See Eric Uphill, *JEOL* 6 (1967), 393-420.

[150] *Ancient Egyptian Religion* (London, 1952), 43; cf. R. T. Rundle Clark, *Myth and Symbol in Ancient Egypt* (London, 1959), 86.

[151] *Ancient Egyptian Coffin Texts* (hereafter *CT*), I, 85.

[152] Gardiner, *Egn. Gr.* 133, § 178.

[153] *Wb*. III, 280, 1.

[154] Cf. *Wb*. III, 265, 6 for *ḫpr m* giving a mathematical result.

[155] Cf. E. Otto, *Saeculum* 14 (1963), 274f. ('Altägyptischer Polytheismus: Eine Beschreibung').

[156] Cf. Faulkner, ad loc. I, 112.

[157] Cf. my *Origins of Osiris and his Cult*, 12; Faulkner, *Pyr.* 120.

[158] See Faulkner, *JNES* 25 (1966), 161.

[159] The expression consciously projects a triad; cf. *Pyr.* 363f, P: *He (the King) will be your third in Heliopolis* (or, *as a Heliopolitan*). The other two are Sothis his sister (cf. 363a, P) and Harakhty or Rê. Faulkner, however, p.76 n.6, omits Sothis.

[160] See the passages quoted by Faulkner, *JNES* 25 (1966), 158-9.

[161] For other examples see my *Conflict*, 23-5.

[162] See *JEA* 36 (1950), Pl.I with Gardiner's discussion; my *Conflict*, 123-4; Brigitte Altenmüller-Kesting, *Reinigungsriten im ägyptischen Kult* (Diss. Hamburg, 1968), 61ff., where it is stated, however, that Seth does not appear otherwise as helper of the dead King in the cult. She quotes other types of purification formulae on pp.47ff. in which Seth does figure.

[163] Cf. Bonnet, *Bilderatlas*, 35, with the cartouche of Sesostris I. For the King in the centre flanked by two deities, cf. the triads of Mycerinus.

[164] Sethe, *Komm*. II, 382.

[165] Cf. *Wb*. III, 239, 15; but many wider meanings are also indicated. Faulkner (p. 101) narrows the sense thus: *for the King is the third at his accession*. A. Piankoff, *The Pyramid of Unas* (Princeton, 1968), 19, renders, *Unas is the third when he appears*, but, as often, appends no note.

[166] Cf. my *Conflict*, 2. Faulkner, 105-6, offers a slightly different interpretation, but the main clause in the fuller text of N is beyond question: it means *The King brings to him his eye ... his testicles ... his arm*. The two texts differ in the opening clause.

[167] Cf. Faulkner, *JEA* 23 (1937), 176.

[168] *Le Papyrus Salt 825* (Brussels, 1965), 176 n.128.

[169] *Pyr.* 110 n.3.

[170] Sethe, *Komm.* III, 49f. thinks that the 2nd feminine singular is intended to address each one of the three goddesses singly. Cf. S. A. B. Mercer, *The Pyramid Texts*, II (New York, 1952), 269. Sethe invokes the use of the singular by the Greek chorus, but in these cases the Leader of the chorus may be involved.

[171] Daressy, *Statues*, 39220, Pl.58.

[172] Ibid. 39221, Pl.58. On triadic groups in bronze with Osiris and his family, see Roeder, *Bronzefiguren*, 490ff.

[173] Cf. in general M. Werbrouck, *Les Pleureuses dans l'Égypte ancienne* (Brussels, 1938).

[174] Cf. my *Conflict*, 15; *CT* III, 260e-g; and often in Osirian literature.

[175] *CT* 309 n. 2.

[176] T. G. Allen, *BD* 56, translates the contextual phrase as *thy light upon me, soul of three*.

[177] Cf. my *Conflict*, 80 n.3; W. Barta, *Das Gespräch eines Mannes mit seinem BA* (Berlin, 1969), 41; Hans Goedicke, *The Report about the Dispute of a Man with his Ba* (Baltimore, 1970), 103ff., where, however, Iesdes is denied a judicial role.

[178] Cf. P. Boylan, *Thoth the Hermes of Egypt* (Oxford, 1922), 201ff.; also M.-T. Derchain-Urtel, *Thot* (Brussels, 1981), 88, on Thoth as *the heart of Rê*, though mainly in relation to cosmic creation. She deals with Thoth's function as a judge on pp.95ff. under the title *T3j-tj-s3b*, pointing above all to his role in civic life; on p.105 she cites A.-P. Zivie, *Hermopolis et le Nome de l'Ibis* (Cairo, 1975), who refers to Thoth as 'Separator of the Two Rivals' on pp.225 and 227.

[179] Cf. Boylan, *Thoth*, 44ff.; my *Conflict*, 82.

[180] See Naville, loc. cit.; also P. Barguet, *Le Livre des morts* (Paris, 1967), 142. Faulkner, *CT* I, 139, gives precedence to the text that mentions Seth.

[181] Cf. Sethe, *ZÄS* 59 (1924), 99.

[182] Cf. ibid., 1.

[183] For the deep family bond thus revealed, see further Jan Zandee, *Death as an Enemy* (Leiden, 1960), 66, and esp. M. Heerma van Voss, 'Hereniging in het hiernamaals volgens Egyptisch geloof', *Pro Regno Pro Sanctuario (Fs. G. van der Leeuw)* (Nijkerk, 1950), 227-32; also Faulkner, *CT*, I, 113f.

[184] Barbara L. Begelsbacher-Fischer, *Untersuchungen zur Götterwelt des alten Reiches* (OBO, 37; Fribourg, 1981); cf. my appreciation in *JEA* 71 (1985), 30-1. She discusses the 'Hathor-triads' of Mycerinus on pp.57f. and 70.

[185] W. Barta, *Aufbau und Bedeutung der altägyptischen Opferformel* (Ägyptologische Forschungen, 24; Glückstadt, 1968), 8, 15, 25. Cf. Begelsbacher-Fischer, op. cit. 256.

2

The Developed Egyptian System

Whereas the New Kingdom reveals an increase in evidence for the triad in sculpture and iconography generally, the same can scarcely be said of the literary sources. Those which deal broadly with non-religious themes can hardly be expected, except incidentally, to refer to groups of deities. I propose to examine various facets of the religious evidence.

1. *The Book of the Dead*

When we consider the Book of the Dead, we confront texts that are specifically religious in purpose, albeit within a restricted funerary orbit. A central figure, naturally, in these texts is the deceased person, and his or her relationship to various deities is a significant matter. The fact that the deceased is regularly called the Osiris So-and-So ensures a favoured relationship to the god who was the sovereign of the realm of the dead. Identity with him in this manner is not, however, always given the expected full meaning. Thus we find in the text of Nebseny for *BD* 104 a picture of the scribe Nebseny kneeling between two enthroned gods, each of whom is called *the Great God*. The scribe is holding a palette and looks a rather insignificant – certainly a subordinate – figure. On the other hand, the two gods are neither of them given distinctive attributes. *Spell for sitting among the Great Gods* is the designation of the spell, and the brief text begins *I have sat among the Great Gods*.[1] Whereas three figures are sometimes shown, they do not constitute a true triad, since Nebseny, a mortal (although Osiris-N), is one of them. Further, the gods are sometimes indicated in the plural.

A clearer category, which is validly triadic, emerges at the end of *BD* 108, which we have discussed in our previous chapter with regard to its form in the *Coffin Texts*. The three *baw* of the West or of the Westerners are named as Atum, Sobek and Hathor (or Seth), and the vignette in the Papyrus of Nebseny shows an indistinctive Atum, Sobek as a crocodile-headed god and Hathor as a seated woman simply.[2] Oddly enough, this spell begins by telling us that Bakhu, of which Sobek is lord, is in the East of the sky and contains a mountain, and that Sobek is in the East of the mountain. The spell goes on to describe Seth's attack on the huge serpent

(Apopis). The *baw* of the Westerners will presumably support this attack, although Bakhu is in the East. Usually the crocodile-god Sobek has Western associations, particularly in the Fayûm at Shedet;[3] many associations with Upper Egypt are also recorded, especially at Kom Ombo.[4]

2. *The Baw as Divine Triads*

The grouping of the *baw* as divine triads has been well analysed by Louis Žabkar,[5] who has documented the groups assigned to Buto, Hieraconpolis, and Heliopolis; and also those called Eastern, Western, and Northern *baw* (but not Southern, although the *baw* of Buto and Hieraconpolis represent this antithesis). According to Žabkar (p.28), the Eastern *baw* probably represent Heliopolis, as opposed to Buto as represented by the Western *baw*; this seems likely, but none of these references (*Pyr.* 159a W; 1209b PMN; 1495c P) is specifically triadic. Indeed Žabkar goes on to refer to Piankoff, *Le Livre du jour et de la nuit*, 3 and 84, where the Eastern *baw* are mentioned as *four* gods who protect the Eastern horizon and Heliopolis.[6] In the *Coffin Texts*, however, as Žabkar points out, the references are to three named gods in this way:

> The *baw* of Heliopolis are Rê, Shu, and Tefnut.
> (*CT* II, 286b–c; cf. *BD* 115, 9–10, Budge)
> The *baw* of Hermopolis are Thoth, Sia, and Atum.
> (*CT* II, 323c–325e; cf. *BD* 116, 6–7, Nav.)
> The *baw* of Buto are Horus, Iemsety, and Hapy.
> (*CT* II, 348b–c; cf. *BD* 112, 14, Nav.)
> The *baw* of Hieraconpolis are Horus, Duamutef, and Qebhsenuef.
> (*CT* II, 361d–362b; cf. *BD* 113, 13, Nav., with vignette showing falcon-headed Horus, but the other two without distinctive attributes)

In the last locus the figures in Lepsius, of the Ptolemaic era, show Horus and Qebhsenuef as falcon-headed, but Duamutef with a head like that of Anubis; cf. Barguet, 150. The *baw* of Hermopolis are shown in the vignette of Nebseny's *BD* as three squatting ibis-headed gods; cf. Faulkner, 109. Obviously, then, they are dominated by Thoth. According to Sethe[7] the naming of three gods, instead of showing simply a plural *baw*, is a slightly later and secondary development; since the plural was indicated at first with a thrice-repeated *ba*-bird, it was felt necessary to give concrete detail about the gods concerned. Whatever the rationale of the process, it is likely that the growing popularity of the triadic idea played a part. The connection with specified places implies a reference to local gods, and it is evident that the link between the place and the leading god of each group is operative with Heliopolis, Hermopolis, Buto, and Hieraconpolis. There are other expressions which allude to the *baw* of places, but these allusions probably refer to dead kings.[8]

3. Osirian Triads

Isis and Nephthys are constantly grouped in triads with a member of the Osirian complex. In Spell 182 of *BD* they are depicted as each leading a triad and flanking a figure of Osiris lying on a catafalque. Isis is followed by Hapy and Duamutef, Nephthys by Iemsety and Qebehsenuef; the four sons of Horus are thus divided between them. The scene is one concerned with the reawakening and regeneration of Osiris,[9] but neither group forms a fixed triad.[10]

Many various groupings of deities occur in sculpture, and the dyad appears often with bronze figures.[11] In the case of Osiris the early family triads clearly explain the frequency in both literature and art of the group Osiris, Isis, and Horus. Osiris is often shown in the centre, but otherwise there is considerable variety of relative location and gesture, and also of individual attributes, whether of form or of geographical affiliation (Fig.2).[12] Horus in these groups is a falcon-headed figure, tall and mature. When Harpocrates joins the group, he is often shown as a naked youth; and Sarapis, in the Ptolemaic era, can replace Osiris (Fig.3).[13] Occasionally a god who has no family connection with Osiris can form one of the triad, as with Khons.[14] In general the prominence of Nephthys is noteworthy, as when Horus is shown between Isis and Nephthys.[15] Of course she does belong to the family: as the youngest of the four children of Geb and Nut, she is a sister of both Isis and Osiris as well as of Seth, to whom she is assigned as wife. Her union with Seth is, however, barren, and Plutarch's version makes her the mother of Anubis through an illicit union with Osiris. Anubis is several times referred to in Egyptian literature as the son of Osiris, but only once as the son of Nephthys.[16] It is in a funerary context that she is closely linked with Isis as one of the Two Kites who bewail the dead Osiris.[17] This role even includes on occasion her participation with Isis in the revival of the dead Osiris[18] – an action which is portrayed as being primarily sexual. Nephthys is certainly given a share also in the sexual longing for Osiris which is fervently expressed in *The Songs of Isis and Nephthys* and in the parallel text of their *Lamentations*.[19] It is difficult to avoid the conclusion that the two goddesses are regarded as sister-wives of Osiris.

Vignettes in *BD* 125 show them as assistants and supporters of the god in his role as judge of the dead. Thus in the papyrus of Hor, of the Ptolemaic era, the enthroned Osiris surveys the weighing of the heart, while behind him stand Isis and Nephthys with one hand raised supportingly.[20] Clearly the goddesses here have a very subordinate role. In these funerary papyri the deceased is often depicted as adoring the gods, whether singly or in groups. Occasionally the Osirian group is a tetrad rather than a triad;[21] and in one scene (Faulkner, 30–1) Hor and his wife

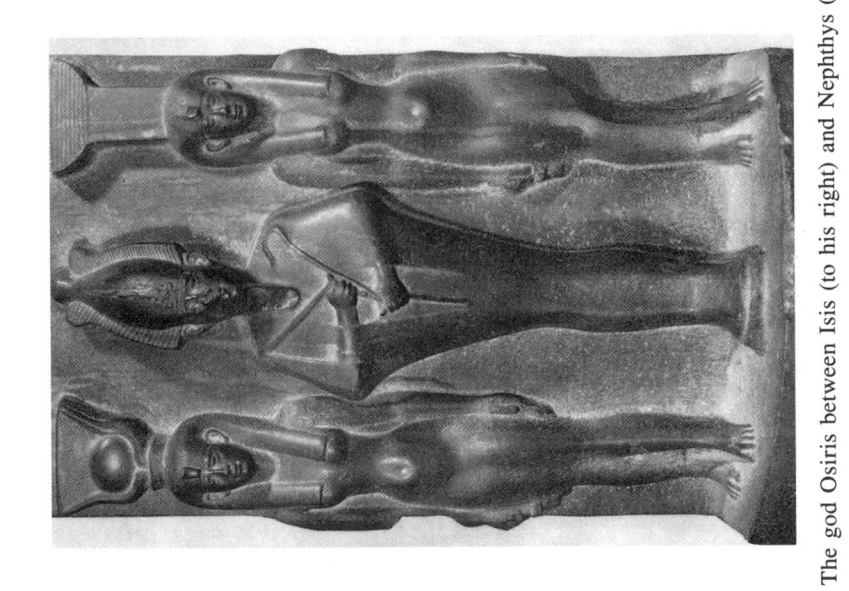

THE DEVELOPED EGYPTIAN SYSTEM 47

Figure 2. Osirian triads

A. The god Osiris between Isis (to his left) and Horus (to his right) B. The god Osiris between Isis (to his right) and Nephthys (to his left)

Figure. 3. Pompeii: Sarapis with Isis and Harpocrates

are shown adoring thirty-five assessors in the judgement. We have noted the often subordinate role of Isis and Nephthys when grouped with Osiris. This is naturally still more marked when they are shown adoring Osiris, as in depictions of Osiris embodied in the *djed*-pillar surmounted by the sun.[22]

We have remarked above (n.15, citing Daressy, *Statues de divinités*, no.39 222, p.305) on an instance where the Theban goddess Mut makes up the triad with Osiris and Isis, thus replacing Nephthys. In fact there is other evidence in the Theban setting for an interesting measure of triadic syncretism. In the temple of Opet at Karnak, which was credited in one tradition as being the birthplace of Osiris as the offspring of the hippopotamus goddess Opet,[23] the Theban triad Amûn, Mut, and Khons is freely merged into that of Osiris, Isis, and Horus. On the northern wall of the central hall the Theban deities are equipped with epithets that identify them in fact with Osiris, Isis, and Horus.[24] Amûn, Mut, and Horus are shown elsewhere with similar epithets; and the young Horus is figured as a young Amûn, the assimilation being now expressed in iconography.[25] The process indicates the increasing power of Osiris in the Ptolemaic era, and also the degree of fluidity which was now possible in theological definitions.[26]

Within the Osirian system there emerges too the phenomenon of the three Horuses. An early distinction was made between the Elder Horus and Horus the Child, and in iconography it was a distinction clearly maintained. Horus the Child or Harpocrates was often figured with Isis and Nephthys.[27] Unlike these (i.e. as a group), the three Horuses revert to the Old Kingdom, and indeed to the royal titulary. Whereas a reference to the falcon-god Anty or Nemty has been seen in the single falcon on the gold sign, the word *bỉk*, 'falcon', has also been invoked and this would more easily apply to the three falcons.[28] Whether *bỉk* or *Ḥr* be involved, the expression of plurality is probably to be seen here. When Horus became the royal god of a united Egypt, many falcon deities were identified with him, and the triple falcon would be a normal way of expressing 'Horuses'.[29] Yet the idea did not prove very persistent. Daressy (*Statues*, no.39 215) wished to explain three plaquettes, each with three Horus figures joined on a base in blue glazed ware, as possibly representing Harpocrates, a hawk-headed Horus, and a Horus with a human head, thus distinguishing their forms. In funerary offerings Horus is sometimes shown three or more times in connection with *ỉdmyt* or *ỉdmy*, types of linen,[30] but the *four torches of red linen* in BD 137 A[31] are associated with the four children of Horus. More apposite to the triple Horus, used again in the plural sense, is the address to Osiris as *Lord of lords, ruler of rulers, sovereign, Horus of the Horuses*.[32] A later development is the use of the winged sun-disc to symbolize Horus, so that its position between two uraei representing Isis and Osiris constitutes an Osirian triad.[33] In his various forms Horus has many local connections, the earliest being with Buto and Hieraconpolis, but the Osirian group as a triad is not topographically attached to a particular centre, although the constituent deities are severally linked in this way – Osiris especially with Abydos and Busiris, Isis with Sebennytos and Philae, but Nephthys has no firm local attachment.

4. Conceptual Triads

In some instances the evolution of the triad is conceptual in origin although related also to a natural phenomenon. Perhaps it is the sun-cult that provides the clearest example. In his study of the hymns to the sun-god in Spell 15 of the *Book of the Dead*, Jan Assmann[34] shows that the theme of these hymns, which he rightly designates as liturgical, is not the person of the sun-god but the process of the sun's course; and this course is related to three phases which are associated with three forms of the sun-god. The phases concern sunrise, the crossing of the sky, and sunset, and they are shown to be reflected in the structure of the hymns. As early as the *Pyramid Texts* the three phases are assigned to Rê in his names of Khepri, Rê, and Atum, where the second name, rather strangely, is that of Rê himself:

> They [the gods] make this King come into being like Rê in this his name of Kheperer.
> You ascend to them like Rê in this his name of Rê.
> You vanish before them like Rê in this his name of Atum [with a pun in *tnm*, 'vanish', and *Tm*].
>
> (*Pyr.* 1695a–c MN)

Faulkner in his translation makes the tenses future, and this is possible as a prediction of the deceased King's blessed prospect. Later the second divine name was varied, such as with Amen-Rê and Harakhty;[35] and the whole scheme is elaborated in a sophisticated way, until by the time of Macrobius there is also a connection with the seasons.[36] The act of worship is likewise related to the three phases of the sun's course, there being services at morn, noon, and evening; and a triple reference is built in – to place (East, mid-heaven, and West), to the divisions of age (child, man, and old man), and to the phases of life (birth, maturity, and death).[37] Nor is it surprising that a triple division of the day is otherwise attested in Egypt, as in the Calendars of Lucky and Unlucky Days.[38] A division of the month into three parts presided over by the decans is a parallel partition, and in this case the origin is clearly in the natural lunar sequence.[39]

The diurnal points and their gods are set out in a text of the Ramesside era (Pleyte-Rossi, Turin P. 133, 10): *I am Khepri in the morning, Rê in the afternoon, Atum in the evening.* Moreover a depiction from the Tomb of Ramesses IX exemplifies the graphic interpretation of this triad as a unit.[40] The sun is shown between earth and heaven, resting on a mountain, and the King is seen on each side offering the Horus-Eye to the sun. Isis is on the left, Nephthys on the right. Bonnet (*Bilderatlas*, 16) states that the sun-god here is represented as *doppelgestaltig*, but since the disc itself denotes the sun, or Rê, there are really three forms here, with Khepri and Atum shown inside the disc. The identity of Atum, admittedly, has been debated. Westendorf, *Sonnenlauf*, 50 (see too his Abb. 37), refers to him as 'der widderköpfige Abendgott', clearly meaning Atum. He also urges that the two eyes which are being presented within the disc symbolize the morning and evening sun; if so, they are attributes of Khepri and Atum, and do not disturb the triadic notion. Jan Zandee, however, as reported by me in ZÄS 100 (1973), 32 n.10, expressed the view that the figure here explained as Atum is the sun-god in his normal form in the underworld, and that there is no warrant for calling him Atum. In *Amduat* and *The Book of Gates* the sun-god in his barque is regularly shown in this form. Discussing the sun-god's image, Hornung in his *Das Buch von den Pforten*, II (1980), 55, notes the designation of him in one locus (2nd Hour, 7th Scene) as $\jmath wf\ R^c$, *the flesh of Rê*, and states, with reference to the ram-headed form, that since the ram can be interpreted as *ba*, the representation indicates two essential aspects of the nocturnal form of the sun-god: he traverses the realm of the dead as a *ba*, yet at the same time as a physical, bodily presence.

The interpretation as a *ba*, however, would appear to conflict with the emphasis on bodily presence, and I prefer Hornung's earlier explanation[41] that the ram's head belongs to the representation of the nocturnal sun; it implies a distinction from the falcon-head of Rê-Harakhty in the day-barque and also from the scarab form of Khepri into which the sun-god changes in the Twelfth Hour of *Amduat*. Textually, as we have seen, there is strong evidence for identifying the evening sun-god with Atum as an ageing deity.[42] Furthermore, Atum is ram-headed in other contexts, although he may have borrowed the attribute from Harsaphes of Heracleopolis.[43]

What is particularly noteworthy about this triad is that it presents one god in three forms or modes. It is the sun-god that appears in three modes, and he is himself named as one of them: Khepri, Rê, Atum. It is a clear example of a modalistic trinity and comparable therefore with the Christian concept.

A broader notion of the triadic division of time into past, present, and future is present in versions of Spell 17 of the *Book of the Dead*. In the earliest versions found in the *Coffin Texts* the stress is on the distinction between Yesterday and Today:

> To me belongs Yesterday, and I know Tomorrow.
> What is the time in which we remain? That is when
> Osiris has been buried and his son Horus is made ruler.
> (*CT* IV, 192a ff.)

A gloss follows: *As for Yesterday, it is Osiris; as for Tomorrow, it is Rê (var. Atum)*.[44] It has been suggested[45] that a triadic formulation appears here with Osiris representing the past, Horus the present and Rê (or, Atum) the future, while the three concepts are united in the present. The latter point is not very clear. If the triadic grouping of past, present, and future is accepted, it can be paralleled in Pleyte and Rossi, *P. Turin* (Dyn. 21), 134, 7: *I am Yesterday, I am Today, I am Tomorrow which has not yet come*, a dictum made by Seth to Horus. One may also compare the inscription assigned by Plutarch (*De Is. et Os.* 9, 354 C) to a seated statue of Athena (= Neïth and Isis) at Saïs: *I am all that has been and is and will be*.[46] So too in Revelation 1: 8 the Lord God is described as he *who is and who was and who is to come, the Almighty*. Yet the passage in *BD*, 17, although it names Horus as the present successor of Osiris, is really rooted in the antithesis of Yesterday and Tomorrow, and this dualism is pointed in the relevant vignette which shows two lions back to back below the sign of the horizon. In the Papyrus of Ani these lions bear the names Tomorrow and Yesterday and thus indicate the same antithesis as that ascribed to Rê and Osiris.[47] The triadic formulation is not therefore conspicuous here. The dualistic opposition, on the other hand, between Osiris and Rê as Yesterday and Tomorrow is analogous to the contrast between the two types of eternity represented by Djet and Neheh.[48] The names Yesterday and Tomorrow as applied to the lions connected with the horizon are a conscious and sophisticated exercise in allegoristic; they clearly derive from the idea of the passage of time from one day to the next and are linked to the sun's course from one horizon to another.

NOTES

[1] Naville's text shows a plural. Cf. the vignette in Barguet (1967), 140, where the deceased is seated before three gods, three doubtless indicating a plural. Earlier forms of the spell are relevant. *CT* VI, 260j shows a plural, but *CT* IV, 65c has *among the two Great Gods* – probably Rê and Osiris.

[2] Cf. Faulkner, 103, for the vignette. Naville displays a Leiden papyrus with Atum here holding an *ankh*-sign, Sobek simply as a seated august figure, and Hathor with

horns, disc and *ankh*-sign.

³ Bonnet, *RÄRG* (1952), 755-9; Claudia Dolzani, *Il dio Sobk* (Rome, 1961), passim; E. Brovarski, *LÄ* V (1984), 995-1031. From the MK onwards the god is constantly shown as crocodile-headed rather than in the earlier theriomorphic form.

⁴ Brovarski, op. cit., 1001ff.

⁵ Louis V. Žabkar, *A Study of the Ba Concept in Ancient Egyptian Texts* (Chicago, 1968), 28-30.

⁶ Cf. Hornung, *Ägyptische Unterweltsbücher* (2nd edn., 1984), 488. The Western *baw* are referred to in Piankoff, op. cit., 89-90 as protecting the Western horizon and Heliopolis. The mention of Heliopolis in each locus seems to upset the pattern.

⁷ *Die Sprüche für das Kennen der Seelen der heiligen Orte* (Leipzig, 1925), 26.

⁸ Cf. Žabkar, op. cit., 30-6.

⁹ L. Speleers, *Rec. trav.* 40 (1923), 86-104 (on a text now in Brussels); Gertrud Thausing, *Der Auferstehungsgedanke in Ägyptischen religiösen Texten* (Leipzig, 1943), 186-8 (a translation with notes); Barguet, *BD* 268; Hornung, *BD* 389 with 520-1.

¹⁰ Nor, of course, does the group showing Nephthys and Isis adoring Rê-Osiris (Hornung, Fig.89, p.384 (= his *Conceptions of God in Ancient Egypt*, 94, from the tomb of Nefertari)).

¹¹ Roeder, *Bronzefiguren*, § 662. The basic import of the dyad as 'Father and Mother' principle is underlined by Westendorf, *ZÄS* 100 (1974), 136-7.

¹² Roeder, ibid., § 664.

¹³ Ibid., no.8871, p.492.

¹⁴ Ibid., no.11 374, p.492. For other Osirian groups v. Bodil Hornemann, *Types of Ancient Egyptian Statuary*, V, 1369 (Isis, Osiris, Horus), a Saïte group in Leiden; 1374 (Horus, Osiris, Isis), of Dyn. 22 at the Louvre. Her no.1380 shows a King between Mut and Amûn (Cairo 42097, Dyn. 18-19), but this is not a divine triad in our sense.

¹⁵ Cairo 39 268 (= Daressy, *Statues de divinités* (1906), 317 (not reproduced)). See also his nos.39 254, 39 260 and 39 262, reproduced on Pl.59. For Osiris, Isis and Nephthys see his nos.39 220 and 39 221 on Pl.58. In his no.39 222 (p.305) the Theban goddess Mut joins Osiris and Isis. Groupings of deities are noted in his Index, pp.415-17; these include seven triads, and five of these are Osirian, showing Osiris, Isis and Horus.

¹⁶ See my *Plutarch's De Iside et Osiride* (1970), 318.

¹⁷ See my *Origins of Osiris and his Cult* (1980), 49-50; and cf. above ch.1, section 6.

¹⁸ Maria Münster, *Untersuchungen zur Göttin Isis* (Berlin, 1968), 149.

¹⁹ Faulkner (on 'The Songs'), *JEA* 22 (1936), 121-40; and *idem* (on 'The Lamentations'), *MIFAO* 66 (1934 (= *Mélanges Maspero*, I)), 337-48. Lana Troy, *Patterns of Queenship* (Uppsala, 1986), 37, says that 'Isis and Nephthys are described as a feminine duality', and goes on to argue that their complementarity refers to two different types of throne embodied in their names. Later (p.146) she designates Isis as 'the female-diurnal-active element' and Nephthys as 'the female-nocturnal-passive' element. See also Hornung in *Studies in Pharaonic Religion and Society*, ed. A. B. Lloyd (London, 1992), 186-8 ('Versuch über Nephthys').

²⁰ Faulkner (ed. Carol Andrews), *BD*, 30. Ibid., 26, from the Papyrus of Ani, only Isis stands behind the god. But in P. Hunefer (ibid., 34) both goddesses are shown.

²¹ Ibid., 122. The deceased pulls a *djed*-pillar before Osiris, Isis, Nephthys and Horus. Cf. Barguet, *BD* 167.

[22] Bonnet, *Bilderatlas*, 6 (= P. Ani, Pl.2); cf. Faulkner, *BD* 6 (P. Hunefer); R. Fazzini, *Egypt, Dynasty XXII–XXV* (Leiden, 1988), Pl.36, 1 (Osorkon II). In the first instance, however, as Bonnet remarks, it is the sun-god that is being worshipped. In Westendorf, *Sonnenlauf*, 79–80 with Figs.69–70, the two goddesses are shown as falcons flanking Osiris.

[23] See C. de Wit, *Les Inscriptions du temple d'Opet à Karnak* (Brussels, 1958), VII; cf. my Comm. ad Plutarch, *De Iside et Osiride*, 300, where a ref. to de Wit's work should have been included.

[24] C. de Wit, op. cit. VIII and 90ff.

[25] Ibid. VIII.

[26] Cf. E. Otto, *Gott und Mensch* (1964), 87.

[27] In Case N of the *Salle des Divinités* in the Cairo Museum I once had occasion to note that faience figurines of Isis, Harpocrates and Nephthys (in this order from left to right) numbered 26, while similar triadic figurines of Nephthys, Harpocrates and Isis numbered 19. In each instance Harpocrates is the central figure.

[28] Jürgen von Beckerath, *Handbuch der ägyptischen Königsnamen* (Munich, 1984), 25–6 with refs. See also *Pyr.* 7a P, 786c P; Maspero, *Rec. trav.* 5 (1884), 167; H. Müller, *Die formale Entwicklung der Titulatur* (Glückstadt, 1938), 60–1.

[29] See my remarks in *ASAE* 56 (1960), 84–5.

[30] *Wb.* I, 153, 15–18; Junker, *Gîza*, I (1929), 177–8; W. S. Smith, *ZÄS* 71 (1935), 136–42.

[31] Budge, 137 A, 28 (Nu); cf. Faulkner, *BD*, 129.

[32] *BD* 185 E (Louvre C 18, Dyn. 19): see Allen, *BD*, 206b S1; cf. *Wb.* III, 123, 13, and above, p.42 n.145.

[33] A. M. El-Khachab, *JEA* 57 (1971), Pl.38, 2 and p.135. The Osirian uraeus is wearing, *pace* El-Khachab, a form of the *atef*-crown, and Horus is represented, not merely by the disc, but by the whole winged disc.

[34] *Liturgische Lieder an den Sonnengott* (MÄS 19; Berlin, 1969), 333ff.

[35] Cf. G. Nagel, *BIFAO* 29 (1929), 99–102. The cult of Atum was not fully merged into that of Rê even in Heliopolis: see L. Kákosy, *LÄ* I (1975), 551.

[36] H. Brugsch, *Religion und Mythologie der alten Aegypter* (Leipzig, 1888), 234.

[37] See J. Assmann, op. cit., 337.

[38] Ibid., 338; A. M. Bakir, *The Cairo Calendar* (Cairo, 1966), 3; for a general survey of some of the mythic content of the nine known calendars see E. Brunner-Traut, 'Mythos im Alltag', *Antaios* 12 (1970), 332–47, reprinted in her *Gelebte Mythen* (3rd edn., 1988), 16–30.

[39] R. A. Parker, *The Calendars of Ancient Egypt* (Chicago, 1950), 54, § 273, referring to the earliest lists in the Middle Kingdom; Parker and Neugebauer, *Egyptian Astronomical Texts*, I (Providence, 1960), 113–15.

[40] Hornung, *Tal der Könige* (Zurich, 1982), 198.

[41] Hornung, *Amduat*, II (1965), 21.

[42] Cf. of Atum, *nḥḥ špss imy 'Iwnw*, the worthy old one in Heliopolis, Assmann, *Re und Amun* (1983), 162, citing K. Myśliwiec, *Studien zum Gott Atum*, II (Hildesheim, 1979).

[43] Kees, *Götterglaube*², 81, 255, 322, where the sun-god's form in *Amduat* and *The Book of Gates* is properly compared. See also Bonnet, *RÄRG*, 731.

[44] Rundle Clark, *Myth and Symbol in Ancient Egypt* (London, 1959), 157ff.; M. Heerma van Voss, *De oudste Versie van Dodenboek 17 a* (Leiden, 1963), 16 and 53ff.; Faulkner, *CT* I (1973), 262ff.

[45] S. G. F. Brandon, *History, Time, and Deity* (Manchester, 1965), 18ff.

[46] Cf. my Comm. ad loc. 284.

[47] Cf. my remarks, *JEA* 53 (1967), 97f. A thorough analysis of this and similar vignettes in relation to the sun's course from East to West is given by Westendorf, *Sonnenlauf*, 18-21 with Figs.10-13.

[48] Westendorf, ibid., 4-5; Assmann, *Zeit und Ewigkeit* (1975), 44; Hornung, *Eranos Jb.* 47 (1978), 291-307. Yesterday and Tomorrow as two lions provide a form of personification (or more exactly of theriomorphization of abstracts) overlooked by Baines in his *Fecundity Figures* (1935), 15. In other contexts, of course, the lion in Egyptian art has royal and divine associations; see Constant de Wit, *Le Rôle et le sens du lion dans l'Égypte ancienne* (Leiden, 1951), 464. Cf. also Assmann, *Ma'at* (Munich, 1990), 169-70. On conceptual triads see further my remarks in *The Intellectual Heritage of Egypt* (Fs. L. Kákosy, ed. U. Luft, Budapest, 1992), 223-8.

3

Amarna Triadic Doctrine

To those who deny that the religion of Amarna achieved the promulgation of a monotheistic belief there is nothing unexpected in the claim that it evolved a triadic doctrine. Triadism, which is so common in Egyptian religion, has initially an essential affinity with polytheism. Yet a recognition of an Amarna monotheism need not be basically imperilled by the ascription to it of triadic notions, especially when the triadism is interpreted as having a structure of inner relevance. One might as plausibly argue that Christian belief imperilled its stress on monotheism by developing its doctrine of the Trinity. The Great Hymn to the Aten, since it rigidly excluded other deities, may rightly be said to inculcate an 'uncompromising monotheism',[1] and is therefore to be distinguished from previous comparable compositions by more than a 'mere nuance'.[2]

Akhenaten himself is conspicuously involved in two of the triadic concepts of his religion. From the standpoint of the history and background of the sun-cult in Egypt, he fulfils the role of the Pharaoh who is the High Priest of the cult. Jan Assmann has given much attention to this tradition,[3] and he stresses the function of the King as one fully initiated into the liturgy of those who accompany the sun-god and into the cult secrets and ritual connections of the sun's course.[4] At the same time he sees the King depicted as the representative of the sun-god on earth, one who is entrusted with the task of preserving the creation through the realization of Maat. A threefold division marks the traditional Egyptian approach to the sun's course, as we have noted: as the morning sun he is Khepri, the scarab-beetle; at noon he is Rê, in the form of a falcon-headed man; and in the evening he is Atum, shown as a man with the double-crown or ram-headed.[5] The triadic division here, as Assmann[6] rightly remarks, does not imply three gods syncretistically fused into one sun-god, but rather one god who in his manifestations to the world appears in three forms.

It is not surprising that Assmann took as the subject of his inaugural lecture at Heidelberg aspects of the Amarna religion.[7] Here he discusses, *inter alia*, the triadic sense of the first 'dogmatic name', to which we shall return. But it might be well to consider first the way in which three beings constitute a closely knit group in a well-known type of representation from Amarna.

1. A Triad of God, King, and Queen

A relief in the Cairo Museum (Fig. 4) shows the sun-god in the form of the solar disc extending rays which end in helping hands to Akhenaten and Nefertiti. A daughter of the royal pair stands behind Nefertiti and raises a sistrum. Although the King is shown as much larger than his Queen, the two are clearly envisaged as being in a special relationship to the sun-god Aten, for he hands an *ankh*-sign to each of them.[8] They are holding offerings in an act of devotion. There are many similar representations,[9] and in view of the subsidiary figures, it may sometimes be questioned whether a title such as 'Die königliche Familie beim Opfer'[10] would not be a more suitable title.

The relative importance assigned to Nefertiti in such scenes also varies, as it does too in the scenes showing the royal pair in the 'Window of Appearances'.[11] Yet the impression that the god Aten is presented as closely linked to the King and Queen, and that the whole triadic group is intended as an object of worship by the people at large, remains strong, especially in the framework of the 'Window of Appearances'.[12] According to Assmann,[13] the triad of God, King, and Queen is thus shown to be the only object of devotion by the people and by individuals. He is here defending the interpretation of the state halls of Akhenaten's palace as part of a *pr h'i*, 'House of Appearance', as opposed to a temple or *pr itn*, 'House of Aten'.[14] He further opines that this triad has been conceived of exactly in the manner of the trinitarian groupings of polytheistic religion – that is, in the forms of a family. If we lay aside the complication that the royal children often appear in the group (a feature that admittedly gives further emphasis to the idea of a family), there are ways in which the Aten–Akhenaten–Nefertiti group differs from most of the Egyptian divine family triads. These usually consist of Father–Mother–Son, as with Osiris–Isis–Horus, Ptah–Sakhmet–Nefertem, Amûn–Mut–Khons, and Khnum–Satis–Anukis. It is true that the feminine component may be less sharply defined, as H. te Velde shows in his remarks on the structure of Egyptian divine triads;[15] and in the case of Anukis the evidence is conflicting.

There are familiar parallels to exemplify the idea of the King's appearance in a group of three of whom the other two are deities. But the Queen does not figure in such a group. The outstanding instances from the Old Kingdom concern Mycerinus. He is shown in a dyad with his wife – a frequent grouping for Kings and private citizens; but the celebrated sculptured triads do not include his wife: they consist of the King, the goddess Hathor and a nome-goddess.[16] Figurines from Karnak show Sethos I between Amûn and Mut;[17] Ramesses II appears with Hathor and Isis;[18] also with Rê-Harakhty and Amen-Rê;[19] Queen Nefertari is seen between

Figure 4. Amarna: Triad of God (Aten), King (Akhenaten), and Queen (Nefertiti)

Hathor and Isis.[20] This kind of group becomes common in the New Kingdom, and a recurring motif is to present the King as the child of the gods.[21] What is distinctive in the Amarna triad is that the King and Queen form two entities in the group.

Yet in some ways a closer analogy is provided, apart from the aspect of triadism, by the tradition in Egyptian art which presents the King and others as being under the protection of a deity or deities. This conception is as old as the Narmer palette, where the goddess Hathor appears on both obverse and reverse; her son Horus is also prominent, clearly in close association with the King. A mural relief showing King Djoser in his *sed*-festival presents, above the monarch, the divine falcon holding the *ankh*-sign; it is, of course, Horus of Behdet giving life to the Pharaoh in his jubilee festival.[22] A chapel of Sesostris I in Karnak portrays the King being conducted by Atum to Amen-Kamutef; above this scene occur the vulture and the falcon with *ankh*-signs in their talons.[23] But it is without doubt the winged sun-disc of Horus of Behdet that comes closest in design and significance to the radiating Aten of Amarna. The form with the sun-disc at the centre of outstretched wings and with enveloping uraei[24] has detailed affinities with the Aten, who also usually carries a uraeus. Solicitude for the persons figured below is sometimes expressed by a down-curving wing; and Hayes[25] suggests that, whereas mortals figured on stelae are often surmounted by two *wedjat*-eyes with a *shenu*-symbol between them, the winged sun-disc is reserved for deities or deified mortals.

A sense of unity between the radiate Aten and the figures of Akhenaten and his wife shown below the sun-god is conveyed by their proximity to the rays. Sometimes the rays are shown reaching towards them, although the royal pair are below the actual impact.[26] More often they are immersed in the rays; and in one case where Nefertiti stands behind her husband, a solicitous ray extends far beyond its expected orbit in order to touch the Queen's crown.[27] A fragmentary sandstone relief now in Hildesheim shows the King's head high among the rays.[28] But, of course, it is the hands with which the rays are equipped that express most clearly the caring beneficence of Aten. It seems that this symbolism first appeared with the Winged Disc.[29]

2. A Shared Priestly and Prophetic Role

In the representations of Aten–Akhenaten–Nefertiti it is certainly made clear that the beneficent rays of the Aten are specially concerned with a blessing proffered to the royal couple and with a bond which binds them to the sun-god in a significant sense.[30] It is natural to connect the unity of the three with the role of Akhenaten as son and prophet of Aten, but with the extension of meaning that Nefertiti now shares the role. This role finds its best-known expression in the Great Hymn to the Aten:

> There is no other who knows thee apart from thy son, Nefer-Kheperu-Rê, Wa-en-Rê. Thou makest him be cognizant of thy plans and of thy might.
> (Sandman, *Texts from the Time of Akhenaten*, 95, 16–17)

Whereas 'son of Rê' is a traditional Pharaonic title, the claim made by Akhenaten goes far beyond the accepted theology, since it posits exclusive knowledge of the sun-god's will.[31] Nefertiti is, of course, completely absent from such statements, but the representations to which we have referred indicate clearly that she is regarded as sharing in the esoteric knowledge vouchsafed to her husband. One might perhaps compare the way in which the Virgin Mary, while absent from the New Testament proclamations about salvation, yet shares with the Saviour the activity of salvation in the practice and developed tradition of the Roman Catholic and Greek Orthodox Churches, becoming almost a co-Saviour.[32] It is true that Akhenaten, in spite of his exalted position, is often shown making offerings to Aten. But only he among men is assigned this function. It is noteworthy, however, that Nefertiti shares the function with him.[33]

There are pointers, at the same time, to her assumption of a more independent role in relation to the god during one phase of her career. It seems likely, during the early part of the reign, that 'there was a separate Aten temple at Karnak for Nefertiti'; here there is 'extreme emphasis' on her role in many ways.[34] She is represented paying homage to Aten on her own, save for the presence of one or two daughters; in these scenes there is no trace of her husband, although it may be an excessive inference to say that 'this worship of the sun god is her exclusive prerogative'.[35] Certainly the addition to her name indicates a doctrinal devotion officially acknowledged. The name Nefertiti has no theological meaning since *The beautiful one is come* presumably refers to the person who bears the name.[36] Nefer-neferu-Aten, *Most beautiful is Aten*,[37] is firmly linked to the god, and might be regarded even as a spiritual correction of the first name: praise of the bearer becomes praise of her god. Further, a special relationship to the god is indicated by the writing of the god's name in reverse in order to make it face the figure of Nefertiti.[38]

For the most part King and Queen participate together in the priestly activities. It is the names that point to a joint prophetic role; and Akhenaten's exclusive claim to knowledge of Aten should probably not be interpreted as debarring Nefertiti from the privilege.[39] The question does arise, none the less, whether the royal pair can possibly be included in a divine triad which is itself an object of worship. If their functions are explained as priestly and prophetic activities on behalf of the god Aten, does not such an explanation make them servants and hierophants of the one deity and prevent their elevation to the level of Aten himself? It seems that Norman Davies[40] was the first to refer to a divine triad at Amarna – 'the three worshipful powers, the Aten, the King, and the Queen'. Praise and worship of Nefertiti are amply attested;[41] but often the three are addressed together. Altars in houses show representations of the King, Queen, and family under the radiate Aten; clearly they are together the object of worship.[42] Processions and public appearances equally concern the triad; and texts exemplify the prayers addressed to them.[43] As for Nefertiti, she supplies the female element which had previously been so conspicuous in various triads and in the great goddesses of Egypt.[44]

It remains true that no intelligent worshipper could have placed these three divine beings on an absolute par; the King and Queen have been exalted to a level of intimate association with Aten, but they are in his service as priests and prophets of the one god. At the same time, the King's daughters may have been associated with less rigid religious tendencies: the Beset-figures of Amarna may impersonate them, although these goddesses can also be located in the company of the sun-god Rê.[45]

3. The Triad of the Early Doctrinal Name

May my father Aten live! is described by Roeder[46] as a kind of *Credo* of the Aten-religion; it is a formula that immediately follows the King's name. It is, however, in the early doctrinal name of Aten that a divine triad figures:

> Rê-Harakhty lives, who rejoices in the horizon in his name as Shu, who is Aten.[47]
> (Sandman, *Texts*, 103ff., 119ff.)

An equation is pointedly made between the three gods Rê-Harakhty, Shu, and Aten. According to Gunn,[48] the name 'proclaims the identity of the Aten with the other purely solar gods of Egypt from the beginning of history'.[49]

The later doctrinal name is a briefer statement which Gunn[50] renders thus:

> Rê lives, ruler of the two horizons, who rejoices in the horizon in his name, Rê the Father who has returned as Aten.
> (Sandman, *Texts*, 119ff.)[51]

A slightly improved version may perhaps read thus:

> Rê lives, ruler of the two horizons, who rejoices in the horizon in his name as Rê my Father, who comes as Aten.

That the double determinative after it, 'father', should be read as $it.i$, 'my father', is an idea revived by Westendorf;[52] and theologically it is an idea that agrees well with Akhenaten's exalted stance in relation to Aten. The last verbal form can be explained as present in reference: 'Rê the father who comes as the sun' is Assmann's version, and he interprets it as the *'parousia'* of the god in his daily appearance to the living.[53] No rigid consistency is shown in the writings of ii, 'come', in the imperfective and perfective active participles;[54] and, in any case, the writings in this context are often much abbreviated. Gunn would obviously see a perfective participle here, Assmann an imperfective. Priority must then be given to the more persuasive force of interpretation. According to Gunn a return of the god Aten is implied. Speaking of the sun-god, he observes that as Amen-Rê he was 'king of the gods'. Gunn continues thus:

> As Horus he was essentially royal. But for a long time his sovereignty had been weakened by the existence of other mighty gods; now, by the agency of his son and prophet, he had attained undisputed supremacy as King of the Universe. The accession of Akhenaten was thus (retrospectively at least) the occasion of a return to kingship for the sun-god, under the name of Aten; and this is what is referred to by the words 'who has returned as Aten' in the later form of the name.
>
> (*JEA* 9 (1923), 176)

He adds in a note (s 6) that 'the king's later personal name "Akhenaten", i.e. "it is well with Aten", may be a direct allusion to this happy restoration'. That the verb ii can mean 'return' is, of course, well established.[55] But the idea of the sun-god's sovereignty being restored *vis-à-vis* other deities, as Gunn argues, is a somewhat expansive interpretation in which the application to rivalry in religion and cult seems hazardous. A cosmic meaning should more probably be sought; and the return may rather be seen, as Assmann views it, as an allusion to the daily reappearance of the departed sun. Catullus expressed it memorably: *soles occidere et redire possunt*. When the name refers to 'Rê my Father who comes (or returns) as Aten', the theological emphasis is clearly on Aten, the form of the sun-god now favoured for special veneration.

The relationship between Rê-Harakhty, Shu, and Aten, which is proclaimed in the earlier name, demands further comment. As in the later name, Aten is mentioned last; but in each case the final position is one of importance, although the earlier name makes Rê-Harakhty paramount. The fact that the name is contained in a cartouche has several implications. It becomes a royal name, proclaiming the kingship of the god Aten. Akhenaten's own royal name, also enclosed in a cartouche, was *Nb-ḫprw-R^c W^c-n-R^c* (*Lord of the forms of Rê, Sole one of Rê*). Rê, be it noted, is twice mentioned – a point worth stressing in view of a recent tendency to remove both Shu and Aten as divine names from the early didactic formula. Gods are often mentioned in official royal names. There seems to be no previous parallel, however, to the proclamation of the sovereignty of a god by enclosing his name in a cartouche. In the Ptolemaic era the practice occurs in the texts of the Edfu temple, where, for example, the text of 'The Winged Disc' refers to Rê in this way. The text begins with a reference to *the King of Upper and Lower Egypt, Rê-Harakhty, may he live for ever and ever.*[56]

Although it refers to three deities, the didactic name is essentially one, and it constitutes a description of the god Aten. The first of the triad, Rê-Harakhty, is a composite name[57] that was well established by the New Kingdom.[58] If it is not recognized as a composite name, the group becomes a tetrad and is thus explained by Gunn:[59]

> The chief purpose of this name seems to be to establish the equation Aten = Shu = Ḥarakhte = Rêʿ, which proclaims the identity of the Aten with the other purely solar gods of Egypt from the beginning of history, and so consolidates and legitimizes his position as the supreme god.

If it be accepted that Rê-Harakhty should be read[60] and that three gods are thus named, the mention of Rê-Harakhty and Shu shows that Akhenaten at this stage was anxious to avoid 'an entire break with the past', as Gunn says, and was keen rather to make 'a direct bid for the adherence of the older solar cults'.

The role of the god Shu in the triad is more problematic. Gunn[61] was doubtful whether '𓆄𓁹, the second member of the Ennead, and 𓆄𓇳 the solar god, are identical'. In the Heliopolitan Enneadic doctrine Shu and his wife Tefnut are the children of Atum, the self-creating sun-god who produces this pair by masturbation or expectoration. In so far as Shu represents air or wind, his cosmic function is not conspicuously solar in essence; nor does that seem to be true of his role in separating heaven and earth. Yet the latter act is one which is envisaged as establishing the celestial course traversed by the sun.[62] Herman te Velde[63] points out that 'Shu, sometimes called the son of Re [*sic*] and sometimes bearing the sun-disk upon his head, separates heaven and earth by bringing light'.[64] *I am he who illumines the darkness for it [the Eye of Atum]* is a dictum of Shu in *Coffin Texts*, II. 5c. Jan Zandee[65] maintains that Shu as god of wind is closely related to Shu as a god of light; and he appositely quotes from another Coffin Text:

> I am the *ba* of Shu, who has become Rê. I have become Rê and Rê has become like me. The heaven was made for me, that I might be lofty.
>
> (*CT IV.* 178f-h)

He also quotes *BD* 98 (Budge 202, 16): *I stand as Shu, I make the sun's ray strong.* It seems that both Shu and the sunlight are viewed as filling the space between heaven and earth; and Shu is presented as one who actively helps the deceased in his ascent to heaven.[66] The close association in origin and function of Atum and Shu makes the Amarna statement of identity regarding Rê-Harakhty and Shu and also regarding Shu and Aten the more understandable; and the claimed identity of Rê and the *ba* of Shu comes closer still.

At the same time Shu is the son of Atum (or now Rê-Harakhty), and Morenz,[67] following Fecht,[68] would see an emphasis on sonship in this triadic formula and would extend the emphasis to include Akhenaten in the sense that his unity with his father is thereby expressed. Indeed Fecht argues that Shu refers directly to Akhenaten here. He further suggests that 'Shu who is Aten' implies a touch of paronomasia, with *ʾItn* recalling *it*, 'father' (pronounced *jāt*), especially if *ʾItn* was pronounced *Jāti*. Akhenaten elsewhere maintained the pride of his position as son of Aten, as we have seen. But it is not easy to see how the doctrinal name exalts him, as son of Aten, to identity with his father. Even if we accept the speculative thesis that the name ends with a thought like 'Shu is Aten (the father)' and supply the additional idea 'and the son of Aten the father is King Akhenaten', the resulting triadism becomes the unity of three generations – Rê-Harakhty and his son Shu, followed by Shu-Aten as the father of the King. The truth is that the third generation finds no direct expression.

Paronomasia is admittedly a frequent occurrence in Egyptian religious texts, but the example alleged to occur here is not apparent in the writing of the words which have been linked. Whereas the sonship of Shu may well be compared with that of Akhenaten – for the King, too, is the son of Rê – yet Shu is not identified with the King, as Morenz[69] maintains, since he is equated with Aten, the King's father. Of such speculations Morenz aptly uses the word 'Klügelei'. One may agree with him that the doctrinal name constitutes a 'modalistic trinity', but his first interpretation is much the most acceptable: the old sun-god Rê-Harakhty is conjoined here with two other forms of his being, namely Shu and Aten, in a triune entity.

Fecht succeeds in showing that Shu as the son and successor of Rê in Heliopolitan doctrine is a deity well suited to adorn a royal cartouche. But where his exposition is particularly revealing is in pointing to the important role attached to Shu in other Amarna texts. He begins with instances where Shu is identified with Akhenaten. In a prayer to Akhenaten in the tomb of the High Priest Meryrê, after Akhenaten has been addressed as the Nile-god Hapy, he is called *Shu by whose glance I live, my* ka *of every day* (Sandman, *Texts*, 16, 9–10). Of course, the impersonal intepretation is not thereby ruled out; indeed Norman Davies[70] here translated *the Light by sight of which I live, my* ka *day by day*. But the fact that another god, Hapy, has been equated with Akhenaten previously suggests that Shu as a deity is meant here. On the other hand, cases where the word is followed by phrases such as *n t3 nb*, *n ḥr nb*, and *n irt nbt*, implying the Shu of all lands, of all men, and of all eyes, might favour the meaning 'Light'. Yet when a prayer states of Shu, *I become strong through hearing thy voice* (Sandman, 172, 13; Fecht, p.106), the personalized god must be intended. Examples in which Akhenaten is likewise identified with Rê (Fecht, pp.106-7) strengthen the argument; no one, it seems, has ventured to explain these occurrences of *rˁ* as an impersonal sun.

Fecht further points out (p.85) that the King is never called Aten, although he is frequently described as *mi itn*, 'like Aten', or *tit itn*, 'image of Aten'. Nor is he equated with Rê-Harakhty. It is when one reaches Fecht's conclusion about Shu's function in the second cartouche that one finds a quite unexpected dictum: he maintains that *šw* in the texts always signifies the King and never the god ('dass *šw* in den Texten stets den König bezeichnet, nie den Gott'); and he adds that *rˁ* also signifies the King occasionally, but can also signify the god. The concept of Shu as son of Rê and as King, it is urged, is confirmed by what the texts reveal about Shu's kingly character. Such a conclusion is not a just inference from the facts which have been so helpfully assembled. In the texts noted the King is sometimes addressed as Shu, sometimes as Rê, and sometimes as Hapy. It does not follow that, whenever these gods are named, it is a means of referring simply to the King. The cartouches are statements about Aten. He is called Rê-Harakhty and Shu, and the latter is equated with Aten. An outstanding Amarna doctrine inculcates the idea that the god Aten is the father of the King. A difficulty therefore arises if Shu is interpreted here as the King. It will mean that the King is identified with his own father.[71] It is far better to explain Shu as the god who is predominantly solar, and to find the element of sonship in his traditional role as son of Atum or Rê-Harakhty. In this way the triad will partly correspond to the ancient Heliopolitan triad of Atum, Shu, and Tefnut, to which the *Coffin Texts* (II.39e) allude when it is said of Atum, *when he was One and became Three*.[72] The new factor is that Aten replaces Tefnut; and the whole triad is presented as the name of Aten – a point which implies an apparent lack of logic, since Aten is also the third member of the triad. Yet an inherent consistency emerges in the emphasis that Aten is one with Shu,[73] who is himself a particular aspect or name of Rê-Harakhty. A strenuous effort is thus apparent to stress the unity of these three gods and the concept that Aten subsumes in his being the deities Rê-Harakhty and Shu.

Here one needs to refer to other possible interpretations. One of these has the effect of demolishing the divine triad above posited. Assmann[74] translates the doctrinal name thus: 'Rê-Harakhty lives, who rejoices in the horizon, in his name as the light which is in the sun.' An early form in an inscription from Gebel Silsila is translated by Gardiner,[75] as 'in his name the sunlight (Egyptian "Shu") which is Aten', where the parenthesis neatly skirts the problem. There is indeed no decisive argument for depersonalizing Shu to *šw*, 'sunlight', here. The absence of the god-determinative is certainly not decisive, for the same absence marks several occurrences of Rê in the Amarna texts.[76] It may also be questioned whether the phrase *m rn.f m*, 'in his name as', is likely to introduce something which is not a proper name – 'light' rather than 'Shu' – although Assmann[77] is careful to point out that 'light' need not be implied as the name of the sun-god, but that his name may be viewed as materializing itself as light. Writing in 1965, Bennett[78] maintained that the retention of Shu in this context had 'largely fallen out of favour'. He notes that Fecht[79] retained the god's name; several others have done so.[80]

In the so-called 'intermediate form'[81] of the early name, the word Shu (or *šw*, 'light') disappears. The name Horus in the first cartouche is written phonetically, and the second cartouche is said to correspond in form to the later name.[82] Julia Samson[83] has republished the two instances of the 'intermediate form' which are found in the Petrie Collection. She states that they show 'that the second cartouche of this intermediate form is identical with that in the later form of the name'. It will be recalled that the later form has, in the second cartouche, 'In his name as Rê the (or, my) Father, who returns as Aten' (*m rn.f m Rʿ it i m Itn*). However, Mrs Samson reads the words of this cartouche in the two instances now republished by her as *m rn.f m iti m itn*. This she does not translate. Presumably it is 'in his name as Father as Aten'. The photograph of UC 351 leaves the reading unclear; but that of UC 098 shows *m rn.f m Rʿ it i m itn* ('in his name as Rê the Father who returns as Aten'). In this case, then, the correspondence is beyond question.

If the end of the second cartouche is translated 'the light which is in the sun' – a possibility, of course – it is evident that both Shu and Aten are now depersonalized and concretized, and only one named god remains – that is, Rê-Harakhty. Clearly this would push back the monotheistic impetus, but there are other pointers to a polytheistic acceptance in the early part of the reign. It is hard to imagine a doctrinal summation more insipid and flat than 'the light which is in the sun'. Admittedly there is much evidence for the glorification of the objective sun-disc in this creed; but equally there is strong evidence for the conviction that a named god Aten is involved, who is often called *ntr ntry*, 'the divine deity'; cf. Sandman, *Texts*, 170, 13, and H. Brunner in *ZÄS* 97 (1971, Fs. W. Wolf), 14. Indeed it is also much stressed that Aten is the father of the King, and there is no escaping the personalism of that relationship, however hard the impersonal objectivity of the central idea is pressed.

Another question which is open to debate is whether *nty m* in the final phrase means *who is* or *who is in*. Bennett[84] states firmly that 'we can delete translations involving the *m* of predication because the phrase *ntỉ m* "which is" is unknown'. He adds, 'at least it does not occur in the *Wörterbuch*'. While this is true (v. *Wb.* I, 352) and while the normal construction after *nty* is an adverbial phrase or Old Perfective, an example with the *m* of predication is quoted by Gardiner[85]: *ỉr nṯr pn nty ḥr.f m ṯsm* (*Urk.* V, 67, 1), 'as to this god whose face is (that of) a dog'. Here the predicative *m* is not linked to the *nty*, but to a new subject *ḥr.f* with the resumptive pronoun; cf. however H.von Deines and W. Westendorf, *Wb. der Medizinischen Texte* (Berlin, 1961), 487-9, especially section f. 'ntj + Nomen (ohne rückbeziehendes Pronomen)', but without the predicative *m*. In *Lebensmüde*, 142, *wnn ms nty ỉm m nṯr ʿnḫ*, 'In truth a man who is yonder will become a living god',[86] although *nty ỉm* is the main subject, the *m* of predication is linked to the verb *wnn*. In the *Instruction of Amenemḥet* we read (ed. Helck, p.24), 'I caused him who had nothing to succeed like him who was somebody', or 'like him who had something'.[87] The last phrase is *mỉ nty wn*; *wn* may be a *sḏm.f* form here,[88] in which case there is no syntactical parallel; but it may be a participle with substantival force, in which case it buttresses the pattern of *nty + nomen*, but without predicative *m*. Assmann in *LÄ* I, 535 n.9 quotes the phrase used elsewhere of the sun-god, *ỉmy ỉtn.f*, 'who is in his disc', where *ỉtn*, as he points out, refers merely to the seat of the sun-god. But it is noteworthy that *ỉm* and not *nty m* is used here. Indeed *ỉmy* is often used in the Coffin Texts to denote the location (named or otherwise) or equipment of deities; see B. Altenmüller, *Synkretismus in den Sargtexten*, 277f.

Consistency within the doctrinal name might suggest another possibility: *Šw nty m ʾItn* may be taken as 'Shu who is as Aten', where the *m* would not be directly predicative in the sense of identity, but with the force of the earlier *m* in the same name: 'in his name as Shu', that is, in the form of, in the manifestation as.[89] Such an interpretation would reinforce the concept of Rê-Harakhty as the basic being who is manifested in another mode as Shu, who in turn is materialized in another mode as Aten.

A partial correspondence in iconography is perhaps supplied by a figure of the god Rê-Harakhty on the stela of 'Kia' which derives from the early part of the reign. In his publication of the stela Aldred[90] states that it shows that 'the image of Rē-Harakhti can appear as a falcon-headed god bearing the early didactic name of the Aten in double cartouches without any accompanying epithets'. It seems doubtful, however, whether the term 'Rê-Harakhty-Aten' should be applied to this falcon-headed god as a 'brief label without any distinguishing epithets'.[91]

It was Anthes[92] who initiated the interpretation of this triad in a manner which removes the divine names Shu and Aten. He also wished to remove the introductory ʿnḫ as a verbal form, reducing its force to that of a sign. Certainly the ʿnḫ is missing from the early cartoucheless form from Gebel Silsila, where the syntax ('first prophet of Rê-Harakhty ...') precludes it; and also from several instances of the developed forms in cartouches. Sethe[93] pointed to cases where incorrect copying caused its omission; and he strongly advocated its full verbal sense as one linked to *m rn.f*: 'Rê-Harakhty lives ... in his name.' Yet he admits that the frequent use of the verb in royal inscriptions of the type 'Horus-N lives' or 'The Good God, King N lives'[94] gave it a merely formal force. Anthes suggests, as alternatives to his view that ʿnḫ is purely a sign or symbol here, a verbal sense as an imperative or the force of a nominal form ('Living One' or 'Life'), but these are not convincing.[95] Assmann[96] wisely keeps the full verbal force ('Es lebt Re-Harachte ...'). Whether *m rn.f* is dependent on the initial ʿnḫ or on the participial *hʿi m 3ḫt*, 'who rejoices on the horizon', is an open question. *M rn.f* is a common phrase that is often related semantically (and sometimes punningly) to a verb that precedes;[97] and such a link tends to favour *hʿi m 3ḫt*, rather than ʿnḫ since Rê-Harakhty exulting on the horizon is likely to be viewed as enacting a quality relating to his name more clearly than by merely living.

Anthes lays great stress on the second preposition *m* in the phrase *m rn.f m šw*. Doubtless he is right in saying that 'in his name of Shu' would normally demand *m rn.f n šw*. But it does not follow that the two prepositions must be syntactically co-ordinated to produce 'who rejoices in his name and in the sunlight'. The second *m* may not be governed in the same way; it probably emphasizes the meaning of identity with the sense of 'in his aspect of', 'in his role of'.[98] We may compare the second *m* of the second name: 'in his name as (*m*) Rê my Father who returns as (*m*) Aten'. Admittedly the second *m* here has its own verb ('returns') to govern it; in the earlier name it seems to be epexegetic to *rn*.

Yet it is the explanation of both *šw* and *ỉtn* as common nouns that is most distinctive of the approach by Anthes. On the former he notes that occasionally translations had used the locution 'Shu (sun)', but that Gardiner's rendering of the inscription from Gebel Silsila had given him satisfaction: 'in his name the sunlight (Egyptian "Shu")'. Gardiner's intention, however, remains mysterious. Was he suggesting that the god Shu here represented sunlight? That is more likely than the idea that a common noun, *šw*, 'sunlight', was involved, although such a noun does of course exist; if Gardiner had meant that, he would presumably not have written 'Shu' with an initial capital. Anthes emphasizes the absence of the god-determinative,[99] but we have noted (n.76) that Amarna texts show no consistency in this matter. Occurring as it does in the second cartouche, which supplies a theological commentary to the simple naming of the god Rê-Harakhty in the first cartouche, where 'rejoicing on the horizon' is also an easily understood formulation,[100] the reference to Shu (or šw),[101] suggests an element of contrast. Anthes[102] is eager to emphasize the meaning of 'sunlight' which šw can bear, but he unwisely posits the attribution of this meaning to the god Shu as the basic etymology of the name. That Shu develops close cosmic kinship to the sun-god Rê has been made clear above; the equation, however, which Anthes proposes would identify him absolutely with the sunlight. The god's name has in fact a different derivation; šwỉ, 'be empty', is the likely source, although šwỉ, 'be dry', may be influential in the development of the meaning eventually assigned to the god.[103]

Turning to the role of Aten in the triad, we note the firm denial by Anthes (p.4) that the word could mean the god at the beginning of the reign; it was only later, he argues, after the transference to El-Amarna, that this meaning was assigned to the word; before that it meant simply 'sun-disc'. The truth is that there are plentiful examples of both meanings even before the reign of Akhenaten.[104] A well-known instance is Sinuhe R 7, of the death of Sehetep-ieb-Rê, ẖnm m 'Itn, 'he was united with Aten', where two manuscripts carry the divine determinative: see Blackman's text, p.3.[105] Of course the two meanings are essentially fused in the god called Aten, just as rꜥ in the sense of 'sun' is behind the name of Rê. In his admirable article 'Aton', Assmann[106] is naturally concerned with this problem. He begins by maintaining that the theology and cult of the god Aten were bound up with the time and person of Amenophis IV and were his achievement. After pointing out that Aten in Amarna is really an abbreviated name, he rejects the equation of him with the term as found in earlier usage. He emphasizes that he is dealing with the god Aten, and his distinctive form as the radiate sun-disc is properly stressed. Discussing the early didactic name, he offers the following interpretation of the second cartouche: '(accessible) in his name (and capable of representation in his form) as daylight, which is in the sun (that is, as "radiate Aten")'. Unlike Anthes, who is prepared to use the personal name in his explanation of the second didactic name,[107] Assmann apparently draws no distinction in this matter, although he favours Fecht's approach. The truth is that royal names in cartouches are consistently based on the names of gods; and this is the tradition here superimposed on the god Aten. Further, the expression m rn.f certainly suggests that a name is to follow; in the first didactic name it may be argued that it precedes mentions of Shu and Aten and in the second mentions of 'Rê my Father' and Aten.[108]

4. Relation to the Basic Aims

If Amarna doctrine is characterized by two triadic formulations – and they are both abundantly attested – their relation to the basic religious aims of Akhenaten is not easily expounded. Indeed Anthes (p.90) opines that theological declarations like the great divine name of Amarna (the first doctrinal name) could be understood in Egypt in manifold ways, as chapter 17 of the Book of the Dead makes clear. In the latter context alternative readings[109] or explanations[110] are, however, expressly pointed to, usually by means of the formula *ky ḏd*. The Amarna texts do not contain such clear pointers; and even when they are present, as in *BD* 17, the question arises whether the interpretations should be accepted as valid. Gardiner[111] once challenged this idea, averring that 'He who desires to grasp the meaning of the 17th chapter will certainly not seek aid from the Egyptian scholia.' Heerma van Voss[112] described this dictum as unjust, and with every apparent reason. The writings of the Egyptians themselves would seem to be the prime source for the correct interpretation of their ideas.

In literature generally the intention of the author may be easily accepted as the final arbiter of interpretation, although the matter is hotly contested in contemporary hermeneutics. Whereas the first Egyptian commentators on *BD* are a little removed from the authors of the text, they[113] are much closer to them than the most sophisticated modern exegete. On the other hand, in the case of Akhenaten and the Amarna texts, the idea of one exclusive interpretation is certainly favoured by the claims which Akhenaten himself made. According to Anthes (p.2) the claim to exclusive validity is typical of Christian theology and is derived from Greek philosophy, and such an approach was alien to Akhenaten in spite of the zeal with which he furthered the essence of his religion in the exclusive claim made for his version of sun-worship. It is the distinction between meaning and significance that opens the way to variety of interpretation. With regard to meaning it is hard to contest Schleiermacher's intentionalist emphasis when he 'sought to restore the sense a text had had for its author and for the original audience'.[114] If some literary works can be said to be 'inexhaustible', this need not imply that the meaning of a particular work is not what the author intended; 'it is perfectly plausible to suppose that what is inexhaustible about a particular literary work is not its meaning but its significance.'[115]

To aim at the establishment of meaning, in this primary sense which links it to intention, seems at the moment demanding enough in the study of the religion of Amarna. For example, how is one to explain the differences between the two doctrinal names? If we believe that the first name comprises a triad of gods, that is evidently not true of the second name, which is usually dated to the ninth year of the reign, the first being not later than the fourth. The second name begins, 'Rê lives, the ruler of the two horizons (lit. the "horizonal" ruler)', where *ḥḳ3 3ḥty* replaces the *Ḥr-3ḥty* of the first name; and it goes on, 'who rejoices in the horizon in his name, Rê my Father who returns as Aten'. Thus both Horus and Shu are eliminated from the second name, whereas Rê himself figures twice, and is connected now only with Aten. The intention appears to be to emphasize still further the monotheistic stress.[116] It is true that *Ḥr-3ḥty* and *ḥḳ3 3ḥty* might be regarded as purely synonymous.[117] But in view of the long-established tradition behind the names Harakhty and Rê-Harakhty, the rare Heqa-akhty is very striking in its purposive break with hallowed convention.

Concurrently there is a break also with the triadic formulation. Yet if this formulation is seen to be inherently modalistic rather than tritheistic, the break here is not so profound. Indeed traces of the modalistic process remain. If Horus and Shu have disappeared, Aten is now presented as a constantly recurring manifestation of Rê.

In both doctrinal names basic importance is assigned to Rê-Harakhty and Rê. Whereas the living cosmic boon that comes from every sunrise is given priority and explained as the gift of life proffered by the helping hands of the radiate Aten, it is surprising that scholars have sought to exclude from this concept any concern for life after death and for moral rectitude. On the latter point Gardiner[118] roundly states that 'a defect of the Doctrine was its complete lack of ethical teaching'. Any doctrine which gave prominence to Rê and to his daughter Maat would not be likely to make such an omission. Further, in Egyptian tradition Rê is the sun-god who not only bestows his blessings during the day, but also by his nightly visit to the realm of the dead provides a guarantee of immortality. It seems that the Amarna texts contain no explicit allusions to the second activity, but it is hard to believe that the prominence of Rê or Rê-Harakhty in the texts can possibly allow a complete *kenosis* of meaning in this respect. These qualities are in fact ascribed to Aten in a number of prayers to which Žabkar[119] has well called attention. A prayer addressed by Tutu to Aten shows great concern for the claims of morality; it couples Akhenaten with Aten in this respect, and it asks for the benefits of a 'goodly burial' with everything implied by that – certainly with a blissful afterlife which is pointedly suggested by the protestations of innocence. A part of Žabkar's translation may be quoted (with very minor changes):

> I have come with praise to Aten, the living and only god ... I have not received reward of lying in order to compel the righteous in favour of the guilty, but I implemented Maat for the King ... I have not set falsehood in my body ... I carried out his [the King's] teaching; there was not found a blameworthy action

of mine in any evil ... [May I live] in adoring his Majesty, being one of his followers. Mayest thou grant that I may be satisfied with seeing thee; my heart prays that thou shouldst assign to me a goodly burial after old age in Akhetaten.[120]

A previous part of the prayer addresses Aten in the second person ('I am come to thee, O living Aten'), and, although adoration of the King is mentioned, the concluding prayer is again addressed to Aten. In other similar compositions the request is sometimes made to the King himself or to the *ka* of the King or Queen. What is clear in the moral assertions, as Žabkar points out, is that the influence of the Osirian judgement is still present, although Osiris himself is not mentioned. Both Rê and Maat were, of course, important in the development of the idea; and the Amarna texts preserve much of the traditional concept of Maat.[121] But Maat is now implemented, as in Tutu's prayer, 'for the King'; and the King is envisaged as testifying to Aten of his follower's integrity – a modified form of the *Totengericht*.[122]

Such associations may well be absent if one accepts an interpretation ending with 'the light which is in the sun', although Rê-Harakhty remains at the beginning. If Shu is admitted as the second member of a triad here, his role in relation to the afterlife should not be excluded; in funerary texts he is seen to be aiding the celestial ascent of the deceased.[123]

If we examine the possible motivation of the triad which binds together the god Aten with the King and Queen, it is the King's desire to glorify himself that perhaps emerges; or a desire, when explained more favourably, to achieve unity with his god in a public ambience. A variation of this intention may be seen in the presence of Aten's doctrinal names within royal cartouches; the King is elevated through the bringing-down of the supreme deity to his level, a notion emphasized by the proximity of the King's own cartouches. The same impulse seems to promote the association of Aten with *sed*-festivals. Several of these allusions are consonant with the traditional concept that such festivals, which affirm the renewal and consolidation of royal power, stem from the favour and beneficence of the gods, in these instances of the god Aten (or Rê) in favour of the King Akhenaten:

> Thine hands hold millions of jubilee festivals for the King.
> (Tomb of Ay; Sandman, *Texts*, 90, 18–91, 1)
> May he (Aten) reward thee with jubilee festivals, like the counting of shore sands.
> (Tomb of Ay; ibid., 92, 12)
> Give him many jubilee festivals and years,
> (Tomb of Meryrê; ibid., 21, 14)
> Give him millions of jubilee festivals.
> (Tomb of Panehesy; ibid., 28, 3; cf. Tomb of Tutu; ibid., 73, 6)

> May Rê give to thee, every time he rises, a multitude of jubilee festivals.
> (Tomb of Meryrê, II; ibid., 32, 10)

By way of contrast, one is rather startled by two expressions which seem to designate the god Aten himself as being the recipient of such festivals:

> Great living Aten, lord of jubilee festivals (*nb ḥbw-sd*).
> (Tomb of Meryrê; ibid., 1, 18)
> Great living Aten, who is in festive jubilee (*imy ḥb-sd*).
> (*Tomb of Ay = The 'Great Hymn'*, ibid., 93, 9)

The former phrase, however, is used of other gods, including Khnum, Sobek and Maat.[124] As for the second phrase, it is sometimes found in the plural,[125] hence the rendering by Davies, 'abiding in the *sed*-festivals'; cf. Gardiner,[126] 'he who is in the Sed-festival', with the suggestion that the near-identity of the King and his god is conveyed, since the *sed*-festival was essentially a 'royal celebration'. Yet a distinction can be maintained even if Gardiner's rendering is accepted: the god Aten is present in the King's jubilee festival in the sense that he has made it possible. *Ḥb-sd* may, none the less, have a less literal meaning here, on the lines of Roeder's[127] 'der in Festfreude ist'. Aten is merged, then, in the King's experience, just as the King's birth and length of existence is equated with those of his god: 'thou (the King) art born as Aten is born, thy lifetime is eternity, the lifetime of Rê' (Tomb of Meryrê; Sandman, 17, 3).[128] The basic idea is, therefore, that of a god ruling in and through the King, an idea facilitated by their relationship as Father and Son. What the Amarna texts and representations convey is a theocracy.[129] The two triadic entities are expressions of the basic idea. An imposing clarity features the triad of Aten, King and Queen: the three are reigning together; not, it is true, as a triad of equal partners, for the god Aten is the sustaining and life-bestowing power under whom the King and Queen rule, although they too are objects of adoration. Less direct is the doctrine of the first didactic name. Aten is here equated with Shu, and the supremacy of Rê-Harakhty is paramount; but Shu as the divine son adumbrates the role of Akhenaten.

NOTES

[1] Cyril Aldred in *CAH*³ II. 2 (1975), 88.

[2] *Idem*, op. cit., 87, following Piankoff in *BIFAO* 62 (1964), 207ff. Cf. Piankoff, *The Shrines of Tut-Ankh-Amon* (New York, Bollingen Series, 40.2, 1955), 12–13, 'a question of a nuance, of a dogmatic finesse'.

[3] See Jan Assmann, *Liturgische Lieder an den Sonnengott* (Berlin, 1969); *idem*,

Der König als Sonnenpriester (ADAIK, 7, Glückstadt, 1970).

[4] Cf. Dieter Müller in *Orientalia* 41 (1972), 446: 'The performed rites closely paralleled the cosmic processes.'

[5] See Jan Assmann, *Ägyptische Hymnen und Gebete* (Zurich, 1975), 47f. The triad is clearly monistic, as the occasional form Khepri-Rê-Atum shows. Cf. H. te Velde in *JEA* 57 (1971), 81.

[6] Ibid. 48. In his masterly study *Ma'at* (Munich, 1990), 231-6 Assmann expounds Amarna's theology as firmly monistic as well as being distinctively cosmic, positive, and anthropocentric.

[7] Jan Assmann, 'Die Häresie des Echnaton: Aspekte der Amarna-Religion', *Saeculum* 23 (1972), 109-26.

[8] Cyril Aldred, *Akhenaten and Nefertiti* (New York, 1973), 56, Fig.33. Cf. Piankoff, *The Shrines of Tut-Ankh-Amon*, 10, Fig.1. It is not only to the King and Queen, however, that the *ankh*-sign is proffered although that is normally the case. In one representation two of their children are also thus provided: see Barbara Lesko, *The Remarkable Women of Ancient Egypt* (Berkeley, 1978), 10, a relief in the Berlin Museum, Charlottenburg (= Aldred, *Akhenaten and Nefertiti*, 102, no.16). But there are three children here in all, and this would leave one of them unprovided for: Aldred thinks that the two *ankh*-signs on each side are intended only for the parents.

[9] See Aldred, op. cit.

[10] Cf. Rainer Hanke, *Amarna-Reliefs aus Hermopolis* (Hildesheim, 1978), 1; cf. 239ff.

[11] Cf. D. B. Redford and R. W. Smith, *The Akhenaten Temple Project*, I (London 1976), 125; Julia Samson, *Amarna, City of Akhenaten and Nefertiti* (London, 1978), 121ff.

[12] The earliest instance is perhaps in the tomb of Ramose: see N. de Garis Davies, *The Tomb of the Vizier Ramose* (London, 1941), Pl.33 and Aldred, op. cit., 35, Fig.17.

[13] In *JNES* 31 (1972), 152 ('Palast oder Tempel?').

[14] See E. P. Uphill, 'The Per Aten at Amarna', *JNES* 29 (1970), 151-66. On p.151 he refers this view to 'the German expedition', but the article cited by him (*JEA* 10 (1924), 299ff.) does not appear to allude to this view.

[15] In *JEA* 57 (1971), 80-6, esp. 84ff.

[16] W. Stevenson Smith, *The Art and Architecture of Ancient Egypt* (Harmondsworth, 1958), Pl.44 B with p.62 for the dyad; for this and the triad see Maspero, tr. Rusch, *Geschichte der Kunst in Ägypten* (Stuttgart, 1913), 82-3; cf. J. R. Harris, *Egyptian Art* (London 1966), Pl.7 with p.35; and above chapter 1, section 4.

[17] G. Daressy, *Statues de divinités* (CCG, 1905-6), no.39210 with Pl.56; cf. nos.39211, 39212, 39213.

[18] Petrie, *Koptos* (London, 1896), 15 with Pl.17.

[19] See D. Wildung in *ZÄS* 99 (1972), 33-41, esp. 34f. with Pl.4.

[20] E. Brunner-Traut in *Universitas* 15 (1960), 607. Cf. Silvio Curto, *Nubien* (Munich, 1966), 332 with Pl.256.

[21] D. Wildung, op. cit., 36.

[22] K. Lange and M. Hirmer, *Egypt: Architecture, Sculpture, Painting*[4] (London, 1968), 401 with Pl.15.

[23] Ibid. 421 with Pl.92; cf. Pls.94 (with falcon above) and 95 (with vulture above). Horus and Nekhbet are the deities thus figured.

[24] Cf. Bonnet, *Bilderatlas* (Leipzig, 1924), no.11; nos.12 and 13 are forms which

centre the scarab beetle instead of the disc. For pre-Amarna forms see Hayes, *Scepter of Egypt*, II (Cambridge, Mass., 1959), 10-11 (with one wing over deified kings), 77, 104-5, 144, 168, 171, 173, 274.

[25] Op. cit., 168; cf. 171.

[26] Aldred, *Akhenaten and Nefertiti*, 69, Fig.45, and 102, no.16.

[27] Ibid., 78, Fig.47. For an example of Nefertiti centred under the Aten see Julia Samson, *Amarna* (1978), 124f.

[28] Hans Kayser, *Die ägyptischen Altertümer im Roemer-Pelizaeus-Museum in Hildesheim* (Hildesheim, 1973), 69 with Abb.44.

[29] Selim Hassan in *ASAE* 38 (1938), 53-61 (on a stela erected for Amenophis II); cf. S. Tawfik in *MDAIK* 29 (1973), 81.

[30] A possibility that the triad was originally reflected in three altars in the House of Hatiay is mentioned by Pendlebury in *The City of Akhenaten*, II (London, 1933), 64; cf. Assmann in *JNES* 31, 153.

[31] Cf. H. Brunner in W. Beyerlin, ed., *Religionsgeschichtliches Textbuch zum Alten Testament* (Göttingen, 1975), 46 n.62. = p.19, n.j in English edn. (1978).

[32] Cf. Cornelis A. de Ridder, *Maria als Miterlöserin?* (Göttingen, 1965; Kirche und Konfession, 5).

[33] Cf. Günther Roeder, *Amarna-Reliefs aus Hermopolis* (Hildesheim, 1969), 375, under 'Gottähnlichkeit des Königs', where the participation of Nefertiti is nevertheless ignored. Julia Samson, *Amarna* (1978), 109ff., discusses 'Nefertiti's Names and Titles'.

[34] Redford and Smith, *The Akhenaten Temple Project*, I, 40ff., esp. 44; cf. Julia Samson, op. cit., 121f.

[35] John A. Wilson in *JNES* 32 (1973), 237 ('Akh-en-Aton and Nefert-iti').

[36] A common name according to Ranke, *Personennamen*, I, 201, 12.

[37] Ranke, ibid., suggests 'schön an Schönheit', but *nfr nfrw* might be regarded as a superlative on the analogy of *wr wrw*, 'greatest of the great' (Gardiner, *Gr.*³ §97). Černý, *Ancient Egyptian Religion* (London, 1952), 63, offered 'Beautiful is the Beauty of Aton', with a displeasing tautology.

[38] S. Tawfik in *MDAIK* 29 (1973), 82ff.; Julia Samson, *Amarna* (1978), 125f., citing Redford's view that the long name derived from very early in the reign. See also Julia Samson on 'Nefertiti's Regality', *JEA* 63 (1977), 88-97, esp. 90-3 ('Scenes of worship'); and cf. Aldred, *Akhenaten and Nefertiti*, 25: 'She had officiated as a sort of high priestess, a virtual equal of the King.'

[39] John A. Wilson in *JNES* 32 (1973), 238 thinks that Nefertiti's religious role belies the claim.

[40] *Rock Tombs of El Amarna*, III (London, 1905), 15. But in one instance the texts there noted venerate Akhenaten, Amenophis III, and Queen Tiy.

[41] Cf. Wilson, op. cit., 239. He observes (p.240) that prayers to her do not include a request for a proper burial, a boon which is mentioned only in prayers to Aten and the King. Otherwise the prayers are similar.

[42] Cf. Erik Hornung, *Conceptions of God in Ancient Egypt* (London, 1983), 248; *idem* in *ZÄS* 97 (1971), 77; Assmann, 'Die Häresie', 123.

[43] E.g. the Great Hymn to the Aten; another hymn is given the title 'Hymn to the Aten and the King' in Miriam Lichtheim, *Ancient Egyptian Literature*, II (Berkeley, 1976), 93; 'and the Queen' should have been added, as the translation duly makes clear.

[44] Cf. Erik Hornung, 'Monotheismus im pharaonischen Ägypten', in Othmar Keel,

ed., *Monotheismus im Alten Israel und seiner Umwelt* (Biblische Beiträge 14, Freiburg, 1980), 83–97, this on p.88.

[45] Kate Bosse-Griffiths, 'A Beset Amulet from the Amarna Period', *JEA* 63 (1977), 98–106, esp. 104ff.

[46] *Amarna-Reliefs*, 292 and 375.

[47] For the likely vocalization *jâti* see G. Fecht, *ZÄS* 85 (1960), 88f.

[48] *JEA* 9 (1923), 174.

[49] Thus claiming his position as the supreme god.

[50] In *JEA* 9 (1923), 176.

[51] For the hieroglyphs, in addition to Sandman, see Gunn, op. cit., 168; see also the refs. in Assmann, *JNES* 31 (1972), 152 n.60.

[52] In *MDAIK* 25 (1969), 202–11.

[53] Assmann, 'Die Häresie', 118.

[54] See Gardiner, *Egn. Gr.*[3] §§ 357 (end) and 359 (end).

[55] *Wb.* I, 37; Faulkner, *Concise Dict.* 10.

[56] Chassinat, *Edfou*, VI, 109, 9. Gunn states of the last phrase, which is used also of the Aten, 'perhaps at no other time applied to a god'; see *JEA* 9, 168. This dictum must therefore be modified. In P. Chester Beatty, I, 1, 6 the name of Wen-nefer (Osiris) is enclosed in a cartouche; cf. I, 14, 8 (also of Osiris).

[57] Gunn, op. cit., 174, misleads when he separates the names as 'Rēʿ lives, Ḥarakhte ...'

[58] It already occurs once in the *Pyramid Texts* (1049 a P) and several times in the Coffin Texts: see B. Altenmüller, *Synkretismus in den Sargtexten* (Wiesbaden, 1975), 103. R. Anthes in *ZÄS* 100 (1974), 77f. points out that elsewhere in the *Pyramid Texts* Rê and Harakhty are named separately.

[59] Op. cit., 174.

[60] Cf. Bonnet, *RÄRG*, 60; Morenz, *Rel.*, 154f.; Assmann, 'Die Häresie', 117.

[61] Op. cit., 175.

[62] H. te Velde, 'The Theme of the Separation of Heaven and Earth in Egyptian Mythology', *Studia Aegyptiaca* 3 (1977), 161–70, esp. 161f.

[63] Op. cit., 163ff.

[64] Cf. J. Zandee in *ZÄS* 100 (1973), 60 and 66f.; cf. *CT* II, 30b: *It is I who make the light of heaven after the darkness*; cf. Zandee in *ZÄS* 101 (1974), 63 and 67. The view that Shu was in origin a personification of the dry, empty atmosphere is presented by W. Barta in *Untersuchungen zum Götterkreis der Neunheit* (MÄS 28, Berlin, 1973), 86, positing a derivation from *šw*, 'be empty' and *šwi̯*, 'be dry'.

[65] *ZÄS* 100 (1973), 67; cf. his remarks in *ZÄS* 99 (1972), 62f.

[66] See Zandee in *ZÄS* 100 (1974), 147.

[67] *Rel.* 154f. See also above n.63.

[68] 'Amarna-Probleme (1–2)' in *ZÄS* 85 (1960), 83–118.

[69] *Rel.*, 155.

[70] *The Rock Tombs of El Amarna*, I (London, 1903), 49.

[71] Familiar, it is true, in Christian doctrine: see John 14: 9ff. The Father, at least, is regarded as being in the Son and at one with him.

[72] Cf. Morenz, *Rel.*, 153.

[73] For Shu in a Memphite triad (Ptah, Shu, and Tefnut) see L. Kákosy in *JEA* 66 (1980), 48–53.

[74] 'Die Häresie', 117.

[75] *Egypt of the Pharaohs* (Oxford, 1961), 218.

[76] See L. V. Žabkar in *JNES* 13 (1954), 93 with n.95.

[77] Op. cit., 117. For the thesis in favour of common nouns here see Anthes in *ZÄS* 90 (1963), 1–6 and Bennett in *JEA* 51 (1965), 207–9.

[78] Op. cit., 208.

[79] Bennett cites *ZÄS* 85 (1960), 103.

[80] Aldred, *Akhenaten and Nefertiti* (New York, 1973), 20, renders the form from Gebel Silsila '... in his aspect of the sun-light which is in the Aten'. But Shu is seen here by J. A. Wilson, *The Culture of Ancient Egypt* (Chicago, 1951), 222; Bonnet, *RÄRG* (1952), 60; Kees, *Götterglaube*² (Berlin, 1956), 370; Morenz, *Rel.* (1960), 154; Piankoff in *BIFAO* 62 (1964), 209; J. Zandee in *ZÄS* 101 (1974), 65; A. M. Badawy in *ZÄS* 102 (1975), 12; M. Lichtheim, *Ancient Egyptian Lit.*, II (Berkeley, 1976), 91. Assmann in *LÄ* I (1975), 530, translates 'als Tageslicht, das in der Sonne ist', but correctly adds in a note to 'Tageslicht' (p.537 n.55), 'Meist als Gott Schu aufgefasst'. Hornung, *Der Eine und die Vielen* (Darmstadt, 1971), 242 (cf. his *Conceptions of God* (1983), 245), takes the view that Shu is meant, but in 'Monotheismus im pharaonischen Ägypten', in Othmar Keel, ed., *Monotheismus im Alten Israel und seiner Umwelt* (Freiburg), 1980), 85, he appears to accept Assmann's interpretation.

[81] The term has no necessary chronological implication, but the form probably belongs in that sense also to a transitional phase.

[82] Fairman in *The City of Akhenaten*, III (1951), 183 with Pl.108; cf. J. Samson, ibid., 231.

[83] *Amarna, City of Akhenaten and Nefertiti*² (1978), 102f.

[84] Op. cit., 208.

[85] *Gr.* § 200, 2.

[86] Cf. J. Gwyn Griffiths in *JEA* 54 (1968, Fs. Černý), 63.

[87] See Helck's note, p.25, citing Gardiner in *Mél. Maspero* (1934), 482 and favouring the second interpretation.

[88] Cf. Gardiner, *Gr.* § 107, 2. M. Hamza, *La Lecture de l'adjectif relatif négatif* (IFAO, 1929), 22, renders, 'j'ai fait arriver celui qui n'est rien comme celui qui est quelque chose.' Cf. Wilson in *ANET*, 418: '... like him, who was (somebody)': M. Lichtheim, *Lit.* I (1973), 136, basically follows Gardiner.

[89] Cf. my remarks in *The Origins of Osiris and his Cult* (Leiden, 1980), 143f.

[90] *JEA* 45 (1959), 22 with Pl.3 and Fig.1.

[91] Ibid., 20.

[92] *ZÄS* 90 (1963), 1–10.

[93] *Beiträge zur Geschichte Amenophis' IV.* (Nachr. Göttingen, 1921), 112 n.3.

[94] Cf. ʿnḫ ḏt after kings' names, probably with optative meaning; Gardiner, *Egn. Gr.* § 313. Gunn, op. cit., 173 n.1, prefers an indicative sense.

[95] Bennett, op. cit., 209, adopts one of these suggestions ('Rēʿ-Ḥerakhty the living'), but without discussion.

[96] 'Die Häresie', 117; cf. *idem* in *LÄ* I, 529, where ʿnḫ is read.

[97] *Wb.* II, 426, 26 and 27.

[98] Fecht, op. cit., 103; cf. Bennett, op. cit., 208; Assmann, 'Die Häresie', 117 n.35, well explains it as denoting 'kultisch zugänglicher, anrufbarer Aspekt'.

[99] The sun-determinative is also lacking in some instances; cf. Sethe, op. cit., 109.

[100] Fecht, op. cit., 103f.

[101] On p.93 n.2 Fecht propounds a vocalization *šaw on the basis of the Greek form Σῶς, but does not explain why the vowel should be *a*. Cf. Hopfner, *Fontes*,

730; Waddell, *Manetho*, 3.

[102] Op. cit., 5.

[103] Cf. Fecht, op. cit., 105.

[104] Sayed Tawfik, 'Aton Studies. 1: Aton before the reign of Akhenaton', *MDAIK* 29 (1973), 77-86. Cf. Bonnet, *RÄRG*, 59-60.

[105] Tawfig, op. cit., 77. Several translators mislead with 'the sun-disc'. It should be, at least, 'the god of the sun-disc'. Assmann in *LÄ* I, 535 n.6, gives instances from the *Coffin Texts* onwards, but would draw a sharp distinction between this meaning of *itn* and that implied by the Amarna doctrine.

[106] *LÄ* I, 526ff.

[107] Anthes, op. cit., 6, ending 'in Vater Re, der im Aton (der Sonnenscheibe) gekommen ist'.

[108] *M rn.f* is often used to denote related cult-forms which have the effect of extending a god's sphere of influence, so that place-names commonly occur in the phrases that follow. Hence its frequent occurrence with Osiris both early and late; cf. my *Origins of Osiris and his Cult* (Leiden, 1980), 136f.; R. O. Faulkner, *An Ancient Egyptian Book of Hours* (Oxford, 1958), x, restoring the title of this text as 'To Osiris in all his names'.

[109] See M. Heerma van Voss, *De oudste Versie van Dodenboek 17a* (Leiden, 1963), 9, showing that earlier readings are thus introduced.

[110] These are sometimes allegorized and mostly concern Rê or Atum; see J. Gwyn Griffiths, *JEA* 53 (1967), 97f.

[111] *ZÄS* 43 (1906), 58f.

[112] Op. cit., *Stellungen*, VI.

[113] Heerma van Voss would locate the earliest in the Ninth or Tenth Dynasty.

[114] Frank Kermode in *London Review of Books*, 20 May 1981, 12, reviewing P. D. Juhl, *Interpretation: An Essay in the Philosophy of Literary Criticism* (Princeton, 1981). Cf. Kermode, *The Genesis of Secrecy* (Harvard, 1979; repr. 1982), 119, on Spinoza's distinction between meaning and truth.

[115] P. D. Juhl, op. cit., as quoted by Kermode in his review. Cf. René Wellek and Austin Warren, *Theory of Literature* (3rd edn., Harmondsworth, 1962; repr. 1973), 41ff., where similar views are rejected.

[116] Cf. Sethe, op. cit., 117; Anthes, op. cit., 6; Assmann in *LÄ*, I, 530.

[117] Cf. Fecht, op. cit., 108. Assmann, ibid., notes the small extent of the graphic changes *vis-à-vis* the first name.

[118] *Egypt of the Pharaohs*, 229.

[119] *JNES* 13 (1954), 94ff. ('Ethics').

[120] Žabkar, op. cit., 94, with refs. to Sandman, *Texts*, 75, 18ff.

[121] As when the King presents Maat to Aten: see Anthes, *Die Maat des Echnaton von Amarna* (Suppl. *JAOS* 14, 1952), 27; cf. Assmann, *Ma'at* (Munich, 1990), 232, pointing to the antithesis of truth and falsehood, the former used of the King's religion, the latter of the traditional polytheistic cults.

[122] Anthes, op. cit., 28.

[123] See above n.66 and Zandee's cited remarks.

[124] *Wb*. III, 59, 11.

[125] Davies, *Rock Tombs of El Amarna*, II, Pl.6 and II, Pl.7 (= Sandman, *Texts*, 24, 9).

[126] *Egypt of the Pharaohs*, 228.

[127] *Urk. Rel.* (Jena, 1923), 62.

[128] Cf. the co-dating of the reign of the King and Aten, suggesting a co-regency, as Assmann notes, 'Die Häresie', 119.

[129] Cf. Assmann in *LÄ* I, 530f.

4
Triadic Topography

From time to time we have referred to the local connections of deities who figure in triadic groups. Most deities in fact have local connections when considered individually. Rather different is the association of a whole triadic group with one place. Perhaps the clearest examples we have encountered are seen in the equation of the *baw* of certain cities with groups of three deities (see above chapter 2.2). In one passage of the *Pyramid Texts* (891aPMN) the King addresses his *city god* (*ntr niwty*), assuring him that the King's *ka* is beside him. Does this mean that his city is regarded as having only one god? No, it probably refers to the foremost of the city's gods. The plural expression *city gods* also occurs often in various texts[1] and might well include reference to triadic groups. It would be unwise, however, to argue a preference for such a meaning, especially as there were other divine groups, such as Enneads of varying sizes, attached to many places.[2]

A theory has none the less been widespread, often in an implicit form, that the establishment of divine triads on a local basis became a conscious part of priestly policy throughout Egypt. It was Erman's view that there was a tendency within a town to forge family links among deities who originally had no such connection, but merely happened to coexist locally.[3] If a great goddess was the neighbour of a deity of less importance, they tended, he avers, to be related as mother and son. Thus at Thebes, Khons becomes the child of Mut; at Dendera, Iehy is the child of Hathor; and at Saïs, Neïth is the mother of the crocodile god Sobek. The presence of an important male deity in the same place brought him similarly into the group as father, thus producing the triads headed by Amûn at Thebes and by Ptah at Memphis (with Sakhmet and the child Nefertem). Such divine families arise, it is suggested, by way of local contiguity, whereas the Osirian triad has a link with mythology. Erman points also to the process of syncretism within localities: in Memphis, for instance, an evolution of Ptah-Sokar is followed, because of the increasing popularity of Osiris, by Ptah–Sokar–Osiris. This is not a modalistic trinity but an amalgamation of three gods, two of whom had previous firm connections with Memphis.

It is not always clear, of course, whether any posited system relates in particular cases to a nome, to its capital, to a town, or to a village within it. Some of the instances concern the capital not merely of a nome but of the whole country. Nor is it surprising that in these instances the capital city, especially Memphis and Thebes, is equipped with several triads. But the smallest of units – the individual temple – may merit attention too. This is precisely how Wiedemann begins his discussion of the theme, remarking that 'the Egyptian temple was dedicated, as a rule, to a single deity' but that honours were also paid to his 'companion deities' who formed a 'cycle of divinities' with him. He goes on to say that 'the cycle being usually three in number, the so-called triads arose, which generally consisted of two gods and one goddess; the goddess being the wife of the chief god, and the third member of the triad being their son'.[4] The examples he proceeds to give are at Thebes, Amûn, Mut, and Khons; at Memphis Ptah, Sakhmet, and Nefertem; at Kom Ombo Sobek, Hathor, and Khons; and at Elephantine Satis, Anukis, and Khnum, although he sees no family relationship in the last group. (He gives differing spellings of the names.) In these examples no relation to particular temples is noted, in spite of the initial emphasis on this. Further, the reference to 'the cycle being usually three in number' ignores the ogdoad at Hermopolis and the many groups of nine and more.

1. The Dyad and Triad at Elephantine

A dualistic pattern often emerges in Egypt owing to the division of the country into the 'Two Lands' and to the attempt to pursue symmetrical entities located in Upper and Lower Egypt. Rather different is the potency of the dyad in individual localities, where a goddess seems often to be attached to the local god, but without the addition of a child.[5] In these cases one of the dyad is female, and in the great majority of triads there is at least one female member, although all-male and all-female triads are known.

A significant and instructive example of a triad which is often given prominence in view of its geographical connections is the grouping of Khnum, Satis, and Anukis at Elephantine. The two goddesses are first grouped triadically in a statuary work which figures Sesostris I in the middle with Satis to his right and Anukis to his left.[6] Later in the Twelfth Dynasty, in the reign of Ammenemes III, an offering is made *to Satis, Mistress of Elephantine, to Khnum, Lord of the Cataract, and to Anukis, Mistress of Sehel.*[7] We have thus a fully fledged divine triad with specific geographical assignments given to each member – the islands of Elephantine and Sehel, and the Cataract itself. It has been tempting in the past to regard this group as a well-established triad, albeit an aberration from the family scheme.[8] Geographically its importance may well reflect the strategic significance of the area at Egypt's southern frontier, as Hornung has emphasized.[9] But the early evidence points to Satis as the deity of central prestige in Elephantine. She is eventually joined there by Anukis, but at first has no connection with Khnum. Only in the Middle Kingdom does Khnum join the goddesses to form a triad, and not until the beginning of the New Kingdom does he appear as the Lord of Elephantine, although he is Lord of the Cataract in a Middle Kingdom text.[10] Dominique Valbelle (p.98) also shows that nothing indicates that Anukis was ever considered as an infant deity. If she sometimes bears the epithets *beloved of her mother and favourite(?) of her mother*, this does not prove that the role of the mother was held by Satis.[11] By the Late Period, on the other hand, Khnum, Satis and Anukis become an accepted triad[12] in which Anukis is the daughter.

From the beginning, as in the *Pyramid Texts* (812a PMNff.), Satis has a suitably warlike character; as Mistress of Elephantine she can repel invaders, and in this capacity she will rebut *him who comes against thee from the South*,[13] shooting with her arrows. When the triad emerges in the Twelfth Dynasty, she presumably preserves this Upper Egyptian ferocity, but inevitably her individuality is softened. Triadic development usually involves subordination, and when we see Sesostris I in the middle of a group with Satis to his right and Anukis to his left, Satis may be rated above Anukis, but the male divine monarch has precedence. The same applies afterwards to Khnum.

A more general consideration arises with regard to the role of the triad. It would not be right to extend the evidence of Elephantine to Egyptian triadism everywhere without further scrutiny, but it is proper to face the question. Does the establishment of divine triads tend to happen later and to follow situations where the groups embrace two deities only or other varying numbers? The somewhat mixed nature of some of the triads suggests a process by which deities who happened to be cultic neighbours were regimented to form a group of three without much regard to the question of whether there were previous links between them and indeed whether there was any real affinity. Sethe points to the very varied elements which were conjoined in the triads of Thebes and Memphis. In Memphis an anthropomorphic god, Ptah, is linked with a lion-goddess Sakhmet and the young god of the lotus-flower, Nefertem. Esna shows a still more bizarre mixture: a ram-headed god, Khnum, is linked with the lion-goddess Menhit ('the slaughterer') and their child is the human Heka ('sorcerer'?).[14] Sethe concludes that triadic groups were developed for the most part relatively late in the historic era, and that changes were eventually introduced, as when Imhotep replaced Nefertem in the Memphite triad in the seventh century or afterwards.[15]

We have seen that Valbelle in her study of Satis and Anukis tends even more strongly in this direction, having found no early evidence of a triad in Elephantine. French scholars indeed have been, in several cases, thus disposed. Sauneron declared that 'triads were never systematically introduced'[16] and Daumas describes them as 'formations relativement tardives et instables', noting the complexity, in some instances, of their antecedents. He points to the triad found at Dendera in the Ptolemaic era – Hathor of Dendera, Horus of Edfu, and Iehy. He then shows that, although there is evidence in earlier times of Iehy being regarded as the son of Hathor, there are conflicting traditions in which the place of Iehy is taken by a form of Horus. Only in the Ptolemaic era does Iehy figure in a triad at Dendera.[17]

2. Triads of One Sex

That the family grouping is by no means invariable[18] is shown by a minority of triads in which three deities of the same sex occur. Kees refers to an example at the end of *BD*, 109, where the *baw* of the Easterners are said to be Rê-Harakhty, the Sun-calf, and the Morning Star.[19] We have considered similar formations (in chapter 2 above) relating to both Easterners and Westerners and also to various places. They all bear the impress of artificially sophisticated groupings, and Kees properly remarks that they cannot easily be linked to temple cults. Among the groups we have cited above there are three in which the triad consists of male deities.

Other groups of three males include the three Nubian deities to whom Ramesses II offers lotuses on a carved scene in the lesser temple of Abu Simbel; they are localized forms of Horus: Horus of Miam, Horus of Bak, and Horus of Buhen (see appendix below, s.v. Abu Simbel). Miam (Aniba) had its own temple of Horus, and Bak (Quban) had an Egyptian fort at the beginning of the Twelfth Dynasty.[20] Three Nubian gods are indicated who have been subsumed under the name of Horus. The fact that they form a triad in no way proves that they represent all the gods of Nubia.[21] Certainly there were in Nubia other more prominent and distinctive deities such as Dedwen and Apedemak,[22] as well as the gods Amûn and Osiris.[23]

In the composite god Ptah–Sokar–Osiris we find again a nexus of three males, but in this case the concept of a single being prevails, as representations indicate (Fig.5).[24] The conjunction of three males is further seen in the triple Horus-falcons and in Khepri, Rê, and Atum, for whom see above chapter 2. It is remarkable, however, that the only apparent instance of three goddesses being thus conjoined concerns three foreign deities: Qudshu, Astarte and Anath. They are named on a relief now in Winchester College and probably of Theban origin. Edwards in his

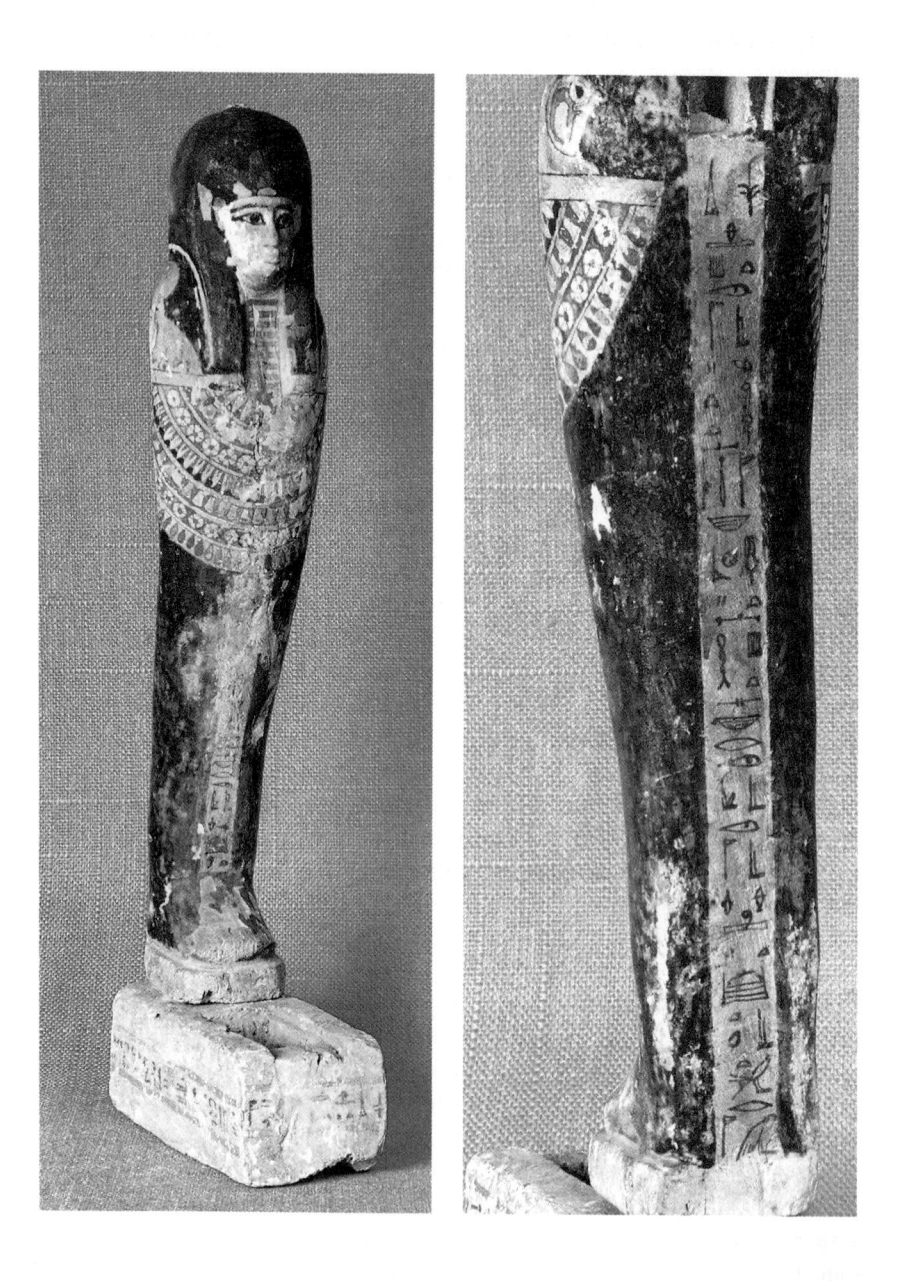

Figure 5. Ptah–Sokar–Osiris: three gods merged into one composite deity

publication of the object reads the name of the deity as Qudshu–Astarte–Anath, 'thus merging into one deity three of the most important goddesses of Western Asia'.[25]

If we ignore the inscriptions, what we see here is a naked goddess standing on a lion, and there are many parallel pieces. (Edwards cites thirteen.) The nudity is chequered by flimsy items, for she wears a head-dress, a collar, thin black bands crossed on the chest, a black girdle, and black bracelets on the lower arms; these elements contrast with the yellow of the body. In her right hand she holds a long lotus plant with a blue flower and red stalk; in her left hand she holds a black serpent. Parallel pieces sometimes show several serpents in one of the hands (two in the left hand of BM no.60308 (= Edwards, Pl.4)). Turning to the inscriptions, we note that the main appellative is given above the goddess, on the right: it is Qudshu or possibly Qadesh, 'Holiness'.[26] Separated from this name, and placed beneath the arms of the goddess, are the two names Anath (below the right arm) and Astarte (below the left arm). The problem is how to relate these three divine names. In other instances the goddess Qudshu is figured with two other named deities who are fully represented on her right and left. One is BM no. 646 which shows the goddess (here named Akent) with Min and Resheph (see Pritchard, *ANEP* (1954), 473, with the notes on p.304; cf. Edwards, p.49). Another also shows Min and Resheph with Qudshu (Louvre C 86 (= Pritchard, 474 with note on pp.304-5)); in this case the inscription includes *Qudshu, lady of heaven and mistress of all the gods*. C. Boreux argued cogently (*Mélanges Dussaud*, 2 (1939), 673-87) that these Syrian deities had been depicted in these and other stelae by Syrian workmen who had migrated to Egypt. The workman named in the relief which mainly concerns us was called Neferhotep, an Egyptian name, but it may have been adopted by a Syrian.

It has been argued by Stadelmann that *Qdš* should be translated 'Holiness', with a genitival sequel relating to the two goddesses named: *the Holiness of Anat* and *the Holiness of Astarte*.[27]

There are, however, four Egyptian examples where Qudshu occurs plainly as the name of the goddess, whatever the original sense of the name may be. Since the two other goddesses named are not actually figured, I now believe that a distinction should be made between the Winchester piece and the examples where full triads are shown. The names Anath and Astarte must be taken as those of subordinated and assimilated deities. Qudshu is the principal name; she has now become a triune goddess, as Edwards claimed, but with the other two deities in the position of mere hypostases. Nor can there be any doubt that both the triadic and the triune aspect is due to Egyptian tradition;[28] in Western Asiatic sources the three goddesses[29] are not thus associated. All three seem to combine the functions of war and love. Although the name Qudshu has the sense of 'holiness' in its Semitic origin, the particular semantic application of 'holy or consecrated one' with reference to a sacred prostitute seems likely, the naked goddess in the representations being regarded as the patroness of such persons. The Ramesside era in Egypt saw a flowering of erotic expression under Syrian influence.[30] Sexuality is certainly conspicuous in the stelae from Deir el-Medina with figures of Qudshu, Resheph and Min, to which we have referred. The first two of these deities are Syrian, but the ithyphallic Min is Egyptian, and, in spite of their varying origin, the three produce a 'triad of sexuality'.[31]

The extreme rarity of the all-female triad is consonant with the lower status of goddesses in the triads generally. In the typical family triad the norm is father, mother, and son, with a duplicated masculine element. The choice of a son and not a daughter probably reflects the dominant predilection in Egypt.[32] Two goddesses sometimes feature in a triad, as with Satis and Anukis, or as with Iunyt and Tenenet at Armant, although Rat-tawy and her son Harprê can also accompany Mont there.[33] Relationships in these cases are unclear – a sign of factitious make-up. Further, Satis and Anukis exemplify a female dyad that precedes the triad.

3. The Principal Theban Triad

Whereas Mentuhotpe II may be regarded as the founder of Thebes at the end of the Eleventh Dynasty when he clinched the supremacy of Thebes over Heracleopolis, it was not until the New Kingdom that the city in the fourth Upper Egyptian nome became the capital, since the Twelfth Dynasty had its capital at Lisht near the entrance to the Fayûm.

The principal divine triad of Thebes consisted of Amûn, Mut, and Khons (Fig. 6A, B), and they were regarded as a group with strong local roots. Devotion to the deities of the city was always a fervent feature of Egyptian religion, and in Thebes the figure of Amûn, as the central deity of the Theban triad, received paramount honour and affection.[34] How ancient Amûn's Theban connections were has been the subject of some debate. In his *Amun und die acht Urgötter von Hermopolis* (1929) Sethe expounded the view that Amûn and his consort Amaunet were part of the Ogdoad of Hermopolis, although perhaps an addendum to the original six couples headed by Nun and Naunet. Hermopolis was therefore Amûn's place of origin. After the Theban armies of the Eleventh Dynasty overcame the last pharaohs of Heracleopolis, they also subdued, according to this theory, the town of Hermopolis and annexed Amûn in the process in order to conciliate the conquered gods, while absorbing their potency likewise thereby. Spirited opposition to such ideas was voiced by

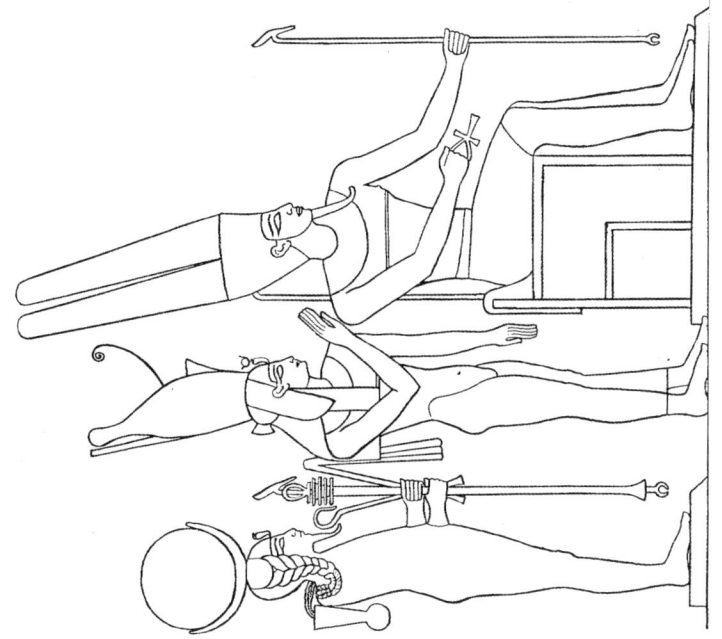

A. Amūn in the centre, Mut to his left, Khons their son to his right

B. A drawing of them, showing their attributes

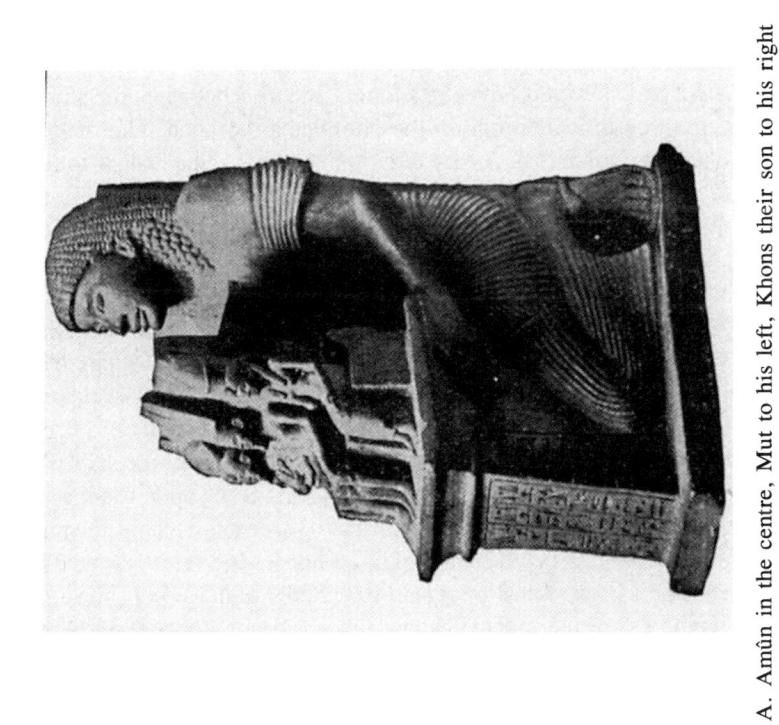

Figure 6. The Principal Theban Triad

Daumas, among others, who maintained the view that Amûn was a very ancient local deity in Karnak.[35] He refers (p.209) to some evidence in the *Pyramid Texts* (especially 446cW) where Amûn and Amaunet are mentioned in a context about offerings, not long after a mention (446a) of Nun and Naunet, the leaders of the Ogdoad of Hermopolis. The other pairs are missing, and the allusion does not help us to decide either way as between Thebes and Hermopolis; it does give Heliopolitan sanction to the antiquity of Amûn, that is all. Nor are the other Pyramid references helpful.[36] We must be content, it seems, to leave the original cult-centre of Amûn an open question.[37] Eventually his temple in Karnak was a grandly conspicuous feature of the religious scene.[38]

South of Amûn's temple was the sacred lake called Isheru, and the Mistress of Isheru was the goddess Mut, to whom a temple was erected in Karnak by Amenophis III. Although no ancient origin can be ascribed to Mut,[39] her roots are entirely Theban, and she becomes attached to Amûn as his consort and as the mother of Khons. The triad are shown together on a relief in the great hypostyle hall, Karnak, where Ramesses II receives emblems of office from Amûn, who is attended by Mut and Khons.[40] While Mut has clear affinities with other goddesses, particularly Sakhmet, Bastet, and Hathor, she borrows from them and does not influence them, so that Bonnet (p.494) can maintain that she was essentially a colourless local goddess. Her liaison with Amûn was doubtless a marriage of convenience, but it had considerable effect on her attributes. As the consort of Amûn in his solar status she becomes *Mistress of Heaven, the Eye of Rê*, and *Great of Magic*. She also becomes the mother of Khons, the youthful moon-god who completes the triad. Her motherhood is clamant in Mut as *the mother of mothers*. She has a vulture head-dress and her name originally meant 'vulture' (cf. *Wb.* III, 53, 15), although it could also mean 'mother'.[41]

As for Khons, he is called *Khons'in Thebes Neferhotep*, where the last epithet perhaps means *rich in grace*.[42] He is sometimes called Khons the Child (*p3 ḥrd*) and he often wears the youthful lock. Of course these features may have resulted from his adoption into the Theban triad. Basically he seems to be a moon-god, as both his name ('the wanderer') and an element in his iconography (the moon-disc on his head) suggest, as also the close connections with Thoth and Iah. It was probably the triadic link that caused the main temple of Khons to be in Karnak in the precinct of Amûn.[43] Two different triads are figured on walls of the small room behind the sanctuary of the temple of Khons. One relief shows Maat being presented by the King to Amen-Rê, Ptah, and Hathor; the other shows a similar presentation to Khons, Thoth, and Osiris. A Ptolemaic origin is suggested, although with possible revision of earlier texts.[44] Numerous other deities are represented, and it is doubtful whether the triadic groupings have any established significance.

It was in the great temple of Luxor, with its three sanctuaries devoted to them, that the three deities of the principal Theban triad were given especial honour. Ramesses II gave this complex its ultimate form, but parts of it were originally erected in the Eighteenth Dynasty.[45]

4. The Theban State Triadic Doctrine

Doctrinally a statement that has had much influence on discussions of Egyptian triads is one found in the Leiden Hymn to Amûn, a hymn which derives from the fifty-second year of the reign of Ramesses II and which was published by Jan Zandee with a Commentary.[46] The statement is translated thus as usual:

> Three are all gods: Amûn, Rê, Ptah. There is no one comparable with them. He who conceals his name as Amûn, he is Rê in countenance, his body is Ptah.
> (Zandee, op. cit. IV, 21-2)

The initial sentence in this translation is perplexing in that it can mean a number of things:

(1) All the gods are three in number. This is plainly false.
(2) All the gods can be represented by the three gods named, because the number three can indicate plurality. A doctrine of triadism would thereby be implied, and in theory would mean that any triad could be similarly interpreted. Conceivably this could apply to any triad of a city or nome in the sense that, although many other deities appear there, the chosen three of the established triad are empowered to subsume them all. If we take a long view of developments, this theory breaks down in the limitation of its validity. Prior to the New Kingdom, the triad is by no means supreme. The dyad, the tetrad, the ogdoad, and especially the ennead are also prevalent.
(3) All the gods (of Thebes) are three in number. This is not valid here because two of the gods named – Rê and Ptah – are not in origin Theban gods. The triad here named contrasts markedly with the Theban triad proper (Amûn, Mut, Khons).
(4) All the gods (of Egypt) are three in number. This enables a pan-Egyptian application of the doctrine of triadism to operate.

The immediate sequel goes on to name the cities associated with these three gods as powerful cities which will last for ever:

> Their cities on earth are established for ever.
> Thebes, Heliopolis, and Memphis until eternity.
> (Ibid.)

Here the emphasis on the importance of the cities invites one to translate the *nbw* of the previous passage, not as *all*, but as *lords*. Either meaning is possible, and when *nbw* follows *ntrw*, 'gods', it is often followed by a genitival phrase indicating the cities or offices ruled by them; but the use is also found absolutely, without an indication of the cities or areas (*Wb.* II, 232, 1),[47] and in the present context the cities are, of course, emphatically named in the sequel. What follows concerns a message from heaven which is heard in Heliopolis and repeated in Memphis; its purpose is to sanction the primacy of the *City of Amûn* – that is, Thebes.

Unlike Thebes, Heliopolis and Memphis were not of contemporary importance. Indeed, Heliopolis owed its significance to the prehistoric era; and Memphis held sway in the Old and Middle Kingdoms. Yet there is some evidence that the state triad thus constituted received worship in the Ramesside era;[48] and Ptah and Rê maintained their prestige. The great temple of Abu Simbel contained four seated statues in the sanctuary, those of Ptah, Amen-Rê, Ramesses II, and Rê-Harakhty. Here we see a tetrad rather than a triad, since Ramesses II is clearly regarded as a god on a par with the state triad.[49]

The inner relationship of the triad as expressed in the Leiden hymn is a matter of some significance. According to John A. Wilson,[50] 'this is a statement of trinity, the three chief gods of Egypt subsumed into one of them, Amon'. E. Otto went further than this, finding here the concepts of both plurality and monism and also the force of three as expressing 'essential qualities': 'the conception of the triad here means the plurality of the gods as such. Three is the first number to signify a plural. But the number three contains at the same time the three components that express the essential qualities of a god – name, appearance, and essence. Amon, Ptah and Ra embody in this sense all the gods, and at the same time they are only aspects of *one* god.'[51] Otto may be right in his enumeration of a god's 'essential qualities', but I have seen no evidence, apart from the present locus, of three being particularly linked to the concept; and even in this locus 'countenance' and 'body' both have to do with appearance, so that essence is omitted.

Whereas the first formulation of the Leiden text points to the idea that Rê and Ptah are aspects of Amûn, suggesting a modalistic approach, afterwards the strong emphasis is on the three gods as lords of separate and independent cities. Morenz concluded that tritheism and not modalism is the dominant idea.[52] One has to agree with this, provided that the modalistic formulation is also acknowledged. Both ideas are present, but there is greater emphasis on the union of the three principal gods of the state.

The other cities mentioned in the Leiden text are, of course, connected with triads of their own. From Memphis probably comes a rare interpretation of the god Apis in which he is equated with three other gods:

> 'Apis, Apis, Apis', that means Ptah, Prê, Harsiesis, who are the lords of the office of sovereign
> ... The three gods denote Apis. Apis is Ptah, Apis is Prê, Apis is Harsiesis.
> (*Demotic Chronicle*, V, 12-13, ed. Spiegelberg, p.12. Cf. below ch.13, section 6)

Clearly we have here the union of three gods in one; the unusual feature is that the god who represents the union is not himself one of the three. Another surprising feature is that Apis, who had an early autonomous cult in Memphis, albeit of modest significance, is here, in the third century BC, given precedence over two very important gods – Ptah and Rê.[53] A further triadic grouping with Osiris-Apis, Atum, and Horus is less clearly formulated.[54]

Not simply a union, but a fusion into a compound deity, concerns triple names like Ptah-Sokar-Osiris. Memphis is the primary cult-centre in this case, but Thebes provides evidence too, and Leclant shows that in one instance here the triple name is assigned the role of *Lord of the Secret Sanctuary (nb štyt)*, rightly referring to him as 'le dieu composite'.[55] Other Theban compounds of this type were Amen-Rê-Month, Amen-Rê-Harakhty, Amen-Rê-Atum, and Rê-Harakhty-Osiris. One embodies a tetrad – Rê-Harakhty-Atum-Osiris.[56]

APPENDIX: A CONSPECTUS

In this topographical list the following brief modes of reference are used:

AEO: Gardiner, *Ancient Egyptian Onomastica* (1947).
Atlas: Baines and Málek, *Atlas of Ancient Egypt* (1980).
Hornung: *Conceptions of God in Ancient Egypt* (tr. Baines, 1983), esp. 217ff.
Kees: *Götterglaube*² (1956), esp. 150ff.
Kees, *Egypt: Ancient Egypt: A Cultural Topography*, ed. T. G. H. James (1961).
Morenz: *Ägyptische Religion* (1960; and tr. 1973, A. E. Keep).
PM: Porter-Moss, *Topographical Bibliography*.
Säve-Söderbergh: *LÄ* II (1977), 686-96.
H. te Velde: *JEA* 57 (1971), 80-6.
W. Westendorf: *ZÄS* 100 (1974), 136-41.

ABU SIMBEL

(1) The lesser temple has a carved representation of three Nubian gods: Horus of Miam, Horus of Bak, and Horus of Buhen. See C. Desroches-Noblecourt and Ch. Kuentz, *Le Petit Temple d'Abou Simbel*, I, 90; II, Pl.104. Temp. Ramesses II. The King is offering lotuses to the triad. Cf. *PM* VII, 116 (33); H. te Velde, 81. Cf. above, p.83.

(2) The lesser temple also has a carved representation of Nefertari offering lotuses to Khnum, Satis, and Anukis. See C. Desroches-Noblecourt and Ch. Kuentz, op. cit. I, 90-1; II, Pls.112, 114. Cf. *PM* VII, 116 (36).

(3) The great temple has four seated statues in the sanctuary: from the left, Ptah, Amen-Rê, Ramesses II, and Rê-Harakhty. See L. Habachi, *Features of the deification of Ramesses II*, 10, Pl.V b. The King is deified here, so that a tetrad is indicated, as Habachi shows. Cf. *PM* VII, 110 (115) and *RÄRG* 1; *Atlas*, 184-5; E. Otto, *LÄ* I (1975), 26, sees here the state triad of the Ramessides (Amûn of Karnak, Ptah of Memphis, and Rê of Heliopolis) in company with the divinized King. H. te Velde, p.81, concurs, but adds that 'the pharaoh seems to represent the unity of this triad.' Usually, however, the deity who expresses the unity is himself one of the triad, as in the Theban state triad with Amûn.

ABÛ-HÔR EAST (AJÛALA)

Mandulis, Osiris, Isis: small temple, Ptolemaic and Roman: A. M. Blackman, *Temple of Dendûr*, 80 with Pl.97, 1; *PM* VII, 39-40.

ABUSIR BAA: v. BUSIRIS

ABUSIR EL MELEQ

This site, near the entrance to the Fayûm, is said to contain scanty remains of a temple of Ptah-Sokar-Osiris of the XXXth Dynasty. Bonnet, *RÄRG*, 2, refers to Scharff's work on Abusir el-Meleq (Leipzig, 1926), 102, Pl.77. Cf. *AEO*, II, 114*.

ABYDOS

(1) In the temple of Sethos I there were three chapels devoted to the Osirian triad – Horus, Osiris–Sethos, and Isis. See R. David, *A Guide to Religious Ritual at Abydos*, 126.

(2) In the same temple there were chapels for the state gods of the three

chief cities – Amûn, Harakhty, and Ptah; *RÄRG*, 3; E. Otto, *Egyptian Art and the Cults of Osiris and Amon*, 52. A total of seven chapels means the dedication of one to the King, and the King seems to be bound up with the two triads.

(3) Ptah–Sokar–Osiris is often mentioned in MK stelae from Abydos: J. Spiegel, *Die Götter von Abydos*, 18ff. and 178 (twenty-four instances).

ACCHO

Ptah, Astarte, Seth. Black stone seal (face): R. Giveon, *The Impact of Egypt on Canaan*, 93 with Fig.46 a–b. Temp. Ramesses II or slightly later.

AJÛALA: v. ABÛ-HÔR EAST

ALEXANDRIA

(1) Sarapis, Isis, Harpocrates: 'the most familiar and best-attested deities of Ptolemaic Alexandria, as later of the Roman city also' – P. M. Fraser, *Ptolemaic Alexandria*, I, 246. Anubis is sometimes found instead of Harpocrates. Fraser says of Isis, Harpocrates and Anubis that they are 'Egyptian deities of respectable, though not of great antiquity'; in fact all three, like Osiris, are of the greatest antiquity since they appear in the *Pyramid Texts* shortly after 2340 BC. Fraser, I, 260–1, points out that in the company of Sarapis, Isis appears as his wife and that 'most shrines dedicated in Alexandria were dedicated to Sarapis and Isis only, and Harpocrates, the child of Osiris and Isis according to the myth, is not included in any of the dedications'. The same is true of the evidence from Delos, and this suggests, according to Fraser, that 'the triadic "family" structure of the Egyptian gods did not develop early' (i.e. in the Ptolemaic world). In art, however, the three deities are figured in a group that shows Harpocrates as a child: J. Leipoldt, *Die Religionen in der Umwelt des Urchristentums*, nos.21 and 22, amulets now in Berlin figuring Sarapis, Isis, and Harpocrates, but without indication of provenance or date. In the same group Harpocrates is shown as a naked boy in a piece bought in Alexandria but not necessarily deriving from there: Roeder, *Ägyptische Bronzefiguren*, 492, no.8871 with Abb.761. The inscription from Chalcis which Harder edited presents Carpocrates (= Harpocrates) explicitly claiming to be the son of Sarapis and Isis: see L. Vidman, *SIRIS*, 88, 2, and *Isis und Sarapis*, 13 (third or fourth century AD).

(2) Sarapis, Isis, Anubis: Fraser, op. cit. I, 246 on their casual grouping in Alexandria and Egypt, although they formed the regular triad in Delos.

(3) Three figures of Harpocrates in a group; probably from Alexandria or elsewhere in Lower Egypt: F. Dunand, *Rel populaire en Égypte romaine*, 255, no. 320 with Pl.104. Roman era. Dunand finds the only parallel in P. Graindor, *Terres cuites de l'Égypte gréco-romaine*, Pl.8, 18.

(4) Agathe Tyche, Arsinöe, Isis, on vases from Alexandria: F. Dunand, *Le Culte d'Isis etc*. I, 35 with n.5, but with the idea that Arsinöe-Isis is meant in a total identification. Dorothy Burr Thompson, *Ptolemaic Oinochoai and Portraits in Faience*, 59, argues that Arsinöe II was regarded as merely associated with Isis in her temple. She errs, however, in saying (p.58) that 'Isis had been a deity of no great importance in early Egyptian religion', especially in that she was writing after Maria Münster's *Untersuchungen zur Göttin Isis*; cf. K. Bosse-Griffiths, *JEA* 61 (1975), 292.

(5) Three goddesses: Demeter, Korê, Dikaiosune (Justice): *OGIS* 83, temp. Ptolemy IV and Arsinöe III. Dikaiosune may refer to Isis; cf. Plut. *De Is. et Os*. 3, 352 B and my Comm. 91; and Fraser, op. cit., I, 241 with n.413 in II, 392; also E. Visser, *Götter und Kulte im ptolemäischen Alexandrien*, 22.

(6) Isis, Horus, Sarapis: a relief of the Roman era now in the Cairo Museum. See Theodor Kraus, 'Alexandrinische Triaden der römischen Kaiserzeit', 97–105, this on pp.97–102 and Pl.XV. The central deity is the elder Horus, Haroëris, shown in military uniform, but Harpocrates is also shown as a small child with Sarapis.

(7) Athena, Sarapis, Heracles. Limestone relief in the Museum of Alexandria. Its provenance is not stated; perhaps from Alexandria itself: Kraus, op. cit., 103–4, Pl.XVIII b.

(8) Isis, Sarapis, Heracles. Dedication from Abuqîr, Ptolemaic. Kraus, op. cit., 104, citing Bottigelli, *Aegyptus* 21 (1941), 10f. and E. Visser, *Götter und Kulte im ptolemäischen Alexandrien*, 89.

(9) Isis, Harpocrates, Dionysus. Paris, Louvre; temp. Hadrian. In this relief the three deities are shown standing, but the bust of Sarapis has been added behind them. See Hornbostel, *Sarapis*, 214–15 with Abb.160. Dionysus was, of course, often identified with Osiris.

(10) Sarapis, Isis, Nilus. From Canopus, two dedications of the third century BC: Fraser, *Ptolemaic Alexandria*, I, 263, and II, 415 n.584.

AMARNA

(1) Aten, Akhenaten, Nefertiti.
(2) Rê-Harakhty, Shu, Aten.
See above chapter 3.

ARMANT (HERMONTHIS)

(1) Mont, Iunyt, Tenenet: M. S. Drower in R. Mond and O. H. Myers, *Temples of Armant*, I, 159, 169; II, Pl.99, 3, where the two goddesses are named together, perhaps to imply one composite goddess. Their names mean 'the Hermonthite' and 'the exalted one'. Cf. *AEO* II, 24*; E. Otto, *Topographie des Thebanischen Gaues*, 89; Kees, 151; 341; Leclant, *Mons. thébains*, 260f; H. te Velde, 84.

(2) Mont-Rê, Rat-tawy, Harprê: E. Otto, *Stierkulte*, 50; *RÄRG* 275; H. te Velde, 84-5. Rat-tawy ('female Rê of the Two Lands') is the female complement of Mont-Rê, and Harprê is their son, thus giving an instance of the family triad.

EL-ASHMUNEIN: v. HERMOPOLIS MAGNA

ASWÂN

Osiris, Isis, Harpocrates: temple of Isis, Ptolemaic, Ptolemy III censes before these three deities: Erich Winter, *Ägyptische Tempelreliefs*, 33-4 with Pl.II.

ATHRIBIS

(1) Horus-Khenty-khety-Osiris who resides in Athribis: Pascal Vernus, *Athribis*, 422f: the composite deity is represented in NK as hawk-headed with the solar disc and the horns of Kem-wer, 'the Great Black', the heraldic bull of Athribis.

(2) Ramesses II with two anthropomorphic deities: P. Vernus, op. cit., 42, Doc. 43: the Pharaoh is seated between the deities, who bear on their heads the solar disc and the uraeus respectively; a monument in red granite, but the text is damaged. Vernus thinks that perhaps Horus Khenty-khety was named.

BAHNASA (OXYRHYNCHUS)

Isis, Osiris Hydreios, Sarapis. Limestone relief, second century AD, now in Leiden. Isis and Sarapis are serpent-bodied, but with human heads and symbols: Hornbostel, *Sarapis*, 297-8 with Abb.310. On the local cults, esp. of Athena-Thoeris, Isis, Sarapis and Osiris, v. W. Otto, *Priester und Tempel*, I, 21; C. H. Roberts, *JEA* 20 (1934), 23-5; Bonnet, *RÄRG* 577-8; they do not show any marked triadism.

BEIT EL-WALI

Ramesses II, Horus of Bak, Isis: rock-temple of Ramesses II, niche in vestibule, with three statues, the King being seated between the two deities and thus being treated as a deity himself, as at Abu Simbel: *PM* VII, 25 (27); *LD* iii, 177 k and Text v, p. 15; cf. *Atlas*, 180.

BUBASTIS (TELL BASTA)

Mention is often made of 'the triad of Bubastis', e.g. Naville, *Bubastis*, 55, naming Atum, Bastet, and Miysis, the last being also seen as Nefertem or Hor-Hekenu. In fact no firmly defined triad emerges. Bastet, an early lion-goddess (later a cat) had her home here and she was known as the mother of the lion-god Miysis: E. Otto, *LÄ* I (1975), 628-30. Bastet was herself regarded as the daughter of Atum and thus equated with Tefnut (*CT* I, 250; cf. Kees in *RÄRG* 81). A triad of Atum, Bastet, and Miysis (or Hor-Hekenu) might thus emerge, but it seems not to be mentioned as such or depicted. If it were attested, it would be interestingly unusual as featuring a father with his daughter and his grandson, a variant of the family triad.

In Naville, op. cit. Pl.39 P the King gives offerings to Bastet and Hor-Hekenu; in Pl.40 A we see a grouping of Amen-Rê, Rê-Harakhty, and Ptah – the only triad figured, and not distinctively Bubastite; Pl.50 C shows Atum, Shu, and Tefnut-Bastet receiving offerings (thus a father, son, and daughter). See further Naville, *Festival-Hall of Osorkon II*, where a great number of deities appear, mainly in the Sed-festival; *RÄRG* 126; 306; L. Habachi, *Tell Basta*; Kitchen, *The Third Intermediate Period in Egypt*, 304; H. te Velde, 83; A. B. Lloyd, *Herodotus II*, Vol.3 96–7.

BUSIRIS (ABUSIR BAA; DJEDU)

Osiris, Isis, Horus: Kees, 151; *Egypt*, 184. Kees regards it as an instance of spatial extensionism, following Maspero in pointing to the proximity of Iseum-Behbet to the north of Busiris in the central Delta. The connections of Horus, on the other hand, were with the Western Delta; his inclusion is mythically motivated since Isis is his mother.

BUTO (TELL EL-FARAÎN)

The *baw* of Buto are Horus, Iemsety, and Hapy: *CT* II, 348 b-c, *BD*, 112 (end), Nav. 112, 14. Cf. *Atlas*, 170.

CANOPUS: v. ALEXANDRIA (10)

CHALCIS

Sarapis, Isis, Anubis: F. Dunand, *Le Culte d'Isis etc.*, II, 28; second century BC. Cf. Hornbostel, *Sarapis*, 336-7 (on this triad at Delos and elsewhere).

DÂBÔD

Isis, Osiris, Horus: temple built in the third century BC, dedicated to Amûn, then to Isis: for the triad, Roeder, *Temples immergés de la Nubie* I, 9, 36-8; *PM* VII, 3 (8), (12). Since 1970 the temple is in a Madrid park: *Atlas*, 180; see also W. Schenkel, *LÄ* I (1975), 997-8.

DEIR EL-MEDINA

(1) Qudshu, Min, Resheph: Louvre C 86; Pritchard, *ANEP* 474 with n. on pp. 304-5; Morenz, *Rel.* 150; R. Stadelmann, *Syrisch-Palästinensische Gottheiten in Ägypten*, 139. Another instance in Otto Koefoed-Petersen, *Les Stèles égyptiennes*, 49 and pp.37f; and again in BM 646 (= Pritchard, *ANEP* 473 with n. on p.304); cf. Edwards, *JNES* 14 (1955), 49.

(2) Qudshu, Anat, Astarte: I. E. S. Edwards, 'A Relief of Qudshu-Astarte-Anath in the Winchester College Collection', 49-51. He sees a nexus of the names, 'thus merging into one deity three of the most important goddesses of Western Asia'; since no Canaanite text mentions this triune goddess, he argues that the threefold syncretism developed in Egypt. The relief was made for the necropolis official Neferhotep, a name common in the Theban necropolis in Dynasties XIX and XX. No. (1) above is also assigned to this period. Stadelmann, op. cit., 115, rejects the syncretistic nexus, preferring to read the names separately. Only one goddess, however, is depicted, and this favours the triune idea. A milieu of Syrian immigrants is perhaps indicated; cf. H. te Velde, 84; and section 2 above.

(3) Amûn, Hathor Lady of the West, Maat, patron goddess of Deir el-Medina: Ptolemaic temple dedicated to these; E. Otto, *Egyptian Art and the Cults of Osiris and Amon*, 68 with Pl.8; Christine Seeber, *Untersuchungen zur Darstellung des Totengerichts* (1976), 29

(4) Sobek, Thoueris, Hathor: Berlev and Hodjash, *Reliefs and Stelae*, 76, temp. Ramesses II. = the triad of Gebel es-Silsila.

DELOS

(1) Sarapis, Isis, Anubis. Ptolemaic. P. Roussel, *Les Cultes égyptiens à*

Délos, nos. 20, 21, 22, 25, 26, 28, et al., from Sarapieion B; also pp.276-9; Fraser, *Ptol. Alex.* I, 262, denying Roussel's claim that Anubis is 'plus effacé'; Hornbostel, *Sarapis*, 336-7.

(2) Arsinöe, Agathe Tyche, Isis. Second century BC. Three goddesses in close relationship: Fraser, op. cit., 241; Dorothy B. Thompson, *Ptol. Oinochoai*, 51. Cf. above Alexandra (4).

DENDERA

(1) Hathor, Harsomtus, Iehy: *AEO* II, 30*; Kees, 151; 304 with Pl.IX b (including the adjacent place Khadi); Hathor here is with her two youthful sons, but Bonnet, *RÄRG* 728, finds that in Khadi Harsomtus, through his link with Rê, is the father of Hathor. Sometimes the King (e.g. Trajan) is identified with Iehy, the young musician-god, in this triad: F. Daumas, *Les Mammisis des temples égyptiens*, 367-8. Cf. H. te Velde, 83 ('highly doubtful' of the claim by Kees); *Atlas*, 113 (with Fig.).

(2) Hathor, Horus of Edfu, Iehy: an ancient triad in Dendera, Daumas, *Les Dieux de l'Égypte*, 58; Bonnet, *RÄRG*, 155. For an early link (Dyn.V) between Hathor and Iehy v. H. G. Fischer, *Dendera in the Third Millennium B.C.*, 44, though this is the Memphite Hathor.

DENDÛR

Arensnuphis, Isis, Harpocrates: temple built temp. Augustus, pronaos, interior south wall: A. M. Blackman, *The Temple of Dendûr*, 77 with Pl.55, Arensnuphis being treated as a form of Osiris. Cf. *PM* VII, 30 (16-17). The temple is now in the MMA. New York: *Atlas*, 181. For Arensnuphis cf. Fritz and Ursula Hintze, *Civilizations of the Old Sudan*, 23 with Pls.90, 98; E. Winter, *LÄ* I (1975), 424f; L.V. Žabkar, *Apedemak, Lion God of Meroe*, 19-20, 129, 84ff; J. Leclant, 'La Religion Méroïtique' (Paris, 1973, in *Journées Internationales d'Études Méroïtiques*), 10.

DERR (ED-DERR)

Rê-Harakhty, Amen-Rê, Ptah: temple built by Ramesses II, removed in 1964 to a new site near Amada. A. M. Blackman, *The Temple of Derr*. The remains of four seated statues in a chapel relate not only to the gods named, but also to Ramesses II himself, recalling Abu Simbel (3). Cf. *Atlas*, 183-4; E. Brunner-Traut, *Ägypten*[4], 752.

DIMAI: v. SOKNOPAIOU NESOS

DJEDET: v. MENDES

DJEDU: v. BUSIRIS

EAST (OF HEAVEN)

Harakhty, the calf Khwrer, the Morning Star: *CT* II, 371b-372a, *I know the souls of the Easterners* (var. *of the East*). *They are*... Cf. *BD*, 109, 10-11 Nav. See further above, ch.2 (2), on the triadic *baw*.

EDFU

(1) Horus, Isis, Osiris. Many scattered refs.: e.g. Fairman, *Triumph of Horus*, 101-5 (from *Edfou* VI). Cf. Kees, 425; W. A. Ward, *JEA* 63 (1977), 64 (a); Pascal Vernus, *LÄ* VI (1986), 326; *AEO* II, 7.

(2) Horus of Behdet, Hathor, Harsomtus: Sylvie Cauville, *La Théologie d'Osiris à Edfou*, 194; H. te Velde, 83. For Harsomtus as a son of Khnum, Berlev and Hodjash, *Reliefs and Stelae*, 184, no.128. *PM* VI, 260 (Index: Edfu) gives 14 refs. to this triad.

(3) Osiris, Isis, Nephthys: S. Cauville, *La Théologie d'Osiris à Edfou*, 194, refers to the many scenes devoted to this group

(4) Horus of Behdet, Hathor, Khons: Kees, 152.

ELEPHANTINE

(1) King (Sesostris I), Satis, Anukis: Statue, L. Habachi, *MDAIK* 31 (1975), 29 with Pl.13 a; cf. D. Valbelle, *Satis et Anoukis*, 3.

(2) Satis, Khnum, Anukis: From Dyn. 12 (Ammenemes III): Valbelle, *Satis et Anoukis*, 5; L. Habachi, *ASAE* 50 (1950), 501-7 and *LÄ* I (1975), 1217-25. Valbelle establishes the primacy of the two goddesses; cf. Kees, 151 and above, section (1).

(3) Yahweh (Yahu), Ashim-bethel, Anath-bethel: Aramaic Papyrus, 419 or 400 BC, about temple-tax: E. G. Kraeling, *The Brooklyn Museum Aramaic Papyri*, 62f., 87ff.; H. L. Ginsberg, *ANET* 491; E. Lipiński in W. Beyerlin (ed.), *Near Eastern Rel. Texts etc.* (1978), 252. For Ashim-bethel cf. 2 Kings 17: 30; Amos 8: 14(?). Černý, *Rel.* (1952), 135, writes of 'a temple of Yahve and his two female companions, Ashima and Anat...', but Ginsberg, loc. cit. sees Ashim-bethel as a male deity; he also believes that the money for the two additional deities was 'doubtless contributed by non-Jews'. B. Porten, *Archives from Elephantine*, 164, shows that Ashim-bethel and Anath-bethel were Aramaean deities, and not hypostatic forms of Yahu.

EPIDAURUS

Isis, Sarapis, Horus-Harpocrates: in the Asclepieion of Epidaurus there was probably a chapel of these three gods (second century AD); F. Dunand, *Le Culte d'Isis*, II, 162 (cf. II, 112 n.6), citing Pausanias, 2. 174, (= Loeb edn. Vol. 1, 2.27.6, p.394 W. H. S. Jones) who says that a chapel was dedicated at Epidaurus to Hygieia, Asclepius, and Apollo under their Egyptian names. (Jones, op. cit., 395, misleads with 'the last two surnamed Egyptian'.)

ESNA

(1) Khnum, Menhit, Heka: Sethe, *Urgeschichte*, 23, who stresses the disparity of the members – a ram-headed Khnum, lion-goddess Menhit, ('slaughterer'), and a young human god Heka ('sorcerer'); cf. Bonnet, *RÄRG*, 451.

(2) Khnum, Neïth, Heka: Sauneron, *LÄ* II (1977), 31, who sees Khnum and Neïth as father and mother, but in some texts regarded as one androgynous being. Cf. *Atlas*, 81; H. te Velde, 84.

(3) Neïth, Khemanefer (crocodile god, son of Neïth), Tutu (Tithoës, chief of messenger gods): Sauneron, *LÄ* II (1977), 31. The temple was begun between 170 and 164 BC and finished under Claudius (41-54 AD).

EUHEMERIA (FAYÛM)

Psosnaus, Pnepheros, Soxis. Ptolemaic era: Th. Kraus, *MDAIK* 19 (1963), 105, citing Bottigelli, *Aegyptus* 22 (1942), 208. Kraus finds here merely a grouping of local gods who are otherwise unrelated, in accord with the earlier Egyptian practice.

FAYÛM

Sobek-Shedty-Horus: 'who resides in the Fayûm', see Ashraf I. Sadek, *Popular Religion in Egypt during the New Kingdom*. Cf. above, section (2), 'Triads of One Sex'.

HELIOPOLIS

(1) Nun, Nut, Rê: W. Barta, *Untersuchungen zum Götterkreis der Neunheit*, 102: this triad was probably the direct cosmological predecessor of the Ennead in Heliopolis. For Nut as an ancient goddess of Heliopolis cf. *Pyr.* 823 d PMN, *rpwt 'Iwnw, Lady of On*, and Faulkner, *Pyr.* 148 n. 2.

(2) *Baw* of this city are Rê, Shu, Tefnut: *CT* II, 286 b–c; cf. *BD*, 115, end (Nu) in Budge; Žabkar, *Study of the Ba Concept*, 29. In P. Leiden I, 350, 21–6, Heliopolis is the city of Rê; cf. *AEO* II, 144*–6*.

HERACLEOPOLIS: v. IHNASYA

HERMONTHIS: v ARMANT

HERMOPOLIS MAGNA (EL-ASHMUNEIN)

Thoth, Sia, Atum are its *baw*: Žabkar, *Study of the Ba Concept*, 29, citing *BD*, 114 and 116. *BD*, 114 does not name them in sequence, but *BD*, 116, 6–7 (Nav.) does: *Thoth the mysterious, Sia (Perception), the knowing, and Atum*. A vignette in *BD*, 114 (Nebseny) shows the three *baw* of Hermopolis as three squatting ibis-headed gods; cf. Faulkner, *BD*, p. 109. Obviously they are dominated by Thoth; but the Ogdoad was of greater import here.

IHNASYA (HERACLEOPOLIS)

Granite statuary triad of Ramesses II with Ptah and Sakhmet. Mostafa El-Alfi, *Sesto Congresso*, I, 167–71, with Pl. Now in the garden of Cairo Museum.

KALABSHA (TALMIS)

Mandulis, Osiris, Isis: great temple of Mandulis built temp. Augustus, now at New Kalabsha near New Aswan dam: PM VII, 11, (1)–(2), pylon, outer doorway; *PM* VII, 15 (29)–(30), the King offers incense to Osiris, Isis, and Horus, but in various scenes several other triadic groups appear, the gods of Philae being esp. to the fore with Mandulis. See also *RÄRG* 765; L. Habachi, *MDAIK* 24 (1969, Fs. Stock), 169–83; H. Stock and K. G. Siegler, *Kalabascha*; J. Leclant, *Orientalia*. 43 (1974), 203 (on the removal of the gate-edifice to a park in Charlottenburg, W. Berlin); D. Arnold, *Die Tempel von Kalabsha*; E. Henfling, *LÄ III* (1980), 295–6; *Atlas*, 180 (with painting of 1839).

KARNAK

(1) Ptah, Hathor, Amûn: temple of Ptah, temp. Tuthmosis III and later: *PM* II², 201 (25), King offers to these three deities; cf. 200 (24).

(2) Amûn, Mut, Khons: the Propylon, Bab el-Abd: *PM* II², 2, Ptolemaic (Euergetes Gate); cf. E. Winter, *Untersuchungen zu den ägypt-*

ischen Tempelreliefs der griechisch-römischen Zeit, 33.

(3) Ptah, Isis-Hathor, Harsomtus-Harsiesis: Ptolemaic, Winter, ibid., pp.29ff. with Abb.3; a text reads *Isis is at his (Ptah's) side as Hathor, and Harsomtus as Harsiesis*, but only Ptah and Hathor are figured in Abb.3.

(4) Mont, Rat-tawy, Harprê: temple of Mut, Ptolemaic, Ptolemy III and Berenice II offer Maat to these three deities: *PM* II², 4, (h)–(i); H. te Velde, 83.

(5) Rê, Tatenen, Hidden-of-name (Osiris?): temple of goddess Opet, Ptolemaic: C. de Wit, *Les Inscriptions du temple d'Opet*, III (1968), 64, I, who argues that the Hidden-of-Name is Osiris, citing Zandee, *Hymnen*, 83, 86; Daumas, *Mammisis*, 434; Derchain, *P. Salt*, 98. H. te Velde, 81, thinks that the Hidden-of-Name is Amûn; cf. Zandee, *Hymnen*, 83. See also *PM* II², 244ff; Morenz, *Rel.* (tr.), 144. Thoth is said in this locus to be *the heart of Rê, the tongue of Tatenen, the throat of Him who is hidden of name*. Te Velde sees Thoth here as being 'the unity of this triad', but Thoth seems rather to have a relation, not to the three as a group, but to each of them singly.

(6) Amen-Rê, Ptah, Hathor: Ptolemaic, small room behind the sanctuary of the Khons temple, with the King (Ptolemy VIII) presenting Maat to figures of these three deities; v. R. A. Parker and L. H. Lesko, 'The Khonsu Cosmogony', *Pyramid Studies etc.*, 168 with Pls.34–5. Doubtless no established triad is implied since various deities receive offerings in triadic groups; cf. *PM* II², 26 (35)–(38); and 32 (101)–(104).

(7) Khons, Thoth, Osiris: the same location and date, Parker and Lesko, ibid. with Pls.36–7.

KÔM OMBO (NUBYT)

A temple which is really two temples, devoted to separate triads. Ptolemaic.

(1) Sobek, Hathor, Khons.
(2) Haroëris, Senetnofret, Panebtawy.

Wiedemann, *Rel.* (London, 1897), 179; J. Baikie, *Egyptian Antiquities in the Nile Valley*, 686; *PM* VI, 179ff.; *AEO* II, 6*; Daumas, *Les Dieux de l'Égypte*, 36–7; A. Gutbub, *Textes fondamentaux de la théologie de Kom Ombo*, passim; *idem*, *LÄ* III (1980), 677–8, with plan of temple; Heike Sternberg, *Mythische Motive und Mythenbildung in den ägyptischen Tempeln und Papyri der griechisch-römischen Zeit*, 115–18. The triads of Kôm Ombo were also honoured at Philae; v. E. Brovarski, *LÄ* V (1984), 1011, citing PM VI, 208.

(3) Osiris, Isis, Nephthys: since Osiris is the leading god of the necropolis of Kôm Ombo, H. Sternberg, op. cit., 116–17.

KONOSSO

Neïth, King, Mont: L. Habachi, 'King Nebhepetre Menthuhotp: His Monuments etc.', 44, Fig.21; the King is Menthuhotep (Nebhepetrê A or B) and is ithyphallic; Neïth and Mont raise hands to him as a sign of blessing. H. te Velde, 84, believes that Min can be the son in a family triad and here sees the Pharaoh 'as the ithyphallic Min-Amun-Kamutef': cf. *PM* V (1937), 254 (par. 4).

LUXOR

Amûn, Mut, Khons: triple shrine or bark-station of the Theban triad, built by Hatshepsut and Tuthmosis III and decorated again by Ramesses II; West shrine, Mut; central shrine, Amûn; East shrine, Khons: *PM* II², 309 with Plan 28 (4); 30; *Atlas*, 87. Cf. L. Habachi, 'The Triple Shrine of the Theban Triad in Luxor Temple', 93-7 and section (3) above. On the Theban deities, *AEO* II, 26*. Not only the barks, but also the relevant cult-images were kept in these chapels: D. Arnold, *Wandrelief und Raumfunktion in ägyptischen Tempeln des Neuen Reiches* (MÄS 2; Berlin, 1962), 32 with Abb.20 and 35, though the latter relief has a more general import (p.113).

MEMPHIS

(1) Ptah, Sakhmet, Nefertem: curved stela, Late Period, provenance unknown, with Ptah in mummified form, Sakhmet lion-headed, Nefertem with sign for Lower Egypt on his head, O. Koefoed-Petersen, *Les Stèles égyptiennes* (1948), 57 with p.43. Cf. Bonnet, *RÄRG* 447 (Ramesside); Kees, 287-8 (canonical triad of Memphis in NK); H. te Velde, 83. For figurines in Cyprus v. G. Clerc et al., *Fouilles de Kition*, II, 117.

(2) Ptah, Shu, Tefnut: L. Kákosy, 'A Memphite Triad', 48-53, gives evidence from the temple of Hibis showing Ptah seated before two *ba*-birds on *djed*-pillars, these two birds being named Shu and Tefnut; also from the temple of Sethos I at Abydos and the tomb of Neferhotep, Saqqâra (Dyn. XIX). Kákosy (p.53) sees the triad as a group with 'traits of both the modalistic and tritheistic triads'; and he finds the Memphite doctrine of creation here conjoined with elements from the Heliopolitan doctrine.

(3) Ptah, Sokar, Osiris as Ptah-Sokar-Osiris. Referred to with a plural pronoun in Leiden V, 108 (MK) and Berlin 7272 (NK); but with a singular pronoun in some texts from the MK, NK and the Ethiopian era: see Morenz, *Rel. (Tr.)* 143 and 315 notes 20 and 21. Cf. Leclant, *Monuments thébains*, 269 n.4.

(4) Ptah, Prê, Harsiesis = Apis. Demotic Chronicle (third century BC) ed. Spiegelberg (1914): '*Apis, Apis, Apis*'. *That means Ptah, Prê, Harsiesis ... Apis is Ptah, Apis is Prê, Apis is Harsiesis.* Morenz, *Rel. (Tr.)* 143, says that 'the unity of the three gods in Apis' is being claimed, with the intent of enhancing the power of Apis through his association thus with important gods. Apis therefore incorporates three gods. It should be added, however, that Apis is identified with each of the three gods separately; the net result is a tetrad in which one deity is equated with each member of a triad. In the Christian Trinity, on the other hand, with its doctrine of *Three in One and One in Three*, the triadic structure remains unless one posits, as some have done, a quaternity – the one substance and the three persons.

(5) Amûn, Rê, Ptah: In P. Leiden, I, 350, IV, 21–26 it is Memphis that is linked with Ptah. See further s.v. THEBES.

(6) Osiris–Apis, Atum, Horus: after their names in a text from the Serapeum (Dyn. XIX) occur the words *at the same time (n sp), the Great God*. See Morenz, *Rel. (Tr.)* 143 with 316 n.23, citing E. Otto, *Stierkulte* (1938), 32 and Mariette, *Sérapéum*, III, Pl.8. It seems that the triad here achieves unity in *the Great God*, probably Osiris.

MENDES (DJEDET: TELL EL-RUBA)

(1) Ptah, Amen-Rê, Banebdedet: curved stela of Nekhet-Amûn, *the royal scribe of Banebdedet* (the Ram, Lord of Mendes), probably from Mendes, Dyn. XVIII–XIX: O. Koefoed-Petersen, *Les Stèles égyptiennes*, 30 with p.26.

(2) Hatmehit (dolphin-goddess), Banebdedet, Harpocrates: H. De Meulenaere, *Mendes II*, 178–80 ('the Mendesian triad'). Late Period and Ptolemaic. But no example is cited.

(3) Osiris-Hemag, Isis, Harpocrates: De Meulenaere, ibid., 180. Ptolemaic.

MESOPOTAMIA

Isis–Thermuthis, Sarapis, Isis Lactans: E 14268, Louvre, Roman era, (second–third century AD), gold pendant bought in Mossul; v. Th. Kraus, *MDAIK* 19 (1963), 105 with Pl. XVIII a. He cites H. W. Müller, *Münch. Jb.* 14 (1963), 31f. with Abb.27, which I have not seen.

MIT RAHINA

Ptah–Sokar–Apis, temple of: statue of Harenhap, probably Dyn. XXVI, in Berlin (East) Museum, 10289: *PMM* III², part 2, fasc. 3 (1981), 867 (par. 5)

MUSAWWARAT ES-SUFRA (SUDAN: MEROË)

(1) Amûn, Sebiumeker, Arensnuphis: Amûn in the centre is ram-headed. Fritz and Ursula Hintze, *Civilizations of the Old Sudan*, 23 with Pl.98. Third century BC. The sculptured heads are joined; cf. P. L. Shinnie, *Meroe*, 143 (but of a sextet of gods).

(2) Amûn, Shu, Tefnut: F. and U. Hintze, op. cit., 23 with Pls.100 and 101. Third century BC. Amûn, in the centre, is ram-headed; Shu and Tefnut have each the head of a lion. On other deities here see F. Hintze, *LÄ* IV (1982), 226–8; and L. V. Žabkar, *Apedemak*, passim.

NAQA (S. OF MUSAWWARAT ES-SUFRA)

Apedemak, Isis, Horus: S. Wall of Lion-temple (*c.* fourth century BC); L. V. Žabkar, *Apedemak*, 9, 14, 17, 20, with Pls.3, 4, comparing treatment of the Theban Triad; cf. P. L. Shinnie, *Meroe*, 89; J. Leclant in *Les Syncrétismes*, ed. M. Simon, 142–4 with Pl.7, 2.

NOME, IVTH UPPER EGYPTIAN.

Mont, Sobek, Wenw: Helck, *Gaue*, 11; 79, MK.

OXYRHYNCHUS: v. BAHNASA

PHILAE

(1) Osiris, Isis, Harpocrates: temple of Isis, Ptolemaic, Birth-house; H. Junker and E. Winter, *Das Geburtshaus des Tempels der Isis in Philae*, 64, 124, 140, 308. As expected in this famous temple of Isis, the Osirian triad prevails, though with many variations; cf. section 3 in ch. 2 above. So too in H. Junker, *Der grosse Pylon des Tempels der Isis in Philä*.

(2) Khnum, Sothis, Anukis: Junker and Winter, op. cit., 36.

(3) Arensnuphis, Thoth-Rê of Pnubs, Amen-Rê: ibid., 218.

(4) Khnum, Hathor, Harpocrates: ibid., 24, 138. This exemplifies the many Osirian variations; Khnum replaces Osiris, and Hathor Isis. The many forms of Horus account for other changes.

(5) Harpocrates, Second Harpocrates, Meret: ibid., 318. A feature of several of these triads is the doubling of one of the deities, obviously in an urge to fill up the number to three.

(6) Shu-Arensnuphis, Tefnut: temple of Arensnuphis, near a grouping of Khnum, Sothis, Anukis: PM VI, 210, Room II, (45), (46). Yet Osiris, Isis, Horus appear in (49)–(51).

(7) Osiris–Onnophris, Isis, Imhotep: temple of Imhotep: PM VI, 213, (60).

The above constitute a selection only of the triadic groupings attested. On Philae there were temples of Isis, Arensnuphis, Mandulis, Imhotep, Hathor and Augustus; since the building of the High Dam the temples have been moved to the adjacent island of Agilkia; cf. *Atlas*, 73.

In his *Hymns to Isis in Her Temple at Philae*, Louis V. Žabkar has published with a translation and commentary eight hieroglyphic hymns to Isis which derive from the time of Ptolemy II Philadelphus (284–246 BC). In these hymns there is constant mention of the ties which bind Isis, Osiris, and Horus, but Isis is 'always the predominant member of this divine triad' (p.129).

QADESH

Qadesh on the Orontes has sometimes been connected with the goddess Qudshu who appears in two triads in Egypt: v. DEIR EL-MEDINA (1) and (2). The name is more properly derived from the Semitic קדוש (*qadhôsh*), 'sacred, holy', from which words meaning 'consecrated, dedicated' are derived, with an application sometimes to temple prostitutes.

EL-QALA.

NE of Qift (Coptos), a small temple for Min, Isis, and Horus was built by Claudius (AD 41–54). *Atlas* 111; 109 (map).

ROME

Harpocrates, Isis, Anubis: lamp, Roman, R. E. Witt, *Isis in the Graeco-Roman World*, Pl.38 (BM). Cf. M. Malaise, *Inventaire préliminaire des documents égyptiens découverts en Italie*, 234, no.437 (but with four figures); J. Leipoldt, *Die Religionen in der Umwelt des Urchristentums*, 21, 22 (amulets figuring the same triad).

SAÏS

(1) Ptah, Sakhmet, Weret-hekaw: statuette no. E 25.980, Louvre; from Eastern Delta, temp. Ramesses II; see El-Sayed, *Documents relatifs à Saïs et ses divinités*, 28ff., Doc. 2. Neïth stands on the right facing these three. El-Sayed sees her as the presiding deity who is greeting the triad, perhaps in a local temple.

(2) Amûn, Shepenwepet II (god's wife of Amûn), Nitocris: a theolog-

ical triad at the basis of the Saïte (26th) Dynasty; J. Leclant, *Monuments thébains*, 359ff.; Černý, *Rel.* 133.

SEHEL

Satis, King, Anukis: relief, Brooklyn Museum 77. 194 (seen by the writer, 19 September 1978), from Sehel, temp. Sobek-hotpe III (Dyn. XIII, c. 1744 BC). The King is shown twice in the centre: on the left he presents a libation vessel to the goddess Satis of Elephantine; on the right he presents one to the goddess Anukis of Sehel Island. The King is probably not to be regarded as one of a triad here; Satis and Anukis are the basic dyad in this context; v. D. Valbelle, *Satis et Anoukis*, 87ff.; cf. ELEPHANTINE above.

SESEBI

Mut, Khons, Amen-Rê: triple temple built by Sethos I and perhaps dedicated to the Theban triad; the name of Mut was found on part of a door-jamb: A. M. Blackman, *JEA* 23 (1937), 147; *PM* VII, 172; *Atlas*, 187. D. N. Edwards, *JEA* 80 (1994), 159ff. uses the forms 'Sesibi' and 'Sesi'.

SILSILA, GEBEL ES-

(1) Sobek, Thoueris, Nut: R. Caminos and T. G. H. James, *Gebel es-Silsilah. I. The Shrines*, 34. Sobek is the presiding deity; he is the *lord of Silsilah*, 22. Haroëris is named with Sobek in a joint cult, 32.

(2) Thoueris, Thoth, Nut: *AEO* II, 6*.

(3) Amen-Rê, Mut, Khons: Ramesses III offers Maat to them on a stela: *PM* V, 213f.; on a rock stela Sobek is added to the Theban triad: *PM* V, 213.

On a stela which is probably from Deir el-Medina the group Sobek, Thoueris, Hathor appears: v. Berlev and Hodjash, *Reliefs and Stelae*, 137 and above DEIR EL-MEDINA (4). See also Bonnet, *RÄRG* 716. None of the cults is earlier than NK.

SOKNOPAIOU NESOS (DIMAI; FAYÛM)

Isis Sononaei, Harpocrates, Premarres: Ptolemaic; Th. Kraus, *MDAIK* 19 (1963), 105, citing Bottigelli, *Aegyptus* 22 (1942), 188. Kraus finds here merely a grouping of local gods who are otherwise unrelated, in accord with the earlier Egyptian practice. Premarres is from Marres, a cult name of Ammenemes III (Neb-maat-rê), esp. popular in the Fayûm; cf. D. J. Crawford, *Kerkeosiris*, 133. For Dimai v. *PM* IV, 96-7.

TANIS (SAN EL-HAGAR)

Amûn, Mut, Khons: Late Period, black granite statue of a priest, Djehor, who holds small statues of the Theban Triad; Cairo Museum, 700, Borchardt, *Statuen*, III, 42-3 with Pl.129; *PM* IV, 26. For the 'great temple of Amun' here v. *Atlas*, 176-7.

TELL BASTA: v. BUBASTIS

TELL EL-FARAÎN: v. BUTO

THEBES

(1) Amûn, Mut, Khons: figured together, with Ramesses II, in the great hypostyle hall, Karnak: Charles F. Nims, *Thebes of the Pharaohs*, Pl.34; for other frequent occurrences here *PM* II^2 (1972), 41ff. and also (in other Theban locations as well) ibid., 569 (Index). Cf. above KARNAK (2); with sections (3) and (4) of this chapter. See further, O. Koefoed-Petersen, *Cat. des statues et statuettes égyptiennes*, 78 with Pls.89-90 and p.48, Dyn. XIX-XX, probably from the Theban area; Brooklyn Museum, 37. 277 E (seen by the writer 19 September 1978), fragment of long ivory-topped staff, Dyn. XIX, where a soldier and chief artist of Amûn is shown at the top worshipping the Theban Triad; in Wreszinski, *Atlas*, II, Pl.51 the Pharaoh (Sethos I) leads captives to the Triad (a ref. I owe to Dr Clive Broadhurst).

For other relevant remarks see Kees, 149-50; H. te Velde, 83; E. Otto, 'Amun', *LÄ* I (1975), 237-48; H. Brunner, 'Chons', *LÄ* I (1975), 960-3; H. te Velde, 'Mut', *LÄ* IV (1982), 246-8; R. Fazzini, 'Mut-Tempel Karnak (Mut Precinct)', *LÄ* IV (1982), 248-51; *idem*, *Egypt, Dynasty XXII-XXV*, Pl.29. 1.

(2) Amûn, Rê, Ptah: a state triad representing Thebes, Heliopolis and Memphis: see above, section (4).

(3) Amûn, King, Mut: Daressy, *Statues de divinités*, 39210 with Pl.56, Karnak, Sethos I; cf. nos. 39211, 39212, 39213 (all from Karnak, but not in Pls.). The King seems to replace Khons.

(4) Amûn, Mut, Horus: C. De Wit, *Opet III* (1968), 149, pointing also to the equation of Amûn with Osiris and of Mut with Isis-Hathor; cf. E. Otto, *Gott und Mensch*, 87.

(5) Mut, Amûn, Mont: statue of priest Wesir-wer in green slate, holding three divine figures; from Karnak, Dyn. XXX; Brooklyn 55. 175 and Cairo Museum J.E. 38064; B. V. Bothmer et al., *Egyptian Sculpture of the Late Period*, 105-6, no.83 with Pl.79; R. Fazzini, *Images for Eternity*, 120, no.104 c.

Figure 7. The crowning of Philometor: a performative triad

(6) Amen-Rê-Atum: Leclant, *Monuments thébains*, 240, 306, 318.
(7) Amen-Rê-Harakhty: Leclant, ibid., 240, 306, 307, 318.
(8) Amen-Rê-Mont: Leclant, ibid., XVIII, 85ff, 108, 318.
(9) Rê-Harakhty-Osiris: Leclant, ibid., 285, 318.

THEBES: v. also ARMANT; DEIR EL-MEDINA; KARNAK; LUXOR.

WEST

Atum, Sobek, Hathor: they are the *baw* of the Westerners: *BD*, 108, 14–15 Nav. Nebseny. The vignette (cf. Faulkner, *BD*, p.103) shows an undistinctive Atum, Sobek as a crocodile-headed god and Hathor as seated woman simply. Cf. above sections (1) and (2) in chapter 2.

UNSPECIFIED

There are types of triads which enjoy widespread currency and cannot easily be linked to a single location. This is true, for instance, of the Osirian triads, and of those which feature the King in the centre of a ritual action performed by two deities. The latter type might be termed 'performative triads'; examples are the 'Purification of Pharaoh' or 'Uniting the Two Lands',[57] rites both related to coronation (Fig. 7).

NOTES

[1] *Wb.* II, 212, 10.
[2] W. Barta, *Untersuchungen zum Götterkreis der Neunheit* (1973), 59–60. Brugsch's idea that the triads were simply local forms of the Heliopolitan Ennead is rightly rejected by Kees, *Götterglaube*, 150.
[3] Erman, *Rel.* (1934, tr. H. Wild, 1952), 71–2.
[4] A Wiedemann, *Rel.* (1897), 103. In his *Das alte Ägypten* (Heidelberg, 1920) the treatment of religion is very brief, but he wisely comments (p.360) on its lack of system and its indifference to inner contradictions.
[5] Kees, *Götterglaube*, 152, gives several instances, some of which, however, are dyads of mother and child.
[6] L. Habachi, *MDAIK* 31 (1975), 29 and Pl.13 a.
[7] Dominique Valbelle, *Satis et Anoukis*. DAIK (Mainz am Rhein, 1981), 5; cf. *PM* V, 247. The Egyptian form is ʿAnuqet.
[8] Cf. Kees, op. cit., 151.
[9] Hornung, *Conceptions of God*, 69–70. Cf. J. Málek in Baines and Málek, *Atlas of Ancient Egypt* (1980), 72.
[10] See Dominique Valbelle, op. cit., 5. On Khnum's lack of early connections with Elephantine cf. B. L. Begelsbacher-Fischer, *Untersuchungen zur Götterwelt des Alten Reiches* (1981), 42–9.

[11] Cf. L. Habachi, *ASAE* 50 (1950), 501-7 ('Was Anukis considered as the wife of Khnum or as his daughter?'). The second alternative is supported there; the only difference from other triads, it is argued, is that the child is a daughter, not a son.

[12] Cf. Junker and Winter, *Geburtshaus*, 62. Anukis is here called *the mother of the god*. Ibid., 170 Khnum, Sothis, and Anukis are grouped.

[13] Thus a Coffin Text from El Bersheh of Dyn. 12: *CT* IV, 89j ff. See Valbelle, op. cit., 2.

[14] Sometimes Nebtu or Isis-Nebtu replaces Menhit; cf. Sauneron, *Esna III* (Cairo, 1968), no.361.

[15] K. Sethe, *Urgeschichte* (1930), 23-4. Cf. Erman's view, cited above n.3. Kees, *Götterglaube*, 151-2, rejects the earlier view that triads were a consistently used currency and he proceeds to emphasize other groups such as Enneads. He avers too (p.152) that the pair consisting of a local god with a goddess subordinated to him was more important than the triad. His further statement that when triads were eventually evolved, they were of lesser cultic significance is open to question.

[16] Sauneron in Posener, *Dict.* 290.

[17] F. Daumas, *Les Dieux de l'Égypte* (1965), 30-1.

[18] Contrast Sauneron's dictum, loc. cit.: 'A triad was a secondary group, arranged in an invariable pattern (father, mother and son), of the gods of a city who might earlier have been independent.'

[19] Kees, *Götterglaube*, 152; Faulkner, *BD* 102 with vignette of P. Nebseny on p.104; Allen, *BD* 86.

[20] Málek in *Atlas of Ancient Egypt*, 181-3.

[21] Or 'the many Nubian deities', H. te Velde, *JEA* 57 (1971), 81.

[22] See L. V. Žabkar, *Apedemak, Lion God of Meroe* (Warminster, 1975), ch.6, 79ff. with a detailed discussion of Egyptian-Nubian syncretism.

[23] Fritz Hintze and Ursula Hintze, *Civilizations of the Old Sudan* (Leipzig, 1968), 18 (for Amûn); for Osiris see p.26 and Pl.122. The many and varied falcon-deities are discussed by Žabkar, op. cit., 73.

[24] H. te Velde, op. cit., 81; cf. K. Bosse-Griffiths, 'Problems with Ptah-Sokar-Osiris Figures', *4th International Congress of Egyptology, Abstracts* (Munich, 1985), 26.

[25] I. E. S. Edwards, *JNES* 14 (1955), 49-51, this remark on pp. 50-1.

[26] Cf. W. F. Albright, *Yahweh and the Gods of Canaan* (London, 1968), 106. Earlier, in *The Archaeology of Palestine and the Bible* (New York, 1932), 96, he had proposed the meaning 'courtesan'.

[27] Rainer Stadelmann, *Syrisch-Palästinensische Gottheiten in Ägypten* (Leiden, 1967), 115. Cf. my remarks, *JEA* 55 (1969), 230. For Astarte in a triad with Ptah and Seth see R. Giveon, *The Impact of Egypt on Canaan* (Freiburg, 1978), 93 with Pl.46 a-b. Astarte's role in Egypt is fully expounded by Leclant, *Syria* 37 (1960), 1-67.

[28] Edwards, op. cit., 51; Morenz, *Rel.*, 150.

[29] Anath and Astarte are sometimes merged: see Edwards, op. cit., 51 with n.16.

[30] W. Helck, 'Zum Auftreten fremder Götter in Ägypten', *Oriens Antiquus* 5 (1966), 1-14, esp. 9. Cf. Stadelmann, op. cit., 116 and 150. Albright, *The Archaeology of Palestine and the Bible*, 88, would give phallic force to Qudshu's serpents. Helck, *Beziehungen*[2] (1971), 463-6 gives a full and able account.

[31] H. te Velde, *JEA* 57 (1971), 84. For other figures of Qudshu with Resheph and Min v. Hodjash and Berlev, *The Egyptian Reliefs and Stelae* (Moscow, 1982), 75 with notes. No. 74 shows Qudshu on her own.

[32] 'The ideal child was undoubtedly a son'; H. te Velde, ibid., 85. He discusses the female element in some detail.

[33] J. Leclant, *Recherches sur les monuments thébains* (Cairo, 1965), 260f.

[34] Cf. several quotations given by Assmann, *Theologie*, 29-33.

[35] F. Daumas, 'L'Origine d'Amon de Karnak', *BIFAO* 65 (1967), 201-14.

[36] In 1540b P the deceased King is *as the son of Geb upon the throne of Amûn*. In 1712b MN the gods Ha, Min, and Sokar are mentioned together; one text (N) has *Amûn* instead of *Min*, which recalls Wainwright's view that Amûn and Min were originally identical: see *JEA* 49 (1963), 21-3.

[37] E. Otto, *Osiris and Amon* (1968), 80, refers to the likely action of Mentuhotep in transferring artists from Heracleopolis to Thebes, but concedes that no evidence points to an earlier cult centre of Amûn on Theban soil. In *LÄ* I (1975), 237-8 he deals with varying views of the god's origin.

[38] Cf. Charles F. Nims, *Thebes of the Pharaohs* (London, 1965), 69ff.

[39] Bonnet, *RÄRG*, 492; H. te Velde, *LÄ* IV (1982), 246.

[40] Nims, op. cit., 34.

[41] Cf. Bonnet and te Velde, opp. citt. and Leclant, *Monuments thébains*, 246-53 (on the titles cited above and on this triad generally). He emphasizes the influence of Hathor and Sakhmet on Mut (p.247).

[42] Leclant, op. cit., 248 n.7. He also discusses the many other epicleseis of Khons.

[43] E. Otto, *Osiris and Amon*, 96; cf. Nims, *Thebes*, 114ff. with Pl.63 (cf. Pl.29).

[44] See R. A. Parker and L. H. Lesko in *Pyramid Studies and Other Essays presented to I. E. S. Edwards* (London, 1988), 168-75 with Pls.34-7. Pl.34 does not include the figure of Hathor.

[45] E. Otto, op. cit., 97ff. with Figs.13-14 and Pls.28-36; L. Habachi, 'The Triple Shrine of the Theban Triad in Luxor Temple', *MDAIK* 20 (1965), 93-7.

[46] J. Zandee, *De Hymnen aan Amon van Papyrus Leiden*, I, 350 (OMRO 28; Leiden, 1947).

[47] Cf. my remarks in *ZÄS* 100 (1973), 30-1. See also *Pyr.* 613b TM, *the White Crown, The Mistress*; *Nefer-ti*, 57 (= ed. Helck, XII, 9), *the Heliopolitan district, the birthplace of the Lord God* (*ntr nb*) - it is certainly not the birthplace of *every god*; Sinuhe B 210: *and the gods who are the Lords of the Beloved Land and the Islands of the Sea* (thus Simpson, *Lit.* 69); cf. D. Meeks, *Ann. Lex.* III (1979 and 1982), 160, for *nb* 'maître', of a god.

[48] Cf. Brunner, 'Egyptian Texts', 25. For Amûn grouped with Ptah and Prê in the preamble of letters see A. M. Bakir, *Egyptian Epistolography* (Cairo, 1970), 57; Mut and Khons occasionally replace Ptah and Prê.

[49] PM VII, 110 (115); Bonnet, *RÄRG*, 1; L. Habachi, *Features of the Deification of Ramesses II* (ADAIK 5, 1969), 10 with Pl.V b; E. Otto, *LÄ* I (1975), 26.

[50] *ANET* 369 n.11. Cf. Gardiner, *ZÄS* 42 (1905), 35-6; Erman, *Sitzb. Berlin* 1923, 73; Zandee, *Hymnen aan Amon*, 87; te Velde, *JEA* 57 (1971), 81-2; Westendorf, *ZÄS* 100 (1974), 139; Säve-Söderbergh, *LÄ* II (1977), 692.

[51] E. Otto, *Osiris and Amon*, 52.

[52] Morenz, *Rel.* 152 (p.144 in Ann Keep's tr.). Cf. my remarks in *ZÄS* 100 (1973), 31.

[53] Cf. Morenz, *Rel.* 150-1 (p.143 of tr.).

[54] See Mariette, *Le Sérapéum de Memphis*, III, Pl.8; E. Otto, *Stierkulte*, 32; Morenz, loc. cit.; and my remarks in *ZÄS* 100 (1973), 30.

[55] Leclant, *Monuments thébains*, 269 n. 4.

[56] Ibid. 318.

[57] Cf. above ch.3, section 1; and Erik Hornung, 'Die Anfänge von Monotheismus und Trinität in Ägypten' in *Der eine Gott und der dreieine Gott*, ed. Karl Rahner (Munich, 1983), 61, noting the instances where the King or Seth or Osiris are added to the state triad. Hornung's title is slightly ambiguous, but he ends his study with the claim that Egyptian theologians during the second millennium provided the earliest examples in human history of both monotheism (with Akhenaten) and of trinitarianism.

Early Indian religion presents a rival trinity in the latter half of the second millennium: see the cosmic role of the god Agni (ch.6, sections 2 and 5). Wendy Doniger O'Flaherty, *Textual Sources for the Study of Hinduism* (Manchester, 1988), 1, refers to the *Rig-Veda* as 'the earliest Indian text', composed 'in around 1000 B.C.' Gonda favours the twelfth century for the oldest part: v. chapter 6 n.2. In that case, the Egyptian tradition has priority.

Part II
MESOPOTAMIA AND ADJACENT AREAS

5

Mesopotamia: Types and Regions

Already in the Early Dynastic period of Mesopotamian culture (*c.* 2800–2400 BC) as many as four thousand deities are named in texts.[1] They are frequently mentioned in divine lists, but it is not often that they are systematically grouped. In a country of independent city-states it was natural that prominence should be given to the association of deities with particular cities. An international Assyriological conference held in Rome in June 1974 was devoted primarily to the theme of the panthea of the Ancient Near East, and it is not surprising that several of the published papers give a good deal of attention to local aspects of the cults.[2]

1. *Cosmic Groups*

A group of three gods encountered in texts relating to Sumerian religion consists of An (in Akkadian Anu), Enlil, and Enki. An, king of heaven, was connected with the city of Uruk, and he represented sovereignty. Enlil, 'Lord of Wind', is the son of An. Enki is 'Lord of Earth' or 'Lord of the subterranean region'; he is likewise a son of An, and is also called Ea '(god of) the house of water'.[3] The triad is first attested in the Isin-Larsa period (2006–1894 BC).[4] It has clear cosmological connotations with its references to heaven, wind, and earth, and corresponds in this respect to the roles in Egyptian mythology of Nut, goddess of heaven, Geb, god of earth, and Shu, god of the atmosphere which separates heaven and earth. Charles-F. Jean[5] refers to the Egyptian group as a triad, and it is so represented iconographically, although in the designations of the Ennead, as in the *Pyramid Texts* (e.g. 1655 a–b), Shu is mentioned with his consort Tefnut. As far as the cosmogonic divisions are concerned there is a parallel too in the early Indian triad of Agni, Vāyu, and Sūrya.[6] The Sumerian group is not treated with any rigid consistency. In one list Enki appears at the head, but King Rim-Sin of Larsa often mentions the triad in the order An, Enlil, and Enki.[7] In the same period at Nippur Enlil often heads the list; understandably so, since Nippur was his sacred city.[8] Neither cosmological features nor factors of family relationship are conspicuous in the period studied by Charles-F. Jean. An emerges as a rather vague figure. Enlil is described as an aggressive bull and a god of fertility. Enki appears not only as lord of the Earth but also as a god of wisdom. All three members of the triad are provided with consorts through whom they become creator-gods. Whereas Enlil in these texts is said to be the son of An, the origin of Enki–Ea is not referred to. However, in the *Enuma elish*, the poem concerned with creation which derives from a later era (the first Babylonian dynasty, probably), the god An (now called Anu) is said to have engendered Ea, whereas the origin of Enlil is not mentioned.[9] It is not clear, therefore, that the triad consists of a father and two sons. A female element is lacking in the triad itself, although it is present in their spouses.

At this point it may be well to consider the use of the term 'triad' of such a group. H. W. F. Saggs[10] comments on the matter thus:

> Though the term 'triad' is often applied (as it is elsewhere in this book) to the three gods Anu, Enlil and Enki considered together, it can be misleading if 'triad' is to mean anything more specific theologically than three gods of roughly equal rank. In many respects Enki stands apart from Anu and Enlil, and the conception of a triad (in the more precise sense of three deities whose inter-relationship is of the essence of their natures) is certainly not present in Sumerian religion.

Of his two definitions – 'three gods of roughly equal rank' and 'three deities whose inter-relationship is of the essence of their natures' – the former will prove the more useful in our treatment. We shall encounter a wide variety of triadic divine groups which will differ very much in both relationship (that is, within the group) and symbolism. It will be reasonable to demand, however, that any group so designated will not be attested only sporadically, but will occur with sufficient frequency to enable one to assume that the ancients regarded the three as forming a firmly established grouping. Not that any triad in this sense is likely to be static. Changes in its composition and significance may be expected with the lapse of time.

2. *An Astral Triad*

Using the evidence of personal names before Ur III, J. J. M. Roberts[11] names a number of astral deities as occurring frequently; and he states that three of them, which compose the triad sun, moon, and Venus – Shamash, Suen, and Ishtar – 'are three of the four deities which occur most often in the Old Semitic personal names'. He goes on to urge that since these three names occur in other Semitic languages too, even if the name Suen may not be originally Semitic, the importance of this triad among the early Semitic inhabitants of Mesopotamia probably reflects 'a dominant role for the astral deities during the Proto-Semitic period'. At this point he advances an attractive sociological hypothesis:

> This would agree nicely with the commonly assumed semi-nomadic background of the early Semites, for the veneration of the heavenly bodies appears to be a religious response typical of semi-nomadic herdsmen or shepherds, but highly untypical of settled farming communities.

In support thereof he cites[12] discussions by Thorkild Jacobsen[13] in which it is maintained that 'the astral aspect in the Sumerian pantheon comes from the areas where cattle or sheep herding is the main occupation'. Jacobsen's distinctions, however, seem somewhat bold. He speaks of 'Southern Cowherds' Gods' and of the 'Central Grasslands Shepherds' Gods'. It seems more likely that when farming communities enabled cities to be founded in both Mesopotamia and Egypt, features of earlier nomadic life were not abruptly abandoned, but a mixed farming economy emerged. Another embarrassment accompanies the triadic claim by Roberts: his evidence comes from proper names, and he does not make it clear whether the astral deities mentioned occur together *as a triad*. That the triad does, however, occur in other ways is stated by Jacobsen[14] in a dictum which relates it to an earlier Sumerian group; he has mentioned Akkadian personal names of the period of the dynasty of Agade and just before:

> They show the presence of a not very clearly defined major god Il and of the astral triad Sin, god of the moon; Shamash, deity of the sun, seemingly a goddess; and Ashtar, later Ishtar, goddess of the morning and evening star. The deities of this triad were identified with the Sumerian deities Nanna, Utu, and Inanna respectively and merged into them.

Yet in discussing a 'herdsman's pantheon, a family of gods headed by Nanna of Ur' and a 'separate family of Ninhursaga to the north of them', Jacobsen says that a 'prominence of astral deities' is characteristic for this pantheon of herdsmen; and he gives them as 'Nanna, the moon; Utu, the sun; Inanna, the morning and evening star; and seemingly An, the sky'. One doubts, therefore, whether a triad is firmly indicated. Is it a tetrad rather? Again, the family relationships of gods seem to be often mentioned, but the grouping of father, mother, and son does not crystallize into an established triad.

3. *City Groupings*

A significant feature of the early religion of Mesopotamia is the way in which topographical phenomena were deified. Mountains, rivers, temples, and cities were thus treated.[15] The addition of an epithet *of the mountain* to the name of a god, such as *Inanna of the mountain* may refer to a sanctuary on a mountain; but in other cases the mountain itself is treated as an independent, albeit lesser, divinity.[16] The deification of cities was also expressed by the early Semites, and Roberts[17] suggests that it was because they were 'awed by their first encounters with the great cities of Mesopotamia'.

However that may be, the religious role of the city is conspicuous. Every city must have its patron deity; and in marked contrast to Egyptian usage, where the divine patrons usually constitute a triad, the Sumerians and their successors assigned to each city one, and only one, protecting deity. According to royal hymns assigned in date to Ur III and the Isin-Larsa era, the king of all Sumer was nominated by his city-god or an associated deity in an assembly of the gods at Nippur where An and Enlil presided.[18] The relationship of the city-ruler to the presiding deity of the city is exemplified in a hymn to the goddess Baba which ends with a prayer on behalf of Gudea, ruler of Lagash:[19]

> Baba, thou hast raised thy glance in the divine Council, thou
>   hast clad him with joy,
> Thou hast called the good one to thine heart, the shepherd
>   Gudea:
> Mother Baba, in thy city Lagash will he ever praise thee!

The city-god of Eridu, situated in an area of marshlands, was Enki. Of the early gods of this region Jacobsen[20] says that 'they belong to a single family, that of Enki in Eridu'. He goes on to show how Enki was credited with the organization of agriculture. We have seen that Enki sometimes figures in a triad.

That the concept of the allocation of cities to particular deities is early is shown by the Sumerian flood myth, where an unnamed god is said to arrange this:[21]

> [He] founded ... cities in ...,
> Gave them their names, apportioned the capitals:
> The first of these cities, Eridu, he gave to the leader Nudimmud,
> The second, Badtibira, he gave to the 'nugig',
> The third, Larag, he gave to Pabilsag,[22]
> The fourth, Sippar, he gave to the hero Utu,
> The fifth, Šuruppak, he gave to Sud.
> He gave the names to these cities, apportioned the capitals.

Nudimmud here is a name borne by Enki, and Utu is the sun-god, who is known as the patron of both Sippar and Larsa.[23] But normally, it seems, the principle was 'one city, one deity'. This text, incidentally, attributes the creation of mankind to a divine triad:[24]

> After An, Enlil, (and) Ninḫursag[25]

Had created the black-headed people,
Animals multiplied everywhere;

Kramer,[26] however, translates the group as 'Anu, Enlil, Enki, and Ninursag', clearly reading one section differently and thus making the group a tetrad. Other texts similarly assign the emergence of man to various deities who symbolize the primeval sea, from which heaven and earth emerged; when they were separated by the air, there developed, it was thought, plant and animal life, to be followed by the appearance of man.[27] However that may be, the protecting god of the city is a guardian especially of the city's king who is himself in a position sanctioned by the gods.[28] Indeed Gudea of Lagash (c. 2143–2124 BC) is called 'the prince of the city, the god of his city', and the latter phrase is used of the kings of Akkad.[29]

Successive changes in the imperial set-up naturally brought changes in the dominant deities. Thus with the rise of Assyria the national god Ashur gradually supplants the Babylonian supreme deity Marduk; he does so even in an Assyrian form of the creation epic *Enûma elish* (*When on high*).[30] Within the Akkadian orbit, however, it seems that a measure of continuity prevailed with regard to the cosmic divinities.

4. *Hittites, Hurrians, Ugarites*

Although living outside Mesopotamia proper, the peoples of Asia Minor, Syria, and Palestine were much exposed to cultural winds from the East. In the case of the Hittites there was also a diversity of inner strains, including the Hattian, Hurrian, Luwian, Semitic, and Indo-European elements; and the equation of deities of different origin often occurred through syncretism. In his book *Some Aspects of Hittite Religion* (1977) O. R. Gurney devotes his first chapter to 'The Pantheon', and his detailed analysis does not reveal marked triadic groupings. We find that the goddess Ishtar is constantly accompanied by the attendant goddesses Ninatta and Kulitta.[31] Ishtar was, of course, the principal Babylonian goddess, deriving from the Sumerian Inanna, sovereign of heaven, and prominent too among the Assyrians;[32] her attendant deities are clearly subordinate in function. A text for the erection of a new palace groups together the Weather-god, the Throne-goddess, and 'Our God', the last-named being equated with the Sun-god.[33] Another group, mentioned on tablets from Alalakh, consists of Hebat, queen of heaven, the Weather-god of Aleppo, and Ishtar; the background is now Hurrian.[34] Two deities, Istustaya and Papaya, who are primeval Netherworld goddesses, are described as *spinning the king's years*; the Greek Moirae also spin the thread of life, and are clearly comparable, but they are three in number.[35]

At the head of the Hurrian pantheon was Teshub, king of heaven, depicted as a bull; with his consort Hebat (or Hepat), queen of heaven, and their son Sharruma he leads a family triad,[36] although the addition of their daughter Allanzu makes the family larger.[37] Another triadic group figures in a Hittite translation of a West Semitic myth: they are Baal, Elkunirsha, and Ashertu (= Asherah). In this myth Ashertu is the wife of Elkunirsha, but tries to seduce the young god Baal in the manner of Potiphar's wife.[38] We are concerned here, however, with a situation-group in a myth rather than with a triad of beings who receive cultic veneration together.

Mythologically rich is also the material from Ugarit itself. Baal is certainly conspicuous here in the fertility cult, together with his consort Anath. A long text which places the god El in the centre lauds him as the progenitor of seven fertility deities who are to ensure seven-year cycles of abundance; indeed the heptad stamps itself on the text both structurally and in some of the mythic detail.[39] Yet the triad appears in several Ugaritic loci referring to the daughters of Baal: they are three, by name Pidrai, Tallai, and Arsai, symbolizing respectively light, dew-and-rain, and earth.[40] They may function as both daughters and consorts of Baal – primarily daughters, with the term *banât-*, but with no rigid exclusion of the sexual meaning. The triad of Allah's daughters in pre-Islamic Arab thought is said to reflect the earlier group.[41] One passage describes Baal as dwelling on the peaks of the mountain of the North and looking at his daughters; here the girls seem to serve a purely cosmic purpose.[42] Another allusion to the three[43] has invited the comment by H. L. Ginsberg that 'the three names mean "Flashie (or, Lightningette) daughter of Light, Dewie daughter of Distillation, Earthie daughter of ..."' He adds that 'they are Baal's wives or daughters, and Baal is the god of rain and dew and "The Prince, Lord of the Earth"'.

Such triadisms, it should be noted, are rare and sporadic in this area. The Hebrew tradition is discussed in our part IV.

5. *Heliopolis-Baalbek*

During the first century AD a huge temple of Hadad-Jupiter was erected at Heliopolis-Baalbek in Syria. A divine triad was prominent there, as shown by the evidence of iconography and epigraphy; it appears also in Arabia and Phoenicia and in various European cities of the Roman imperial era. A typical dedication was *Iovi Veneri Mercurio*.[44] Usually Jupiter Heliopolitanus was shown as the central figure with Venus and Mercury flanking him, although one of these two paredroi sometimes occupied the centre. Mercury was presented as the son of Jupiter and Venus, but the three names referred really to the Semitic deities Hadad (or Adad),

Atargatis (the Syrian goddess), and a god variously identified as Simios[45] and Nabu.[46] Whereas Hadad was essentially a god of storm and rain, the dedications mostly address this central figure in terms suited to Jupiter – *despotês, kurios, hupatos, Augustus*, and *rex deorum* – clearly the marks of omnipotence and universality.[47] It has been questioned whether one is justified in calling this group a 'triad'; the term 'trio' is preferred.[48] But the distinction between 'trio' and 'triad' is not at all apparent, although the suggestion is made that affiliation or functionalism should be viewed as the hallmark of a triad. Certainly such types are common, as are others.[49] Frequency of attestation is clearly a *sine qua non*, and Hajjar[50] gives a list of twenty-one epigraphical and iconographical testimonies proving the veneration in Roman Heliopolis of 'une triade organisée', comprising Jupiter, Venus, and Mercury.

6. *Palmyra*

As examples of functional triads Palmyra is said to provide two: Bel, Yarhibol, and Aglibol, with the partly similar Baalshamin, Aglibol, and Malakbel.[51] In both instances the schema is found to consist of a major god with two acolyte deities who are figured with moon-god and sun-god features. The Palmyrene pantheon is almost exclusively male. Comparable to the instances cited is obviously the Mesopotamian grouping of Sin (god of the moon), Shamash (god of the sun), and Ashtar (later Ishtar, goddess of the morning and evening star), but with a female element; see above section 2.[52] The Palmyra triads relate to the first three centuries AD in a region where the Babylonian pantheon continued to hold some sway over both Roman Syria and western Parthia.[53] A relief from the court of the temple of Bel in Palmyra shows Baalshamin in the centre flanked by Aglibol the moon god and Malakbel;[54] the astral qualities of the two acolyte deities are indicated by their rayed diadems. Baalshamin was a god of heaven,[55] so that this triad had a celestial unity, Malakbel ('King Bel') being connected with the sun. For the most part the Palmyrene triads consisted of male deities only, and eventually these were addressed in generalizing epithets only, such as 'the kindly', 'the merciful', 'lord of the world', as opposed to specific names, suggesting an incipient weakening of polytheism.[56]

NOTES

[1]H. W. F. Saggs, *The Greatness that was Babylon* (London, 1962; repr. 1966), 328. Cf. Th. Jacobsen, *Towards the Image of Tammuz* (Cambridge, Mass., 1970), 21.

[2]See *Orientalia* 45 (1976), 1–226.
[3]Saggs, op. cit., 328–30.
[4]Charles-F. Jean, *La Religion sumérienne* (Paris, 1931), 46 n.10. They are mentioned previously, but not together as a group.
[5]'La Grande Triade divine An, ᵈEn-lil, ᵈEn-ki', *Rev. Hist. Rel.* 110 (1934), 113–39, this point on p.115 n.3. See also H. te Velde, 'The theme of the separation of heaven and earth in Egyptian mythology', *Studia Aegyptiaca* 3 (1977), 161–7.
[6]See below ch. 6, section 2.
[7]Charles-F. Jean, op. cit., 134.
[8]Ibid., 116.
[9]Ibid. 138–9. D. Nielsen, *Der dreieinige Gott*, I (Copenhagen, 1922), 14, stresses that this triad was not taken over in Semitic tradition. The task of separating the Sumerian and Akkadian elements in the early religion of Mesopotamia is still unfinished: see J. J. M. Roberts, *The Earliest Semitic Pantheon* (Baltimore, 1972), 1ff. with the refs. on p.9.
[10]*The Greatness that was Babylon*, 330.
[11]*The Earliest Semitic Pantheon*, 57.
[12]Ibid., 120 n.484.
[13]Including his *Toward the Image of Tammuz*, 27.
[14]Ibid., 34.
[15]J. J. M. Roberts, op. cit., 58ff.
[16]See E. Douglas Van Buren, 'Mountain-Gods', *Orientalia*, 12 (1943), 76–84.
[17]Op. cit., 59.
[18]Jacobsen, *Toward the Image of Tammuz*, 140.
[19]A. Falkenstein and W. von Soden, *Sumerische und Akkadische Hymnen und Gebete* (Zurich, 1953), 87.
[20]*Toward the Image of Tammuz*, 27.
[21]Translation by M. Civil, 'The Sumerian Flood Story', in W. G. Lambert and A. R. Millard, *Atra-ḫasīs: The Babylonian Story of the Flood* (Oxford, 1969), 141, lines 91–8. Cf. C. J. Gadd, *Ideas of Divine Rule in the Ancient East* (London, 1948), 5.
[22]S. N. Kramer in *ANET*³ 43 reads the name as Endurbilhursag, but M. Civil, op. cit., 170 n.95 points out that 'Pabilsag is well attested as the god of Larag'.
[23]Kramer, ibid., n.35.
[24]Civil, op. cit., 141, lines 47–9.
[25]Here = mankind rather than the people of Sumer and Babylon; see Kramer and Civil, locis cit.
[26]*ANET*³, 43.
[27]S. N. Kramer, *Sumerian Mythology* (Philadelphia, 1944), 73–5.
[28]Cf. Ivan Engnell, *Studies in Divine Kingship in the Ancient Near East* (1943, 2nd edn. Oxford, 1967), 21. On p.23 he speaks of the king's 'identity with the god'. For a different approach see H. Frankfort, *Kingship and the Gods* (Chicago, 1948), 295ff.; he finds here association rather than identity.
[29]A. Falkenstein in *Reallexikon der Assyriologie und vorderasiatischen Archäologie* 3 (1971), 679, where the deification of Gudea during his lifetime is left an open question.
[30]Thorkild Jacobsen, *The Treasures of Darkness* (New Haven, 1976), 167; cf. E. A. Speiser, *ANET*³, 62, notes 28, 30.
[31]O. R. Gurney, *Some Aspects of Hittite Religion* (Oxford, 1977), 5, 16, 18.

[32]Cf. Gurney, *The Hittites* (Harmondsworth, 1952 and later reprints), 157, quoting a Hittite text: *Ishtar dwells in Nineveh.*
[33]Gurney, *Some Aspects*, 9–10.
[34]Ibid. 13. Cf. Gernot Wilhelm (tr. J. Barnes), *The Hurrians* (Warminster, 1989), 49ff.
[35]Cf. Hans G. Güterbock, 'Hittite Mythology', in *Mythologies of the Ancient World*, ed. S. N. Kramer (New York, 1961), 149, rightly rejecting an Indo-European origin. For the text cf. A. Goetze, *ANET*³, 357.
[36]William J. Fulco, *Encycl. of Religion*, ed. M. Eliade, 6 (1987), 534 ('Hurrian Religion'). Cf. G. Wilhelm, op. cit., 50f.; he also refers to a triad Tesshup-Hepat-Shawushka, the last deity being a great goddess in the Mitanni kingdom.
[37]Gurney, *Some Aspects*, 14, 17, 19–22.
[38]Harry A. Hoffner, Jr. in *Unity and Diversity*, ed. H. Goedicke and J. J. M. Roberts (Baltimore, 1975), 141f., and in M. Eliade, op. cit., 411; cf. A. Goetze, *ANET*³, 519.
[39]Cyrus H. Gordon, 'Canaanite Mythology', in *Mythologies of the Ancient World* (1961), ed. S. N. Kramer, esp. 185–6; cf. W. Röllig, *Altorientalische Literaturen* (Wiesbaden, 1978), 258.
[40]Gordon, ibid., 196.
[41]Gordon, ibid., 217 n.7, cites *Moslem World* 33, 1 (1943) for 'The Daughters of Baal and Allah', which I have not been able to consult.
[42]Cf. Karl-Heinz Bernhardt, *Near Eastern Religious Texts*, ed. W. Beyerlin (1978), 193; Gordon, op. cit., 196. The photograph of Gebel el-Aqra, north of Ugarit, in W. Röllig, op. cit., 263, gives a vivid idea of the locale. Cf. too S. H. Hooke, *Middle Eastern Mythology* (Harmondsworth, 1963), 82.
[43]H. L. Ginsberg, *ANET*³, 131, e. II AB with n.12.
[44]Youssef Hajjar, *La Triade d'Héliopolis-Baalbek* (Leiden, 1977), II, 512. Two volumes of the work appeared as EPRO 59; a third volume was published in Montreal in 1985.
[45]Ibid. II, 456, citing R. Dussaud. Cf. R. A. Oden, Jr., *Studies in Lucian's De Syria Dea* (Missoula, Mont. 1977), 116ff., referring to the similar triad at Hierapolis in Syria.
[46]Jonas C. Greenfield in *Numen* 38 (1991), 272.
[47]Hajjar, op. cit. II, 513.
[48]Greenfield, op. cit., 272.
[49]Hajjar, op. cit. III, 180, refers to astral, cosmic, and family triads.
[50]In *Numen* 38 (1991), 270.
[51]Greenfield, op. cit., 272 (also citing Hajjar).
[52]Uncogently questioned by Greenfield, ibid.
[53]Malcolm A. R. Colledge, *The Parthians* (London, 1967), 104.
[54]Ibid., Pl.39 with p.228. Each of the three figures wears oriental tunics and trousers over cuirasses of Hellenistic form. The relief is dated to *c* .AD 50.
[55]Bertholet, *Wb. Rel.*, 436, s.v. Palmyra. For Baal-shamayim, 'the lord of heaven', cf. E. Lipiński on the Zakkur inscription from Afis near Aleppo (*c.* 785 BC) in *Near Eastern Religious Texts*, ed. W. Beyerlin (London, 1978), 230.
[56]Bertholet, ibid.

Part III

THE INDO-EUROPEAN TRADITION

6

Early Indian Religion

1. *A Pre-Aryan Culture*

The earliest literary source for Indian religion is the collection of 1,028 hymns known as the *Rig-Veda Samhita*,[1] and its oldest parts probably derive from north-west India in the twelfth centuty BC.[2] Archaeologically a much earlier civilization is attested in the discoveries at Mohenjo-Daro and Harappa. It is a civilization that antedates the coming of the Aryan population. It is not surprising, therefore, that theories which would connect aspects of the religion of the Veda with this earlier culture are regarded as speculative.

A dancing-girl with half-closed eyes represented in a bronze figure from Mohenjo-Daro[3] and a male figure in steatite from the same site, which has similar half-closed eyes[4] may naturally evoke much later manifestations,[5] although a direct line of succession is hard to establish. The most convincing instance of a possible ancient antecedent of a deity well known later is the figure already cited which can be related to the god Shiva. Sir John Marshall[6] describes the figure as 'recognizable at once as a prototype of the historic Śiva'. This figure is carved on a seal at the top of which is an inscription of seven letters. A pair of large curved horns adorns his head and they meet in the centre to merge into a crown. The figure is seated on a low throne and his legs are bent beneath him; he is accompanied by animals – an elephant, tiger, buffalo, and rhinoceros – while two deer are shown under the throne. He is apparently shown with erect phallus.[7] What is relevant to our theme is that he has three faces, although Marshall[8] avers that 'it is possible that a fourth is to be understood at the back'. In support of the interpretation implying three faces Marshall states that 'in historic times Śiva was portrayed with one, three, four, or five faces and always with three eyes' and also that 'the familiar triad of Śiva, Brahmā and Viṣṇu is habitually represented by a three-faced image'.[9] Shiva with three faces as an independent deity who is not associated with Brahma and Vishnu is said not to be frequently represented in historic times, although such figures are not rare.[10] Marshall,[11] however, questions whether the three-faced deity on the ancient seal is not 'a syncretic form of three deities rolled into one' in the sense that the cult of the proto-Shiva had been amalgamated with other cults, a fact signified by giving him three faces. He then avers that 'the conception of the triad or trinity is a very old one in India, though it was possibly not until the historic period that it assumed a philosophic aspect'. Yet Marshall finally opts for the view that 'in the first instance the god was provided with a plurality of faces in token of his all-seeing nature; that these images afterwards suggested the *trimūrtis* of Śiva, Brahmā, and Vishṇu; and that the latter in their turn subsequently inspired such images as those referred to above (that is, the images of historic times)'.

The triadic idea is attested also for this early era – about the middle of the third millennium BC – by a seal from Mohenjo-Daro which figures an animal with three heads, those of a bison, unicorn, and ibex.[12] There are others of comparable composition, but interpretation must be speculative. Citing the 'triple, interlaced tigers' of another seal, Marshall suggests that they may embody 'the conception of a triply powerful demon, though, on the other hand, it may be nothing more than a fanciful design of the kind that Indian imagination has always delighted in'. Nor does he exclude a third possibility – 'that these triple-headed creatures represent triads of zoomorphic deities, just as the three-faced god may also represent a triad'.[13]

If doubts attend the precise interpretation of these triadic features, in general it is not feasible to deny the possible persistence or re-emergence of elements of the ancient religions. A clear example is that which concerns phallus-worship. According to the testimony of the *Vedas*, this was not a feature of the religion of the Vedic Aryans, but it was a part of the cults of the peoples conquered by them. Yet in the later religion it is prominent in the worship of Shiva, so that a reversion to the pre-Aryan religion is probably implied.[14] At the same time the theme of divine triads may be regarded as one which is common to all periods of Indian religion. In the later *Upanishads* they are the subject of a sophisticated doctrine centred on the principle of the absolute – *brahman* or *ātman*; the triad Brahma, Rudra, and Vishnu are presented as forms of the absolute, which is itself regarded as incorporeal.[15]

2. *Divine Groupings and Functional Divisions in the* Rig-Veda

Although the *Rig-Veda* does not reveal a developed doctrine of three forms (*trimūrti*) regarded as manifestations of a supreme spirit, it anticipates in some ways the formal aspects of this belief which became characteristic of classical Hinduism, as A. B. Keith shows in his study of 'Trimurti' in *ERE* 12 (1921), 457–8, referring to the triad Brahma,

Figure 8. Shiva-Trimūrti. Colossal rock-sculpture at Elephanta Island near Bombay

Vishnu, and Shiva (Fig. 8).[16] Three areas are regarded as important in the *Rig-Veda*: sky, air, and earth; and these areas are related to the three forms of Agni, the god of fire, since he is regarded as the sun, as lightning, and as fire. A contradictory relationship appears in a prayer quoted by A. B. Keith:[17]

> May Sūrya protect us from the sky, Vāta from the air, Agni from the earthly regions.
>
> (*RV* 10, 158, 1)

for Agni seems now to be related only to the earth. Nor is it clear that this illustrates 'a tendency to reduce all the gods to manifestations of three chief deities, each representative of the three divisions, sky, air, and earth'. Certainly these divisions are often prominent in divine contexts.

A functional or spatial reference may apply also to groups of two deities or to dual deities, as Jan Gonda shows in his book *The Dual Deities in the Religion of the Veda*. Here Gonda is especially concerned with dual compounds which he describes (p.5) as 'copulative compounds which consist of two co-ordinated nouns in the dual, each with its own accent, e.g. mitrá-váruṇa "Varuṇa and Mitra"'. One wonders whether the 'and' is in place here, for he points out (p.11) that in the ritual texts dual deities are 'worshipped and spoken of as if they were single divine persons'. This is a phenomenon that frequently occurs in Ancient Egypt. As early as the *Pyramid Texts* we meet formations like Rê-Atum. The Vedic examples refer sometimes to contrasted functions or regions such as man and wife, or heaven and earth, and Gonda's chapter-headings indicate this: 'Heaven-and-Earth; Sun-and-Moon; Dawn-and-Night (Dusk); Mitra-and-Varuna; Indra-and-Vāyu'. Yet he points out (p.9) that 'with a few exceptions ... these double deities are couples of male divinities and in this they are clearly distinguished from such well-known divine couples as the Greek Zeus and Hera as well as from the post-Vedic pairs of gods and their śaktis'.

Returning to the triadic groups and their possible relation to sky, air, and earth, we note that according to A. B. Keith,[18] as we have seen, one school of Indian interpreters taught that 'the whole of the deities could be reduced to three, Agni on earth, Vāyu in the air, or, in place of Vāyu, Indra, and Sūrya in the heaven'. Here, then, the deities may vary although the connected divisions are the same. We referred earlier to the three forms of Agni, god of fire, as sun, as lightning, and as fire, the last of the forms being related usually to altar-fire on earth. Although the functions and the spheres of operation may seem purely physical, Agni is described in one hymn (*RV* 1, 1, 8) as the *bright protector of truth* or *of order*, perhaps as the enemy of darkness when the latter symbolizes falsehood and deceit;[19] and Paul Thieme[20] shows how the natural forces which are personified in the deities of the *Rig-Veda* are often assigned ethical motivations. He also shows how a religion without temples and images impelled the poets to lavish details of appearance and function on the deities addressed.

After maintaining that the threefold division of the universe related to Agni is 'the earliest Indian triad, the centre of much mystical speculation', H. D. Griswold[21] points out that he is described as having three heads (1, 146, 1), three stations, tongues, bodies (3, 20, 2),[22] three dwellings (8, 39, 8), and three kindlings[23] (3, 2, 9). It seems reasonable to infer, as Griswold does, that the three stations and dwellings of Agni imply the sky, mid-air, and earth. But the reference of the three heads, kindlings, and tongues to 'altar-fire, lightning and sun' seems more doubtful. Geldner[24] refers to an explanation of the three heads as alluding to the three pressings of Soma or to the three fires. Doubtless an allusion to the fires comes more easily since Agni is 'a thoroughly transparent Sondergott – "he of the fire"'.[25] It was a feature of the earliest Indian religion, as we have seen, to conceive of fantastic divine forms, such as a deity with three faces. Speculation follows the mythopoeic phase, and this is clearly true of the threefold nature of Agni, as the variety of the speculations shows.

Even the basic spatial divisions are not rigidly adhered to. A variant appears in an early hymn which tells of Agni's three births:

> His three births embrace them (the singers) [in spirit],
> the one in the sea, the one in the heaven,
> (the one?) in the waters. (Knowing) the eastern
> region of the earthly spaces, he has rightly divided the times.
>
> (*RV* 1, 95, 3)

Geldner, whose version has been followed, refers to an explanation of the triple division which sees in the three areas an underwater fire in the sea, the sun in the heaven, and lightning in the air (although the waters are referred to in the third place – the waters of a thunderstorm, perhaps). In another hymn the births are described in this way:

> Threefold are these his highest true (Births), the longed-for births of the god Agni.
> Concealed in endless (Darkness?) is he come, the pure, bright, gleaming lord.
>
> (*RV* 4, 1, 7)

Griswold (op. cit., 150) renders the stanza thus:

> Threefold are those, the highest, true, and lovely,
> The births of this god Agni. Close enveloped
> Within the infinite has he come hither,
> The shining, gleaming and resplendent Aryan.

In *RV* 10, 45, 1 an allusion to the three births of Agni contains reference to the heaven, the scene of the first birth, to the earth, the abode of men, and to water. Some consistency therefore emerges.

The three areas, heaven, air, and earth, are naturally regarded as containing not only forms of Agni, but other gods too. A total of thirty-three major gods is normally given in the *Rig-Veda*. These are divided into three groups of eleven distributed to the three regions.[26] In view of his threefold nature which relates to three cosmic regions, Agni not only represents a conceptual triad; he remains a unified deity in spite of his three aspects or forms, and so can be described as 'the earliest Indian trinity'.[27]

Another deity who is credited in the *Rig-Veda* with an activity of a rather curiously triple character is Vishnu, Indra's warrior comrade. Macdonell[28] states that 'the central feature of his nature consists in his three steps, connected with which are his exclusive epithets "wide-going" (uru-gāyá) and "wide-striding" (uru-kramá)'; and a typical allusion is thus rendered by R. C. Zaehner in his *Hindu Scriptures*, 4:

> I will now proclaim the manly powers of Vishnu
> Who measured out earth's broad expanses,
> Propped up the highest place of meeting;
> Three steps he paced, the widely striding!
>
> (*RV* 1, 154, 1)

The highest place of meeting will refer to the heaven; and other allusions make it likely that Vishnu's three steps are viewed as taking him through the three cosmic divisions of earth, air, and heaven which are mentioned elsewhere in these texts. See A. A. Macdonell, *Vedic Reader*, 31; Griswold, *The Religion of the Rigveda*, 283, who opts for 'the three levels, sunrise, mid-air and zenith'; Wendy D. O'Flaherty, *Hindu Myths*, 176, who remarks that the highest of the three *padas* is Vishnu's heaven. J. Gonda, *Triads in the Vedas*, 25, tends to regard three here as expressing the idea of totality, implying thus that Vishnu traversed the whole earth or even universe; cf. his *Viṣṇuism and Śivaism* (London, 1970), 7–8.

3. *Impersonal Triadic Groupings*

In his elaborate survey *Triads in the Veda*, Jan Gonda gives a good deal of attention, initially, to the concept of three as a potent and numinous number. While we are not in this study aiming at a comprehensive view of such matters, save in so far as they affect the concept of a divine triad or trinity, clearly they have a general relevance to our theme. The inclusion of pre-Christian traditions in many areas means that some startling similarities emerge from areas which are widely separated. In our survey of the Egyptian scene we noted the predominance of four and seven as sacred or typical numbers. Gonda begins his book with a reference to an article by E. Washburn Hopkins,[29] who stated that 'the most revered cardinals of the Rig-Veda are three and seven'. For his own part Gonda (p.6) aims at 'a discussion of the numeral three and the various triads occurring in Vedic literature'. He is using the word 'triads' in its widest sense.

His discussion of general or universal considerations is nevertheless of some relevance. Aristotle's[30] sophisticated belief that three implies a beginning, a middle, and an end, and therefore expresses the idea of completion is, of course, not relevant to the early phases of our inquiry. But his statement includes a reference to the usage of 'nature'.[31]

> For, as the Pythagoreans say, the world and all that is in it is determined by the number three, since beginning and middle and end give the number of an 'all', and the number they give is the triad. And so, having taken these three from nature as (so to speak) laws of it, we make further use of the number three in the worship of the Gods.

J. L. Stocks (op. cit., n.4) states that 'oaths, for instance, normally appeal to three Gods, as in the Homeric appeal to Zeus, Athene, and Apollo', but the reference may well be wider, in the sense of envisaging formalized divine triads.

The usage of 'nature' in the sense that certain numbers are provided in the world around us may be reasonably adduced in relation to prehistoric societies who have not left written evidence of the way they think about numbers. At least round or typical numbers can sometimes be traced to their origin in this way, although the definition of what comes naturally is not always beyond debate. Hermann Usener[32] suggested that the sense of completion or perfection attached to the number three originated with prehistoric man, who could not count beyond three. One might suppose that, since the fingers of the hand were used to count, the number ten would have been quickly achieved. But Usener cites a number of cases among modern primitives where finger-numbering is practised, and yet where three is the maximum reached and where three is therefore tantamount to plurality. Among Australian tribes which are ethnologically the oldest a 'pair system' is found with numerals for 'one' and 'two' and no more, but with a practice of forming the following numerals by addition to the pair: $3 = 2 + 1$; $4 = 2 + 2$; $5 = 2 + 2 + 1$.[33] In such a system it is clear that three has no special position; two is the important number. Yet it would be unwise to postulate for prehistoric man a uniform stage of numeracy. It is likely, for instance, that the Egyptians developed a calendar before the emergence of writing, probably basing it on the regularity of the Nile-inundation; they must have recorded the number of days between inundations by a simple method of notching strokes.[34] Nor does a primitive system based on three necessarily imply an inability to achieve numbers beyond that.

E. Washburn Hopkins, like Kurt Sethe, thought that a potent force in the elevation of three came from 'obvious threes around us', such as earth, air, and sky; land, water, and air; sun, moon, and stars.[35] Such an approach would have to admit, however, that there are many 'obvious twos', such as father and mother, heaven and earth, sun and moon, hot and cold, light and dark, good and evil. Indeed the evolution of opposites in qualities would seem to be a universal feature of thought. In the Vedic system such pairs are frequent and are often treated as coexisting.[36] That such dualisms could be notionally extended to embrace a triadic grouping is exemplified on an intellectual level by Aristotle's doctrine of the ethical mean: every virtue is regarded as a mean between two extremes, as courage stands between foolhardiness and cowardice. Not dissimilar is the triadic grouping in the Buddhist teaching about the middle path.[37]

A poem in the *Rig-Veda* (4, 27) describes 'the rape of *Soma*', the sacred intoxicating drink which is personified in the poem and speaks in the first part, telling how it was brought down from heaven by an eagle.[38] The god Indra is exhorted to drink freely of it. Later texts cited by Gonda (p.10) refer to two daily pressings and libations of *Soma*, and tell how Indra came to the gods to remind them that several other things were in threes, and that there was a saying *three times among the gods*. When the gods refused, Indra made a third pressing himself and so instituted three daily pressings. Now sayings such as that attributed to Indra can be paralleled in many cultures, even up to modern times. A few popular examples are:

Third time does the trick (Eng.).
Aller guten Dinge sind drei.
Dreimal ist Bubenrecht (Germ. Cf. Usener, *Dreiheit*, 1).
Alle goede dingen bestaan in drieën (Dutch: All good things consist of three. Cf. Gonda, p.21).
Tri chynnig i Gymro (Welsh: Three tries for a Welshman).

Yet the three daily pressings of *Soma* may revert ritually to the three divisions of day – morning, noon, and evening – cited by V. F. Hopper[39] as a natural 'triplicity'. One could, admittedly, look on the noon-zenith of the sun as dividing the day into two; but the phenomena of sunrise and sunset contribute to the division into three.[40]

Periodic triads are pointed to by Gonda (pp.27f.), such as three days and three nights. The most important group of this kind is that of the three seasons; and the *Rig-Veda*, according to him, 'often alludes to a triad, mentioning spring, summer and autumn in one and the same stanza' (pp.109f.). Whether this triple division is imposed by nature is questionable. The cycle of crops is that of sowing, maturity, and dormancy. But Usener[41] can say that nature herself divides the year into summer and winter; and he shows that among the Greeks and the Germans this was the original division of the year.

A large number of triadic groupings have been assembled by Gonda, but for the most part they are not inherently connected with the portrayals of the nature of the gods. He shows that in ritual there was a veritable plethora of triple elements which often have reference to the threefold universe.

4. *The Three-headed Gods*

We have seen that the god Agni in the *Rig-Veda* is credited with a number of triple attributes, including three heads, and that these can be interpreted as referring to three types of fire, as Gonda shows (pp.43f.). He collects many other triple aspects of Agni, including his three lifetimes (*RV* 3, 17, 3, where Geldner says 'drei Leben oder drei Lebensalter'). A problem with the three heads is that Agni is also said to be endowed with three bodies (*RV* 3, 20, 2). One later tradition portrays him as passing from gods to men and in so doing as laying down his three bodies in the separate divisions of the universe, the earth, air, and sky.[42] Are we then to imagine that the three heads are attached to the three bodies? If we judge from the numerous examples of three-headed deities in the later art of India, such as those assembled in Willibald Kirfel's *Die dreiköpfige Gottheit*, then the three heads must be assumed to emerge from one body.

Another deity to whom the *Rig-Veda* assigns three faces, as well as three bellies and three udders (*RV* 3, 56, 3), is the bull Viśvarūpa, who is also at times, as in the description cited, regarded as a cow. Gonda (p. 105) rejects Geldner's suggestion (*Rig-Veda*, I, 403) that the three threes here constitute a 'Spielerei mit der Dreizahl'; he thinks that they are intended, rather, to 'underline the animal's absolute excellence'. Visually, at any rate, there is an element of playful fancy in the resultant picture. According to Griswold[43] 'Viśvarūpa is used in a pregnant sense "shaping all forms", as well as "possessing all forms"; hence "Omniform".' The god Soma too has three heads (*RV* 9, 73, 1). In one hymn (*RV* 10, 8, 8) the three-headed Viśvarūpa is attacked and slain by Trita Āptya ('the third one of the water') who is urged on by Indra; and it is Indra himself who then cuts off the three heads.[44]

The theme of the three-headed deity is richly represented in many other cultures, and the best comprehensive treatment of it is that of Kirfel's *Die dreiköpfige Gottheit*. He challenges (p.187) Usener's view that the type with three bodies comes first and that the three-headed divine figure is a secondary formation drawn from this basic type. Kirfel provides detailed evidence, too, not only for the widespread occurrence of the idea in the iconography of the ancient world, but also for its reappearance in Christian art, mainly in symbolic representations of the Trinity. At the same time the Christian tradition provides instances of three faces being ascribed to evil and the Devil: see Kirfel, Pl.61, 185-6, thirteenth and fifteenth centuries.

5. *Groups of Three Deities*

It has been observed above that an early fundamental grouping of deities was that of Sūrya, Vāta, and Agni, who were assigned respectively to the sky, air, and earth, although Agni himself, as sun, lightning, and fire, is also assigned to these areas.

Gonda (p.42) states that 'identity of a triad and oneness means triunity' and goes on to say that 'ideas verging on a sort of doctrine of a union of three divinities or sacred objects are not absent'. He then paraphrases a passage from the *Śatapatha-Brāhmana* according to which 'the gods came in a threefold way (*tredhā*) to consist of one deity (*ekadevatyā abhavan*), because Agni, Soma and Indra are said to be all (the totality of) the deities (*sarvā devatāḥ*)'. Here, then, three gods become one, and they also seem to represent all deities.

In the early literature the idea of a deity possessing three functions or qualities is certainly more common than that of groups of three deities conceptually associated. An example additional to those noted above, several of which concern Agni, are three forms and names ascribed to the same god: see Gonda, pp.44f.

Whereas the gods in general are grouped into two hostile divisions – the Devas or gods and the Asuras or demons – there is a division of the gods themselves which corresponds to the tripartition of the universe. This produces the three classes of the celestial Ādityas, the aerial Rudras, and the terrestrial Vasus.[45] According to Gonda[46] 'groups of three gods are not rare'; and the statement is carefully worded. They are certainly not as frequent as the dominance of triple concepts in ritual and ideology might lead one to expect. Gonda begins with examples where the grouping is 'more or less incidental', and refers to an episode where the gods are said to fashion an arrow to attack the citadels of the Asuras. Agni, we are told, was the point of the arrow, Soma its barb, and Vishnu its shaft. That the triad was not basic is shown by the fact, adduced by

Gonda (p.65 n.134), that in another account there are four gods, the fourth being Varuna, who is equated with the feathers.

The grouping of Mitra, Aryaman, and Varuna is of a different order. They are sons of Aditi, goddess of heaven, and are mentioned in a hymn to her:

> Great should be the protection of the three (gods),
> the heavenly protection of Mitra and Aryaman,
> unassailable the protection of Varuna.
>
> (*RV* 10, 185, 1)[47]

According to Paul Thieme,[48] Mitra is the god who, in these texts, protects the idea of contract or covenant, while Aryaman protects the sense of hospitality. Georges Dumézil[49] explored the ideology of these two gods in the light of other Indo-European religions; he discusses, among other themes, 'Celeritas et Gravitas', 'Romulus et Numa', 'Ahura et Miθra', '*Wôdhanaz et *Tîwaz', finding in these pairs a parallel antithesis. Romulus, for instance, is the warrior and city-founder, Numa the man of peace and founder of religious institutions. For Dumézil the parallel to Numa is Mitra; and Varuna corresponds to Romulus. Incidentally, the Vedic pair are gods, the Roman pair human kings, though semi-legendary. Dumézil follows an unusual method when he pursues a theme in several Indo-European cultures simultaneously on a broad front. In a statement which does not confine itself to the Sanskrit tradition he draws the following antithesis:

> Mitra est le souverain sous son aspect raisonnant, clair, réglé, calme, bienveillant, sacerdotal; Varuṇa est le souverain sous son aspect assaillant, sombre, inspiré, violent, terrible, guerrier.
>
> (*Mitra-Varuna*³ (1948), 85)

Paul Thieme[50] appears to make a valid criticism when he notes that the adjectives used here do not correspond to the language used of these gods either in the *Rig-Veda* or in later literature. He points out, for instance, that both Mitra and Varuna are called 'merciful' in *RV* 1, 136, 1.[51] Be that as it may, we are here examining the possibility that Mitra, Aryaman, and Varuna are regarded as a triad. Another passage suggests this:

> For through thee, Agni, have Varuna, the protector of law, Mitra and Aryaman, the noble in gifts, achieved self-confidence ...
>
> (*RV* 1, 141, 9)

Thieme[52] transliterates and translates thus:

> tráyā hy àgne váruṇo dhṛtávrato mitráḥ śāśadre aryamā sudānavaḥ

> Through thee, O Agni, Varuṇa of firm vows, Mitra, [and] Aryaman are resplendent [as being] of good wetness.

The bestowal of rain is the theme, and Thieme shows that the three gods Varuna, Mitra, and Aryaman are regarded here as givers of rain, the quality being elsewhere often associated with Varuna. Yet Thieme establishes that in *RV* 5, 67, 1 and 8, 26, 11 this triad is really divided into two groups – Varuna on the one hand, and Mitra and Aryaman on the other, these latter two being interpreted as 'the contract (God Contract) which is hospitality (God Hospitality)'. If this explanation is valid, then the triad here presented is one which contains a dyad. This can be true, of course, of many divine triads. Those which comprise father, mother, and child exhibit a dyad in the father and mother. If the Christian Trinity be explained as having a dominant member in God the Father, with Christ and the Holy Spirit regarded as emanations of him, then the two emanations constitute a subordinate dyad.[53]

Gonda (p.67) notes the presence of some other triads in the *Rig-Veda*. In one hymn (*RV* 9, 67, 26) he finds the poet calling on three gods to purify him and other worshippers; these gods are Savitar, Soma, and Agni, the first of these being the 'Stimulator God' who is invoked in *RV* 3, 62, 10 in a prayer which asks him to stimulate the thoughts of worshippers.[54] In *RV* 10, 85, 40f. the three gods Soma, the Gandharva, and Agni are named; the second of these was a celestial deity and guardian of the *Soma*. It seems doubtful, however, whether the last two instances should be regarded as established triads.

A group of divine craftsmen, the three Ribhus – Ribhu, Vāja and Vibhvan – are, on the other hand, several times treated as a group; and although they are of minor grade compared with Tvashtar, the divine artificer-in-chief, they are said to help him in his works.[55] They are roughly reminiscent of Jabal, Jubal, and Tubal, who are said in Genesis 4: 20ff. to be makers of tents, musical instruments, and metal objects.

In *RV* 3, 56, 5, Agni is said to be *trimātá*, 'the child of three mothers'; and allusion is made also there to three divine women who live in the waters. These goddesses appear too in *RV* 10, 114, 2. Their identity seems uncertain, but Gonda can point (p.69) to triads of goddesses in later texts, such as the three Sarasvatīs.

In *RV* 10, 45, 2 we find the words *We know thy threefold three (forms), O Agni; we know thy forms which are divided in many places*. They are explained as referring to the three worlds, which are themselves sometimes divided into three.[56] Gonda (pp.65f.) sees in a later explanation – (*We know*) *Agni, Vāyu, Āditya, these are (thy) three in three forms* – a 'tendency to trinitarianism'. He also sees (p.70) a 'modalistic trinity' occasionally in the Brāhmanas, as in *He (Indra) said: 'Three are these "bodies" (forms) of my own that have strength.'* Three special functions are then assigned to the three, and the statement is said to explain the rite of offering a cake on eleven dishes three times to these three aspects of Indra. The total of dishes will allude to the thirty-three gods.

6. *The Role of the Three Social Classes*

In a hymn to the Asvins, twin horse-gods who are comparable to the Dioscuri, reference is made to three ranks in society:

> Strengthen the priesthood and strengthen the thoughts. Slay the evil spirits, drive away diseases. In accord with Ushas and Sūrya drink, O Asvins, the *Soma* of the one who presses. Slay etc.
>
> Strengthen the rank of the princes and strengthen the men of war. Slay etc.
>
> Strengthen the cows and strengthen the people. Slay etc.
>
> (*RV* 8, 35, 16-18)

See Geldner, II, 349 and Gonda, p.127. The latter renders the first part of 16 thus: *Resuscitate (animate) the bráhman* (rather than Geldner's 'Geistlichkeit') *and resuscitate the poetic inspirations* ... H. Oldenberg[57] notes that *bráhmā* (plur.) should not be conjectured since *kṣatrám* follows in 17. M. Mayrhofer[58] gives a basic early meaning of 'Formung, Gestaltung, Formulierung' to *bráhma*, following a fine analysis by Thieme;[59] as a masculine the word then means 'singer, poet, priest'. Gonda's proposal is 'power'.[60] It certainly suits the present context if it means here 'power of inspiration'.[61]

The meaning of the other terms relating here to social divisions is not, happily, contested. In 17 *kṣatrám*, which means 'might, power, supremacy', represents collectively the princes or noblemen, the *kṣatriyas*. In 18 *viśaḥ* is a term for the Aryan people in general, but specifically in the sense of the lower orders; Geldner indeed gives 'Untertanen'. He refers (II, 349n.) to 8, 37, 1 and 7 for other allusions to three social divisions. In 8, 37, 1, a hymn to Indra, the god is told that he has 'helped this priesthood in the struggles'; and in 8, 37, 7 that he alone 'helped Trasadasyu[62] in the slaughter of men, strengthening the ruling powers'. These allusions, however, are not as revealing as *RV* 8, 35, 16-18. Here it is clear, as Gonda[63] explains, that divine inspiration is connected with the first class, the brahmans, power with the second class, the warrior-princes, and cattle-breeding with the third class. He adds that

> Brahman priests were, in the times of the Ṛgveda, not necessarily members of an hereditary class and the term *brahmán-* could, in all probability, be applied to all those who were distinguished by special genius or virtue, and were specialized in the performance of rites or who for some reason were deemed specially receptive of 'divine inspiration'.

Three social classes are at any rate presented here, however loose the distinction between them might have been. It is remarkable that Geldner, whose knowledge of these texts has perhaps not been surpassed, could not refer to a single detailed parallel. Yet Georges Dumézil[64] could maintain with some confidence that from the time of the redaction of these hymns society was thought of as composed of priests, warriors and stockbreeders, and that the abstract terms used of them indicated the formulation of a hierarchical system.

Dumézil begins his argument in this book by pointing to the systematic division into *four* classes which prevailed in India after the age of the *Rig-Veda*. The fourth class he dismisses as not having been a part of the primal division since it represented the conquered elements after Aryan sovereignty. But the other three classes are seen as a feature of early Aryan society, and even of the undivided Indo-European society. He lists them thus;

(1)   The *brāhmaṇa*, priests.
(2)   The *kṣatriya* (or *rājanya*), warriors.
(3)   The *vaiśya*, who are concerned with labour, commerce, and the production of material goods.

The person who presides over the whole society is the king, *rājan*, although he comes from the second class. Heredity decides his choice, and indeed the position of others in their classes. Endogamy also prevails as a natural corollary. Dumézil indicates his debt to an Indian scholar, V. M. Apte, who in 1940 showed on the basis of the first nine books of the *Rig-Veda* (especially on 8, 35, 16–18, which we have discussed above) that this was the original tripartite division of society. Apte gave a short account of the theory in his book *Social and Religious Life in the Grihya Sutras*, which was first published in Bombay in 1939,[65] and which begins with a discussion of 'The Rig-Veda Period' (pp.1–3). Dumézil then continues with a wide-ranging discourse which embraces the Avestan social classes and those of the Scythians, Celts, Romans, Ionians, and Egyptians, although the last-named people, who were obviously not of Indo-European origin, belong to the treatment only because Tuthmosis IV had married an Aryan princess of the Mitanni, a daughter of Artatama. It would be wise, one feels, at this point to deviate from Dumézil's method in one way. Rather than survey the whole field simultaneously, as he does, we shall discuss his theory in relation to the separate cultures as they arise; and the basic question we shall treat is the possible relation between a social tripartition and the emergence of divine triads.

There have been many criticisms of Dumézil's general method.

Perhaps the most telling, and certainly the most engaging, is the study by John Brough, 'The Tripartite Ideology of the Indo-Europeans: An Experiment in Method'.[66] After quoting the concession made by Dumézil when he states that the tripartite social division is not be interpreted too rigidly in terms of social reality, he notes the claim that the division is reflected in theological and mythological structures. Thus Mitra represents the first class, Indra the second, and the twin Asvins the third. Triplicity in many other matters is similarly related. Brough makes an important point when he stresses Dumézil's argument that the 'tendency to think of things in groups of three ... is held to be, not merely Indo-European, but characteristically and exclusively Indo-European'. He quotes a paragraph from Dumézil (p.16) to justify the summary he gives. Brough then examines the Old Testament from the point of view of the tripartite hypothesis, and finds a surprising number of correspondences. Beginning with aspects of God, he observes that the God of the Covenant can be assigned to the first class (aspect Mitra); the jealous God, the God of the penitential Psalms, to the same category (aspect Varuna); the Lord mighty in battle to the second category; the God who produces food for man to the third category.

Turning to the treatment of the legendary history of Rome, Brough notes that the three tribes are regarded as representing the three functional classes in the order Ramnes, Luceres, and Titienses. The twelve tribes of Israel are then shown to be presented by Jacob in Genesis 49 in a way that 'neatly allocates them, four to each of the three "fonctions"'. Brough follows with impressively subtle parallels from Hebrew sources in the manner of the 'lost mythology' which Dumézil claims to retrieve for the Romans. David is shown to have analogies with Romulus and, through his friendship with Jonathan, with the twin Vedic Asvins. An exceptional situation is sometimes explained by Dumézil by invoking outside influence. Thus Brough summarizes one argument by saying that the Egyptian Pharaoh Tuthmosis IV 'was unable to think of the device of a standing army until his Indo-European wife put the idea into his head'. Solomon's mother, Bathsheba, we are reminded, was originally the wife of Uriah the Hittite – a path of influence which might explain the correspondences adduced. This is a point which might characterize Brough's study as a 'burlesque' of Dumézil's method; and he himself mentions the possibility. For the most part, however, it is something much more serious, and one must agree with Brough's final emphasis (p.84):

> The more general we make our categories, the greater the probability will be that an impressive quantity of data can be classified under these categories; but at the same time the chance of our results being significant will be diminished.

The three 'fonctions' practically cover, in fact, all human activities.

A crucial matter, from our point of view, is whether the Vedic divine triads or other triadic groupings can be shown to be related to the three social divisions. In a discussion of the thirty-three gods of the *Rig-Veda* Dumézil[67] explains them, albeit with some hesitation, as representing a divine society which is conceived in accordance with the image of Aryan society and which is sometimes divided into three groups of ten, completed by three supplementary units. For this last procedure he compares the thirty-three representatives of the Comitia Curiata in Rome, thirty of whom (3 × 10) stand for the early tribes, characterized by him as 'fonctionelles', the Ramnes, Luceres, and Titienses, the number being made up by three augurs. Gonda[68] justly points out that the thirty-three gods of the *Rig-Veda* are three groups of eleven and that they are assigned to heaven, air, and earth. In his note on the dictum Dumézil[69] argues that the three divisions of the world are themselves related ('en rapport avec') to the three functions, though he does not say how. He goes on to say that the Indo-Iranian character of the thirty-three gods is warranted by the Avestan concept of the 'thirty-three *ratu*' or protective spirits. The two comparisons illustrate the unevenness of Dumézil's method. The second is perfectly acceptable and convincing, since he is comparing like with like (divine beings). But in the comparison with the Roman Comitia Curiata he has been beguiled by the numeral coincidence in which thirty-three figures, and the equation is almost absurd since the Roman parallel is not at all concerned with gods and does not show three groups of eleven.

We referred above to the group of three divine artisan-gods, the Ribhus. Clearly the triadic sense here cannot refer to three classes since all three have the same function.[70] While artisans are not specifically included in the tripartite social doctrine, the Vedic hymns refer to carpenters, wheelwrights, blacksmiths, tanners, and weavers.[71] In an allusion to artisans Dumézil[72] cites only Greek writers (Strabo, Plato, and Plutarch); but he doubtless regards artisans as subsumed within the wide range of activities ascribed by him to the Nasatya or Asvins as deities who secure health, fecundity, abundance in people and property, and well-being in a temporal sense.[73]

It is doubtful whether the idea of a rigid departmentalism of activity was assigned to the three classes; and still less is this true of gods who might be associated with them. The second class, the *kṣatriyas*, is the warrior class and also produces the king; but he is, in theory at least, the military commander.[74] Yet there are many allusions to the third class, the people (*vaiśyas*), fighting in war.[75] At the same time the king is closely connected with the priestly class. The three classes, as opposed to the fourth (the *śudras*), have the interesting adjective *dvija*, 'twice-born', applied to them, 'in the sense that they participate in initiation, second birth, and in the religious life in general'.[76] But the first two classes are often elevated above the third, and the king must have his Brahman, his *purohita*, going before him:

> He (the king) lives comfortably in his own palace; the earth (Ilā) ever brings increase to him; before the king the people bow down of themselves; with him goes the High Priest in front.
>
> (*RV* 4, 50, 8)[77]

Other hymns, as we have seen, portray the people as not only bowing in obeisance before the king, but also actively serving his warlike purposes. What can happen, according to Dumézil,[78] is that 'the god or king of the second function mobilizes into his service the gods of the third function or some heroes born within it', although in the process he has been violating 'the rules of the first function'. He also finds, following Wikander, two types of warrior gods in the early Indian tradition: Vāyu, of almost monstrous physical vigour, who is neither handsome nor too intelligent, but relies on the brute force of his two arms and a club; Indra, on the other hand, is the civilized superman who deploys sophisticated weapons and is withal both perceptive and moral in his attitudes.[79] A weakness of this theory is that it concedes that such a dichotomy has been almost entirely deleted in the *Rig-Veda* in favour of Indra, although it is said to be adumbrated in the later *Mahābhārata*.

The theory which attaches great importance to the three social classes has been discussed at length by Gonda in his *Triads in the Veda* and elsewhere.[80] In one respect Dumézil has corrected an overstatement: Gonda[81] referred to his 'contention that the triad of social classes has been the determining factor that has brought about numerous other triads, the example imitated by the Indians in creating a variety of triadic groupings'. Dumézil[82] points out that he had used a less far-reaching phrase: 'L'Inde a mis les trois classes de la société, avec leurs trois principes, en rapport avec les nombreuses triades de notions soit préexistantes, soit créées pour la circonstance.'[83] Even so, the sentence is quite comprehensive in its force. It does not, admittedly, refer to gods, but that claim is explicitly made elsewhere. The gods related by Dumézil to the three classes are as follows:

(1) Varuna and Mitra, regarded as two aspects of the first function.
(2) Indra, with Vāyu representing another aspect of warlike divinity.
(3) The Asvins, supported by various lesser deities.

Whereas the relation of the posited functions may be accepted, it is important to recognize that these deities are not presented as any kind of divine triad. Indra (or Vāyu) occurs, as we have seen, in a divine triad (with Agni and Sūrya), but the connection of this group is with air, earth, and sky respectively. Gonda[84] states that a suggestion is possible 'that the deities Varuṇa–Mitra, Indra, the Aśvins – or their companions or substitutes as "functional gods" – are sometimes combined to constitute a triad'. But he quotes no example of this. He quotes one saying

> I bear both Varuṇa and Mitra, Indra and Agni, the Aśvins.
>
> (*RV* 10, 125, 1)

but this can be regarded as a triad only in the sense of three pairs. He is probably right, however, when he states (p.196) that it was 'the cosmic triad, and not the social tripartition' that was basic. The cosmic divisions are clearly indicated, at any rate, in relation to the gods. Whether they affected triadic notions in general is more doubtful.

In a book devoted to Dumézil's theories, C. Scott Littleton[85] comes to the conclusion that the theory of 'an inherited, tripartite ideology' is 'substantially correct'. He further believes (p.224) that it is possible 'to make a strong case for the uniqueness of the I.E. ideology strictly from the standpoint of myth and religion ...' He also states (p.222), following Stuart Piggott, that what is uniquely Indo-European is the 'formal recognition' of a tripartite division of functions. Our analysis of early Indian texts shows that such recognition is rare, although it does occur. As applied to the gods, its significance is cosmic rather than social. The verdict of Richard Gombrich[86] in a review of Dumézil's *Les Dieux Souverains des Indo-Européens* may here be quoted:

> I think that we may have to abandon the one big theory in favour of several smaller theories. Very likely the Indo-Europeans (and certainly the Indo-Iranians) thought in terms of three social functions and three classes of men, and very likely these three also formed a hierarchy. But the content of the tripartition may never have been completely uniform; the gods may never have fitted the categories; and in particular the concepts of sovereignty were a different story, which not all societies brought into the same (or any?) relation with their theories of social structure. Popular ideologies are just not always that consistent.

'The gods may never have fitted the categories': this is the relevant point.

If Dumézil did not succeed, except in rare contexts, in his attempt to establish his theory of social tripartition in relation to divine triadism, this does not invalidate his many other conclusions. His comparative study of early Indo-European traditions brought welcome illumination to obscure areas of Roman religion. A brilliant example is his interpretation of the rites of Mater Matuta, the Matralia on 11 June, by the invocation of Vedic prototypes: in both, the goddess of Dawn repels the darkness, an act symbolized when the *bonae matres* slap and push a slave woman and when, in the *Rig-Veda*, a heroic archer chases his enemies.[87]

NOTES

[1] Arthur Berriedale Keith, *The Religion and Philosophy of the Veda and Upanishads* (Harvard Oriental Series, 31, Cambridge, Mass., 1925), 1ff.

[2] Jan Gonda, *Die Religionen Indiens*. I: *Veda und älterer Hinduismus* (Die Religionen der Menschheit, 11; Stuttgart, 1960), 9. R. C. Majumdar in *Studies in the Cultural History of India* (Agra, 1965), 9, says that 'the consensus of opinion is in favour of referring at least the bulk of the R̥gveda to about 1500 B.C.'

[3] Sir John Marshall, *Mohenjo-Daro and the Indus Civilization*, III (London, 1931), Pl.94, 6-8 and I, 345.

[4] Ibid. III, Pl.98.

[5] R. Chanda's view is cited in I, 375 n.1, maintaining that the second figure is a yogī. A seal from Harappa, shown on Pl.12, 17 (facing p. 52) is also said to represent 'Siva in the posture of a yogī'.

[6] Op. cit. I, 52; see Pl.12, 17. W. Kirfel, *Die dreiköpfige Gottheit* (Bonn, 1948), Pl.8, 17, reproduces it with the rather bold caption 'Plakette mit dem dreiköpfigen Shiva aus Mohenjo-daro'.

[7] Marshall, ibid., is not certain (it may be 'the end of the waistband'). A. Pusalker in *The Vedic Age* (History and Culture of the Indian People, I; London, 1951), 187, refers to its *penis erectus*, and the photograph seems to indicate a stylized form of penis with testicles.

[8] Op. cit. I, 53 n.1.

[9] Cf. Alain Daniélou, *Hindu Polytheism* (London, 1964), Pl.1 (facing p.192), a relief in Orissa province of the eleventh century AD.

[10] Cf. P. Banerjee, *Early Indian Religions* (Delhi, 1973), 26-7 with refs.

[11] Op. cit. I, 53. Cf. Sukumari Bhattacharji, *The Indian Theogony* (Cambridge, 1970), 112.

[12] Marshall, op. cit. I, 67 and Pl.12, 24.

[13] Ibid., 67 n.1. Cf. Kirfel, *Die dreiköpfige Gottheit*, Pl.8, 18 and 19.

[14] See R. C. Zaehner, *Hinduism* (Oxford, 1962; repr. 1975), 15f.

[15] A. B. Keith in *ERE* 12 (1921), 457. Cf. J. Mascaró, *The Upanishads* (Harmondsworth, 1965), 11.

[16] Cf. H. von Stietencron in *Der Name Gottes* (Düsseldorf, 1975), 57; and his remarks on the lore of the spiritual principle developed in the *Upanishads*, 53 n.8; and Franklin Edgerton, *The Beginnings of Indian Philosophy* (London, 1965), 359, on *Trivarga*, group of three abstracts.

[17] Op. cit., 457. The best, and the only complete, modern translation of the *Rig-Veda* is said to be that by Karl Friedrich Geldner, *Der Rig-Veda* (Harvard Oriental Series, Vols.33-5, with an Index in Vol.36; Cambridge, Mass., 1951 and 1957). He also adds a running Commentary. In Vol.III, 387 he ends the present locus differently from the version quoted above: 'Sūrya soll uns vor dem Himmel schützen, der Wind vor dem Luftreich, Agni uns vor den irdischen (Leuten)!' But by supplying 'Leuten' he breaks the spatial pattern of the other references. For a version of a selection see Wendy Doniger O'Flaherty, *The Rig Veda* (Harmondsworth, 1981; repr. 1984); cf. her *Hindu Myths* (Harmondsworth, 1975).

[18] *The Religion and Philosophy of the Veda and Upanishads*, 86.

[19] Cf. Paul Thieme, *Gedichte aus dem Rig-Veda* (Stuttgart, Reclam, 1964), 16 n.8. Geldner translates *Hüter des rechten Brauches*. Macdonell, *Vedic Reader for Students* (Oxford, 1917; repr. 1951), 9, says that '*r̥tá* means the regular order of nature ...;

then, on one hand, the regular course of sacrifice (rite); on the other, moral order (right), a sense replaced in Skt. by dharma'. He adds that 'Agni is specially the guardian of ṛtá in the ritual sense ...', and so translates *the shining guardian of order.*

[20] Ibid., 8f.

[21] *The Religion of the Rigveda* (London, 1923; repr. Delhi, 1971), 150.

[22] Also, in Geldner's version, three seeds or sperms.

[23] I.e., pieces of burning wood.

[24] *Der Rig-Veda*, I, 204n. to 1, 145, 1.

[25] Griswold, op. cit., 151. Cf. Thieme, *Gedichte aus dem Rig-Veda*, 7, comparing Lat. *ignis*. The tongue and limbs of Agni naturally denote his flames; see Macdonell, *Vedic Reader*, xviii. For a general discussion of his role see Louis Renou, *Vedic India* (Delhi, 1971), 68-9.

[26] Macdonell, loc. cit.

[27] Ibid., 2.

[28] Ibid., 30.

[29] 'The Holy Numbers of the Rig-Veda' in *Oriental Studies. A Selection of the Papers read before the Oriental Club of Philadelphia, 1888-1894.* (Boston, 1894), 141-59. The quotation is from p.141.

[30] *De caelo*, 1. 268a12. Aristotle is here citing the view of the Pythagoreans.

[31] The translation is that of J. L. Stocks (Oxford, 1922). Cf. that by W. K. C. Guthrie (Loeb, 1939; repr. 1953), p.5.

[32] *Dreiheit*. (Bonn, 1903; repr. Darmstadt, 1966), 358ff. It appeared first in the journal *Rheinisches Museum* 58 (1903), in several parts, and the pagination is that of the journal.

[33] See P. Wilhelm Schmidt in *Encyc. Brit.* (1959), s.v. Numeral Systems.

[34] See my *Origins of Osiris and his Cult* (1980), 114ff. and the works there cited.

[35] Op. cit., 145. Cf. Gonda, *Triads in the Vedas*, 7f.

[36] Gonda, op. cit., 9.

[37] Cf. T. R. V. Murti, *The Central Philosophy of Buddhism* (London, 1955), 7-8, where, however, the 'Middle Path' is given a rather wider application: 'The middle path is the non-acceptance of the two extremes ... The middle path is the avoidance of both the dogmatism of realism ... and the scepticism of Nihilism ...'

[38] So Geldner, I, 457 and Griswold, op. cit., 216; cf. Maurice Bloomfield, *The Religion of the Veda* (New York, 1908), 146. Paul Thieme, *Gedichte aus dem Rig-Veda*, 41, renders the word 'der Falke'.

[39] *Medieval Number Symbolism* (New York, 1938), 7. The book devotes a good deal of attention to the ancient world.

[40] Cf. the pronouncement of a magical incantation at morning, noon, and evening prescribed in Babylonian medical texts: see Johannes Hehn, *Siebenzahl und Sabbat bei den Babyloniern und im Alten Testament* (Leipzig, 1907), 67-8. Vedic oblations with similar reference are mentioned by Gonda, op. cit., 37.

[41] *Dreiheit*, 337. Cf. above Introduction 4ff.

[42] See Gonda, *Triads in the Veda*, 62.

[43] *The Religion of the Rigveda*, 275 n.6.

[44] Cf. Gonda, op. cit., 106; Usener, *Dreiheit*, 168f.; Kirfel, *Die dreiköpfige Gottheit*, 31.

[45] A. A. Macdonell, *Vedic Mythology* (Strasbourg, 1897), 5. The later Bhagavadgītā shows a monistic emphasis in relation to Krishna or Brahman, but

divine pluralism occurs too, though not, it seems, in triadic groups. Cf. Cyril G. Williams, *Y Fendigaid Gân* (Cardiff, 1991), 5.

[46] *Triads in the Vedas*, 65.

[47] Thus Geldner. The order Varuna, Mitra, and Aryaman is given by Ralph T. H. Griffith, *The Hymns of the Rigveda*, II (3rd edn., Benares, 1926), 608. Aditi is sometimes treated as masculine: see A. Bergaigne, *La Religion védique*, III (Paris, 1963), 92.

[48] *Der Fremdling im Ṛgveda* (Abh. DKM, 23, 2; Leipzig, 1938; repr. Nendeln, 1966), 106.

[49] *Mitra-Varuna* (3rd edn., Paris, 1948; 1st edn. 1939).

[50] *Mitra and Aryaman* (*Transactions of the Connecticut Acad.*, 41; New Haven, 1957), 6ff.

[51] Geldner, I, 190, uses the adjective 'barmherzig'. The hymn is addressed to these two gods.

[52] *Mitra and Aryaman*, 10.

[53] Cf. Gonda, *Triads in the Veda*, 8 n.22 with the reference to a dictum by V. F. Hopper.

[54] One stanza is 'the celebrated Sāvitrī stanza which has been a morning prayer in India for more than three thousand years'. Thus A. A. Macdonell, *Vedic Reader*, 10.

[55] Cf. Griswold, *Religion of the Rigveda*, 276, citing 1, 20, 6; 1, 161, 5; cf. 10, 53, 9. See also Macdonell, *Vedic Mythology*, 131; and Gonda, op. cit., 68.

[56] Cf. Geldner, III, 201.

[57] *Ṛgveda: Textkritische und exegetische Noten* (Abh. Göttingen, 13; Berlin, 1912), 106.

[58] *Kurzgefasstes etymologisches Wb. des Altindischen*, II (Heidelberg, 1963), 452.

[59] In *ZDMG* 102 (1952), 91–129.

[60] *Selected Studies*, II (1975), 26.

[61] Mayrhofer, *Wb.* I (1956), 284–5.

[62] Indra is said to have conferred gold and cattle on him. He is regarded as a semi-historical warrior. See Macdonell, *Vedic Mythology*, 146-7; Hermann Oldenberg, *Die Religion des Veda* (1917; repr. Darmstadt, 1970), 151, deriving his name from the pre-Aryan Dasyus.

[63] *The Vision of the Vedic Poets* (The Hague, 1963), 120.

[64] *L'Idéologie tripartie des Indo-Européens* (Coll. Latomus, 31; Brussels, 1958), 7f.

[65] It was reprinted in 1954. Apte is also the author of *Ṛgveda Mantras in their Ritual Setting in the Gṛhyasūtras* (repr. from the *Bull. of the Deccan College Research Institute*, I; n.d.).

[66] *Bull. of the School of Oriental and African Studies, University of London* 22 (1959), 69–85.

[67] *L'Idéologie tripartie*, 18.

[68] *Selected Studies*, I, 541.

[69] Op. cit., 96.

[70] *Ribhu* means 'skilled'; cf. Louis Renou, *Vedic India* (Classical India, III; Delhi, 1971), 72, §143.

[71] Ibid. 133, §253.

[72] *L'Idéologie tripartie*, 16.

[73] Ibid., 39. Cf. Gonda, *Triads in the Veda*, 154-5, on the position of blacksmiths and chariot-makers. He shows that later Sanskrit commentators had difficulty in classifying the various craftsmen, and tended to exclude them from the three higher orders.

[74] L. Renou, *Vedic India*, 130-1.

[75] Gonda, op. cit., 152.

[76] Louis Dumont, *Homo Hierarchicus: The Caste System and its Implications*, tr. Mark Sainsbury (The Nature of Human Society Series; London, 1970), 67.

[77] Cf. Geldner, I, 481; Macdonell, *Vedic Mythology*, 96, who translates *purohita* as 'domestic priest'; L. Renou, *Vedic India*, 69 ('chaplain'); L. Dumont, *Religion, Politics and History in India*, 65, who states that 'the *purohita* is to the king as thought is to will, as Mitra is to Varuna'. Clearly a Dumézilian touch.

[78] *The Destiny of the Warrior*, tr. A. Hiltebeitel (Chicago, 1970), 45.

[79] Dumézil, *L'Idéologie tripartie*, 76-7.

[80] See especially his remarks in *Selected Studies*, I (Leiden, 1975), 531-45 (= *Mnemosyne* 13 (1960), 1-15).

[81] *Triads in the Vedas*, 206, cf. 177.

[82] *Les Dieux souverains des Indo-Européens* (Paris, 1977), 252-3.

[83] In fact Gonda quotes the sentence after his statement on p.206.

[84] *Triads in the Veda*, 199.

[85] *The New Comparative Mythology* (rev. edn., Berkeley, 1973), 221.

[86] *The Times Literary Supplement*, 3 February 1978, p.144. Cf. his emphasis on the many possible interpretations of the Veda in his inaugural lecture, *On Being Sanskritic* (Oxford, 1978), 25. The four classes of post-Vedic society are well discussed by A. L. Basham, *The Wonder that was India* (3rd rev. edn., London, 1967; repr. 1988), 35ff. and in more detail 137ff. On p.310 he treats of the doctrine of the *Trimūrti* or triple form (cf. above section 2), and states that the parallel between the Hindu trinity and that of Christianity is in fact 'not very close'; the former, he avers (p.311), was 'an artificial growth, and had little real influence'. Basham's first edition is dated 1954; he was writing of course before the studies by Dumézil.

[87] Dumézil (tr. Krapp), *Archaic Roman Religion*, I (Chicago, 1970), 47ff. In a work which subjects Dumézil's whole *oeuvre* to a critical examination, Wouter W. Belier finds in it 'a progressive loss of verifiable and predictive content' while rejecting the tripartite ideology; see his *Decayed Gods: Origin and Development of Georges Dumézil's 'Idéologie Tripartie'* (Leiden, 1991), and cf. the review by K. Dowden in *CR* 43 (1993), 97-8.

7

Iran

1. *A Variety of Groupings*

In its early phases the religion of Iran is closely linked to that of India, as we have already remarked from time to time in the previous section. Of course it develops several distinctive facets, and it is well known for its dualistic approach. Its theological and ethical system is heavily coloured by the idea of two opposed forces, and its pantheon is broadly patterned in relation to these forces. This does not exclude a variety of groupings among the gods, but it does mean usually that they are ordered in degrees of subordination to the leading deities. Thus in Zoroastrian doctrine the supreme deity was Ahura Mazdâ, and he was deemed to have created lesser divine beings, chief among whom were the six Amesha Spentas, the six Bounteous Immortals.[1] These were grouped with their creator in a heptad, but were regarded as independent beings and not as mere aspects of Ahura Mazdâ.[2] Groupings of two deities are also common, and the Indian conjoining of Mitra and Varuna persists in the Iranian nexus of Mithra and Ahura, also found as a compound.[3]

According to Nyberg (op. cit., 225) the grouping of Ahura Mazdâ with Khshathra and Armaiti in the Gāthās (Yasna 47, 1. 4) implies the subordination of the other two deities to Ahura Mazdâ since the instrumental forms are used with their names, while the supreme god has the Nominative, so that the meaning *with Khshathra and Armaiti* emerges. Later translators, however, prefer to interpret these two appellatives as abstracts, as S. Insler does: *The Wise One in rule is Lord through piety.*[4] Here *piety* renders *armaiti*. Nor is the gulf between the versions really so startling. Mary Boyce observes that 'reverence for deities who personified "abstractions" appears a dominant feature of Indo-Iranian worship'.[5] In origin Armaiti was a goddess of earth, and her quality of 'devotion' and 'obedience' maintains this link with nature, although the Gāthās may bring the abstract idea to the fore[6] in view of the Zoroastrian playing down of the other deities.

2. *Three Divine Judges*

The importance of three in Iranian ritual is exemplified in funerary rites which last, in the first place, for three days.[7] More significant is the ethical demarcation of Thought, Word, and Deed, a triadic grouping that figures in the concept of judgement. It is a logical division of human behaviour, and appears in the opening of Yasna 47, although 'striving' (*mainyu*) is also stressed there.[8] Still more relevant to our purpose is the implementation of judgement at death by three divine judges – Mithra, Sraosha, and Rashnu – and it is Rashnu who holds the balance in which good and evil are assessed. It should be noted that these details are not given in the Gāthās. They appear in a translation of a long part of the *Mēnōk i Khrat* which Zaehner[9] provides, and this is a Pahlavi work deriving from the ninth century AD. The concept of the Saoshyant, the Saviour of humanity, albeit human himself, also takes on a triple form, but not in the early material.[10]

3. Zervanism and the Tetrad

By the fourth century BC the rise of Zervanism is attested, with its worship of Zurvân, the god of Time.[11] A striking feature of this movement's theology was its preference for the tetrad. It developed a belief in a tetradic board of Creator-gods – Ohrmazd, Time, Space, and Wisdom; or Ohrmazd, Light, Religion, and Time.[12] A 'tetrad of fate' and a 'terrestrial tetrad' were also elaborated, as Nyberg showed, and the four creator-gods were eventually paralleled in the Manichaean tetrad of God (Zurvân), Light, Power, and Wisdom.[13] It is doubtful whether Zervanite ideas, as distinct from those of Zoroastrianism, had any measure of influence on Judaism and Christianity. In eschatology the influence of Zoroastrianism was considerable, and the thousand-year element in the various patterns of prognosis was a feature of both systems. The concept of godhead was a different matter, and orthodox Zoroastrianism was firm on the monotheistic stress. It was hardly proper, therefore, for Miles Menander Dawson[14] to describe the Zoroastrian concept as 'a sevenfold Godhead, composed of the Amesha Spentas'[15] and to juxtapose the Christian idea as 'a triune Godhead, composed of Father, Son and Holy Spirit'.

4. Mithraism

We have noted that three judges appear in the later Iranian tradition, attested in the ninth century AD, concerning a trial after death.[16] Western Mithraism, which reached its apogee in the second and third centuries AD, does not seem to know of this triad, although the concept of a ritual trial or ordeal was prominent in its procedures; among these the fire ordeals clearly point to Iranian origins.[17] Two figures who frequently appear in the bull-slaying scenes are those of the torch-bearers Cautes and Cautopates, the former with a torch pointing upwards and the latter with it pointing downwards. Sunrise and sunset may be thus symbolized.[18] Since they flank the bull-slaying scene in which Mithras himself is the main figure,[19] they can be regarded as forming a triad with the god. Vermaseren, arguing in support of this idea, invokes some iconographical instances of triadism, such as a tree figured at Dieburg 'with three heads wearing Phrygian caps';[20] there is no clear context to identify the figures as Cautes, Mithras, and Cautopates, but the idea is supported.[21] The etymology of the names Cautes and Cautopates seems likely to be Iranian, although the precise roots have been debated.[22] By the fourth century AD Mithras was certainly regarded by some, notably by pseudo-Dionysius the Areopagite, as 'three-formed' or 'triple' (*triplasios*).[23] At the same time the two torch-bearers have all the appearance of being in origin a pair of complementary twins, parallel in some ways to the Dioscuri.[24]

The cult of Mithras was certainly known to several of the early Christian writers. Tertullian refers to the 'lions' of Mithras as reflecting the fiery aspect of nature; he has just mentioned Osiris as relating to its fertility.[25] He attacks the baptismal rites of both Isis and Mithras[26] and portrays Mithraic rites with a sword and wreath[27] and with features of a sacred meal.[28] Justin Martyr (*Apol.* I. 66) also compares the Eucharist with the Mithraic communion meal, although he ascribes the latter to the imitative urges of 'wicked demons'.[29] Before that Justin (I. 65) mentions thr trinitarian formula used in the first Eucharist of the newly baptized, but here he adduces no Mithraic parallel.

A Mithraic triad, 'Saturnus-Aion, Sol Invictus, and Mithra', has been posited by W. O. Moeller in a study of the 'Rotas–Sator' square.[30] In one version of this magical square found in a graffito from Pompeii (*CIL* IV, 8622, 8623) he finds the name 'Sautranus', which he not unreasonably equates with 'Saturnus', stating that he 'may have been specifically the high god of Mithraism, who was called by many names: Saturnus, Kronus, Chronus, Saeculum, Aion, and Zervan Akarana' (p.5). Although 'high god' is now an outmoded term, the dominance of this figure in Mithraic groupings is evident. Moeller also sees in the 'Rotas–Sator' complex a number of geometric symbols: the 'circle of eternal return' or of 'the unity of the Godhead'; and the triangle as 'the symbol of both the female element and of a trinity'; he sees the triangle also as a symbol of 'the past, present, and future' (pp.30–1). Plato is cited for such ideas; Plutarch (*De Is. et Os.* 56) also refers to Plato when he regards the most beautiful triangle as suggestive of Osiris, Isis, and Horus; see my Comm. ad loc., p.509. Here, then, there is nothing inherently Mithraic.

NOTES

[1] Mary Boyce, *A History of Zoroastrianism*, I (Leiden, 1975), 194. Cf. Plutarch, *De Is. et Os.* 47 and my Comm. ad loc. (p.476).

[2] Bernhard Geiger, *Die Aməša Spəntas* (Vienna, 1916), 85f., discussing the functions assigned to them. Cf. Boyce, op. cit., 202.

[3] H. S. Nyberg (tr. H. H. Schaeder), *Die Religionen des Alten Iran* (1938; repr. Osnabrück, 1966), 97f. and 224. Boyce, op. cit., 31, remarks that 'no member of the Avestan or Vedic pantheon is ever seen in isolation'.

[4] S. Insler, *The Gāthās of Zarathustra* (Leiden, 1975), I, 89. Cf. Helmut Humbach, *Die Gathas des Zarathustra* (Heidelberg, 1959), I, 136, but with a slightly different sense: *Kundig durch seine Macht und durch seine Gemäßheit ist der Lebensherr.*

[5] Boyce, op. cit. I, 203.

[6] Herman Lommel, 'Symbolik der Elemente in der zoroastrischen Religion' (1959) in *Zarathustra*, ed. B. Schlerath (Wege der Forschung 169, Darmstadt, 1970), 262-3; cf. Boyce, op. cit. I, 206f.

[7] Boyce, op. cit. I, 121; cf. 312 on 'threefold cleansings' and 258 on dawn, noon, and night as three important ritual times. There is a parallel in Egypt: see above ch.2, section 4 ('Conceptual Triads').

[8] Humbach, *Die Gathas*, I, 55-6; cf. Boyce, op. cit. I, 241. Miles Menander Dawson, *The Ethical Religion of Zoroaster* (New York, 1931), 105ff. gives primacy to 'the Good Mind and the Right'.

[9] R. C. Zaehner, *The Dawn and Twilight of Zoroastrianism* (London, 1961), 302-5. I have discussed Iranian ideas of judgement in some detail in my book *The Divine Verdict* (Leiden, 1991), 40-6, 243ff. See also Zaehner, *Zurvan* (Oxford, 1955), 102 and 321. Boyce, op. cit. I, 241, uses the phrase 'the tradition' to cover the much later works.

[10] Boyce, op. cit. I, 285. In Yasna 48, 9, 4 Zoroaster regards himself as the one who will save: see Humbach, I, 140 and Insler, 92, and cf. Zaehner, *Dawn*, 59.

[11] Zaehner, *Zurvan*, 20ff.; Boyce, *Hist. Zor.* II (1982), 235ff.

[12] Zaehner, *Zurvan*, 204ff.

[13] Ibid., 205. Boyce, *Hist. Zor.* II, 236-7, dwells on 'Zurvan's quaternity' as a subdivision of the 'Great Year' into four periods of 3,000 years each. For other Zervanite tetrads see Zaehner, op. cit., 491 (Index s.v.).

[14] *The Ethical Religion of Zoroaster* (1931), xxi.

[15] J. Duchesne-Guillemin, *The Western Response to Zoroaster* (Oxford, 1958), 51, says of 'the one god' that 'all the functions of the old gods (were) either submitted to him or absorbed into him'.

[16] Cf. above section 2 and my remarks in *The Divine Verdict* (1991), 256.

[17] Ibid. 332-7. Cf. J. Gwyn Griffiths, 'The Concept of Divine Judgement in the Mystery Religions', in *La soteriologia dei culti orientali nell'impero romano*, ed. U. Bianchi and M. J. Vermaseren (Leiden, 1982), 209-13.

[18] Vermaseren, *Mithras, the Secret God* (London, 1963), 73. David Ulansey, *The Origins of the Mithraic Mysteries* (New York, 1989), 62-5, argues that the association of the two figures with a bull's head and a scorpion respectively suggests that they represent the spring and autumn equinoxes – a quite cogent idea.

[19] E.g. R. Merkelbach, *Mithras* (Hain, 1984), 320, Abb.71 (Bononia) and many others assembled by him.

[20] Vermaseren, op cit., 74 with Fig.14.

[21] Merkelbach, op. cit., 358 with Abb.122. That the three heads represent 'the totality of life', as L. A. Campbell, *Mithraic Iconography and Ideology* (Leiden, 1968), 194, argues, adducing the Arbor Vitae, is to be doubted.

[22] See Martin Schwartz in *Mithraic Studies*, ed. J. R. Hinnells (Manchester, 1976), II, 406–23, and Ilya Gershevitch, *The Avestan Hymn to Mithra* (Cambridge, 1959), 68ff., who regards the two torch-bearers as lesser forms of Mithra.

[23] Vermaseren, op. cit., 73. Another Mithraic triad (Saturn, Sol, and Luna) may be present in G. Grimm, *Kunst der Ptolemäer- und Römerzeit im Ägyptischen Museum Kairo* (Cairo, 1975), Pl.73, no.38 with p.11.

[24] Cf. Ulansey, op. cit., 112ff.; also Campbell, op. cit., 141.

[25] Tertullian, *Adv. Marcionem*, I. 13. 5.

[26] *Id. De Baptismo*, 5. 1.

[27] *Id. De Corona*, 15. Cf. Vermaseren, *Mithras, the Secret God*, 145; Merkelbach, *Mithras*, 95f.

[28] Tertullian, *De Praescript. haeret.*, 40.

[29] Cf. Stevenson, *A New Eusebius*, 67.

[30] W. O. Moeller, *The Mithraic Origin and Meanings of the Rotas-Sator Square* (EPRO 38, Leiden, 1973), 1, 5, 30f.

8

Greece

In the *Clouds* of Aristophanes (423–4) Socrates at one point tells his reluctant pupil Strepsiades:[1]

> Then from now on you'll believe in no other gods but ours – the holy trinity of Chaos, Clouds, and Talk.

Socrates is of course pictured in this play as the iconoclastic modernist who exults in poking fun at the traditional religion as well as the conventional education.

1. *Accepted Triads*

Chaos, Clouds, and Talk implies a belief in more respectable triads; in v.627 Socrates similarly swears *By Respiration, Chaos, and Air*! Later an accepted triad is invoked when Pasias and Strepsiades clash thus (1234f.):

> *Pasias*: Swear by all the gods you've had no money from me.
> *Strepsiades*: Gods! What are you talking about?
> *Pasias*: I mean Zeus, Hermes, and Poseidon.

There might be a hint here, comparable to the Egyptian tradition, that three important gods may typify or represent the pantheon. More likely is the reflex of one of the triadic groups constantly invoked in oaths, of which Usener gives a lengthy list (pp.17–24), citing Zeus, Apollo, and Demeter as the triad used in official oaths at Athens (p.19, 4). Usener's survey provides a wide range of Greek divine triads both male and female and also of cosmic or elemental groupings such as Aether, Chaos, and Erebus, or Fire, Water, and Earth. He shows that female triads include sinister beings like the Erinyes, the Harpies, the Sirens, and the Maenads, but also the more pleasing types such as the Graces and the Hesperides. This type he engagingly follows into the Christian heaven which welcomed the three daughters of Sophia (Pistis, Elpis, Agape – Fides, Spes, Caritas), the three sisters Agape, Theophila, and Domna, and even three mothers called Mary (p.11 with refs.). Nor does he omit to take a glance at the closely comparable *Matres* and *Matronae* of Roman–Germanic and Celtic tradition.

A distinct category is supplied by deities who join in the campaign against evil and disease. But why should they do this in threes? Simply, one supposes, because this was so ubiquitous a trend. Yet Usener concedes (p.14) that Asclepius and Hygieia were an ancient dyad long maintained as such. Eventually, it is true, Asclepius is shown to have figured in a number of triadic groups, some of which also include Hygieia. Tutelary deities of the city states were often triadic in grouping, the most celebrated being a group outside Greece itself – the Roman Capitol's Jupiter Optimus Maximus, Juno, and Minerva. In the Council-house of Athens there were images of Zeus Boulaios, Apollo, and Demos; and Pausanias, who records this (1. 3. 5), states that in the same place (the Agora) was a sanctuary to the Mother of the gods. But he gives prominence (1. 25. 7) also to Athena Polias, the city's true guardian deity.

Usener's account of the deities invoked in oaths has a revealing comment (pp.22–3) on the influence of the scepticism which arose in the era of the Sophists; it transpires that the first result was not a radical rejection of the divine invocations, but a show of disillusion concerning the sufficiency of the triad. Now the number of deities is increased, as though quantity were deemed to make up for a lack of quality, sometimes by the appending of an additional triad.

2. *Divine Children in Triads*

Apollo, Artemis, Leto, a triad in which the mother's name follows those of her two children, is shown by Usener in a second catalogue (p.24) to have some variety in the order of the names; in one instance from Eretria the mother's name comes first. How far indeed is the family triad important in Greek theology? Zeus, Hera, and Ares form a group of father, mother, and son, but they are not particularly conspicuous as a group, one reason being the presence of other offspring, and another, perhaps, the many infidelities of the mythological Zeus. The Eleusinian triad, especially Demeter, Kore, and Pluto, carried an intense appeal, as Usener shows (pp.25–6). It is strange that in his analysis (pp.4–6) of the Hesiodic triads he concentrates on the triadism of the children of the gods.[2] A contrast is discernible between this emphasis and the father–mother–child unit of the Egyptian tradition. Even in the evolution from the grouping of two to that of three, of which Usener (pp.323ff.) sees many instances, it is noteworthy that the idea of family incrementation expressed by the father–mother–child group is mostly missing. If Zeus and Hera are the most important pair of gods, thus forming 'the archetype of the married couple', their impact is often negative, while Apollo and Artemis, as 'a brother–sister pair free from sexual tensions', make up a popular group, and in their case the link with their mother Leto does produce a well-established triad.[3]

3. *Triple Features and the Triune Concept*

At first sight another contrast with Egypt is that the Greeks did not produce triads which included the triune concept. Yet it may be present indirectly in their evolution of triple-equipped forms. A deity is shown with three heads or three of some other corporal element. Usener (pp.162-89) gave some attention to this phenomenon, but it was Williband Kirfel in his *Die dreiköpfige Gottheit* who made it the theme of an expansive study; I have discussed aspects of this work in chapter 6, section 4 above. In Greek religion the goddess Hecate is the best-known instance. She was shown in art as a figure with three heads facing in different directions; and the great Pergamon frieze shows her also with six arms: she is attacking a bearded giant and her arms are suitably equipped, for in her right hands are a huge torch, a spear, and a two-edged sword; one of the left hands holds a sword-scabbard, while the other two left hands hold a great shield against the fiercely attacking serpents, one of which is biting the lower part of the shield.[4] Whatever the underlying idea may be, it is clear in this particular case that the triple appearance of head and arm serves to fortify the combative force of the goddess Hecate, just as the three heads of the hell-hound Cerberus make him more hellish, and that in spite of the element of unreality which inevitably results. Literature confirms Hecate's triplicity. Vergil (*Aen.* 4. 511) calls her *tergeminam*, 'threefold', and Ovid, *Fasti* (1. 141) says that her image on the crossways had three faces, thus having a very practical purpose: *ora vides Hecates in tres vertentia partes*.[5] Apuleius *(Metam.* 11. 2) applies the expression *triformi facie* to Proserpina, and this goddess is linked with Artemis and Hecate in their sway over hell.[6]

The claimed priority of the three-headed forms (as opposed to the forms with three separate bodies) is buttressed by Kirfel (p.105) in his technical remarks, which follow Overbeck, on the Hecate of the Pergamon frieze, a work of the second century BC. The artist, he maintains, had originally aimed at sculpting one Hecate figure, but the difficulty of representing three heads and six arms constrained him to produce a semblance of three figures. When the three figures are clearly shaped in a group, as in a bronze piece of the Roman era[7] now in Paris (Kirfel, p.109 with Abb.94), it is significant that three aspects of Hecate are represented – the domains of heaven, the earth, and the underworld, pertaining strictly to Selene, Artemis, and Hecate and suggested respectively by the moon-crescent, a bunch of flowers, and a serpent, all placed on the head.

Whichever mode be given priority, one must ask what is the basic reason for the repetition of the same form, albeit with some slight differentials. Repetition, as it happens, is a fond technique of modern advertising. As I write these words in the Bodleian Library, I recall the light supper which I have just taken in an Oxford 'Wimpy Café'. On the table before me was a coloured paper strip depicting three(!) bright figures all entitled *Mr Wimpy*. The hamburger which I ate was enclosed in a paper on which was printed *WIMPY Hamburger* – twenty times. WIMPY was also printed on the paper serviettes. One recalls the dictum that if a thing is repeated often enough, it is sure to be widely believed. But countersuggestion is also possible, and the quality of the hamburger may seem more important.

An intensified potency was evidently a part of the ancient aim for the figures in question. The epithet in Hermes Trismegistos, ultimately of Egyptian origin, illustrates the urge, but it is not confined to the number three, as the case of Cerberus amply shows. Hesiod (*Theog.* 312) was the first to name him, and he gives him fifty heads, not three. In Pindar and Horace he gets a hundred heads as well as a hundred snakes on the heads, while the tragedians reduce the number to three (see H. von Geisau, *Kl. Pauly* 3 (1969), 197–8 for refs.). In art the number of the heads is usually two or three, and here, as M. L. West remarks (ad *Theog.* 312, p.253), the reasons may be purely practical. Other polycephalic monsters show a similar variety, and what they also have in common is their sinister ferocity. Cerberus is the *dread dog* (*Theog.* 769), and the same quality marks Typhon and the Hydra, both usually credited with a hundred heads, and Geryon with his three heads or three bodies. (Cf. T. H. Gaster on 'Monsters', *Encycl. of Rel.*, 10 (1987), 76–80, esp. 79; only a minority of these beings are seen to be benign in nature.) It is a strongly persistent tradition, which is found in the glut of mythical beings presented in the Book of Revelation and inaugurated by the *four living creatures, full of eyes in front and behind* (4: 6), each having also six wings. Even the Lamb has *seven horns and seven eyes* (5: 6); and we see *a great red dragon, with seven heads and ten horns, and seven diadems upon his heads* (12: 3; cf. the beast in 13: 1). In this book seven is clearly the preferred number, and whereas there are direct affinities with Ezekiel, Isaiah, and Daniel, the ultimate debt goes beyond these to Babylon's myth of Marduk and the dragon Tiamat or to the Egyptian myths of combat against Seth or Apopis, areas where many-headed monsters occur. See especially A. Yarbro Collins, *The Combat Myth in the Book of Revelation* (Harvard Diss., Missoula, Mont., 1976), 77.

In such data the presence of a triune concept is not easy to demonstrate. In the case of Hecate the occasional differentiation of the three figures suggests one deity with differing manifestations in the manner of modalism. What is interesting is that Usener (p.180 with Fig. on p.188) was able to provide Christian parallels: a small church in the region of the Upper Anio (Vallepietra) is dedicated to the Santissima Trinità and used to attract a host of visitors on Trinity Sunday (perhaps it still does). An old picture in this church derives from the early period of Italian painting and follows a Byzantine prototype, depicting the Trinity by means of three bearded heads of identical similarity: all three give a picture of the Saviour. Another Italian picture cited by him (p.181) presents three similar figures, but with slight variations – God the Father has a higher seat and each figure bears a distinguishing mark on the breast, the Father having an open eye in a triangle, the Holy Spirit the dove, and the Son the lamb of God. In Christian art there were frequent symbols of the Trinity, and Usener was not suggesting a direct line of influence from the triadic types of Greek religion. Indeed his parallels include several items from later centuries, and among them (p.181) is the type attested in the fifteenth and sixteenth centuries in which one head with three faces is depicted.

In his *Die dreiköpfige Gottheit* Kirfel devotes an admirably detailed chapter (ch.9, pp.147–73) to the three-headed and three-faced forms of the Christian Middle Ages. He points out (p.147) that such forms were used to illustrate not only the Holy Trinity, but also ideas of wisdom, time, and even of evil. His examples concerning the Trinity include a relief by Donatello (1386–1466) in the Church of Orsanmichele in Florence (see his pp.148–9 with his Pl.53, Abb.152). Here three separate heads are shown, one frontally and the other two in profile. They suggest persons of a similar age, but bear no distinguishing marks, save that the face presented frontally may be thought to be that of God the Father. Each head is topped by a rayed wreath and merges above into a disc which is flanked by wings in a manner, as Kirfel duly recognized, reminiscent of the Egyptian Winged Disc.

A Florentine edition (1491) of Dante's *Divina Commedia* includes a woodcut which shows the enthroned triune God holding the world-globe in his left hand; at the sides of his head, shown frontally, are two other heads shown in profile and much smaller. They are also differentiated in other ways: the bearded face to the right of the central figure is clearly that of the Son, while the more youthful face to his left is that of the Holy Spirit. What is striking is that the three faces are enclosed within a right-angled triangle, obviously symbolical of the Trinity of beings on a par. Another symbolic type displays one head with three faces, but sometimes with only four eyes. In this artistic evolution the most unexpected phase is undoubtedly the application of the symbolism to the concept of evil, and even to the Devil himself. The very same types emerge, including the use of the symbolical triangle. In an example from a manuscript in Paris (Kirfel, pp.150–1 with Abb.186) Satan is shown with three faces, but also with a number of demonic heads attached to his apparel. The resulting monstrosity recalls, for Kirfel, the phrase 'Satan Trismégiste' used by Baudelaire in his *Fleurs du Mal*. At the beginning of the sixteenth century Matthias Grünewald produced a more naturalistic study of evil; again a three-headed man is presented, and a debt to the religious tradition is implied, without any radical parody of the Trinity (see Kirfel, (pp.160-1 with Abb.189).

Such parallels can be related to early Greek representations. In them, for the most part, the prime motive is intensification. Hecate stands as an exception, for with her, as in some Christian interpretations of the Trinity, the basic intention is modalistic: three aspects of one deity are being shown.

A fondness for a grouping of three is found in a number of mythological reliefs, mainly of a votive character and belonging mostly to the later fifth century BC. In these a theme is presented by choosing three of the protagonists, and the underlying myth is concerned usually with attitudes to death and immortality. The prominent groups are as follows:

(1) Orpheus, Eurydice, Hermes
(2) Heracles, Theseus, Peirithöos
(3) Medea and the Peliades
(4) Heracles and the Hesperides

Available only in later copies, these works, in spite of their triadism, do not concern divine triads; indeed, the figures are mostly heroes rather than deities. See further E. Berger in *Lex. der Alten Welt* (1965), 775 s.v. 'Dreifigurenreliefs'.

4. *The Philosophical Tradition*

The triune concept can be clearly seen in the Greek philosophical tradition, most manifestly perhaps in Neoplatonist writings. Thus Proclus (*Ad Tim.* 178 B) proclaims the threefold sanctity of the soul in that both the monad and the triad can apply to it: its essential being is both one and triple and its existence, harmony, and form are all present one in the other.[8] As one who wrote in the fifth century AD Proclus cannot qualify as a likely candidate to have influenced formative thinking on the Trinity. Thr truth is, however, that Neoplatonist writings were teeming with triads and that Proclus was himself deploying previous authors in this area, such as Plato, Plotinus, Iamblichus, and the compiler-authors of the Chaldaean Oracles. In his use of Plato, Proclus in the first book of his *Platonic Theology* offers triadic sets of divine attributes; thus from the *Phaedo* 80 A-B he derives the triads 'divine-immortal-intelligible' and 'unitary-indissoluble-self-identical', relating them to one another and also to the basic triad of 'Being-Life-Intelligence'.[9] R. T. Wallis[10] warns us against equating the Neoplatonic triads with the Hegelian system of thesis–antithesis–synthesis, showing that there is a vital difference in that the Hegelian scheme has the final phase producing a conclusion, whereas to the Neoplatonists the middle term is significant as a link between two extremes.

Our theme prompts us to proceed to another warning: the Neoplatonist triads are groupings of abstractions. Such groupings admittedly occur in the New Testament, as in Faith, Hope, and Love (1 Cor. 13: 13). They are prominent in the Gospel of Matthew in other ways too. First, in the general structural sense, for 'the five major Matthean discourses are largely made up of triads';[11] so also in many episodic details, such as the three temptations of Jesus and the three denials of Peter. Other numbers are significant as well, especially two, seven, and fourteen.[12] Davies and Allison conclude (p.86) that 'Matthew's penchant for numbers would thus appear to place him squarely in the Jewish world, and perhaps specifically in the world of the rabbis'; they cite many instances from the Mishnah. In the case of Matthew as an author this conclusion may well convince, but the ubiquity of triadic groupings in the Greek tradition, and indeed in many others, undermines any suggestion of their being exclusively Jewish. A marked and significant contrast, however, can be seen in the Christian Trinity: here we have a linking, not of three abstractions, but of three divine beings – unless one regards the Holy Spirit as an abstraction. Certainly the Holy Spirit, while eventually defined as a person, has a disparate character.

5. *Three Gods in Unity*

A triune interpretation of three gods was sometimes featured in the annals of Greek religion. In a wider sense there appears from time to time the idea of one god as existing behind the plethoric variety of polytheism. It is a well-known trait of Plato's thought that he refers often to 'the gods', but also to 'the god', implying God in the monotheistic sense. Before that we find in Aeschylus (*Prom.* 210) the idea that whereas Mother Earth has many names (Themis is also given there), she has one form. Later in the play (515, ed. Mark Griffith) Prometheus asks, *Who then is the helmsman of Necessity?* to which the Chorus reply, *The three-formed Moirai (Fates) and the remembering Erinyes (Furies).* The three Fates, Clotho, Lachesis, and Atropos, are doubtless regarded as united in function, but the Furies also share in the unity of concept, with the suggestion that Fate, as embodied in them, is stronger than Zeus himself.[13]

A stress on unity is certainly present in the type of formula which became popular in the Hellenistic and Roman eras, including those in a Christian context. A cult in Canopus is attested by an inscription on a marble altar from Schedia which includes a dedication to *Zeus Helius the Great Sarapis* (*SB* 349; cf. Nilsson, *Gesch. Gr. Rel.* II³ (1974), 512 n.2). Although three gods are named here in a composite manner to indicate identity, the number is often two, as in Zeus Helius or Zeus Sarapis; another popular triad, at the same time, is Helius-Osiris-Sarapis. Prefixing the word *One* to such groups, as in Εἷς Ζεὺς Σάραπις invites a more distinctive interpretation to which attention was called by Weinreich in 1919 (*Neue Urkunden zur Sarapis-Religion*) and very thoroughly by Erik Peterson in his ΕΙΣ ΘΕΟΣ (Göttingen, 1926). Peterson elaborates on the several functional uses of the formulae: they can serve as an acclamation of faith or miracle, as concomitants of magic, healing, and sorcery; and on a higher level they can affirm syncretistic unity (e.g. that Zeus, Helius, and Sarapis are really one and the same god, with a suggestion, perhaps, that the last two are elevated thereby; cf. R. MacMullen, *Paganism in the Roman Empire* (1981), 83-4); or a basic monotheism, especially when *One God* begins the formula (see Peterson, p.305). For the latter formulation there are Egyptian antecedents, as Peterson duly points out. A good example comes from an amulet of the first or second century AD which is now in the British Museum. It is a green triangular stone showing a triad of deities described thus in the accompanying inscription:

> One is Baït, one is Hathor, one is Akori; one is their power. Be greeted by me, father of the world, be greeted by me, God in three forms.
> (Usener, op. cit., 36; O. Weinreich, op. cit., 28; W. Spiegelberg, *Arch. Rel.* 21 (1922), 225-7; H. Gressmann, *Die orientalischen Religionen im hellenistischen-römischen Zeitalter* (1930), 51-3; Morenz, *Rel.* (1960), 270)

The deities mentioned are Egyptian, the goddess Hathor being the best known; Baït is a form of *bi̓k*, the falcon-god Horus: Akori is more enigmatic – figured as a winged serpent, possibly a variant form of Hathor. Crystal clarity informs the doctrine proclaimed: the cosmic father has three forms, but the three deities are fused into one and the greeting is to a single unified being who is *God in three forms* (τρίμορφε Θεός). So striking is the parallel to Christian doctrine that one is bound to ask: is Christian influence present here?

The authors I have cited unite in denying this. If the Abraxas gem is not later than 200 AD, then it precedes the full evolution of the Christian creed. Most powerful of the arguments is that of Morenz: not only is the object evidently Egyptian, but Egypt provides plentiful antecedents of the doctrine presented. It is true that the idea of trinitarian monotheism, the term used by Gressmann, was already in vogue to some extent. At the beginning of the third century Tertullian had been positing the creed of one substance in three persons, with a specific application to the

Trinity; and in his *De Pallio*, 4, he invokes the example of Geryon, the three-headed Greek monster, and talks of *Geryon ter unus*, 'triply one', meaning that the three heads do not impinge on the unity of his being. When Martial (*Ep.* 5. 24. 15) praises a famous gladiator called Hermes as *ter unus*, his first meaning is probably that he is tantamount to 'three men in one'; perhaps an allusion to Hermes Trismegistos is also subtly present, but scarcely a theological echo.

6. *The Twelve Gods*

In spite of the frequency of Greek divine triads, it is doubtful whether the Greeks, when thinking of the organization of their traditional pantheon, recalled instantly this type of grouping. They were much more likely to think of the often officially sanctioned Twelve Gods; and the widespread vogue of this classification has been elaborately established of late.[14] The theory that the Twelve Gods began as anonymous local daemons or heroes is rejected by Charlotte R. Long and she tends to favour the claim of Otto Weinreich[15] that the Twelve were in origin the Olympian gods of Attic tradition; at least she opines (p.140) that the Attic Twelve 'seem to have been major, named Greek gods from the start'. In the fifth century BC Thucydides (6.54.6-7 (= Long, p. 62)) refers to the dedication of the Altar of the Twelve Gods in the Agora, and Herodotus (2. 4. 1-2) assigns an Egyptian origin to the whole concept, relating it to the twelve months: see Long, p.50, and other allusions by this author. I have suggested[16] that on the Egyptian side Herodotus was thinking of the expanded Enneads which sometimes appear.

What is more relevant to the present study is the persistent flourishing of the cult in the second century AD. It was now mainly under the aegis of Rome that this happened. The Twelve had been officially honoured in Rome itself, in the Forum, the Roman equivalents of the Greek Twelve being deployed (see Long, pp.236-7). Outside Rome too, and throughout the imperial domains, the Twelve in the guise of the Olympians were a firmly established order, 'recognized by all who shared the Greek and Roman cultural heritage, almost a cliché'.[17] At the same time they were brought into contact ideologically with astral, Mithraic and Egyptian systems.

NOTES

[1] Tr. H. J. and P. E. Easterling.

[2] Cf. M. L. West, *Hesiod, Theogony* (Oxford, 1966), 36 n.2, pointing out that the Olympian Twelve do not appear as such in Hesiod.

[3] Burkert, *Greek Rel.* (1985), 219.

[4] J. Overbeck, *Geschichte der griechischen Plastik*, II (3rd edn., Leipzig, 1882), Fig.132 C; H. Kähler, *Der grosse Fries von Pergamon* (Berlin, 1948), Pl.6; Eva Maria Schmidt, *Der grosse Altar zu Pergamon* (Leipzig, 1961), 27 with Pls.15 and 59. For this and other representations see also Roscher in his *Lex. Myth.* I (1887), 1902-9.

[5] Cf. Keune in Roscher, *Lex. Myth.* V (1915), 1108-9 s.v. Triformis; he ascribes this quality not only to Hecate and Cerberus, but also to Libera (Proserpina), the Chimaira, the Geryones, and the Sphinx. Kirfel, *Die dreiköpfige Gottheit*, 104, points to instances in which Hecate has three distinct bodies, a type to which he denies priority.

[6] Cf. my *Apuleius: The Isis-Book*, 118.

[7] Another example cited by him on p.110 with Abb.99 is a group of three marble figures from Aegina arranged around a pillar and assigned to the fourth century BC.

[8] Cf. Usener, p.36, quoting also Proclus, *Theol. Plat.* 3. 21. Cf. Proclus, *Elements of Theology*, 197, with its emphasis on the unity of the soul in spite of a certain plurality; see E. R. Dodds ad loc. (Oxford, 1933), 301.

[9] *Platonic Theol.* I, 26-7. See further R. T. Wallis, *Neoplatonism* (London, 1972), 130.

[10] Ibid.

[11] W. D. Davies and Dale C. Allison, ICC Comm. (Edinburgh, 1988), I, 66.

[12] Ibid. 85-7.

[13] Cf. D. J. Conacher, *Aeschylus' Prometheus Bound* (Toronto, 1980), 53-4; cf. Usener, 36.

[14] Charlotte R. Long, *The Twelve Gods of Greece and Rome* (EPRO 107; Leiden, 1987).

[15] 'Zwölfgötter', Roscher, *Lex. Myth.* VI (1937), 764-848.

[16] J. Gwyn Griffiths, *JHS* 75 (1955), 21-3; cf. A. B. Lloyd, *Herodotus II, Comm.*, II (Leiden, 1976), 28-9, 201-2; and Long, 147ff.

[17] Long, 275 and the chapter which follows ('The Zenith of the Roman Empire'). On the nameless early Greek phase see Otto Kern, *Die Religion der Griechen*, I (Berlin, 1926), 132.

9

Rome and Etruria

The Romans, as we have just seen, took over the Greek order of Twelve Gods, replacing the individual deities with Roman equivalents. At the same time they gave pre-eminence to the Capitoline triad, Jupiter, Mars, and Quirinus.

1. *The Capitoline Triad*

This all-male triad truly reflects Rome's patriarchal social basis, although the religious terminology sometimes tries to leave the question of gender open or to reveal an uncertainty. Thus liturgical formulae use the phrase *whether god or goddess* (*sive deus sive dea*). A shield kept at the Capitol bore the inscription *To the Genius of Rome, whether male or female* (*Genio Romae, sive mas sive femina*): we are told of this by Servius in a note to *Aeneid* 2. 451.[1]

This uncertainty might be traced to a 'primitive' element in Roman religion. Dumézil prefers to see in it a mark of the Roman juridical spirit and an urge to be careful and prudent. On occasion the urge to specify the double gender element is apparent: thus there were sanctuaries to *Male Fortune* and to *Female Fortune* (*Fortuna virilis, Fortuna muliebris*). The festival of the Matralia, on 11 June, was devoted to Mater Matuta, goddess of Dawn, and it was open to women only, and still further restricted – woman who had been married but once (*univirae*). The rites included driving out a slave woman with slaps and blows, and Dumézil (pp.47ff.) successfully invoked the dawn goddess of the Vedic Indians to explain this: the goddess Uṣás drives back the shadows of night.

A question naturally raised in connection with Jupiter, Mars, and Quirinus, the triad centred on the Capitol, is whether it was a special phenomenon attached exclusively to Rome, or whether there were comparable triads among other Latin peoples. A very clear parallel has emerged, actually, among the Umbrians: at Iguvium was honoured the triad Iou, Mart, and Vofiono, to whom the common epithet Grabovio was applied. While the meaning of Grabovio remains obscure, Vofiono is claimed to correspond closely to Quirinus. The interpretation of the two triads is inevitably linked to the general approach adopted. According to Dumézil, the idea of the tripartition of functions is closely bound up with the Capitoline triad, and I have discussed this theory, including Roman ramifications, in chapter 6 above ('Early Indian Religion'). Another matter affects the interpretation of the Umbrian triad. The traditional view has accepted Quirinus as the god of the Sabine component, and in his chapter 6 Dumézil attacks the whole theory that Rome was formed by the union of Latins and Sabines, the former being of Indo-European, and the latter of Mediterranean, origin. Dumézil rejects the idea of a dual origin; to him the Sabines were also Indo-Europeans.

An etymological argument has, nevertheless, been adduced in favour of the Sabine origin of Quirinus: this is the claimed connection with the Sabine city of Cures,[2] and also the link between Rome's *collis Quirinalis* and an impact from the same direction. Whether the name of the hill antedates that of the god is of course a debated point.[3] What Dumézil is anxious to demolish is the belief in an early Sabine settlement on the Quirinal and the whole dualistic theory of Roman religion that goes with it. If we accept his act of demolition, then the way is cleared for the imposition of the Indo-European interpretation of both the Capitoline and the Umbrian triads.

The functions posited by him might be conceded in the case of Quirinus because the third function, which covers a wider and less definable sphere, can be easily assigned to him. Dumézil (p.246) invokes the form **Couirino-* as the acceptable etymology which points to 'the patron of men considered in their organic totality'; he 'watches over the existence, the well-being, and the continuance of this social mass', and his *flamen* therefore takes care of the mature grain. Whereas R. M. Ogilvie[4] pointed out that other functions of Quirinus are unknown, he concedes that the Consualia, Robigalia, and Fornacalia are concerned with grain. Presumably the attributes of the Umbrian Vofiono were similar. Formerly connected with the Latin *voveo*, Umbrian *vufru*, the god was associated with vows, but Pisani, followed by Poultney, proposed derivation from **Leudh-iōn-*, from the same root as that found in the German *Leute*; so that it has been concluded that 'the name is therefore from the same root as L. *Līber*, and like Dionysus and Etr. *Fufluns* the god is one of vegetation and growth'.[5] Certainly the context in VI b 19 of the Tablets of Iguvium favours the conceptual link portrayed. A priest has to sacrifice before the Veian Gate three oxen to Vofionus Grabovius, and the text goes on to specify that the sacrifice should be accompanied by wine or mead and by grain and parts of particular cakes.[6] One feels that here the ritual detail is a firmer guide than etymology; the only slight doubt that arises is that some of the objects named, expecially wine, are concomitants of sacrifice to other gods. On the Roman Quirinus one encounters a contrary view: 'Quirinus is a god of war; he was the war-god of the community of the Quirinal' (Altheim, op. cit., 138) – a view that accepts the theory of the 'two communities'.

The cult of Quirinus in Rome was without doubt of ancient origin since it was included in the Calendar of Numa. Perhaps the epithet Grabovius, which the Umbrian Vofiono shares with the other members of the triad, points to an early sky-god Grabo; this belief is sustained by a suggestion that he was worshipped on mountains. In Rome the priest of Quirinus was no ordinary priest: the *flamen Quirinalis* belonged to the *flamines maiores*, and Pfiffig's notion[7] that a chthonic *numen* stands behind Quirinus seems reasonable enough. But he is surprisingly abrupt and peremptory in his rebuttal of the claim that the Umbrian Vofiono (and presumably the Roman Quirinus) can represent the farming peasantry, thus locating him in the third class of an Indo-European category. He avers that this alleged sociological construction is everything other than Indo-European, quite apart from the fact that the early stage of Mars can scarcely designate him as a god of war.[8]

At this point a note on scholarly etiquette seems called for. I referred to Pfiffig's rebuttal as 'abrupt and peremptory' because one would expect the theory of religious and social tripartition, which has received such wide attention, to be treated with some detail and constraint. Dumézil (p.149 n.2) refers with contempt to Pfiffig's reaction: 'the author is one of those who understand Etruscan.' Unhappily Dumézil is often guilty of such attitudes, and it is surprising to find a fervent admirer making the claim that his work is marked by a serenity which prefers the simple indication of deficiencies to aggressive polemic.[9] In a reference to 'dendolatry', Dumézil says that he borrows the word 'from one of the worst descriptions ever made of a religion, based on a purely archaeological dossier: G. Glotz, *La Civilisation égéenne* (1923), pp. 263-95'.[10] This unduly offensive remark at once raises the suspicion that Dumézil himself tended to neglect archaeology in favour of philology; the latter field certainly had primacy for him, particularly in his use of Vedic texts. Yet he does take archaeological evidence into account.[11] Still more offensive, and regularly so, are the allusions to the Latinists Carl Koch and Kurt Latte. Against Latte he conducts what amounts to a running battle; indeed Ogilvie in his review of *Archaic Roman Religion* ends by saying that 'the book is spoilt by a persistent vendetta against Kurt Latte'.[12] The same flaw was evident in his treatment of the noted Indologist Paul Thieme in *L'Idéologie tripartie des Indo-Européens* (Brussels, 1958), 108-18 ('Aryaman et Paul Thieme'). I have not noticed that French scholarship is especially exposed to extremes of controversy. It is an approach that can enliven the writing and sharpen the issues, but it is not conducive to calm appraisal. In fairness one must admit that Dumézil writes more extensively *ad rem* than *ad hominem*.

If we return to the problem of Mars, mentioned as such by Pfiffig (above), it is abundantly clear that by the third century BC he was identified with Ares, the Greek god of war, and that this led to the conferment of various warlike functions, such as the custody of the sacred shields, the *ancilia*; these shields were shaken on a declaration of war and the cry went up, *Mars, awake (Mars, vigila)!*[13] Considerable earlier evidence, though, connects him with agriculture. In the rite of the purification of the fields, the *Ambarvalia*, it was he who presided; and in the rite of the Equus October it was Mars who received the sacrifice of the horse. He figures in prayers for fertility in the Elder Cato's *De agricultura* and in other documents relating to work in the fields.[14] He was a god shared by the Italic peoples,[15] and like Quirinus he embodied several functions.[16] Eventually these functions were related to the fertility of the earth and to war, and the earliest evidence favours the former functions. The theory of functional tripartition, since it is linked to the primary Indo-European tradition, must evidently be especially concerned with the earliest stratum of the available material. Whereas the tablets of Iguvium are 'not earlier than the beginning of the 3rd century' (Poultney, p.24), the prayer of the Arval Brethren is usually dated to the fifth century and is thus 'the oldest surviving Latin prayer';[17] it seeks the aid of the Lars and of Mars (in three forms) to ward off ravages from the land and secure its fertility. here Kurt Latte[18] prefers an emphasis on Mars as a wild and hostile power against which the fields must be guarded; it is more likely that his help is sought as a friendly defender who also needs to be sated with the produce of the earth. What emerges is that Mars was not in origin simply a god of war. Ogilvie's view[19] that he was 'the principal god of early Rome' has something to commend it, in particular the fact that he stands at the head of the foundation legend, as Livy presents it, as the divine father of Romulus and Remus.

It is true that Jupiter occupies the central position in the Capitoline triad. He was in origin the exclusive god of heaven whose priest was forbidden to touch anything of chthonic import such as graves, goats, dogs, and beans.[20] His role became more expansive and he dominated the Capitoline triad, occupying the central chapel in the grand temple on the Capitol.

2. *The Etruscan Triads*

Before the rise of Rome it was the Etruscans who established the most imposing culture in Italy; it flourished from the eighth to the fourth century, but was itself an amalgam of various strains – the Anatolian,[21] the Italic and the Greek as well as the more distinctively Etruscan. Their religion was much concerned with eschatology, but a number of triadic groups appeared which did not have this association. Of special significance was their involvement in the Capitoline triad.

As we have noted, the group in which Jupiter, Mars, and Quirinus were joined was the earliest important Roman triad and its original centre was the Quirinal. Towards the end of the sixth century BC, perhaps at the time of the expulsion of the Tarquins, a temple in bold Etruscan style was dedicated on the Capitol.[22] Its presiding deities were Jupiter Optimus Maximus, Juno, and Minerva, corresponding to the Etruscan Tinia (the supreme god of heaven), Uni, and Menerva. This was doubtless the acme of Etruscan influence on Rome. Towards the same time the she-wolf which was to adorn the Capitol was removed from Etruria to Rome and became the city's perennial symbol in a splendid example of Etruscan animal art.[23]

An obvious feature of the Etruscan triad is the marked increase in the female element, and this is consonant with the comparative prominence of women in representations of various performances, games, and spectacles. Here the contrast with both Greek and Roman life is striking and goes some way to explain the charge of immorality made by Greek and Roman writers against the women of Etruria.[24] At the same time we must not overlook the impact of Greek religion on the Etruscans, particularly in the development of their pantheon; the shaping of their anthropomorphic iconography is probably indebted to the Greeks. This happened in the case of Tinia (Jupiter), who was assimilated to Zeus, and of Uni (Juno), who was patterned on Hera; and Menerva (Minerva) was equated with Athena.[25] Yet it is significant that Greek religion does not provide a triad with Zeus, Hera, and Athena, so that my point about the strong female element remains a valid mark of Etruscan predilection.[26]

While there are allusions in Latin literature to Etruscan divine colleges consisting of twelve or nine gods, a grouping of a god and goddess occurs more than once, as in the infernal dyads Aita and Phersipnai, Mantus and Mania.[27] Yet the central triad of Tinia, Uni, and Menerva may have been worshipped in Etruscan temples generally, since the triple cult-cells of most temples seem to point in this direction. Three such cult-cells, intended to house the statue of the deity, are attested for the early shrine of Juno Curitis in Falerii, the Capitolium of Signia, and the temple of Orvieto.[28] Perhaps in each case it was the Capitoline triad that was thus honoured.[29] But it is possible that various local triads are implied. According to Servius (ad *Aeneid*, 1. 422) Etruscan ritual rules ordained that whenever a city was founded, shrines should be raised in honour of the Capitoline triad. The archaeological record has often revealed the three *cellae* implied by this rule, although not invariably. Two temples at Marzabotto do not contain such an arrangement.[30]

In apparent contrast to the heavenly Capitoline triad (headed at least by the supreme sky-god) was the grouping of the powers of the earth, Ceres, Liber, and Libera, to whom a temple was dedicated on the Aventine in 493 BC. These were deities of Italic origin, but direct Greek influence is discernible from the impress of Demeter, Persephone, and Dionysus (or Iacchus). In this case the Etruscans were not the intermediaries of Greek influence.[31]

'The Religion of the Etruscans' is the title of an Appendix by Dumézil in his book on *Archaic Roman Religion* (pp.625-96). It perhaps follows irreversibly from his theory of Indo-European heritage that he is eager to play down the role of the Etruscans. Indeed he tells us at once (p.625) that 'Rome's debt to Etruria is not so great as it is usually portrayed'. He pays some attention to the Jupiter-Juno-Minerva triad, but queries its antiquity (p.684); he is also sceptical about the triadism inherent in the three *cellae* of the temples (p.685). R. M. Ogilvie, on the other hand, believes that in several areas, including religion, Etruscan influence was 'all-pervasive'.[32] That seems to me a more just assessment, provided one allows for the fact that in its later phase this influence became a channel for the spread of Greek religion and mythology; and Ogilvie was actually discussing there the early religion of Rome.

NOTES

[1] Cf. Georges Dumézil (tr. P. Krapp), *Archaic Roman Religion* (2 vols., Chicago, 1970), I, 43. On the other hand, the male and female elements were sometimes contrasted; cf. Franz Altheim (tr. H. Mattingly), *A History of Roman Religion* (London, 1938), 404, referring to both ideology and ritual.

[2] Hülsen, *RE* s.v. Cures (1900), 1814, citing *Cures Sabini* (Livy, 1. 18. 1) - an association 'no longer defended', says Dumézil (p.160 n.19).

[3] See Kurt Latte, *Römische Religionsgeschichte* (Munich, 1960), 113; and Dumézil, op. cit., 77 (the pagination in his two volumes is consecutive). The name was explained by Kretschmer as being originally *co-uiri-um*, 'assembly of the men', regarded as plausible by H. J. Rose, *OCD*² (1970), 908.

[4] Reviewing Dumézil's work in *Antiquaries Journal* 52 (1972), 211-13, this on p. 212.

[5] James Wilson Poultney, *The Bronze Tablets of Iguvium* (Baltimore, 1959), 260, adding that etymological equivalence between *Vofionus* and *Quirinus* is impossible, and that it is desirable to have a representative of the farming class as the third member of the Iguvine triad. The latter dictum is an unhappy example of theory almost dictating to etymology.

[6] Thus Ambros J. Pfiffig, *Religio Iguvina* (Vienna, 1964), 40.

[7] Ibid., 41.

[8] Ibid.

[9] Robert Schilling, *Nouvelle École*, 21-2 (1972-3), 91, in an article on 'Georges Dumézil et la religion romaine'. Cf. his contribution on 'Roman Religion: The Early Period', in *The Encycl. of Religion* ed. M. Eliade, 12 (1987), 445-61, esp. 452. In

Dumézil, *Camillus* (tr., Berkeley, 1980), 29, the editor, Udo Strutynski, fails to praise D. without a scornful dismissal of the 'offerings of H. J. Rose, H. Wagenvoort, and Kurt Latte'.

[10] Dumézil, *Archaic Roman Religion*, 26 n.9.

[11] Cf. on the *ancilia*, pp.146, 214, claimed to relate to the Capitoline triad.

[12] According to A. Momigliano, Dumézil favoured Nazi intellectuals, and Latte was of Jewish origin. I refer to a comment made privately; but cf. Momigliano's *Studies of Historiography* (London, 1969), 234, 246.

[13] R. M. Ogilvie, *Early Rome and the Etruscans* (Glasgow, 1976), 36, citing Servius on *Aeneid*, 8. 3.

[14] Ibid. For detailed allusions see F. C. Grant, *Ancient Roman Religion* (New York, 1958), 7-8 (Iguvium Tablets), 16-17 ('The Nerio of Mars in Ancient Prayers'), 17-18 ('The Song of the Arval Brothers'), 36-7 (Cato on expiation for the field borders).

[15] Kurt Latte, *Kleine Schriften* (Munich, 1968), 82, pointing to his warlike role in Iguvium, VI, 60 ff., but admitting the contrasting, if unexplained, role in the Arval Song. F. Altheim, op. cit., 139-40 does not convince in his attempt to deny the equation of Mavors and Marmar with Mars, Cf. H. J. Rose, *Ancient Roman Religion* (London, 1949), 62-7.

[16] Carol Koch, *Religion: Studien zu Kult und Glauben der Römer* (Nuremberg, 1960), 19.

[17] Robert E. A. Palmer, *Roman Religion and Roman Empire: Five Essays* (Philadelphia, 1974), 92.

[18] *Römische Religionsgeschichte*, 66. On this point Dumézil (p.229) seems to agree: Mars 'is only the watchful god, in no way involved in the mysterious processes which perpetuate vegetable life'.

[19] *Early Rome and the Etruscans*, 36.

[20] Aulus Gellius, *Noctes Att.* 10. 15; cf. Grant, op. cit., 30-2; Carl Koch, op. cit., 8.

[21] Hugh Hencken, *Tarquinia and Etruscan Origins* (London, 1968), 165, thinks that 'present evidence is against it' (i.e. the theory of a migration). Yet there are features of Etruscan religious practices, such as divination, which are hard to explain without assuming an original contact with Mesopotamia. On the diversity of the gods see Emeline Richardson, *The Etruscans* (Chicago, 1964), 232-4.

[22] Ogilvie, op. cit., 37, 84-5; cf. M. Pallottino, *The Etruscans* (Harmondsworth, 1955), 90.

[23] Raymond Bloch, *The Etruscans* (London, 1958), 171-2; Kurt Pfister, *Die Etrusker* (Munich, 1940), 78, the bronze figure which he dates to about 500 BC.

[24] R. Bloch, op. cit., 58.

[25] M. Pallottino, *The Etruscans*, 160.

[26] The position of women in Etruria is treated in deail by Altheim, *Hist. of Roman Rel.*, 50-64, 82-3. He points out (p.53) that the Etruscan hero, Herulus, appears as the son of a divine mother and only so; he also refers to sepulchral inscriptions which mention descent of the dead only on the mother's side.

[27] Pallottino, op. cit., 161-2. The early presence of the Etruscan language in Rome is significant: 'Rome of the Tarquins was bilingual': Ogilvie, op. cit., 50.

[28] Altheim, op. cit., 234.

[29] A. Bertholet, *Wb. der Religionen* (3rd edn., rev. K. Goldammer, 1976), 167; J. Heurgon, *OCD*[2] (1970), 913.

[30] Altheim, op. cit., 235.

[31] Ibid., 269; H. J. Rose, *Ancient Roman Rel.*, 71-2; Ogilvie, op. cit., 107; Stewart Perowne, *Roman Mythology* (London, 1969), 58 with Pl. on p.55 (Liber and Libera only). Cf. Cicero, *De nat. deorum*, 2. 62.

[32] *Antiquaries Journal* 52 (1972), 212.

10

The Celtic and Germanic Peoples

If Dumézil was not able to do much business with the Etruscans, the situation was very different in his approach to the Celtic and Germanic peoples. With these, especially the former, he found abundant material which seemed to allow his theories almost to luxuriate. Quite apart from his or anyone else's theories, divine triadism is certainly attested among both groups.

1. *The Celtic Three Brothers*

A problem with some of the material is that of chronology. In the present study our *terminus ad quem* is around AD 500, and most of the literary Celtic material is not earlier than the tenth century in terms of manuscript composition. I am referring here to material in the Celtic languages rather than to writings in Latin and Greek. The question is not so simple, of course, since a written composition deriving from the tenth century may embody much earlier traditions. Further, any possible connection with the Indo-European heritage must assume the survival of myths and ideas from very distant ages and areas.

One of the important mythological cycles in Irish is the *Tuatha Dé Danann* ('The Peoples of the Goddess Danann'), where the goddess is called *the mother of the gods*, but where the recorders of the narrative in the eleventh century were uncertain as to whether the *Tuatha*, themselves, the 'Peoples', should be regarded as men or demons or fallen gods.[1] A part of the cycle is concerned with the hero Cúchulainn, who is said in his first combat to have overcome the three sons of Nechta; after this he brings the three severed heads in a state of battle *furor* and then faces sexual trials and immersion into three huge vats of cold water – clearly a process of initiation. An early Indo-European theme is here recognized by Dumézil: 'the combat, fraught with consequences, of a god or hero against an adversary endowed with some form of triplicity'.[2] He compares, in particular, the account given by Livy (1. 24ff.) of how, in the reign of Tullus Hostilius, three Roman brothers fought with the Curiatii, three Alban brothers, the two sets being also triplets; the Curiatii were killed, as were two of the Roman brothers, and the survivor, Horatius, then killed his sister Horatia, who was betrothed to one of the Curiatii; he was condemned to death, but acquitted after an appeal. Apart from the element of triplicity, no detailed correspondence emerges here. Nor does the ultimate source, claimed to be in Indian mythology, provide it. The god Indra is said to overcome his monstrous three-headed enemy, either by himself or aided by Trita Āptya; since the tricephal was a brahman, the grave crime of brahmanicide is involved, and an element of kinship is said to colour the Indian as well as the Roman story (i.e. kinship between the opposing sides).[3]

A parallel is also seen in the Welsh *Mabinogi* of Math son of Mathonwy, where the 'Children of Don' (Gwydion, Efeidd, Gilfaethwy, Gofannon, and Amaethon) are five brothers joined by a sister, Arianrhod.[4] One might have expected Dumézil to be inhibited by the lack of triadism here. Not at all! He now examines the question of how far the five brothers incorporate the functions of the Indo-European heritage (defined on his p.4 as 'sovereignty, force, and fecundity') and finds (p.144) that with 'The Children of Don' the distribution of the three functions is 'more complete than that of the chiefs of the Irish "Tribes of the goddess Dana", to whom they correspond'. Gwydion is a sorcerer, Gofannon a blacksmith and Amaethon a ploughman; so the first serves the function of sovereignty while the other two serve the third function. Efeidd deputizes for King Math in the company of Gilfaethwy, so that these two seem to fulfil the first function, save that Gilfaethwy is said (p.146) to assure 'the existence of the warrior function'. The trouble with this schematization is that no human activity would seem to fall outside the orbit of the categories.

The story of Math includes various animal transformations wrought by magic; the three sons of Gilfaethwy, the eminent warriors, thus become a wolf, a hart, and a pig (Bleiddwn, Hyddwn, Hychtwn). In sum, the Irish and Welsh tales present mythical figures who are sometimes in groups of three; these figures may be gods perhaps or demigods; but a firmly etched divine triad does not appear. A group of three stories entitled *Tri Truaighe na Sgéalaigheachta* (Three Sorrows of Instruction) is said to present three heroes in each story; they belong to the mythological tradition, but with no suggestion that they have divine status: see J. E. Caerwyn Williams, *Traddodiad Llenyddol Iwerddon*, 105.

In a remarkable study, 'L'Unité en trois personnes chez les Celtes', the Celtic scholar J. Vendryes presented an unexpected interpretation of the theme of the three brothers.[5] He wisely begins with a recognition, citing Usener, that the importance of three is 'un fait universel'. He goes on to claim that in Ireland a type of triad appears in which three persons, usually three brothers who may also be triplets, appear as the multiplication in three instances of one and the same personage. The triads cited by him are not all brothers, but among the latter groups are instances of three brothers who bear the same name save for the addition of distinctive epithets or else names which are rigidly united by meaning or form. In the second group Vendryes places (p.235) the three sons of the goddess Danu, Brian, Iuchar, and Iucharba – an example where one of the brothers has a name which differs from those of the other two. Alliteration often marks the groups. Thus the nine cup-bearers of the Tuatha Dé Danann are given in sets of three: Delt, Drucht, and Daithe; Tae, Talom, and Trog; Glei, Glan, and Glési (p.235 n.1). In the instances where one name differs from the others it is argued that the person thus treated imparts his character to the whole group; the two others are but shadows of him in the sense that they always go where he goes and pattern their behaviour on his. An instance is seen in the adventure of the sons of Uisliu: among them it is only Noise, the lover of Derdriu, who has a marked character. When they die, Derdriu mourns them together. It seems that the original legend concerns one person who presents himself in three corporal forms.[6]

When the three brothers are triplets, a similar conclusion seems to be still more cogent. Rather bizarre, however, is the idea (p.237) that one person can be the son of three fathers; one of the killers of Cúchulainn, we are told, was called Lugaid and bore the nickname ('surnom') of *Mac Tri Con*, 'Son of Three Dogs' – a pointer, it is suggested, to a triple personality. One wonders whether this is not rather a contemptuous rhetorical flourish. Summing up the Irish evidence, Vendryes (p.238) remarks that the dominant trait of the theme which displays three triplet brothers is the unity of the person; this is expressed, he urges, by the indivisibility of the personality of the three brothers and also by the fact that only one among them has a defined personality, the other two being indistinguishable from him. It seems to me that in this part of his study Vendryes neglected to consider the possible biological basis of the theme. It is well known that twins are often hard to distinguish from one another. The whole theme does not arise, therefore, from the concept of the unity of the personality expressing itself in three forms, but rather from the triple forms which seem to point to a unity. Further, there would be a strong literary constraint preventing the development of three divergent personalities; to attempt this would have added much complexity to the stories, especially if each brother were allowed to pursue separate courses of action.

Turning to Welsh terrain, Vendryes notes (p.239) the odd triad in the Red Book of Hergest (p.302, 11), where it is said that Arthur had three chief queens (*teir prif riein*) who all three of them bore the name Gwenhwyfar. This occurs in the 'Triads' of the book; the differing names of their fathers are then given. Now the legends do not usually bear out the idea of a triple Gwenhwyfar; she is a somewhat wayward figure, it is true, featuring in abductions and adultery (see *The Oxford Companion to Welsh Literature*, ed. M. Stephens, 1986, 237), but preserves in her inconstancy a firm unitary character. It has been suggested that a threefold goddess lies behind the early triad.[7] It is possible, though, as Rachel Bromwich points out in her admirable study of the Triads (p.156) that the thirteenth-century Arthurian Romance preserves a hint at least of a double personality: in the vulgate *Merlin* and *Lancelot* appear the characters of the True and False *Guineveres*. She also mentions (p.155) the possible interpretation of the Triad as a witticism, presumably a light-hearted way of portraying an inconstant woman.

The rest of the study by Vendryes deals with the tricephalic god of the Celtic Gauls, which I discuss below.

2. *The Female Triad: Matres, Matronae, Matrae*

Another feature of the Celtic tradition is happily well attested and unequivocally interpreted. A triad of goddesses is often presented in both art and literature. A 'Fertility Goddess' or 'Mother Goddess' was a conspicuous figure in the religion of south-eastern Europe in the Neolithic and Chalcolithic eras assigned to the seventh, sixth, and fifth millennia BC. In spite of some complexities of symbolism (e.g. the dotted lozenge design above the abdomen), triadic designs are absent.[8] Yet the cult of three Mothers, *Matres* or *Matronae* or *Matrae*, probably arose from this ancient tradition, although these Latin terms point to epigraphic sources in the Celtic lands of the Roman Empire, where iconography also throws light on the character of the deities.[9]

While the *matronae* in a human sense play an important part in some ritual episodes of Roman religion, for instance in the *Matralia* (cf. above ch. 9 ad init.), the Celtic goddesses thus named are presented as bestowers of both physical and vegetative fertility. They are not invariably shown in groups of three; sometimes a group of two is seen, and occasionally a single female fertility figure.[10] The continental examples are for the most part earlier than those found in Britain, and it seems doubtful whether the variation of the names according to different regions (thus the *Matrae* do not appear in Gallia Cisalpina) leads to any firm differentials beyond local popularity. The *Matronae* were very popular also among Germanic peoples, especially in the Rhineland, possibly through Roman influence, although simple folk are often involved in the dedications.[11]

Often represented sitting together in a small shrine, they are shown holding in their laps baskets with fruit or bread or a horn of plenty; and sometimes a child in swaddling-clothes.[12] Those carrying a child are obviously the true *Matres* in the primal role of motherhood. As bearers of food and sustenance they have a role contrary to their probable function in the society to which they belong, for the males were undoubtedly the providers of food. We see here a clear indication of the identity of these female figures: they represent Mother Earth, who bestows fertility in vegetation. The fusion of this role with that of sexual productivity was not of course difficult.

The suggestion has been made[13] that these female triads show contrasting attitudes, being sometimes benign and sometimes hostile. There can be little doubt that the former attitude is the prevailing one. A good example, cited and displayed by Anne Ross (Pl.IX),[14] is that from Corinium Dobunnorum (Cirencester) (Fig. 9A). It is true that the three goddesses here present a certain dignity ('stiff and prim, as British as they can be'),[15] but their mild beneficence concurs with the gifts in their laps (loaves, cakes and fruit). The group from Ancaster (Sheppard Frere, Pl.30 a), where the middle head is missing, bears a rather sterner look, but no trace of hostility (Fig. 9B). A sculptured triad from Bathwick near Bath is cited by Anne Ross[16] as an example of an expression of hatred; the eyes have been represented deliberately as large, we are told, while mouths have been omitted from the faces, 'giving the impression of the hardened personality of a being that threatened humanity'; the same impression is assigned to a number of the groups of three mother-goddesses made in Britain. A problem here is that the artistic power of the sculpture is limited, and therefore intepretation is not easy; the groups are the products of simple people and many often arise from the narrow circle of the family, as Jan de Vries (p.123) believes. I cannot accept that any of the groups were envisaged as threatening humanity in general. If a hostile attitude is sensed, it probably comes from the concept of the mother-goddesses as protectors of the family or clan, fear being aroused by an apotropaic strength.

A field of rich affinities is opened up by the inviting comparisons in Irish or Welsh mythology. In the Irish *Lebor Gabála Érenn* ('The Book of the Taking of Ireland') the female triad Ériu, Banba, and Fótla is prominent, and they ask the invaders to perpetuate their names in the land;[17] their attitude to the invaders varies, since they are both friendly and hostile. Other important triads are the Brigits and the Macha, the latter being war goddesses. In the early Welsh tradition the goddess Modron, whose name derives from Matrona, is the mother of Maponos or Mabon, and her son is known as Mabon fab Modron, thus giving priority to the mother.[18]

3. *Male Triads*

When Lucan describes Julius Caesar withdrawing troops from the

A. Relief from Corinium Dobunnorum (Cirencester)

B. Relief from Ancaster, Lincs.

Figure 9. Triads of Celtic mother-goddesses

provinces in order to prepare for Pharsalus, he portrays the pleasure of the conquered peoples, including *those who appease ruthless Teutates with cruel blood, and Esus who instils terror with his savage offering-slabs, and Taranis, whose altar is no more gentle than that of Scythian Diana*:

> Et quibus inmitis placatur sanguine diro
> Teutates horrensque feris altaribus Esus
> Et Taranis Scythicae non mitior ara Dianae.

He goes on to depict the relaxed peace and joy of the bards and Druids. The elements of the names Teutates[19] and Esus[20] are well attested in Gaulish personal names; and Taranis is of undoubted Celtic origin, relating to the Irish *torann* and the Welsh with the Breton *taran*, 'thunder', thus pointing, it seems, to a Celtic sky-god.[21] What is problematic is whether Lucan intended to portray a triad. Jan de Vries remarks on the metrical exigencies which may well have influenced his choice of these three; and Powell[22] even speaks of the 'misunderstanding or indifference' which led the poet to give 'inordinate prominence' to these three. Nor do the Roman equations given by scholiasts on Lucan (Taranis = Dispater and Jupiter, Teutates and Esus both = Mercury and Mars)[23] help to fix a triadic norm. Further, it is not clear whether Lucan intends a group of merely local validity or one of more general sway.[24] As the Celtic Jupiter, Taranis ('Thunderer') is several times accompanied by the eagle and the wheel symbol, as Anne Ross (p.347) shows.

Male triads are more plentiful in early Irish myth, as we saw in the discussion of the 'Three Brothers'. The god Lug or Lugos, whose name figures in the town Lugdunum, the modern Lyon, and in fourteen other town-names, among them Liegnitz in Silesia and Leiden in Holland, may be implicated in a triadic group which perhaps includes his two brothers.[25] Dedications to the Lugoves were found in Spain and Switzerland, and a Spanish dedication from Osma was made on behalf of a guild of cobblers. The god's interpretation as the Roman Mercury is thus illumined as well as his connection with Gwydion and Llew Llaw Gyffes, who appear in the guise of cobblers in *Math fab Mathonwy*. Jan de Vries[26] argues, however, that two Christian martyrs who became patrons of shoemakers were successors of a heathen pair of gods, so that a divine dyad, rather than a triad, is the antecedent group, with Lug as the more prominent of the two.

4. *The Tricephaloi*

It was Roman Gaul that provided the numerous sculptured representations of a god with three heads or three faces;[27] in the latter case there is no separation of the triple forms, as with the three-faced bearded deity on a vase from Bavay (Nord).[28] Thirty such representations (including the two types) have been noted,[29] eleven of which derive from the region of Reims, so that M. L. Sjoestedt[30] thought in terms of a distinctive god of the Remi. He is sometimes figured with other gods; an altar in Reims shows him with Apollo and Mercury,[31] thus producing a double triadism, as in the altar from Malmaison which shows him with a god and goddess who may represent Mercury and Rosmerta, the latter a Celtic goddess of fertility.

The wide distribution of this type of god seems to exclude a particular connection with Reims; some sporadic examples have appeared even in Britain and Ireland.[32] Irish myth also knows of a monstrous three-headed creature called Three-headed Ellén.[33] Birds and animals often entered into the picture, and triadism colours this amalgam at times; a bronze from Maiden Castle portrays the presiding deity as 'a Trinity of Bull, Female, and Owl',[34] although Anne Ross[35] sees there 'a three-horned bull surmounted by three human busts'. Ross has found evidence even of a triphallic motif. Following Pierre Lambrechts,[36] she discusses (op. cit., 167 n.116) a bronze statuette from Tongres in Belgium: a seated figure holds a purse in one hand and a bird in the other. Ross continues thus:

> The figure was originally *triphallic*. The penis has disappeared but a phallus is placed on the top of the head and the nose is likewise replaced by a phallus. The phallus on the head has a small trough for suspension. Lambrechts lists other figures having phalloi coming from their heads.

The fragmentary state of the object is unfortunate, and the head-phallus and nose-phallus appear to be bizarre aberrations; they also tend to contradict the main argument in another work by Lambrechts[37] in which he establishes the prominence of the head in Celtic art, sometimes in mere size and often in the ignoring of the rest of the body. The total absence of the phallic character, it is argued (p.71), contrasts with the emphasis of the classical Hermae, but with the implication that the phallus is incorporated in the head in the manner of *pars pro toto*. Certainly an emphasis on the head is evident in the tricephaloi (pp.83–90), but with no hint of a phallic presence, unless the equation with Mercury might point to a Hermes in the Priapic sense (p.89).[38]

It is rather surprising that triadism in the Celtic tradition has often been regarded as something distinctive of it. The wider contexts I have been considering rebut this firmly; it is not even distinctively Indo-European; it is universal.[39] As for the particular theme of three-headed or three-faced beings, it is conspicuous in early Indian religion (see above, ch. 6, section 4) and is found also in the Greek tradition (see above, ch. 8, section 3). The pre-Christian Slavs of Eastern Europe worshipped a three-headed deity named Triglav, from *tri*, 'three', and *glava*, 'head'.[40] Although the convention was taken over by Christian art to symbolize the Trinity, as also was the mode of depicting three separate beings, the main urge in the early examples, including the Celtic creations, was to express intensified potency. A relief of the goddess Coventina from Carrawburgh on Hadrian's Wall (now in the Chesters Museum) shows her 'triplicated to express her power',[41] although other reliefs represent her without the triple form.[42]

Occasionally the three-headed god is shown squatting cross-legged in the so-called Buddhic posture.[43] The feature is found with various gods and goddesses who are without the tricephalic form, the best-known example being Cernunnos on the Gundestrup cauldron (see Mac Cana, p.38). From classical writers it is known that the Celts used little furniture and so sat cross-legged on the ground; the more mystical explanations are thus not needed.[44]

5. *Aphoristic Triads*

Both Ireland and Wales produced collections of aphoristic or gnomic triads. They are of much later origin than the material we have been discussing,[45] but sometimes they echo early myth and history. This is less prevalent in the Irish triads, of which a collection derives from the ninth century; in them the tone is more gnomic and sententious.[46] The Welsh triads are found in manuscripts of the thirteenth and fourteenth centuries; a long period of oral transmission is likely before that.[47] The triple form[48] implies a didactic and mnemonic urge, and the thematic field embraced 'stories which concerned the national past alike of the people of Wales and of the lost northern territory which was still remembered in the Middle Ages as a former home of the British race'.[49] But who are the characters embodied in these triads? Do they include divine beings? These are the questions that relate to our theme. Dr Bromwich (p.lxvii) says that the characters are 'figures of the early Welsh semi-mythological tradition'; also figures who represent the medieval Welsh view of the country's leaders in pre-Saxon times, as well as those belonging to the 'British Heroic Age of the sixth and seventh centuries'.[50] One should not therefore expect direct allusions to deities. I have referred above (section 1 n.7) to a triple Gwenhwyfar, who belongs to the heroic Arthurian cycle. The ever-resourceful Anne Ross has claimed to have dug out a real god from some of the triads. She refers to

> three bull-protectors of the Island of Britain (Triad 6)
> three bull-chieftains of the Island of Britain (Triad 7)

three bull-spectres of the Island of Britain (Triad 63)

Whereas Rachel Bromwich is content to note that *tarw* ('bull') is 'a common metaphor for a warrior in early poetry',[51] Anne Ross refers to 'the widespread propitiation especially in northern Britain of a horned warrior god'; she concedes that the use of *tarw* to describe a warrior is 'purely conventional in Welsh verse', but 'may have derived from the earlier mythology in which the tribal god was conceived of in northern Britain as, amongst other things, a bull-horned warrior', adding that most of the characters named in the contexts are part of northern British genealogies.[52] It is an attractive proposal which is worth pondering. It is a pity that epigraphy does not supply a name for this bull-horned warrior-god.

6. *Triads of Northern Europe*

I have remarked above (section 2, 'The Female Triad') that the triad of mother-goddesses was popular among the German tribes. Indeed the veneration of these deities was not less prevalent among them than among the Celts.[53] The Romans too had evidently become enamoured of these goddesses and had doubtless contributed to the spread of their cult. Yet the high incidence of the dedications in Gaul and Britain points to a Celtic origin. If we wish to apply Dumézil's tripartition of functions, these groups are obviously not themselves divisible, but together they will fulfil part of the third function of providing sustenance. The scheme does not work out very tidily, though. At the head of the first function, which includes sovereign power with juridical control and magical potency, are the deities Mitra-Varuna in India, Týr-Odin among the Germans, and Nodens-Teutates among the Celts. The second function of warlike power is represented, claims de Vries further,[54] by Indra-Donar-Taranis, but the truth is that there are many more competitors for this type of post, especially in the Celtic area, as Anne Ross[55] makes abundantly clear in her chapter on 'The Warrior God in Britain'.

In discussing evidence from northern Europe I am using the geographical term in its wider sense to include Germany together with the Baltic and Scandinavian countries,[56] and I am naturally more interested in the earlier material than in the rich mythological store compiled by the Icelandic writer Snorri Sturluson (AD 1179–1241) in the work now known as the Prose Edda. The Poetic Edda, perhaps composed in Norway, is of slightly earlier origin, while the *Gesta Danorum* of Saxo Grammaticus belongs to the late twelfth and early thirteenth centuries; but we have to turn to the classical writers and to archaeology for light on the religion of the German tribes in prior ages.

Julius Caesar attributes a basic triad to German religious thought, saying that *they count as gods only those beings whom they see and whose help they openly receive – the Sun, the Fire-god, and the Moon; the others they have not known of even by report*:

> Deorum numero eos solos ducunt, quos cernunt et quorum aperte opibus iuvantur, Solem, et Vulcanum et Lunam, reliquos ne fama quidam acceperunt.
> (*De Bello Gallico*, 6. 21. 2)

Sol and Luna are clearly personified here, and there is a slight incoherence in the naming of Vulcanus rather than Ignis; but the meaning is not in doubt. One might have expected Terra in the list.[57] The statement has little value since it arises partly from the factitious contrast which Caesar presents as between Gauls and Germans; it is a black-and-white contrast which contravenes reality.[58] He was of course recording the first Roman contacts with German tribes, and it was essentially a fleeting encounter.[59] Caesar has in fact been getting low marks lately. His personal knowledge of the Celts in Gaul must have been extensive, but his account of them relies largely on previous writers, in particular Poseidonius.[60] This, however, was a constant habit of classical writers, so that it is not fair to berate him on this score. Even the accuracy of his record of Celtic personal names has been questioned, but here again a defence is possible, since members of his staff who sent his despatches to the Senate in Rome may have committed the errors.[61] His Germanic triad of crude natural powers reflects his prejudice against tribes whom he regarded as simple barbarians.

The attitude of Tacitus more than a hundred years later was very different. He also elaborates a contrast, but now it is between the primitive purity of the Germans and the luxury-loving corruption of the Romans. It is a contrast that naturally leads to exaggeration in a double direction. Tacitus also leans on previous writers, especially, it seems, on the now lost *Bella Germanica* of the elder Pliny; he also profited, at the same time, from information supplied orally by Romans who had campaigned in the regions described. His remarks on religion begin in chapter 9, where he tells us that *among the gods they especially revere Mercury, to whom they deem it right to sacrifice on fixed days even with human victims*. Then he states that *they propitiate Hercules and Mars with acceptable animal victims*:

> Deorum maxime Mercurium colunt, cui certis diebus humanis quoque hostiis litare fas habent. Herculem ac Martem concessis animalibus placant.
> (Tacitus, *Germ*. 9. 1)

The reference to Mercury is strikingly paralleled not only by Caesar's statement about the Gauls (*DBG* 6. 17: *Deum maxime Mercurium colunt*) but also by the dictum of Herodotus (5. 7) about the Thracian chiefs:

Among the gods they especially revere Hermes. Poseidonius as the intermediary source probably explains the parallelism.[62]

It is of course evident that the Roman appellations cover the names of leading German deities. Mercury is for Wodan or Odin (cf. Eng. Wednesday); Hercules for Donar or Thor (cf. Eng. Thursday); and Mars for Týr or Tîwaz (cf. Eng. Tuesday).[63] Tacitus is dealing here with the German tribes of the West, and the many dedications to Mercury in this region often show epithets added to the god's name which have Germanic and geographical significance confirming this.[64]

A more difficult question is whether these three deities constituted a triad and whether Tacitus intended to convey that. They are named, be it noted, in separate though consecutive sentences; and then we are told that *some of the Suebi sacrifice also to Isis*. The chapter ends with general remarks on German religion: there are no temples or images, and groves and glades are consecrated. In his opening sentences Tacitus may well have chosen to name the three chief gods, but it is not clear that he regarded them as a closely linked group. A number of votive inscriptions were interpreted by Zangemeister as implying that Mercurius, Hercules, and Mars formed 'a fixed triad of Germanic divinities', but this view has been challenged.[65] It has been remarked[66] that 'Mercury is flanked by Mars and Hercules'; yet the Latin of Tacitus does not give this impression, although the mention of the types of offerings made does link Mercury and the other two gods.

An undoubted triad is provided by Tacitus before this, in his chapter 2, where he describes the divine ancestors of the three principal Germanic groups of tribes: he tells us that they were the three sons of Mannus, himself the son of the god Tuisto, who was born from the earth and was apparently bisexual. Further offspring of Mannus were said to account for other tribes. A poetic tradition is cited as the source of this account, and it is doubtful whether it implies a kind of amphictyonic bond of three groups, still less that a social division is meant.[67]

A triad attested for the Swedish great temple at Uppsala is that of Odin, Thor, and Freyr, described by Adam of Bremen (ob. *c.* AD 1081) in his *Gesta*, 4. 26-7 (he calls them Thor, Wodan, and Fricco). The third of this group was shown as a hugely phallic deity (*cuius etiam simulacrum fingunt cum ingenti priapo*);[68] he was regarded as a god of male fertility who was the founder of the Swedish royal dynasty. From Adam of Bremen and from Saxo have come portrayals of human sacrifices, lascivious dances, obscene songs and dramatic orgies which were said to be part of the pagan rites at Uppsala; these portrayals recall those given by Tacitus (*Germ.* 40) of the rites relating to the goddess of Mother Earth, Nerthus, among northern Germanic tribes.[69] Remains of Uppsala's splendid temple have long since vanished, but in Gamla Uppsala one can still inspect (as I did in June 1984) the 'royal mounds', where three early Swedish kings are said to be buried. Nor have the three deities once honoured in the temple lost all their appeal. Professor R. Holthoer informed me that in the aura of the last century's romantic nationalism it was common for families and societies to gather in Gamla Uppsala in scenes of warm festivity when the wine flowed freely in honour of Odin, Thor, and Frö (Freyr).

According to Adam of Bremen's account of the temple of Uppsala, Thor was the most potent of the triad. He says that *in this temple, entirely decorated with gold, the people worship statues of three gods, in such a way that the most powerful of them, Thor, occupies the throne in the centre of the seated group of three; on each side of him Wodan and Fricco have their places*:

> In hoc templo, quod totum ex auro paratum est, statuas trium deorum veneratur populus, ita ut potentissimus eorum Thor in medio solium habet triclinio; hinc et inde locum possident Wodan et Fricco.
> (*Adami Gesta Hammaburgensis Ecclesiae Pontificum*, Hanover, 1876, 4. 26, p.174)

He then proceeds to dwell on the functions of the three:

> Thor: thunder and lightning, rain and wind; repelling plague and famine.
> Wodan: *furor*, waging war.
> Fricco: peace and pleasure, sexual potency, fertility in marriage.

These details caused considerable trouble to Dumézil in an attempt to apply his triple functional division.[70] The main problem is that Thor is presented as the most powerful of the gods and as the deity who occupies the central position. Dumézil argues that the true hierarchy of Uppsala is in the order Odin, Thor, Freyr. Thor's hammer, he urges, has been misinterpreted as a sceptre, thus evoking the sceptre of Jupiter. An error of interpretation, according to him, underlies the account, since the Indo-European scheme demands that the first function, that of sovereignty, be assigned to Odin. Dumézil accepts that Adam visited Uppsala, but it has been maintained[71] that his description is 'not that of an eye-witness', since a Christian informant must have contributed some details. Yet the primacy of Thor rather than Odin in this region is supported by other evidence.[72] Whereas an early Germanic tradition puts Odin in front, as the Tacitean dictum about Mercury makes clear, one must allow for varying regional emphases and reject Dumézil's attempt to press Adam's account into a dogmatic straitjacket.

NOTES

[1] For a detailed discussion of the cycle see Alwyn Rees and Brinley Rees, *Celtic Heritage* (London, 1961), 28ff. Jan de Vries, *Keltische Religion* (Stuttgart, 1961), 151ff. denies any historical import.

[2] Dumézil, *The Destiny of the Warrior* (tr.; Chicago, 1970), 11. On the account in Livy see R. M. Ogilvie, *Comm. on Books 1-5* (Oxford, 1965), 109, who finds the closest parallel in the Irish legend of Cúchulainn.

[3] Dumézil, op. cit., 13ff. Trita Āptya is 'the third one of the water'; cf. Wendy D. O'Flaherty, *Hindu Myths* (Harmondsworth, 1975), 71, 355; and eadem, *The Rig Veda* (Harmondsworth, 1981), 87-8.

[4] See W. J. Gruffydd, *Math vab Mathonwy* (Cardiff, 1928), 46ff. (following a text and translation); cf. Alwyn and Brinley Rees, op. cit., 50ff.

[5] J. Vendryes, *Choix d'études linguistiques et Celtiques* (Paris, 1952), 233-46.

[6] D. Ellis Evans, *Gorchest y Celtiaid yn yr Hen Fyd* (Inaugural Lecture, Swansea, 1975), 24, appears to accept this view. Alwyn and Brinley Rees, *Celtic Heritage*, 186-204, devote a whole chapter to 'Numbers' without a mention of this theory, although three is discussed sporadically elsewhere.

[7] Rachel Bromwich, *Trioedd Ynys Prydain: The Welsh Triads* (2nd edn., Cardiff, 1978), 154 (Triad 56); Anne Ross, *Pagan Celtic Britain* (London, 1967; repr. 1974), 267.

[8] Marija Gimbutas, *The Goddesses and Gods of Old Europe, 6500-3500 B.C.* (new edn., London, 1982), 152ff. E. Anati in *Archaeology and Fertility Cult in the Ancient Mediterranean*, ed. A. Bonanno (Amsterdam, 1986), 2-15, shows that the term 'fertility cult' usually refers to the productivity of nature or to human procreation, but that evidence of a cult is often missing.

[9] Jan Filip, *Celtic Civilization and Its Heritage* (Prague, 1962), 176, 184.

[10] Jan de Vries, *Keltische Rel.*, 120; D. Ellis Evans, *Gorchest y Celtiaid*, 24. Examples of a single figure were found at Carrawburgh, Northumberland, and at Bewcastle, Cumberland: v. Anne Ross, op. cit., 265, 269.

[11] J. de Vries, op. cit., 121; idem, *Kelten und Germanen* (Berne, 1960), 94; cf. H. D. Rankin, *Celts and the Classical World* (London, 1987), 268, remarking that 'in Christian times they possibly became the three Maries in some places'.

[12] Jan Filip, *Celtic Civilization etc.*, 184, Fig.49, 3; Anne Ross, *Pagan Celtic Britain*, 269, Fig.133; 270, Figs.134-6.

[13] Anne Ross, in *Y Gwareiddiad Celtaidd*, ed. Geraint Bowen (Llandysul, 1987), 109-10.

[14] A better reproduction is given in Sheppard Frere, *Britannia* (London, 1967), Pl.29 b. The *Matronae Aufaniae* sculptured on a monument in Bonn (AD 164) shows a comparative magnificence of style and demeanour, but strong Roman artistic influence evidently accounts for this; v. Hans Lehner, *Die Ausgrabung in und bei der Münsterkirche in Bonn* (Bolzano, 1931), 16ff. with Pls.5-6; cf. the very dignified *Matronae* on a monument from Cologne: Fritz Fremersdorf, *Inschriften und Bildwerke aus Römischer Zeit* (Cologne, 1956), 5, no.240 with Pl.4.

[15] I. A. Richmond, *Roman Britain* (Harmondsworth, 1955), 190-1.

[16] Op. cit. (n.13 above), 100. She does not unhappily provide a photograph. But see Miranda Green, *The Gods of the Celts* (Gloucester, 1986), 209, Fig.92.

[17] Anne Ross, *Pagan Celtic Britain*, 266; cf. T. G. E. Powell, *The Celts* (London, 1958), 124.

[18] D. Ellis Evans, *Gorchest y Celtiaid*, 24; Anne Ross, op. cit., 270; A. and B. Rees, *Celtic Heritage*, 264. Probably quite unconnected with the mother-goddesses is the triad of hooded deities shown in a relief from Housesteads, Northumberland: v. Anne Ross, op. cit., 380 with Pl.90. She cites other parallel groups, but is unclear about their function. Even their sex is uncertain and they are not known outside Britain. See further J. M. C. Toynbee, *Art in Britain under the Romans* (Oxford, 1964), 105 and 177-8. These *genii cucullati* are said by her (p.105) to be 'godlets of fertility and the other world'. Of thirteen examples in relief, eight are triads. In one instance (her Pl.44 a), where their cloaks are short, they carry an egg, 'the widespread symbol of life and immortality'. It is doubtful whether this rare revelation should be applied to the whole series.

[19] See the full and authoritative record by D. Ellis Evans, *Gaulish Personal Names* (Oxford, 1967), 266-9. The element *Teuto-* is shown to be cognate with the Irish *túath*, 'people' and Welsh *tud*, 'country'; cf. his p.117 on Teutomatus and Anne Ross, op. cit., 225. The debate on Celtic identity (language v. material culture) is admirably dealt with by Ellis Evans in *Arch. Camb.* 140 (1991), 1-16.

[20] Ibid., 200-2, with attention to the many theories of its etymology, among which is Latin *herus*, 'master'; cf. J. de Vries, *Keltische Rel.*, 97ff.

[21] J. de Vries, op. cit., 63.

[22] Cf. T. G. E. Powell, *The Celts*, 128.

[23] The ambivalence is defended by Ross, op. cit., 352.

[24] Jan Filip, *Celtic Civilization*, 176, thinks that the names might be applicable to 'almost any tribal deity'.

[25] Powell, op. cit., 125.

[26] *Keltische Rel.*, 50-2.

[27] Powell, ibid.

[28] Cabinet des Médailles, Bibliothèque Nationale, Paris; v. Proinsias Mac Cana, *Celtic Mythology* (London, 1970), 48-9 (with photograph).

[29] J. de Vries, op. cit., 158-63, with map on p.159.

[30] (Tr. Myles Dillon), *Gods and Heroes of the Celts* (London, 1949), 16.

[31] J. de Vries, op. cit., 159.

[32] Anne Ross, *Pagan Celtic Britain*, 107-12.

[33] Ibid., 159, 335.

[34] I. A. Richmond, *Roman Britain*, 195; cf. 142.

[35] Op. cit., 299 n.44. Cf. J. C. M. Toynbee, *Art in Britain under the Romans*, 103: 'three-horned bull (probably Tarvos Trigaranus)'; in all ' a quartet of curious Celtic divinities'. For a reproduction see R. E. M. Wheeler, *Maiden Castle, Dorset* (Oxford, 1943), Pl.31 (cf. pp.75-6) and Ross, op. cit., Pl.72 C.

[36] *Antiquité Classique* 10 (1941), 71-6 ('Note sur une statuette en bronze de Mercure'). Phallic amulets were very common, as Hans Herter showed in his masterly survey in *RE*, s.v. 'Phallos' (1938), 1681-748, and they were found often in tombs. Lambrechts assigns to his figure an apotropaic and magical force, and for the triplicity he cites W. Deonna's phrase 'la répétition d'intensité'. The phallic nature of the three items is not certain, however.

[37] *L'Exaltation de la tête dans la pensée et dans l'art des Celtes* (Diss. Arch. Gandenses, 2; Bruges, 1954).

[38] J. de Vries, op. cit., 44 points to other associations of Mercury with the phallus but plays down the importance of the bronze from Tongres. Marie-Louise Sjoestedt (tr. M. Dillon), *Gods and Heroes of the Celts* (new edn., Berkeley, 1982), 28, finds

in the stele from Malmaison, where Tricephalus is associated with Mercury and Rosmerta, evidence of the idea that Tricephalus is dominating the other two – 'a triumph for the Remi'.

[39] Rightly stressed by Proinsias Mac Cana, *Celtic Mythology*, 48.

[40] Marija Gimbutas in *Encycl Rel.*, ed. M. Eliade, 15 (1987), 53. Cf. C. H. Meyer, *Fontes hist. rel. Slavicae* (Berlin, 1931), 26, quoting Herbordus (AD 1159), *Dialogus de vita Ottonis*, 2. 30: *Erat autem ibi simulacrum triceps, quod in uno corpore tria capita habens Triglaus vocabatur*; and many other refs. on p.106 (Index).

[41] J. Collingwood Bruce, *Handbook to the Roman Wall* (10th edn., ed. I. A. Richmond, Newcastle, 1947), 104 with Fig.; cf. Richmond, *Roman Britain*, 196; Anne Ross, op. cit., 268 ('a trio of nymphs').

[42] E.g. Proinsias Mac Cana, op. cit., 79.

[43] Ibid. 44–5 (a figure found near Autun).

[44] J. de Vries, *Keltische Rel.*, 165–6. Yet the Cernunnos figure has magical potency in other ways; cf. Jan Filip, *Celtic Civilization*, 176.

[45] Anne Ross, op. cit., 43.

[46] For a gnomic collection ascribed to a judge, Morann, and dated to the eighth century, see J. E. Caerwyn Williams, *Traddodiad Llenyddol Iwerddon*, 49; cf. P. Mac Cana, op. cit., 48; H. D. Rankin, *Celts and the Classical World*, 70.

[47] Rachel Bromwich, *Trioedd Ynys Prydain* (2nd edn., 1978), lxv ff.; also by the same author, '*Trioedd Ynys Prydain*' in *Welsh Literature and Scholarship* (G. J. Williams Memorial Lecture, Cardiff, 1969), 4.

[48] Cf. two artistic Celtic motifs – the *triquetra* and the triskel. Cf. D. Ellis Evans, *Gorchest y Celtiaid*, 28–9, 30–1, with refs. The triangular motif occurs in prehistoric Ireland: v. Joseph Raftery, *Prehistoric Ireland* (London, 1951), 110, 139f. Both triskel and triangle design are also found, however, in the prehistoric continental record, and the second motif appears in Hittite and Phrygian art: v. Nancy K. Sandars, *Prehistoric Art in Europe* (1968), 275–7 and 315 n.50; cf. *Antiquity* 45 (1971), 103–12. On St. Patrick's use of the trefoil or shamrock as a symbol of the Trinity see Ferguson, *Signs and Symbols etc.* 29.

[49] R. Bromwich, op. cit. (1978), lxv.

[50] Cf. Ceri W. Lewis in *A Guide to Welsh Literature*, I, ed. Jarman and Hughes (Swansea, 1976), 141: 'a kind of catalogue of the names of the traditional heroes, classified in groups of three ...'

[51] R. Bromwich, op. cit., 11.

[52] Anne Ross, *Pagan Celtic Britain*, 219–29 n.108. She discusses the warrior god of the northern region on pp.249ff. He is 'frequently horned', 'often naked and phallic', suggesting a concern with war and fertility. The lack of inscriptions in the representations prevents a firm appellation.

[53] J. de Vries, *Keltische Rel.*, 121; also the detailed exposé in his *Altgermanische Religionsgeschichte*, II (Berlin, 1957), 288–97, where he points (p.291) to the many localizing epithets which are Germanic.

[54] *Idem, Kelten und Germanen*, 93–4.

[55] *Pagan Celtic Britain*, 221ff.

[56] There is some divergence of usage in this matter. Thus H. R. Ellis Davidson, *Gods and Myths of Northern Europe* (Harmondsworth, 1964; repr. 1979), 14, says that 'Northern heathenism, that is, the pre-Christian beliefs of Germanic peoples and the Scandinavians, came to an end in the eleventh century'; she gives little attention,

however, to the early religion of the German tribes, and is mainly concerned with the Scandinavian pantheon. In their book *Germanische und Baltische Religion* (Stuttgart, 1975) Åke V. Ström and Haralds Biezais prefer to make a division on the lines of their title. E. O. G. Turville-Petre, *Myth and Religion of the North* (London, 1964) gives as a subtitle *The Religion of Ancient Scandinavia*, and the latter term normally includes Norway, Sweden, Denmark, Finland, Iceland and the Faeroe Islands. The peoples embraced, apart from the Finns and the Lapps, speak related Germanic languages.

[57] Fr. Kraner and W. Dittenberger (9th edn., rev. H. Meusel, Berlin, 1920; repr. 1961) ad loc., p.180.

[58] J. de Vries, *Kelten und Germanen*, 94–5.

[59] Idem, *Altgermanische Rel.-Geschichte*, I (1956), 29.

[60] James J. Tierney, *The Celtic Ethnography of Posidonius* (*Proc. Royal Irish Academy* 60, 1960); also his 'The Celts and the Classical Authors', in *The Celts*, ed. J. Raftery (Cork, 1964), 23–33. In the former work (p.216) he points out that the distinction of Gaul and German was unknown to Posidonius; to him the Germans were 'merely the most savage and farthest removed of the Celts'.

[61] D. Ellis Evans, *Gaulish Personal Names*, 21–2.

[62] J. G. C. Anderson in his Comm. (Oxford, 1938), xxxi, discussing Norden's demonstration of the influence of Herodotus on this work. On the latter's love of antithesis see Alan B. Lloyd, *Herodotus Book II*, Vol.I (Leiden, 1975), 149ff.

[63] J. de Vries, *Altgermanische Rel.-Geschichte*, II (1957), 27–8 (Mercury), 107–33 (Hercules), 10–11 (Mars). Cf. Anderson, op. cit., 74–5; Dumézil, *Les Dieux des Germains* (Paris, 1959), 27–9, where Caesar's Vulcan is equated with Thor.

[64] J. de Vries, ibid., II, 29ff. Rudolf Much, *Die Germania des Tacitus* (3rd edn., ed. H. Jankuhn, Heidelberg, 1967), 172, shows that the worship of Mercurius–Wotan was not confined to the Germans of the Rhineland.

[65] Anderson, op. cit., 73 with refs. R. Much, op. cit., 176, thinks that Tacitus is presenting a divine triad and that it corresponds to the old Saxon baptismal vow naming Thuner, Woden, and Saxnōt, save that these three do not generally stand at the head.

[66] Edgar C. Polomé, 'Germanic Religion', in *Encyl. Rel.*, ed. M. Eliade, 5 (1987), 520–36, this on p.531.

[67] J. de Vries, op. cit. I, 485–6; cf. Polomé, op cit., 531.

[68] J. de Vries, ibid. I, 131; II, 182ff.

[69] Cf. Wilhelm Grönbech, *Kultur und Religion der Germanen*, II (5th edn., Stuttgart, 1954), 246–7. Nerthus derives from a Celtic root, Gaulish *nerto*, 'power', being cognate with Irish *nert* and Welsh *nerth*: v. D. Ellis Evans, *Gaulish Personal Names*, 237.

[70] Dumézil, *Les Dieux des Germains* (Paris, 1959), 5–6, 107ff.; idem, *Les Dieux souverains des Indo-Européens* (Paris, 1977), 186–9 ('La triade des dieux d'Upsal').

[71] E. O. G. Turville-Petre, *Myth and Religion of the North* (1964), 245. He also cites the view of S. Lindquist that the account is that of one who had seen the temple from a distance.

[72] Brian Branston, *Gods of the North* (London, 1955), 111–12, says that Odin was not finally accepted as chief god 'at any one time by all the Northmen'. Cf. Turville-Petre, op. cit., 75: 'in the eyes of many Norsemen, particularly in western regions, Thór, the thunderer, was the noblest and most powerful of gods'; cf. p.90, of the same deity: 'the god held in greatest veneration'.

Part IV

THE MATRIX OF THE CHRISTIAN DOCTRINE

11

Possible Hebraic Antecedents

The influence of Hebrew thought on Christian doctrine is so evidently potent in many ways that there has been a natural urge to ask whether the Christian doctrine of the Trinity has its origin in Hebrew or Jewish ideas. In this examination we confront, to begin with, the whole question of the concept of God in the Hebrew mind.

1. *Divine Pluralism in the Old Testament*

The very first verse in the Old Testament (Gen. 1: 1) tells us that *in the beginning God created the heavens and the earth,* where the Hebrew word for *God* is *'elohîm* – a plural form. In Gen. 2: 4 the term *Lord God* (*Yahweh 'Elohîm*) is used of the same act, and frequently throughout the Old Testament these two appellations appear; in the latter case the name Yahweh results in the treatment of the phrase as singular, while *'elohîm* by itself is treated formally as a singular (see Koehler and Baumgartner, *Lexicon,*[3] s.v.) save when it refers to other gods.

Certainly the stress on the unity of God is fervently and constantly made, as in the famed liturgical injunction, *Hear, O Israel: the Lord our God is one Lord* (or, *the Lord is our God, the Lord alone.* Deut. 6: 4). How, then, was the plural form of the word for 'God' regarded? If there was an ancient background to this plural, with a reference to the many gods worshipped of old, the likelihood is that the realization of that background had long been forgotten. At the same time, the religion of Israel in its early phases was not monotheistic; Yahweh, the god of Israel, was regarded as very much superior to other gods, but the existence of other gods was not denied. In this henotheistic approach the force of the plurality in the term implies that the standing of Yahweh makes him 'supreme among the gods or "Holy Ones" ';[1] perhaps even as subsuming the power of all other gods within himself, if we regard *'elohîm* as a 'quantitative' plural in the manner of *mayîm,* 'water', as the mass of individual rain drops.[2]

The best discussion of this pluralistic facet is probably that by Aubrey R. Johnson.[3] He deals with points such as the one which arises in Gen. 11: 7, in the story of Babel's Tower, where it is said that Yahweh declared, *Let us go down, and there confound their language.* It is the same problem as that in several other well-known loci, as in:

Then God said, 'Let us make man in our image.'
(Gen. 1: 26)
And I heard the voice of the Lord saying, 'Whom shall I send, and who will go for us?'
(Isa. 6: 8)

On the Genesis quotation Claus Westermann in his Commentary (tr., 1984, p.145) is content to invoke the grammatical formula, 'the plural of deliberation in the cohortative'. The basic explanation goes deeper than this: the Israelite uses fluidity of reference in these passages because *'elohîm* can mean the Many or the One (Johnson, op. cit., 28). In Isaiah 6: 8 the phrase *for us* has been connected with *the council of the Holy Ones* (Ps. 89: 7), but Otto Kaiser points out in his Commentary (2nd edn., tr. Bowden, London, 1983, 131 n.70) that no council or court is mentioned in the context, only the seraphîm (6: 2; perhaps in origin the Egyptian winged Uraei: v. Othmar Keel, *Jahwe-Visionen und Siegelkunst,* 70ff.). Yet Kaiser resorts, like Westermann, to the 'plural of deliberation'.

2. *Abraham and the Three Visitors*

Pluralism in the concept of God is plainly present in the Old Testament, but there is no trace of triadism in the passages so far cited. Such a trace, and even a hint of anticipation of the Christian doctrine, is sometimes seen in the account of Abraham's being visited by three beings (Fig. 10) who represent Yahweh (Gen. 18: 1-16) and who bring him the promise of a son to Sarah. Although the visitors are said in verse 2 to be *three men,* they are sometimes referred to as angels,[4] and indeed they are thus described in 19: 1 and 15 in the context of their visit to Sodom. What is not entirely clear is the relationship between Yahweh and these three beings. Is he identified with one of them? Or does he appear in all three? The latter view is supported by Gerhard von Rad, who proceeds to compare traditions in other religions concerning divine visitations; he cites the Greek myth about the childless Hyrieus in Boeotia, who was said to be visited by Zeus, Poseidon, and Hermes, three gods by whose help he was rewarded with the birth of a son, Orion.[5] The Hebrew tradition was probably of ancient origin and connected with Abraham's association with Hebron.[6] Von Rad (p.206) remarks that 'the interpretation given by the early church that the trinity of visitors is a reference to the Trinity has been universally abandoned by recent exegesis'. That may well be so,

Figure 10. Abraham by the oak of Mamre encounters Three Visitors. Words ascribed to him are TRES VIDI UNUM ADORAVI. (I saw three, I worshipped One).

but it by no means excludes the possibility that such traditions influenced the early process by which the doctrine of the Trinity was shaped.

Whereas Philo (*De Abrahamo,* 131-2) interpreted Abraham's three visitors as a triple vision of one single God, several of the Church Fathers offered a Trinitarian explanation, notably Augustine, who saw the whole Trinity in Abraham's visitors, but in Lot's the Son and the Holy Trinity.[7] According to Justin Martyr (*Dial.* 56) Abraham's three visitors were two angels and Christ himself. Unlike Augustine, Justin Martyr, writing as he did in the second century AD, witnessed the age when the Christian doctrine was still in its formative stage. Accordingly he shows some vagueness on the matter, as when he refers in his *Apology* (1. 6) to God and to *the Son who came from him and taught us these things, and the army of good angels who follow him and are being made like unto him; and the prophetic Spirit too.* He thus affixes an apocalyptic expression about Jesus and the angels to an early Trinitarian formula.[8] Yet elsewhere he can be less equivocal, as when he portrays Christ in these terms:

> We are sure that he is the Son of the true God, and hold him the second in order, with the Spirit of prophecy in the third place.
> (Justin Martyr, *Apol.* I. 13)[9]

3. *The Extension of Divine Personality and the Creative Word*

There is another way in which an idea of plurality may be assigned to God. Some of his most conspicuous attributes may take on such a distinctively forceful character that they invite a definition which gives them the status of separate entities. The crucial question is whether such entities achieve the rank of persons in their own right. If that happens, then a doctrine of plurality, if not of trinity, can be said to emerge. A further possible development may result from this stage if reciprocal converse and reaction occurs between the beings thus embraced within the supreme deity. The Christian Trinity certainly implied a vital spiritual relationship between the son and the Father.[10]

Of basic significance in the earliest Hebrew tradition was the divine Word (*dâbhâr*). The verbal form is used of God's Word in the act of creation: *And God said, 'Let there be light.'* (Gen. 1: 3; cf. 6, 9, 11, 14, 20); and the noun is used in the Psalms, 33: 6: *By the word of the Lord the heavens were made.* God's creative Word gives way in the prophetic writings to the divine Word which was transmitted to the prophets; indeed this transmission is regarded as the *sine qua non* of the high prophetic process, as the constant formula *Thus says Yahweh* shows; the cultic prophet's ecstasy also claimed divine instigation, but it was institutionally based rather than charismatic (if Weber's distinction is followed, although it seems actually to have combined the two aspects).[11]

We are told in the Wisdom of Solomon (*c.* 100–50 BC), in a reference to the slaying of the first-born in Egypt, that God's Word was the agent:

> Thine almighty Word leaped from thy royal throne in heaven, a stern warrior into the midst of that doomed land.
>
> (Wisd. 18: 15)

A partial source is seen in 1 Chron. 21: 15ff., where Jerusalem is threatened by God; there, however, the agent is the destroying angel, and one can scarcely avoid the impression that in Wisdom the Word, the Logos, is being treated as a person. There has been a constant tendency to deny this with the argument that 'the personification of the Logos is purely poetical'.[12] Hosea 6: 5 is compared[13] (*I have slain them by the words of my mouth*) and Jeremiah 23: 29 (*Is not my word like fire, says the Lord*), but no clear personification is apparent in either of these loci. Nor do they suffice to rebut the theory that Wisdom here shows a pre-Philonic use of the Philonic Logos. Philo was writing more than fifty years later, probably, and the divine Logos figured constantly in his thought. Yet it would be unwise to maintain that a doctrine of the Logos was unkown to Alexandria before his time; the impact of Platonic and Stoic ideology had ensured its presence. Philo was faithful to Judaism in his stress on the unity of God, although it has been rightly said[14] that 'he does hint at a threefold apprehension of God', if only as 'three aspects of the one supreme and only God'.

Before this the Greeks from Heracleitus to Plato had been much concerned with the concept of the Logos, and with the advent of Stoicism had added elaborately distinctive ideas, particularly that of the *Logos Spermatikos,* the creative Word (often in the plural, of 'generative prinicples'). Philo was of course wide open to the thrust of such an idea, like Alexandrians before him, and it is significant that he was able to designate the Logos as a 'Second God'.[15] By the time we reach the Prologue of John's Gospel the Word is the creative force that produced the cosmos; but it is now identified with Jesus Christ, who has his own status as a divine being (*and the Word was God*). The doctrine of creation by the Word of God was familiar to Egyptians in *The Memphite Theology,* a work which ascribed the origin of the world to the effective utterance of Ptah, the god of Memphis.[16] It appears also in Gnostic writings: see Zandee, ibid., 38.

The Word as a person is manifestly present in the Egyptian process by which Hu (Speech) came to be regarded as a separate being or hypostasis; it is also present in the Book of Wisdom and in Philo's work.

4. *Wisdom*

Wisdom is another concept which eventually leads in a similar direction. In Hebrew thought wisdom is often given a practical emphasis, but its origin is regarded as divine. Wisdom, furthermore, is sometimes also presented as a person. In chapter 8 of Proverbs, Wisdom calls and cries aloud, standing *beside the gates in front of the town* (8: 13). She proclaims her early and divine origin:

> The Lord created me at the beginning of his work, the first of his acts of old. Ages ago I was set up, at the first, before the beginning of the earth.
>
> (Prov. 8: 22–3)

Here the word for Wisdom is *khokmâ*. As William McKane points out (ad loc., 351), there is a contrast here with the preceding passage, which depicts 'Wisdom's role in a historical community, as the adviser of kings, as politician and instructress of men in the good life ...'; now the theme is much wider – 'the place and precedence of Wisdom in a cosmological context'. It appears too that *procreated* rather than *created* is a more likely meaning of the verb *qny* here, as McKane shows; if so, Wisdom is being regarded as the daughter of the Lord, although McKane does not seem to accept that. He does, however, refer to Herbert Donner's very relevant study of this chapter ('Die religionsgeschichtlichen Ursprünge von Prov. Sal. 8'), where it is suggested that the Egyptian concept of Maat has been influential through the medium of the Jewish settlement at Elephantine. Donner remarks on the function of this goddess, who personifies the abstraction 'Truth', 'Justice', 'Cosmic Order', as an escort of the sun-god Rê. What he seems to have missed is that Maat was also regarded as the daughter of Rê: v. Kees, *Götterglaube*, 248 and Westendorf, *MIO* 2 (1954), 168, also Assmann, *Ma'at*, 161ff. This adds point to the parallel.

In some ways the role of Wisdom in chapter 7 of the Wisdom of Solomon is similar. The writer emphasizes his own mortal origins, but associates Wisdom (Sophia) with God:

> Therefore I prayed, and understanding [φρόνησις] was given me;
> I called upon God, and the spirit of wisdom [πνεῦμα σοφίας] came to me.
>
> (Wisd. 7: 7)

We are told later that *Wisdom, the fashioner of all things,* taught him:

> For in her there is a spirit that is intelligent, holy, unique, manifold, subtle, mobile, clear, unpolluted ...
>
> (ibid., 7: 22)

Wisdom claims (Prov. 8: 30) of God's work in creation, *then I was beside him, like a master workman* (or, *little child*, the more likely meaning, cf. H. Gese, *RGG* 6 (1962), 1576); cf. her claim to extol herself *in the assembly of the Most High* (Sir. 24: 2). None of these passages justifies the pallid interpretation, so often advanced, of an exercise of poetic personification. Citing Sir. 24: 1-2, Edmund J. Fortman admits that 'it can seem that wisdom is a person, a conscious agent', but adds that 'only God's own activity' is denoted and that wisdom was not regarded as 'a person to be addressed'.[17] The latter point is valid; yet the portrayals quoted show Wisdom as having a conscious life of her own and therefore constituting an 'extension of divine personality'.[18]

A further consideration arises here: the figure of the goddess Isis may well stand behind the Sophia of the Wisdom of Solomon. Plutarch, who was writing probably a little before AD 120, states that Isis was a goddess *exceptionally wise and devoted to wisdom (De Is. et Os.* 2, 351 E). Her association with wisdom is proclaimed in several earlier Greek sources, including the Aretalogy from Andros, which is dated to the first century BC.[19] A long record of Egyptian tradition precedes this evidence, and the Book of Wisdom's catalogue of the knowledge conferred by Sophia is reminiscent of the praise of Isis in 'The Story of Isis and Rê' in Papyrus Turin 131.[20] Even in the earlier wisdom literature of Israel the influence of 'International Wisdom' is palpably a dominating force, as William McKane shows in his fine Commentary on Proverbs. By the middle of the first century BC the scholarly Jews of Alexandria were wide open to the influence of Platonism and Stoicism (the latter via Poseidonius mainly), and the picture of Sophia was coloured accordingly. This does not mean that the Jewish element has been completely swamped; indeed proposals have been made to see parallels of some themes in the documents from Qumrân,[21] especially the theme of the Teacher of Righteousness as there conveyed.

Whether Sophia here reflects an early form of the Valentinian Gnostic myth about her is not an easy question. The myth is given by Hippolytus, *Ref. Haer.* 6. 30. 6ff. (ed. M. Marcovich, Berlin, 1986, 240ff.) and has been discussed by G. C. Stead[22] and George W. MacRae;[23] the former of these two suggests an origin in the ideology represented by Philo, while MacRae argues for a source in the Genesis account of the fall of Eve. MacRae refers also to the 'concept of personal Wisdom within Judaism itself', and puts forward the belief (pp.86-7) that its origin lies 'in a combination of the late Jewish tendency toward the hypostatization of divine attributes and the widespread ancient myths of the female deity, especially the Isis myths'. On this last point he cites the references in H. Conzelmann's article, 'Die Mutter der Weisheit'.[24]

In a penetrating and wide-ranging study Conzelmann begins by noting that Bultmann had characterized Logos and Wisdom as 'siblings, shoots from one mythical root'. He points out that in Egypt, the personified Maat is honoured in the cult. but has no genuine myth; and finds difficulty in Wisdom's sexual aspects: she is Wife, Mother, Beloved, Virgin; i.e. Isis, Ishtar, Aphrodite; and Psyche, Demeter and Kore. The goddess who combines these qualities, especially in the Hellenistic era, is Isis, who is equated with many other deities, as the epithet 'many-named' shows. He then maintains that Sirach 24: 3ff., while Wisdom has been identified with the Torah, gives in verses 3-7 a 'hymn to Isis', only slightly adapted from the Aretalogies of Isis. Sophia/Isis is given Egyptian attributes. The adjective μόνη, 'alone', is seen to be significant, and present in Gnostic transformation in the *hubris* of Sophia; she is also a Sea-goddess. It is shown that the Aretalogies also connect Isis with law and justice. He concludes with remarks on Aelius Aristides 45. 17 (*In Sarapim*), where Wisdom thinly veils Isis; and he compares the depersonalizing of Isis in the poem of Mesomedes. This is a compelling study; yet it has a major weakness in that almost everything seems to begin in the Hellenistic era. There are rich and ancient Egyptian antecedents to Isis in the role of Wisdom. The best recent discussion of the Isiac Aretalogies is that of Louis V. Žabkar, *Hymns to Isis in Her Temple at Philae,* 135-60.

In the themes relating to the Word and to Wisdom, it is clear that they are both sometimes treated as persons; since they are also aspects of God, these usages contribute to the idea of the plurality of God. Yet neither the Word nor Wisdom occurs in a pre-Christian triad; the Word, of course, as the Christ–Logos, becomes an important member of the Christian Trinity.

5. *The Role of Rûach as Spirit*

The Hebrew *rûach,* 'spirit', conveys another concept which invites the same questions as those addressed to Word and Wisdom. It has perhaps greater importance in that it has often been regarded as the direct ancestor of the *Pneuma*, 'Spirit', which figures in the Trinity.

The word *rûach* derives from a verbal root meaning 'blow' or 'breathe' and its primary senses are 'wind' or 'breath'. It is used of the 'breath of life' in man, and occasionally the Septuagint translates it as *pnoë* (πνοή) or *psychê* (ψυχή); much the most frequent translation, though, is *pneuma* (πνεῦμα), *anemos* (ἄνεμος), 'wind', being also found often. As an element in human psychology *rûach* is open to good or evil impulses. Our theme naturally draws us to the very frequent term *Spirit of God*. This is sometimes used of physical phenomena such as the wind and the Life-breath in man. More often it is used of the divine energy which inspires man with spiritual ecstasy and understanding, and the writings of the prophets give vivid examples of this elevated activity; in the non-literary cultic prophets it was doubtless on a lower level. Nor is it surprising that the Spirit of God is sometimes equated with God's presence, since it exemplifies God's personal activity:

> Cast me not away from thy presence, and take not thy holy Spirit from me.
> (Ps. 51: 11)
> Whither shall I go from thy Spirit? Or where shall I flee from thy presence?
> (Ps. 139: 7)
> Work, for I am with you, says the Lord of hosts ...
> My Spirit abides among you; fear not.
> (Hag. 2: 4–5)

It has been rightly remarked[25] that 'these functions of the Spirit imply that it is nothing less than the personal activity of God' and that the Spirit of God or the holy Spirit is in such passages 'explicitly made synonymous with God's own presence'.

Yet the same author (Geoffrey Lampe) does not hesitate to call attention to 'other and less rewarding conceptions of the Spirit of God in the Old Testament'. These include the idea of mysterious and manic possession which negates the realization of a personal encounter with God's Spirit. Inspiration was a feature of the prophetic experience, as I have noted, although the canonical prophets did not accept this as a mechanical transmission; even the words ascribed to David (2 Sam. 23: 2) – *The Spirit of the Lord has spoken through me, and his word is on my lips* – need not imply the imposition of an outside force in the manner of a medium's performance in a trance. The phenomenon is of course widespread and can be witnessed in connection with Islamic Sufism; in the ancient world the whole Dionysiac tradition favoured it, while Plato in his *Ion* was prepared to interpret poetic inspiration as divine possession, *enthousiasmos*.

By way of contrast the Book of Wisdom (7: 22–30) identifies the *intelligent and holy Spirit* with Wisdom itself, and makes the Spirit thus an intermediary, as an active agent, between God and the world.[26] Such a role suits the occasionally Messianic association assigned to it, as when Isaiah (11: 2) says of the future shoot from the stock of Jesse that *the Spirit of the Lord shall rest upon him,* a Spirit then defined as wisdom, understanding, counsel, might, knowledge, and fear of the Lord, a sextet of attributes. In the same book (Isa. 61: 1) the writer (or a successor) states, *The Spirit of the Lord is upon me, because the Lord has anointed me to bring good tidings to the afflicted* ... While the idea of anointing points to the Messiah, the prophet's personal spiritual claim is more probably intended. A divine sanction is also given to the chosen Servant:

Behold my servant, whom I uphold ... I have put my Spirit upon him (Isa. 42: 1). In most of these contexts the Spirit can hardly be said to act as an independent person; its activity is rather a mark of God's beneficent intervention.

6. *Philo on* Pneuma

Writing as he was at the beginning of the Christian era, Philo of Alexandria, a pious Jew, is a figure of considerable importance. Although he did not know Hebrew, he was much concerned with the exegesis of the Old Testament, indulging heavily in allegoristic; in this task he naturally used the Greek of the Septuagint. At the same time he was deeply steeped in Platonist, Stoic and Neopythagorean thought, and Logos, as the ruling rationalism of the universe, was basic to his mind. He regards Logos as the constant higher law, but for the same principle he often uses the term *Pneuma,* Spirit; *Sophia,* Wisdom, is another associated term. When he is discussing the Logos in relation to man he tends to prefer the word *Pneuma.*[27] To him, as to the Stoics, the word can have a certain physical property. The Stoics regarded it as a kind of fire and ascribed the quality of tension (*tonos*) to it. Philo follows Stoic teaching in his view of 'tensional movement'.[28] The idea of *pneuma* as a material substance, a sort of gas, appears to have influenced Paul to some extent.[29] Yet in Philo the most frequent stress is on divine inspiration, leading eventually perhaps to a theory of 'absolute inspiration'.[30]

His thought on the roles of Spirit, Wisdom, and Word raises the question of the plurality of divine attributes which have become hypostases. He emphasizes the monism of God and in so doing he merges biblical terminology into that of Greek philosophy. His basic belief is that 'God is the One or Monad, the ultimate ground of being beyond all multiplicity'.[31] At the same time, however, Philo finds in the plural *let us make man* (Gen. 1: 26) a suggestion that in the creation of man God was aided by subordinate powers and further finds this to be in agreement with Plato's doctrine in the *Timaeus* (41) that such powers had made the mortal part of man. A satisfying solution to a dire problem resulted: if inferior angels shared in the creation, this explains the existence of evil.[32] Quite apart from these subordinate powers, Philo in his *De Cherubim* 26–8, and elsewhere presents a concept of God which is itself triadic. To this I hope to return a little later.

Philo's treatment of the Spirit's role does not reveal a conscious inhibition in his mind that God's unity is being compromised. Here we may compare the attitude divulged in early Rabbinic literature. To the Rabbis the Holy Spirit, strictly so termed, is a post-biblical idea, although the expression occurs in Psalms 51: 11 and Isaiah 63: 10; but they use the term to explain the divine inspiration of the Scriptures. What is significant, however, is that they sometimes regard the Holy Spirit as a being who is in some way separate from God, as when the Pesikta Rabbati 3. 4 presents God addressing the Holy Spirit about Joseph and his sons.[33] The same kind of separation applies occasionally to their treatment of the Shekina and the Heavenly Voice. If the attributes and manifestations of God function to some extent as speaking partners in the heavenly council, this process, it is argued, does not in the slightest degree place the unity of God in doubt.[34] Yet it is admitted that it assigns many faces to the divine reality; and this means that it probably prepared the way for, and indeed actively encouraged, as did Philo's attitude, the idea of plurality in God's being.

7. *The Function of Angels*

Reference has been made above (section 2) to the difficulties raised in the Genesis account of how Abraham was visited by men or angels. I have also referred there and in section 5 to Philo's concept of the angelic role. It is well known that a process of elaboration occurred in Jewish thought about angels. Whereas Isaiah (6: 2, 6) is content to refer to seraphim without naming them, albeit with a portrayal that points to Egypt, Daniel (3: 28; 6: 22; 10: 2ff.) refers to the angel of God, but twice he names the angel Gabriel (8: 16; 9: 21) and twice (10: 13, 21) the angel Michael. All these angelic persons may properly be described as 'heavenly beings so clearly subordinate to God that they in no way compromise His unity or uniqueness', since they merely 'did God's errands'.[35] In the subsequent elaboration angels were not only more frequently named; they were also given special assignments. This is true of the systems developed in the Pseudepigrapha and the Rabbinic literature; and Sandmel mentions an idea 'that Israel is led by God himself, and only the foreign nations by angels'.[36]

The later multiplicity of angels in Jewish thought probably reflects a degree of Zoroastrian influence; certainly there is a contrast in early Hebraic thinking, where *the angel of the Lord*, as in Gen. 16: 7ff., denotes an appearance of God himself in human form. It is significant that Zoroastrianism also exemplifies a tension between monism and a plurality of divine beings who are closely related to the one God. This begins with the bond between Ahura Mazdâ and his Holy Spirit, Spenta Mainyu, 'who is both his active agent and yet one with him, indivisible and yet distinct'.[37] A similar relationship operates with the Amesha Spentas, 'Holy Immortals', the six lesser divinities produced by Ahura Mazdâ to aid him in the task of creating the world. Monism and pluralism result in a paradox of the type we have noted in some Hebrew contexts:

> As transcendent Beings the Six hypostatise aspects of God's own nature, and are so close to him that in the Gathas Zarathushtra addresses Ahura Mazda sometimes as 'Thou', sometimes (when he apprehends him together with one or more of the Beings) with the plural 'You'.
>
> (Mary Boyce, ibid.)[38]

In the early Christian centuries such ideas, especially when familiar in Judaism, must have facilitated the definition of monotheism in pluralistic terms.

I referred earlier to the use of the plural *'Elohîm* to allude to God. The difficulty of assessing the precise nuance in the mind of the writer is illustrated by the so-called *'Elohîm*-psalter (Psalms 42–83) of the post-exilic period. The remarkable fact about these psalms is that almost invariably they use the term *'Ehohîm* instead of Yahweh.[39] Such distinctive consistency might suggest a doctrinal nuance, but commentators have been reluctant to define it.

In any case, the thrust of the plurality implied in this concept cannot easily be equated with a structural trend in favour of a triadic divine framework. Here there was no simple evolution. Far more significant is the likely Judaic origin of the prominence of the Holy Spirit in the importance of *Rûach*. It is attested in a passage of the Qumrân *Community Rule* (III, IV).[40] Although the Greek concept of *pneuma* became a potent parallel influence, it did not replace *Rûach,* even if the interaction of the two ideas resulted in a refinement of the spiritual content.[41] In the New Testament, as we have noted, the Hebraic tradition is vibrantly maintained.

NOTES

[1] Aubrey R. Johnson, *The Cultic Prophet and Israel's Psalmody* (Cardiff, 1979), 79.

[2] George A. F. Knight, *A Christian Theology of the Old Testament* (London, 1959), 66–7. Cf. his *A Biblical Approach to the Doctrine of the Trinity* (Edinburgh, 1953).

[3] A. R. Johnson, *The One and the Many in the Israelite Conception of God* (2nd edn., Cardiff, 1961).

[4] E.g. S. R. Driver, *The Book of Genesis* (12th edn., London, 1926), 191.

[5] Gerhard von Rad, *Genesis* (3rd edn., London, 1972), 205. See Ovid, *Fasti,* 5. 495ff.; cf. H. J. Rose, *Handbook of Greek Mythology,* 115–16 with n.54 on p.131 (for further sources); A. Schachter, *Cults of Boiotia,* II (London, 1986), 193. The legend ascribes an odd device to the three gods: they urinated on an ox-hide, ordering it to be buried in the earth for ten lunar months; a child was then born from the earth. It was named Urion, after 'urinate' οὐρεῖν, a name later changed to Orion.

[6] Cf. Otto Eissfeldt, *Die Genesis der Genesis* (Tübingen, 1958), 50, pointing to

pre-Israelite times. He refers to the three men as three heavenly beings ('drei himmlische Wesen').

[7] Augustine, *De Trinitate*, 2. 19–22. Gen. 19 mentions two angels only.

[8] Cf. Philip Carrington, *The Early Christian Church*, II: *The Second Christian Century* (Cambridge, 1957), 114–15. H. Lietzmann, *Hist. of the Early Church*, II (tr. B. L. Woolf, London, 1949), 185, says that Justin 'adds belief in the angels in order to prove to pagans how far removed were Christians from the bald monotheism which pagans derided as atheism'.

[9] Tr. Henry Bettenson, *The Early Christian Fathers* (Oxford, 1956; repr. 1969), 59. Cf. *Apol.* I. 67 (ibid. 62) ... *we bless the Maker of all things through his Son Jesus Christ and through Holy Spirit.*

[10] Cf. Arthur W. Wainwright, *The Trinity in the New Testament* (London, 1962; rev. 1969), 38: 'There was a dialogue within the Godhead.'

[11] Klaus Koch (tr. M. Kohl), *The Prophets*, I (London, 1982), 24 and 152 on the Word which impelled the literary prophet. ('It is *dynamis* – effective word.')

[12] J. A. F. Gregg, *The Wisdom of Solomon* (Cambridge, 1909), xxxviii.

[13] Samuel Holmes ad loc. in *The Apocrypha and Pseudepigrapha of the Old Testament*, ed. R. H. Charles, I (Oxford, 1913), 565 n.15. The work is not included in *The Apocryphal Old Testament*, ed. H. F. D. Sparks (Oxford, 1984).

[14] R. Travers Herford, *Talmud and Apocrypha* (London, 1933), 311.

[15] Cohn-Wendland, I, 107, 28f. Cf. E. Fuchs in *Rel. in Geschichte und Gegenwart*, 4 (3rd edn., Tübingen, 1960), 436. Walter Kasper, *Der Gott Jesu Christi* (2nd edn., Mainz, 1983), 230, believes that John's Prologue is indebted to Philo's Jewish Hellenism and that in this the Old Testament concept of Wisdom was linked to the Logos-philosophy of the Greeks.

[16] Cf. my 'Faith of the Pharaonic Period', in *Classical Mediterranean Spirituality*, ed. A. H. Armstrong (New York, 1986), 9. For many other examples see Jan Zandee, 'Das Schöpferwort im alten Ägypten', in *Verbum (Fs. H. W. Obbink)* (Utrecht, 1964). 33–66. He quotes (p.37) a NK text from Thebes in which Rê is said to have *created everything through his word*. He also shows that Hu and Sia, Speech and Understanding, were at first attributes of Rê, but developed into independent beings.

[17] Edmund J. Fortman, *The Triune God* (London, 1972), 5.

[18] A. W. Wainwright, *The Trinity in the New Testament*, 34.

[19] J. Gwyn Griffiths, *Plutarch's De Iside et Osiride*, 256–7.

[20] Ibid. 256 n.1 (*She was not ignorant of anything in heaven and earth*). Cf. my *Apuleius: The Isis-Book*, 247; Louis V. Žabkar, *Hymns to Isis in Her Temple at Philae*, 119 *(Isis, Great in magical power)*.

[21] J. Fichtner, *RGG* 5 (1962), 1344 s.v. Salomo-Weisheit.

[22] 'The Valentinian Myth of Sophia', *JTS* 20 (1969), 75–104. The myth is also related in a Coptic document from Nag Hammâdi: v. John D. Turner in *The Nag Hammadi Library in English*, ed. James M. Robinson (3rd edn., Leiden, 1988), 482ff.

[23] 'The Jewish Background of the Gnostic Sophia Myth', *NT* 12 (1970), 86–101.

[24] In *The Future of Our Religious Past (Essays in Honour of R. Bultmann)*, ed. James M. Robinson (London, 1971), 230–43 (tr. from *Zeit und Geschichte*, Tübingen, 1964).

[25] G. W. H. Lampe, *God as Spirit* (Bampton Lectures, 1976; Oxford, 1977), 49–50.

[26] Cf. Lampe, ibid., 42.

[27] Erwin R. Goodenough, *An Introduction to Philo Judaeus* (New Haven, 1940), 155.

[28] S. Sambursky, *Physics of the Stoics* (London, 1959), 29, with refs. to the phrase *tonike kinesis* (τονικὴ κίνησις) which Philo uses metaphorically to describe the propagation of the word of the Lord. Cf. J. M. Rist, *Stoic Philosophy* (Cambridge, 1969), 86; A. A. Long, *Hellenistic Philosophy* (London, 1974), 157.

[29] W. D. Davies, *Paul and Rabbinic Judaism,* 183, referring to 1 Cor. 15: 44; but he then cites Rabbinic sources for a similar idea. For Philo's implicit reliance on the Stoic theory of *pneuma* see David Winston, *Philo of Alexandria* (London, 1981), 19. John Dillon, ibid., xiii, regards Philo as combining 'Stoicizing Platonism with a Pythagorean-influenced view of the transcendence of God, and of the significance of Number ... '

[30] Martin Hengel (tr. Bowden), *Judaism and Hellenism,* II (London, 1974), 108 n.384. Philo believed that the Septuagint translation was divinely inspired (*V. Mos.* 2. 40); cf. H. Chadwick in *Cambridge History of Later Greek and Early Medieval Philosophy,* ed. A. H. Armstrong (1967), 137. In the locus cited Philo maintains that the Greek translations have kept close to the purest of spirits, the spirit (*pneuma*) of Moses.

[31] H. Chadwick, op. cit., 141, with many refs.

[32] Ibid., 145–6, Cf. David Winston, op. cit., 62–4 (Philo on Angels, Souls, and Daemons).

[33] Reinhard Neudecker, 'Die vielen Gesichter des einen Gottes. Zur Gotteserfahrung im rabbinischen Judentum', in *Der eine Gott und der dreieine Gott*, ed. Karl Rahner (Munich and Zurich, 1983), 86–116, esp. 104–9. I have used Neudecker's translation of the locus in *Pesikta Rabbati*.

[34] Ibid.

[35] Samuel Sandmel, *Judaism and Christian Beginnings* (New York, 1978), 171.

[36] Ibid. 172.

[37] Mary Boyce, *Zoroastrianism* (Manchester, 1984), 12.

[38] Cf. Plutarch, *De Iside et Osiride,* 46–7, and my Comm. ad loc. 470ff.; also quoted by Boyce, op. cit., 108–9.

[39] Cf. Gunther Wanke in *Cambridge History of Judaism,* I (1984), 162–88, esp. 185; and on *'Elohîm,* Yahweh, and *theos* cf. Nicholas Lash, *Believing Three Ways in One God* (London, 1992), 26–7.

[40] G. Vermes, *The Dead Sea Scrolls in English,* 75–7, with mention of the *spirit of holiness,* but also of a spirit of falsehood. For the duality cf. Mary Boyce, *A History of Zoroastrianism,* III (Leiden, 1991), 423ff., who adduces Zoroastrian parallels.

[41] Manfred Görg, 'Ptolemäische Theologie in der Septuaginta', in *Das ptolemäische Ägypten,* ed. H. Maehler and V. M. Strocka (Mainz, 1978), 183. The account of creation in Genesis has led some theologians, notably Karl Barth, to find an analogy in the relation between man and woman there portrayed to the relation of the Three Persons of the Trinity of God. But a retrospectively Trinitarian interpretation of the Genesis locus (1: 27 ... *in his own image* ... *male and female he created them*) in an analogical sense is certainly not acceptable. Cf. James Barr, *Biblical Faith and Natural Theology* (Oxford, 1993), 159 and 163.

12

The Evolved Christian Creed

At this point it will be relevant to give an account, albeit in briefest outline, of the Christian Trinitarian doctrine as it evolved.

1. The New Testament

The New Testament does not explicitly present a doctrine of the Trinity, but it names together several times God or the Father, Jesus Christ or the Son, and the Holy Spirit. The two most familiar examples are the baptismal command and the apostolic salutation:

> Go therefore and make disciples of all nations, baptizing them in the name of the Father and of the Son and of the Holy Spirit.
> (Matt. 28: 19)
> The grace of the Lord Jesus Christ and the love of God and the fellowship of the Holy Spirit be with you all.
> (2 Cor. 13: 14)

The same Spirit, the same Lord, and *the same God* are invoked in 1 Cor. 12: 4-6; cf. 2 Thess. 2: 13. A similar collocation occurs in 1 Peter 1: 1-2 and in Jude 20-1, but the latter epistle derives from the second century, when the triadic formula became common.[1]

On the other hand, the New Testament gives considerable prominence to the role of Jesus as the Son of God.[2] The Gospel of John, in particular, gives much attention to this relationship, and he emphasizes the unity of Jesus and God.[3] In the Synoptic Gospels, too, the relationship is highlighted in the accounts of the baptism and transfiguration of Jesus. Paul shows full awareness of the bond of Father and Son, often suggesting that the latter's status in his earthly life is an inferior one. Similarly, the writer to the Hebrews explains the mission of Jesus as essentially a role of his sonship.[4] Difficulties arise when the Son is also regarded as the pre-existing Logos, since the idea of his incarnation is then scarcely compatible with the unity of God.[5] It is clear, at the same time, that the New Testament is more concerned with the doctrine of the divine Father and Son than with that which also includes the Holy Spirit; its emphasis is binitarian rather than trinitarian.[6]

To some extent this implies that the Holy Spirit is not accorded a significant position, and it is revealing that Cullmann, for example, in his study of the Christology of the New Testament, has very little to say about the role of the Spirit. It may well be urged that the experience of the Spirit in the early Church was a factor which inevitably exalted the role of the Spirit, thus contributing to the need for a clarifying doctrine.[7] In the New Testament itself the term *pneuma* is not attributed to Christ, but is used only of the 'activity of God among Christians *through Christ*'.[8] The Spirit of God impels and controls the Christian advocate as it did the early Hebrew prophets, the difference now being in the idea that the Spirit is mediated through Christ.[9]

2. The Process of Definition

It was in the following centuries that the process of clarification and dogmatization occurred, and in this process a particular concern was the definition of the relationship between the three persons of the Trinity. The Councils of Nicaea (325), Constantinople (381), and Chalcedon (451), made the main credal pronouncements, and they were largely instigated by the various theological challenges that had arisen, especially from the direction, at first, of Arianism. This is clear in the creed of Nicaea, which is concerned above all with the relationship between God and his Son:[10]

> We believe in one God, Father Almighty, the Maker of all things visible and invisible. And in one Lord Jesus Christ, the Word of God, God from God, Light from Light, Life from Life, Only-begotten Son, first-born of all creation, before all the ages begotten from the Father, by Whom also all things were made; Who for our salvation was incarnate, and lived among men, and suffered, and rose again the third day, and ascended to the Father, and will come again in glory to judge living and dead. And we believe also in One Holy Spirit.

Eusebius goes on to record the addition of the words *begotten not made, Consubstantial with the Father*. The Arians, in contrast, had regarded Christ as a subordinate, created Deity.

The Council of Constantinople, on the other hand, sought to refute the teachings of Macedonius, who applied Arian ideas to the Holy Spirit, holding that, although the Son was equal to the Father in substance and status, the Holy Spirit was inferior to both, being a creature. Now the belief is stressed in *the Holy Spirit ... who with the Father and Son together is worshipped and glorified*.[11] In 451 the Chalcedonian definition of the faith incorporated the creeds of Nicaea and Constantinople. In effect it reiterated Tertullian's formula 'One Substance, Three Persons' – a fact which reminds us that the creeds were shaped not only in the formal Councils of the Church, but also by many individual theologians, culminating in Augustine's *De Trinitate*. The exact relationship between the Holy Spirit and the other two members of the Trinity continued, however, to cause perplexity. The Chalcedonian creed affirmed belief in *the Holy Spirit, the Lord and Giver of life, Who proceeds from the Father*.[12] and it was not till AD 589 that the Western Church, at the Third Council of Toledo, added the famous words *filioque, and the Son*, the addition being then opposed by the Eastern Church. Support for this idea of the 'Double Procession' of the Holy Spirit is found in John 16: 13-15, words which indicate the link of the Spirit to both Father and Son.

3. Individual Contributors

I have mentioned the importance of individual contributors to the formation of the doctrine. Clearly it is relevant, in any attempt to trace the sources of the doctrine, to assess the kind of influences to which they were severally exposed. Whereas Justin Martyr, who taught at Ephesus, attempted a synthesis of classical and Christian approaches, his contribution to this theme was slight (cf. above ch. 11, section 2).

[i] *Tertullian*

A pioneer formulator, Tertullian, was of pagan parentage and lived mostly in Carthage in the Roman province of Africa. He was trained as a lawyer, and although only his Latin works have survived, he was doubtless well versed in Greek literature also. His importance relates not only to the theory of the Trinity, but to Latin Christian terminology in general. He it is who inaugurated the use of the word *trinitas*, in his *Treatise against Praxeas* (2. 32: *unitatem in trinitatem disponit*; cf. 8. 46; and 11. 63-4, *distinctio trinitatis*).[13] Probably he was translating the Greek word τριάς,[14] which seems to have been first used of the Christian Trinity by Theophilus of Antioch in his *Ad Autolycum*, 2. 15, where he says that *the three days which precede the luminaries* (πρὸ τῶν φωστήρων) *are types of the Trinity, God and His Word and His Wisdom*.[15] He was writing before AD 183 (the likely date of his death; Bardy, p.15); and Tertullian's *Against Praxeas* was written perhaps in AD 213 (Ernest Evans, p.18). If Tertullian was using *trinitas* to translate the Greek τριάς, which had already been applied to the Trinity, the question arises whether τριάς had been used by the Greeks to refer to their own divine triads, thus suggesting a transition from a polytheistic world. Lexicography (LSJ 1816) does not record a similar Greek usage until the third or fourth century AD, when Zosimus the Alchemist wrote of the mystical Man from heaven who combined the attributes of God, Angel, and suffering man (ἄνθρωπος παθητός).[16]

There were many triadic groups of deities in the Greek and Roman systems, as Usener and Lease were able to show. Usener[17] counted fifteen divine triads in Hesiod's *Theogony* alone; they include male triads such as the Cyclops, and female triads such as the Moirae. Lease[18] was more interested in triadic sequences in magic and ritual, but he too devotes some attention (pp.57-8) to divine triads, as well as to the various theories of origin.[19] Tertullian, however, does not seem usually concerned with their triads of deities with the exception of Egypt. In his work *On Idolatry* he happens to mention (chapter 10) the list of seven idols (*tabula septem idolorum*) known to every schoolmaster,[20] just as he elaborates on the gods associated with doors. Of his acquaintance with the classical literary sources there can be little doubt.[21] The truth is, of course, that these sources do not give prominence, except in separate and particular contexts, to the triadic divine groups. One of the authors cited by Tertullian is Herodotus, who refers in his second book (2. 4. 2 etc.) to a comparison of the Greek and Egyptian orders of gods, ascribing to the Greeks a superior order of Twelve Gods and presumably comparing forms of the Egyptian Ennead. Whereas an order of twelve deities can include four triads, such a division is not suggested by Herodotus.[22]

Tertullian shows considerable familiarity with Osiris and Isis. There are several mentions of them – in the *De corona* (7), the *De Pallio* (3) and the *Adversus Marcionem* (I. 13), the last locus providing detailed reference to the joyful rite of the discovery of Osiris after death: *cum gaudio invenitur*; see Hopfner, *Fontes*, 378-83 for a convenient compendium of these sources. The discovery is featured by Plutarch in chapter 39 of his *De Iside et Osiride*: '*Osiris has been found!*' See my Commentary ad loc., p.452. In his *Apology* (6. 8, ed. Waltzing², 1961) Tertullian refers to the triad Sarapis, Isis, and Harpocrates but seems to add Hermes-Thoth to the group (*Cum suo cynocephalo*). In the *De Anima* (15. 5) he appears to allude to the Egyptian Hermetic writings: see J. H. Waszink ad loc. (Amsterdam, 1947), p.228, and Garth Fowden, *The Egyptian Hermes* (Cambridge, 1986), 198. The Osirian triads were evidently the most prominent; and Isis, Horus (or Harpocrates), Nephthys, and Anubis, who come at times to make up the triad, scarcely impinge on the patriarchal supremacy of Osiris. In Plutarch's *De Iside et Osiride* Osiris is unequivocally given the first place even by Isiac devotees, for the final aim of the sacred rites is said to be *the knowledge of the First and the Lord*, who is near and with Isis and united to her. Later in the second century AD Isis might seem to challenge the primacy of Osiris in book XI of the *Metamorphoses* of Apuleius. Yet if Isis dominates the glittering radiance of that narrative, it should be noted that Lucius at the end awaits the climactic experience of initiation into the rites of Osiris at Rome. See my remarks in *Apuleius of Madauros: The*

Isis-Book (Leiden, 1975), 341. For the importance of Osiris in the Roman cult see Fabio Mora, *Prosopografia Isiaca* (EPRO 113; Leiden, 1990), II, 106ff. and 116. On the Plutarchian passage see my *Plutarch's De Iside et Osiride* (1970), 120-1 and 262; on pp.33 ff. of the Introduction I discuss the relative importance of Isis and Osiris in Egyptian religion and in the Graeco-Roman cult.

Greek influence was most evident in Alexandria in the work of Clement and Origen. Of these it has been said that 'both were profoundly influenced, in their attempts to understand and expound the triune Godhead, by the revived, or "middle" Platonism fashionable at this time at Alexandria'.[23] It was ready to accept intermediary divinities below the rank of the Supreme God.

Plutarch's thought provides a clear example, for in his most mature phase he embraces a pluralistic theology.[24] A lesser member of this group was the anti-Christian Celsus, whose Ἀληθὴς Λόγος was summarized by Origen in his *Contra Celsum*. Here (7. 42) Celsus mentions the three ways of knowing God – synthesis, analysis, and analogy – and Dillon (p.401) admits the similarity to a dictum of Albinus in his *Didascalos* (164. 31ff.). Albinus did not mean to imply that God can be known, as with Plotinus, through an ecstatic experience or *unio mystica*; his three ways are dialectical processes.[25] Whether Celsus was following Albinus is uncertain.[26] They were both writing, at any rate, at a time when the theology of the Trinity was being developed, and the impact of the Middle Platonists should not be ignored.[27]

[ii] *Clement of Alexandria*

A feature of the writings of Clement of Alexandria was the attention he gave to the role of the Holy Spirit.[28] Greek thought had clearly influenced him to some extent, but already the synthesis of the Greek and Hebraic traditions had been at work. Philo had himself propagated the basic dogma that the teaching of Plato ultimately derived from Moses; and Justin had declared that Plato had deduced from hints in the Pentateuch that the idea of a divine triad of supreme beings was necessary.[29] Henry Chadwick rightly remarks (loc. cit.) that the dictum of Justin foreshadows 'the coming together of the Christian Trinity with that of Neoplatonism'. It should be noted, though, by way of caution, that Chadwick (like his predecessor Charles Bigg on *The Christian Platonists of Alexandria*) is expressly discussing these themes in the light of the classical tradition, as his title shows.[30] In the Holy Spirit Clement saw a distinct hypostasis (*Paed.* 1. 6. 42; 3. 12. 101 and elsewhere),[31] although he has little to say on the relation between the Spirit and the other two members of the Trinity. His belief that the Holy Spirit, with the Logos, speaks through the prophets, was by then a familiar tenet; not so his emphasis on the Holy Spirit as an agent of purification who sanctifies soul and body (*Quis dives salvetur*, 34 – an odd combination: *buttressed by the power of God the Father and the blood of God the Son and the dew of the Holy Spirit*, but without adding *God* to describe the Spirit; cf. *Strom.* 4. 26. 163).[32] Yet Clement's Platonism does not enable him to accept the implication of Plato's third member of his trinity, that is, the World Spirit, which is said to include the soul of man as a part. The indwelling of God in man, through the Holy Spirit, is not to imply the indwelling of God's essence, only the impact of his power.

Clement has a good deal more to say of the relation between the Father and the Son; the distinction between them is pointed, but their unity is also stressed:

> O the Great God! O the perfect child! Son in Father and Father in Son.
> (Clement Alex., *Paed.* 1. 5. 24)

It has been well remarked[33] that Clement was concerned 'to emphasise the transcendence of the former (the Father) and the immanence and condescension of the latter (the Son)' and also to 'maintain the unity of the Godhead'. It may be added that his views here concur with those of the Johannine writings in the New Testament.

Taught in Alexandria by Pantaenus, a Christian convert from Stoicism, Clement embellishes his works with many literary quotations mostly culled from handbooks. But in spite of a suspicion of artificiality in all this, he 'belongs to the world he is addressing'.[34] His debt to previous works in Greek includes the considerable debt to Philo. Chadwick (p.141 n.65) observes that this debt 'is large but measurable and is not to be exaggerated'. He proceeds to define several clear examples. In the meantime a Dutch scholar has examined the matter in meticulous detail: see Annewies van den Hoek, *Clement of Alexandria and his Use of Philo in the Stromateis: An Early Christian Reshaping of a Jewish Model (Suppl. Vigiliae Christianae,* 3; Leiden, 1988). She concluded (p.210) that Clement refers to twenty-five of the thirty-two known treatises of Philo; she also divides the borrowing into two types – the scattered and the sustained. A clear instance of the latter type is seen in book II of the *Stromateis:* it seems that Clement here 'went through Philo's treatise *De Virtutibus* from beginning to end', every section of the treatise being given a few lines. If the borrowings are sometimes rather mechanical, Clement was yet 'capable of subtly turning the words of Philo to serve his own purposes' (p.215). A significant comparison is of the references to God and creation (pp.225–7). It is not surprising that Clement gives to these themes a 'Christological dimension': Philo gives to God a central position; in Clement this shifts 'in favor of Christ'. In general, this confirms the accepted view of Philo's deep influence on the Christian Platonists of Alexandria; on the course of Middle Platonism,[35] on the other hand, or on Jewish thought (paradoxically)[36] his influence was negligible.

[iii] *Origen*

Although born of (*c.* AD 185) and nurtured by Christian parents, Origen became versed in Greek philosophy, having attended the lectures of the Neoplatonist Ammonius Saccas, who also taught Plotinus a little later. But he strove to learn Hebrew too, perhaps without mastering it,[37] and gave to the Hebrew of the Old Testament a prominent place in his *Hexapla*, recording both the original Hebrew and various Greek transliterations of it. In this task he was helped by a Jewish Christian who had been trained as a rabbi and who is referred to by Origen as *the Hebrew*, without naming him. He probably influenced him profoundly also in wider matters of interpretation; and since Alexandrian Jews were not normally versed in Hebrew, this person was something of a *rara avis*. Among interpretations ascribed by Origen to him is the idea that the two seraphim in Isaiah 6 represent the Son and the Holy Spirit.

Parental influence, at the same time, should not be discounted. In the sixth book (ch.1) of his *History of the Church* Eusebius names Origen's father as Leonides, though with the qualification that he is usually given this name. The father is presented as a cultured Greek who had been converted to Christianity and became a Christian martyr; the name Leonides of course suits this sequence of events. The mother's name is not given, and it has been surmised that she was an Egyptian of Jewish origin.[38] Her Jewish connections would certainly explain Origen's success in deploying the aid of a learned Hebrew scholar. As for an Egyptian background, the name Origen suggests this – 'son of Horus' or 'of the race of Horus' – although its honorific allusion to an Egyptian god (the son of Osiris and Isis) does not guarantee an early parental zeal for Egyptian religion. Henry Chadwick[39] says of this matter:

> The name 'Origen' has been derived by some from the name of the Egyptian god Horus, the suggestion being that he was born on the anniversary day of that god; and, if this be correct, it would go far to show that at the time of his birth, his parents, or at least his father, were pagans. That this was probably so, other facts serve to suggest.

He goes on to refer to the martyrdom of Origen's father in the persecution of AD 202, directed against proselytizing Jews and Christians. Chadwick's phrase 'derived by some' is puzzling; I am not aware that any other etymology has been proposed for 'Origen'. The name undoubtedly refers to Horus, but it occurs with other Christians,[40] so that a purposive religious reference cannot be pressed, not even in the sense cited by Chadwick. Origen also bore the cognomen Adamantius, 'man of steel or diamond', which was probably a real name and not an honorific addition.[41]

Origen's immensely varied writings included a distinctive contribution to Trinitarian thought, his main exposition being given in his *De Principiis*. He is much concerned with the relationship of the Father and the Son. To him God is the supreme, transcendent, and omnipotent being; but he is also the Father, and no one can be a father without the existence of a child, and Christ is God's only and eternally begotten Son:

> The existence of the Son derives from the Father, but not in time, nor does it have any beginning, except in the sense that it starts from God himself.
> (*De Princ.* 1. 2. 10)[42]

Although the Son is thus begotten by an eternal act, so that it cannot be said that *there was (a time) when he was not*, yet his status is a derivative one. He is divine, he is God, but a *Second God* (δεύτερος θεός; *C. Cels.* 5. 39).[43] J. N. D. Kelly[44] remarks that 'the parallel with Albinus, who believed in a supreme Father Who organized matter through a second God (whom he, however, identified with the World-Soul), is striking'. A similar idea is found, however, in an earlier writer from Alexandria – Philo; indeed he uses the same phrase, invoking a *Second God*: see above ch.11, section 3. Platonism is a big influence, of course, on both Philo and Origen; and in the latter's thought, as Kelly shows, the Son is regarded as embracing a plurality of 'aspects' (ἐπίνοιαι) which represent Plato's eternal forms. Yet the Christian Trinity is always concerned with divine beings rather than abstractions; and the primacy of the Father may well reflect rather the dominant role of Osiris in the Egyptian triad which constantly faced all Alexandrians.

In some ways Origen equates the Holy Spirit with the Father and the Son: *he is ever with the Father and the Son; like the Father and the Son he always is, and was, and will be.*[45] Sanctification is the primary function assigned by Origen to the Spirit, and the idea of eternal generation is also a quality which joins the Spirit closely to the Father and the Son. The three, according to him, are three distinct Persons; he uses the term *hupostasis*, whether of essence or existence. He is particularly anxious to define the relationship of the Son to the Father: as Persons they are distinct beings and yet at one. In the *Dialogue with Heraclides* (122) he says that *we need have no fear of saying that in one sense there are two Gods, while in another there is one God.*[46] It is clear, though, that God the Father remains the supreme source. It is He, also, that is viewed as providing the graces of the Spirit, but they are mediated by Christ. It appears, then, that Origen's Trinity is tritheistic, 'a triad of disparate beings'; at least it has a manifestly pluralist strain.[47]

Its subordinationist character is also very clear. A moderate expression of it is seen in part of his Commentary on Hebrews: *But the Son and the Spirit are also in their degrees divine, possessing, though derivatively, all the characteristics of deity.* (tr. Kelly, ibid.). Origin sees his eternal and adorable Triad in Old Testament anticipations: if Isaiah's seraphim (6: 3) describe the Lord of hosts as *Holy, holy, holy,* they are alluding to the Triad; if Habakkuk (3: 2, in the Septuagint) says of the Lord, *thou shalt be known between the two living creatures),* these beings refer to Christ and the Holy Spirit.[48] A quotation of Origen in Justinian, *Epistula ad Menam,* gives a sharper edge to the subordinationist idea:

> The Son is inferior in relation to the Father, since he touches only things endowed with reason; for he is subordinate to the Father. The Holy Spirit is still lower in degree, pertaining only to the saints.
> (tr. H. Bettenson, *The Early Christian Fathers,* 239)

Origen supported the Son's inferiority with a reference to the opening of John's Gospel, where the Son is not ὁ θεός but simply θεός. Both Kelly (p.132) and Trigg (p.99) appear to accept this argument, but it is a false one, since the predicate in Hellenistic Greek often sheds the article.[49] Origen's view of the Holy Spirit went further in the same direction: although regarded as a third eternally existing divine hypostasis, the Spirit is seen as subordinate to the Son. The whole doctrine of Trinitarian subordinationism was eventually rejected decisively by the Church, together with other of Origen's tenets; in his own age, none the less, it could not be condemned as unorthodox. It was a marked feature, be it noted, of the great majority of Egyptian divine triads.

Although he spent some years at Caesarea, where Greek and Jewish influences were potent, it was Alexandria that had the major impact on Origen. It is moreover significant that it was there that his ideas were supported most strongly in later times, especially by Didymus the Blind and Evagrius Ponticus. The Cappadocian Fathers were more selective in their Origenist sympathies.[50] Subordinationism was rejected by them, but the Father, as the primary source of Godhead, was regarded as imparting His being to the two other Persons. Gregory of Nyssa, towards the end of the fourth century, was able to refer to *one and the same Person of the Father, out of Whom the Son is begotten and the Spirit proceeds.*[51]

[iv] *Athanasius*
Before this, Alexandrian influences were again represented in the career

and work of Athanasius, who became bishop of Alexandria. In the same city Arius was a priest, and it was his subordinationist Trinitarianism that instigated the great doctrinal controversy in the course of which Arius was condemned both at a Council in Alexandria and in the General Council of Nicaea in 325. To Arius and his supporters Christ was the Son of God and as such was created by the Father and was not eternal. It was Athanasius who led the opposition to this doctrine, maintaining that the Father and the Son were equal in their eternity and in their being or substance; the term *homoousios* was used of the latter concept, while the Eastern Churches, clinging to Arianism, preferred the term *homoiousios*, 'similar in being'.

Like Arius, though for different reasons, Paul of Samosata on the Upper Euphrates was condemned; he was furthermore deposed from his position as bishop of Antioch. He was virtually a unitarian in his insistence on unconditional monotheism as fundamental.[52] Sabellianism was also condemned by Athanasius,[53] as by Origen before him. Sabellius had rejected the idea that Christ was God's pre-existent Logos; emphasizing the monarchy of God, he developed the modalistic[54] approach to the Trinity, regarding the Son and the Spirit as modes of being of God the Father. Sabellius even spoke of the 'Son-Father' (υἱοπάτωρ) as the divine Person who is both Father and Son: see Lampe, *Patristic Greek Lexicon*, 1426.[55] This stress on the unity of the Father and the Son led to the objection that it meant Patripassianism, with God seen as suffering on the Cross in the Son. There was an attempt, supported by Athanasius, to steer a middle course between Arianism and Sabellianism.[56]

These attempts at definition reflect the lack of precision found in New Testament sources. Thus Paul maintains the centrality of the one God who is Father and Creator:

> For although there may be so-called gods in heaven or on earth – as indeed there are many 'gods' and many 'Lords' – yet for us there is one God, the Father, from whom we are all things, and for whom we exist, and one Lord, Jesus Christ, through whom are all things and through whom we exist.
>
> (1. Cor. 8: 5–6 RSV)

Although Christ is here regarded as pre-existent and as sharing in the work of creation, he is plainly regarded also as subordinate to the Father. The latter is said to be εἷς Θεός, while Christ is εἷς Κύριος – a noble but inferior status.[57]

Athanasius and his contemporaries developed a rigid system which, on this matter, was not consonant with the teaching of Paul. To Athanasius the three Persons were separate and co-equal hypostases. A certain antithesis eventually marked the teachings of the rival theological schools of Alexandria and Antioch. Its simplest distinction was a stress on the divinity of Christ at Alexandria with a corresponding stress at Antioch on the reality of his humanity. This debate does not impinge on the Trinitarian question save in so far as it is concerned with the relationship of the Father and the Son. An early representative of the Syrian tradition, Ignatius of Antioch, condemned the Docetism of his age for its idea that Christ had not really possessed a human body on earth, but only the appearance of one. Writing about AD 110, he occasionally expressed himself in Trinitarian terms, as in his Letter to the Magnesians (13: see H. Bettenson, *The Early Christian Fathers*, 43).

Much later Nestorius, who began his ecclesiastical career as a monk in Syria and became bishop of Constantinople in AD 428, took a leading part in the controversy about *Theotokos* ('Mother of God' or 'God-bearer'), as used of the Virgin Mary, maintaining that *Christotokos* ('Mother of Christ') would be more suitably used of her role. In maintaining this he was really seeking to rebut the claim of Apollinarius (also a Syrian by birth, but much under Alexandrian influence) that Christ's divinity meant his being devoid of all human spirit or thought. Nestorianism, on the other hand, meant that Christ was to be envisaged as really two persons, the divine and human. The idea of Mary as the *Theotokos*, it may be added, has a remarkable parallel in Egyptian religion, for Isis often has the title *Mother of the God*: cf. Witt, *Isis in the Graeco-Roman World* (1971), 273, though he omits to point out that *the God* in Egyptian myth is Horus the son of Isis; see also Louis V. Žabkar, *Hymns to Isis in Her Temple at Philae* (1988), 22-3.

[v] *Philo's Trinity*
The dependence of the Alexandrian theologians on the Platonic tradition has often been stressed. Philo may well come into the picture here, as we have noted (above, ch.11, section 5). Goodenough[58] has elaborated on the Philonic ideology, comparing it with that of the Kabbalistic literature. He regards Philo's Logos as parallel to the Kabbalah's concept of the Heavenly Man, in origin an Iranian concept; and he maintains (p.361) that 'the distinctive contribution of Hellenistic Judaism was to identify the Gayomart – Heavenly Man –, Adam of the East, with the Greek Logos, and thereby with the κόσμος νοητός of Platonism' and that 'the Logos as the Son of God, or Primal Man, in Philo became the prototypal man in the Platonic sense'.

Since the Kabbalah did not come into literary shape before the eleventh century, such comparisons are not so profitable, and in his later study, *An Introduction to Philo Judaeus* (1940), Goodenough has much less to say about this area, although he elaborates on Philo's idea that 'God and the Powers together constitute a sevenfold deity' (p.137). Within the heptad is a triad – the Logos, Goodness, and Sovereignty; and of these Goodness is also described as the Creative Power and Sovereignty as the Ruling Power. A brief exposition by Philo states the idea thus:

> The voice told me that with the one God who truly Is are two all-high and primary powers, Goodness and Sovereignty. Through his Goodness he engendered all that is, and through his Sovereignty he rules what he has engendered, but a third, uniting both is intermediating Logos, for it is through Logos that God is both ruler and good.
>
> (Philo, *De Cherubim*, 27–8)[59]

It has been suggested[60] that here Goodness and Sovereignty correspond to the Unlimited (*apeiron*) and Limit (*peras*) of Plato's *Philebus* (23 C–31 A). There the discussion concerns the definition of 'the good'; pleasure is gradually rejected in this quest, while the Unlimited and the Limit are invoked in an effort to give the second place to intelligence (*nous*).[61] The alleged correspondence seems to apply only to the triadic structure.

Plato himself certainly emphasized the presence of unity in diversity, especially in the *Philebus* (as in 16 C). A concern with the reconciliation of monad and triad is apparent in the Neoplatonists, but their triads are often groupings of abstractions (see my remarks above, ch. 8, section 4). A Platonist flavour may appear in the words of Dionysius of Alexandria: *We both expand the Monad into the Triad without dividing It.*[62] Yet an exact analogue to the Trinity is not provided by any phase of Platonism. The threefold sanctity ascribed to the soul, for instance (above ch. 8, section 4), does not relate to the Godhead; nor, of course, does the trichotomy of man into body, soul and reason. Philo comes closer, but in his Logos doctrine the impress of Stoicism is clear.

[vi] *Plotinus*
The triadism of Plotinus is explicitly based on the dialogues of Plato.[63] Below the supreme One or the Good are ranged the universal Mind (*Nous*) and the universal Soul (*Psuchê*). That there is a graded hierarchy of powers is shown by the experience of mystic union with the One – *a flight of the Alone to the Alone*; the other entities are helpful, but the union is only with the One.[64] It has been maintained[65] that there is no gradation of powers and that all are subsumed in the One. Pistorius quotes *Enneads*, 3.9.1: *But to others it will seem that the three are one* ... (Armstrong, Loeb, 408–9); the force of *others*, however, points to a differing view. Plotinus also speaks of Matter (ὕλη) as a fourth level of reality, but he does not regard it as a hypostasis.[66] Jan Zandee,[67] in an admirable study, has pointed to many parallels between the terminology of Plotinus and that of some Gnostic writings, especially parallels concerned with the One (pp.7–13). Yet his conclusion is very cautious:

he does not posit a dependence of either on the other, but argues that they have a common source in Middle Platonism (p.41). A possible point of contact between Plotinus and Origen has also been mentioned,[68] with reference to the relation of Father and Son.

It is here relevant that a fourth-century Neoplatonist, Marius Victorinus, a pupil of Porphyry, wrote a theology of the Trinity which is coloured with Plotinian concepts.[69] His God, at the same time, is the living personal God of the Bible and his triadic constitution of the Godhead presents a being with three powers – being, living, understanding (*esse, vivere, intelligere*).[70] It would of course be misleading to interpret this as a mark of early Neoplatonist influence on the evolution of the Christian doctrine since it does not belong to the formative era.

NOTES

[1] Cf. Arthur W. Wainwright, *The Trinity in the New Testament*, 245.

[2] Ibid. ch.10, 171ff. ('Father and Son'). Martin Hengel (tr. Bowden), *The Son of God* (London, 1976), 59ff. pays special attention to the early confession in Rom. 1: 3f., where the idea is linked to the resurrection.

[3] Cf. R. Bultmann (tr. L. D. Smith), *Faith and Understanding*, I (London, 1966), 282. In *The Religion of Jesus the Jew* (London, 1993), 210, Geza Vermes makes the valid point that the Jesus of the Synoptic Gospels 'would no doubt have been mystified' by doctrines such as that of the Trinity.

[4] Cf. Oscar Cullmann (tr.), *The Christology of the New Testament* (London, 2nd edn., 1963), 304.

[5] 'When Jesus is identified with the pre-existent Son, belief in a true incarnation of God in Jesus is weakened.' Thus G. W. H. Lampe, *God as Spirit* (Oxford, 1977), 142.

[6] Earlier studies tended to ignore the binitarian concern; cf. Leonard Hodgson, *The Doctrine of the Trinity* (2nd edn., Welwyn, 1944). A later study, H. P. Owen, *Christian Theism* (Edinburgh, 1984), devotes a chapter (pp.53ff.) to 'The Triune God', but in the previous chapter discusses 'belief in a divine Dyad – in God the Father and God the Son, who became man in Christ' (p.53).

[7] Cf. Reginald H. Fuller, *The Foundations of New Testament Christology* (London, 1965), 244.

[8] C. F. D. Moule, *The Origin of Christology* (Cambridge, 1977), 155; see also Lampe, *God as Spirit*, 222-8. David Brown, *The Divine Trinity* (London, 1985), 16, remarks on the popularity of Moule's binitarian exposition of the NT in his book *The Holy Spirit* (London, 1978).

[9] Moule, *The Holy Spirit*, 63. He cites Rev. 1: 10, where the inspiration is ascribed to the condition of being 'in Spirit' on the Lord's day.

[10] J. Stevenson, *A New Eusebius* (London, 1957), 365.

[11] Charles J. Hefele, *History of the Councils of the Church*, II (Edinburgh, 1876), 350; cf. Kelly, *Early Christian Doctrines*, 88, 238.

[12] J. Stevenson *Creeds, Councils and Controversies* (London, 1966; repr. 1972), 335.

[13] Ed. A. Gerlo, Corpus Christianorum, Series Lat. II (1954): cf. Ernest Evans, *Tertullian's Treatise against Praxeas* (London, 1948). Cf. his mention of the *trinitas unius divinitatis* in *De Pud.* 21. 16, on which see Hugo Koch, *RE* (1934), 825. Before Tertullian a Trinitarian emphasis appears in the work of Irenaeus, the Greek theologian from Asia Minor, but with primacy given to the Godhead of the Father and little explication of the status of the Son and the Spirit as coequal Persons: see J. N. D. Kelly, *Early Christian Doctrines* (5th edn., London, 1977; repr. 1985), 107–8. Yet Hippolytus affirmed the existence of a plurality in the Godhead: *Though alone, He was multiple*: see Kelly, p.111.

[14] Cf. H. Lietzmann (tr. B. L. Woolf), *History of the Early Church,* II (London, 1949), 224.

[15] Gustave Bardy, *Théophile d'Antioche: trois livres à Autolycus* (Sources Chrétiennes, Paris, 1948, tr. Jean Sender). Cf. Lampe, *Patristic Greek Lex.* (1961), 1404.

[16] M. Berthelot, *Collection des anciens alchimistes grecs,* 11 (Paris, 1888), 230.

[17] 'Dreiheit', 4 (*Rhein. Mus.* 58, 1903), 4; repr. 1966.

[18] 'The number Three, Mysterious, Mystic, Magic', *Class. Phil.* 14 (1919), 56–73.

[19] Among these is the idea that the origin of the conception of a trinity may be phallic. See his p.70 n.3, referring presumably to the penis and the two testicles. Lease cites Richard M. Meyer, *Altgermanische Religionsgeschichte* (Leipzig, 1910), 68, with 52 and 486. In these passages, however, Meyer refers to phallic objects and images as being prevalent, but without any mention of a triadic idea.

[20] . H. Waszink and J. C. M. van Winden, *Tertullianus, De idolatria* (Leiden, 1987), 38–9 and Comm. on p.185.

[21] T. D. Barnes, *Tertullian: A Historical and Literary Study* (Oxford, 1971; rev. 1985), ch.13, 187ff., 'A Pagan Education'. After discussing some doubts and uncertainties about the handling of Greek sources, his verdict (p.204) is positive: 'Tertullian recovers his credit as a learned man.'

[22] J. Gwyn Griffiths, 'The Orders of Gods in Greece and Egypt (according to Herodotus)', *JHS* 75 (1955), 21–3; cf. A. B. Lloyd, *Herodotus II,* II (Leiden, 1976), 201–2.

[23] Kelly, *Early Christian Doctrines,* 127.

[24] J. Gwyn Griffiths, *Plutarch's De Iside et Osiride,* 20–8. Cf. John Dillon, *The Middle Platonists* (London, 1977), 202ff., but with a restrictive emphasis on 'dualism'. It really goes beyond this, especially in the demonology.

[25] R. E. Witt, *Albinus and the History of Middle Platonism* (Cambridge, 1937), 133. See also his remarks in *Gnomon* 51 (1979), 382–5.

[26] Dillon, op. cit., 401.

[27] R. E. Witt, *Gnomon* 51 (1979), 383, is rightly critical of Dillon on this point.

[28] Charles Bigg, *The Christian Platonists of Alexandria* (Oxford, 1913; rev. edn., 1968), 100ff. Biggs misleads here when he says that 'Philo had no Trinity, unless the World be counted as the third term'. See above ch.11, section 5.

[29] Henry Chadwick, *Early Christian Thought and the Classical Tradition* (Oxford, 1966; repr. 1984), 15.

[30] Cf. his equally fine study on 'Philo and the Beginnings of Christian Thought', in *The Cambridge History of Late Greek and Early Medieval Philosophy* (1967), 137–92, which has chapters on Justin, Clement and Origen.

[31] Charles Bigg, op. cit., 100 n.3. My refs. are to Stählin's text, rev. Ursula Treu (Berlin, 1972); and with some works to the same editors' 2nd edn. (Berlin, 1970).

[32] Cf. Bigg, op. cit., 101.

[33] E. F. Osborn, *The Philosophy of Clement of Alexandria* (Texts and Studies, n.s. 3) (Cambridge, 1957), 40.

[34] Henry Chadwick, *Early Christian Thought*, 36.

[35] John Dillon, *The Middle Platonists*, 144.

[36] Samuel Sandmel, *Philo's Place in Judaism* (Cincinnati, 1956), 210-14; Philo is 'outside the ultimately dominant rabbinic Judaism' and he gives 'a marginal aberrative version of Judaism'.

[37] Joseph Wilson Trigg, *Origen* (London, 1985), 80-4.

[38] W. H. C. Frend, *The Early Church* (London, 1965; repr. 1971), 97.

[39] In Oulton and Chadwick, *Alexandrian Christianity* (London, 1954), 171.

[40] Hal Koch, 'Origenes (Alex.)', *RE* (1942), 1037. The religious force often atrophies in later generations of theophorous names.

[41] Hal Koch, loc. cit. Cf. Henry Crouzel, in *Encycl. Rel.* ed. M. Eliade, 11 (1987), 108, and in his *Origen* (tr. A. S. Worrall, Edinburgh, 1989), xi.

[42] Tr. H. Bettenson, *The Early Christian Fathers*, 232.

[43] See Kelly, *Early Christian Doctrines*, 128, for a detailed and admirable analysis of Origen's thought on the Trinity. On the other Origen, the pagan and Neoplatonist, see Trigg, op. cit., 259-60.

[44] Ibid. Cf. H. Chadwick on *C. Cels.* 5. 39, p.296 of his tr. with notes (Cambridge, 1965; repr. 1980).

[45] *Comm. in Ep. ad Romanos*, 6. 7 (ad fin.); tr. H. Bettenson, op. cit., 227.

[46] Tr. Henry Chadwick in *Alexandrian Christianity*, 438.

[47] Kelly, op. cit., 131. He rejects the first formulation.

[48] *De Princ.* 1. 3. 4, tr. H. Bettenson, op. cit., 229. On Abraham's three visitors Origen's view is similar to that of Justin Martyr (Christ and two angels are meant); cf. above ch.11, section 2, and Wainwright, *The Trinity and the New Testament*, 28 n.1.

[49] See J. Gwyn Griffiths, 'A Note on the Anarthrous Predicate in Hellenistic Greek', *Expository Times* 62 (1951), 314-16; also the remarks of Bruce M. Metzger, ibid. 63 (1952), 125-6, pointing to the researches of E. C. Colwell, who showed that the article was most often omitted in the predicate when it preceded the verb.

[50] J. W. Trigg, *Origen*, 249; Kelly, op. cit., 263ff.

[51] Kelly, 265.

[52] Kelly, 117-19; H. Lietzmann, *History of the Early Church*, III, 102.

[53] Kelly, 267.

[54] Historians of dogma have classified this trend as Modalist Monarchianism, demarcating it from Dynamistic Monarchianism, which regarded Jesus as being endowed with divine power (*dunamis*). See R. S. Franks, *The Doctrine of the Trinity* (London, 1953), 77-8; Bernard Lonergan, *The Way to Nicea* (London, 1976), 36-9. The term 'economic Trinity' has also been used of this view, the Trinity being seen as a vehicle of revelation.

[55] Cf. J. W. Trigg, *Origen*, 79.

[56] Kelly, op. cit., 271.

[57] Frederick C. Grant, *Roman Hellenism and the New Testament* (Edinburgh, 1962), 154. He refers also to 1 Cor. 11; 3, *the head of Christ is God*. F. F. Bruce ad loc. (the first locus quoted) in the New Century Bible, London, 1971, 80, thinks that Paul may here be quoting 'a primitive "binitarian" confession'. Greek parallels to the idea of God as a perfect being who is the beginning, end, and middle of all

things are cited by Edmund Spiess, *Logos Spermaticós* (Leipzig, 1871), 266ff. (esp. Plato, *Laws,* IV, 716 A ff.)

[58] *By Light, Light* (New Haven, 1935), 360ff. He also gives a good deal of attention to Philo's remarks on Abraham's triad of visitors.

[59] Tr. David Winston, *Philo of Alexandria* (1981), 89 with refs. cited by him on p.23.

[60] Winston, op. cit., 23. On p.310 n.68 he quotes Philebus, 27 B-C and compares 'a similar triadic configuration in the mysticism of the Zohar'.

[61] Cf. J. C. B. Gosling, *Plato, Philebus* (Oxford, 1975), xiv ff. He prefers to translate the terms as 'indeterminate' and 'determinant' (p.14).

[62] Kelly, *Early Christian Doctrines*, 136.

[63] Cf. *Enneads*, 3. 5. 8, ed. A. H. Armstrong (Loeb, 1967), 194ff. with the editor's remarks on p.197 n.4. See also Armstrong, *The Architecture of the Intelligible Universe in the Philosophy of Plotinus* (Cambridge, 1940), 109-20.

[64] Cf. Armstrong, ibid. 46-7: 'The way to the mystic union is for Plotinus through the knowledge of the One in multiplicity; the path to the One lies through the realm of Νοῦς.'

[65] P. V. Pistorius, *Plotinus and Neoplatonism* (Cambridge, 1952), 60-1.

[66] *Enneads,* 3. 6. 6ff. (Armstrong, 232ff.). Cf. Jan Zandee, *The Terminology of Plotinus and of some Gnostic Writings, mainly the Fourth Treatise of the Jung Codex* (Istanbul, 1961), 5. Cf. Pistorius, op. cit., 117ff.

[67] Op. cit.

[68] A. H. Armstrong in *Cambridge Hist. of Later Greek Philosophy,* 236 n.1.

[69] See Mary T. Clark, 'The Neoplatonism of Marius Victorinus the Christian', in *Neoplatonism and Early Christian Thought (In honour of A. H. Armstrong)*, ed. H. J. Blumenthal and R. A. Markus (London, 1981), 153-8.

[70] Kelly, *Early Christian Doctrines*, 270-1.

13

The Likely Sources

I have devoted some space to the Greek, especially the Neoplatonist, background. The influence of Greek terminology is apparent from time to time in Christian writings about the Trinity, and since these writings were mostly in Greek up to the time of Augustine, it was inevitable that the Greek philosophical and religious tradition should be reflected. Its philosophical rigour is unquestioned and at its best it rivals Plato himself, although in the case of Plotinus there is sometimes a lack of clarity and consistency. When we consider, however, the development of the doctrine of the Trinity, we are dealing with a religious phenomenon in which the Godhead is seen as a group of three divine beings; and it is as a religious phenomenon that Neoplatonism, in spite of its many triadic concepts, seems rather removed from the Christian approach.

1. Abstractions and Divine Beings

One clear mark of this gulf is the sophisticated concern with abstractions which characterizes Neoplatonism. *The One* is a neuter concept: τὸ ἕν. The Christian Trinity, on the other hand, is primarily presented as a group of divine personal beings. It is true that the Holy Spirit might be regarded as originally a divine quality or attribute, but in Christian experience it achieves the rank of a personal being. Again, the Logos is often used to describe Christ as the second member of the Trinity; but Christ is pre-eminently a person, even one of historical validity.

In the case of Plotinus there is hardly a shred of a personalist ideology in his analysis of the triad which is ruled by the One as the First Principle. It is in his experience of mystic union with the One that the matter may be otherwise interpreted. Is this simply union with the Absolute in a purely monistic sense? Or does the love of God in a spiritual and religious sense pervade the experience?[1] The latter interpretation must be the favoured one,[2] and it is confirmed by the analogy of erotic love which Plotinus invokes. In *Enneads,* 5. 3. 17 he refers to the eager longing of the soul (female) for the One, when *the soul suddenly takes light*: see Armstrong, Vol.5 (Loeb, 1984), 130–5. In *Enneads,* 5. 5. 12 occurs the phrase, in this connection, *the waking of love* (τοῦ ἔρωτος ἡ ἔγερσις): see Armstrong's note on pp.192-3 n.1 and the remarks of E. R. Dodds in his *Pagan and Christian in an Age of Anxiety* (Cambridge, 1965), 89. The idea of Beauty (τὸ καλόν) plays a part in such contexts, as is clear in 6. 2. 18, on which see Armstrong's remarks on p.162 n.1 of his Vol.6 (1988).

It is well known that Plotinus also used the term *theos, God,* of *the One*; but he used it too of the Second Hypostasis, Nous, so that the title *theos,* while it suggests a more personal designation, is not necessarily a more august one.[3] According to John M. Rist (op. cit., 178) Plotinus uses ὁ θεός both of *the One* and of the other hypostases; also θεός without the article. It may be questioned whether Rist was aware of the rule about the absence of the article in predication to which I have referred above. Of greater import is his comparison of the terms used by Origen of the first two Persons of the Trinity – ὁ πρῶτος θεός of the Father, while the Second Person, Logos, is described as δεύτερος. But the precise analogue here is in Numenius of Apamea in Syria, the second-century Greek philosopher who described Plato as an Atticizing Moses; he was perhaps of non-Greek origin, his name, like that of Porphyry, being a Greek version of a Semitic original. He showed much interest in the teachings of the Brahmans, the Jews, the Persian Magi, and the Egyptians. A key figure in the affinities revealed is the Alexandrian Ammonius Saccas, teacher not only of Plotinus but also of Origen (perhaps too of the Pagan Origen); the class would devote some time to the writings of Numenius. Eventually Plotinus was active in Rome, becoming friendly with senators; but among his circle were a dominant group of people of Oriental origin.[4]

The Trinitarian scheme is found already in the second century in the works of Clement of Alexandria; and *The Teachings of Silvanus,* found in a Nag Hammâdi Codex (VII (4)) of the fourth century, provides many passages that are ideologically comparable.[5] Prominence is given to God as Mind; and Zandee shows that God as Mind appears in Clement, *Strom.* 4. 25: 155. 2 (Stählin and Früchtel): *Now the Mind is the place of ideas, and God is Mind.* Clement has referred previously to Plato, and clearly the line of thought and category carries on to Plotinus. See further below section 2.

Greek scholars have no difficulty in pursuing such affiliations. Sometimes, however, they have shown a certain aversion to recognizing the influence of traditions other than Greek – an unwise stance when dealing with the Hellenistic or Roman eras. An instance appears in the interpretation of *Enneads,* 5. 1. 6, where Plotinus describes the quality of prayer:

> But let us first call upon God himself, not with the spoken word, but stretching

ourselves out by means of our soul in prayer towards him, since this is the way in which we are able to pray to him, alone to the Alone. While he, then, is on his own in the inner temple, as it were, remaining in stillness, beyond all things, the beholder must look at what might be called the stationary images which are already external to him ...
(Plotinus, *Enneads*, 5. 1. 6, tr. Michael Atkinson (1983), lviii)[6]

Reference is made to statuary in temples. I have quoted Atkinson's translation because his comments on the passage merit attention (his pp.132-3). He states that 'Ha. suggests in his note to this passage that P. was thinking of worship in an Egyptian temple' (Ha. = Pierre Hadot). Atkinson agrees that Plotinus knew about Egyptian temples; he compares ἐν τοῖς ἱεροῖς (5. 8. 6; 6-7) and concedes that 'Egyptian temples did contain an inner sanctuary and a surrounding courtyard in which statues of gods were placed'. He then points out that such a layout is also found in the temple at Eleusis, and argues that some sort of mystery religion must be in the mind of Plotinus here, noting that a purification process was an essential part of Eleusinian initiation. But the very same thing could be claimed for the mystery cult of Isis, as both Plutarch and Apuleius make clear. Atkinson's remarks might well make us forget that Plotinus was probably born in Lycopolis (Asyut) in Middle Egypt and was a Hellenized Egyptian. This does not mean that the invocation of Eleusis should be ruled out; but the brusque dismissal of Hadot's suggestion is not acceptable.

In fact one of the rare allusions made by Plotinus to religious observances relates to a temple of Isis which he visited in Rome – a salutary reminder that the cult of the goddess was then widely popular in the Graeco-Roman world. Porphyry gives this account of the incident:

Plotinus certainly possessed by birth something more than other men. An Egyptian priest who came to Rome and made his acquaintance through a friend wanted to give a display of his occult wisdom and asked Plotinus to come and see a visible manifestation of his own companion spirit evoked. Plotinus readily consented and the evocation took place in the temple of Isis: the Egyptian said it was the only pure spot he could find in Rome. When the spirit was summoned to appear, a god came and not a being of the spirit order, and the Egyptian said 'Blessed are you, who have a god for your spirit and not a companion of the subordinate order'.
(Armstrong, Loeb, Vol.1 (1966), 32-5 (= Porphyry, *Life of Plotinus*, 10))

We are then told that no further converse was possible because the friend who was assisting strangled the birds which he was holding as a protection. Mention is made afterwards of the treatise of Plotinus, *On our Allotted Guardian Spirit*.

Although the incident is located in a Roman temple of Isis (probably the Iseum in the Campus Martius which Lucius in the *Metamorphoses* of Apuleius (11. 26) is said to attend; cf. my remarks ad loc. p.327), the episode seems not to belong to the Mysteries of Isis.[7] It should be noted that Plotinus *readily consented* to the priest's invitation, so that Armstrong's[8] comment is not easy to accept – 'there is no evidence to show in what frame of mind he went, or how interested he was in the proceedings' – save for his last clause. The episode was ably, though one-sidedly, expounded by E. R. Dodds,[9] who was impelled by an obsessive urge to protect Plotinus from the taint of theurgy, the idea that the gods could be influenced through ritual practices. He rightly invoked the parallel in *PGM* 7, 505–28 (*Meeting with your own daimon*), for which see now H. D. Betz (ed.), *The Greek Magical Papyri in Translation* (Chicago, 1986), 131–2, with the remarks by Betz in *History of Religions* 21 (1981), 160–2, relating it to the Delphic maxim *Know Yourself*.[10] A part of the spell is patently Egyptian in origin, as is shown by the invocation *O master of all, holy Scarab*.[11]

The possible debt of Plotinus to other non-Greek influences has also been mooted. Armstrong's essay on 'Plotinus and India'[12] is an admirable example of how such themes should be treated. He concedes the possibility of Indian influence in view of the attested intercourse at that time between Alexandria and India; there are conceptual parallels, but these ideas of Plotinus can be fully explained within the Greek philosophical tradition.

2. The Ubiquitous Divine Triads

If the triads of Neoplatonism have only a marginal influence, relating mainly to terminology, they exemplify the urge to think in terms of triadism, albeit for the most part in a philosophical rather than in a religious mode. The expositors and shapers of early Christian doctrine lived, none the less, in a world of worshippers who were very familiar with the idea of groups of three divinities. It is in this religious milieu of the first three centuries that the sources of the doctrine are probably to be sought, at least as far as its formal and structural aspects are concerned.

In presenting his theory of a paramount Egyptian influence, Siegfried Morenz laid great stress on the contemporary widespread vogue of the Egyptian divine triads, although he eagerly included earlier evidence too. These triads were popular not only in Egypt itself, but also, in the case of certain cults, in many other lands of the Eastern Mediterranean. Morenz, however, tends to focus his quest on Egypt, and in so doing denies the presence of trinitarian analogues in other countries, at least in neighbouring lands.[13] He concludes that 'if such a search is undertaken, it will yield a negative result for all territories except Egypt'. What

Morenz was looking for was the precise formula of 'Three in One', the tri-unity which is prominent in both Egyptian and Christian theology.

Of divine triads there is a profusion everywhere. Such is clear from the researches, among others, of J. Hehn, Carl Clemen, H. Usener and W. Kirfel. Among these Carl Clemen formulated distinctions which are still valid in any consideration of religious influences.[14] He accepts Deissmann's demarcation of the analogical and the genealogical. He accepts an external influence as valid if a particular religious idea cannot be explained completely from within the religious culture concerned, especially if the idea is demonstrable in another religion which has temporal priority. He attaches importance also to the manner in which a religious idea is transmitted: it must be comprehensible and practically possible.[15]

The last point plainly implies that the areas which mostly concern our theme are those bordering on the Eastern Mediterranean with the proviso that outlying regions, such as Mesopotamia, should also be seen as culturally influential. If we consider the centres most potent in the literature of early Christianity, then Palestine, Syria, and Egypt must be given precedence, and within them Jerusalem, Antioch, and Alexandria. The impact of Greek thought should obviously not be excluded from the account, and this was exerted mainly in Alexandria, although the same city provided abundant channels for other religious movements, particularly that of Egypt itself. Some of these movements were essentially international in their spatial scope as well as in their oecumenical intercourse, such as in the popular Mystery Religions. Theologically there was a tendency in them to apportion the principal attention to one particular deity, such as Mithras or Isis, but associated deities easily contributed to attractive groupings. These of course are not always triadic. The dyad is often popular, as with Isis and Osiris (or Sarapis), although Horus makes up a still more popular triadic group. The same can be said of Demeter and Korê, with Triptolemus acting as a third related member.

The diagnostic test of tri-unity which Morenz wished to apply in his discussion of possible sources is not originally apparent in the Christian doctrine itself. In the New Testament we have seen the stress on bi-unity in the Johannine expositions (e.g. John 17: 21: *even as thou, Father, art in me, and I in thee* ...) and elsewhere. But tri-unity seems to be expressed first in Tertullian's formula in the second century, *Una substantia, tres personae.* (Cf. above ch.12, section 3 (i) and his use of the word *trinitas*.) If the comparative material seems to provide no precise parallels, the question does arise whether the vast array of tricephalic gods assembled by Kirfel amounts to a notion that three gods are thus regarded as a unity. A conspicuous possibility is found in the

Indian idea of the Trimūrti (see above ch.6, sections 1 and 2). Our survey of this evidence has led to a different approach: one god is here given a triplicate form, and the parallel is only with the modalistic interpretation of the Christian doctrine. It is true, as we have seen, that this iconographic feature later influenced some artistic expressions of the Trinity; it does not follow at all that it influenced the early evolution of the dogma.

It is worth noting at this point that Morenz concerned himself only with the structural make-up of the Trinity and especially with the internal relationship of its members. He explicitly debars himself from a consideration of the Trinity's substance:

> In order to avoid any gross misunderstanding, we must at once emphasize that the substance of the Christian Trinity is of course Biblical: Father, Son and Holy Ghost. The three are mentioned alongside one another in the New Testament, probably for liturgical reasons. But one essential point is still lacking for the Trinity in the proper sense: the concept or notion of such a combination.
>
> (Morenz, *Rel.* 271 (= tr. 255))

The wisdom of this self-imposed limitation may be open to question. Some theories have certainly adduced parallels which emphasize functional similarities in the roles of some of the deities implicated. Clemen[16] offered a valuable survey of certain of these theories. He cites that of F. D. H. Zimmern (1896 and later) who invoked the Babylonian triad of Ea, Marduk and the fire-god Gibil (or Girru or Musku), with a stress on the role of the last figure as a fire-god who is an intercessor, a paraclete, recalling the New Testament idea of the Holy Spirit as a being associated with fire (cf. Acts 2: 3, *tongues as of fire*). The fiery association of divine beings is commonly found in the Old Testament[17] as elsewhere; and the Paraclete is a term used of Christ as well as of the Holy Spirit in the New Testament. After remarking that triads of gods are extremely common in Babylonish, Johannes Hehn[18] refers to Anu, Bel, and Ea as the best-known. Among others mentioned by him are Ea, Marduk, and Nebo; and in an attempt to identify Nebo with the Spirit he adduces the name of a speaker in a text – Nabû – as one which recalls the word *nabhi'*, 'prophet', in Hebrew; and the prophets, he reminds us, were inspired by the Spirit.[19] Such interpretations are patently overlaid with speculation. Whereas Hehn can maintain (pp.70–1) that among the Babylonians the number three can denote fullness and completion, it is significant that when he looks for an accompanying sense of unity (the three being regarded as one), he has to cite Usener's examples from the Roman era (Martial on the gladiator Hermes, Tertullian on Geryon, and the Egyptian amulet with Baït, Hathor, and Akori; cf. above ch.8, section 5). One assumes that he had not encountered tri-unity in the Akkadian material. Another problem in this context is the question of how familiar the Christian writers of the early centuries were with that material. Direct familiarity is unlikely, but some knowledge could be garnered in classical sources. Berossus, who had been a priest of Marduk in Babylon, probably lived later in Cos, a Greek island, and in the third century BC produced his *Babyloniaca* in Greek, from which Josephus was able to quote. Babylon also features prominently, of course, in the Old Testament. Numenius, the non-Christian author of the second century AD, had cast his net widely, but his catholicity was a rare phenomenon. In the first book of his work *On the Good* he states that his aim is to use Plato and Pythagoras, but that he will also introduce doctrines of illustrious nations which agree with Plato; and here he names the Brahmans, the Jews, the Magi, and the Egyptians. A kind of 'doctrine of three gods' is seen in his work; also the idea that the soul at the time of its descent can acquire *pneuma* from the planets. But few clear traces of oriental doctrines have been found in his extant writings.[20]

At the end of his critical and valuable survey Clemen (p.208) is content with positing, rather feebly, the impact of 'the widespread predilection for the triad'. Such a very loose formulation is scarcely a revealing position to take. It only serves to show how wise Morenz was in concentrating on the distinctive feature of tri-unity. Our own survey has produced a range of many types of divine triads, the most basic in many cultures being the family grouping. If the Christian doctrine reached a firm definition in the fourth century, versions of it prevailed from the second century onwards, and in spite of their variety these versions could be covered by the term used by Hugo Gressmann – 'trinitarian monotheism'.[21] In his discussion of this theme he raised what he regarded as the decisive question: did there exist at that time, in the first or second century after Christ, a religion in which the triad of divine beings was regarded as a unity? The New Testament, he argues, gives only certain trinitarian suggestions. It emphasizes the relationship of God the Father and Christ as His Son, but it is in no way self-evident that the Holy Spirit must be the third being in the Trinity; for a long time indeed, according to Gressmann, 'the Church' had struggled with 'the Spirit' for this place. It is not entirely clear what he meant by this struggle. The Church certainly occupied an exalted place in the early thought of Christians. In the second century Tertullian refers to the Church as the bride of Christ who is mentioned in Solomon's *Song*; to him the Church is also the ruler and mother (*domina mater ecclesia*).[22] Sometimes the mother image was perhaps reflected in ritual: the baptized received milk mixed with honey to symbolize their sustenance as children of Mother Church.[23] Earlier in the second century Irenaeus had seen the Church as taking on the role of the Chosen People as the New Israel; to him she was also *the great and glorious body of Christ*[24] She had a close link too with the Holy Spirit as the special vehicle of spiritual gifts;[25] and according to Irenaeus, *where the Church is, there is the Spirit of God; and where the Spirit of God is, there is the Church and all grace.*[26] In spite of this loftily high regard for the Church, no formulaic expression of a triadic function appears unless one is prepared to argue that the close association with the Spirit brings the Church into the Trinity.

Gressmann further urges that the strongest drive in the direction of Trinitarianism (though not necessarily towards the choice of the Spirit) was derived from Egyptian religion. Here the evidence adduced by him includes material which we have already cited: Tertullian on Geryon (*De Pallio*, 4); Martial on the gladiator Hermes (*Ep.* 5. 24); and the amulet showing Baït, Hathor and Akori. He rightly avers that this amulet, deriving perhaps from the first or second century AD, is not a product influenced by Christianity, but one familiar to Graeco-Egyptian theologians who had recourse to magic (the inscription is in Greek). He then refers to the well-known acclamations of monotheism linked to plurality which are associated with both Sarapis and Isis, the latter being addressed as *una quae es omnia* (*CIL*, X, 1, 3800 (= Vidman, *SIRIS*, 502, from Capua, first–second century AD)).

Reverting to the exaltation of the Church, one needs to note that it occurs also in some Christian Gnostic writings. In the second-century Valentinian system of Ptolemaeus, the perfect pre-existent Aeon, who is the Forefather, produces Depth and Silence, then Mind and Truth. Logos and Life were then produced, and *from the union of Logos and Life were emitted Man and Church.*[27]

In *The Teachings of Silvanus*, a Coptic writing from Nag Hammâdi (VII (4), 15–118, 7), which has been dated to the first half of the fourth century AD,[28] allusion is made to the work of the Holy Spirit and of Mind:

And all were made new through the Holy Spirit (πνεῦμα) and the Mind (νοῦς).
(*Silvanus*, 112. 25–7, tr. Zandee, op. cit., 117)

Zandee compares an earlier dictum in the same text (102. 15) which states that *to know who God is, Reason (λόγος) and Mind (νοῦς) are male names*. Here Christ is mentioned in preceding lines. The Trinity, then, is here viewed as comprising Christ and God the Father as two differentiated beings. Yet the Holy Spirit figures in the dictum first cited above. A state of doctrinal uncertainty is apparent, and in spite of the fourth-century date Zandee (ibid.) says that the context of the work is 'in many respects reminiscent of second century hellenized Christianity as it is known from Justin Martyr and the teachers of the Alexandrian School'. He also says that 'like Clement, Silvanus can be compared with Philo, their forerunner in combining hellenistic and Biblical thought'.

Logos and Nous in this tract are regarded as attributes or constituent beings of God the Father, and are described as *male names*, perhaps on merely grammatical grounds. The work is not Gnostic in character, and Zandee (p.117) rightly reminds us that God is also called Nous in the theology of Clement of Alexandria. The part played by Nous in the triadic ideology of both Philo and Plotinus has been discussed above in chapter 12.

3. Gnosticism and the Female Element

Triads in the non-Christian religions give constant prominence to the female element, sometimes in all-female groups, as with the Celtic *matronae,* but more frequently in the groups based on the family. Isis is the supreme paradigm of the latter type, and it is significant that marriage oaths for Greeks in the Fayûm name the deities Osiris, Isis, and Horus.[29] Among the Greeks generally Demeter, grouped with Persephone (Korê) and Triptolemus, exemplified the pattern. Nor should one ignore, in considering these categories, the concept of the male–female element. It is found, for instance, in the Valentinian Gnostic text by Ptolemaeus from which we quoted above. It is there said of the beings Depth, Mind, Logos, and Man, that *each of them is male–female.*[30]

A view of the Holy Spirit as female is provided by the Coptic Gospel of Philip:

> Some said: Mary conceived of the Holy Spirit. They are in error. What they are saying they do not know. When did a woman ever conceive of a woman?
> (Gospel of Philip, 103, 23–6)[31]

Wilson[32] remarks that 'the passage rejects the doctrine that Mary conceived by the Holy Ghost, on the ground that the Spirit itself is female (a view held by the Ophites and the Valentinians, and due in part to the fact that the Hebrew *ruah* is feminine)'. K. H. Kuhn[33] also says that 'the Spirit in Hebrew and Aramaic is feminine'; he adds that the Spirit is often given female names in Gnostic texts, such as 'Sophia', 'Prounikos' (lewd), 'Zoë' (life) and 'Mother of all'. It has been pointed out[34] that various groups in the second century (in addition to those mentioned above) rejected the virginal conception of Jesus: these included the Ebionites, the Cerinthians and the Elchesaites. Strangely enough, the idea of a virgin birth is found in a Christian Arabic Sibylline prophecy:[35]

> At the end of four hundred years after the Orthodox Kingdom a woman from the tribe of Dan shall conceive of [another] woman.

In this case, however, the fruit of the miraculous birth is the Antichrist; and an ideological connection between this prophecy and the denial in the Gospel of Philip is quite unlikely. In other sections (82-3; Wilson, pp.145-8) this gospel accepts Christ's virginal conception, and the importance of Sophia in the text (in Logion 55 she is *the mother of the angels*) may well have promoted the idea of a female Holy Spirit.

The great invisible spirit is mentioned in the *Sophia Jesu Christi* (Berlin Gnostic P. 125. 4-5) and also in the Coptic Gospel of the Egyptians from Nag Hammâdi as one of its titles – *The Sacred Book of the great invisible spirit*.[36] Whether these allusions concern the third person of the Christian Trinity is in doubt; 'the supreme being of a gnostic system' may be implied.[37] In the Coptic Gospel of the Egyptians *the great invisible spirit* is identified with the transcendent God, from whom issues a series of glorious beings, beginning with the great trinity of Father, Mother Barbelo, and Son.[38] Barbelo is equated with Sophia, an important figure in many of these writings. In the fourth tractate of the Jung Codex Sophia is, however, treated as male and as one of the Aeons; her male character is a confusing feature and perhaps results from her being identified with the Logos.[39] The Wisdom of Solomon, as we noted in chapter 11, gives prominence to Sophia, and some Isiac attributes are ascribed to her. Philo was much absorbed with the same figure, and he expresses the same paradoxical interpretation of Sophia as that found in the Jung Codex: he raises the question as to why the name of Sophia is feminine while her nature is masculine. It is because, he avers, she endows souls with learning, knowledge, and insight, and at the same time sows and procreates good and praiseworthy deeds.[40]

In Valentinian Gnosis Sophia stands in close association with Christ as a saviour-figure. Yet she shares with Isis the intrinsic imperfection of matter and the created world, as Plutarch was able to opine.[41] She is identified in various writings with both the Logos and with Pneuma, and here the Stoic impress is marked. At the same time she has experienced a spiritual fall, and this is why George MacRae felt able to invoke the figure of Eve as her prototype (see above chapter 11, section 3), although he accepted too a measure of influence from the direction of Hellenistic Judaism, including an interest in Isis.

Remarking on the fact that many Gnostic texts 'speak of God as a dyad who embraces both masculine and feminine elements', Elaine Pagels suggests that in this respect, although these texts are 'unmistakably related to a Jewish heritage', they seem to contravene the tradition of a God who is 'monistic and masculine'.[42] Before this Dr Pagels says that 'one might expect that these texts would show the influence of archaic pagan traditions of the Mother Goddess', but it is very strange that she does not, in spite of this rather vague pointer, discuss the rich Pharaonic background in which the 'Father–Mother' idea is prominent.[43] This background is embellished, *inter multa alia,* by celebrated texts from Amarna. Of special interest, none the less, is the passage from the Apocryphon of John to which she draws attention (her p.74). Here John is said to have a vision which assuages his grief after the crucifixion; he sees a likeness of three forms, and to a question by him the vision replies thus:

> He said to me, 'John, John, why do you doubt, and why are you afraid? You are not unfamiliar with this likeness, are you? That is to say, be not timid! I am the one who [is with you (pl.)] for ever. I [am the Father]; I am the Mother; I am the Son.'
> (Apocryphon of John, II 2. 9–14; tr. F. Wisse in *The Nag Hammadi Library in English,* 99)

This group of three recalls the family triad which was ubiquitously popular. Or can we see here 'another version of the Trinity'?[44] There are difficulties in this view, particularly in the fact that the term Holy Spirit is applied to God himself as *the Father of the All ... the invisible Spirit* (II 2. 29–34; *NHL* 100); cf. Wilson, *Studies in the Gospel of Thomas* (1960), ad Logion 44. It might be argued, admittedly, that, in the pericope adduced above, the vision is itself personified in *He said to me ...* and that he proceeds to identify himself with each member of the triad, the Father, Mother, and Son – a unity, thus, with three aspects. But Walter Till regards Christ as the speaker,[45] although Christ is presumably the Son. This triad is also mentioned by Irenaeus (*Adv. Haer.* I. 29. 3), but with no further detail.[46] Now Irenaeus belongs to the end of the second century, and the Apocryphon of John must also have its ultimate origin in those years. We would not, therefore, expect a fully-fledged Trinitarianism to be familiar at that time. Indeed the Apocryphon has such a profusion of spiritual beings, whose relationship is quite complex, that a clear dogmatic schema can scarcely be claimed for it. A lack of clarity attaches also to some of the central figures; and this problem occurs elsewhere too. In the Gospel of the Hebrews Jesus is said to mention *my mother, the Holy Spirit.*[47] If the Virgin Mary is thus the Holy Spirit, this rather contradicts the more general view of the Spirit as Sophia or Mother-figure, although in some Catholic ideology one senses a desire to see the Mother of God, the Theotokos, as an unofficial member of the Trinity, perhaps as an associate of the Holy Spirit.[48]

A saying in the Gospel of Philip makes an unusual claim:

> When we were Hebrews we were orphans and had only our mother, but when

we became Christians we had both father and mother.
(Gospel of Philip, II 52. 20-4 (= *NHL* 132))

Wilson, ad loc. (1962, p.68), offers a clue to this difficult statement from the Valentinian theory: 'Sophia attempted to produce by herself, without her consort, and the result was a formless abortion; but from this the world derives, and all that is in it.' He then shows that as a Hebrew, the Gnostic was a child of Sophia only; but when formed by the Saviour, by becoming a Christian, he is now the child of a husband and a bride-chamber.[49] It follows that 'father and mother' in this context form a different idea from that of the 'Father–Mother' concept of a unique deity fulfilling the primal role in creation.

A female Holy Spirit[50] did not, at any rate, achieve any permanent status. In spite of the negative end of the Gospel of Thomas, which maintains, in words assigned to Jesus, that only by becoming a male can a woman enter the Kingdom of Heaven, there is much in the Gnostic writings that favours the female role, whether female *per se* or as part of the androgynous 'Mother–Father' being. There is evidence too for an active female participation in the Gnostic communities, as Dr Pagels shows in her able chapter on 'God the Father, God the Mother' in *The Gnostic Gospels,* 71ff. She points out also that Clement of Alexandria, unlike Tertullian, actively supported participation by women. Among the orthodox, however, his viewpoint was exceptional. In the theological sequel it is clear that a female Holy Spirit does not survive. Nor does Trinitarian iconography show any trace of this feminine character. In early Christian art the Trinity is represented by the Hand of God, the Lamb, and the Dove.[51] It was doubtless the New Testament accounts of the Baptism of Jesus that provided the equation of Dove and Holy Spirit (Fig. 11). In Mark 1: 9–11 it is said that Jesus, when rising from the water, saw the heavens being opened and the Spirit (*pneuma*) descending on him like a dove, where the latter term is the feminine *peristera*. Matthew 3: 16 has a similar allusion to the dove, but refers to the Spirit as *the Spirit of God*. Luke 3: 22 says that *the Holy Spirit descended upon him in bodily form as a dove*. The exact origin of the link between Dove and Holy Spirit is not easily located. In Israelite ritual practice the dove was a common offering, but with no particular symbolism. Operative, perhaps, was the beneficent symbolism of the dove which brought to Noah the olive leaf as the happy sign of the Flood's end (Gen. 8: 8ff). Less apposite is *my dove, my perfect one* (S. of S. 5: 2) as a term of affection, or even *innocent as doves* (Matt. 10: 16). Genesis, however supplies another possible affinity when it tells us that *the Spirit of God was moving over the face of the waters* (Gen. 1: 2). Here a Rabbinic interpretation suggests 'like a dove which broods over her young but does not touch them'.[52] Yet the

Figure 11. The Trinity in the Baptism of Jesus

allusion in Genesis does not contain the word *iônâh;* the Spirit is there, but not the dove. Jonah the prophet bears the bird's name, and indeed the suggestion has been made that the baptismal dove in John's account (1: 32) is a hidden reference to the prophet and therefore is 'an assertion of universal mission at the very beginning of the ministry of Jesus'.[53] There is no hint, though, of such subtlety in John's account, which is distinctive in one way: here it is said that John the Baptist saw the dove,[54] whereas the Synoptics suggest an ecstatic and subjective vision by Jesus.[55] The exact significance of the Dove–Spirit experience, and more particularly of its source, may lie in a Judaic tradition which is no longer accessible.[56]

The dove persists in depictions of the Trinity, often in conjunction with a human form. Thus an English miniature of the eleventh century shows God and the Son in a group with a female figure whose crown is surmounted by the dove (Fig. 12). This female figure is, however, carrying the Christ-child in her arms and is therefore the Madonna; the Holy Spirit here probably points to the miraculous conception, but is also part of the Trinitarian group.[57] A painting by Velázquez in the Prado portrays the Coronation of Mary; the Father and Son hold the crown above her head and the Spirit appears as a dove in a blaze of light above the crown.[58] In paintings of Pentecost the Spirit appears simply as rays of light or as flames.[59] While the white dove is the favoured form, the three Persons are shown in anthropomorphic mode and in one triplicate figure when the oneness or unity of God is being expressed.[60] A good example is provided by an icon from Siebenbürgen in Romania which portrays a divine figure with three faces (Fig. 13).[61] More often three separate figures are depicted, the Holy Spirit being sometimes given a more youthful form than Father and Son. I have discussed some of these triple depictions above in chapter 8, section 3 ('Triple Features and the Triune Concept'). What is especially of interest is that the Spirit is always presented as male, thus contravening earlier suggestions of her female status. Yet one must bear in mind that in Renaissance art and afterwards the Virgin Mary is given exceptional prominence,[62] perhaps as a kind of compensation, whether conscious or unconscious, for the loss of the female component in the triumphant all-male Trinity.

4. The Missionary Motive

In the early Christian centuries the interrelationship of religions revealed very varied tones and nuances. Borrowings from one cult to another were freely sanctioned by the popular polytheism which was a legacy not only of the Graeco-Roman world but also of cults in the Near and Middle East. The tolerance which prevailed in this way was not, of course, an

Figure 12. The Trinity with the Madonna as Holy Spirit.

Figure 13. The Trinity as God with three visages

all-embracing attitude. In the Mystery Cults a certain exclusivism persisted, and can be seen, perhaps, most plainly in the exacting rules of Eleusis. A sharp contrast to the prevailing tolerance was manifest in both Judaism and Christianity, where the claims of monotheism produced tensions *vis-à-vis* the pagan environment. Within that milieu, none the less, symbiosis was by and large the order of the day. Whereas T. R. Glover's book, *The Conflict of Religions in the Early Roman Empire,* still has potential to stimulate, its leitmotif is rather misleading.[63] In earlier times, for instance, it had been difficult, and indeed dangerous, to seek the introduction of Oriental cults into Greek and Roman cities (especially of the cults marked by orgiastic rites); the whole temper of the early and later Roman Empire enabled the active support of several of these cults to be arranged even by the imperial authorities. Adherents of the pagan religions, as a result, rarely displayed a sense of vicious hostility to one another.[64]

The case was different with early Christian attitudes, and the question arises whether the religious ambience of the times led to psychological pressure, in the evolution of doctrine, towards the formulation of a Trinitarian dogma. A further question is whether the situation favoured the possibility of Christian borrowing from pagan cults and ideas in order to serve a missionary purpose. Such a process, it might be thought, would make Christianity more presentable to people brought up on polytheistic beliefs. Trinitarianism would modify the uncompromising monotheism of the primal creed. An appeal to Jews, on the other hand, could not well be built on the same basis.

Polytheism with its man-made idols is the object of frequent scornful attacks in both Old and New Testaments; and extra-biblical Christian writers maintained these attacks unremittingly. Yet they became implicated in the trend to construct a pluralistic monotheism. While the New Testament presents the figure of Christ as the Son of God,[65] from the beginning of the second century he is portrayed as 'the God of Christians'.[66] A problem arose here, for in the Roman Empire apotheosis was decided by the Senate in Rome, and a limited form was accorded to Augustus.[67] A similar status marked both Greek and Egyptian traditions. The early Church stood by its rigid monotheism, nevertheless, when faced with the ruler-cult, and thus evoked periods of dire persecution. A certain inconsistency[68] is apparent here, and still more so when the end of the second century saw the elevation of the Holy Spirit as a divinity, not merely as an abstract spiritual force but as a divine personal being.[69]

In view of this it may seem surprising that in the contemporary debate between pagan and Christian writers the trinitarian trend is not heeded. The target of the pagan attack is monotheism, as when Origen complains that *Celsus imagines that it makes no difference whether we call Zeus the Most High, or Zen, or Adonai, or Sabaoth, or Amoun like the Egyptians, or Papaeus like the Scythians* ...[70] It is clear that Celsus is here reflecting the Stoic doctrine which enabled the old polytheism to be reconciled with a kind of monotheism, as Chadwick[71] points out, quoting also the dictum of the Platonizing sophist Maximus of Tyre, a contemporary of Celsus: *the gods are one nature, but many names*. In his reply to Celsus, Origen remarks on the nature of divine names and their magical quality; the names Sabaoth and Adonai, according to him, are concerned with *a certain mysterious divine science that is related to the Creator of the universe*.

Popular charges against Christianity included those relating to magical practices, incest and cannibalism, but writers such as Celsus did not descend to this level. Well versed as he was in Greek philosophy, particularly that of Plato and its sequel in Middle Platonism, Celsus was tolerant of most religions, but firmly opposed to both Judaism and Christianity – religions which themselves showed little tolerance of the polytheistic creeds.[72] A telling point is made by Celsus when he refers to the anomaly seen by him in the divine status given by Christians to Christ; to him it contradicts the stress on monotheism:

> If these men worshipped no other God but one, perhaps they would have had a valid argument against the others (i.e. adherents of polytheism). But in fact they worship to an extravagant degree this man who appeared recently, and yet think it is not inconsistent with monotheism if they also worship His servant.
> (Origen, *C. Celsum*, VIII. 12, tr. H. Chadwick, p.460)[73]

Although Origen replies with a reference to the unity of the Father and Son, as in John 10: 30 (*I and the Father are one*), he himself elsewhere (ibid. V. 39) calls Christ a *second God*: see, for a detailed discussion, our remarks above, chapter 11, section 3 (ii) on Origen. It is noteworthy that Celsus here does not adduce the divine Holy Spirit as further evidence for his point; the Third Person of the Trinity had not yet achieved such prominence.[74]

The defence of polytheistic beliefs is a frequent mark of the literary opponents of the Christian faith. Celsus does this, as we have noted, by claiming that the vast pantheon of deities worshipped by most people is really a concourse of daemons and that behind them is one divine reality. Among the other major opponents – Lucian the satirist, Porphyry and Julian – the first-named ridiculed pagan cults as well. His portrait of Peregrinus Proteus, a charlatan who became a Christian in pursuit of material gain, has been dubbed 'a vivid and cruel portrait',[75] but it presents Christians as generous, if gullible. Lucian includes little of theological interest; Christians believe firmly in immortality, but they are guilty of divinizing a man: *they still worship that great man, the fellow who was crucified in Palestine, for bringing this new cult into the world.*[76] According to Lucian, Peregrinus himself was called *a new Socrates* by his Christian admirers; but he also says that *they revered him as a god*. These people, he adds, while they regard themselves as all brothers of one another, *have transgressed once for all by denying the Greek gods and by worshipping that crucified sophist himself and living under his laws.*[77] In his *Alexander* Lucian groups Christians with Epicureans as being atheists (*atheoi*) since they rejected the accepted world of religion and the worship of gods. Alexander is presented as primarily opposed to the Epicureans, and perhaps this view can be assigned to Lucian also. Yet in the *Peregrinus* (11ff.) the doctrine of Christians is termed an 'amazing wisdom' (θαυμαστὴ σοφία) which implies that Lucian saw it as a sort of curiosity.[78]

The charge of atheism occurs again and again in the pagan attacks on Christianity, and its precise meaning varies somewhat. In the *Peregrinus*, as we have seen, the charge is specified by the taunt of *denying the Greek gods* and worshipping *that crucified sophist himself*. In effect this is the onus of the charge in the early centuries. It does not denote an absolute rejection of belief in God or the gods, but a rejection, rather, of belief in the accepted gods of the state. Such a limitation in the scope of the idea goes back in fact to the trials of Anaxagoras, Protagoras, Diagoras and Socrates in the latter part of the fifth century BC. *Asebeia*, 'impiety', was the key word of the charge and it included the rejection of the gods of the state. Socrates certainly held religious beliefs, but Diagoras was a true atheist.[79] In the Roman era it was a fairly loose term of abuse,[80] which tended to ignore the Christian claim to worship the true God, not to mention the claim embedded in the Trinity. It is of interest that Justin Martyr in a refutation of the charge of atheism goes on to mention the Christian worship of the Father, Son, and Holy Spirit, though not in a set formula.[81] Otherwise the Trinity does not figure much in the debate between the opposing sides. Indeed, as the fourth century approaches one senses that the most fierce debates occur within the Christian camp, thus evoking, towards the end of the century, the comment ascribed by Ammianus Marcellinus (22. 5. 4) to Julian, that even wild beasts are less savage to men than are Christians to each other.[82]

Only fragments of the *Symmikta Zetemata* of Porphyry are extant. He was a known opponent of Christianity, but the fragments of this work relate to the views of Nemesius, bishop of Emesa, who was writing about AD 390, on the question of the two natures conjoined in Christ. The wider question of the union of body and soul was a theme which Porphyry had discussed at length with his teacher Plotinus (see *Vita Plot.* 13. 11) and

Nemesius claims that Porphyry's views confirmed his own theory that the transcendental can coexist with the earthly body, although Nemesius rejects Porphyry's belief in the *apatheia* of the soul.[83]

Porphyry's *Contra Christianos* was a large work in fifteen books, written by him in Sicily about AD 270 soon before or after the death of his teacher Plotinus. Only fragments are extant and they were edited with a masterly Commentary by Harnack in 1916.[84] It stands with the attack by Celsus as the most learned and comprehensive polemic against Christianity. About the same time, as Harnack (p.3) points out, Porphyry wrote his letter to the Egyptian priest Anebo, and he slated the religion of Egypt, at least its worship of daemons, although in a more measured manner, which indulges in questions and ironical remarks. When Christianity became Rome's official religion, Porphyry's work was proscribed, and in AD 448 the proscription was renewed (see Harnack, p.5) by Theodosius II and Valentinian III. Later on, Julian's anti-Christian work probably borrowed from Porphyry to some extent; so did Hierocles, the supporter of Diocletian's persecution in 303. Harnack gives a convenient Index in summary form to the numerous passages edited by him, and his list opens with the attack on the atheism of Christians: they are neither Greeks nor barbarians, but atheists and anarchists. Most of the lemmata relate to the New Testament, its evangelists and apostles, and also to the writers of the Old Testament. They are all denigrated for their lack of trustworthiness and objectivity, particular incidents, especially miraculous tales, being scornfully rejected. The parts dealing with belief and dogma are more relevant to our theme. Can we expect Porphyry to attack the doctrine of the Trinity? He was writing at a time when the matter was being tensely debated within the Church. In section 76 Porphyry rebuts the Christian rejection of polytheism by saying that Christians themselves accept polytheism since their lore about Angels really amounts to that. The reference is to Matthew 22: 29ff., where Jesus says that in the resurrection there will be no marrying or giving in marriage, but they will be *like the Angels in heaven*. Furthermore, says Porphyry, Holy Scripture itself assumes the existence of many gods; allusions are to Exodus 22: 28, Deuteronomy 13: 2, and 1 Corinthians 8: 5f. The last-noted locus, with its reference to the many alleged gods and lords in heaven and earth, contrasts the Father who is the *one God* of the Christian. Perhaps, in spite of the *legomenoi theoi* of this passage, one might concede a henotheistic concept here (as opposed to the monotheistic). Certainly that is true of the Old Testament allusions. In section 85 Porphyry maintains that God has no son; and in 86 he attacks the Logos-doctrine of Christianity, which of course involves the son. One would expect such remarks to lead on to a discussion of the Trinity. If the omission seems extraordinary in view of the doctrine's prominence by this time, we have to remember that the *Contra Christianos* is not extant as a complete work. The extracts collected are from other authors, so that no firm conclusion is possible about Porphyry's knowledge or ignorance of the doctrine.

Although by Julian's reign Trinitarianism was a fully endorsed and established Christian tenet, it is rather strange that it is missing, for the most part, in this emperor's works. Julian was himself close to the Neoplatonists, whose pantheon, by and large, was ordered in such a way as to elevate a supreme deity with a range of subordinate deities below him. The feature of Christian belief and ritual which especially riled Julian was the Edict of Constantius in AD 341: *Cesset superstitio, sacrificiorum aboleatur insania.*[85] A measure of tolerance was introduced by Julian,[86] and he became, in relation to the second clause of the quoted edict, a fanatical performer of massive sacrifices himself. While he 'ultimately rejected the whole of the doctrinal foundation of Christianity',[87] after being a Christian until his twentieth year, he seemed then to be in search of an explicit theological doctrine.[88] In this search he was perhaps open to Christian ideas, and among these the doctrine of the Trinity has been mentioned as a possible example.[89] In his Hymn to King Helios (Orations, IV) Julian distinguishes three manifestations of Helios as a god: (1) The Intelligible (*noêtos*) World, the One, who is identified with Plato's the Good; (2) The Intellectual (*noeros*) World; (3) The World of Sense-perception (*aisthêtos*).[90] This division, according to Edward J. Martin, is 'singularly like the Christian Trinity with the Father in Heaven, the Son, the Logos or Mediator to the Soul of man, and the Holy Spirit, the active guide in the world of sense'. Hence he finds here 'a suspicion of Christian influence on Julian's scheme, more unconscious perhaps than in the case of his church organisation, but not the less vital'. In this unconvincing suggestion Martin diverts the Christian doctrine to suit his argument. To describe the Holy Spirit as 'the active guide in the world of sense' goes beyond the accepted interpretations ('the world of the soul' would be more correct). Again, the Platonic character of the first being is plain; indeed it is expressly noted.[91] In fact Platonism and its sequel probably provides the whole of this triad, save that a mention in Julian's context of a Fifth Substance may point to Aristotle, *De caelo* (1. 3. 270b), which is also echoed by Iamblichus, the Fifth Substance being seen by Julian as a guardian of the One and as culminating in the beams of the Sun.[92]

In his tract *Against the Galileans*[93] Julian freely uses the arguments of both Celsus and Porphyry, while in his wider philosophical and religious views he is especially indebted to Iamblichus.[94] The attack on the Christians again says little of the Trinity, but derides the claimed monotheism of Christians, alleging that in fact they worship God's illegitimate son as God (159 E, p.362 Wright, *ton nothon huion*). In one place (291 A, p.402 Wright) he does, however, cite the command in Matthew 28: 19 which concerns baptism in the name of the Trinity, and therefore, according to Julian, cuts across Mosaic monotheism.

Equally noteworthy is the reluctance of Christian defenders of the faith to dilate on this doctrinal tenet. Justin Martyr, as we have seen, mentions the doctrine, and adds an emphasis on the Angels – perhaps 'in order to prove to pagans how far removed were Christians from the bald monotheism which pagans derided as atheism'.[95] Justin makes no explicit statement, though, to this effect; and the Apologists, including also Tatian, Athenagoras, and Theophilus, were 'highly confused' in their thought on this doctrine.[96] If Irenaeus was more explicitly Trinitarian, his emphasis was on God the Father as a single personage, reflecting an urge to guard the principle of monotheism.[97] Here, then, the motive of countering pagan charges is missing. In Tertullian's work, on the other hand, we see an attempt to equate the emphasis on monotheism with the idea of the monad embodied in the Roman emperor. The parallel is pursued to the point of arguing that God's essential unity is not endangered by the belief that a triple form is found within it, since the unity of the imperial government allowed the co-operation with it of a number of agencies.[98] A change of attitude on this question was perhaps bound to happen, for Augustine himself was not so sure that 'one God in heaven should be mirrored by one king on earth'.[99] In making this remark Momigliano was discussing 'the disadvantages of monotheism for a universal state', but as Erik Peterson[100] pointed out, it was the orthodox doctrine of the Trinity that especially threatened the Roman Empire's political theology. The idea that God's kingdom provided a parallel to the rule of Rome's emperor had been favoured by Origen and Eusebius; by the fourth century, however, the fierce debates which focused on the Trinity, and in particular on the status of Christ, had all but pulverized the parallel. When Diocletian established his tetrarchy in AD 293, a centrifugal trend set in, and when Constantine established his court in Constantinople in 330, the unitary potency of Rome was ended.[101] While these changes were eventually in some cases instrumental in making the emperor more accessible to Christian and other appellants, it would be rash to relate such changes too closely to theological ideas. It might, of course, be argued that a politico-religious parallel of a kind persisted when God the Father was seen to share his sovereignty with the two other members of the Trinity, just as the imperial sovereignty of the emperor was to some extent decentralized. But I am not aware that this parallel featured in the theological discussions about the Trinity.

The Christian missionary motive, with its doctrinal implications, should be linked rather to the geographical and ethnic character of the communities which were first approached. It is clear that in many ways the pattern of early activity followed the lines revealed in the New Testament concerning the missionary work of Paul and the other apostles. The synagogues of the Diaspora were the first important targets, and only afterwards was contact usually essayed with the surrounding Gentile peoples. One result of the initial thrust was an eagerness to deploy the narratives of the Old Testament, often with allegorical interpretations, thus finding in the Scriptures prefigurations of Christian doctrine and Church history.[102] Abraham's three visitors, as we have noted above (ch. 11, section 2), were seen as prefiguring the Trinity. It has been rightly maintained,[103] of the early Christian mission, that it 'entered the Hellenistic world from the background of the Diaspora synagogue'; also that 'it was only because the Diaspora synagogues were spread like a thick net over the entire area of the Mediterranean that Christianity could expand over the whole *oikumene* within one generation'.

The general attitude of missionary activity was clearly conditioned by these facts. As presented by the Synoptic Evangelists, Jesus himself came not to destroy, but to fulfil, and there are suggestions that he was regarded as a new Moses.[104] Paul was also full of respect for the Hebraic faith, even if his conviction that Jesus was in some ways to replace the Torah was bound to provoke opposition. Furthermore, the first Christians in the early Church were themselves Jews, and when the time came to define their Christology more sharply, they felt impelled to preserve the basic monotheism of their inherited faith. In this they faced a certain tension because of some pluralistic trends of that faith. At the same time the non-Jewish sector of their contemporary world was steeped in polytheistic and triadic traditions; and Arnold Toynbee has ascribed a conscious motivation to Christians in the sense of an appeal to this religious milieu:[105]

> Christianity made Jewish monotheism acceptable to Greek and Roman polytheists, who were already feeling their way doubtfully towards monotheism, by diluting this with a tincture of polytheism in the doctrine of the Trinity, with a tincture of Graeco-Roman man-worship in the deification of Jesus; and, no doubt, this was one of the causes of Christianity's sensational success in converting the great non-Jewish majority of the population of the Roman Empire.

Toynbee here is dealing with broad generalities, and his method is rather facile. To say that Greek and Roman polytheists were then 'feeling their way doubtfully towards monotheism' can be misleading unless specific schools of thought are referred to. For instance, the constant emphasis of Stoic writers was to seek to reconcile a belief in the gods with a basic monotheism. At the same time there were Epicureans, Sceptics and atheists whose attitude to religion was hostile. Plutarch was a fairly representative Greek thinker in the second century and he explicitly declared his belief that there was *one reason* and *one providence* behind the variety of beings worshipped as gods.[106] In another place[107] Toynbee sees a Christian assimilation to the cults of Cybele, Isis, and Jupiter Dolichenus; and here he does venture into some detail. Referring to the competing missionary religions, he says that 'Christianity has incorporated in itself some of their constituent elements such as the Isiac and Cybelene forms of the worship of the Great Mother and the Mithraic and Dolichenian ideal of the Church Militant'. The latter ideal was shared also by the Isis cult, as is shown by the emphasis on the *sancta militia* in Apuleius, *Metam.* 15 (ad fin.) and my remarks ad loc. (p.354f.).

Still, Toynbee's broad-brush approach is more acceptable than that of Jacquetta Hawkes, who dismisses trinitarian ideas scornfully in a discussion of Cretan religion. She is trying to answer the question whether the divinity of the Cretans was one goddess or many. 'It is puzzling', she says, 'that people who can understand a monotheistic religion in which the divinity may be represented as a young man, an old man and a dove, and in which this three-in-one enjoys an obscure and changing relationship with a woman who is both mother and virgin, should expect a precise intellectual answer to this question.'[108] Admittedly, these remarks occur in a popularizing work which indulges in a flashy and slap-happy style.

The mission motive was not, of course, limited to Jews and Christians, although their proselytizing energies were often resented. Opposing ideas clashed too within the Church itself, and it seems that Paul's opponents in Corinth were (in his First Letter) Christian Gnostics and (in his Second Letter) Hellenistic Jewish Christians.[109] Other religious cults were also often propagandist in tone. Pilgrimages, pageants and parades were the stock-in-trade of their appeal, with music, colourful garments, images and dance enhancing the exciting allure.[110] Polytheism featured attractively too and was often shorn of any exclusivist aspect. Christianity lacked this type of appeal. In its monotheistic form it seemed bizarre, for the One God was invisible and without an image. Moreover, its apologetic writings could be read by only a minority,[111] and were perhaps intended mainly for internal consumption.

Firm evidence seems to be lacking for the provision of a Trinitarian emphasis in order to meet the pressure of a polytheistic milieu. The pressure was itself an indirect force, but it must have been there. We may compare the idea propagated in recent years within the Roman Catholic Church and introduced to it by the Jesuits: it is called 'inculturation' and has been defined as 'the creative and dynamic relationship between the Christian message and a culture or cultures'; the same author[112] remarks that 'the Christian Faith cannot exist except in a cultural form'. To honour that principle actively in current missionary practice is plainly a wise policy, and its first classic example was the address delivered to the Athenians by Paul, as recorded (doubtless very loosely) by the author of the Acts. It is, and was, a policy which in its very nature implies a two-way intellectual traffic, for the Christian propagandist both offers and receives a distinctive cultural and spiritual message. It is fairly clear that a similar idea, without any formal definitions or plans, impelled the religious adherents of the early centuries to offer in the open marketplace of cult and creeds whatever salvation they believed in. On the popular and public stage Christianity could not display very much save in times of persecution, when the courage to face death in terrible ways proclaimed the most impressive witness to their faith. Only a minority, as we noted, could appreciate the defence of this faith in literary media, but the sporadic persecutions could evoke both a grudging admiration and a searing hatred,[113] the latter reaction being a type of behaviourism, since killers become haters of their victims. The literary debate, as we have seen, was not much concerned with the Trinity except when certain interpretations of the Old Testament were at issue. An example of this in the inner-Christian debate concerned the exegesis of the Seraphim in Isaiah 6: 2, where three sets of wings are assigned to each. The number of the Seraphim was questioned by Jerome after Origen had suggested that they were two. The Alexandrian theologians were particularly engrossed with Isaiah's chapter 6, the Seraphic triple cry of *Holy* being related to the Trinity by Athanasius and by Didymus of Alexandria.[114]

In Alexandria we would expect the motivation of an appeal to the *literati* among the Greeks. Certainly those who followed the Platonic tradition would be familiar with triadic structures, albeit in rather abstract formulations. The Alexandrian Jews were a more firmly defined group, and to them the importance of Philo was undoubtedly a factor; he was himself very ready to deploy Middle Platonism in his exegesis of parts of the Old Testament, which included an emphasis on the pluralism of *Let us make* ... in Genesis 1: 26, thus enabling him to see God as creator being aided by His two subordinates Logos and Sophia. Yet in his *On the Creation*, 170-1 (Loeb, Vol.I, 1929, 134) he stresses that *God is one* (ὅτι θεὸς εἷς ἐστι).[115] Both Clement of Alexandria and Origen were steeped in Greek philosophical ideas, and it is possible that, like Christian theologians after them, they regarded, as part of the missionary requirements of their task, a presentation of the faith which would attract the interest of the Middle Platonists.[116] The doctrine of the divine Trinity would not seem utterly alien, certainly, to believers in the Platonic tradition. The Neoplatonist Porphyry included in his thought the triad of the One, Mind, and Soul, and also that of Being, Life, and Intelligence. Whether these thought-structures should be described as 'trinities'[117] is, however, questionable. The triune concept does not seem to characterize their inner relationships. Nor is it present in the triadic systems of Philo, whose creed has been described as a 'fundamentally strict monotheism'.[118] As for Arius, in spite of the fury of the later debate, he began with an affirmation (with Euzoïus) that the Trinitarian faith rests on Scripture, in particular on the dominican command concerning baptism in Matthew 28: 19; and Rowan Williams portrays him as 'a theological conservative'.[119]

5. Alexandrian Christians and Egyptian Religion

The possible influence of Egypt on early theological developments is to some extent linked to the evolution of Gnosticism. In the second century Valentinus made a profound impact. He was a native of Egypt although he lived for some time in Rome and perhaps in Cyprus. Another significant figure was Basilides, who taught at Alexandria in the middle of the second century. Both these theologians are now classified as Gnostics, but they exemplify the possible early influence of Egyptian religion in Alexandria.[120] Basilides took the view that all suffering is a just punishment for sin, adding that it may be punishment for sin committed in an earlier life.[121] Punishment to the third and fourth generation, as stated in the Old Testament, is invoked, but in accordance with the belief in metempsychosis, which is here of Pythagorean rather than Egyptian origin. An Egyptian connection clearly emerges, however, in the custom followed by the Basilidians in celebrating the feast of the Baptism of Christ; they conducted a nocturnal rite preceding the day itself. This was observed on 6 and 10 January in accordance with the ancient feast of Osiris when holy water was drawn by all from the Nile during the night.[122] This may correspond to the ceremony described by Plutarch in chapter 39 of his *De Iside et Osiride*.[123]

More important figures for the evolution of Christian doctrine were Clement of Alexandria and Origen, both wide open not only to classical culture but also to that of Egypt. It is remarkable how the impact of the latter has been virtually ignored by historians of Christian dogmatics. This is true of the fine study by Jean Daniélou which explicitly addresses 'Hellenistic Culture',[124] where the term is related mainly to Greek philosophy save for the inclusion of Old Testament and Gnostic concerns. It is also avowedly true of Henry Chadwick's *Early Christian Thought and the Classical Tradition* (1966; repr. 1990), which treats principally of Justin, Clement, and Origen. It is also true of the admirable standard work, *Early Christian Doctrines,* by J. D. N. Kelly, to which the present study is heavily indebted. What is more surprising is that Siegfried Morenz, although pleading the cause of Egyptian influence, has little to say about the abundant evidence that connects both Clement and Origen with this cultural area. Admittedly, he places them prominently in the line of the Alexandrian heritage.

We have seen above (ch.12, section 3 (ii)) that Clement's contribution to Trinitarianism was slight and that it included an emphasis on the bond between the Father and the Son. In one place (*Strom.* V. 14, p.116, 1) he invokes Homer as a revered source who also groups Father and Son.[125] Another feature of his view of the Trinity is its apparent subordinationism: the Son is subordinate to the Father and the Spirit to the Son. Kelly[126] seeks to defend this feature by maintaining that 'it implies no inequality of being, but is the corollary of his Platonic conception of a graded hierarchy'. In spite of such explicit allusions to Greek literature (he also invokes Euripides for a similar grouping), the question arises whether Clement was also influenced by his knowledge of actual religious dyads or triads. Greek religion provided a Father and Son in Uranus and Cronus as well as in Cronus and Zeus – both ill-fated relationships. An outstanding Egyptian group was seen in Osiris and Horus, often within the triad which included the mother Isis. The extent of Clement's interest in the Egyptian pantheon is shown by Hopfner's valued collection of allusions by Greek and Latin authors.[127] Here the allusions made by Clement take up nearly eight pages of the text (pp.365-73) and they betray a lively interest. He cites Aristotle on Apollo[128] as the son of Hephaestus and Athena, with the addition of other genealogies which end with Libys as the son of Ammon; they are all triadic family groups. Clement shows a particular interest in the Egyptian god Apis and the connection between him and Sarapis. He cites[129] Leo Pellaeus, a writer of the fourth century BC and his book *Concerning the Gods of Egypt*. His citations of earlier authors are of course a marked feature of his writing, although we may agree that 'Clement never loses his Christianity in a sea of Hellenism';[130] nor indeed of Egyptianism. His sea of Hellenism does, however, contain many fish of Egyptian and other non-Greek genera. On the god Apis he is anxious to tell us[131] that the divine bull after death and embalmment was placed in a coffin (*soros*) and because of this was called Soroapis. The first element in Sarapis was probably *Osir-,* and Clement[132] ascribes the form Osirapis as the origin to Athenodorus of Tarsus, a Stoic friend of Cicero.

Clement's general attitude to Egyptian religion is naturally not favourable. He remarks[133] that the error of idolatry is ancient, while the truth is new; here he proceeds to refer to claims of high antiquity made by the Phrygians, the Arcadians and the Egyptians. The facile deification of Alexander as the son of Ammon[134] evokes a light tone, as with several Greek writers; and the Egyptian animal cults are likewise tilted at. A more sympathetic approach is found[135] in Clement's splendidly detailed account of an Egyptian religious procession; it deals though, more with the priestly participants than with the deities honoured. In his *Protrepticus* Clement makes a scathingly elaborate attack on Greek mythology and religion, especially on the Eleusinian Mysteries, claiming that their ritual core was concerned with sexual symbols. His allusions to Egyptian rites are much more temperate, as when he refers (2. 21f.) to the illogical nature of their lamentations for the gods, or again (4. 43) to the funeral rites of Osiris and Apis. We must remember, at the same time, that this work is specifically addressed to the Greeks; it is an *Exhortation to the Greeks,* so that the contrast loses force.

Origen's contribution to Christian doctrine is of greater import, and his interest in Egyptian religion is reflected in Hopfner's *Fontes,* pp.352-4 (Celsus), 386 (Numenius), and 437-41. Many allusions occur in his *Contra Celsum,* a work which has been translated and annotated by Henry Chadwick (Cambridge, 1953; repr. with corrections, 1980) and later by Marcel Borret in five volumes (Paris, 1967-76), the last of which contains a General Introduction and a detailed Index.[136] Origen's basic presentation of Egypt's religious practices is one which to some extent follows the account given by Herodotus in his second book:

> Αἰθιόπων μὲν οἱ Μερόην οἰκοῦντες Δία καὶ Διόνυσον μόνους σέβουσιν, Ἀράβιοι δὲ τὴν Οὐρανίαν καὶ Διόνυσον τούτους μόνους, Αἰγύπτιοι δὲ πάντες μὲν Ὄσιρίν τε καὶ Ἶσιν, Σαῖται δὲ Ἀθηναν, Ναυκρατῖται δὲ οὐ πάλαι ἀρξάμενοι ὠνόμασαν Σάραπιν καὶ οἱ λοιποὶ κατὰ νομοὺς ὡς ἕκαστοι.[137]
>
> (Origen, *C.Cels.* V. 34, Borret p.102 (= Hopfner, *Fontes,* 353))
>
> (The Ethiopians who inhabit Meroë worship only Zeus and Dionysus, the Arabs Urania and Dionysus and these only. All the Egyptians worship Osiris and Isis, while the Saïtes worship Athena, and the Naucratites, though not since so long, have invoked Sarapis; the others differ in the different regions.)

The primacy throughout Egypt ascribed to Osiris and Isis is noteworthy. After the above remarks Origen refers to the various abstentions from animal food which also differ in different localities; these details are likewise the staple material of previous Greek and Latin descriptions of Egypt. In one passage (*C. Cels.* V. 41) Origen assigns to Celsus a statement which bears a remarkably universalist tone; and a similar passage occurs later (V. 45). I have discussed these passages in section 4 of this chapter (above). Marcel Borret (Vol.I, p.135 n.3) remarks on the reminiscence of Plato in the idea that the many gods bear names of what is really one God. In his reply Origen defended the distinctive force of some of these names, particularly in those of Hebrew origin.

In his *Contra Celsum* (v. 37-8 (= Chadwick, pp.294f.)) Origen has more to say about Osiris and Isis: he denies their divinity and rejects the view of the people of Saïs that Athena (perhaps for Neïth) should be connected with them. He refers also to the religious view of the people of Naucratis; in earlier times, he notes, they worshipped other gods, but recently have taken to worship Sarapis, *a new god,* whose existence must be rejected. He remarks too that he has read about the formation of Sarapis in Numenius the Pythagorean. His familiarity with the myths and interpretations relating to Osiris and Isis is shown by his allusion to the allegorical explanation (a method espoused by Origen himself) of Osiris as water and Isis as earth; cf. Plutarch, *De Is. et Os.* 32, 363 D and my Comm. 420f.; and F. Zimmermann, *Die ägyptische Religion nach der Darstellung der Kirchenschriftsteller und die ägyptischen Denkmäler* (Paderborn, 1912), 43 and 49, the latter locus with sceptical comments on the attribution to Isis (by Christian writers) of the powers of fertility and chastity.

6. The Triune Emphasis in the Graeco-Egyptian Milieu

At this point it would be well to look in closer detail, especially from the standpoint of the Hellenistic and Roman eras, at the possibility of Egyptian influence and its distinctive character. Aspects of the triadic doctrines of the New Kingdom were discussed in chapter 4, sections 3 and 4, with reference to the Theban state triad; again in chapter 8, sections 3 and 5, Greek triadic forms were assessed in relation to the idea of the unity of three gods. Greek ideology was plainly important in the work of the Alexandrian theologians; at the same time their familiarity with the Egyptian pantheon has been exemplified. Moreover, my 'Conspectus' of Egyptian triadic occurrences in chapter 4, appendix, shows that from the New Kingdom onwards the divine triad achieved massive poplurarity. No one who lived in Egypt during the Hellenistic and Roman eras could possibly have avoided noticing this religious phenomenon.

Towards the end of the nineteenth century the French Egyptologist Émile Amélineau stood out as an exponent of the importance of Egyptian religion. In a volume[138] devoted to the evaluation of moral ideas in Ancient Egypt, he deals with the ordering of the pantheon, pointing to the early importance of the Ennead, but maintaining that the Ennead was eventually dethroned and replaced by the Triad; and he sees the Triad as always consisting of Father, Mother, and Child.[139] 'Toujours' here is an overstatement; we have seen that the triads of Mycerinus (ch.1, section 4), conceptual triads (ch.2, section 4), a triad of God, King, and Queen (ch.3, section 1), and triads of one sex (ch.4, section 2), were all deviations from the family group. He then refers to this concept as 'cette idée qui présage la Trinité chrétienne et qui serait même tout à fait semblable'. Here his use of the word 'présage' is commendably cautious; but the suggested similarity is of course impaired by the presence of the Holy Spirit instead of the Mother, and this is why, perhaps, he goes on to remark on the fact that in Hebrew the word for the Spirit is feminine, rendered by the Greek translators as *pneuma*. In fact, the idea of a female Holy Spirit was developed in Christian Gnostic thought, as we saw in section 3 of the present chapter.

After Amélineau the conviction of a bond between Egyptian triads and Christian Trinity seems to have waned for some time. W. Max Müller[140] posited the triad as a primal form, averring that 'the development of the ennead (perhaps a triple triad in source) is obviously much later' – a dictum that is doubly misleading since the Heliopolitan Ennead is found in the Pyramid Texts, unlike any triadic group (although a triadic schema sometimes emerges) and since this Ennead is essentially a grouping of four marital pairs headed by Atum:

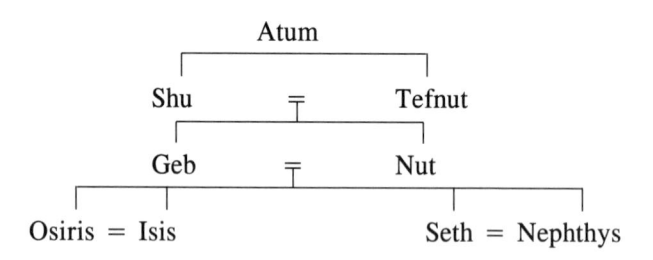

```
                    Atum
           ┌──────────┴──────────┐
         Shu         =         Tefnut
           ┌──────────┴──────────┐
         Geb         =          Nut
     ┌─────┴─────┐         ┌─────┴─────┐
  Osiris  =  Isis         Seth  =  Nephthys
```

See *Pyr.* 1655 a–b, referring to *the Great Ennead of Gods which is in Heliopolis*. The relationship of these deities is provided by other allusions.[141] We have seen that one early text groups Atum and his two offspring as the One who became Three, but the continued marital couplings are not presented triadically in relation to their parentage.

In an impressively original study published in 1939 Helmuth Jacobsohn sought to establish the existence of a trinitarian doctrine under the Pharaohs of the New Kingdom, the theologians of that era having developed it, he claimed, *ad maiorem gloriam* of the kings whom they served.[142] The theory is much concerned with the title *Ka Mut-ef*, 'Bull of His Mother', which was applied to the gods Amûn and Min and also to Horus and Min-Amûn, often with a sexual meaning.[143] The clear intent of the phrase is to indicate the self-procreation of the god and the idea that no god existed before him.[144] Jacobsohn argues that *Ka Mut-ef* points to both the power of the *ka* and the fecundity of the bull, and accordingly represents divine procreative power. As a result he sees a trinity at work, that of 'Gott-König-Ka', in the sense that God the father, the King as his son, and the *ka* as the creative link between father and son, form a unity.[145] Further, he sees the figure of the father as including the royal ancestors. The close grouping of father and son in such contexts had long since been perceived by Emmanuel de Rougé,[146] and it finds a parallel in the binitarianism of the New Testament. If Jacobsohn sees a trinity in the New-Kingdom material, it should be stressed that it is a purely subjective postulate. He does not quote a text which portrays the group thus – not even as a constantly evoked triad, leave alone a trinity.[147] The latter term may be conceded in a context where the three powers are envisaged as unified – envisaged, that is, by the author.[148]

In his final section Jacobsohn maintains that historical religious links run from the 'trinitarian' creator-god of the ancient Egyptians over the Graeco-Egyptian mysticism which he sees in both Philo and Plutarch up to the divine Trinity of the New Testament. Like Morenz after him, however, he underlines the fact (p.64) that he is dealing not with the essence of the Christian revelation, but with the origin of the forms. Even so, a parallelism between the Holy Spirit and the *ka* of *Ka Mut-ef* is a difficult equation, although they both represent a divine creative force. In fact Jacobsohn is dealing mainly with the Egyptian doctrine of divine procreation and incarnation, and the best exposition is now that of Hellmut Brunner.[149]

Whereas studies of Egyptian religion had given some attention to the evolution of the divine triad, and particularly to the prominence of the Theban triad in the New Kingdom with its doctrine of a unity of three gods,[150] it was Siegfried Morenz who revived with a degree of elaboration the idea that Egyptian triadism had some influence on Christian thought. He went further than this, for he maintained that the concept of three-in-one and one-in-three, as seen in the Trinity, was specifically of Egyptian origin. Gardiner[151] had described the Theban grouping of Amûn, Rê and Ptah with the words 'trinity as a unity' – a slightly tautologous phrase if we consider the eventual meaning of 'trinity' (see *Shorter OED* s.v. 3; and Introduction above, init.). Similar was the view of Jan Zandee, who edited the relevant hymns from a papyrus now in Leiden;[152] but he was wary of suggesting any connection with the Christian Trinity.

Morenz first gave detailed attention to this theme in a lecture presented in 1956 to the Leipzig Academy on 'Egyptian Trinities. Their Presuppositions and Continued Influence'.[153] After commenting on the widespread occurrence of triads everywhere, he points to the extreme rarity of trinitarian formulations. Egyptian theologians, however, are claimed to have expressed the idea in their earliest religious literature and to have continued to do so up to the Roman imperial era (now also through the medium of Greek). The following subdivisions of the material are suggested by him:

(1) Representative trinities, with three as a representation of plurality.
(2) Trinities of being, with a unity of the primal god and the first created pair.
(3) Trinities with a threefold division and with a reunification of a divine being.
(4) Trinities with an equation of gods, that is, with a simultaneous identification of three gods with the purpose of heightening their power.
(5) Eventually appears a trinity of generations.

While the precise meaning of (5) is not explained, it is maintained that with the exception of (2), which is confined to one trinitarian expression, the groups reveal themselves as particular examples of a general tendency of Egyptian theologians, whose basic problem was to reconcile the pluralism and monism of their historically formed pantheon (nos.1 and 4) and to whom also the phenomenon of splitting a god's being was not unfamiliar (no.3). The inner threefold divisions of trinities and their numerically important character are seen as typical expressions of Egyptian religious thought.

Morenz found nothing like this in the ancient countries of the Eastern Mediterranean; neither Mesopotamia nor Syria offered a parallel. Nothing similar, he adds, was to be expected from Israel and Judaism, nor from the Greeks before the Hellenistic era and late antiquity, when philosophy was secularized and taken from the service of religion. Accordingly, he urges, inquiries concerning the elements of the Christian Trinity must be directed to Egypt. While the substance of the doctrine is biblical, the whole idea of trinity as a feature of structural religious thought is not so. Furthermore, historical reasons, it is urged, favour Egypt's impact, in particular the vitality of Egyptian theology in the imperial era and the significance of Alexandria for early Christian theology.

These views were developed by Morenz in his *Ägyptische Religion* (1960),[154] which appeared later in French and English translations. In other works he gave little attention to the theme.[155] There are patent weaknesses in his exposition, and it would be invidious to enlarge on them, particularly as the present study, while attempting to fill in the huge gaps left by him, was yet stimulated by his work. One of the gaps, certainly, was his failure to note the way in which previous Egyptologists, especially Amélineau, had espoused the basic idea of Egypt's influence on Christian Trinitarianism. On the early developments in Egypt Morenz is very brief and selective. He refers (*Religion*, 153) to the locus in *Coffin Texts*, II, 39 b–e, where it is said of Atum, *when he was One and became Three*.[156] In his Academy lecture at Leipzig Morenz rightly demarks that locus as being a merely incidental expression of trinitarianism; the group there mentioned did not become a standard or typical triad. Morenz ignored the other triadic manifestations produced in the Old Kingdom, including groups in statuary and the triads of Mycerinus, as well as the prehistoric evidence. For these see my chapter 1. At the same time my conclusion stands that it was not until the New Kingdom that the triad achieved extensive popularity in Egypt. That it was also sometimes imbued with the triune concept cannot well be controverted. It was true of the Theban state triads, as we have seen, and Morenz correctly describes its character as tritheistic rather than modalistic, although the two ideas seem to coexist. Tritheism is evident when a man is said to be high-priest of the three gods Rê, Ptah, and Amûn at Thebes, the three titles being mentioned separately;[157] but a modalistic form appears when Amûn is said to be Rê in his countenance and Ptah in his body.

While the family triad, popular especially with Osirian groups, was a favourite in Egypt, several triads were not of this type, particularly triads of one sex (see ch.4, section 2 above). The all-male triad at Memphis, Ptah–Sokar–Osiris, is an example of this, the group being often treated as a singular. What is implied in this usage is a syncretistic unity rather than a group of still separate gods: see Jean Leclant, *Recherches sur les monuments thébains de la XXVe dynastie dite éthiopienne,* 269 n.4. In this dynasty Ptah-Sokar-Osiris is called 'Lord of the Secret Sanctuary' (*nb štyt*), and Leclant[158] refers to him as 'le dieu composite'. Other groupings in vogue at that time (*c.* 690 BC) were Amen-Rê-Month, Amen-Rê-Harakhty, Amen-Rê-Atum, Rê-Harakhty-Osiris, and even Rê-Harakhty-Atum – Osiris.[159] While the last-named breaks with the triadic pattern, the others form a composite unity and as such are rather different from the Trinity; yet they are clearly on the high road to trinitarianism.

The curt dismissal by Morenz of the influence of Greek philosophy may be partly due to its very brevity. In the summary of his Leipzig lecture he refers to the secularization of Greek philosophy in the Hellenistic era and later and to its removal from the service of religious belief. A similar dictum appears in his *Religion* 271 (= tr. 256, but wrongly rendered): in Greece theology was totally sterilized in the sixth century through the departure of philosophy from the religious sphere. He is clearly thinking of the lack of systematic thought thereafter in relation to the deities of the Greek pantheon. Yet the suggestion that Greek philosophy was consequently bereft of any religious interest or significance is quite unacceptable. Plato's work was profoundly religious in its basic perceptions, and what is crucially relevant to our theme is that the formative era of Christian Trinitarian thought was one in which Middle Platonism and Neoplatonism exerted demonstrable influence on the language and ideology of Christian theologians. In particular, the triadic systems of these movements predisposed the Alexandrian theologians to adopt similar religious structures. In this connection Morenz (*Religion*, 271 (= tr. 256)) rightly recognizes the importance of Philo, citing his exegesis of the three visitors at Mamre (Gen. 18: 2): *one can be three and three can be one, because by a higher principle they are one* (Philo, *Quaest. in Genesim*, 4. 2); see also my remarks in chapter 11, section 2, and David Winston, *Philo of Alexandria* (London, 1981), 90.

In his final presentation Morenz wisely concentrates on the evidence of later origin. Impressive as is the tri-unity of the Theban Hymn to Amûn, it dates after all to an era well over a thousand years before the early Christian centuries, and with the eclipse of Thebes as a capital city its continued impact had long ceased. It is true that the many triads of the Book of the Dead, especially the Osirian groups, remained familiar in the Ptolemaic era and in the Roman era in reduced measure. But they do not normally show the triune concept. Among the later attestations, including those cited by Morenz and others, are the following:

(1) The Demotic Chronicle, third century BC:
'Apis, Apis, Apis': that means, Ptah, Prê, Harsiesis, who are the lords of the office of sovereign ... The three gods denote Apis. Apis is Ptah, Apis is Prê, Apis is Harsiesis.

> (Spiegelberg, *Die sogenannte Demotische Chronik*, Leipzig, 1914, V, 12–13, p.20. Cf. Morenz, *Rel.* 151 = tr. 143; and above ch.4, section 4.)

Apis is identified with three other gods, two of whom are of great import (Ptah and Rê). There are loud tones of theological supremacy (for Apis). A unity of three-in-one is thus proclaimed, but the One (Apis) yet stands outside the triad.

(2) Temple of Opet, Karnak, third century BC:
Thoth is described as *the heart of Rê, the tongue of Ta-Tenen, the throat of Hidden-of-name*.

> (C. de Wit, *Les Inscriptions du temple d'Opet à Karnak*, Brussels, 1958, 119 and 167; and his Comm., ibid. III, 1968, 133 n.262. Cf. Morenz, *Rel.* 152 = tr. 144; and above ch.4, Appendix, s.v. Karnak, 5)

As in (1), the lauded god is outside the triad.

(3) Gate of Euergetes, Karnak, third century BC:

THE LIKELY SOURCES 257

The features and names of (2) are assigned to the god Khons.

(Urk. VIII, 47, 58b. Cf. C. de Wit, Comm. ibid.; *ZÄS* 100 (1973), 31)

The heart of Rê denotes his intelligence, aptly applied to Thoth, but not to Khons. Triple divine attributes are united in the god first named, but again he is outside the triad.

(4) Martial, *Epigr.* 5. 24. 15,[160] *c.* AD 98:
Hermes omnia solus et ter unus.

Hermes who is alone all things and three times one.

(Usener, *Dreiheit* (1903; repr. 1966), 36; Reitzenstein, *Mysterienreligionen* (3rd edn., 1927), 27f., comparing *Isis, quae es omnia;* H. S. Versnel, *Ter Unus* (1990), 206ff.; and above, ch.8, section 5; also below section 7)

(5) Dedication in Egyptian quarry of Mons Claudianus in the Eastern Desert, in NE of Qena, AD 117:
Διὶ Ἡλίῳ μεγάλῳ Σαράπιδι

To Zeus Helius the great Sarapis.

(*OGIS* 678; L. Vidman, *Isis und Sarapis bei den Griechen und Römern* (1970), 116, with other examples)

(6) Dedicatory inscription of a temple in Luxor, 24 January AD 126. Similar to (5)

(Vidman, ibid. with n.47, citing Leclant, *Orientalia* 20 (1951), 456. The date was the birthday of Hadrian.)

It is significant that these triadic groups are first attested in Egypt. However, the group is sometimes found as two, sometimes four. Cf. *Iovi Serapi* at Ostia, AD 127, Vidman, *SIRIS,* 553; M. F. Squarciapino, *I culti orientali ad Ostia* (Leiden, 1962), 21; M. Malaise, *Inventaire* (Leiden, 1972), 71, Ostia 16. The theme of syncretistic unity in various conjoined forms, whether dyadic, triadic or tetradic, is clearly present.

(7) First–second century AD.

εἷς βαΐτ, εἷς Ἀθώρ, μία τῶν βία, εἷς δὲ Ἄκωρι.
χαῖρε πάτερ κόσμου. χαῖρε τρίμορφε θεός.

One is Baït, one is Hathor, one is Akori, one is their power; be greeted by me, father of the world, be greeted by me, God in three forms.

(Kaibel, *Epigr. Gr.* (1878), 1139. 'Amuletum Aegyptium'. For references see above chapter 8, section 5. Add Versnel, *Ter Unus* (1990), 236f. and below section 7)

(8) Tertullian, *De Pallio,* 4. 3, *c.* AD 210:
Ubi Geryon ter unus?

Where is Geryon, the three-times one?

Tertullian is consciously echoing Martial's very rare phrase in no.4 above and dismissing the claims of the three-headed monster Geryon. Neither author is presenting an analogue to the Christian idea of Trinity, but each mirrors the current interest in trinitarian thought. Cf. Versnel, *Ter Unus,* 247, although he differs on the latter point; and above ch.8, section 5 (ad fin.).

(9) Mithraeum in a room of the Baths of Caracalla in Rome, after AD 212:
Εἷς Ζεὺς Σάραπις Ἥλιος κοσμοκράτωρ ἀνείκητος.

One is Zeus Sarapis Helius, ruler of the world, invincible.

Later, probably after the death of Caracalla in AD 217, *Sarapis* was replaced by *Mitras*.

Vidman, *SIRIS,* 389 and *Isis und Sarapis* (1970), 147. Cf. Otto Weinreich, *Neue Urkunden zur Sarapis-Religion* (1919), 17ff.; A. D. Nock, *Conversion* (1933), 134; Morenz, *Rel.* (1960), 270 = tr. 254f.; M. J. Vermaseren, *Mithras, the Secret God* (1963), 49; M. Malaise, *Inventaire* (1972), Rome 108, pp.143–4, and *Conditions,* (1972) 442.

(10) Julian, *Or.* IV, p.175, 23 Hertlein, fourth century AD (= W. Cave Wright (Loeb, 1913; repr. 1980), III, 368f.)

εἷς Ζεύς, εἷς Ἀίδης, εἷς Ἥλιός ἐστι Σάραπις

One is Zeus, one is Hades, one is Helius Sarapis.

Wright renders: (For this god (Apollo) declares), 'Zeus, Hades, Helios Serapis, three gods in one godhead!'

See Erik Peterson, *EIS THEOS* (1926), 241. For Julian's attack on the Christian Trinity as a denial of Mosaic monotheism see above, ch.13, section 4.

It should be pointed out that while the material selected above includes in each case an Egyptian element, the examples are typical and representative and could be augmented. On the other hand, the henotheistic formulae beginning with εἷς, as Peterson showed, run into hundreds of instances and are by no means confined to triadic groups or to an Egyptian background. The henotheistic formulae in Greek reflected an emphasis which had been strengthened within the Greek tradition, but Weinreich in his *Neue Urkunden* (1919), 28, after citing the Orphic verses in which Zeus, Hades, Helius, and Dionysus are lauded as one (a tetrad, be it noted (see Kern, 239 b), with εἷς before each name), went on to underline the significance of the fact that in Egypt such formulae were used to designate trinities, as in no.7 above.

Rather different from the use of εἷς in these locutions is that of εἷς καὶ μόνος or εἷς μόνος or ἓν καὶ μόνον referring to a divinity. Here the intention is not to indicate unity with other deities but a quite contrary emphasis: the unique and supreme status of the god named. In the fourth volume of his *La Révélation d'Hermès Trismégiste* (2nd edn., Paris, 1954) A. J. Festugière devotes his second chapter to 'L'un transcendant aux nombres' (pp.18ff.), beginning with the arithmological speculations in Hermetism and with the 'one and only' formula. He refers to the Corpus Hermeticum 1.4 (p.49, 4, ed. Nock and Festugière), where the Demiurge is said to have created everything, being the *one and only*. In his note ad loc. Festugière cites other occurrences of the phrase and regards the meaning as pointing to the uniqueness and solitude of the creator-god; in the much fuller discussion previously cited he proceeds to treat of Philo's related ideas and the Pythagorean speculations of his time. The idea of a creator-god who produces everything on his own is conspicuous in Egypt, for Atum procreates without a consort; a parallel concept is the existence, in the beginning, of an androgynous creator. In spite of this evidence Festugière insists that the idea of the 'one and only', as found in the Greek material analysed by him, is Pythagorean in origin; he rejects likewise all suggestions of oriental influence on Stoicism.

Iamblichus, *De Mysteriis* (8. 3; Des Places, p.197) is quoted (p.39) on the precedence of the One over a plurality of deities, with a clear reference to the Ogdoad of Hermopolis, but Festugière says that Iamblichus refers to the Egyptians, 'mais reproduit en fait la doctrine pythagoricienne de Modêratus'. He thus fails to locate the origin in Egypt, where the tradition is early. Rather strangely, Versnel in *Ter Unus* (1990), 243 n.180, interprets Festugière as arguing, apropos of εἷς καὶ μόνος, 'for an Egyptian origin'.

Of interest here is that Morenz has adduced a precise parallel in Egyptian usage. He refers (*Rel.* 259f. = Tr. 254f.) to the amulet with *One is Baït ...* (= no.7 above) and compares early Christian formulations such as *for us there is one God, the Father ... and one Lord, Jesus Christ ...* (1 Cor. 8: 6) and *there is one God, and there is one mediator between God and men, the man Christ Jesus* (1 Tim. 2: 5). Morenz then urges that whereas the amulet with *One is Baït ...* presents a similar idea in an Egyptian–Hellenistic form, it really reverts in origin to the early Egyptian theology (as early as the Eighteenth Dynasty) which asserts that *One is Amûn etc.*, as in the Leiden Hymn to Amûn, where the word w^c is used. It should be added that the Egyptian temple texts of the Graeco-Roman era often express the idea of divine uniqueness with various other expressions such as *there exists not his like* or *there is no other of his kind;* see Eberhard Otto, *Gott und Mensch* (1964), 11–14, where it is properly noted that it would be wrong to attach any monotheistic tendency to such expressions. They are used of the King as well, and also of buildings. Otto shows that they derive from the biographical literature of the Middle Kingdom and are in line with the strongly anthropomorphical picture of the gods that emerges, save that omnipotence and omniscience are often assigned to them. Indeed the very multiplicity of the gods named with the formula results in an obvious enfeebling, if not demolition, of the idea of uniqueness. The same clearly applies to the 'one and only' formula in Greek; but when εἷς alone occurs with the names of several deities, then a different nuance impinges – that of their unified relationship. And when the group is three in number, that means that a trinity is present.

Twenty years later, but with no reference to the work of Morenz, Jean-Pierre Ponsing has repeated some of his arguments in an article entitled 'L'Origine égyptienne de la formule: Un-et-Seul' in *Revue d'histoire et de philosophie religeuses* 60 (1980), 29–34. He begins with comments on Festugière's study, noting that his theory of a Neopythagorean or Neoplatonist origin of the phrase is not buttressed by any texts which actually use it, although the idea of a transcendent God who is unique is found in them. Ponsing argues for an Egyptian source with a quotation, initially, from *PGM* 13, 255–9, a text from probably the fourth century

AD, where the god Helius is said to be placed under the *One-and-Only* who is also described as *the Eternal and Only One*. This text begins with *I am he on the two Cherubim,* and Morton Smith (in H. D. Betz (ed.), *The Greek Magical Papyri in Translation* (1986), 179) rightly designates the prayer as 'a spell of unmistakably Jewish background'. The second part of the spell does, however, reflect the Egyptian idea of the sun's nocturnal journey under the earth. Reverting to earlier sources, Ponsing uses the texts highlighted by Morenz, including the Ramesside Papyrus Leiden 350, although he has recourse only to the early edition by Gardiner in 1905, neglecting entirely the standard edition and commentary published by Zandee in 1947. Yet he very properly quotes from the Cairo Papyrus 58038 (formerly P. Boulaq 17), where Amûn is addressed in a hymn dating from the Eighteenth Dynasty and thus from a period prior to the Amarna literature. Three times in this hymn occurs the phrase $w^c w^c w$ (wrongly transcribed by Ponsing or his printers), *the solitary sole one*, used of the god, and the claim is made that this phrase is an exact counterpart to 'One-and-Only', as opposed to the simple w^c which Morenz had been content to stress in the Leiden text (*One is Amûn etc.*), as we have seen. The parallel is not exact since μόνος is not rendered; yet the general sense is similar. Jan Assmann in his *Re und Amun* (1983), 174, gives the best commentary; he translates the phrase as 'Einziger einsam ist' ('the unique one who is solitary'), comparing the expression in Iamblichus, *De Mysteriis,* 8. 2, Des Places, p.196, used of the One God: *abiding in the solitude of his own one-ness*. The duplicated Egyptian form certainly has an emphatic or intensifying nuance, but cannot be accepted as a precise analogue to εἷς καὶ μόνος.

Ponsing pursues the theme up to the tomb of Petosiris in the fourth century BC and then to the temples of the Graeco-Roman era, using translations by Sauneron and Yoyotte. He ends with a quotation from the *Tractatus Tripartitus,* a Coptic text deriving from a Greek original which has been dated to the second half of the second century AD: see Rudolphe Kasser et al., *Tractatus Tripartitus. Pars I. De Supernis* (Berne, 1973), 37; cf. H. W. Attridge and Dieter Mueller in J. M. Robinson (ed.), *The Nag Hammadi Library in English* (Leiden, 1977), 54ff., and Elaine Pagels, *The Gnostic Gospels* (Harmondsworth, 1982), 57f. The quotation in question tells of the Father, that he existed before anything else; then it says of him that he is *the One who is alone,* rendered by Ponsing as *il est Un-et-Seul* (p.33, quoting two further instances). He slightly turns the expression to bring it closer to εἷς καὶ μόνος but one must accept that the Coptic phrase and its ideology derive directly from the Egyptian material. It is also significant that while Coptic writers were ever ready to borrow Greek terminology, in these examples they did not employ the phrase εἷς καὶ μόνος, preferring instead to quote the native Egyptian phraseology. Ponsing rightly compares these facts with the popular henotheism of the Hermetic tracts and the monotheism of Philo and of Coptic gnosis as well as of Christian writers of the early centuries. He cites Eusebius of Caesarea, *Praep. Evang.* 1. 1. 3 (Gifford, I, p.3), who refers to the Father's one being and nature. Of incidental interest in the *Tractatus Tripartitus* is the allusion (58, 29ff.) to the Church as being pre-existent like the Son and as having issued from the eternal love between Father and Son; see p.40 of the edition by R. Kasser and others and compare above, chapter 13, section 2, on Gressmann's view of the Church as a rival candidate of the Spirit for the third place in the Trinity.

7. A Confluence of Two Traditions

Some controversy has attended the exegis of no.5 in our list of quotations above (*To Zeus Helius the great Sarapis*) and similar statements.[161] The formula often begins with *Heis (One)* as in (7), (9) and (10). Writing in 1926, Erik Peterson in *Heis Theos* (p.239) shows that the formula is found in connection with Mithras and that in this connection its meaning can be syncretistic as well as acclamatory, the latter being according to him (p.241) the original sense of the *Heis Zeus Sarapis* formula. He maintains that the syncretistic interpretation is attested only late and rarely. Peterson's chronology should be noted. He tends to see the origin of the henotheistic formula with Sarapis as occurring in the time of Vespasian (his p.236; cf. Vidman, *Isis und Sarapis* 147). What he regards as 'late' and presumably less significant may be, however, for our purposes of great import since the formative period of the Christian Trinity was the span of the second and third centuries AD. Moreover Peterson totally rejected Weinreich's claim that the syncretistic meaning was of Egyptian origin; it rested hitherto, he maintained, on 'kein einziges Zeugnis'. It will be clear from evidence cited here that attestations of a syncretistic approach are abundant in Egyptian sources. Yet the parallels in Greek and Latin material suggest, for this area, a confluence of two traditions – the Graeco-Roman and the Egyptian. The latter tradition is certainly the earlier and points to the fusion of triad in trinity; but Graeco-Roman expressions of the same idea were likely to be the more influential.

Difficulties have admittedly been raised in the interpretation of (7), *One is Baït etc.* For μία τῶν βία Eitrem[162] suggested reading μί'ἄτων (=αὐτῶν); Kaibel notes that Τωνβία was formerly read. 'One is their force' is the likely meaning. In a study of 'A Vision of Mandulis Aion', a text from the temple of Kalabsha in Nubia (since moved to near Aswân), which dates from the first century AD or later, A. D. Nock[163] quotes our no.7 as a parallel to statements of belief which have pretensions to literary form. He also quotes a text on the Roman wall at Carvoran (probably Hadrianic) which includes the line

Ergo eadem mater diuum, Pax, Virtus, Ceres

(*Carm. lat. epigr.* 24)

Nock opines that 'the tone of these expressions is quite different from acclamations of the εἷς θεός type', but he thinks that the text of our amulet 'approximates'. It is obviously less ambitious, brief as it is, in the literary sense. Indeed, it has been rudely rejected as an authentic source for the existence of trinitarianism outside the Christian model: 'it is inadmissible to base the existence of a trinitarian theology on a single Egyptian amulet of uncertain date and authenticity ...'[164] Versnel, who writes thus, does not discuss the question of date; it seems that the only uncertainty concerns the choice of the first or second century AD. His term 'a single Egyptian amulet' is grossly misleading in view of the profusion of other evidence.[165] On the question of authenticity he cites (p.236 n.148) the dictum of Peterson (op. cit., 240 n.2), 'geradezu falsch'; but Peterson, while he regards the text as corrupt, does not reject the authenticity of the amulet *in toto;* his expression denotes a rejection rather of Spiegelberg's view on priestly trinitarian speculations in Egypt. If anything, Spiegelberg understated the strength of the evidence here.

The metre and syntax of our amuletic text are said to be suspect. Neither is perfect, but this class of document scarcely leads one to expect linguistic perfection.[166] No breath of suspicion is aroused by Campbell Bonner in his discussion,[167] although he admits that μία τῶν βία, *one is their power,* is a locution placed before its logical position, since the three deities named must be included in its force. Bonner suggests that the third of these, Akori ('Coptic *achōri,* serpent') may imply Wadjet, goddess of Buto; probably Spiegelberg, in referring to the serpent goddess Buto, really meant that. In the second line, although two goddesses are named in the first, the triad is addressed as a masculine *father of the cosmos* and specifically as *a god in three forms.* Here one must agree with Bonner in his appraisal of 'an approach toward a trinitarian monotheism', although he questions whether a strict monotheism is implied.[168]

Before looking once more at our no.4 (Martial, 5. 25. 15) a tribute is due to Versnel's able and richly informative treatment in his book *Ter Unus* (1990) which takes its title from the last line of Martial's poem.[169] At the same time one must demur to the author's resolute refusal even to discuss trinitarian ideas in this context. These are his words:

> Now that we are going to tackle the problem of the meaning of *ter unus,* I would first and foremost exclude from the discussion one suggestion, put forward by

> Reitzenstein and Usener, namely the supposed relation to the Christian idea of trinity in the dogmatic sense of 'three persons in one God'. Any history of dogma can inform us that after a long and laborious genesis this doctrine of trinity did not receive its definite form until the latter half of the fourth century.
> (Versnel, op. cit., 233.)

While the present writer shares Versnel's Christian convictions, the implicit suggestion that there is anything eternally sacrosanct about the dogma defined in the fourth century is calculated to interfere with an honest examination of how the process was achieved. It is true that the final definition gained enduring success and properly reflected the Church's experience of the Holy Spirit; but the debate produced some deplorable decisions. The most shameful of these was undoubtedly the eventual condemnation of Origen's teaching; even Jerome joined in this although he had earlier described Origen as 'the greatest teacher of the Church since the apostles'.[170] The condemnation of Pelagius in the early fifth century was a comparable misfortune.[171]

To return to Martial's *ter unus*. Several explanations seem possible. The gladiatorial context suggests an allusion to three kinds of gladiators: Martial's hero has excelled in all three arts and he is 'three times one' in the sense that, although one person, he combines the three prowesses in himself.[172] The idea of 'three in one' is clearly present here in a factual way. However, wider ideas may coexist with this initial point. Since the gladiator's name is Hermes, the triplicity invites an association with Hermes Trismegistos. While Martial is unlikely to have imbibed much, if anything, of the ideology attached to the Egyptian Hermes, he was very probably aware of the importance of three in relation to him.[173] Perhaps he was thinking of a god with three facets or triple force. No direct connection with Christian Trinitarianism would be implied, but there would be a parallel interest in the approach. It has been remarked[174] that 'the name τρισμέγιστος cries out, as it were, for a trinitarian interpretation'. In origin, however, the name has the force of a superlative, and that applies also to the Egyptian prototypes. The Greek name became established in the Roman era, and it was only in the sixth century that Joannes Malalas attributes to Hermes Trismegistos three very great powers (δυνάμεις), but one divinity (μίαν δὲ θεότητα).[175] It is true that Thoth figures in a triad at Hermopolis Magna, where he is grouped with the goddess Nehmet-away and their son Nefer-Hor (or Hor-Nefer);[176] and in the 'Strasbourg Cosmogony', a papyrus of the fourth century AD, he forms a generational triad with his father Zeus and his son Logos.[177] Again, in contexts concerned with posthumous judgement, Thoth is often grouped with Horus and Anubis in the procedure of weighing the heart, mainly as the divine Recorder.[178] Yet all this amounts to triadism and not trinitarianism. The same is true, for the most part, of similar features in the Hermetic writings. Thus in the *Korê Kosmou* (*CH* IV, 23, 11) Phusis is said to be impregnated by Ponos, producing a daughter Heuresis – a typically Greek group where Nature, Labour, and Discovery bear the impress of Stoicism. At the same time the framework of the work focuses on Isis, Horus, and Osiris; and Hermes is said to share the secrets of Osiris. It is the inner logic of Martial's Hermes poem that justifies Usener's use of it as a witness to a trinitarian trend.[179] A combination of three powers in one being is plainly thought of, and Hermes Trismegistos may have supplied a paradigm, albeit not substantiated in actual tradition about him.

8. Relationships in the Interior Structure

The fact that Tertullian in his *De pallio* (4. 3; cf. above, ch.13, section 6, quotation no.8) alludes to Martial's epigram with a reference to the triplicate monster Geryon, whom he describes as *Geryon ter unus,* shows that Tertullian, at any rate, is far from comparing the Trinity with such a concept. Yet the question does arise as to whether such concepts had an indirect influence on Christian writers. Cerberus, Chimaera, and Hecate were other Greek beings imagined as possessing three bodies or features; and similar phenomena appear in several other cultures.

The internal relationships of the three units thus conjoined plainly stress the idea of unity since the three bodies are regarded merely as modes of the essential divine entity. At the same time distinctions are sometimes made, as in the case of the Greek (perhaps Carian in origin) Hecate. As goddess of triple crossroads she has statues with three forms, perhaps in order to survey the three roads simultaneously; but her three faces are sometimes connected with three different personalities – Selene in heaven, Artemis on earth, Hecate in hell.[180] Such demarcations are scarcely possible, one might think, with the three heads of the dog Cerberus; he is hellish and canine through and through. Yet Macrobius gives him heads of lion, wolf, and dog, and supplies associations with the present, past and future.[181]

Such phenomena, however, are widespread; and early Indian religion, as was indicated in our chapter 6, provides plentiful examples, including *trimūrti,* 'three forms' (section 2 there) and deities with three heads (section 4). There are groups of three deities too, and Gonda (our section 5) finds an instance in the *Śatapatha-Brāhmana* of the idea of a unified deity being seen in them. The *Brāhmanas* are late Vedic texts dating perhaps to about 900 BC,[182] and Gonda's citation seems to be a rather incidental occurrence. Naturally the general question of Indian influence in the early Christian centuries arises here. Intercourse by way of trade (at least indirectly) between India and Alexandria is well attested for the Ptolemaic era;[183] and it flourished in the Roman era. A keen interest in Indian affairs is revealed by Strabo's book XV as well as in the account given by Philostratus of the life of Apollonius of Tyana. A striking fact is that King Ashoka, emperor of India *c.* 270–230 BC, who had been converted to Buddhism, sent embassies (whom H. Idris Bell preferred to term 'missionaries') to the court of Ptolemy II Philadelphus in Alexandria as to the courts of other Greek monarchs.[184] That Ashoka was a keen propagandist for his religion is certainly shown by his Rock Edicts. Whether Indian influence can be discerned in the thought of Plotinus is a matter of debate. Parallels are conceded by Armstrong,[185] but he finds antecedents in earlier Greek philosophy. It is relevant to note that both Origen[186] and Numenius[187] showed an interest in Indian religion, but precise details are lacking. Divine triads are often featured in this material, but no firm concept of triunity seems to emerge.

A mark of the unity in the evolved Christian doctrine is its indivisible character. There is a stress on 'the one Triune God who is in himself wholly Father, wholly Son and wholly Spirit, without division in the unity of his being'.[188] Torrance adds that in the fourth century Nicene theologians preserved the Trinity 'from Judaising tendencies in a Sabellian contraction of the three Persons into an undifferentiated unity and preserving the Unity from Hellenising tendencies in an Arian severance of the three Persons by a diversity of natures'. While this may well be true of the dominant fourth-century attitudes, the earlier formative stages of the second and third centuries reveal a different approach. By and large, the sequence postulated was from a primal Monad to a Dyad: God the Father-Creator became the Son in the historical Jesus and after the latter's ascension assumed the role of the Holy Spirit, the successive forms comprising an *oikonomia* which served the cause of divine revelation and eventually achieved a Triad which was also a Trinity.[189]

A conspicuous trait of the early formulation is its subordinationism. In one sense it was a logical development of New Testament doctrine which presents Christ as the Son of God and as His close associate. The Son's relationship to the Father is by nature one of subordination; otherwise the words 'Son' and 'Father' lose their initial force, since the one is, by definition, created by the other. In a chapter on 'The Triune God' John Macquarrie notes 'the paradoxical character of the trinitarian formula and the need to maintain a balance between the thought of the one "substance" and the three "persons"', and finds these points expressed in the words of the *Quicunque vult,* the so-called Athanasian creed: 'neither confounding the persons nor dividing the substance'.[190] Macquarrie is concerned more with a theological defence of the doctrine than with its historical evolution. When the latter theme is considered, it is seen that the early theologians were very ready to assign subordinate roles to both the Son and the Holy Spirit. In varying degrees this is true of the beliefs held by Ignatius, Justin, Tatian, Hermas, Theophilus of Antioch, Athenagoras and Irenaeus, although the figures of the Logos and Wisdom sometimes complicate the schema.[191] Tertullian, on the other hand, was able to counter the problems of subordinationism and modalism by positing that the One God is not a monadic One, but a unity differentiated within itself; the Logos comes from God through the act of eternal generation, thus becoming the Son; and the Son and the Father are *distincti* but not *divisi*. To Tertullian the Holy Spirit is sent by the Father through the Son. The formula which later prevailed is thus anticipated.[192] As for Clement and Origen, their subordinationism is palpably proclaimed; see above chapter 12, section 3 (ii and iii). At Antioch several Christian thinkers went further in this direction, for a 'low Christology' was in vogue there, holding with the Jewish-Christian Ebionites that Christ was 'a simple, ordinary person, a man justified by progress in character and that alone' and that he was 'born of the intercourse of a man with Mary'.[193] Ignatius of Antioch, in contrast, does not go thus far; he is credited with a 'high Christology', for his Christ, while inferior in status, is regarded as pre-existent with the Father and indubitably divine. The contrary view is represented to some degree by Theophilus of Antioch, Paul of Samosata and Serapion of Antioch.

The idea of parity of status among members of the Trinity, coupled with that of their unity, evidently causes difficulties; and Augustine states in his *De Trinitate* (1. 5. 2–4, Mountain–Glorie, p.36) that 'some are disturbed when they hear that the Father is God and the Son is God, and the Holy Spirit is God, and yet that this Trinity is not three gods but one God'.[194] Earlier Christian writers eschewed this idea of parity, assigning firm precedence to God the Father. If we ask where was the source of that conviction, the first obvious answer is that the Hebraic tradition was the primary influence. We have referred to the Ebionites at Antioch; probably they were Jewish Christians who rejected the divinity of Christ.[195] Yet other possible sources, including most of the traditions of various religions, shared, remarkably enough, this emphasis of the primacy of the Supreme God. The differing phases of Platonism certainly displayed it; so did Aristotle's idea of God as the 'unmoved mover'. In Middle Platonism and Neoplatonism the elevation of the Supreme God is heightened by the idea that the material world is evil, so that its creation must be assigned to a Demiurge who is lower in status. A parallel development occurs in the works of Gnostic writers who envisage a veritable *pleroma* of beings to bridge the gap between God and man; and the Judaic Hellenism of Philo can be said to fuse high ethical monotheism with the transcendentalist theology of Platonism; at the same time he presents a notion of a great chain of being whose diversity is held together by the immanent power of the Logos.[196]

The field of influence seems thus to be wide open when we seek to explain the subordinationist element in early Trinitarianism. It is a field that also includes Egyptian religion. Osiris and Isis were recognized by Origen, as we have seen (chapter 12, 3 (iii)) as the best known generally of Egyptian deities. Tertullian also shows much familiarity with them, referring in detail to a particular rite in the Osirian ceremonies in which the discovery of Osiris after his death is joyously celebrated; he alludes as well to the triad of Sarapis, Isis, and Harpocrates: see above chapter 12, 3(i).

More problematic from the viewpoint of possible influence is the nature of the Egyptian triple-named deities, whose structure at first sight suggests a parity of beings fused into one entity. Outstandingly popular in the Ptolemaic and Roman eras was Ptah–Sokar–Osiris, a deity centred in Memphis. A statuette with a Demotic inscription, perhaps of the third century BC, states that *Pi-heri-pa-shai, the son of Pakhois, will serve (šms) Ptah–Sokar–Osiris for ever and ever (š3' nḥ ḏt)*.[197] Spiegelberg says that the statuette bearing this inscription is one of Osiris; but as Kate Bosse-Griffiths reminds me, this composite deity is generally portrayed in the form of Osiris.[198] An indication of the importance of Ptah–Sokar–Osiris is found in one of the papyri of Nesmin, a Ptolemaic writing edited by Faysa Haikal (PBM 10209; Brussels, 1970 and 1972) and dating probably to about 350 BC. It was written for the Festival of the Valley near Thebes, but Haikal states (Vol.II, p.14) that 'the decline of *Amūn* in Thebes was counter-balanced by the rise in favour of Ptah–Sokar–Osiris'. Such formations, while ostensibly offering an egalitarian triad, often sought to elevate the status of one particular god by association. In this case Sokar was the god probably destined for such elevation. Ptah and Osiris were much more prominent, and although Ptah and Sokar were especially connected with Memphis, it was Sokar who stood to gain most from this triadic grouping.[199] In Egyptian, of course, the names are not hyphenated, but follow each other in asyndeton. In the Pushkin Fine Arts Museum, Moscow, which I visited in September 1986, there is a stela (Moscow I la 5608) dated to the Thirteenth Dynasty in which the names Ptah Sokar Osiris are followed by Horus Hemen; Svetlana Hodjash and Oleg Berlev have shown that the first three names pertain to one deity and the other two to another one.[200]

Within Egypt the influence of the native religious tradition was generally deeply pervasive, although with marked local preferences, and this remained true in the Graeco-Roman era to a lesser, but still considerable degree. The priestly personnel were a significant factor. The Greek papyri found in Oxyrhynchus invite, initially, a Greek interpretation, but the example of P. Oxy. 1380, with its long aretalogy of Isis, reveals a preponderantly Egyptian background. Many temples have been attested for Oxyrhynchus, and it is of some import that the priests and priestesses there all bear Egyptian names.[201] There was, further, a broad base of Graeco-Egyptian bilingualism – not of course among the populace at large, but among the *literati,* especially the priesthood.[202] Such remarks buttress the idea of Egyptian influence on the build-up of the interior relationships of the Trinity, particularly in the early stage of graded relationships which allow one dominant figure. But a similar characteristic in the Judaic, Greek, Gnostic and Indian traditions leaves the question rather open.

NOTES

[1] Cf. R. C. Zaehner, *Concordant Discord* (Gifford Lectures, Oxford, 1970), 203–5.

[2] A. H. Armstrong, in *Cambridge History of Later Greek Philosophy*, 263: '... the mysticism of Plotinus is not "monistic" but "theistic".'

[3] See John M. Rist, 'Theos and the One in Some Texts of Plotinus', *Mediaeval Studies* 24 (1962), 169–80; also Michael Atkinson, *Plotinus: Ennead V.1 On the Three Principal Hypostases* (Oxford, 1983), 1–2. The Good (τὸ ἀγαθόν), used also of the One, is likewise neuter, but the whole concept relates to 'a Principle Who corresponds more closely than anything else in Greek philosophy to what we mean by God' (Armstrong, *Plotinus*, London, 1953, 30).

[4] J. M. Rist, *Plotinus: The Road to Reality* (Cambridge, 1967), 7: 'we must not forget that the larger section of his group was always of Oriental origin.' On Numenius see E. R. Dodds in *Les Sources de Plotin, Entretiens,* V (1960), 3–32 and Philip Merlan in *Camb. Hist. of Later Greek Philosophy,* 96–106.

[5] See J. Zandee, *'The Teachings of Silvanus' and Clement of Alexandria: A New Document of Alexandrian Theology* (Leiden, 1977), 1–2.

[6] Cf. A. H. Armstrong (Loeb), 29.

[7] See S. Eitrem, *Symb. Oslo.* 22 (1942), 49–79, esp. 62ff.

[8] *Camb. Hist. of Later Greek Philosophy,* 208.

[9] *The Greeks and the Irrational* (Berkeley, 1963), 289–91 ('A Séance in the Iseum').

[10] Garth Fowden, *The Egyptian Hermes* (Cambridge, 1986), 87 n.54, regards the link as 'excessively ingenious'.

[11] See Jan Bergman in *The Greek Magical Papyri in Translation* (1986), 132 nn.83–4, and also in *Studies in Egyptian Religion (Fs. J. Zandee)* (Leiden, 1982), 28–37.

[12] *CQ* 30 (1936), 22–8 (= the first essay in his *Plotinian and Christian Studies* (Variorum Reprints, London, 1979)).

[13] Morenz, *Rel.* 270ff. (= tr. 255ff.).

[14] Carl Clemen (tr. R. G. Nisbet), *Primitive Christianity and its Non-Jewish Sources* (Edinburgh, 1912), 204ff.

[15] Cf. Christoph Elsas, in *Encycl. Rel.,* ed. M. Eliade, s.v. 'Clemen, Carl', 3

(1987), 532-3.

[16] *Primitive Christianity,* 205ff.

[17] Gustav Krüger, *Das Dogma von der Dreieinigkeit und Gottmenschheit* (Tübingen, 1905), 51. Krüger rejects the suggestions of external influence, whether Babylonian or Egyptian.

[18] J. Hehn, *Siebenzahl und Sabbat bei den Babyloniern und im alten Testament* (Leipziger Semitistische Studien, II, 5; Leipzig, 1907), 63. In spite of his title Hehn devotes a substantial section (pp.63-75) to the significance of three among the Babylonians and in the Old Testament.

[19] Clemen, op. cit., 206, citing Hehn's *Hymnen und Gebete an Marduk* (1903), 23f.

[20] Philip Merlan, in *Camb. Hist. of Later Greek Philosophy* (1967), 96ff.

[21] H. Gressmann, *Die orientalischen Religionen im hellenistisch-römischen Zeitalter* (Berlin, 1930), 50.

[22] Kelly, *Early Christian Doctrines,* 200 with refs. He finds in the thought of the mother 'more than the germ of the later axiom that only he who has the Church for his mother can have God for his Father'.

[23] James Moffatt, *The First Five Centuries of the Church* (London, 1938), 49, referring especially to Marcionite communions. Cf. 1 Cor. 3: 2: *I fed you with milk.* He mentions another possible meaning: 'to symbolize their entrance into the promised land of God'.

[24] H. Bettenson, *The Early Christian Fathers,* 93-4. Both these ideas have, of course, biblical bases.

[25] Ibid. 93.

[26] Kelly, op. cit., 192; cf. Frend, *The Early Church,* 79.

[27] Irenaeus, *Adv. Haer.* I. 1, tr. Robert M. Grant, *Gnosticism: An Anthology* (London, 1961), 163.

[28] See. J. Zandee, *'The Teachings of Silvanus' and Clement of Alexandria,* 1. He notes that Martin Krause dates it to the third quarter of the same century.

[29] Sharon. K. Heyob, *The Cult of Isis among Women in the Graeco-Roman World* (EPRO 51, Leiden, 1975), 43 with n.23.

[30] R. M. Grant, *Gnosticism,* 164. Cf. *Poimandres* 9 (= *Corp. Herm.* I. 9. 16): *Nous the God, being male and female* (ἀρρενόθηλυς). Cf. Thomas M. Scott, *Egyptian Elements in the Hermetic Literature* (D. Theol. Thesis, Harvard, 1987, unpubl.), 33f., where two other Hermetic refs. to God's bisexuality are quoted. For a searching analysis of this theme in Egyptian religion and Gnosticism see Jan Zandee, 'Der androgyne Gott in Ägypten: ein Erscheinungsbild des Weltschöpfers', in *Ägypten und Altes Testament,* 14. *Religion im Erbe Ägyptens,* ed. M. Görg (Fs. A. Böhlig, Wiesbaden, 1988), 240-78. To Zandee's account could be added the evidence of the Pyramid Texts; see my *Origins of Osiris and his Cult,* 195. After noting the several parallels in the Egyptian tradition, Zandee points to one basic contrast; unlike Gnosticism, that tradition viewed the created world as wholly good. In Greek religion the androgynous idea was often expressed in art: cf. Marie Delcourt, *Hermaphrodite* (Paris, 1958), passim. This is rarely found in Egyptian art: see John Baines, *Fecundity Figures* (Warminster, 1985), 120f.

[31] Tr. R. McL. Wilson, *The Gospel of Philip* (London, 1962), 80. Cf. Martin Krause and K. H. Kuhn in Werner Foerster, *Gnosis,* II, ed. R. McL. Wilson (Oxford, 1974), 81.

[32] Ibid.

[33] Ibid.

[34] Brian McNeil, *JTS* 29 (1978), 143-6 ('New Light on Gospel of Philip 17').

[35] Brian McNeil, op. cit., 144, quoting from R. Y. Ebied and M. J. L. Young, *Oriens Christianus* 60 (1976), 92.

[36] R. McL. Wilson, 'The Spirit in Gnostic Literature', in *Christ and Spirit in the New Testament*, ed. B. Lindars and S. S. Smalley (In honour of C. F. D. Moule, Cambridge, 1973), 345-55, this on p.355.

[37] Wilson, ibid.

[38] A. Böhlig and F. Wisse in *The Nag Hammadi Library in English*, ed. J. M. Robinson (Leiden, 1977), 195, ascribing the work to the Sethian Gnostics.

[39] See J. Zandee, 'Die Person der Sophia in der vierten Schrift des Codex Jung', in *The Origins of Gnosticism*, ed. U. Bianchi (Leiden, 1967), 203-14.

[40] Zandee, ibid., 210, quoting from Philo, *De fuga et inventione*, 50.

[41] See my *Plutarch's De Iside et Osiride*, 48f.

[42] Elaine Pagels, *The Gnostic Gospels* (Harmondsworth, 1982; first publ. 1979), 72.

[43] On p.82 she does refer to the cults of the Great Mother and of Isis; also to the fact that 'in Egypt, women had attained, by the first century AD a relatively advanced state of emancipation, socially, politically, and legally'.

[44] E. Pagels, op. cit., 74.

[45] Cf. Walter Till's translation in R. M. Grant, *Gnosticism*, 70. Bertil Gärtner, *The Theology of the Gospel according to Thomas* (tr. E. J. Sharpe, New York, 1961), 138, says, 'But Christ comes down to him in a revelation, in a threefold form, and the form which is the heavenly Christ says to him ...' But the context does not name Christ, although prior passages refer to him.

[46] See Martin Krause in W. Foerster, *Gnosis*, I, 105 and also his comparison of the Apocryphon of John with the account in Irenaeus on pp.100-3.

[47] E. Hennecke, ed. W. Schneemelcher, tr. and ed. R. McL. Wilson, *New Testament Apocrypha*, I (London, 1963), 164, section 3. Cf. E. Pagels, *The Gnostic Gospels*, 74, where the Gospel of Thomas is also adduced (*NHL*, 129, on the gift of life by the true Mother).

[48] The BV Mary is described rather as a 'Co-Saviour' by Cornelis A. de Ridder, *Maria als Miterlöserin* (Göttingen, 1965), 125.ff., where he uses the term *Corredemptrix*. G. van der Leeuw, *Religion in Essence* (1964, p.170), citing Heiler, says that 'the trinity of Jesus, Mary, and Joseph may be regarded as "the trinity of Catholic popular piety"'.

[49] Cf. M. Marcovich, *Studies in Graeco-Roman Religions and Gnosticism* (Leiden, 1988), 167, on 'the redemption of the pneumatics through the Bridal Chamber ... well known to the Valentinians ...'

[50] Cf. Hans Leisegang, *Die Gnosis* (Leipzig, 1924), 30; and Hans Jonas, *The Gnostic Religion* (2nd edn., Boston, 1963), 72, on the Ruha d'Qudsha, 'Holy Spirit', understood as female but regarded as 'the demonic mother of the Planets in Mandaean doctrine'.

[51] M. D. Beck, 'Trinität in der Kunst', in *RGG* VI (1962), 1038-41.

[52] J. C. Fenton, *The Gospel of St Matthew* (Harmondsworth, 1963; repr. 1974), 59; cf. G. W. H. Lampe, *The Seal of the Spirit* (2nd edn. 1967), 36.

[53] John Marsh, *The Gospel of St John* (Harmondsworth, 1968; repr. 1974), 125, citing with approval the view of Dr G. F. Knight in his Torch Comm. on Jonah.

[54] Raymond E. Brown in his Comm. (New York, 1966), 66, says that 'John's

claim that John the Baptist alone saw the Spirit, is relatively modest'. But John's dictum does not preclude a vision by others, notably by Jesus.

[55] Cf. R. E. O. White in *Christian Baptism,* ed. A. Gilmore (London, 1959), 89; also D. R. Griffiths, ibid., 149ff. on the Johannine material.

[56] Cf. D. E. Nineham in his Comm. on Mark (Harmondsworth, 1963; repr. 1975), 61: 'it no doubt rests on some dove symbolism current in late Judaism but no longer known to us.'

[57] Heinrich Schipperges, *Dreifaltigkeit* (Freiburg, 1954), 10 with Pl.18.

[58] Ibid. 5 with Pl.6.

[59] George Ferguson, *Signs and Symbols in Christian Art* (New York, 1966), 94.

[60] Ibid.

[61] Schipperges, *Dreifaltigkeit,* 9f. with Pl.17.

[62] Ferguson, op. cit., 94: 'With the exception of Christ, no other figure is so frequently portrayed in Renaissance art as the Virign Mary.'

[63] '... to follow the conflict of ideals, not in the abstract but as they show themselves in character and personality ...' (from the Preface).

[64] J. Gwyn Griffiths, 'Hellenistic Religions', in *Religions of Antiquity,* ed. Robert M. Seltzer (New York, 1989), 237–58, esp. 252. The term 'conflict' is aptly used by A. Momigliano in the book edited by him, *Conflict between Paganism and Christianity in the Fourth Century* (Oxford, 1963), but the opposing sides are properly defined.

[65] A title not claimed, it seems, by Jesus himself in the Synoptic Gospels. See R. H. Fuller, *The Foundations of New Testament Christology* (1965; repr. Glasgow, 1976), 114f. Cf. Pennar Davies, *Y Brenin Alltud* (Llandybïe, 1974), 15ff.

[66] G. L. Prestige, *Fathers and Heretics* (1940; repr. 1968), 27; cf. p.41 on the 'bacillus of god-making'.

[67] The phrase *Augusto Deo* in an inscription from Thinissut in N. Africa does not, however, imply this; v. D. Fishwick in *Hommages Vermaseren,* I (Leiden, 1978), 375–80, who see in it 'a formula for an (unnamed) Augustan god'.

[68] Cf. H. S. Versnel, *Inconsistencies in Greek and Roman Religion,* I: *Ter Unus* (Leiden, 1990), 61, on a 'contradiction in the Greek ruler-cult'.

[69] Prestige, op. cit., 27f.; cf. Kelly, *Early Christian Doctrines,* 88ff. on the appearance, at this time, of the 'triadic pattern' in the works of Ignatius, Justin and in the *Didache.*

[70] Henry Chadwick, *Origen Contra Celsum* (Cambridge, 1953; revised 1965 and 1980), V. 45, p.299.

[71] Ibid., XVII. In the same century Plutarch, *De Is. et Os.* 67, avers that in spite of the varying names among different peoples, one reason and one providence is the ruling power; see my note ad loc. p.532f.

[72] Cf. Ramsay MacMullen, *Christianizing the Roman Empire (AD 100–400)* (New Haven, 1984), 17: 'By contrast (to the pagan religions), Christianity presented ideas that demanded a choice, not tolerance.'

[73] Cf. H. Bettenson, *The Early Christian Fathers,* 242–3; J. W. Trigg, *Origen,* 219.

[74] Cf. Christopher Stead, *Divine Substance* (Oxford, 1977), 178.

[75] Henry Chadwick, *The Early Church* (Harmondsworth, 1967; repr. 1971), 57. Barry Baldwin, *Studies in Lucian* (Toronto, 1973), 105, remarks that 'for all we can tell, the Lucian picture of Peregrinus may be a total caricature'. Cf. Graham Anderson, *Lucian* (Leiden, 1976), 52ff. on parody and caricature in this portrait. That

may be so, but the attack on the deification of Christ is found also in Celsus, as we have just noted. Jennifer Hall, *Lucian's Satire* (New York, 1981), 212–13, discusses this passage (*De morte Peregrini*, 11–13) with a greater readiness to accept its portrait of Christians.

[76] Tr. Paul Turner, *Lucian, Satirical Sketches* (Harmondsworth, 1961), 11; the work itself is not included in the volume. For *this new cult*, Glover, *Conflict of Religions*, 212, has *this new mystery; teletē* can certainly mean that.

[77] Tr. A. M. Harmon, *Lucian* V (Loeb CL), section 13, pp.14–15; cf. J. Stevenson, *A New Eusebius* (London, 1968; repr. 1970), 135; unchanged in Frend's revised edn. (1987), 129.

[78] H. D. Betz, *Lukian von Samosata und das Neue Testament* (Berlin, 1961), 7, compares 1 Cor. 2: 7 and Col. 2: 23. The latter, however, has a pejorative sense. Harmon renders Lucian's phrase as 'wondrous-lore'. One feels that it may be tinged with a little irony.

[79] F. Jacoby, *Diagoras Ὁ Ἄθεος* (Abh. Berlin, 1959, no.3), 15: 'Diagoras was a straightforward and complete atheist, who bluntly declared that gods did not exist at all.' He was outlawed by verdict of an Athenian court of law in 416/415 BC (ibid., 17). For an admirable discussion of the whole theme see H. S. Versnel, *Ter Unus* (1990), 123ff.

[80] Ramsay MacMullen, *Paganism in the Roman Empire,* 5ff. *Away with the Atheists* was a cry heard before the martyrdom of Polycarp in AD 155 or 156: see J. Stevenson, *A New Eusebius*, 19 (= rev. Frend, 24).

[81] Stevenson, ibid., 62f. (= rev. Frend, 60).

[82] J. Stevenson, *Creeds, Councils and Controversies*, 63 (section 42); John Matthews, *The Roman Empire of Ammianus* (London, 1989), 445; Lietzmann, *Hist. of the Early Church*, III, 266 (with a slightly differing translation based on a variant reading).

[83] Heinrich Dörrie, *Porphyrios' 'Symmikta Zetemata'* (Munich, 1959), 18f., 39, 100–3. On Porphyry's view of the 'separation of soul from body' cf. Andrew Smith, *Porphyry's Place in the Neoplatonic Tradition* (The Hague, 1974), 20ff.

[84] Adolf von Harnack, *Porphyrius 'Gegen Christen', 15 Bücher Zeugnisse, Fragmenta, und Referate* (Abh. Berlin, 1916. Einzelausgabe).

[85] Robert Browning, *The Emperor Julian* (London, 1975), 159.

[86] But with special favours to non-Christians; cf. Kurt Latte in *Julian Apostata*, ed. R. Klein (Wege der Forschung, 509; Darmstadt, 1978), 124ff., in an essay from 1928; see also G.W. Bowersock, *Julian the Apostate* (London, 1978), 70.

[87] Polymnia Athanassiadi-Fowden, *Julian and Hellenism* (Oxford, 1981), 24.

[88] Browning, op. cit., 167, suggesting that in this he was influenced by Christian example.

[89] Edward J. Martin, *The Emperor Julian: An Essay on his Relations with the Christian Religion* (London, 1919), 92ff.

[90] Julian, *Or.* IV. 132 C ff. See Wilmer Cave Wright (Loeb CL), I (London, 1913), 358ff.

[91] Wright cites Plato, *Republic*, 508ff. for this notion (the 'Form of the Good' as exemplified in the role of the sun); cf. A. E. Taylor, *Plato, the Man and his Work* (7th edn., London, 1960; repr. 1971), 286.

[92] Wright, op. cit., 357 n.4 and 359 n.1.

[93] Wright, Vol.III (Loeb, 1923), 313ff.

[94] Hans Raeder, 'Kaiser Julian als Philosoph und religiöser Reformator', in *Julian*

Apostata (Wege der Forschung, 509, 1978, this essay from 1944), 209. He finds a deviation from Plato in the Helios Hymn (the locus discussed above).

[95] Lietzmann, *Hist. of the Early Church,* II (2nd edn. 1949), 185.

[96] Kelly, *Early Christian Doctrines,* 103.

[97] Ibid., 107f. Cf. Irenaeus on 'The Rule of Faith' in Stevenson, *A New Eusebius,* 115f. (= rev. Frend, 111–12). He is anxious to refute heretics rather than pagans.

[98] Tertullian, *Adv. Praxean,* ed. Kroymann and Ern. Evans (1954), 3.

[99] Momigliano, *On Pagans, Jews, and Christians* (1987), 153.

[100] *Der Monotheismus als politisches Problem* (Leipzig, 1935), 95ff. 'Die orthodoxe Trinitätslehre bedrohte in der Tat die politische Theologie des Imperium Romanum' (p.96).

[101] On both these developments, and the antecedent processes which obviated any sudden break, see Fergus Millar, *The Emperor in the Roman World* (London, 1977), 40ff.; cf. idem, *The Roman Empire and its Neighbours* (2nd edn., 1981), 128, on the effects of the emperor's departure to Constantinople.

[102] Jean Daniélou, 'Christianity as a Missionary Religion', in *The Crucible of Christianity,* ed. A. J. Toynbee (1969), 293–8, esp. 296.

[103] Leonhard Goppelt (tr. R. A. Guelich), *Apostolic and Post-apostolic Times* (London, 1970), 81–2.

[104] W. D. Davies, *The Setting of the Sermon on the Mount* (Cambridge, 1964), 25f. ('New Exodus and New Moses').

[105] A. J. Toynbee (ed.), *The Crucible of Christianity* (London, 1969), 13, in an Introduction to the volume.

[106] Plutarch, *De Is. et Os.* 67, 377 E ff. and my remarks ad loc., p.532f., pointing to the Stoic influence on a belief which was not rigidly monotheistic.

[107] Toynbee, op. cit., 11.

[108] Jacquetta Hawkes, *Dawn of the Gods,* (London, 1968), 135.

[109] Dieter Georgi, *The Opponents of Paul in Second Corinthians* (Edinburgh, 1987), 317. He deals with missionary activity on pp.27ff., 83ff., and 164ff.

[110] R. MacMullen, *Paganism in the Roman Empire,* 27–8.

[111] R. MacMullen, *Christianizing the Roman Empire,* 21. He points also to the 'unimportance of dogma' and to the likelihood that 'three quarters or more of the population were illiterate'.

[112] Aylward Shorter, *Towards a Theology of Inculturation* (London, 1988), 11–12.

[113] Jean Daniélou speaks also, in the context of persecution, of 'a new pagan mysticism animated by a passionate hatred of Christianity'. See Toynbee, op. cit., 298 a.

[114] Georg Kretschmar, *Studien zur frühchristlichen Trinitätstheologie* (Beiträge zur historischen Theologie, 21; Tübingen, 1956), 78f. He shows that later Theophilus of Alexandria made a bitter attack on what he regarded as Origen's excessive fondness for allegoristic. Rather strangely, Kretschmar begins his study with the 'Non-Trinitarians' of the fourth century, including Eusebius of Caesarea, who used the Trinitarian formula, but in his own thought recognized only God and the Logos, the Spirit being seen by him as the first creation of the Son.

[115] That Philo was indebted in his ideas of the Monad and the Dyad to Eudorus of Alexandria is urged by John Dillon, *The Middle Platonists* (1977), 128. But Philo never mentions Eudorus, a Platonist of the first century BC, and the ascription seems unlikely. Cf. Robert Grant, *Gods and the One God* (London, 1986), 85.

[116] Cf. J. P. Mackey in Alan Richardson and John Bowden, *A New Dictionary of Christian Theology* (London, 1983; repr. 1987), 582.

[117] Ibid. 583.

[118] Rowan Williams, *Arius: Heresy and Tradition* (London, 1987), 121. On p.117f. he challenges the view of Wolfson that Arius was responsible for a 'reversion to the original view of Philo on the Logos'. The passage of Philo's *On the Creation* cited above proclaims a firm monotheism, but elsewhere Logos and Sophia, both divine entities, blur the picture.

[119] Op. cit., 232.

[120] Cf. Morenz, *Rel.* 272 (= tr. 256f.). On Basilides v. H. Lietzmann, *Hist. of the Early Church* (tr. Woolf), I (1961), 280, with a note, derived from Clement of Alexandria, that Basilides made missionary journeys through the nomes of the Delta.

[121] Lietzmann, op. cit., 281.

[122] Ibid., 283, citing Clem. Alex. *Strom.* 1. 21 (p.146, 1-2).

[123] Cf. my Comm. ad loc. (1970), 448ff.

[124] Jean Daniélou (tr. J. A. Baker), *Gospel Message and Hellenistic Culture* (= Vol.II of his *Hist. of Early Christian Doctrine Before the Council of Nicaea* (London, 1973)).

[125] Cf. Daniélou, op. cit., 89-90.

[126] Kelly, *Early Christian Doctrines,* 127f.

[127] Th. Hopfner, *Fontes historiae religionis Aegyptiacae* (Bonn, 1922) (= *Fontes* hereafter).

[128] *Protr.* 2. 27. 3; Stählin and Treu, p.21, 5-9 (= *Fontes,* 55).

[129] *Strom.* 1. 21, p.68, 18ff. (= *Fontes,* 59).

[130] Henry Chadwick, *Early Christian Thought and the Classical Tradition* (Oxford, 1966; repr. 1990), 38.

[131] *Strom.* 1. 21, p.68, 23ff. (= *Fontes,* 74).

[132] *Protr.* 4. 48, p.37, 20ff. (= *Fontes,* 89).

[133] *Protr.* 1. 6, p.7, 6ff.

[134] *Protr.* 4. 54, p.42, 7ff.

[135] *Strom.* 6. 4. p.448, 24ff.; cf. my *Plutarch's De Iside et Osiride* (1970), 437f.

[136] Another French scholar who has contributed richly is Pierre Nautin. See his *Origène: Sa vie et son oeuvre* (Paris, 1977).

[137] Following the emendation κατὰ νομούς by Koetschau and Hopfner; it agrees with the regional distinctions of the previous dicta. Borret prefers νόμους with a reference to varying laws.

[138] É. Amélineau, *Essai sur l'évolution historique et philosophique des idées morales dans l'Égypte ancienne* (Bibliothèque de l'École des hautes études. Sciences religieuses, VIe vol., Paris, 1895).

[139] Ibid. 408. A. Wiedemann, *Religion of the Ancient Egyptians* (London, 1897), 105, assumed the priority of the triad ('Later it (the triad) expanded into an ennead ...'). Cf. P. Le Page Renouf, *Lectures on the Origin and Growth of Religion* (3rd edn., London, 1893), 83, on Triads and Enneads; Ed. Naville (tr. Colin Campbell), *The Old Egyptian Faith* (London, 1909), 138 (on the family triad). An outline of the views of early Egyptologists on Egyptian religion is given by E. A. Wallis Budge, *From Fetish to God in Ancient Egypt* (London, 1934; repr. New York, 1988), 52ff. Several of these early scholars are said to have regarded the essence of Egyptian religion, in spite of the many gods, as having been monotheistic.

[140] *Egyptian Mythology* (The Mythology of All Races, Vol.12, Boston, 1918), 20 and 215f.

[141] Cf. above ch.1, section 6, and my remarks in *ZÄS* 100 (1973), 28f.

[142] H. Jacobsohn, *Die dogmatische Stellung des Königs in der Theologie der alten Ägypter* (Ägyptologische Forschungen, 8; Glückstadt, 1939; 2nd unchanged edn., 1955), esp. 58ff. and the Third Part, 62–71.

[143] Cf. J. Gwyn Griffiths, *Conflict of Horus and Seth* (1960), 91.

[144] Bonnet, *RÄRG*, 364. Frankfort, *Kingship and the Gods* (1948), 180, prefers to give the idea a forward view: 'But the notion of a god who begets himself on his own mother became in Egypt a theological figure of thought expressing immortality.'

[145] Jacobsohn, op. cit., 58.

[146] See Jean Sainte Fare Garnot, *Religions égyptiennes antiques* (Paris, 1952), 65, quoting from E. de Rougé, *Bibliothèque Égyptologique*, III (1856), 332.

[147] He uses the phrase 'Dreieinigkeit Gott–König–Ka' (p.58). Ibid., n.12 he cites two representations which he regards as depicting this divine trinity. They do show the activities relating to divine procreation, but with no clear triadic phasing.

[148] Samuel A. B. Mercer, *The Religion of Ancient Egypt* (London, 1949), 285, rightly rebukes modern scholars who sometimes use the term 'trinity' when 'triad' will suffice.

[149] H. Brunner, *Die Geburt des Gottkönigs* (Wiesbaden, 1964). The doctrine persisted into post-pharaonic times: see J. Gwyn Griffiths, 'Apocalyptic in the Hellenistic Era', in *Apocalypticism in the Mediterranean World and the Near East*, ed. D. Hellholm (Tübingen, 2nd edn., 1989), 273–93. For the parallel with Christianity in the idea of the 'Son of God' see Emma Brunner-Traut, *Gelebte Mythen* (3rd edn., Darmstadt, 1981), 31–59, and cf. Martin Hengel, *The Son of God* (London, 1976), 23. Hengel believes that Jewish Hellenistic thought was a more important formative factor.

[150] Cf. Jean Sainte Fare Garnot, *La Vie religieuse dans l'ancienne Égypte* (Paris, 1948), 84, noting the boldness of the theologians who produced, under the Ramessides, syncretistic speculations like 'la conception de la trinité-unité Amon-Rê-Ptah'.

[151] A. H. Gardiner in *ZÄS* 42 (1905), 36 and in Sitzb. Berlin, 1923, 73.

[152] Jan Zandee, *De Hymnen aan Amon van P. Leiden I, 350* (Leiden, 1948), IV, 21–2.

[153] 'Ägyptische Trinitäten. Ihre Voraussetzungen und ihr Fortwirken'. A summary appears in *Deutsche Literaturzeitung* 78 (1957), 373–4, of which Morenz favoured me with a copy. It seems that the full text, due to appear in the Leipzig Akademie's Sitzungsberichten, was never published. After his death in 1970 a collection of his studies was edited by Elke Blumenthal and Siegfried Herrmann under the title *Religion und Geschichte des alten Ägypten* (Weimar, 1975), but none of his discussions of trinities appears here. A bibliography of his works is given by Angela Heller in *ZÄS* 99 (1972, his Gedenkschrift), IV ff. and includes (no.48) the summary of his Academy lecture, but with no thematic sequel. Morenz had kindly given me *separata* of several of his publications.

[154] Pp.150ff. and 270ff. (= tr. 142ff. and 255ff).

[155] This is true of Siegfried Morenz, *Gott und Mensch im alten Ägypten* (Heidelberg, 1963; 2nd enlarged edn., ed. Elke Blumenthal, Leipzig, 1984). See however his contribution to *RGG³* (1957), 'Ägypten IV. Im christlichen Altertum'; and his article 'Fortwirken altägyptischer Elemente in christlichen Zeit', in *Koptische Kunst: Christentum am Nil* (Essen, 1963), 54–9.

[156] Cf. above ch.1, section 6.

[157] Maj Sandman Holmberg, *The God Ptah* (Lund. 1946), 226f.

[158] Leclant, *Recherches sur les monuments thébains de la XXVe dynastie dite éthiopienne* (Cairo, 1965), 269 n.4. Cf. my remarks in *ZÄS* 100 (1973), 29; and above ch.4, section 4.

[159] Leclant, op. cit., 318. Amen-Rê-Harakhty is similarly treated in Late Ramesside letters: see A. M. Bakir, *Egyptian Epistolography* (Cairo, 1970), 59.

[160] Cf. above ch.8, section 5.

[161] Cf. ibid. For Harpocrates as Helius in early Christian art see El-Khachab in *JEA* 57 (1971), 137, with Pl. 37, 20 where the cross is shown on the winged disc.

[162] *Symb. Osl.* 10 (1932), 155.

[163] Nock, *Essays*, I (Oxford, 1972; repr. 1986), 399 (first publ. 1934).

[164] H. S. Versnel, *Ter Unus* (Leiden, 1990), 237.

[165] On p.236 n.149 he kindly cites my article in *ZÄS* 100 (1973), 28-32, but with no discussion. He does not refer at all to the studies of Morenz.

[166] Cf. my review of Versnel's book in *The Classical Review* 42 (1992), 90-2, and see further Campbell Bonner, *Studies in Magical Amulets* (Ann Arbor, 1950), 333 ('Grammatical Details').

[167] Op. cit., 175f.

[168] Cf. Françoise Dunand in *Les Syncrétismes*, ed. M. Simon (1975), 163, and Versnel, op. cit., 236 n.148.

[169] Versnel's discussion, pp.206-51, covers the whole poem.

[170] Henry Chadwick, *Early Christian Thought and the Classical Tradition* (1966; repr. 1990), 97 and 155 n.7.

[171] B. R. Rees, *Pelagius, the Reluctant Heretic* (1988), 130-1, showing that when the Synod of Diospolis in AD 415 had pronounced in favour of Pelagius, Augustine campaigned successfully against him. On pp.135ff. Rees translates material relating to the Synod and here (p.138) Pelagius maintains his belief in 'the Trinity of the one substance'. Peter Brown, *The Making of Late Antiquity* (Cambridge, Mass., 1978), 98, contrasts the 'perfectionism' latent in the teaching of Origen and Pelagius with the 'ascetic sensibility' of the fourth and fifth centuries.

[172] Cf. L. Friedlaender ad loc. (Leipzig, 1886), I, 402; Walter C. A. Ker (Loeb CL, Vol.I, 1919; repr. 1930), 315: Versnel, *Ter Unus*, 242. The poem itself details the three types.

[173] Conceded by Versnel, op. cit., 242; cf. Garth Fowden, *The Egyptian Hermes* (1986 and 1993), 26ff. and 216f. on the evolution of the term *Trismegistos*. For the anterior Egyptian terms see J. Quaegebeur in *Hommages Daumas* (Montpellier, 1986), II, 525-44.

[174] By Versnel, op. cit., 236.

[175] Hopfner, *Fontes*, 712; cf. Versnel, ibid., n.150.

[176] Bonnet, *RÄRG*, 512; J. Parlebas, *Die Göttin Nehmet-awaj* (Kehl, 1984), 102.

[177] Daria Gigli Piccardi, *La 'Cosmogonia di Strasburgo'* (Studi e Testi, 10, Florence, 1990), 30ff.; cf. Fowden, *The Egyptian Hermes*, 175.

[178] See my remarks in *The Divine Verdict* (Leiden, 1991), 326.

[179] *Dreiheit*, 36. Reitzenstein, *Hellenist. Mysterienrel.* (3rd edn., 1927), 27, was too confident when he explained the allusion as seeking to ridicule Hermes as the triune god of the world; he compares (and contrasts) the acclamation *Isis, quae es omnia*. Versnel, op. cit., 250, opts for a superlative force of *ter*: 'most (*ter*) exceptional (*unus*)' - a rather insipid conclusion.

[180] H. J. Rose, *Handbook of Greek Mythology* (6th edn., 1958), 121-2; cf. Fritz Graf in J. Bremmer (ed.), *Interpretations of Greek Mythology* (London, 1988), 100

and 106; and above, ch.6, section 4.

[181] Ugo Bianchi, *La religione greca* (1975), 252; cf. Otto Kern, *Die Religion der Griechen* (2nd edn., Berlin, 1963, originally 1938), 215; cf. also above ch.8, section 4, pointing to the idea of intensified potency.

[182] Wendy Doniger O'Flaherty, *Textual Sources for the Study of Hinduism* (Manchester, 1988), 2; cf. A. L. Basham, *The Wonder that was India* (3rd edn., London, 1954; repr. 1988), 241.

[183] Sir William Tarn and G. T. Griffith, *Hellenistic Civilisation* (3rd edn., London, 1952), 245ff.; A. H. Armstrong in *CQ* 30 (1936), 23; P. M. Fraser, *Ptolemaic Alexandria* (Oxford, 1972), I, 180, refers to 'a limited amount' of indirect trade in the third and second centuries BC. In the Roman era, however, direct contact was possible, as the *Periplus Maris Erythraei* shows; cf. Fraser, I, 174.

[184] A. L. Basham, 'Aśoka', *Encyclopedia of Religion,* ed. M. Eliade, 1 (New York, 1987), 466–9, esp. 467; cf. H. Idris Bell, *Egypt from Alexander the Great to the Arab Conquest* (Oxford, 1948), 53; F. W. Walbank, *The Hellenistic World* (Glasgow, 1981), 61f. Vegetarianism is mentioned in the Rock Edicts of Ashoka, some of which are in Greek and Aramaic and others in Greek only, in Kandahar: see Fraser, op. cit., I, 181, and for the Rock Edicts in general see Trevor Ling, *The Buddha* (Harmondsworth, 1976), 187ff., pointing to the emphasis on non-violence to living beings, which meant the forbidding of animal slaughter for food (with some exceptions) or for sacrifices – the priniciple of *ahimsa;* cf. A. L. Basham, *The Wonder that was India,* 53f.

[185] Op. cit., in n.183; cf. above ch.13, section 1; also Armstrong's remarks in *Cambridge Hist. of Later Greek and Early Medieval Philosophy* (1967), 8 and 200.

[186] See above ch.13, section 4, where he is quoting and discussing Celsus.

[187] See above ch.13, section 1, with an allusion to the Brahmans.

[188] Thomas F. Torrance, *The Trinitarian Faith: The Evangelical Theology of the Ancient Catholic Church* (Edinburgh, 1988), 64. Here he is paraphrasing Athanasius.

[189] Martin Werner, *Entstehung des christlichen Dogmas* (Berne and Leipzig, 1941; repr. Stuttgart, 1959), 602. He detects Gnostic influence in the structure. He also finds an early tradition which presents the Son of Man as a 'prince of angels', an emphasis rejected by Wilhelm Michaelis in *Zur Engelchristologie im Urchristentum* (Basle, 1942), 85f.

[190] J. Macquarrie, *Principles of Christian Theology* (revised edn., London, 1977), 193.

[191] Kelly, *Early Christian Doctrines,* ch.IV ('The Divine Triad'), 83–108. On p.101 he remarks that the aim of the Apologists was 'to safeguard the monotheism which they considered indispensable'.

[192] Cf. J. Moltmann, *The Trinity and the Kingdom of God* (London, 1981), 137.

[193] Robert Grant, *Gods and the One God* (1986), 135, quoting Eusebius, *Eccles. Hist.* 3. 27; Grant's chapter is entitled 'Divergent Christologies at Antioch'. On the traditions of Antioch see also A. J. Festugière, *Antioche païenne et chrétienne* (Paris, 1959), which gives attention, for the most part, to the fourth-century sophist Libanius. The tensions between Jews and Christians in Antioch are dealt with by Wayne A. Meeks and Robert L. Wilken in *Jews and Christians in Antioch in the first four centuries of the Common Era* (Missoula, Mont., 1978), 13–52. Antiochene doctrines are discussed in detail by D. S. Wallace-Hadrill, *Christian Antioch* (Cambridge, 1982), 67ff. ('The doctrine of the nature of God'). In *JRS* 61 (1971). 1–17 Fergus Millar raises the interesting possibility of a cultural clash (Aramaic and

Greek) in the stance of Paul of Samosata.

[194] Cf. Alan Richardson, *Creeds in the Making* (London, 1941; repr. 1972), 60, who goes on to deny the idea that 'three separate personalities' are meant; the 'social doctrine' of the Trinity must, he argues, invite the charge of Tritheism, the Godhead being held to be a society of persons.

[195] Cf. R. P. C. Hanson, *The Search for the Christian Doctrine of God* (Edinburgh, 1988), 115. On Jewish groups at Antioch who gave difficulties to Paul cf. Peter Richardson, *Israel in the Apostolic Church* (Cambridge, 1969), 93ff.

[196] Henry Chadwick in A. H. Armstrong (ed.), *Cambridge Hist. of Later Greek and Medieval Philosophy* (1967), 140-3.

[197] W. Spiegelberg, *Demotica* II (20-34), Sitzb. München 1928, 41.

[198] Cf. K. Bosse-Griffiths, 'Problems with Ptah–Sokar–Osiris Figures', *4th International Congress of Egyptology: Abstracts,* ed. S. Schoske (Munich, 1985), 26; Budge, *The Mummy* (1925; repr. 1987), 382ff. pointing also to the dyadic form Osiris–Sokar, still in the image of Osiris. D. P. Silverman in *Religion in Ancient Egypt,* ed. B. E. Shafer (London, 1991), 51, says that Sokar was 'eventually syncretized with Osiris'; the most popular form, though, included the name Ptah as well.

[199] See also above ch.4, section 2 ('Triads of One Sex') and ch.4, appendix, s.v. Memphis. The three are naturally linked in their functions as funerary gods; cf. J. Leclant in *Les Syncrétismes*, ed. F. Dunand and P. Lévêque (Leiden, 1975), 12.

[200] See their article in *Altorientalische Forschungen*, III (Berlin, 1975), 5–18, this stela on pp.5–11 with Pl.1; also their monumental publication, *Reliefs and Stelae in the Pushkin Museum of Fine Arts Moscow* (Leningrad, 1982), no.38, Stela of Dedi-wi-sen-i. On the early links of the three gods see Gaballa and Kitchen in *Orientalia* 38 (1969), 1–76, esp. 23.

[201] Naphtali Lewis, *Life in Egypt under Roman Rule* (Oxford, 1983), 87. The early attestation of Christianity in Egypt is also mentioned by the same author, p.100, noting that the earliest papyrus fragments of Gospels and other Christian books found in Middle and Upper Egypt date from 'about AD 100 or not long after'.

[202] Morenz in *RGG* I³ (1957), 121ff. ('Ägypten: Im christlichen Altertum'): cf. J. W. B. Barns, *Egyptians and Greeks* (Oxford, 1973, Inaugural Lecture), 13.

14

Concluding Remarks

In the course of our survey many parallels have emerged to the idea of divine groupings of three, and also to the pattern in which such groupings are arranged. Since our principal aim is to trace the likely formative influences and sources relating to the Christian doctrine of the Trinity, it is clear that considerations of time and place produce a historical exclusion of many, indeed of most, of the parallel systems evoked. For instance, both Celts and Germans produced notable divine triads, but neither of these peoples was historically placed to influence Christian thought. There were Celts in Galatia when Paul was active there; but no suggestion has appeared of the impact of Celtic beliefs from this source. In Britain the early Celtic Church was able to send bishops to the Synod of Arles in AD 314; and in the early fifth century Pelagianism had support, and indeed its origin, there,[1] but this is too late for the timetable of our theme. As for the Germans, their contact with the early spread of Christianity was still more unlikely.

Furthermore the field is restricted in another way. The search for sources and impacts will not be profitably pursued in the finished product of doctrinal exposition, which occurred in fact after long years of acrimonious debate, in particular between Arians and Athanasians. Rather will it be more wisely focused on earlier stages of the Christian discussion, before a fixed formula was approved of. Theologians were then aiming at a more precise definition of the theme. At a later stage, Augustine in the early fifth century wrote his classic *De Trinitate*, often with a mirror of the final controversies, but with few pointers to the formative phases. Even Novatian, the third-century presbyter at Rome, who wrote his own *De Trinitate*, is not so revealing about the earlier impulsions, although he agrees with Tertullian in his emphasis on the economic doctrine of the Trinity. An apposite title, from the viewpoint here adopted, is that of a recent study[2] – *The Search for the Christian Doctrine of God* – although its scope is also limited to the final phase, as its subtitle shows (*The Arian Controversy, 318–381*). In his assessment of Greek philosophical influences Hanson[3] opines that 'no philosophical necessity pressed here', adding that 'the Neo-Platonic three *hypostases* perhaps eased the situation a little, but they had comparatively little effect on the thought of the Cappadocians here'. He points to the importance, in the general doctrinal movement, of the recognition of the full divinity of the Son; still more important, in his view, was the recognition of the Holy Spirit's divinity, for 'to refuse divinity to the Spirit would have been to leave Jesus Christ as an isolated, inexplicable, enigma . . . or as a deified man.'[4]

The main formative influences, in my view, came from the heritage of Israel and Judaism, from phases of Greek philosophy, and from Egyptian theological doctrines, with the proviso that these mainstreams sometimes experienced an interflux in the sense of accepting forms and ideas from one another. In previous discussions Egypt is for the most part missing from the count, so that this facet of the present study must claim to be its most distinctive contribution. Under Egypt I include Gnosticism, although the origin of its various strands is much debated; I also include the Graeco-Egyptian amalgam which had a decisive impact.

1. The Heritage of Israel and Judaism

Without question Judaism demands primacy in this matter, and especially its interpretation of Hebraic tradition. If we adopt the Aristotelian distinction of substance and form, then the substance may be regarded as coming from Judaism, while the other contributions are concerned with form.[5] The distinction must not, of course, be explained too superficially; aspects of the form can certainly enrich the basic concept. It is true that the Old Testament offers no doctrine of divine Trinity, although early Christian writers were anxious to see in it anticipations of the doctrine, particularly in the account of the three Visitors who came to Abraham at Mamre (see above ch.11, section 2) and in the triple *Holy* cry of Isaiah's Seraphim. The role of Angels was also interpreted sometimes in this way (see ch.11, section 6). Such interpretations are retrospective performances rather like the attempts to find allusions to Christ in the redemptive Messiah-figures of the Old Testament. In a somewhat different category are suggestions in the Old Testament that God should be thought of in a pluralistic sense, particularly in the plural term 'Elohîm and in such a basic sentence, in the context of divine creation, as *Let us make man in our own image* (Gen. 1: 26), on which Lloyd R. Bailey[6] remarks that the plural 'may be a majestic plural, or else refer to the minor divine beings thought to surround God, like courtiers of a human king'. While such expressions lead to the idea that an extension of personality is applied to God and that a trinitarian concept is thus intellectually prepared for, the main impulse in the direction of the later doctrine lies elsewhere in the heritage of Israel.

This is in the Hebraic concept of the role of the Spirit (*Ruach*). It was a role of basic import in the idea of the divine creation of the world and also in that of the spiritual power bestowed by God on the prophets. Whereas it was a belief in late Judaism that the spirit of prophecy had been extinguished,[7] the experience of the early Church points to a powerful resurgence of the belief, as in the account of Acts (2: 17, 20f.), which expressly refers to the words of Joel (2: 28–32):

> Thereafter the day shall come when I will pour out my spirit on all mankind; your sons and your daughters shall prophesy ...
>
> (Joel 2: 28.)

Nor was this only a Pentecost event; it was a continuing experience recorded frequently in the New Testament and necessitating, obviously, a theology which gave adequate room to the Holy Spirit. A. D. Nock was no Hebrew scholar, but this does not excuse his failure to recognize the Hebraic origin of the idea. He does refer, quite properly, to Stoic analogues concerning the divine reason that permeates the universe and also to the divine *Nous* in Hermetic writings as well as to Iranian parallels.[8] He refers briefly to Philo, and I have tried to show (above ch.11, section 5) that Philo's exposition of *Pneuma* must have been significant in the evolution of Trinitarianism. It was a product of Hellenistic Judaism which probably influenced Christian writers, especially Clement of Alexandria.

2. Phases of Greek Philosophy

The impact of Greek philosophy on the doctrine is more difficult to assess because of the varying attitudes of early Christian writers when faced with the rich spiritual heritage of Greek thought. It was rare to find a dismissal of the claims of Israel. In the second century Marcion was an outstanding example: he rejected the Old Testament because he saw the dominance of the Law in it as fully contrary to the Christian Gospel of Love. In the same century the Christian Apologist Tatian made a wholesale attack on the philosophy of the Greeks and indeed on Greek civilization in general.[9] His teacher, Justin Martyr, was, rather strangely, a sympathetic student of Greek literature. Tertullian, however, was another fierce opponent of pagan philosophy. Otherwise, particularly in Alexandria, the early Christian teachers followed the example of Philo in their attempts to combine their knowledge of Platonist ideas with their veneration of the Hebrew Scriptures. The systems of Middle Platonism and of Neoplatonism were alike much enamoured of triadic groupings, and before that Philo had developed a similar schema of his own. Admirers of any or all of these writings must inevitably have been favourably disposed, in a general sense, to the Trinitarian trend within Christianity. This was true of Justin Martyr, Irenaeus, Theophilus of Antioch, and particularly of Clement of Alexandria and Origen.

The intellectual and spiritual acme of Neoplatonism was achieved by Plotinus in the third century, and this impressive achievement in itself invites us to support the idea that Christian thinkers were attracted to, and sought to emulate, the Greek systems. Yet the first decisive phases in the shaping of Trinitarianism occurred before the time of Plotinus, so that the question must be addressed to his precursors. It has been argued[10] that Greek philosophical parallels were probably influential in view of two facts:

> First, the Greeks were interested, as the Hebrews were not, in triadic patterns as such ... (Plato, *Timaeus*, 31 B, and Aristotle, *Physics* I. 6 are adduced).

> Secondly, the Greeks indisputably did evolve a theological Trinity on their own lines; the only question is whether the development took place early enough to affect the beginnings of Christian theology. Such a Trinity is well known in Plotinus in the third century; it is also quite clearly traceable in Numenius at the end of the second.

Stead goes on to suggest that 'it can perhaps be brought down to the first century if we accept a report by Simplicius which deals with the Pythagorean philosopher Moderatus, who lived early enough to be mentioned by Plutarch'. He further says of Moderatus that he 'introduces an absolute or pure One, a second One who (like Philo's Logos) is the (complex of) Ideas, and a third One which is Soul, and presumably the World-Soul, since it is called the origin of all sensible things'.[11] Here the mention of Philo implies that the chronological emphasis is misplaced; so does the information under the first point. Surely the early Christian writers, at least several of them, were familiar with philosophical triads not only in Philo's works but also in Plato. Indeed, Plato's *Timaeus*, as Stead himself points out, was of fundamental significance.

What one often finds in the Greek triadic systems is a schematic ordering of abstractions in contrast to the personal grouping of the Christian Trinity, in which, admittedly, the Holy Spirit begins as a numinous force rather than as an acknowledged person; and here the definition of 'person' is itself a problem. Can the One or the Good in the Neoplatonic system be assigned any personal attributes? In the case of Plotinus there are two apparently contradictory attitudes. A. H. Armstrong, who is probably his best expositor today, is able to say, on the one hand, that 'in Plotinus' universe the relationship between God and the soul is not the personal and dramatic one which exists for the Christian. The action of the One is impersonal, indifferent and universal.'[12] On the other hand,

Armstrong is able to interpolate 'not so impersonal, perhaps, after all, in some of his descriptions of the mystical union, VI. vii. 35 or VI. ix. 11' (the references are to the *Enneads*).[13]

What is apparently missing in the Greek philosophical triads is the principle of tri-unity in the sense of Tertullian's *una substantia, tres personae*. The groups are regarded as forming a close association, but without the idea of consubstantiality or of individual separateness as implied by *personae*.

3. Egyptian and Graeco-Egyptian Theological Systems

Egypt does not figure in most previous treatments of Trinitarianism, as we have seen. Usener and Reitzenstein are exceptions; so of course is Morenz. A more recent exception is seen in a book by Peter Gerlitz which expressly deals with non-Christian influences on the development of the Christian dogma of the Trinity.[14] Gerlitz devotes his first part (pp.9ff.) to 'the external structure of the Trinity', a theme which I discuss (in what follows) as 'the interior structure' with its inner relationships. (There is nothing troublous in the accidental inversion of the terms.) He properly gives attention (pp.14ff.) to the binitarian tradition in early Christianity up to the appearance of Tertullian – a well-chosen mark.

What is especially relevant to our presentation is his chapter II in this section, devoted to 'the Orient in its influence on the form of the Christian triad' (pp.19ff.). He begins with the startling dictum that oriental–early-Christian thought had never been able to develop a Trinity, but only, at most, a Triad. It was Greek philosophy, he maintains, that first offered the prerequisites for thinking on trinitarian lines; but Greek mythology provided, in his view, a rich background with vivid examples, from Hecate to Geryon, even if Tertullian is sarcastic about the latter. At the same time he refers to Hermes Trismegistus as 'the "trinitarian God" of the Hellenistic mystery-cults' without offering a detailed explanation of this idea. The early Egyptian tradition of trinitarian groups is here ignored, although it is touched on later. Yet he makes a valid point in noting a contrast (p.21) in Egypt, Babylon and Phoenicia: here groups of three deities tend to form a family. Considering Osiris, Isis, and Horus, though wrongly dating their origin to the fifth millennium, Gerlitz recognizes their importance in the doctrine of birth, death, and resurrection, as well as in the theology of divine incarnation in the God-King; here he stresses Jacobsohn's contribution, but unwisely ascribes to Isis (p.22) an inferior role in accordance with 'the oriental slave-status of woman' ('auf Grund der orientalischen Sklavenstellung der Frau'). No one who knows Ancient Egypt well could write like that. It was a patriarchal society, but the status of women was considerably higher than, for instance, among the Greeks.

Gerlitz is far too ready to see a parallel to the Trinity in Jacobsohn's theology of the *ka-mutef* which finds a trinity in the concept of God–King–Ka; it is a trinity imposed on the doctrine, as I have tried to show in chapter 13, section 6 above. That the *ka* was later identified with the Christian *pneuma* cannot be established, although several allusions in Greek magical papyri do use *psuchê* with the sense of *ba* (not of *ka*), as in *You are the psuchê of the daemon of Osiris*; see Gerlitz, p.26 and Reitzenstein, *Die hellenistischen Mysterien-religionen* (3rd edn., Leipzig, 1927), 309. Much more significant, though barely touched on here (p.27) is the trinity of the gods Amûn, Rê, and Ptah, as expressed in P. Leiden I, 350; IV, 21f.: these gods form a 'Homousie' in which the personal existence of each individual god is preserved. Here Gerlitz refers to Morenz's contribution to *RGG*, I³, 123 ('Ägypten im christlichen Altertum') but not to his *Ägyptische Religion*, which gives so much more detail. The latter work was published in 1960; although Gerlitz's book appeared in 1963, it is based on a thesis presented in the summer of 1960 in Marburg. The revised and enlarged form referred to in the Foreword did not unhappily extend to a knowledge of later works by Morenz.

If Gerlitz disappoints, therefore, in his assessment of Egypt's contribution, he has valuable comments on triadism in other areas. These include Babylon, Ugarit, the Jews of Elephantine, Iran, and especially (pp.35ff.) the doctrine of Trikāya in Mahayana Buddhism and Hinduism. Trikāya is said to involve the three forms of the Buddha's body. Parallels are seen in the doctrine of salvation (p.44), particularly with the Christian trichotomy of the earthly body of Christ, the heavenly glorified body, and the eternal Logos-Christ. No direct influence, however, is claimed, not even on the Alexandrian Ammonius Saccas. Nor are the triads of the other areas based on any trinitarian ideas.

From here on (pp.48ff.) Gerlitz treats of the inner evolution of the Trinitarian doctrine, taking as his first theme the development of Logos-Christology. A momentous external influence was evidently exerted in this connection by Stoicism, in which Logos-doctrine is refined under the adjectives *endiathetos*, *prophorikos*, and *spermatikos*. The force of these impacts is traced in some detail, but other possibilities are not neglected. A Babylonian hypothesis relating to Ea and his son Marduk is considered (pp.92f.): it regards Mummu, the creator of heaven and earth, as the prototype of the Logos – a theory rejected by Gerlitz and scarcely supported by Th. Jacobsen's analysis of the epic *Enûma elish* in *The Treasures of Darkness* (1976), 170f., where the name is explained as 'original form'. A stronger prototype appears in Egypt in the *Memphite Theology*, where the divine utterance is the creative element. A similar role assigned to Hermes-Thoth is regarded as a more cogent factor (cf. Plutarch, *De Is. et Os.* 54, cited (as 53) on p.95 n.1); and the influential figure of Philo is highly assessed, and rightly so. A possible Mithraic connection is also adduced (p.104 n.2) with an allusion to Mithra, Cautes, and Cautopates as designations of one and the same person.[15]

If some of these judgements seem extreme,[16] the section on the development of *Pneumatologie* (pp.120ff.) refers rewardingly to several parallels. Gerlitz attaches much importance to the influence of the 'oriental Mother-goddess' on the evolution of the idea of a female Holy Spirit in early Christianity. His terminology here is rather expansive in view of the fact that the 'oriental Mother-goddess' assumes so many divergent forms and names. The goddess Isis could probably be subsumed under this heading, and her connection with Logos and Sophia in Jewish Hellenistic thought is well attested. Gerlitz (p.130) is properly aware of this; he quotes Clement of Alexandria, *Strom*. VI. 16 (now Stählin and Früchtel, 4th edn., 1985, Vol.II, 507, 3ff.) averring that 'the Mother is not the being from which we have come, nor, as others have propounded, the Church, but the divine gnosis and Wisdom, as Solomon says, calling Wisdom the Mother of the just'. Gerlitz here aptly cites a dictum of Reitzenstein observing that Isis is at once Sophia and Mother.[17] He shows (p.143ff.) that the Church, at the same time, was sometimes regarded as the Mother, as in the allegorical treatment of Galatians 4: 21ff.

In general terms, Gerlitz sees an impact made by the formal aspects of triadism in the cosmic and mythical traditions in which triads are usually ordered hierarchically. His regards the emphasis on the Father-God in the New Testament in a monotheistic sense as deriving from Israel's developed doctrine; the status of the Son becomes consequently a matter for debate since that status is inherently inferior and is at first explained even as that of an *angelos*; even when divinity is ascribed, it is that of a second (*deuteros*), as in Origen's exposition. Yet the Stoic–Philonic doctrine of the Logos confers cosmic import on the Son, while the concept of the Holy Spirit is shown to be much indebted to the Oriental emphasis on the role of the Mother-goddess. On the other hand the inner relationships of the Persons of the Trinity show the impress of Platonic and Aristotelian categories, particularly in the terms *ousia, hypostasis, homoousios, idea*, and *eikôn*. The final emphasis on the consubstantiality of the Persons is seen to make large concessions to Neoplatonism.[18] At this point Gerlitz stresses his view that the dogma of the Trinity was erected from the most divergent building-stones gathered from the cults and the religious philosophies of the contemporary world. While he does not think that the word 'syncretism' suffices to explain the process, he deems it wrong to claim, as G. L. Prestige did (in *God in Patristic Thought*, London, 1936, p.xv), that the dogma 'was reached by true rational development'. Of course a rational debate (though often irrational in its vehemence) had preceded the finally agreed dogma, but external influences had played a vital part.

The most distinctive feature of the dogma was the belief in tri-unity, and it has been shown above that this was prevalent long since in the make-up of Egyptian triadism. A striking early instance is found in Spell 80 of the *Coffin Texts*, which may derive from the early part of the second millennium BC; here the primal creator-god Atum is said to have engendered in Heliopolis the divine pair Shu and Tefnut, *when he* (Atum) *was one and when he became three*. I have offered a detailed discussion above in chapter 1, section 6; the resulting concept is rightly described by Jan Assmann, *Ma'at* (Munich, 1990), 167, as 'eine Art Drei-Einheit'. Gerlitz has made brief mentions only of this significant heritage. When it came to bear on the credal decisions of the first four centuries, it found expression, for the most part, in Greek data of various types. It certainly affected many instances of the Greek *One God* formula in which Egyptian deities figure, although other examples are neither triadic in form nor Egyptian in content; see above chapter 13, section 6. In its final stage, therefore, it could be described as a Graeco-Egyptian influence; more precisely, perhaps, as Graeco-Roman–Egyptian, although the Roman element is much indebted to the Greek.

4. *Unity and Equality*

If unity, and in particular tri-unity, is an emphasis of the early doctrine, a question that clearly arises is whether unity implies equality. If it does, we must look for a possible ideological source. If it does not, sources of unequal unity must likewise be sought.

The doctrine of three in one and one in three could theoretically be explained as implying equality if it could be applied to any one of the three. If three persons or entities are united in one, a principle of equality must mean that any one of them must be seen to embrace or include the other two. Similarly the idea of one in three, if equality is the principle, should be applicable to any one of the three. We look in vain for the affirmation of equality in early Trinitarian formulations. In the developed postulates, as when the Nicene faith was reiterated at the Council of Constantinople in AD 381, there was an urge to stress that both the Spirit and the Son shared the substance of the Father. Yet there were some variations of emphasis. The Cappadocian Fathers produced the formula 'one *ousia* in three *hupostaseis*', thus emphasizing the three separate beings rather than the Godhead which is shared by them. But the rejection of *homoiousion*, 'of like substance', in favour of *homoousion*, 'of the same substance', meant that the Godhead was now deemed to be closer to both Son and Spirit. The idea of the 'co-inherence' or *perichoresis* of the three Persons was thus promoted since their identity of nature was accepted. Kelly remarks, at the same time, that 'while all subordinationism is excluded, the Father remains in the eyes of the Cappadocians the source, fountain-head or principle of the Godhead'.[19] In earlier phases, as in the *trinitas* expounded by Tertullian, the dominance of the Father is forcefully expressed. Any notion of equality is thus rendered unacceptable.

The mainstream influences which we have been considering all contain a prominent element which is a serious obstacle to the idea of equality in a triadic divine group.

(1) Judaism inherits a tradition which reflects a progression from henotheism to monotheism. Even the henotheistic (or monolatrous) Decalogue shows no trace of whittling down the dominance of the supreme divine power, and when monotheism becomes the established creed, the relation of the one and only God to ancillary beings, such as Angels, never compromises the ruling power of the dominant figure. Judaic monotheism was inherited by Islam, and it is a striking fact that those who proclaim that Allah is great (*Allah akbar*) and that there is no other God apart from him, Muhammed being carefully defined as his Prophet only, regard the Christian idea of God as a Trinity as something outrageous, although some aspects of the Christian tradition are regarded sympathetically. Within Judaism itself there is also opposition to it, apart from the rejection of the basic claims relating to Christ.

(2) Greek religion remained officially polytheistic, but there was no egalitarian treatment of deities. Zeus maintained, for the most part, his supremacy. Of course the crude polytheism of Greek worship (including that of many alien cults subsumed) was an object of constant vilification by both Jews and Christians. Greek philosophy, on the other hand, was much admired by both these groups, as the work of Philo and Origen amply illustrates. Yet the dominance of a supreme being is ever evident. In the late Hellenistic mental milieu the transcendency of the supreme being, often termed the One or the Good, was a cardinal belief; he was a God remote from the universe and incomprehensible to the human mind.[20] It is true that in Neoplatonism there are other divine categories and that some kind of unity binds the whole system together. But the Demiurge who creates the earth is sharply distinguished from the perfect and absolute One. Still further removed from the One were the other divinely ordered participants in this system. Even more elaborate in their hierarchical divisions were the systems of the various Gnostic movements, although some of these gave a more exalted status to the feminine constituents, both divine and human. Equality in the divine sphere is conspicuously absent.

Theoretically, the possibility of an idea of equality in the Trinity might depend on the concept of their being true Persons. If Neoplatonism was a deciding factor, then personalism must be ruled out as far as God himself is concerned. While Plotinus often uses 'personal language' about encounters with the One, yet his doctrine that God is infinite and unknowable means that 'we cannot say that God is a person'.[21] See my remarks on 'Abstractions and Divine Beings' in section 1 of chapter 13.

(3) The Egyptian and Graeco-Egyptian ideology has been shown to include expressions of a belief that is clearly trinitarian. In the early Egyptian record the primacy of one central figure is often evident. This is so in four of the five extant triads of Mycerinus, where the God-King himself is in the centre; and in the fifth of these exquisite sculptures Hathor is the central figure, shown as the divine mother of the Horus-King. See chapter 1, section 4 and the Frontispiece. The same principle is followed in the Atum-Shu-Tefnut group where Atum is the father and creator in Spell 80 of the *Coffin Texts*. In the Osirian triads (ch. 2, section 3) Osiris himself is often in the centre between Isis and Horus or Isis and Nephthys, but a considerable variety in divine personnel marks the structure of these groups. The primacy of Aten is manifest in the Amarna triad of Aten, King, and Queen (ch. 3), while in the King's first didactic name Aten is equated with two other gods.

Something different emerges in the New-Kingdom Theban triad of Rê, Ptah, and Amûn, since this group seems to suggest a sense of parity of status for the three gods and also for the areas of the kingdom where they were prominent – Rê at Heliopolis, Ptah at Memphis and Amûn at Thebes, these three cities being specifically mentioned in the Theban Hymn to Amûn. Doubtless Amûn was tacitly given priority, and this was expressly the case when Amûn was said to be Rê in his countenance and Ptah in his body. Triadic composites such as Ptah–Sokar–Osiris suggest an apparent parity of status, the three deities being merged in a syncretistic unity; but the gods of Memphis, Ptah and Sokar, were probably invested with greater authority through being linked to Osiris, and the resulting iconography was Osirian. In Egypt such a process was frequently at work in examples of syncretistic linkage, the lesser deities being afforded a heightened importance through association with a more august deity. This applies even to the One-God formula of the Roman era: unity and equality (even identification) are implied by this, as in Julian's *One is Zeus, one is Hades, one is Helius Sarapis*. Three gods are thus conjoined in one divinity; probably the last-named stood to gain from the original conjunction.

If we look at the whole gamut of our assembled triads, we find the superior import of one central figure being often expressed. A good example is the triad of Heliopolis-Baalbek, which is attested not only there but in many other regions of the Roman Empire. The central figure is Hadad-Jupiter, whose two paredroi are usually named as Venus and Mercury, concealing the Semitic names Atargatis (the Syrian goddess) and Simios or Nabu (see above ch. 5, section 5). In the Indian tradition triads are often related to cosmic, spatial, functional and social divisions, and for the most part an egalitarian principle seems to prevail, save for the clear primacy of the priestly Brahman class. Three gods of equal rank are sometimes conveyed by Mesopotamian groupings, but the dominant deity of a city often assumes priority. While the *matres* or *matronae* of the Celtic pantheon are outside the likely sphere of influence, they exhibit obvious equality when depicted as three stereotyped figures with similar attributes such as baskets of fruit or provisions, although the repetitive features make them less interesting. Local names occur when a single figure is shown, as with Rosmerta and Sirona, and it has been argued that the triple figures express mere intensification of the idea of fertility, or more precisely of a primal mother-goddess: see Miranda Green, *The Gods of the Celts* (1986), 208. The Celtic veneration of triplets is of course a direct expression of equality, in this case of members of a male group. (See above ch. 10, sections 1-3.) Occasionally even Christian iconography is content to depict the Trinity as three undifferentiated male figures, implying tritheism – a mode rebuked by Benedict XIV in 1745.[22] Probably the impact of Greek triadism was responsible for this, although a figure with three heads or faces was more common in that tradition. On the whole the Christian approach was concerned to preserve the distinctive monarchianism of the One God. This concern has characterized Eastern Orthodoxy in particular; and it is in sympathy with it that a Jesuit writer has declared that Trinitarianism is 'the Christian way of being a monotheist'.[23]

5. A Christian Innovation

By and large the triadism of the ancient religions allowed the primacy of one central figure. In Egypt this was true of the popular Osirian triads, although the three Horuses and the three *baw* rather exceptionally comprise repeated figures on a par.[24] In the New Testament, before the explicit embrace of Trinitarianism, the close relationship of the Father and the Son of necessity implied the primacy of the Father, and this was true afterwards of the earliest phases of the doctrine of the Trinity. The movement towards the idea of the unity of three divine persons was marked, first of all, by the recognition of the divinity of Christ; then of the divinity of the Holy Spirit.

In the third century the theory of Modal Monarchianism or Sabellianism interpreted the relationship of the Three as implying three modes of existence of the central Godhead. A sequence of revelation was seen to have been at work: God was initially the Father-Creator, revealing himself in the tasks of creation; then he revealed himself in the Son as the historical Christ; after the Resurrection and Ascension of Christ, it was in the Holy Spirit that God was deemed to reveal himself. In this way a doctrine of a revelatory or 'economic Trinity' was evolved, the *oikonomia* referring to 'functional organisation' (Lampe, *Patristic Lex.* (1961), 941 B. 3). Such a doctrine, while it rejected any possible charge of positing three separate divine beings, clearly gave the Son and the Spirit a subordinate status as being only modes or aspects of the Father. Here there is a close parallel with some of the Egyptian trinitarian models; and the Graeco-Egyptian expressions of this doctrine probably exerted a crucial influence at this stage, in the second and third centuries AD, particularly on the theologians of Alexandria.

Subordinationism, which was so frequently a feature of non-Christian triadic structures, and also of early Christian Trinitarianism itself, was firmly rejected in the creeds of Nicaea and Constantinople, the Son being now declared to be of the same substance as the Father. The equal divine status of the Three was affirmed in the *Quicunque Vult* (the 'Athanasian' Creed), which derives probably from the middle of the fifth century:[25]

So the Father is God; the Son is God; and the Holy Spirit is God. And yet they are not three Gods, but one God.

Co-eternity is also ascribed to the Three. The doctrine that the Holy Spirit proceeds from the Father and from the Son (*Filioque*), which was promulgated by the Third Council of Toledo in AD 589, found the Eastern Churches rejecting the latter emphasis, although the Western interpretation also implied that the Spirit proceeds from the Father *through* the Son, an idea inculcated already by Tertullian. This was the position expressly adhered to by the Eastern Churches.[26] A greater cohesion within the Trinity was thus envisaged. Augustine's appeal to analogies with the structure of the human soul contributed further to the idea of a 'psychological Trinity'. Treating the Three Persons as separate individuals in converse with one another led to a still more fervid 'social doctrine' of the Trinity.

The term περιχώρησις, 'interpenetration', lit. 'going around', was first used of the Trinity in pseudo-Cyril, *Trin.* 10 (Lampe, *Patristic Lex.* 1078, C) and it conveys a similar concept. The idea, although not the term itself, was urged by the Cappadocian Fathers when they emphasized the co-inherence and mutual relation of the Three Persons.[27] According to this doctrine the Triune God is worshipped as 'an ineffable Communion of Persons, in whom the Persons are who they are in their mutual or "perichoretic" relations with one another in one and the same divine Being'.[28] Gregory Nazianzen was using the term *hupostaseis*, as in his *Orationes* 31. 9, avowing his aim that *the distinction of the Three*

Persons (hupostaseis) *may be preserved in the one nature and dignity of the Godhead.*[29] A troublous problem, often noted, is the rendering of the terms *hupostasis* and *persona* by 'person'; and it has been maintained that 'we ought frankly to admit that we know nothing of personality possessing three distinct centres of consciousness'.[30]

If we compare the early phases of Trinitarianism, where the status of the Son and the Spirit is regarded as being below that of the Father, we see that the doctrine which posits the equality of the Three constitutes an innovation. It is a doctrine that is also contrary to the general trend of triadism in other cultures, where one central divine figure is usually dominant; and this applies as well to the trinities of the Egyptian and Graeco-Egyptian tradition which probably made an impact in the second and third centuries. Here it is of interest and relevance that Gregory Nazianzen appeals to the analogy of the family in order to fortify his argument concerning the equality and consubstantiality of the Trinity. The family he adduces is a little unexpected: it is Adam, Eve, and Seth, in accordance with the tradition recorded in Genesis 4: 25 that Seth was born as the third son of Adam and Eve after the murder of Abel; here it is said of Eve that *she bore a son and called his name Seth, for she said 'God has appointed for me another child instead of Abel, for Cain slew him'*, where the Hebrew words for *Seth* and *appointed* show paronomasia. Gregory Nazianzen[31] makes rather strange use of this ancient tradition:

> What was Adam? A creature of God. What then was Eve? A fragment of the creature. And what was Seth? The offspring of both. Does it then seem to you that creature and fragment and begotten are the same thing? Of course it does not. But were not these persons consubstantial? Of course they were. Well then, here is an acknowledged fact that different persons may have the same substance.

He then concedes that he is dealing mainly with human beings, but argues against those who reject the idea that the Spirit can be consubstantial with God; they should, he urges, *admit from human examples the possibility of our position*. He has adduced, of course, a mere analogy. It is rather striking, though, that the analogy is based on the idea of the family and that this is a feature of divine triadism in many diverse settings.

Much recent writing on the Trinity has been concerned to elaborate on the 'social doctrine' or 'inner Trinitarianism', and it is no part of the present study to pursue this line of thought unless the question of possible external influence suggests itself. Discussing the idea of *perichôrêsis*, Moltmann rightly maintains that 'two different categories of analogy have always been used for the eternal life of the Trinity: the category of the individual person, and the category of community.'[32] He shows that precedence was given in the West to the first category, following Augustine's psychological approach, but that the Eastern Orthodox emphasis was on the unity and fellowship of the Persons, following the Cappadocian Fathers and promoting the idea that 'the image of the family is a favourite one for the unity of the Trinity: three Persons – one family'.

Yet no human family is possible without a female element; there must be a mother as well as a father. In Gregory Nazianzen's scriptural analogy the mother is of course Eve. If the Trinity in fact is an all-male group, the Father image is open to be modified in the sense that 'a father who both begets and bears his son is not merely a father in the male sense' but a 'motherly father too' or at the same time 'the fatherly Mother of his only begotten Son'.[33] This kind of interpretation was not favoured by Paul's *kephalê*-ideology in 1 Corinthians 11: 3: *the head of every man is Christ, the head of a woman is her husband, and the head of Christ is God*,[34] which was unhappily espoused by Augustine, although its triad of God, Christ, and man did not prove dogmatically influential. Further, there was an evident weakness in Gregory Nazianzen's invocation of Adam, Eve, and Seth. It does not belong to the original creation story and figures only in the Priestly Record.[35] Yet that record adds import to the status of woman when it says that God created His image on earth male and female; for *on the day when God created human beings, he made them in his own likeness; he created them male and female* (Gen. 5: 1–2; cf. Gen. 1: 27). For female human beings this is a distinct amelioration of the tradition (in Gen. 2: 22) that God made Eve out of a rib extracted from Adam. If we leave early myth, however seriously it was taken by exponents of the divine purpose, we must concede that *the fellowship of the Holy Spirit* was an ardent and dynamic experience in the annals of the Church. It is a part of the triple benediction such as that which concludes Paul's second letter to the Corinthians: *The Grace of the Lord Jesus Christ, and the love of God, and fellowship of* (or, *in*) *the Holy Spirit, be with you all* (2 Cor. 13: 14); and here is found its fullest form. The final phrase indicates the full ambience of the fellowship: it embraces all believers, both male and female, and all social classes, including slaves. As a feminine noun *koinônia* seems to endow the Spirit with female force. It also suggests a communion freed from the idea of domination and opposed therefore to the essence of *monarchia*, although the latter term was often applied to the Trinity. Moreover it indirectly suggests a communion and converse not only of the human participants but also of the divine Persons named.

The concept of a female Holy Spirit became one of the lost causes of early Trinitarianism,[36] but it was revived in later times by Count N. L. Zinzendorf (AD 1700–60), who envisaged the Trinity as a family. Here, however, the status of Mary as the *Theotokos* enters into the thought.

'Through the relationship of Christians to Jesus, "His Mother" (the Spirit) becomes "Our Mother".'[37] While the idea of the Trinity as a divine family consisting of Father, Mother, and Child finds little support either in the New Testament or in later doctrine, apart from the Gnostic deviation, it can be argued that if it is favoured, the 'Motherhood of God', on a par with His Fatherhood, is thereby implied.[38]

We have seen that the figure of Isis was influential in the early stages of this idea, mainly through her identification with the Judaic and Hellenistic concepts of Wisdom and Logos. At a later stage Syria made a contribution, but it is not acceptable to claim that 'the designation of the Holy Spirit as Mother is of Syrian origin'.[39] One must admittedly accept that the Fifty 'Spiritual Homilies' formerly ascribed to 'Macarius the Egyptian' should now be attributed in some measure to Symeon of Mesopotamia. They are associated with the Messalians, the pietistic sect of 'praying people' who first emerged in Mesopotamia after about AD 350 and later spread to Syria, Asia Minor and Egypt.[40] In his study of the theology of Macarius/Symeon[41] the use of the double name by Hermann Dörries pointed to the strange duplication of ascription.[42] It was only in 1920 that the Belgian Benedictine scholar L. Villecourt found in the famous 'Fifty Homilies' sentences that had been recognized in 431 at Ephesus as betraying a Messalian origin. Their author's home was probably in the region of the Upper Euphrates; his culture was Greek and he chose the life of a monk with like companions. In his written work he was concerned with the force of evil, with prayer, and with the Spirit of God. To him the Spirit is the Spirit of Christ, and the Last Judgement is exemplified by the pericope of Matthew 25: 31ff., where Symeon follows the Evangelist verbatim.[43] But to him the fate of the world is decided within the individual soul. He quotes Augustine (*nos sumus tempora*) and is therefore writing after him.[44]

The role of Macarius remains rather unclear. His famed spirituality is assumed as a background force which is ill-defined: 'Makarios bleibt der stille Partner des Theologen Symeon.'[45] In a long epistle Symeon defends orthodox Trinitarian belief (Dörries, 328ff.) and emphasizes the birth of Christ from a Virgin (p.331). Elsewhere he presents the Holy Spirit in the image of a Mother who succours the needs of a crying, helpless child (p.161); and he returns to this image and that of the family in his treatment of the Holy Spirit.[46] In particular he portrays the fellowship of the Holy Spirit as implying a conjunction and union with the heavenly nature without which the soul is naked, imperfect and polluted.[47] Again, the Spirit is the heavenly Mother who understands and helps her stammering children, while the scriptural idea of ecstatic utterance is also present.[48] Certainly the preference for the mother-image strikes one as rather odd in some passages, as when the grief of a mother for her dead only-begotten son is compared with that of the *nous* when the divine soul dies;[49] the 'only-begotten' (*monogenês*) has specific reference to the Father.

In the fourth century Ephrem the Syrian was also giving special honour to women in his writings, composing *hymns for virgins* and proving *a second Moses for women folk* in that he allowed them to proffer praise.[50] Sebastian Brock shows that Ephrem was writing before Egyptian monasticism had come to northern Syria and Mesopotamia in the last decades of the fourth century; he describes his milieu as 'Syrian proto-monasticism' in which an ascetic ideal of virginity was upheld with reference to two groups – 'virgins', that is, celibate men and women, and 'holy ones', that is, married people who had renounced sexual intercourse.[51] From this viewpoint prominence is given to the idea of Christ as the Bridegroom, applied to both the Church collectively and individual members. Unexpected ideas can result from this biblical and Semitic source which is allied now to Christian thinking. Thus an exegesis of Genesis 2: 24 (*Therefore a man leaves his father and his mother and cleaves to his wife*) by Aphrahat, the Syriac Church Father who was writing in the early fourth century, includes an allusion to the Holy Spirit as a man's Mother:[52]

> What father and mother does he leave when he takes a wife? The sense is this: as long as a man has not yet taken a wife, he loves and honours God his Father and the Holy Spirit his Mother; but when a person takes a wife, he leaves his Father and Mother – in the sense indicated just now – and his mind is caught up with this world ...
> (Aphrahat, *Demonstrations*, 19. 10, tr. S. Brock)

The Virgin Mary received special devotion in the Syrian tradition, but without a general equation with the Holy Spirit.[53] It is true also that 'Christ's female companions are given a major role in the Gnostic gospels',[54] and that texts of the assumption legend relating to Mary are found in both Coptic and Syriac.[55] 'Sister Mary' is contrasted favourably with 'Mother Eve' in a Syriac poem which praises Ephrem for providing *hymns for virgins*.[56] It was in the sixth century that the doctrine of the corporeal assumption of the Virgin Mary was developed, but neither this nor the later doctrine of her Immaculate Conception had any clear Trinitarian implication. Yet the attribution of eternal virginity and sinlessness, as well as the occasional designation as *Co-redemptrix* (with the Saviour), suggest an approach to divinization; so does the fact that the Virgin Mary is often addressed in fervent prayer: *Ave Maria, gratia plena*!

As for the idea of *perichôrêsis*, it has continued to flourish in various ways. The advocates of 'Process Theology' favour the concept of 'the dynamic character of reality'. Among Greek thinkers it is Heracleitus who appeals to them with his dictum that all things are in flux, rather than Parmenides with his affirmation of the 'primacy of being over becoming and of absoluteness over relativity';[57] or Aristotle with his elevation of the absolute and immutable[58] and his concept of God as the unmoved mover. In Christian thought the doctrines of the Incarnation and the Trinity imply a sequence of divine revelation which has clear affinities with the approach of 'Process Theology'. Analogies have been found too in aspects of modern cosmological theories, particularly in the idea, implied by the general theory of relativity, that 'space and time are now dynamic quantities',[59] and that the universe is expanding through a process of continuous creation.[60] There is no precise parallel, naturally, to these ideas in the ancient world, although the notion of *creatio continua* has been applied to the inexhaustible life-giving potency of the Aten as portrayed in the Great Hymn of Akhenaten to his Sun-god.[61] In spite of the gulf of millennia one may justly compare the words of Teilhard de Chardin:[62] 'Creation has never ceased. Its act is a great continuous movement spread out over the totality of time. It is still going on.' Less easy to accept is his assumption that the sequence of creation, beginning with a self-sufficient First Being, denoted 'a primeval multiplicity which converges towards a final unity',[63] the last point being his famous 'Christ-Omega'. Particularly difficult is the second moment in the sequence: 'according to revelation, there was a moment of internal diversity and union in the divine life understood as "trinitization" rather than static unity.'[64] The reference apparently is to the development of the Trinity as a 'revealed' doctrine; in what sense that is feasible is not clear, unless the early debates within the Church are admitted to the category of revelation.

Interior relationships within the Trinity have been expounded by advocates of 'Process Theology'. An understanding of the role of the three Persons is clearly basic to such thinking, and the contribution of Augustine is seen to be significant since he appealed to the analogy of 'man, mind, and soul'.[65] The three faculties of man's spirit are defined as 'memory, intellection, and that love of self which is identical with the ecstatic love of God', where *voluntas* is expanded from the full context; and Thomas Aquinas is regarded as complementing this approach with his insistence that 'within the Trinitarian life of God, into the very notion of person, there enters the idea of relation: the Persons are subsistent relations'.[66] Walter Stokes sees God's benevolent *voluntas* as being exemplified by 'an eternal, free decision to create this universe'; and this is seen as leading to his 'self-revelation in time and history' and thus transcending any action completed in the past. The door is thus open for changing emphases and applications. Gone is the immutable and timeless Absolute of Greek philosophy; God is 'in the world and the world in him', an idea encapsulated in the term 'pan-en-theism', expressing 'the interpenetration of God and the world while at the same time not identifying God with the world'.[67]

Before the advent of the 'Process School' the early concept of mutual indwelling of Father, Son, and Holy Spirit had continued to receive attention, although the attitudes of theologians in the nineteenth and twentieth centuries have sometimes been far from favourable. In America W. Newton Clarke and Williams Adams Brown rejected the doctrines of internal relations and *perichôrêsis* as well as other aspects of the traditional formulae.[68] Ideas about the inner-Trinitarian relations were also rejected by Emil Brunner, who averred too that the concept of *substantia* had no place in a Christian theology and that placing the three Persons beside one another was contrary to the Biblical emphasis on their successive roles.[69] Catholic theologians, on the other hand, have emphasized the doctrine of the inner divine processions, including the 'double procession' of the Spirit, from the Father and from the Son according to the Western Church. The idea of the indwelling or interpenetration of the Persons is presented in two slightly differing aspects. One takes on a static stance by which the Persons rest in one another (*circuminsessio*), the other 'in more dynamic terms as indicating the eternal interchange and flow of life and activity (*perichoresis, circumincessio*)' suggests lively converse.[70] It is true that facets of this doctrine have aroused apprehension. If the Three Persons are regarded as communicating with each other and also with man, the danger arises, it has been urged, of 'a crude tritheism, not of course explicit but nonetheless very deeply embedded, which is a much greater danger than a Sabellian modalism'.[71]

The term 'Social Trinity' is sometimes used of the trend I have been discussing, and the suggestion has been made that the concept of plurality of Persons in God was based on 'the Christian experience of fellowship, *agape*, in the new community' and that 'the fellowship, or κοινωνία, of the Spirit in the new community is referred back to a transcendent fellowship of Persons in the life of God'.[72] But Lionel Thornton was careful to trace its origin to Christ's avowed relationship to his Father; this relationship was stressed particularly in John's Gospel, but is mentioned too in the Synoptic Gospels. Thornton was ready to use the term Persons of the Trinity, but not the term Personality. His analogy in the fellowship of the early Christian community is less convincing if large numbers are envisaged; the smaller groups of the 'House-Church' lead more naturally to the transference of the idea.[73]

Attitudes to this theme are not divided, be it noted, on Protestant vs. Roman Catholic lines. Whereas 'Process Theology' seems to have won more adherents in the latter camp, 'Inner Trinitarianism' has found many Protestant supporters. Even Karl Barth, whose stress on the absolute transcendence and otherness of God is well known, was able to sum up his

Trinitarian belief with an emphasis on the inner relationship:[74] 'In God Himself this Love is the love of the Father to the Son, of the Son to the Father. This eternal love within God Himself is the Holy Spirit.' To him the human community in a general sense offers a reflection of the divine community, the Trinity.[75]

Barth's use of the phrase 'eternal love within God Himself' raises the question of how far Inner Trinitarianism is seen to concern an essential and eternal relationship as opposed to one which is active and vital at the present time. Of course the two concepts can coexist, but the 'Process School' lays more emphasis on the vitality of present converse and influence. Barth was admittedly able to underline the continuing dynamism of the impact of the Spirit,[76] but a theologian such as Norman Pittenger goes further when he argues that the 'substance philosophy' can no longer be maintained 'when we come to see that "a thing *is* what it *does*" (Whitehead) ... and when we have to do not with substances but with events or occasions or (again to quote Whitehead) "actual entities" which are essentially "becomings" rather than "beings"'.[77] Without allying himself to the 'Process School', Jürgen Moltmann regards 'the perichoretic unity of the Triune God' as one which is 'open to human beings and the world' and goes on to speak of the 'open Trinity'.[78] Rejecting Barth's 'Trinitarian Monarchy' and also Rahner's theory of 'Threefold Self-Communication', he espouses 'the eternal *perichoresis* of Father, Son and Spirit', believing that communion or fellowship is the 'nature and the purpose of the triune God'.[79] Consistently with this he rejects too Pannenberg's emphasis on 'the monarchy of the Father'[80] and goes on to urge that the equality inherent in the Trinitarian notion of communion means that 'the mutual *perichoresis* of the three divine persons is in fact an expression of communication which is free from domination'.[81] Here he is thinking particularly of male domination. In the course of these arguments Moltmann fails to convince on some specific points, as for instance in his suggestion that 'neither male nor female' in Galatians 3: 29 implies 'an androgynous kind' of human being. He rightly puts this bizarre[82] idea in the form of a question. Yet he incisively cuts through to the implications of accepted dogma, as in his discussion of the birth of the only-begotten Son from the Father, showing that the Council of Toledo in AD 675 inculcated a 'motherly Father' when it declared that the Son was created *from the womb of the Father* (*de Patris utero*).[83]

The parity thus attributed to inner-Trinitarian relations is contrary to the general mode of triadic systems in other cultures and constitutes, as I have already suggested, a Christian innovation. In several expositions, as in those by Moltmann and Pittenger, it has a double attraction: it invokes the experience of the past in the history of doctrinal developments and in the faith of the Church, while at the same time opening the way to the vitality of present and future spiritual impacts. As far as the invocation of the past is concerned, it is true that analogies can be readily supplied from the triads of other religions, provided one includes myth, legend and ritual in the idea of the past. Thus a popular Greek triad, often depicted in painting and sculpture, comprised Demeter, Persephone and Triptolemus. According to early myth Persephone was the daughter of Demeter and Zeus. Triptolemus was the youthful god (or hero), apparently not related in kinship, charged by Demeter with the task of spreading the knowledge of agriculture, and a relief found at Eleusis shows Demeter and Persephone in the act of blessing the mission entrusted to the young god.[84] It is significant that Plutarch, when he discussed the myth and functions of Demeter and Persephone in his *De facie in orbe lunae* (942 D ff., 27), is interested mainly in ascribing Demeter's domain to the earth (and corn) and that of Persephone to the moon, which he sees as the abode of the good after death.[85] Plutarch does not mention Triptolemus here; perhaps he was regarded as a young hero-figure attached to the two goddesses.[86] But elsewhere Plutarch shows a special interest, possibly deriving from experience as an initiate, in the Osirian triad which features Osiris, Isis, and Horus. To him Isis is now the leading figure of the triad; and after describing the terrible deeds of the hostile Typhon he proceeds to praise the example given by Isis in her wise and brave actions:

> The sister and wife of Osiris, however, as his helper quenched and stopped Typhon's mad frenzy, nor did she allow the contests and struggles which she had undertaken, her wanderings and her many deeds of wisdom and bravery, to be engulfed in oblivion and silence, but into the most sacred rites she infused images, suggestions and representations of her experiences at that time, and so she consecrated at once a pattern of piety and an encouragement to men and women overtaken by similar misfortunes.
> (Plutarch, *De Iside et Osiride*, 361 D, 27)[87]

In his account of the legend (chs. 12-20) Plutarch has given the details which support his eloquent claim. These include the murder and dismemberment of Osiris, the birth of Horus and the victory of Horus over Typhon. Isis is said to have achieved sexual union with Osiris after his death, thus producing Harpocrates. While the credibility of certain 'outrageous episodes' is rebutted, Plutarch regards the account as being, for the most part, a record of actual events. He is therefore appealing, to use Christian parlance, to a revelation made in history. He is presenting an ardent *credo* which calls for an *imitatio Isidis*, for she is the *pattern of piety* which is worthy of emulation.[88]

Some half a century later, in the second century Apuleius was giving expression to a similar attitude with even greater fervour and colour, although he lacks the triadic content. In his 'Little Aretalogy' (*Metam.* 11.

5-6) he allows Isis to predicate of herself universal sway as the mother of the universe who is adored by the whole world in varied forms; and goddesses[89] identified with her are then named. After this she promises to Lucius release from his asinine form and extended happiness in this world and the next, on condition that he will vow to serve the goddess diligently and worthily. In chapter 25 of the same book Apuleius presents the prayer of gratitude which Lucius offers to Isis after his renewal of human form and his initiation. It is an exquisite prayer, hailed by Norden as the best example of a prose doxology; in fact it is beautifully poetic in style.[90] Yet it is remarkably bare of any allusions to the inner themes of the Isiac story, being content to praise her for her cosmic sovereignty, including her control of seas, stars and all forms of animal life. She is admittedly said to be *the holy and eternal saviour of the human race*, one who brings *the sweet love of a mother* (*dulcem matris adfectionem*) to the trials of the unfortunate. Such an expression might have led, one would have thought, to her famed role as mother of Harpocrates. That is not the case; nor does Apuleius give other allusions to the legend, although it is sometimes implied. It is true that a grand climax is promised at the end, for Lucius is heading for Rome to receive initiation into the cult of the supreme god Osiris. But Osiris is given no mention before the concluding chapters.

Plutarch and Apuleius, as second-century classical authors, might be expected to provide analogies, albeit in a limited sense, to the Trinitarian thought of the same era. While Apuleius is a strong witness to the vibrant ethos of the living Isiac religion, it is Plutarch who shows an affinity in this doctrinal area. His chapter 27, quoted above, presents a synoptic view of the Osirian triad as portrayed in the sequences of the mythic record. It is obviously subordinationist in that Isis is given pre-eminence over both Osiris and Horus, although her helpful actions for both of them are expressed or implied. Yet the treatise as a whole gives pride of place to Osiris. Subordinationism was a marked element of second- and third-century Trinitarianism as developed by Tertullian, Clement of Alexandria and Origen. It was only later that the doctrine of *perichôrêsis* was able to expunge the subordinationist element. Now the sense of parity, equality and converse between the Three Persons, and also between them and the human believers, was fervently accepted. The converse embedded in the mythic record was a part of the Isiac approach. At this point, however, a major difference in the ancient traditions emerges. The second Person of the Trinity is firmly anchored to history in the evidence for the earthly life of Christ. It is true that Plutarch believed that Osiris was an early king of Egypt; but there is an overwhelming weight of evidence to show that he was in origin a god who was assigned sovereignty over the realm of the dead,[91] a view credited by Plutarch in his chapter 78 to contemporary priests.

CONCLUDING REMARKS 301

Figure 14. Rome: Sarapis with Isis (in two forms) and Harpocrates

The second century of the Christian era was a century when the cult of Isis reached a high mark of popularity in the Roman Empire.[92] At an earlier stage the cult had Osiris as its central figure, and the several divine triads associated with the cult often give him this position, although Sarapis tends to displace him in the Ptolemaic era. I have tried to show, however, that the triune emphasis in the treatment of triads became a widespread phenomenon in the second and third centuries. Examples of it are often connected with Egyptian religion as presented in Greek sources (see my ch.13, section 6) and they are by no means confined to Osirian or Isiac contexts. In Egypt a strong early tradition supported the idea, especially after the beginning of the New Kingdom from about 1550 BC. In the early Christian centuries a general trend towards triadism in religion was potently furthered by phases of Platonism; and in this connection the impact of Hellenistic Judaism, particularly in the works of Philo, was a significant factor. But the idea of tri-unity was rarely evident in such systems. Here the Egyptian tradition was, in my view, a decisive influence on Christian interpretations of the Trinity, and Alexandria was very open to the force of this tradition. Greek tradition was also influential there. To some extent it presented aspects of the native tradition which it had subsumed; but in addition it conveyed the urgency of the contemporary Greek desire to find unity in the diversity of the pantheon. A cross-cultural confluence is therefore evident in this process.

In both the Ptolemaic and Roman eras the god Sarapis achieved amazing popularity in the pattern of the Osirian triad throughout the Graeco-Roman world (Fig.14).[93] He often replaces Osiris, but himself bears a facet of the character of Osiris, as the derivation of his name from the Egyptian *Wsir-ḥp* clearly shows, where the second element points to the Memphite bull-god Apis. In fact the term Osiris-Apis was a regular name in the old religion for the immortalized dead Apis.[94] In iconography, however, a good degree of Hellenization occurred, including the measure of corn, the *calathus*, seen on the head of Sarapis. Whereas the god shared an anthropomorphic visage with Osiris, features of Pluto, Dionysus, Zeus, Helius and Osiris-Aion are sometimes assigned to him, and these doubtless added to his popular appeal, particularly outside Egypt (Fig. 15).[95] According to Plutarch (*De Is. et Os.* 362 B, 28) *Sarapis is common to all* (πᾶσι κοινός), *and this is true also of Osiris, as the initiates know*. In a meticulous study of the Sarapieion in Memphis, the cult of Sarapis is well described as 'that Greek masterpiece of adaptation of an old Egyptian cult'.[96] In general function he acted as a saviour god who could fend against present perils as well as against the dangers of death; he was a healer and comforter and one who at the same time guaranteed fertility and strength. Several of these qualities he shared with both Osiris and Isis.

Figure 15.
A. The remains of the temple of Isis on the island of Delos
B. Above, the author admires her statue, albeit now headless, at the back of the cella

Our present concern, though, is with his triadic function: what precisely does he contribute to the group which links him with Isis and Harpocrates? (Or, at Delos, with Isis and Anubis – see Fig. 15). His frequent identification with Osiris implies giving him the role of *paredros* to Isis and thus also that of father of Harpocrates. But the mythology of all this remains attached to Osiris only.[97] Yet Isis appears often as the wife of Sarapis, and in Alexandria most shrines dedicated to them were dedicated to Sarapis and Isis only with no mention of Harpocrates.[98] The triadic group is represented in art, but only in a minority of objects. More often Isis and Sarapis are figured as a dyad, as on a slate palette in the Cairo Museum;[99] but the great majority of the massive collection garnered by Hornbostel concern the single figure of the god himself. Harpocrates occurs with Isis-Pharia and an uncertain figure on a gem in Cairo.[100] If such a figure were recognized as Sarapis, he would undoubtedly be interpreted as the father of Harpocrates. When Anubis occurs with Sarapis and Isis (sometimes in Alexandria and often in Delos), his role is probably that of a helper of Isis.

Our theme has its immediate setting, evidently, in the Roman imperial era, and in Alexandria triadism continued to flourish at that time. Although the Sarapieion at Memphis marked the origin of Sarapis, the Alexandrian temple was at the heart of the city which saw the clash and competition of creeds, as well as, sometimes, their cohesion and interpenetration. In both Memphis and Alexandria a degree of continuity clearly prevailed as between the Ptolemaic and Roman eras. In an Epilogue to *Memphis under the Ptolemies* (1988), 266ff. Dorothy J. Thompson remarks on the continuity in some external and economic facets of life in Memphis and on the 'apparent reconciliation of the Memphite clergy with the new Roman emperor'. Thus the Apis cult continued to enjoy favour. Although she does not make special mention of it, a marked feature of her previous chapter on 'The Sarapieion' can also be assumed to have persisted. This was the easy interplay of the two languages, Egyptian and Greek; and the 'Dream of Nectanebo', which she rightly describes as 'this Greek version of an essentially Egyptian tale', is an excellent example of the bilingual approach which made literary and religious influences possible in a two-way traffic.[101]

The status of Sarapis was strengthened in Alexandria during the Roman era by his elevation to be patron god of the city. It was in Alexandria too that the Emperor Vespasian in AD 69 was said to have effected miraculous healings of lameness and blindness as Sarapis incarnate; in the Egyptian tradition Isis is the main upholder of healing magic which Sarapis now shares, as the Sarapis-Hymn of Aelius Aristides makes very clear. Yet the most striking feature of the cult, as of the Osirian deities in general, was its popularity throughout the countries of the Roman world. In the Aegean area Sarapis was more conspicuous, while in the West Osiris retained some importance; in this era, however, Isis tended to be dominant, and in most areas the triadic grouping of deities was frequent, although with some variation in the choice of deities associated with Isis.[102]

The far-flung extent of this religious orbit demands recognition in terms of influence, and particularly on the early Christian shapers of doctrine. Mention has been made above (ch.12, section 3(i)) of Tertullian's familiarity with Graeco-Egyptian triadism. In his *Apology* (6. 8) he bemoans the fact that Sarapis, Isis, and Harpocrates had earlier been evicted with contempt from the Capitol in Rome, but now have enjoyed the highest honour and esteem (*summam maiestatem*). For that matter we know that in his own native Carthage there was a temple of Sarapis in the second century – during Tertullian's lifetime.[103] Indeed the visual evidence for these cults, in the form of temples,[104] statuary, coins, amulets, lamps and inscriptions, was so widespread and richly pervasive that the most casual observers must have been aware of them. To exponents of religious belief of whatever creed, they must have held acute interest, even when that might be tinged with contempt. For Christian would-be-trinitarians it was evidence writ large in the contemporary environment. Indeed it could not easily be avoided. Nor should we ignore the related impact of the living cult as expressed in festivals and processions. In this respect the flamboyant and emotional appeal of the Isis cult has been unforgettably conveyed by Apuleius, with a local reference to the cult in Cenchreae near Corinth. That scenario could have been witnessed in numerous other places in both East and West, albeit often with less colourful elaboration, probably, than that depicted by the African author, who was an adept literary artist. Several of the General or Oecumenical Councils of the Church were held in Asia Minor, a region where Sarapis and Isis were especially popular; the lesser Synods were held in more scattered areas. Attenders at these meetings, including the bishops, must have been fully aware of the religious situation in their own areas, and the increasing power of Christianity was doubtless not the only topic of conversation.

It has to be admitted, though, that the processional displays of the Egyptian cults as portrayed by Apuleius, Plutarch and Clement of Alexandria do not include clear allusions to triadism. Perhaps that would have been difficult. Yet we know that Isis was adored as a loving mother at the centre of a family triad, and as such she figured in statuary and amulets. Furthermore, to theologically inclined observers the message of *Isis, una quae es omnia* and like expressions would not have been lost, with its emphasis on unity in plurality. In the case of Sarapis the εἷς θεός formula, often followed by the name of three gods (and at times by two or four) marked a trinitarian idea, the purely elevatory sense being replaced in the second century and later by an emphasis on henotheism and unity, as in *One is Zeus Sarapis Helius, ruler of the world, invincible* (Rome, c. AD 212; cf. above, ch.13, section 6, no.9). In such contexts there is a clear debt also to the syncretistic urge which is evident in Greek writings of the Hellenistic and Roman eras.[105]

Our survey has shown that the grouping of deities in triads was a favourite practice in many parts of the ancient world. Other numerical groupings were also favoured, particularly those of two, four, seven and nine deities. The dyad has special relevance to the importance of the triad, since the addition of one (a child, say, of parents, or a deity also revered locally) converts it into a triad. Types of iconography contributed in some degree to such an evolution. In both Egypt and Sumeria an antithetic group of two figures often meant that they were facing a central figure, so that a group of three actually emerges.[106]

But how significant are divine triads in the history of religions? After a critical review of a work devoted to the triad of Heliopolis-Baalbek,[107] Jonas C. Greenfield opines that there are 'many scholars who no longer take triads that seriously', adding that 'this is an inheritance of a previous generation who sought, it would seem, for a *Sitz im Leben* for the trinity'.[108] The last point has some force, and it is true of part of the motivation behind the present study. Greenfield is also anxious to restrict the application of the term 'triad'. He rightly remarks that 'affiliation' is often indicated, while other triads are 'functional'. He is ready to refer to the group at Heliopolis-Baalbek as a 'trio' but not as a 'triad'. In view of the many other types of triad which have appeared, the validity of such a distinction must be questioned.[109] The only practical procedure is to grant the status of triad to any set of three deities who are grouped together frequently enough in literature or art (or both) to be regarded as forming an established group (see above, Introduction).

In this theme we encounter a wide-ranging manifestation of human thought and imagination about the divine; and quite apart from its occurrence in Christian faith and doctrine it has a deep intrinsic interest wherever it appears. As Herman te Velde has remarked, the triad should not be dismissed as a secondary religious phenomenon, for 'theological treatment of the religious tradition, such as grouping gods into triads, is no less an element of religion than certain aspects and developments of cult and devotion.'[110]

Structurally the heritage of Israel and Judaism prepared Christian minds for the idea that unity and plurality could characterize the divine, even if the idea was not as a rule on specifically triadic lines. The role of the Holy Spirit was directly derived from this source. But for the highly distinctive idea of tri-unity we must turn to Egypt, where the New-Kingdom theology began to treat the triad as a trinity. In the early Christian centuries this development was endorsed by Greek influence: the Platonic triadic systems sometimes came close to the dimension of trinitarianism, and popular Greek syncretism was often ready to regard three deities as one.

NOTES

[1] See B. R. Rees, *Pelagius, a Reluctant Heretic* (London, 1990), xii ff. and 108ff. Also his invaluable sequel, *The Letters of Pelagius and His Followers* (1991), [edited and translated].

[2] By R. P. C. Hanson (Edinburgh, 1988).

[3] Ibid., 874.

[4] Ibid., 875.

[5] *Substance and Illusion in the Christian Fathers* by C. G. Stead (London, 1985) concerns a different second category. In this book (section VI) Stead treats of 'The Origins of the Doctrine of the Trinity' and on pp.514ff. of this Section, 'Of Older Jewish Sources', giving prominence to the image of God enthroned attended by two angels ('either the two Seraphim of Isaiah's vision or the two Cherubim who mount guard over the Ark').

[6] *The New English Bible, Oxford Study Edition*, ed. Samuel Sandmel (New York, 1976). Bailey's remarks are seen ad loc., p.2n. He compares also Gen. 3: 22, *The man has become like one of us, knowing good and evil*; and 11: 7, *Come, let us go down there, and confuse their speech*. Raimundo Panikkar, *The Trinity and the Religious Experience of Man* (New York, 1973), 27, oddly gives precedence to plural notions attached to Indo-European words for God (*deva, theos, Zeus* etc.), but then proceeds to invoke the Semitic *'Elohîm*.

[7] Leonhard Goppelt (tr. D. H. Madvig), *Typos: The Typological Interpretation of the Old Testament in the New* (Grand Rapids, Mich., 1982; German original 1939), 117. On the Old Testament's view of the Spirit see further Jules Lebrereton (tr. A. Thorold), *Hist. of the Dogma of the Trinity*. Vol.I: *The Origins* (London, 1939), 81-9, pointing on p.89 to the intimate unity of Spirit and Wisdom; and on p.116 to the personification of the Spirit, 'frequent enough in the Rabbinical writings'. Cf. H. A. Wolfson, *The Philosophy of the Church Fathers*, Vol.I: *Faith, Trinity, Incarnation* (3rd edn., Cambridge, Mass., 1970), 141ff. He remarks on p.142 that the belief in the Holy Spirit was one of many beliefs which Christianity inherited from Judaism.

[8] A. D. Nock, *Essays on Religion and the Ancient World*, ed. Zeph Stewart (Oxford, 1972; repr. 1986), I, 90. He refers also to Paul's doctrine of the Holy Spirit. For a fuller guide to this doctrine see W. D. Davies, *Paul and Rabbinic Judaism* (new edn., Philadelphia, 1980), ch. 8, 178ff.; cf. *idem*, *The Setting of the Sermon on the Mount* (Cambridge, 1964), 40ff. (on the Spirit in the Rabbinic *Mekilta*) and *Jewish and Pauline Studies* (Philadelphia, 1984), 72ff., with a suggestion that the spread of Christianity may have influenced the *Mekilta*.

[9] Cf. R. A. Markus in *Christian Faith and Greek Philosophy* (London, 1960), 138f. A. H. Armstrong is the author of the first part of this book.

[10] Stead, *Substance and Illusion*, VI, 582ff.

[11] Stead, op. cit. VI, 583. Here he refers to A. H. Armstrong, *Later Greek Philosophy*, 90–5 (= *The Cambridge Hist. of Later Greek and Early Medieval Philosophy*, 1967). The contribution cited is not, however, by Armstrong, but by P. Merlan. Armstrong edited the volume.

[12] A. Hilary Armstrong, *Plotinian and Christian Studies* (Variorum Reprint, London, 1979), VI, 128 (in a paper on 'Salvation, Plotinian and Christian'). See also his *Hellenic and Christian Studies* (Variorum Reprint, London, 1990), esp. VIII: 'The Self-definition of Christianity in relation to Later Platonism'. The attraction of the impersonal approach to God, as attested in Hinduism and Buddhism, is urged by R. Panikkar in *The Trinity and the Religious Experience of Man* (1973), 19ff. He doubts (p.28) 'whether an exclusively personal conception of the godhead does justice to it', avowing too (p.29) that the Upanishads 'point to a religious attitude that is not founded upon faith in a God-Thou ... but in the supra-rational experience of a "Reality" which in some ways "inhales" us into himself'.

[13] Armstrong, *Plotinian and Christian Studies*, VI, 131–2. Cf. his quotation of *Enneads*, VI. vii. 3 on p.128: *The soul loves the Good because it has been moved by Him to love from the beginning.*

[14] Peter Gerlitz, *Ausserchristliche Einflüsse auf die Entwicklung des christlichen Trinitätsdogmas* (Leiden, 1963).

[15] Cumont, *Textes et monuments*, I (Brussels, 1899), 208f. and 3031 are cited; for the former see Vermaseren, *CIMRM* I (The Hague, 1956), 753f.; but the point is not pursued. W. O. Moeller, *The Mithraic Origin and Meanings of the Rotas–Sator Square* (Leiden, 1973), 1, 5, 30f., posits another Mithraic triad (Saturnus–Aion, Sol Invictus, Mithra); see my remarks above, ch.7, section 4.

[16] E.g. p.99: 'Hermes-Thôt ist also so etwas wie der Archetypus des Logosbegriffs ...' Thoth does not have this role in the earliest tradition; see my *Conflict of Horus and Seth* (1960), 81–4 ('The Role of Thoth').

[17] Cf. Pheme Perkins on 'Sophia as Goddess in the Nag Hammadi Codices', in Karen L. King (ed.), *Images of the Feminine in Gnosticism* (Philadelphia, 1988), 96–112.

[18] Cf. R. A. Markus on Marius Victorinus, stating that 'his trinitarian theology is essentially an essay in metaphysics, based on Neoplatonic ontology ...'; *Cambridge Hist. of Later Greek and Early Medieval Philosophy*, 339.

[19] Kelly, *Early Christian Doctrines*, 265. Cf. David Brown, *The Divine Trinity* (London, 1985), 283: 'But, without inequality, it is hard to see how the relation can be the basis for making distinctions within the immanent Trinity.' On 'perichôrêsis' cf. R. J. Feenstra and C. Plantinga, Jr. (ed.), *Trinity, Incarnation, and Atonement* (Notre Dame, Ind., 1989), 4.

[20] Cf. John Whittaker, 'Plutarch, Platonism and Christianity', in *Neoplatonism and Early Christian Thought (In honour of A. H. Armstrong)*, ed. H. J. Blumenthal and R. A. Markus (London, 1981), 50–63, esp. 50.

[21] A. H. Armstrong, *Plotinian and Christian Studies* (1979), XX, 67–8. Cf. R. Panikkar, *Myth, Faith, and Hermeneutics* (New York, 1979), 206, on union and equality or difference in the Trinity: 'Just as the Son and the Spirit are identical with regard to the Father, they are also infinitely different – for nothing finite exists in the Trinity. Strictly speaking, we cannot talk of equality or difference in the heart of the divinity.'

[22] Hans Küng (tr. Ed. Quinn), *On Being a Christian* (London, 1978), 474; cf. above ch.8, section 3.

[23] André Manaranche in his *Le Monothéisme chrétien* (Paris, 1985), as cited by Geoffrey Wainwright in *ET* 98 (1987), 333.

[24] See above ch.2, sections 2-3.

[25] *Book of Common Prayer*, 60, 'Whosoever will be saved ...'; cf. Alan Richardson, *Creeds in the Making* (1972), 121: 'the Holy Spirit is said to be equal to the Father in divinity, majesty, quality and power.'

[26] Kelly, *Early Christian Doctrines*, 263; cf. H. Küng, *On Being a Christian* (1978), 475; J. Moltmann, *The Trinity and the Kingdom of God* (1981), 167. According to Karl Rahner and H. Vorgrimler, *Kleines Theologisches Wb.* (Freiburg, 1962), 110, it was not till about AD 1000 that the added words were acknowledged by Rome.

[27] Kelly, op. cit., 264-5. On p.267 he refers to the view that their doctrine was 'inescapably tritheistic' in spite of their stress on the divine unity.

[28] T. F. Torrance in *Religion, Reason and the Self (In honour of Hywel D. Lewis)*, ed. S. R. Sutherland and T. A. Roberts (Cardiff, 1989), 115, in an essay on 'The Soul and Person, in Theological Perspective'. In his n.23, p.118, he cites passages in the *Orationes* of Gregory Nazianzen 'for the *relational* nature of the divine hypostases'.

[29] Tr. J. Stevenson, *Creeds, Councils and Controversies* (1966), 58.

[30] H. Wheeler Robinson, *The Christian Experience of the Holy Spirit* (3rd edn., Glasgow, 1930), 229. Cf. Nicholas Lash, *Believing Three Ways in One God* (1992), 30ff., arguing against the use of 'Persons' and for the idea of 'three modes of being' in God. Yet the Son was clearly a Person, validated historically.

[31] *Orationes*, 31. 11. Tr. J. Stevenson, op. cit., 58.

[32] J. Moltmann, *The Trinity and the Kingdom of God* (1981), 198-9. He has developed the same interpretation in his *History and the Triune God* (tr. John Bowden, London, 1991), 59ff., where he writes of 'the unique fellowship, communion, of the three persons'.

[33] Moltmann, *The Trinity and the Kingdom of God*, 164.

[34] W. D. Davies, *Jewish and Pauline Studies* (Philadelphia, 1984), 222, questions the relevance of such dicta in any lasting sense. Cf. G. Bornkamm, *Paul* (London, 1971), 205, who finds the whole passage 'oddly obscure'.

[35] Cf. Moltmann, *History and the Triune God* (1991), 61.

[36] Cf. above ch.13, section 3; Peter Gerlitz, *Ausserchristliche Einflüsse* (1963), 120ff.

[37] C. J. Podmore in *JTS* 42 (1991), 776, reviewing Gary Steven Kinkel, *Our Dear Mother the Spirit: An Investigation of Court Zinzendorf's Theology and Praxis* (New York, 1990).

[38] Moltmann, *History and the Triune God* (1991), 64.

[39] Moltmann, ibid. 65.

[40] See esp. Hermann Dörries, *Symeon von Mesopotamia. Die Überlieferung der messalianischen 'Makarios'-Schriften* (Texte und Untersuchungen, 55, Heft 1, Leipzig, 1941), Cf. *ODCC* (rev. edn. 1983), s.v. Macarius, St of Egypt and s.v. Messalians. Yet some of the writings clearly preserve the background and tradition of Egyptian monasticism: see J. Gwyn Griffiths, 'The Impress of Egyptian Religion on the Mediaeval "Dialogue of the Soul and Body"', in *Gegengabe*, ed. I. Gamer-Wallert and W. Helck (Fs. für Emma Brunner-Traut, Tübingen, 1991), 103-18, esp. 117.

[41] Hermann Dörries, *Die Theologie des Makarios/Symeon* (Abh. Göttingen, III, 103, 1978). The author died in 1977.

[42] The variations Makarios, Symeon and Makarios-Symeon are also found in the manuscripts: see ibid., 12.

[43] Dörries, ibid., 313.

[44] Ibid., 22.

[45] Ibid., 12.

[46] Ibid., 200, 210.

[47] Ibid., 237ff. The term 'union' (μίξις) has originally a sexual sense. The Holy Spirit is the female unit in this image.

[48] Ibid., 257ff. and 341. The common speech of all Christians is implied (p.420). For ecstatic utterance see Cyril Williams, *Tongues of the Spirit* (Cardiff, 1981), 25–45, on glossolalia; and J. Gwyn Griffiths, *Atlantis and Egypt with Other Selected Essays* (Cardiff, 1991), 266ff. on claims of xenoglossy in the ancient languages.

[49] Homily 16, 11 (= p. 164, 153), in *Die 50 geistlichen Homilien des Makarios*, ed. H. Dörries, E. Klostermann, M. Kroeger (Patristische Texte und Studien, 4, Berlin, 1964). In his note ad loc. Dörries says that the same comparison occurs in *Apophth. patr. Poimen.* 26.

[50] Sebastian Brock, *Saint Ephrem: Hymns on Paradise* (Crestwood, NY, 1990), 22–3, quoting in this case from another Syriac poet, Jacob of Serugh, who died in AD 521.

[51] Ibid., 26.

[52] Ibid., 28–9. Brock points out that Ephrem's exegesis in his Commentary on Genesis (in Brock's translation on p.206) is quite different. On Aphrahat's importance see F. J. Foakes Jackson, *The History of the Christian Church* (6th edn., Cambridge, 1914), 550f.; on his brand of asceticism see H. Lietzmann, *A History of the Early Church* (tr. B. L. Woolf, London, 1950), 166f.

[53] Kelly, *Early Christian Doctrines*, 495.

[54] W. H. C. Frend, *The Rise of Christianity* (London, 1984), 209.

[55] Ibid., 226 n.98. Whether 'the earliest Mariolatry' (Frend's term) can be said to be Gnostic (ibid., 209) is not so clear; it depends on the force of the term 'Mariolatry'. In the *Gospel of Philip*, as Frend notes, Mary Magdalene is given an important role; and so is Mary the Virgin: cf. above, ch.13, section 3.

[56] Brock, *St Ephrem the Syrian*, 24, quoting from Jacob of Serugh (fifth–sixth century AD).

[57] Ewert H. Cousins in *Process Theology: Basic Writings* (New York, 1971), 7–8. He also refers to similar ideas in Theravada Buddhism with its denial of a permanent static substance; this form of Buddhism probably had its origin in south-east Asia in the early centuries AD.

[58] Cf. Charles Hartshorne, ibid., 48.

[59] Stephen W. Hawking, *A Brief History of Time* (London, 1988), 33.

[60] Ibid., 35–51. Rather different is the idea of linear evolutionism propounded by Teilhard de Chardin, who aims at a 'blend of science and mysticism': see the essays in Ewert H. Cousins, ed., op. cit., 229ff.

[61] Jan Assmann, *Re und Amun* (Freiburg, 1983), 114ff. On p.116 he quotes from the Great Hymn, 'Thou makest millions of new beings (ḫprw) from thyself, the Sole One' (= Sandman, *Texts from the Time of Akhenaten* (Brussels, 1938), 95, 12–13. Cf. Erik Hornung (tr. Baines), *Conceptions of God* (1983), 182, on the 'perpetual renewal' of creation.

[62] From 'Le Milieu mystique', quoted by Ian G. Barbour in Ewert H. Cousins, ed., op. cit., 337.

⁶³ Ian G. Barbour, ibid.

⁶⁴ He also regarded creation, incarnation, and consummation as 'the three fundamental "mysteries" of Christianity': see Hans Küng (tr. Ed. Quinn), *Does God Exist?* (1978; repr. London, 1991), 172, in the course of a valuable critique of Teilhard de Chardin's work, followed by an equally valuable treatment of 'God in process', for which a bibliography is given on p.721 n.52.

⁶⁵ Walter E. Stokes in Ewert H. Cousins, op. cit., 147. More precisely, the spirit (*mens*) of man is given three basic faculties – memory (*memoria*), understanding (*intelligentia*) and will (*voluntas*). The analogy is described by Hans Küng, *On Being a Christian*, 474, as 'ingenious but questionable'; cf. Kelly, *Early Christian Doctrines*, 276ff.

⁶⁶ W. E. Stokes, op. cit., 147.

⁶⁷ Ewert H. Cousins, op. cit., 14.

⁶⁸ Claude Welch, *The Trinity in Contemporary Theology* (London, 1953), 28, having pointed to the potent influence of Ritschl and Schleiermacher. Cf. Alasdair I. C. Heron, *A Century of Protestant Theology* (London, 1980), 23ff.; on 'Process Thought', pp.144ff.

⁶⁹ Welch, op. cit., 69–70.

⁷⁰ Ibid. 116.

⁷¹ Karl Rahner on 'The Triune God' in *A Rahner Reader*, ed. Gerald A. McCool (London, 1975), 142–3. He also mentioned the danger of 'thinking of three different consciousnesses'.

⁷² Lionel S. Thornton, *The Incarnate Lord* (London, 1928), 305, quoted by Claude Welch, op. cit., 136f.

⁷³ Cf. Wayne A. Meeks, *The First Urban Christians* (New Haven, 1983), 29–30.

⁷⁴ Karl Barth (tr. J. S. McNabb), *Credo* (London, 1935), 119; cf. Hugh Ross Mackintosh, *Types of Modern Theology* (London, 1937; repr. 1945), 300f.

⁷⁵ Daniel Day Williams in *Process Theology*, ed. Ewert H. Cousins (1971), 177.

⁷⁶ Karl Barth (tr. Grover Foley), *Evangelical Theology: An Introduction* (London, 1963), 55; 'It was the Spirit whose existence and action make possible and real (and possible and real up to this very day) the existence of Christianity in the world.' Cf. idem (tr. G. W. Bromiley), *The Christian Life: Church Dogmatics*, IV, 4: *Lecture Fragments* (Edinburgh, 1981), 90: 'The Holy Spirit is God himself in his living, his eternally living unity as Father and Son ...'

⁷⁷ Norman Pittenger, *The Lure of Divine Love* (New York, 1979), 133; cf. his *Catholic Faith in a Process Perspective* (New York, 1981), 87, and *Picturing God* (London, 1982), 77 (on God as 'the cosmic Lover').

⁷⁸ J. Moltmann, *History and the Triune God* (1991), 84. He offers a more detailed discussion in his *Trinity and the Kingdom of God* (1981), 171ff., with a mention on p.173 of the doctrine of *the Trinity of love*.

⁷⁹ Idem, *History and the Triune God*, xii.

⁸⁰ Ibid., xix. Cf. W. Pannenberg (tr. L. L. Wilkins and D. A. Priebe), *Jesus – God and Man* (London, 1968), 158ff., where basic import is attached to the distinction between Father and Son as regarded first by the Palestinian community.

⁸¹ Moltmann, *History and the Triune God*, xv.

⁸² I. e. in the context of Paul's thought. The idea of androgyny or hermaphroditism was well known to the Greeks. In Egypt it was sometimes associated with the divine primal creator. See Jan Zandee, 'Der androgyne Gott in Ägypten', in *Ägypten und Altes Testament*, 14. *Religion im Erbe Ägyptens (Fs. A. Böhlig)* ed. M. Görg

(Wiesbaden, 1988), 240-78.

[83] Moltmann, op. cit., 22 and 186 n.4.

[84] Oskar Seyffert, rev. H. Nettleship and J. E. Sandys, *Dict. of Classical Antiquities* (London, 1957), 177, Fig.1 s.v. Demeter. Cf. J. G. Frazer, ed. Mary Douglas and S. MacCormack, *The Illustrated Golden Bough* (London, 1978), 139, with figure of a vase in the BM depicting the same triad.

[85] See the notes by Harold Cherniss in his Loeb edition and translation, Vol.12 (London, 1957), 192-7.

[86] Cf. Erwin Rohde, *Psyche* (10th edn., Tübingen, 1925), I, 283; on p.210 he lists other triadic groups with Demeter. Guthrie, *The Greeks and their Gods* (London, 1954), 103, sees him as 'a youthful attendant and lover' rather like Adonis and Attis. Unlike these, however, Triptolemus has a marked cultural role as a *Sondergott* relating to the production of corn.

[87] Tr. J. Gwyn Griffiths, *Plutarch's De Iside et Osiride* (1970), 159.

[88] Cf. R. E. Witt, *Isis in the Graeco-Roman World* (London, 1971), 134. Friedrich Solmsen, *Isis among the Greeks and Romans* (Cambridge, Mass., 1979), 67, misleads when he says that Plutarch's work tells nothing of 'the help and motherly warmth that people in distress expected when they turned to Isis'.

[89] In the opening lines of ch.5 Isis calls herself *the single form that fuses all gods and goddesses (deorum dearumque facies uniformis)*, but no gods are afterwards named. See my note ad loc. in *Apuleius ...: The Isis-Book* (1975), 143-4. We have here a clear instance of unity in plurality.

[90] See my remarks ibid., 320ff.

[91] J. Gwyn Griffiths, *The Origins of Osiris and his Cult* (Leiden, 1980), 23 and 208.

[92] This century, Jean Leclant said, *est isaïque par excellence*. See R. E. Witt, 'The Importance of Isis for the Fathers', *Studia Patristica* 8 (Berlin, 1966), 135.

[93] See P. M. Fraser, *Ptolemaic Alexandria* (Oxford, 1972), 246ff., where he deals mainly with the theology of the Sarapis-cult, but also with its origins. See also his studies in *Op. Athen.* III (1960), 1-54 and VII (1965), 23-45.

[94] Cf. D. J. Crawford in *Studies in Ptolemaic Memphis* (Louvain, 1980), 7, noting also the alternative Apis-Osiris; also Morenz, *Rel.* (1960), 260.

[95] John E. Stambaugh, *Sarapis under the Early Ptolemies* (EPRO 25; Leiden, 1972), 14ff.

[96] Dorothy J. (Crawford-)Thompson, *Memphis under the Ptolemies* (Princeton, 1988). 213.

[97] Cf. J. E. Stambaugh, op. cit., 36ff.

[98] Fraser, op. cit., 261. Cf. above, after ch.4, 'Conspectus', s.v. Alexandria (1).

[99] Wilhelm Hornbostel, *Sarapis* (EPRO 32; Leiden, 1973), Abb.306 a/b (Pl.188) and pp. 287, 401. It belongs to the Roman era.

[100] Ibid., 303f. with allusions to a triadic group in which Sarapis is accompanied by two female deities, one of whom is Isis. Cf. Th. Kraus, *MDAIK* 19 (1963), 77-105 and above, 'Conspectus' after ch.4. s.v. Alexandria.

[101] Cf. Erich Winter in *Das ptolemäische Ägypten*, ed. H. Maehler and V. M. Strocka (Mainz, 1978), 185, on points of contact between Greek and Egyptian literati.

[102] Sometimes a tetrad emerges, as when Harpocrates joins Sarapis, Isis, and Anubis: see Fabio Mora, *Prosopografia Isiaca*, II (Leiden, 1990), 33f.; cf. Fraser, 'Two Studies' (*Op. Athen.* III, 1960), 32 n.5, for an instance of Apis in this fourth role. On Harpocrates in triads cf. A. M. El-Khachab, *JEA* 57 (1971), 143f.

[103] L. Vidman, *SIRIS* 326, with related inscriptions, nos.770ff.; cf. Mora, op. cit. I, 512f.

[104] Cf. Regina Salditt-Trappmann, *Tempel der ägyptischen Götter in Griechenland und an der Westküste Kleinasiens* (EPRO 15, Leiden, 1970). See also the detailed surveys by Françoise Dunand, Michel Malaise and L. Vidman, for which see Bibl. J. Leclant and G. Clerc, *IBIS* (4 vols., EPRO 18, Leiden, 1972-91) is also of basic import, dealing as it does with the diffusion of these and other Egyptian cults.

[105] Cf. Keith Ward, *A Vision to Pursue* (London, 1991), 8, on the 'revision' which occurred in the third and fourth centuries, 'when the concepts of Hellenistic philosophy were introduced to give shape to classical doctrines of Jesus as the "second person of the Trinity"'. See too his remarks on pp.111-12 and 194.

[106] See above ch.3, section 3. Several striking examples are given by W. L. Dulière in his *De la dyade à l'unité par la triade* (Paris, 1965), 146-9, with figures from Sumerian and Egyptian art. He compares the use of anthropomorphic but winged cherubim in Christian art, facing a central figure of Christ in his Fig.81, p.148. My copy of this book had been presented by the author to the late Dr Ramsey, archbishop of Canterbury.

[107] Youssef Hajjar, *La Triade d'Héliopolis-Baalbek* (2 vols., Leiden, 1977; and Vol.3, Montreal, 1985), Cf. above, ch.5, section 5.

[108] *Numen* 38 (1991), 272. The review itself appeared ibid. 37 (1990), 280-3.

[109] Cf. above, ch.5, section 5.

[110] H. te Velde, *JEA* 57 (1971), 80.

Appendix: The Pallid Pantheon of Ancient China

The early leaders of Chinese religious thought offer a varied ideology that is richly attractive, but in general its tone can be said to be philosophical rather than religious. This becomes particularly evident when we try to discover whether any system of structural order of divine beings was evolved.

In the sixth or fifth century BC Confucius defined wisdom thus:

> To work for the things the common people have a right to and to keep one's distance from the gods and spirits while showing them reverence can be called wisdom.
>
> (Confucius, *Analects*, 11. 12)[1]

In view of such sayings it is easy to understand the remark of a Sinologist that 'Confucianism is rather like a secular religion invented by a benevolent agnostic for the harmonious functioning of a human beehive'.[2] Nor is it surprising that the works of Confucius and his adherents do not proffer details about *the gods and spirits* from whom he wished to distance himself. Allusions to the divine will and purpose often use the term *T'ien*, 'Heaven', and the same is true of the literature associated with the impressive movements encountered in Mohism and Taoism, as in Mo Tzu's, *T'ien Ming* (*The Will of Heaven*).[3] In this tract Mo Tzu refers to four righteous kings who received special praise because *above they honoured Heaven, in the middle realm they served the spirits, and below they loved men.*[4] Three areas are presented here – Heaven, the middle realm, and the earth. Of these the middle realm is apparently the abode of the spirits, but Heaven is the ruling power; and when Mo Tzu states (Watson, p.93) that *obedience to the will of Heaven is the standard of righteousness*, he seems to be ascribing to Heaven the status of a personal God.[5] There is no separate ascription of the three areas to different divinities, and it is maintained that 'only later, when the depersonalized *t'ien* becomes the Highest in a trinity of Heaven, Earth, and Man, that we might ascribe a God-like power to the Supreme Ruler'.[6] Here the term 'trinity' is used rather loosely, not applying even to divine beings (apart perhaps from Heaven), although the three entities are significant powers. In the first century BC the lexicographer Hsü Shen explained the Chinese character 王 (*wang*, meaning 'king') as the being who mediates between the three powers Heaven, Earth, and man.[7]

In a study devoted mainly to the situation in the nineteenth and twentieth centuries AD, the author remarks on 'the shortage of factual data on Chinese religion' in spite of the ubiquity of temples, shrines and family cults.[8] With regard to the ancient world the situation is inevitably more difficult, and for two reasons. Not only are sources of information far more restricted; religious cults in these sources tend to be smothered by the sway of great doctrinal protagonists. The pantheon was multitudinous enough, even without counting the results of the spread of a Chinese form of Indian Buddhism from the first century AD onwards.[9] Nature deities abounded in an aftermath of animism; so did culture heroes, often of local origin; if there were many agrarian deities, so also were there many for artisans and technicians in an urban setting. Of basic and central import was the ancestor-cult.[10] The very complexity of these systems of belief with their far-flung local attachments was an inhibiting factor in the establishment of divine figures in a widely acceptable framework. The feudal system admittedly linked itself firmly to the general belief in *T'ien*, Heaven; its sovereign carried the title of King, *Wang*; and 'he might be also called *T'ien Wang*, which may be translated as King by the grace of Heaven.'[11] He also bore the title *T'ien Tzu, Son of Heaven*, which conferred a divine mandate on his dynasty. Yet the learned bureaucracies which bolstered up such a system refrained from shaping a structural order of deities; or perhaps they simply failed because of the immensity and complexity of the task. Certainly they did not show any marked predilection for triadic structures.

Such structures did appear, it is true. With the advent of Buddhism a triad appeared consisting of Buddha, the *Dharma* (Law), and the *Sangha* (priesthood).[12] 'Three great principles' were seen in essence, breath, and spirit; and three lives of rebirth in past, present, and future.[13] During the third century AD, Tao, 'The Way', regarded as the originator of all life and worshipped as The One and The Greatest One, was enlarged into a triad which embodied the three stages of creation.[14] It remains true, however, that the triad which exerted the deepest impact on the Chinese mind was the result of Confucian thought. It consists of the Three Powers, Heaven, Earth, and Man.[15] Heaven is of course the Supreme Power in the group.[16] Yet an elevated status is conferred on Man, for the doctrine urges that Man should develop his own nature and help others to do so, thus aiding Heaven's activity. With this ability to participate, 'he is able to form a trinity with Heaven and Earth'.[17] One might well demur to calling this a trinity in the full sense. In favour of such an interpretation is the following comment:[18]

The concept that man can share in determining fate stemmed from the Confucian dogma that gave man a high place in the cosmic order. Man, together with Heaven and earth, was a member of the *san kang*, or trinity of the universe. In the Confucian view, the same ethereal substance, *ch'i*, that went into the making of Heaven and earth also went into the making of man ... This same substance was also the innate goodness in man that made him morally and intellectually perfectible to the point at which he could understand the great transforming and nourishing processes of Heaven and earth for the establishment of the foundations of civilized society.

The sharing of one substance recalls the Christian emphasis which began with Tertullian. But sharp differences also appear. The Confucian doctrine is concerned primarily with a cosmic order, as Yang points out in his first sentence. Again, the three entities are disparate in that Man, unlike Heaven and Earth, is animate and personal.

NOTES

[1] D. C. Lau, *Confucius, The Analects* (Harmondsworth, 1979; repr. 1986), 107. Cf. my remarks in *The Divine Verdict* (1991), 147ff.

[2] David Hawkes, *Chinese: Classical, Modern, and Humane* (Oxford, 1961, Inaugural Lecture), 10.

[3] See Burton Watson, *Basic Writings of Mo Tzu, Hsün Tzu, and Han Fei Tzu* (New York, 1967).

[4] Ibid., 81, section 26.

[5] Cf. Laurence G. Thompson, *Chinese Religion* (3rd edn., Belmont, Cal., 1979), 5: 'It is *t'ien* that eventually becomes the customary term for the Supreme Ruler', but with an 'impersonal character'.

[6] Ibid. Thompson adds that *t'ien* or *shang ti*, terms used of Heaven, do not imply a Creator of the universe, but rather a tribal god or 'the High Ancestor of the ruling house'.

[7] I owe this observation to Dr David Hawkes, formerly Professor of Chinese in the University of Oxford.

[8] C. K. Yang, *Religion in Chinese Society* (Berkeley, 1961), 22. On p.20 he quotes Max Weber's dictum on 'a chaotic mass of functional gods' in China.

[9] Cf. Stuart McFarlane, 'Chinese Pantheon' in *Dict. of Religions*, ed. J. R. Hinnells (Harmondsworth, 1984), 85 ('it is impossible to count all the gods and spirits in it'). His brief survey, however, embraces much later periods.

[10] See Marcel Granet (tr. M. Freedman), *The Religion of the Chinese People* (Oxford, 1975), 56ff. On p.54 he remarks that 'China's poverty of myth and divine figures seems extreme', suggesting that restrictions of the language may have been partly responsible. But N. J. Girardot in *Encycl. of Religion*, ed. M. Eliade, 3 (1987), 296-305, supplies detail on early Chinese mythology.

[11] M. Granet, ibid., 65.

[12] R. H. Mathews, *Chinese-English Dictionary* (revised American edn., Cambridge, Mass., 1963), 746f., s.v. SAN, 'Three'. Cf. Granet, op. cit., 139; and

W. E. Soothill, *The Three Religions of China* (2nd edn., Oxford, 1923; repr. Westport, Conn., 1973), 104-5: 'The Trinity of the Mahāyāna school is defined in various ways and differs from the general Buddhist Trikāya ...' The latter refers to the *Three Bodies* of the Buddha, a concept formulated towards the end of the third century AD. On the role of the indigenous Chinese priesthood cf. Max Weber, *The Religion of China* (Glencoe, Ill., 1951), 177, remarking on their patronage of 'most of the old folk deities'.

[13] R. H. Mathews, op. cit., 746. Cf. the reference to 'The Triad Society', a secret society in modern times for which see C. K. Yang, *Religion in Chinese Society* (1961), 62ff.

[14] Werner Eichhorn, 'Taoism', in *The Concise Encycl. of Living Faiths*, ed. R. C. Zaehner (2nd edn., 1971; repr. 1983), 378, observes that 'some would take this to show the influence of the Christian Trinity'.

[15] R. H. Mathews, loc. cit. Cf. the remark by David Hawkes cited in n.7 above.

[16] W. E. Soothill, *The Three Religions of China*, 170, refers to 'that ternion of Powers, Heaven, Earth, and Man, which has become a leading article in the Chinese creed'. He adds that 'it is not necessary to assume that Confucius means that man is equal to God'.

[17] Soothill, ibid.

[18] C. K. Yang, *Religion in Chinese Society* (1961), 273. On p.418 n.47, he cites in support E. R. and K. Hughes, *Religion in China* (London, 1950), 56-7. Cf. Confucius, *Analects*, 7. 23: *The Master said, 'Heaven is author of the virtue (te) that is in me'* (= Lau, p. 89 with comment on p. 11).

Sectional Bibliography

GENERAL

Bertholet, Alfred, with von Campenhausen, Hans Freiherr. *Wörterbuch der Religionen* (*Wb. Rel.*), 3rd edn., newly revised by Kurt Goldammer. Stuttgart, 1976.
Beyerlin, Walter (ed.) (tr. John Bowden). *Near Eastern Religious Texts relating to the Old Testament*. London, 1978 (German edn., 1975).
Bianchi, Ugo, and Vermaseren, M. J. (eds.). *La soteriologia dei culti orientali nell' impero romano* (EPRO 92). Leiden, 1982.
Buren, E. Douglas Van. 'Mountain-Gods'. *Orientalia* 12 (1943), 76–84.
Chantraine, Heinrich. 'Trias'. *Der kleine Pauly* 5 (1975), 944.
Evans-Pritchard, E. E. *Theories of Primitive Religion*. Oxford, 1965; repr. 1972.
Finegan, Jack. *The Archaeology of World Religions*. Princeton, 1952.
Frazer, Sir James George (ed. Mary Douglas and Sabine MacCormack.) *The Illustrated Golden Bough*. London, 1978.
Fulton, W. 'Trinity'. Hastings, *ERE* 12 (1921), 458–62.
——'Tritheism'. Ibid., 462–4.
Gennep, Arnold van (tr. Rodney Needham). *The Semi-Scholars*. London, 1967. (Paris, 1911).
Goedicke, H., and Roberts, J. J. M. (eds.). *Unity and Diversity: Essays in the History, Literature, and Religion of the Ancient Near East*. Baltimore, 1975.
Goldammer, Kurt. *Die Formenwelt des Religiösen. Grundriss der systematischen Religionswissenschaft*. Stuttgart, 1960.
Gwyn Griffiths, John. *The Divine Verdict: A Study of Divine Judgement in the Ancient Religions* (Studies in the History of Religions. Supplements to *Numen*, 52). Leiden, 1991.
Hawkes, Jacquetta. *Dawn of the Gods*. London, 1968.
Hawking, Stephen W. *A Brief History of Time*. London, 1988.
Heiler, Friedrich. *Erscheinungsformen und Wesen der Religion. Die Religionen der Menschheit*, ed. C. M. Schröder, Vol.I. Stuttgart, 1961.
Hooke, S. H. *Middle Eastern Mythology*. Harmondsworth, 1963.
Hopper, Vincent Foster. *Medieval Number Symbolism* (Columbia University Studies in English and Comparative Literature, 132). New York, 1938.
Juhl, P. D. *Interpretation: An Essay in the Philosophy of Literary Criticism*. Princeton, 1981.
Kermode, Frank. *The Genesis of Secrecy*. Cambridge, Mass., 1979; repr. 1982.
Kirfel, Willibald. *Die dreiköpfige Gottheit. Archäologisch-ethnologischer Streifzug durch die Ikonographie der Religionen*. Bonn, 1948.
Leeuw, G. van der (tr. J. E. Turner). *Religion in Essence and Manifestation*, 2nd edn. London, 1964.

Meek, Theophile James. 'The Origin of the Trinity'. *American Journal of Semitic Languages and Literatures* 40 (1924), 145-6 (review of D. Nielsen, *Der dreieinige Gott*, Vol.I).
Murray, James, et al. *The Oxford English Dictionary*. Oxford, 1933. For 2nd edn. v. Simpson, J. A.
Needham, Rodney. *Belief, Language and Experience*. Oxford, 1972.
——(ed). *Right and Left*. Chicago, 1973.
——*Structure and Sentiment*. Chicago, 1962.
Nielsen, Ditlef. *Der dreieinige Gott in religionshistorischer Beleuchtung*. Vol.I: *Die drei göttlichen Personen*. Vol.II: *Die drei Naturgottheiten*. Copenhagen, 1922 and 1942.
Pettazzoni, Raffaele. (tr. H. J. Rose). *The All-knowing God*. London, 1956.
——(tr. E. A. Voretzsch). *Der allwissende Gott*. Frankfurt am am Main, 1960.
Pritchard, James B. (ed.). *The Ancient Near East in Pictures relating to the Old Testament (ANEP)*. Princeton, 1954.
——*Ancient Near Eastern Texts Relating to the Old Testament (ANET)*, 3rd edn. with Supplement. Princeton, 1969.
Revesz, Géza. *Die Trias. Analyse der dualen und trialen Systeme*. Munich, 1957.
Ringgren, Helmer. *Word and Wisdom: Studies in the Hypostatization of Divine Qualities and Functions in the Ancient Near East*. Lund, 1947.
Roberts, J. J. M. v. Goedicke, H.
Schmidt, P. Wilhelm. 'Numeral Systems', in *Encycl. Brit.* (1959), s.v.
Schwabacher, W. 'Trias' in *Lexikon der alten Welt* (Zurich, 1965), 3121.
——(tr. (H. J. Rose). *The Origin and Growth of Religion*, 2nd edn. London, 1935.
Simpson, J. A. and Weiner, E. S. C. *The Oxford English Dictionary*, 2nd edn. Oxford, 1989.
Usener, Hermann. *Dreiheit*. Repr. from *Rheinisches Museum* 58 (1903). Bonn, 1903; repr. Darmstadt, 1966.
Vermaseren, M. J. v. Bianchi, Ugo.
Warren, Austin. v. Wellek, René.
Weiner, E. S. C. v. Simpson, J. A.
Wellek, René, and Warren, Austin. *Theory of Literature*, 3rd edn. Harmondsworth, 1962, repr. 1973.

PART I *EGYPT*

Abubakr, A. M. *Untersuchungen über die ägyptischen Kronen*. Glückstadt, 1937.
Albright, William F. *The Archaeology of Palestine and the Bible*. New York, 1932.
——*Yahweh and the Gods of Canaan*. London, 1968.
Aldred, Cyril. *Akhenaten and Nefertiti*. New York, 1973.
——*Akhenaten, King of Egypt*. London, 1991.
——'The Beginning of the El-'Amarna Period'. *JEA* 45 (1959), 19-33.
——'Egypt: The Amarna Period and the End of the Eighteenth Dynasty', in *CAH²·* II (1975), 3-60.
——*Egypt to the End of the Old Kingdom*. London, 1965.
Allam, Schafik. *Beiträge zum Hathorkult bis zum Ende des Mittleren Reiches* (MÄS 4). Berlin, 1963.
Allen, Thomas George. *The Book of the Dead or Going forth by Day* (Studies in Ancient Oriental Civilization, 37). Chicago, 1974.

Altenmüller, Brigitte. 'Anubis'. *LÄ* I (1975), 327-33.
——(Altenmüller-Kesting). *Reinigungsriten im ägyptischen Kult.* Diss. Hamburg, 1968.
—— *Synkretismus in den Sargtexten.* Wiesbaden, 1975.
Altenmüller, Hartwig. *Die Apotropaia und die Götter Mittelägyptens.* Diss. Munich, 1965.
——'Denkmal memphitischer Theologie'. *LÄ* I (1975), 1065-9.
——*Die Texte zum Begräbnisritual in den Pyramiden des alten Reiches.* Wiesbaden, 1972.
Andrews, Carol A. v. Faulkner, R. O.
Anthes, Rudolf. 'Harachti und Re in den Pyramidentexten'. *ZÄS* 100, Heft 2 (1974), 77-82.
——'... in seinem Namen und im Sonnenlicht'. *ZÄS* 90 (1963), 1-10.
——*Die Maat des Echnaton von Amarna.* Suppl. *JAOS* 14, Boston, 1952.
Arnold, Dieter. *Die Tempel von Kalabsha.* Wiesbaden, 1975.
——*Wandrelief und Raumfunktion in ägyptischen Tempeln des Neuen Reiches* (MÄS 2). Berlin, 1962.
Assmann, Jan. *Ägypten: Theologie und Frömmigkeit einer frühen Hochkultur.* Stuttgart, 1984. 2nd Edn. (unchanged), 1991.
——*Ägyptische Hymnen und Gebete.* Zurich, 1975.
——'Aton'. *LÄ* I (1975), 526-40.
——'Atonheiligtümer'. *LÄ* I (1975), 542-9.
——'Die Häresie des Echnaton: Aspekte der Amarna-Religion'. *Saeculum* 23 (1972), 109-26.
——*Der König als Sonnenpriester* (ADAIK 7). Glückstadt, 1970.
——*Liturgische Lieder an den Sonnengott* (MÄS 19). Berlin, 1969.
——*Ma'at. Gerechtigkeit und Unsterblichkeit im Alten Ägypten.* Munich, 1990.
——'Palast oder Tempel?' *JNES* 31 (1972), 152.
——*Re und Amun* (OBO 51). Fribourg, 1983.
——*Zeit und Ewigkeit im alten Ägypten.* Abh. Heidelberg, 1975.
Badawy, Alexander M. 'The Names Per Ḥaʿy/Gem-Aten of the Great Temple at 'Amarna'. *ZÄS* 102 (1975), 10-13.
Baer, Klaus. *Rank and Title in the Old Kingdom.* Chicago, 1960.
Baikie, James. *Egyptian Antiquities in the Nile Valley.* London, 1932.
Baines, John. *Fecundity Figures.* Warminster, 1985.
——and Málek, Jaromír. *Atlas of Ancient Egypt.* Oxford, 1980.
——v. Hornung, Erik.
Bakir, Abd el-Mohsen. *The Cairo Calendar.* Cairo, 1966.
——*Egyptian Epistolography.* Cairo, 1970.
Barguet, Paul. *Le Livre des morts des anciens Égyptiens.* Paris, 1967.
Barta, Winfried. *Die altägyptische Opferliste* (MÄS 3). Berlin, 1963.
——*Aufbau und Bedeutung der altägyptischen Opferformel.* Glückstadt, 1968.
——*Das Gespräch eines Mannes mit seinem BA* (MÄS 18). Berlin, 1969.
——*Untersuchungen zum Götterkreis der Neunheit* (MÄS 28). Munich, 1973.
Baumgartel, Elise J. *The Cultures of Prehistoric Egypt*, I: 1947; revised 2nd edn., London, 1955. II: London, 1960.
Beckerath, Jürgen von. *Handbuch der ägyptischen Königsnamen* (MÄS 20). Munich, 1984.
Begelsbacher-Fischer, Barbara L. *Untersuchungen zur Götterwelt des Alten Reiches* (OBO 37). Fribourg, 1981.
Bennett, John. 'Notes on the "Aten"'. *JEA* 51 (1965), 206-7.

Berlev, Oleg, and Hodjash, Svetlana. *The Egyptian Reliefs and Stelae in the Pushkin Museum of Fine Arts, Moscow.* Leningrad, 1982.
Blackman, A. M. *Temple of Dendûr.* Cairo, 1911.
——*Temple of Derr.* Cairo, 1913.
Bleeker, C. J. *Hathor and Thoth.* Leiden, 1975.
Bonnet, Hans. *Bilderatlas zur Religionsgeschichte,* in D. Hans Haas (ed.), *Ägyptische Religion* (Leipzig, 1924), 2-4.
——*Reallexikon der ägyptischen Religionsgeschichte (RÄRG).* Berlin, 1952; 2nd edn., Berlin and New York, 1971 (unchanged).
Borchardt, Ludwig. *Das Grabdenkmal des Königs Ne-user-reʿ.* Leipzig, 1907.
——*Das Grabdenkmal des Königs Śa3ḥu-reʿ,* Vol.II. Leipzig, 1913.
——*Statuen und Statuetten von Königen und Privatleuten* (Cairo CG). Berlin, 1911.
Boreux, Charles. *Guide-Catalogue Sommaire.* Louvre, Paris, 1932.
——'Quelques remarques sur les "pseudo-groupes" égyptiens', in *Mélanges Maspero* (Cairo, 1935-8), I, ii, 805-15.
Bosse-Griffiths, Kate. 'Problems with Ptah-Sokar-Osiris Figures', in *4th International Congress of Egyptology, Abstracts,* ed. Sylvia Schoske (Munich, 1985), 26.
——'A Beset Amulet from the Amarna Period'. *JEA* 63 (1977), 98-106.
Bothmer, Bernard V., et al. *Egyptian Sculpture of the Late Period.* Brooklyn, 1960.
——'Notes on the Mycerinus Triad'. *Bulletin of the Museum of Fine Arts* (Boston) 48 (1950), 10-17.
Bottigelli, Pia. 'Repertorio topografico dei templi e dei sacerdoti dell'Egitto tolemaico, II'. *Aegyptus* 22 (1942), 177-215.
Boylan, Patrick. *Thoth the Hermes of Egypt.* Oxford, 1922.
Brandon, S. G. F. *History, Time, and Deity.* Manchester, 1965.
Brovarski, Edward. 'Sobek'. *LÄ* V (1984), 995-1031.
Brugsch, Heinrich Karl. *Religion und Mythologie der alten Aegypter.* Leipzig, 1888; 2nd edn., Leipzig, 1891.
Brunner, Hellmut. 'Egyptian Texts' in *Near Eastern Religious Texts Relating to the Old Testament,* ed. W. Beyerlin, tr. J. Bowden (London, 1978), 1-67.
——*Altägyptische Weisheit. Lehren für das Leben.* Zurich, 1988.
——*Das hörende Herz. Kleine Schriften,* ed. W. Röllig (OBO 80). Fribourg, 1988.
——*Die Geburt des Gottkönigs.* Wiesbaden, 1964.
Brunner-Traut, Emma. *Ägypten,* 4th edn. Stuttgart, 1982.
——'Das Drama am Nil'. *Universitas* 15 (1960), 599-612.
——Fs. für: *Gegengabe,* ed. I. Gamer-Wallert and W. Helck. Tübingen, 1991.
——*Gelebte Mythen,* 3rd edn. Darmstadt, 1988.
——'Mythos im Alltag'. *Antaios* 12 (1970), 332-47.
Brunton, Guy. v. Petrie, W. M. F.
Buck, Adriaan de. *The Egyptian Coffin Texts,* Vols.I-VI. Chicago, 1935-56.
Bullard, Roger A. *The Hypostasis of the Archons.* Patristische Texte und Studien, 10. Berlin, 1970.
Burney, Ethel W. v. Moss, Rosalind L. B.
Capart, Jean. *L'Art égyptien: Études et histoire,* I. Brussels, 1924.
——*Recueil de monuments égyptiens.* Brussels, 1902.
Cauville, Sylvie. *La Théologie d'Osiris à Edfou.* Cairo, 1983.
Černý, Jaroslav. *Ancient Egyptian Religion.* London, 1952.
Chassinat, Émile. *Le Temple d'Edfou,* 14 vols. (MIFAO). Cairo, 1892-1934.
Clark, R. T. Rundle. *Myth and Symbol in Ancient Egypt.* London, 1959.
Clerc, Gisèle, et al. *Fouilles de Kition,* II. Nicosia, 1976.

——v. Leclant, Jean.
Crawford, Dorothy J. *Kerkeosiris*. Cambridge, 1971.
——(= Thompson). *Memphis under the Ptolemies*. Princeton, 1988.
Curto, Silvio. *Nubien*. Munich, 1966.
Daressy, Georges. *Statues de divinités*, 2 vols. (Cairo CG). Cairo, 1906.
Daumas, François. *La Civilisation de l'Égypte pharaonique*. Paris, 1965.
——*Les Dieux de l'Égypte* ('Que sais-je?', 1194). Paris, 1965.
——*Les Mammisis des temples égyptiens*. Paris, 1958.
——'L'Origine d'Amon de Karnak'. *BIFAO* 65 (1967), 201–14.
David, Rosalie. *The Ancient Egyptians: Religious Beliefs and Practices*. London, 1982.
——*A Guide to Religious Ritual at Abydos*, 2nd edn. Warminster, 1981.
Davies, Norman de Garis. *The Rock Tombs of El Amarna*, 6 vols. London, 1903–8.
——*The Tomb of the Vizier Ramose*. London, 1941.
Deines, H. von, and Westendorf, Wolfhart. *Wörterbuch der medizinischen Texte*. Berlin, 1962.
Derchain, Philippe. *Hathor Quadrifrons*. Istanbul, 1972.
——*Le Papyrus Salt 825, rituel pour le conservation de la vie en Égypte*, 2 vols. Brussels, 1965.
Derchain-Urtel, Maria-Theresia. *Thot* (Rites égyptiens, 3). Brussels, 1981.
Desroches-Noblecourt, Christiane, and Kuentz, Charles. *Le Petit Temple d'Abou Simbel*. Cairo, 1968.
Dolzani, Claudia. *Il dio Sobk*. Rome, 1961.
Drioton, Étienne. On 'Bull of the Ennead'. *ASAE* 45 (1945), 53–4.
——'Un syllogisme dans un texte magique égyptien', in *Mélanges Mariette* (Cairo, 1961), 173–5.
Dunand, Françoise. *Le Culte d'Isis dans le bassin oriental de la Méditerranée*, 3 vols. (EPRO 26). Leiden, 1973.
——*Religion populaire en Égypte romaine* (EPRO 67). Leiden, 1979.
——'Le Syncrétisme isiaque à la fin de l'époque hellénistique', in *Les Syncrétismes dans les religions grecque et romaine*, ed. Marcel Simon (Paris, 1973), 79–93.
Dunham, Dows, and Simpson, William Kelly. *The Mastaba of Queen Mersyankh III*. Boston, 1974.
Edel, Elmar. *Altägyptische Grammatik*, 2 vols. (Analecta Orientalia, 34 and 39). Rome, 1955 and 1964.
——and Wenig, S. *Die Jahreszeiten-reliefs aus dem Sonnenheiligtum des Königs Neuser-re*. Berlin, 1974.
Edwards, I. E. S. (ed.) *Introductory Guide to the Egyptian Collection*. The British Museum, London, 1964; repr. 1975.
——*The Pyramids of Egypt*, revised edn. London, 1961.
——'A Relief of Qudshu-Astarte-Anath in the Winchester College Collection'. *JNES* 14 (1955), 49–51.
El-Alfi, Mostafa. 'Une triade de Ramsès II', in *Sesto Congresso Internazionale di Egittologia. Atti*, I (Turin, 1992), 167–71.
El-Sayed, Ramadan. *Documents relatifs à Saïs et ses divinités*. Cairo, 1975.
Emery, W. B. *Archaic Egypt*. Harmondsworth, 1961.
Erman, Adolf. *Die Religion der Ägypter*. Berlin, 1934.
——(tr. Henri Wild). *La Religion des Égyptiens* (tr. of previous work). Paris, 1952.
Evers, Hans Gerhard. *Staat aus dem Stein*, 2 vols. Munich, 1929.
Fairman, Herbert W. *The Triumph of Horus*. London, 1974.
Faulkner, Raymond O. *The Ancient Egyptian Coffin Texts*, 3 vols. Warminster, 1973–8.

—— *The Ancient Egyptian Pyramid Texts*. Oxford, 1969.
—— *The Ancient Egyptian Book of the Dead*. New York, 1972; revised edn., rev. Carol Andrews. London, 1985.
—— *An Ancient Egyptian Book of Hours*. Oxford, 1958.
—— 'The Bremner-Rhind Papyrus, I'. *JEA* 22 (1936), 121-40.
—— *A Concise Dictionary of Middle Egyptian*. Oxford, 1962.
—— 'The King and the Star-religion in the Pyramid Texts'. *JNES* 25 (1966), 153-61.
—— 'The Lamentations of Isis and Nephthys', in *Mélanges Maspero*, I (Cairo, 1934), 337-48.
—— *The Plural and Dual in Old Egyptian*. Brussels, 1929.
Fazzini, Richard A. *Egypt. Dynasty XXII–XXV* (Iconography of Religions, 16, 10). Leiden, 1988.
—— *Images for Eternity*. Brooklyn, 1975.
Fecht, Gerhard. 'Amarna-Probleme (1-2)'. *ZÄS* (1960), 83-118.
Firth, Cecil M., and Gunn, Battiscombe. *Excavations at Saqqara. Teti Pyramid Cemeteries*. Cairo, 1926.
—— and Quibell, J. E. *Excavations at Saqqara. The Step Pyramid*, 2 vols. Cairo, 1935, 1936.
Fischer, Henry George. *Dendera in the Third Millennium B.C.* New York, 1968.
—— v. Terrace, E. L. B.
Fisher, Clarence Stanley. 'The Harvard University-Museum of Fine Arts Egyptian Expedition'. *Bulletin of the Museum of Fine Arts (Boston)* 11 (1913), 19-22.
Franke, Detlef. *Altägyptische Verwandtschaftsbezeichnungen im Mittleren Reich*. Hamburg, 1983.
Frankfort, Henri. *Kingship and the Gods*. Chicago, 1948.
—— v. Pendlebury, J. D. S.
Fraser, Peter Marshall. 'Current Problems concerning the Early History of the Cult of Sarapis'. *Opuscula Atheniensia* VII (1967), 23-45.
—— *Ptolemaic Alexandria*, 3 vols. Oxford, 1972.
—— 'Two Studies on the Cult of Sarapis in the Hellenistic World'. *Opuscula Atheniensia* III (1960), 1-54.
Gardiner, Sir Alan H. *Ancient Egyptian Onomastica*, 3 vols. Oxford, 1947; repr. 1968.
—— 'The Baptism of Pharaoh'. *JEA* 36 (1950), 3-12.
—— *Egypt of the Pharaohs*. Oxford, 1961.
—— *Egyptian Grammar*, 3rd edn. Oxford, 1957.
—— 'Horus the Beḥdetite'. *JEA* 30 (1944), 25-60.
Gauthier, Henri. *Le Livre des rois d'Égypte*, 5 vols. Cairo, 1907-17.
Gautier, J.-E., and Jéquier, G. *Fouilles de Licht*. Cairo, 1902.
Gayet, Albert. *Le Temple de Louxor*. Paris, 1894.
Gimbutas, Marija. *The Goddesses and Gods of Old Europe, 6500-3500 B.C.*, new edn. London, 1982.
Giveon, Raphael. *The Impact of Egypt on Canaan* (OBO 20). Fribourg, 1978.
Goedicke, Hans. *The Report about the Dispute of a Man with his Ba*. Baltimore, 1970.
Graindor, Paul. *Terres cuites de l'Égypte gréco-romaine*. Antwerp, 1939.
Griffith, F. Ll., and Thompson, Herbert. *The Demotic Magical Papyrus of London and Leiden*. London, 1904; repr. New York, 1974.
Grundmann, Walter. v. Leipoldt, Johannes.
Gunn, Battiscombe. 'Notes on the Aten and his Names'. *JEA* 9 (1923), 168-76.
—— v. Firth, Cecil M.

Gutbub, Adolphe. *Textes fondamentaux de la théologie de Kom Ombo*. Cairo, 1973.
Gwyn Griffiths, John. 'Allegory in Greece and Egypt'. *JEA* 53 (1967), 79-102; also in *idem*, *Atlantis and Egypt with Other Selected Essays* (Cardiff, 1991), 295-324.
——*Apuleius of Madauros: The Isis-Book* (EPRO 39). Leiden, 1975.
——'βασιλεὺς βασιλέων: Remarks on the History of a Title'. *Class. Phil.* 48 (1953), 145-54; also in *idem*, *Atlantis and Egypt* (1991), 252-65.
——*The Conflict of Horus and Seth: From Egyptian and Classical Sources*. Liverpool, 1960.
——'The Death of Cleopatra VII'. *JEA* 47 (1961), 113-18; also in *Atlantis and Egypt* (1991), 47-54.
——'The Faith of the Pharaonic Period', in *Classical Mediterranean Spirituality*, ed. A. H. Armstrong (New York, 1986), 3-38.
——'The Impress of Egyptian Religion on the Mediaeval "Dialogue of the Soul and Body"', in *Gegengabe (Fs. für Emma Brunner-Traut)* (Tübingen, 1991) 103-18.
——*The Origins of Osiris and his Cult*. Studies in the History of Religions (Supplements to *Numen*, 40). Leiden, 1980.
——*Plutarch's De Iside et Osiride*, edited with a translation and Commentary. Cardiff, 1970.
——'A Possible Anticipation of the Triad in Prehistoric Egypt', in *Les Religions de la préhistoire* (Valcamonica Symposium, 1972) (Capo di Ponte, 1975), 317-22.
——'The Relative *nty* with Generic Reference'. *JEA* (1968, for J. Černý), 60-6.
——'Remarks on the Horian Elements in the Royal Titulary'. *ASAE* 56 (1959), 63-86.
——'Some Remarks on the Enneads of Gods'. *Orientalia* 28 (1959), 34-56.
Haarlem, W. M. Van. 'A Functional Analysis of Ancient Egyptian Amulets', in *Sesto Congresso Internaz. di Egittologia. Atti*, I (Turin, 1992), 237-40 with Tav.VII, 2.
Habachi, Labib. 'Divinities Adored in the Area of Kalabsha'. *MDAIK* 24 (1969, Fs. H. Stock), 169-83.
——*Features of the Deification of Ramesses II*. Cairo. 1969.
——'King Nebhepetre Menthuhotp: His Monuments etc.' *MDAIK* 19 (1963), 16-52.
——*Tell Basta*. Cairo, 1957.
——'The Triple Shrine of the Theban Triad in Luxor Temple'. *MDAIK* 20 (1965), 93-7.
——'Was Anukis Considered as the Wife of Khnum or as his Daughter?' *ASAE* 50 (1950), 501-7.
Hamza, Mahmud. *La Lecture de l'adjectif relatif négatif etc.* Cairo, 1929.
Hanke, Rainer. *Amarna-Reliefs aus Hermopolis*. Hildesheim, 1978.
Harris, J. R. *Egyptian Art*. London, 1966.
Hassan, Selim. *Excavations at Gîza, 1929-30*. Oxford, 1932.
——'A Representation of the Solar Disk with Human Hands ...' *ASAE* 38 (1938), 53ff.
Hayes, William C. *The Scepter of Egypt*, II. Cambridge, Mass., 1959.
Heerma van Voss, M. S. H. G. 'Hereniging in het hiernamaals volgens Egyptisch geloof', in *Pro Regno Pro Sanctuario (Fs. G. van der Leeuw)* (Nijkerk, 1950), 227-32.
——*De oudste Versie van Dodenboek 17 a*. Leiden, 1963.
Helck, Wolfgang. *Die altägyptischen Gaue*. Wiesbaden, 1974.
——*Die Beziehungen Ägyptens zu Vorderasien in 3. and 2. Jahrtausend v. chr*, 2nd edn. Wiesbaden, 1971.
——*Der Text der 'Lehre Amenemhets I. für seinen Sohn'* (Kleine ägyptische Texte). Wiesbaden, 1969.

—— *Untersuchungen zu den Beamtentiteln des ägyptischen alten Reiches*. Glückstadt, 1954.
—— 'Zum Auftreten fremder Götter in Ägypten'. *Oriens Antiquus* 5 (1966), 1–14.
Henfling, E. 'Kalabscha'. *LÄ* III (1980), 295–6.
Hintze, Fritz, and Hintze, Ursula. *Civilizations of the Old Sudan*. Leipzig, 1968.
Hirmer, M. v. Lange, Karl.
Hodjash, S. I. and Pavlov, V. V. *Egypetskaya plastyka malikh form*. Moscow, 1985.
Hodjash, Svetlana. v. Berlev, Oleg.
Hopfner, Theodor. *Fontes historiae religionis Aegyptiacae*. Bonn, 1922–5.
Hornbostel, Wilhelm. *Sarapis* (EPRO 32). Leiden, 1973.
Hornemann, Bodil. *Types of Ancient Egyptian Statuary*, 7 vols. (boxes). Munksgaard, 1951.
Hornung, Erik. *Ägyptische Unterweltsbücher*, 2nd edn. Zurich, 1984.
—— *Das Amduat*, 2 vols. Wiesbaden, 1963–7.
—— 'Die Anfänge von Monotheismus und Trinität in Ägypten', in *Der eine Gott und der dreieine Gott*, ed. Karl Rahner (Munich, 1983; Katholische Akademie Freiburg), 48–66.
—— (tr. John Baines). *Conceptions of God in Ancient Egypt*. London, 1983.
—— *Der Eine und die Vielen*. Darmstadt, 1971.
—— 'Gedanken zur Kunst der Amarnazeit'. *ZÄS* 97 (1971), 74–8.
—— 'Monotheismus im pharaonischen Ägypten', in *Monotheismus im Alten Israel und seiner Umwelt*, ed. Othmar Keel (Freiburg, 1980), 83–97.
—— and Staehelin, Elisabeth. *Studien zum Sedfest* (Aegyptiaca Helvetica, I). Geneva, 1974.
—— *Tal der Könige*. Zurich, 1982.
—— *Das Totenbuch der Ägypter*. Zurich, 1979.
—— 'Versuch über Nephthys', in *Studies in Pharaonic Religion and Society*, ed. Alan B. Lloyd (London, 1992), 186–9.
—— 'Zeitliches Jenseits im Alten Ägypten'. *Eranos Jb.* 47 (1978), 291–307.
James, T. G. H. *British Museum: Hieroglyphic Texts from Egyptian Stelae*, I, 2nd edn. London, 1961.
—— *Gebel es-Silsilah*. I: *The Shrines*. London, 1963.
Jéquier, G. v. Gautier, J.-E.
Junge, Friedrich. 'Isis und die ägyptischen Mysterien', in *Aspekte der spätägyptischen Religion*, ed. W. Westendorf (Wiesbaden, 1979), 93–115.
Junker, Hermann. *Gîza, I–XII*. Vienna, 1929–55.
—— *Der grosse Pylon des Tempels der Isis in Philä*. Vienna, 1958.
—— and Winter, Erich. *Das Geburtshaus des Tempels der Isis in Philä*. Vienna, 1965.
Kaiser, Werner. 'Die Entstehung des gesamtägyptischen Staates'. *ZÄS* 91 (1964), 117–25.
Kákosy, László. 'Atum'. *LÄ* I (1975), 550–2.
—— 'A Memphite Triad'. *JEA* 66 (1980), 48–53.
—— *Selected Papers*. Budapest, 1981.
—— Studies Presented to, ed. Ulrich Luft: *The Intellectual Heritage of Egypt*. Budapest, 1992.
Kaplony, Peter. 'Der Titel *wnwr(w)* nach Spruch 820 der Sargtexte'. *MIO* 11 (1966), 137–63.
Kayser, Hans. *Die ägyptischen Altertümer im Roemer-Pelizaeus-Museum in Hildesheim*. Hildesheim, 1973.
Kees, Hermann (ed. T. G. H. James). *Ancient Egypt: A Cultural Topography*. London, 1961.

——*Der Götterglaube im Alten Ägypten*, 2nd edn. Berlin, 1956.
El-Khachab, A. M. 'Some Gem-Amulets depicting Harpocrates seated on a Lotus Flower'. *JEA* 57 (1971), 132-45.
Kitchen, Kenneth A. *The Third Intermediate Period in Egypt*. Warminster, 1973.
——*Ramesside Inscriptions*, 6 vols. Oxford, 1968-83.
Koefoed-Petersen, Otto. *Catalogue des sarcophages et cercueils égyptiens*. Copenhagen, 1951.
——*Catalogue des statues et statuettes égyptiennes*. Copenhagen, 1950.
——*Les Stèles égyptiennes*. Copenhagen, 1948.
Kraeling, E. G. *The Brooklyn Museum Aramaic Papyri*. New Haven, 1953.
Kraus, Theodor. 'Alexandrinische Triaden der römischen Kaiserzeit'. *MDAIK* 19 (1963), 97-105.
Kuentz, Charles. v. Desroches-Noblecourt, C.
Kurth, Dieter. *Den Himmel stützen*. Brussels, 1975.
Lange, Karl, and Hirmer, M. *Egypt: Architecture, Sculpture, Painting*, 4th edn. London, 1968.
Lauer, Jean-Philippe. *Saqqara*. London, 1976.
Leclant, Jean. 'Aspects du syncrétisme méroïtique', in *Les Syncrétismes dans les religions grecque et romaine*, ed. Marcel Simon (Paris, 1973), 135-45.
——'Astarté à cheval après les représentations égyptiennes'. *Syria* 37 (1960), 1-67.
——*Recherches sur les monuments thébains de la XXVe dynastie dite éthiopienne*. Cairo, 1965.
——and Clerc, Gisèle. *Inventaire bibliographique des Isiaca*, 4 vols. (EPRO 18). Leiden, 1972-91.
Lefebvre, Gustave. *Grammaire de l'égyptien classique*. Cairo, 1940.
Legrain, Georges. *Statues et statuettes de rois et de particuliers*, 3 vols. (Cairo CG). Cairo, 1906-14.
Leipoldt, Johannes. *Die Religionen in der Umwelt des Urchristentums*, in *Bilderatlas*, ed. D. Hans Haas, (Leipzig, 1926), 7-11.
——and Grundmann, Walter. *Umwelt des Urchristentums*. III: *Bilder zum neutestamentlichen Zeitalter*, 2nd edn. Berlin, 1967.
Lesko, Barbara. *The Remarkable Women of Ancient Egypt*. Berkeley, 1978.
Lesko, Leonard H. *The Ancient Egyptian Book of Two Ways*. Berkeley, 1972.
——v. Parker, Richard A.
Lichtheim, Miriam. *Ancient Egyptian Literature*, 3 vols. Berkeley, 1973-80.
Lillesø, Ebba K. 'Two Wooden Uraei'. *JEA* 61 (1975), 137-46.
Lloyd, Alan B. *Herodotus Book II*, 3 vols. (EPRO 43). Leiden, 1975-87.
Luft, Ulrich. *Beiträge zur Historisierung der Götterwelt und der Mythenschreibung*. Budapest, 1978.
——(ed.). *The Intellectual Heritage of Egypt: Studies presented to L. Kákosy*. Budapest, 1992.
Maehler, Herwig, and Strocka, Volker Michael (eds.). *Das ptolemäische Ägypten*. Mainz, 1978.
Malaise, Michel. *Inventaire préliminaire des documents égyptiens découverts en Italie* (EPRO 21). Leiden, 1972. Also his sequel in EPRO 22 (1972).
Málek, Jaromír. Editor of Porter-Moss-Burney, *Topographical Bibliography*, 2nd edn., from 1974 (v. Moss et al.).
——v. Baines, John.
Mariette, Auguste. *Le Sérapéum de Memphis*. Paris, 1857.
——(ed. G. Maspero). *Le Sérapéum de Memphis*. Paris, 1882.
Maspero, Gaston (tr. A. Rusch). *Geschichte der Kunst in Ägypten*. Stuttgart, 1913.

Meeks, Dimitri. 'Génies, anges, démons en Égypte', in *Génies, Anges, et Démons* (Sources Orientales, 8). Paris, 1971.
Mercer, Samuel A. B. *The Pyramid Texts in Translation and Commentary*, 4 vols. (New York, 1952).
——*The Religion of Ancient Egypt*. London, 1949.
Meulenaere, Herman de. *Mendes, II*. Warminster, 1976.
Möller, Georg. v. Scharff, Alexander.
Mogensen, Maria. *Inscriptions hiéroglyphiques du musée national de Copenhague*. Copenhagen, 1918.
Mond, Robert, and Myers, O. H. *Temples of Armant*, 2 vols. London, 1940.
Morenz, Siegfried. *Ägyptische Religion*. Stuttgart, 1960; repr. 1977.
——(tr. Ann E. Keep). *Egyptian Religion*. London, 1973.
——(ed. Elke Blumenthal et al.). *Religion und Geschichte des alten Ägypten*. Weimar, 1975.
Moss, Rosalind L. B., Porter, Bertha and Burney, Ethel W. *Topographical Bibliography of Ancient Egyptian Hieroglyphic Texts, Reliefs and Paintings*, 7 vols. Oxord, 1927–51; 2nd edn. from 1960 (see also s.v. Málek).
Müller, Hans-Wolfgang. *Ägyptische Kunst*. Frankfurt am Main, 1970.
Müller, Hugo. *Die formale Entwicklung der Titulatur der ägyptischen Könige*. Glückstadt, 1938.
Münster, Maria. *Untersuchungen zur Göttin Isis* (MÄS 11). Berlin, 1968.
Myśliwiec, K. *Studien zum Gott Atum*, 2 vols. Hildesheim, 1978–9.
Nagel, Georg. 'Un papyrus funéraire de la fin du nouvel empire, Louvre 3292 (inv.)'. *BIFAO* 29 (1929), 1–127.
Nagel, Peter. *Das Wesen der Archonten aus Codex II der gnostische Bibliothek von Nag Hammadi*. Halle, 1970.
Naville, Édouard H. *Das Aegyptische Todtenbuch der XVIII. bis XX. Dynastie*, 3 vols. Berlin, 1886; repr. Graz, 1971.
——*Bubastis*. London, 1891.
——*The Festival-Hall of Osorkon II in the Great Temple of Bubastis*. London, 1892.
Neugebauer, Otto. v. Parker, R. A.
Nims, Charles F. *Thebes of the Pharaohs*. London, 1965.
Otto, Eberhard. 'Altägyptischer Polytheismus. Eine Beschreibung'. *Saeculum* 14 (1963), 274f.
——*Beiträge zur Geschichte der Stierkulte in Aegypten*. Leipzig, 1938.
——(tr. Kate Bosse-Griffiths) *Egyptian Art: The Cults of Osiris and Amon*. London, 1967.
——*Gott und Mensch nach den ägyptischen Tempelinschriften der griechischrömischen Zeit*. Abh. Heidelberg, 1964.
——'Die Lehre von den beiden Ländern Ägyptens in der ägyptischen Religionsgeschichte'. *Analecta Orientalia* 17 (1938), 10–35.
——*Topographie des thebanischen Gaues*. Berlin, 1972.
Otto, Walter. *Priester und Tempel im hellenistischen Ägypten*, 2 vols. Leipzig, 1905–8.
Page, Anthea. *Egyptian Sculpture, Archaic to Saite, from the Petrie Collection*. Warminster, 1976.
Parker, Richard A. *The Calendars of Ancient Egypt*. Chicago, 1950.
——and Neugebauer, Otto. *Egyptian Astronomical Texts*, I. Providence, 1960.
——and Lesko, L. H. 'The Khonsu Cosmogony', in *Pyramid Studies and Other Essays presented to I. E. S. Edwards*, ed. John Baines et al. (London, 1988), 168–75.

Pavlov, V.V. v. Hodjash, S. I.
Pendlebury, J. D. S. and Frankfort, Henri. *The City of Akhenaten*, part II. London, 1933; part III, London, 1951.
Petrie, W. M. Flinders. *Ceremonial Slate Palettes*. London, 1953.
——*Deshasheh*. London, 1898, repr. 1989.
——*A History of Egypt*, Vol.I, 10th edn. London, 1923.
——*Koptos*. London, 1896.
——*Medum*. London, 1892.
——*The Royal Tombs of the First Dynasty*. London, 1900, 1901.
——and Brunton, Guy. *Sedment*, 2 vols. London, 1924.
Piankoff, Alexandre. 'Les Grandes Compositions religieuses du nouvel empire et la réforme d'Amarna'. *BIFAO* 62 (1964), 207–18.
——*The Pyramid of Unas*. Princeton, 1968.
——*The Shrines of Tut-Ankh-Amon*. New York, 1955.
Porten, Bezalel. *Archives from Elephantine*. Berkeley, 1968.
Porter, Bertha. v. Moss, Rosalind L. B.
Posener, Georges (ed.). *A Dictionary of Egyptian Civilization* (tr.). London, 1962.
Quibell, J. E. *Hierakonpolis*, parts I and II. London, 1900, 1902.
——v. Firth, Cecil M.
Quirke, Stephen *Ancient Egyptian Religion*. London, 1992.
Ranke, Hermann. *Die ägyptischen Personennamen (PN)*, 2 vols. Glückstadt, 1935–52.
Redford, D. B. *Akhenaten: The Heretic King*. Princeton, 1984; repr. 1987.
——and Smith, R. W. *The Akhenaten Temple Project*, I. London, 1976.
Reisner, George A. *Mycerinus: The Temples of the Third Pyramid at Giza*, Cambridge, Mass., 1931.
Ricke, Herbert. *Beiträge zur ägyptischen Bauforschung und Altertumskunde*, 4. Zurich, 1944.
Roberts, Colin H. 'Two Papyri from Oxyrhynchus'. *JEA* 20 (1934), 20–8.
Robinson, James M. (ed.). *The Nag Hammadi Library in English*. Leiden, 1977.
Roeder, Günther. *Ägyptische Bronzefiguren*, 2 vols. Berlin, 1956.
——*Die ägyptische Religion in Texten und Bildern*, 4 vols. Zurich, 1959–69.
——*Amarna-Reliefs aus Hermopolis*. Hildesheim, 1969.
——*Temples immergés de la Nubie*, I. Cairo, 1911.
——*Urkunden zur Religion des alten Ägypten*. Jena, 1923.
Roussel, Pierre. *Les Cultes égyptiens à Délos*, 2 vols. Paris, 1915–16.
Sadek, Ashraf I. *Popular Religion in Egypt during the New Kingdom*. Hildesheim, 1988.
Samson, Julia. *Amarna. City of Akhenaten and Nefertiti*. London, 1978.
——'Nefertiti's Regality'. *JEA* 63 (1977), 88–97.
Sander-Hansen, C. E. *Studien zur Grammatik der Pyramidentexten*. Copenhagen, 1956.
Sandman, Maj. *Texts from the time of Akhenaten*. Brussels, 1938.
Sauneron, Serge. *Le Temple d'Esna*, Vols.I–V. Cairo, 1959–69.
——'Triad', in *A Dictionary of Egyptian Civilization*, ed. Georges Posener (tr.) (London, 1962), 290.
Säve-Söderbergh, Torgny. 'Götterkreise'. *LÄ* II (1977), 686–96.
Schäfer, Gerd. *'König der Könige' – 'Lied der Lieder'*. Abh. Heidelberg, 1974.
Scharff, Alexander (ed.). *Die archaeologischen Ergebnisse des vorgeschichtlichen Gräberfeldes von Abusir el-Meleq nach den Aufzeichnungen Georg Möllers*. Leipzig, 1926.

Schott, Siegfried. *Hieroglyphen*. Abh. Mainz, 1950. Wiesbaden, 1951.
——*Mythe und Mythenbildung im alten Ägypten*. Leipzig, 1945.
Sethe, Kurt H. *Die altaegyptischen Pyramidentexte*, 4 vols. Leipzig, 1908-22.
——*Amun und die acht Urgötter von Hermopolis*. Abh. Berlin, 1929.
——*Beiträge zur Geschichte Amenophis' IV*. Nachr. Göttingen, 1921.
——'Die Sprüche für das Kennen der Seelen der heiligen Orte'. *ZÄS* 59 (1924), 73-99; also printed separately, Leipzig, 1925.
——*Übersetzung und Kommentar zu den altägyptischen Pyramidentexten*, 6 vols. Glückstadt, 1935-62.
——*Urgeschichte und älteste Religion der Ägypter*. Leipzig, 1930.
——*Von Zahlen und Zahlworten bei den alten Ägyptern*. Strasbourg, 1916.
Settgast, J. *Untersuchungen zu altägyptischen Bestattungsdarstellungen*. Glückstadt, 1963.
Shinnie, P. L. *Meroe*. London, 1967.
Siegler, K. G. v. Stock, Hanns.
Simpson, William Kelly. (ed.) *The Literature of Ancient Egypt*. New Haven, 1972.
——v. Dunham, Dows.
Smith, William Stevenson. *The Art and Architecture of Ancient Egypt*. Harmondsworth, 1958.
——*A History of Egyptian Sculpture and Painting in the Old Kingdom*. Oxford, 1946.
——'The Old Kingdom in Egypt and the Beginning of the First Intermediate Period', in *CAH* I (1965, revised edn.), 3-73.
Spiegel, Joachim. *Die Götter von Abydos*. Wiesbaden, 1973.
Spiegelberg, Wilhelm. 'Der Gott Bait in dem Trinitäts-Amulett des Britischen Museums', *Archiv für Religionswissenschaft* 21 (1922), 225-7.
——*Die sogenannte Demotische Chronik* (Demotische Studien, 7). Leipzig, 1914.
Stadelmann, Rainer. *Syrisch-Palästinensische Gottheiten in Ägypten*. Leiden, 1967.
Staehelin, Elisabeth. v. Hornung, Erik.
Steindorff, Georg. *Catalogue of the Egyptian Sculpture in the Walters Art Gallery*. Baltimore, 1946.
Sternberg, Heike. *Mythische Motive und Mythenbildung in den ägyptischen Tempeln und Papyri der griechisch-römischen Zeit*. Wiesbaden, 1985.
Stock, Hanns and Siegler, K. G. *Kalabscha*. Wiesbaden, 1965.
Strocka, Volker Michael. v. Maehler, Herwig.
Tawfik, Sayed. 'Aton Studies. 1. Aton before the Reign of Akhenaton'. *MDAIK* 29 (1973), 77-86.
——'Aton Studies. 3. Back Again to Nefer-nefru-Aton'. *MDAIK* 31 (1975), 159-60.
Terrace, E. L. B. and Fischer, Henry George. *Treasures of the Cairo Museum*. London, 1970.
Thausing, Gertrud. *Der Auferstehungsgedanke in ägyptischen religiösen Texten*. Leipzig, 1943.
Thompson, Dorothy Burr. *Ptolemaic Oinochoai and Portraits in Faience*. Oxford, 1973.
Thompson, Dorothy J. (= Crawford). *Memphis under the Ptolemies*. Princeton, 1988.
Thompson, Sir Herbert. v. Griffith, F. Ll.
Troy, Lana. *Patterns of Queenship*. Uppsala, 1986.
Ucko, Peter J. *Anthropomorphic Figurines*. London, 1968.
Uphill, Eric. 'The Nine Bows'. *JEOL* 6 (1967), 393-420.
——'The Per Aten at Amarna'. *JNES* 29 (1970), 151-66.
Valbelle, Dominique. *Satis et Anoukis*. Mainz, 1981.

Vandier, Jacques. *Manuel d'archéologie égyptienne*, 4 vols. Paris, 1952–64.
Velde, Herman te. 'The Structure of Egyptian Divine Triads'. *JEA* 57 (1971), 80–6.
——'The Theme of the Separation of Heaven and Earth in Egyptian Mythology'. *Studia Aegyptiaca* 3 (1977), 161–7.
Vernus, Pascal. *Athribis*. Cairo, 1978.
Vidman, Ladislaus. *Isis und Sarapis bei den Griechen und Römern*. Berlin, 1970.
——*Sylloge inscriptionum religionis Isiacae et Sarapiacae (SIRIS)*. Berlin, 1969.
Visser, Elizabeth. *Götter und Kulte im ptolemäischen Alexandrien*. Amsterdam, 1938.
Waddell, W. G. *Manetho* (Loeb CL). London, 1940.
Wainwright, G. A. 'The Origin of Amūn'. *JEA* 49 (1963), 21–3.
Wenig, S. v. Edel, Elmar.
Werbrouck, Marcelle. *Les Pleureuses dans l'Égypte ancienne*. Brussels, 1938.
Westendorf, Wolfhart. *Altägyptische Darstellungen des Sonnenlaufes auf der abschüssigen Himmelsbahn* (MÄS 10). Berlin, 1966.
——'Das angebliche Doppeldeterminativ (Gott und König) beim Wort "Vater" in den Texten der Amarnazeit'. *MDAIK* 25 (1969), 202–11.
——'Eine auf die Maat anspielende Form des Osirisnamens'. *MIO* 2 (1954), 165–82.
——(tr. L. Mins). *Painting, Sculpture and Architecture of Ancient Egypt*. New York, 1968.
——'Zweiheit, Dreiheit und Einheit in der altägyptischen Theologie'. *ZÄS* 100, Heft 2 (1974), 136–41.
——v. Deines, H. von.
——(ed.). *Aspekte der spätägyptischen Religion*. Wiesbaden, 1979.
Wiedemann, Alfred. *Das alte Ägypten*. Heidelberg, 1920.
——*Religion of the Ancient Egyptians*. London, 1897.
Wild, Henri. v. Erman, Adolf.
Wildung, Dietrich. 'Ramses, die grosse Sonne Ägyptens'. *ZÄS* 99 (1972), 33–41.
Wilson, John A. 'Akh-en-Aton and Nefert-iti'. *JNES* 32 (1973), 235–41.
——*The Culture of Ancient Egypt*. Chicago, 1951.
——Translations of Egyptian Texts in James B. Pritchard (ed.), *Ancient Near Eastern Texts relating to the Old Testament (ANET)*, 3rd edn., with Supplement. Princeton, 1969.
Winter, Erich. *Untersuchungen zu den ägyptischen Tempelreliefs der griechisch-römischen Zeit*. Vienna, 1968.
——v. Junker, Hermann.
Wit, Constant de. *Les Inscriptions de temple d'Opet à Karnak*. Brussels, 1958.
——*Oud Egyptische Kunst*, 2nd revised edn. Luxor, n.d.
——*Le Rôle et le sens du lion dans l'Égypte*. Leiden, 1951.
Witt, R. E. *Isis in the Graeco-Roman World*. London, 1971.
Wolf, Walther. *Die Kunst Aegyptens*. Stuttgart, 1957.
Wood, Wendy. 'A Reconstruction of the Triads of King Mycerinus'. *JEA* 60 (1974), 82–93.
Żabkar, Louis V. *Apedemak, Lion God of Meroe*. Warminster, 1975.
——*Hymns to Isis in her Temple at Philae*. Hanover, NH, and London, 1988.
——*A Study of the Ba Concept in Ancient Egyptian Texts*. Chicago, 1968.
——'The Theocracy of Amarna and the Doctrine of the Ba'. *JNES* 13 (1954), 87–101.
Zandee, Jan. 'Der androgyne Gott in Ägypten: ein Erscheinungsbild des Weltschöpfers', in *Ägypten und Altes Testament*, 14: *Religion im Erbe Ägyptens*, ed. M. Görg (Fs. A. Böhlig) (Wiesbaden, 1988), 240–78.
——*Death as an Enemy according to Ancient Egyptian Conceptions*. Leiden, 1960.
——*De Hymnen aan Amon van Papyrus Leiden, I. 350*. Leiden, 1947.

——'Sargtexte, Spruch 76'. *ZÄS* 100 (1973), 60–71.
——'Sargtexte, Spruch 80'. *ZÄS* 101 (1974), 62–79.
——'Das Schöpferwort im alten Ägypten', in *Verbum (Fs. H. W. Obbink)* (Utrecht, 1964), 33–66.
Zivie, A.-P. *Hermopolis et le Nome de l'Ibis*. Cairo, 1975.

PART II MESOPOTAMIA AND ADJACENT AREAS

CHAPTER 5 *MESOPOTAMIA: TYPES AND REGIONS*

Bernhardt Karl-Heinz. 'Ugaritic Texts', in *Near Eastern Religious Texts*, ed. W. Beyerlin (London, 1978), 185–226.
Buren, E. Douglas Van. 'Mountain-Gods'. *Orientalia* 12 (1943), 76–84.
Civil, M. 'The Sumerian Flood Story', in W. G. Lambert and A. R. Millard, *Atraḫasīs: The Babylonian Story of the Flood* (Oxford, 1969), 138ff.
Colledge, Malcolm A. R. *The Parthians*. London, 1967.
Engnell, Ivan. *Studies in Divine Kingship in the Ancient Near East*, 2nd edn. Oxford, 1967.
Falkenstein, A. and Soden, W. von. *Sumerische und Akkadische Hymnen und Gebete*. Zurich, 1953.
Frankfort, Henri. *Cylinder Seals*. London, 1939; repr. 1965.
——*Kingship and the Gods*. Chicago, 1948.
Fulco, William J. 'Hurrian Religion', in *Encycl. of Religion*, ed. M. Eliade, 6 (1987), 533–5.
Gadd, C. J. *Ideas of Divine Rule in the Ancient East*. London, 1948.
Ginsberg, H. L. 'Ugaritic Myths, Epics, and Legends'. *ANET*[3] (1969), 129–55.
Goetze, Albrecht. 'Hittite Rituals, Incantations, and Description of Festivals'. *ANET*[3] (1969), 346–61.
Gordon, Cyrus H. 'Canaanite Mythology', in *Mythologies of the Ancient World*, ed. S. N. Kramer (New York, 1961), 181–218.
Güterbock, Hans G. 'Hittite Mythology', in *Mythologies of the Ancient World*, ed. S. N. Kramer (New York, 1961), 141–79.
Gurney, O. R. *The Hittites*. Harmondsworth, 1952 and later.
——*Some Aspects of Hittite Religion*. Oxford, 1977.
Hajjar, Youssef. *La Triade d'Héliopolis-Baalbek*, 2 vols. Leiden, 1977; vol. 3 Montreal, 1985.
Hehn, Johannes. *Siebenzahl und Sabbat bei den Babyloniern und im Alten Testament* (with 'Bedeuting der Dreizahl', 63–75). Leipzig, 1907.
Hoffner, Harry A., Jr. 'Hittite Mythological Texts: A Survey', in *Unity and Diversity*, ed. H. Goedicke and J. J. M. Roberts (Baltimore, 1975), 136–45.
Jacobsen, Thorkild (ed. William L. Moran). *Toward the Image of Tammuz*. Cambridge, Mass., 1970.
——*The Treasures of Darkness*. New Haven, 1976.
Jean, Charles-F. 'La Grande Triade divine An, ᵈEn-lil, ᵈEn-ki, sous les dynasties d'Isin-Larsa, 2186–1925'. *Rev. Hist. Rel.* 110 (1934), 113–39.
——*La Religion sumérienne*. Paris, 1931.
Kramer, Samuel N. *Sumerian Mythology*. Philadelphia, 1944.
——(ed.) *Mythologies of the Ancient World*. New York, 1961.

—— 'Mythology of Sumer and Akkad', in *Mythologies of the Ancient World*, ed. S. N. Kramer (New York, 1961), 93–137.
—— 'Sumerian Myths and Epic Tales'. *ANET*³ (1969), 37–59.
Lambert, W. G. and Millard, A. R. *Atra-ḫasīs. The Babylonian Story of the Flood*, with 'The Sumerian Flood Story' by M. Civil. Oxford, 1969.
—— 'The Historical Development of the Mesopotamian Pantheon: A Study in Sophisticated Polytheism', in *Unity and Diversity*, ed. H. Goedicke and J. J. M. Roberts (Baltimore, 1975), 191–200.
Lipiński, E. 'North Semitic Texts from the First Millennium BC', in *Near Eastern Religious Texts*, ed. W. Beyerlin (London, 1978), 227–68.
Millard, A. R. v. Lambert, W. G.
Moortgat, Anton. *Die Kunst des alten Mesopotamien*. Cologne, 1967.
Oden, R. A., Jr. *Studies in Lucian's De Syria Dea*. Missoula, Mont. 1977.
Roberts, J. J. M. *The Earliest Semitic Pantheon: A Study of the Semitic Deities attested in Mesopotamia before Ur III*. Baltimore, 1972.
Röllig, Wolfgang (ed.). *Altorientalische Literaturen*. Wiesbaden, 1978.
—— 'Die ugaritische Literatur', in *Altorientalische Literaturen*, ed. W. Röllig (1978), 255–71.
Saggs, H. W. F. *The Greatness that was Babylon*. London, 1962; repr. 1966.
Soden, W. von, with E. Ebeling, B. Meissner, E. Weidner and D. O. Edzard. *Reallexikon der Assyriologie und vorderasiatischen Archäologie*, 7 vols. Berlin, 1928–87.
—— v. Falkenstein, A.
Speiser, E. A. 'Akkadian Myths and Epics: The Creation Epic.' *ANET*³ (1969), 60–72.
Wilhelm, Gernot (tr. J. Barnes). *The Hurrians*. Warminster, 1989.

PART III THE INDO-EUROPEAN TRADITION

CHAPTER 6 *EARLY INDIAN RELIGION*

Apte, V. M. *Ṛgveda Mantras in their Ritual Setting in the Gryasūtras*. Repr. from the *Bull. of the Deccan College Research Inst*. I, n.d.
—— *Social and Religious Life in the Grihya Sutras*. Bombay, 1939; repr. 1954.
Banerjee, P. *Early Indian Religions*. Delhi, 1973.
Basham, A. L. *The Wonder that was India*, 3rd revised edn. London, 1967; repr. 1988.
Belier, Wouter W. *Decayed Gods: Origin and Development of Georges Dumézil's 'Idéologie Tripartie'* (Studies in Greek and Roman Religion, 7). Leiden, 1991.
Benoist, Alan de (ed.). *Georges Dumézil et les études indo-européennes. Nouvelle École* 21-2 (1972-3).
Bergaigne, Abel. *La Religion védique d'après les hymnes du Rig-Veda*, 4 vols., 2nd edn. Paris, 1963.
Bhattacharji, Sukumari. *The Indian Theogony: A Comparative Study of Indian Mythology from the Vedas to the Purāṇas*. Cambridge, 1970.
Bloomfield, Maurice. *The Religion of the Veda*. New York, 1908.
Brough, John. 'The Tripartite Ideology of the Indo-Europeans: An Experiment in Method'. *Bull. of the School of Oriental and African Studies* 22 (1959), 69–86.

Daniélou, Alain. *Hindu Polytheism*. London, 1964.
Dumézil, Georges (tr. A. Hiltebeitel). *The Destiny of the Warrior*. Chicago, 1970.
——*Les Dieux souverains des Indo-Européens*. Paris, 1977.
——*L'Idéologie tripartie des Indo-Européens*. Brussels, 1958.
——*Mitra-Varuna*. Paris, 1939; 3rd edn., Paris, 1948.
——*Mythe et épopée. L'Idéologie des trois fonctions dans les épopées des peuples indo-européens*, 2 vols. Paris, 1968.
——*Le Troisième Souverain. Essai sur le dieu indo-iranien Aryaman et sur la formation de l'historie mythique de l'Irlande*. Paris, 1949.
Dumont, Louis. *La Civilisation indienne et nous*. Paris, 1964.
——(tr. Mark Sainsbury.) *Homo hierarchicus: The Caste System and its Implications*. London, 1970.
Edgerton, Franklin. *The Beginnings of Indian Philosophy*. London, 1965.
Embree, Ainslie T. *The Hindu Tradition: Readings in Oriental Thought*. New York, 1972.
Geldner, Karl Friedrich. *Der Rig-Veda. Aus dem Sanskrit ins Deutsche übersetzt und mit einem laufenden Kommentar versehen*, 4 vols. (Harvard Oriental Series, Vols. 33-6). Cambridge, Mass., 1951-7.
Gombrich, Richard. 'Dyads, triads, and Aryans'. *Times Literary Supplement*, 3 February 1978, p.144.
——*On Being Sanskritic* (Inaugural Lecture). Oxford, 1978.
Gonda, Jan. *Aspects of Early Viṣṇuism*. Utrecht, 1954.
——*The Dual Deities in the Religion of the Veda*. Amsterdam, 1974.
——*Old Indian. Handbuch der Orientalistik*. II. 1: *Die indischen Sprachen*. Leiden, 1971.
——*Die Religionen Indiens*. I: *Veda und älterer Hinduismus*. Stuttgart, 1960.
——*Selected Studies*, 5 vols. Leiden, 1975.
——'Some Observations on Dumézil's Views of Indo-European Mythology'. *Mnemosyne* 4 (1960), 1-15; repr. in Gonda, *Selected Studies*, I (Leiden, 1975), 531-45.
——*Triads in the Veda*. Amsterdam, 1976.
——*The Vedic God Mitra*. Leiden, 1972.
——*The Vision of the Vedic Poets*. The Hague, 1963.
——*Viṣṇuism and Śivaism: A Comparison* (Jordan Lectures, 1969). London, 1970.
Griffith, Ralph T. H. *The Hymns of the Rigveda*, 2 vols., 3rd edn. Benares, 1920.
Griswold, H. D. *The Religion of the Rigveda*. London, 1923; repr. Delhi, 1971.
Hinüber, O. von. Review of J. Gonda, *Old Indian* (Leiden, 1971). *OLZ* 72 (1977), 205-7.
Hopkins, E. Washburn. 'The Holy Numbers of the Rig-Veda'. *Oriental Studies* (Oriental Club of Philadelphia, Boston, 1894), 141-59.
Hopper, Vincent Foster. v. I. General.
Jaini, P. S. 'Karma and the Problem of Rebirth in Jainism', in *Karma and Rebirth in Classical Indian Traditions*, ed. Wendy Doniger O'Flaherty (Berkeley, 1980), 217-38.
Keith, A. Berriedale. *The Religion and Philosophy of the Veda and Upanishads*, 2 vols. Cambridge, Mass., 1925.
——'Trimūrti'. Hastings, *ERE* 12 (1921), 457-8.
Littleton, C. Scott. *The New Comparative Mythology: An Anthropological Assessment of the Theories of Georges Dumézil*. Berkeley, 1966; revised edn., Berkeley, 1973.
Macdonnell, Arthur A. *The Vedic Mythology*. Strasbourg, 1897; repr. Delhi, 1971.
——*Vedic Reader for Students*. Oxford, 1917; repr. 1951.

Mackay, Ernest. *Early Indus Civilizations*. London, 1948.
Majumdar, R. O. *Studies in the Cultural History of India*. Agra, 1965.
Marshall, Sir John. *Mohenjo-daro and the Indus Civilization*, 3 vols. London, 1931.
Mascaró, Juan. *The Upanishads*. Harmondsworth, 1965.
Matilal, Bimal Krishna. *The Logical Illumination of Indian Mysticism* (Inaugural Lecture). Oxford, 1977.
Mayrhofer, M. *Kurzgefasstes etymologisches Wörterbuch des Altindischen*. Heidelberg, 1956; repr. 1963.
Moeller, Volker. 'Trinität', in *Die Mythologie der vedischen Religion und des Hinduismus* (= *Wörterbuch der Mythologie*, ed. H. W. Haussig, I. 8). Stuttgart, 1966.
Murti, T. R. V. *The Central Philosophy of Buddhism*. London, 1955.
O'Flaherty, Wendy Doniger. *Dreams, Illusion, and Other Realities*. Chicago, 1984.
——*Hindu Myths: A Source-book translated from the Sanskrit*. Harmondsworth, 1975; repr. 1976.
——(ed.) *Karma and Rebirth in Classical Indian Traditions*. Berkeley, 1980.
——*The Origins of Evil in Hindu Mythology*. Berkeley, 1976.
——*The Rig Veda*. Harmondsworth, 1981; repr. 1984.
——*Sexual Metaphors and Animal Symbols in Indian Mythology*. Oxford, 1980
——*Textual Sources for the Study of Hinduism*. Manchester, 1988.
Oldenberg, Hermann. *Ṛgveda: Textkritische und exegetische Noten* (Abh. Göttingen, 13). Berlin, 1912.
——*Die Religion des Veda*. 1917; repr. Darmstadt, 1970.
Piggott, Stuart. *Prehistoric India*. Harmondsworth, 1950.
Pusalker, A. *The Vedic Age: History and Culture of the Indian People*, I. London, 1951.
Radhakrishnan, S. *The Hindu View of Life*. London, 1927; repr. 1960.
——*Religion and Culture*. New Delhi, 1968.
Renou, Louis. *Bibliographie védique*. Paris, 1931.
——(tr. Ph. Spratt.) *The Civilization of Ancient India*, 2nd edn. Calcutta, 1954.
——*Les Écoles védiques et la formation du veda*. Paris, 1947.
——*Vedic India* (*Classical India*, Vol.3). Delhi, 1971.
Schulberg, Lucille. *Indien. Reiche zwischen Indus und Ganges*. Reinbek bei Hamburg, 1971.
Sen, Kshiti Mohan. *Hinduism*. Harmondsworth, 1961; repr. 1987.
Stietencron, Heinrich von. 'Name und Manifestation Gottes in Indien', in *Der Name Gottes*, ed. H. von Stietencron (Düsseldorf, 1975), 50–65.
Thieme, Paul. 'Bráhman'. *ZDMG* 102 (1952), 91–129.
——*Der Fremdling im Ṛgveda*. Leipzig, 1938; repr. Nendeln, 1966.
——*Gedichte aus dem Rig-Veda*. Stuttgart, 1964.
——*Mitra and Aryaman*. New Haven, 1957.
Williams, Cyril G. *Crefyddau'r Dwyrain* (Religions of the East). Cardiff, 1968.
——*Y Fendigaid Gân*. Cyfieithiad o'r Bhagavadgītā (tr. with notes and Introduction). Cardiff, 1991.
——'World Negation and World-Maintenance: Some Hindu Perspectives'. *Scottish Journal of Religious Studies* 8 (1987), 22–40.
Zaehner, R. C. *Hinduism*. Oxford, 1962; repr. 1975.
——(tr.) *Hindu Scriptures*. London, 1966.
Zimmer, Heinrich (ed. Joseph Campbell). *Myths and Symbols in Indian Art and Civilization*. New York, 1946; repr. 1953.

CHAPTER 7 *IRAN*

Boyce, Mary. *A History of Zoroastrianism.* I, Leiden, 1975; II, Leiden, 1982; III, Leiden, 1991, with Frantz Grenet.
——*Zoroastrianism. Textual Sources for the Study of Religion.* Manchester, 1984.
Campbell, L. A. *Mithraic Iconography and Ideology* (EPRO 11). Leiden, 1968.
Cumont, Franz. *Textes et monuments figurés relatifs aux mystères de Mithra,* 2 vols. Brussels, 1896-9.
Dawson, Miles Menander. *The Ethical Religion of Zoroaster.* New York, 1931.
Duchesne-Guillemin, J. *The Western Response to Zoroaster.* Oxford, 1958.
Geiger, Bernhard. *Die Ameša Spentas.* Vienna, 1916.
Gershevitch, Ilya. *The Avestan Hymn to Mithra.* Cambridge, 1959.
Grenet, Frantz. v. Boyce, Mary.
Grimm, Günter. *Kunst der Ptolemäer- und Römerzeit im ägyptischen Museum Kairo.* Cairo, 1975.
Gwyn Griffiths, John. *The Divine Verdict.* Leiden, 1991.
Hinnells, J. R. (ed.). *Mithraic Studies,* 2 vols. Manchester, 1976.
Humbach, Helmut. *Die Gathas des Zarathustra.* Heidelberg, 1959.
Insler, S. *The Gāthās of-Zarathustra* (Acta Iranica, 8). Leiden, 1975.
Lommel, Herman. 'Symbolik der Elemente in der zoroastrischen Religion', in *Zarathustra,* ed. B. Schlerath (Darmstadt, 1970), 262-3.
Merkelbach, Reinhold. *Mithras.* Hain, 1984.
Moeller, W. O. *The Mithraic Origin and Meanings of the Rotas-Sator Square* (EPRO 38). Leiden, 1973.
Schlerath, B. (ed.). *Zarathustra* (Wege der Forschung, 169). Darmstadt, 1970.
Schwartz, Martin. v. Hinnells, J. R. (ed.), *Mithraic Studies.*
Stevenson, J. *A New Eusebius.* London, 1957; repr. 1970.
Ulansey, David. *The Origins of the Mithraic Mysteries.* New York, 1989.
Vermaseren, Maarten J. *Corpus inscriptionum et monumentorum religionis Mithriacae,* 2 vols. The Hague, 1956-60.
——*Mithras, the Secret God.* London, 1963.
Zaehner, R. C. *The Dawn and Twilight of Zoroastrianism.* London, 1961.
——*Zurvan: A Zoroastrian Dilemma.* Oxford, 1955.

CHAPTER 8 *GREECE*

Anderson, Graham. *Lucian.* Leiden, 1976.
Armstrong, Arthur Hilary. *The Architecture of the Intelligible Universe in the Philosophy of Plotinus.* Cambridge, 1940.
——(ed.) *Cambridge History of Later Greek and Early Medieval Philosophy.* Cambridge, 1967.
——*Hellenic and Christian Studies* (Variorum Reprints). London, 1990.
——*Plotinian and Christian Studies* (Variorum Reprints). London, 1979.
——*Plotinus.* London, 1953.
——'Plotinus', in *Cambridge History of Later Greek Philosophy* (1967), 195-268.
——(tr.) *Plotinus* (Loeb CL), 7 vols. London, 1966-88.
——'Plotinus and India'. *CQ* 30 (1936), 22-8 (= the first essay in his *Plotinian and*

Christian Studies (1979)).
Atkinson, Michael. *Plotinus: Ennead V.1 on the Three Principal Hypostases*. Oxford, 1983.
Baldwin, Barry. *Studies in Lucian*. Toronto, 1973.
Bergman, Jan. 'Ancient Egyptian Theogony in a Greek Magical Papyrus', in *Studies in Egyptian Religion (Fs. J. Zandee)* (Leiden, 1982), 28-37.
——*Ich bin Isis*. Uppsala, 1968.
Betz, Hans Dieter (ed.) *The Greek Magical Papyri in Translation*. Chicago, 1986.
Burkert, Walter. *Ancient Mystery Cults*. Cambridge, Mass., 1987.
——(tr. J. Raffan). *Greek Religion: Archaic and Classical*. Oxford, 1985.
Conacher, D. J. *Aeschylus' Prometheus Bound*. Toronto, 1980.
Delcourt, Marie. *Hermaphrodite*. Paris, 1958.
Diels, Hermann. *Die Fragmente der Vorsokratiker*, 6th edn., revised by Walther Kranz, 3 vols. Berlin, 1951-2.
——*Sibyllinische Blätter*. Berlin, 1890.
Dillon, John. *The Middle Platonists*. London, 1977.
Dittenberger, W. *Orientis Graeci inscriptiones selectae*, 2 vols. Leipzig, 1903-5; repr. Hildesheim, 1960.
Dodds, E. R. *The Greeks and the Irrational*. Berkeley, 1963.
——'Numenius and Ammonius', *Les Sources de Plotin*. Entretiens Hardt V (1960), 3-32.
——*Proclus, Elements of Theology*. Oxford, 1933; 2nd edn., 1963.
Dörrie, Heinrich. *Porphyrios' 'Symmikta Zetemata'*. Munich, 1959.
——'Hypostasis' (Nachr. Göttingen, 1955), 35-92.
Fowden, Garth. *The Egyptian Hermes*. Cambridge, 1986; revised edn. 1993.
Gomperz, Theodor. *Festschrift Theodor Gomperz*. Vienna, 1902.
Gosling, J. C. B. *Plato, Philebus*. Oxford, 1975.
Gressmann, Hugo. *Die orientalischen Religionen im hellenistisch-römischen Zeitalter*. Berlin, 1930.
Guthrie, W. K. C. *Aristotle, De caelo* (Loeb CL). London, 1939; repr. 1953.
——*The Greeks and their Gods*. London, 1954.
Gwyn Griffiths, John. *Apuleius of Madauros: The Isis-Book* (EPRO 39). Leiden, 1975.
——'Hellenistic Religions', in *Religions of Antiquity*, ed. Robert M. Seltzer (New York, 1989), 237-58.
——'The Orders of Gods in Greece and Egypt'. *JHS* 75 (1955), 21-3.
——*Plutarch's De Iside et Osiride*. Cardiff, 1970.
Hall, Jennifer. *Lucian's Satire*. New York, 1981.
Heyob, Sharon K. *The Cult of Isis among Women in the Graeco-Roman World* (EPRO 51). Leiden, 1975.
Jacoby, Felix. *Diagoras,ὁ Ἄθεος*. Berlin, 1959.
Kähler, H. *Der grosse Fries von Pergamon*. Berlin, 1948.
Kern, Otto. *Die Religion der Griechen*, Vols.I and II. Berlin, 1926, 1935.
Lampe, G. W. H. *A Patristic Greek Lexicon*. Oxford, 1961.
Lease, Emory B. 'The Number Three, Mysterious, Mystic, Magic'. *Class. Phil.* 14 (1919), 56-73.
Lloyd, Alan B. *Herodotus Book II*, 3 vols. (EPRO 43). Leiden, 1975-87.
——'Herodotus on Egyptians and Libyans'. *Entretiens Hardt* XXXV (1990), 215-53.
Lloyd, G. E. R. *Polarity and Analogy: Two Types of Argumentation in Early Greek Thought*. Cambridge, 1966.
Long, A. A. *Hellenistic Philosophy*. London, 1974.
Long, Charlotte R. *The Twelve Gods of Greece and Rome* (EPRO 107). Leiden, 1987.

LSJ v. Abbreviations.
Marcovich, Miroslav. *Studies in Graeco-Roman Religions and Gnosticism*. Leiden, 1988.
Merlan, Philip. 'Numenius', in *Cambridge History of Later Greek and Early Medieval Philosophy* (1967), 96–106.
Overbeck, J. *Geschichte der griechischen Plastik*, II, 3rd edn. Leipzig, 1882.
Pistorius, O. V. *Plotinus and Neoplatonism*. Cambridge, 1952.
Rist, John M. *Plotinus: The Road to Reality*. Cambridge, 1967.
—— *Stoic Philosophy*. Cambridge, 1969.
—— 'Theos and the One in Some Texts of Plotinus'. *Mediaeval Studies* 24 (1962), 169–80.
Rohde, Erwin. *Psyche*, 10th edn. Tübingen, 1925.
Roscher, W. H. *Ausführliches Lexikon der griechischen und römischen Mythologie* (*Lex. Myth.*), 6 vols. Leipzig and Berlin, 1884–1937.
—— 'Zwölfgötter', in *Lex. Myth.* VI (1937), 764–848.
Rose, H. J. *Handbook of Greek Mythology*, 6th edn. London, 1958.
Schachter, Albert. *Cults of Boiotia*, Vols. 1, 2, 3, 4. London, 1981–94.
Schmidt, Eva Maria. *Der grosse Altar zu Pergamon*. Leipzig, 1961.
Scott, Thomas M. *Egyptian Elements in the Hermetic Literature*, D.Theol. thesis, Harvard, 1987. Unpubl.
Seyffert, Oskar (rev. H. Nettleship and J. E. Sandys). *Dictionary of Classical Antiquities*. London, 1957.
Solmsen, Friedrich. *Isis among the Greeks and Romans*. Cambridge, Mass., 1979.
Smith, Andrew. *Porphyry's Place in the Neoplatonic Tradition*. The Hague, 1974.
Sophocles, E. A. *Greek Lexicon of the Roman and Byzantine Periods*, 1887; repr. New York, 1957.
Staudacher, Willibald. *Die Trennung von Himmel und Erde*. Tübingen, 1942; repr. Darmstadt, 1968.
Stocks, J. L. *Aristotle, De caelo*, tr. with Commentary. Oxford, 1922.
Szepes, E. 'Trinities in the Homeric Demeter-Hymn'. *Annales Universitatis Scientiarum Budapestinensis, Sectio Classica* 3 (1975), 23–38.
Taylor, A. E., *Plato, the Man and his Work*, 7th edn. London, 1960; repr. 1971.
Turner, Paul (tr.) *Lucian, Satirical Sketches*. Harmondsworth, 1961.
Usener, Hermann. v. I. General.
Versnel, H. S. *Inconsistencies in Greek and Roman Religion*. I: *Ter Unus*. Leiden, 1990. II. *Tradition and Reversal in Myth and Ritual*, (1993).
Wallis, R. T. *Neoplatonism*. London, 1972.
Weinreich, Otto. 'Tria Fata', in Roscher, *Lex. Myth.* (1922), s.v., 1099.
West, M. L. *Hesiod, Theogony*. Oxford, 1966.
Witt, R. E. *Albinus and the History of Middle Platonism*. Cambridge, 1937.
—— 'Hypostasis', in *Amicitiae Corolla (Fs. J. Rendel Harris)*, ed. H. G. Wood (London, 1933), 319–43.
—— *Isis in the Graeco-Roman World*. London, 1971.
Wood, H. G. (ed.). *Amicitiae Corolla (Fs. J. Rendel Harris)*. London, 1933.
Zandee, Jan. *The Terminology of Plotinus and of some Gnostic Writings, mainly the Fourth Treatise of the Jung Codex*. Istanbul, 1961.

CHAPTER 9 *ROME AND ETRURIA*

Altheim, Franz (tr. H. Mattingly). *A History of Roman Religion*. London, 1938.

Athanassiadi-Fowden, Polymnia. *Julian and Hellenism*. Oxford, 1981.
Belier, Wouter W. *Decayed Gods: Origin and Development of Georges Dumézil's 'Idéologie Tripartie'* (Studies in Greek and Roman Religion, 7). Leiden, 1991.
Bloch, Raymond. *The Etruscans*. London, 1958.
Bowersock, G. W. *Julian the Apostate*. London, 1978.
Browning, Robert. *The Emperor Julian*. London, 1975.
Dumézil, Georges (tr. P. Krapp). *Archaic Roman Religion*, 2 vols. Chicago, 1970.
——(tr.). *Camillus*. Berkeley, 1980.
——*L'Idéologie tripartie des Indo-Européens*. Brussels, 1958.
Fishwick, Duncan. 'AUGUSTUS DEUS and DEUS AUGUSTUS', in *Hommages Vermaseren*, I (Leiden, 1978), 375-80.
——*The Imperial Cult in the Latin West*, 2 vols. (EPRO 108). Leiden, 1987.
Grant, F. C. *Ancient Roman Religion*. New York, 1957.
Gwyn Griffiths, John. *Apuleius of Madauros: The Isis-Book* (EPRO 39). Leiden, 1975.
Hencken, Hugh. *Tarquinia and the Etruscan Origins*. London, 1968.
Heurgon, Jacques. 'Religion, Etruscan', in *OCD*[2] (1970), 912-13.
Klein, R. (ed.) *Julian Apostata* (Wege der Forschung, 509), with an essay by Kurt Latte. Darmstadt, 1978.
Koch, Carl. *Religio: Studien zu Kult und Glauben der Römer*. Nuremberg, 1960.
Latham, R. E. *Revised Mediaeval Latin Word-List*. London, 1965.
Latte, Kurt. *Kleine Schriften*. Munich, 1968.
——*Römische Religionsgeschichte*. Munich, 1960.
——v. Klein, R. (ed.)
MacMullen, Ramsay. *Paganism in the Roman Empire*. New Haven, 1981; rev. edn. 1982.
Martin, Edward J. *The Emperor Julian: An Essay on his Relations with the Christian Religion*. London, 1919.
Matthews, John. *The Roman Empire of Ammianus*. London, 1989.
Mayani, Zacharie (tr. Patrick Evans). *The Etruscans Begin to Speak*. London, 1961.
Millar, Fergus. *The Emperor in the Roman World*. London, 1977.
——*The Roman Empire and its Neighbours*, 2nd edn. London, 1981.
——'Paul of Samosata, Zenobia, and Aurelian: The Church, Local Culture and Political Allegiance in Third-century Syria'. *JRS* 61 (1971), 1-17.
Ogilvie, R. M. *Early Rome and the Etruscans*. Glasgow, 1976.
——*Livy: Commentary on Books 1-5*. Oxford, 1965.
——Review of Dumézil, *Archaic Roman Religion*. *Antiquaries Journal* 52 (1972), 211-13.
Pallottino, Massimo. *The Etruscans*. Harmondsworth, 1955.
Palmer, Robert E. A. *Roman Religion and Roman Empire: Five Essays*. Philadelphia, 1974.
Perowne, Stuart. *Roman Mythology*. London, 1969.
Pfiffig, Ambros J. *Religio Iguvina*. Vienna, 1964.
Pfister, Kurt. *Die Etrusker*. Munich, 1940.
Poultney, James Wilson. *The Bronze Tablets of Iguvium*. Baltimore, 1959.
Raeder, Hans. 'Kaiser Julian als Philosoph und religiöser Reformator', in *Julian Apostata*, ed. R. Klein (1978), 209ff.
Richardson, Emeline. *The Etruscans*. Chicago, 1964.
Rose, H. J. *Ancient Roman Religion*. London, 1949.
——'Quirinus', in *OCD*[2] (1970), 908.
Schilling, Robert. 'Georges Dumézil et la religion romaine'. *Nouvelle École* 21-2 (1972-3), 91ff.

——'Roman Religion: The Early Period', in *Encycl. of Religion*, ed. M. Eliade, 12 (1987), 445–61.
Solmsen, Friedrich. *Isis among the Greeks and Romans*. Cambridge, Mass., 1979.
Souter, A. *A Glossary of Later Latin to 600 A.D.* Oxford, 1949.
Strutynski, Udo (ed.). *Georges Dumézil, Camillus*. Berkeley, 1980.
Tschudin, Peter Friedrich. *Isis in Rom*. Diss. Basle. Aarau, 1962.
Wright, Wilmer Cave (ed.). *Julian, Orationes* (Loeb CL), Vol.I. London, 1913; Vol.III, 1923.

CHAPTER 10 THE CELTIC AND GERMANIC PEOPLES

Alcock, Leslie. 'Celtic Archaeology and Art', in *Celtic Studies in Wales*, ed. Elwyn Davies (Cardiff, 1963), 3–46.
Anati, E. 'Fertility Cults', in *Archaeology and Fertility Cult in the Ancient Mediterranean*, ed. A. Bonanno (Amsterdam, 1986), 2–15.
Anderson, J. G. C. *Tacitus, Germania*. Oxford, 1938.
Biezais, Haralds. v. Ström, Åke V,
Bonanno, A. v. Anati, E.
Bowen, Geraint (ed.). *Y Gwareiddiad Celtaidd*. Llandysul, 1987.
Branston, Brian. *Gods of the North*. London, 1955.
Bromwich, Rachel. *Trioedd Ynys Prydain: The Welsh Triads*, 2nd edn. Cardiff, 1978.
——'*Trioedd Ynys Prydain*', in *Welsh Literature and Scholarship* (G. J. Williams Memorial Lecture). Cardiff, 1969.
Bruce, J. Collingwood (ed. I. A. Richmond). *Handbook to the Roman Wall*, 10th edn. Newcastle, 1947.
Davidson, H. R. Ellis, *Gods and Myths of Northern Europe*. Harmondsworth, 1964; repr. 1979.
Davies, Pennar. *Rhwng Chwedl a Chredo*. Cardiff, 1966.
Dittenberger, W. v. Kraner, Fr.
Dumézil, Georges. (tr.) *The Destiny of the Warrior*. Chicago, 1970.
——*Les Dieux des Germains*. Paris, 1959.
——*Les Dieux souverains des Indo-Européens*. Paris, 1977.
Evans, D. Ellis. 'Y Brydain Rufeinig', in *Y Gwareiddiad Celtaidd*, ed. Geraint Bowen (1987), 65–100.
——'Celticity, Identity and the Study of Language – Facts, Speculation, and Legend'. *Arch. Camb.* 140 (1991), 1–16.
——'Celts and Germans'. *Bull. of the Board of Celtic Studies*, 29 (1981), 230f.
——*Gaulish Personal Names*. Oxford, 1967.
——*Gorchest y Celtiaid yn yr Hen Fyd* (Inaugural Lecture). Swansea, 1975.
Filip, Jan. *Celtic Civilization and its Heritage*. Prague, 1962.
Ford, Patrick J. v. Williams, J. E. Caerwyn.
Fremersdorf, Fritz. *Inschriften und Bildwerke aus römischer Zeit*. Cologne, 1956.
Frere, Sheppard. *Britannia*. London, 1967.
Green, Miranda. *The Gods of the Celts*. Gloucester, 1986.
Grönbech, Wilhelm. *Kultur und Religion der Germanen*. Vol.II, 5th edn. Stuttgart, 1954.
Gruffydd, W. J. *Math vab Mathonwy*. Cardiff, 1928.
Herter, Hans. 'Phallos'. *RE* (1938), 1681–1748.
Kraner, Fr., and Dittenberger, W. *Caesar, De Bello Gallico*, 9th edn., rev. by H. Meusel. Berlin, 1920; repr. 1961.

Lambrechts, Pierre. *L'Exaltaton de la tête dans la pensée et dans l'art des Celtes.* (Diss. Arch. Gandenses, 2). Bruges, 1954.

——'Note sur une statuette en bronze de Mercure'. *Antiquité Classique* 10 (1941), 71-6.

Lehner, Hans. *Die Ausgrabung in und bei der Münsterkirche in Bonn.* Bolzano, 1931.

Lewis, Ceri W. 'The Court Poets: Their Function, Status and Craft', in *A Guide to Welsh Literature*, Vol.I, ed. A. O. H. Jarman and G. R. Hughes (Swansea, 1976), 123-56.

Mac Cana, Proinsias. *Celtic Mythology.* London, 1970.

Meyer, C. H. *Fontes historiae religionis Slavicae.* Berlin, 1931.

Meyer, Richard M. *Altgermanische Religionsgeschichte.* Leipzig, 1910.

Much, Rudolf. *Die Germania des Tacitus*, 3rd edn., ed. H. Jankuhn. Heidelberg, 1967.

O'Flaherty, Wendy Doniger. *Hindu Myths.* Harmondsworth, 1975.

——*The Rig Veda.* Harmondsworth, 1981; repr. 1984.

Ogilvie, R. M. *Livy: Commentary on Books 1-5.* Oxford, 1965.

Polomé, Edgar C. 'Germanic Religion' in *Encycl. Rel.*, ed. M. Eliade, 5 (1987), 520-36.

Powell, T. G. E. *The Celts.* London, 1958.

Price, Glanville (ed.). *The Celtic Connection* (Princess Grace Irish Library, Monaco, 6). Gerrards Cross, 1992.

Raftery, Joseph. (ed.) *The Celts.* Cork, 1964.

——*Prehistoric Ireland.* London, 1951.

Rankin, H. D. *Celts and the Classical World.* London, 1987.

Rees, Alwyn and Brinley. *Celtic Heritage.* London, 1961.

Richmond, I. A. *Roman Britain.* Harmondsworth, 1955.

Ross, Anne. 'Y Diwylliant Celtaidd', in *Y Gwareiddiad Celtaidd*, ed. Geraint Bowen (1987), 101-11.

——*Pagan Celtic Britain.* London, 1967; repr. 1974.

Sandars, Nancy K. *Prehistoric Art in Europe.* Harmondsworth, 1968.

Sjoestedt, Marie-Louise (tr. Myles Dillon). *Gods and Heroes of the Celts.* London, 1949.

Ström, Åke V. and Biezais, Haralds. *Germanische und Baltische Religion.* Stuttgart, 1975.

Tierney, James J. *The Celtic Ethnography of Posidonius* (Proc. Royal Irish Academy, 60). Dublin, 1960.

——'The Celts and the Classical Authors', in *The Celts*, ed. J. Raftery (Cork, 1964), 23-33.

Toynbee, J. M. C. *Art in Britain under the Romans.* Oxford, 1964.

Turville-Petre, E. O. G. *Myth and Religion of the North.* London, 1964.

Vendryes, J. *Choix d'études linguistiques et celtiques.* Paris, 1952.

Vries, Jan de. *Altgermanische Religionsgeschichte,* Vol.II. Berlin, 1957.

——*Kelten und Germanen.* Berne, 1960.

——*Keltische Religion.* Stuttgart, 1961.

Wheeler, R. E. M. *Maiden Castle, Dorset.* Oxford, 1943.

Williams, J. E. Caerwyn. *The Court Poet in Medieval Ireland.* London, 1972.

——'Medieval Welsh Religious Prose', in *Proc. of the Second International Congress of Celtic Studies* (Cardiff, 1966), 65-97.

——(with Patrick K. Ford) *The Irish Literary Tradition* (Cardiff and Belmont, 1992).

——*Traddodiad Llenyddol Iwerddon.* Cardiff, 1958.

PART IV THE MATRIX OF THE CHRISTIAN DOCTRINE

CHAPTER 11 *POSSIBLE HEBRAIC ANTECEDENTS*

Albright, William F. *Yahweh and the Gods of Canaan* (Jordan Lectures), 1965.
Baumgartner, W. v. Koehler, L.
Charles, R. H. (ed.). *The Apocrypha and Pseudepigrapha of the Old Testament*. Oxford, 1913.
Christen, Robert J. and Hazelton, Harold E. (eds.). *Monotheism and Moses*. Lexington, Mass., 1969.
Conzelmann, H. 'Die Mutter der Weisheit', in *The Future of Our Religious Past (In Honour of R. Bultmann)*, ed. James M. Robinson (London, 1971), 230–43.
Curtiss, Samuel Ives. *Ursemitische Religion im Volksleben des heutigen Orients*, German edn. (based on his travels in Palestine and Syria). Leipzig, 1903.
Davies, William David. *Paul and Rabbinic Judaism*. London, 1948; new edn., Philadelphia, 1980.
——and Finkelstein, Louis. (eds.). *The Cambridge History of Judaism (CHJ)*. Cambridge, 1984ff.
Donner, Herbert. 'Die religionsgeschichtlichen Ursprünge von Prov. Sal. 8'. *ZÄS* 82 (1957), 8–18.
Driver, S. R. *The Book of Genesis*, 12th edn. London, 1926.
Eissfeldt, Otto. *Die Genesis der Genesis*. Tübingen, 1958.
Fichtner, F. 'Salomo-Weisheit'. *RGG* 5 (1962), 1344ff.
Freud, Sigmund. *Der Mann Moses und die monotheistische Religion*. Frankfurt am Main, 1965.
Ginsberg, H. L. 'Aramaic Letters.' *ANET*[3] (1969), 491–2.
Görg, Manfred. 'Ptolemäische Theologie in der Septuaginta', in *Das ptolemäische Ägypten*, ed. H. Maehler and V. M. Strocka, (Mainz, 1978), 177–85.
Goodenough, Erwin R. *An Introduction to Philo Judaeus*. New Haven, 1940.
——*Jewish Symbols in the Greco-Roman Period*, 13 vols. New York, 1953–8.
Gwyn Griffiths, John. 'The Egyptian Derivation of the Name Moses'. *JNES* 12 (1953), 225–31.
Hazelton, Harold E. (ed.). v. Christen, Robert J.
Hehn, Johannes. *Siebenzahl und Sabbat bei den Babyloniern und im Alten Testament*. Leipzig, 1907.
Hengel, Martin (tr. J. Bowden.). *Judaism and Hellenism*, 2 vols. London, 1974
Herford, R. Travers. *Talmud and Apocrypha*. London, 1933.
Johnson, Aubrey R. *The Cultic Prophet and Israel's Psalmody*. Cardiff, 1979.
——*The One and the Many in the Israelite Conception of God*. Cardiff, 1942.
Kaiser, Otto (tr. J. Bowden). *Genesis*, 2nd edn. London, 1983.
Keel, Othmar. *Jahwe-Visionen und Siegelkunst*. Stuttgart, 1977.
——(ed.) *Monotheismus im Alten Israel und seiner Umwelt*. Fribourg, 1980.
——(tr. T. J. Hallett). *The Symbolism of the Biblical World*. London, 1978.
——, et al. *Studien zu den Stempelsiegeln aus Palästina/Israel*, 3 vols. (OBO 67, 88, 100). Fribourg, 1985, 1989, 1990.
Knight, George A. F. *A Christian Theology of the Old Testament*. London, 1959.
Koehler, L., and Baumgartner, W. *Lexicon in Veteris Testamenti libros*, 3rd edn. Leiden, 1967.
Kraeling, E. G. *The Brooklyn Museum Aramaic Papyri*. New Haven, 1953.
MacRae, George W. 'The Jewish Background of the Gnostic Sophia Myth'. *Novum*

Testamentum 12 (1970), 86-101.
McKane, William. *Proverbs: A New Approach*. London, 1970; repr. 1980.
Neudecker, Reinhard. 'Die vielen Gesichter des einen Gottes. Zur Gotteserfahrung im rabbinischen Judentum', in *Der eine Gott und der dreieine Gott*, ed. Karl Rahner (Munich and Zurich, 1983), 86-116.
Porten, Bezalel. *Archives from Elephantine*. Berkeley, 1968.
Rad, Gerhard von. *Genesis*, 3rd edn. London, 1972.
Robinson, James M. (ed.). *The Nag Hammadi Library in English*, 3rd edn. Leiden, 1988.
Sambursky, S. *The Physics of the Stoics*. London, 1959.
Sandmel, Samuel. *Judaism and Christian Beginnings*. New York, 1978.
——*Philo's Place in Judaism*. Cincinnati, 1956.
Schäfer, Gerd. 'König der Könige' - 'Lied der Lieder'. (Abh. Heidelberg, 1974).
Sparks, H. F. D. (ed.). *The Apocryphal Old Testament*. Oxford, 1984.
Stead, C. G 'The Valentinian Myth of Sophia'. *JTS* 20 (1969), 75-104.
Vermes, Geza. *The Dead Sea Scrolls in English*. Harmondsworth, 1962; 3rd edn., 1987.
Wanke, Gunther. 'Prophecy and Psalms in the Persian Period'. *CHJ* I (1984), 162-88.
Westermann, Claus (tr. J. J. Scullion). *Genesis 1-11: A Commentary*. London, 1984.
Winston, David. *Philo of Alexandria*. London, 1981.

CHAPTERS 12, 13, 14   *THE EVOLVED CHRISTIAN CREED; THE LIKELY SOURCES; CONCLUDING REMARKS.*

Albright, William F. *The Archaeology of Palestine*. Harmondsworth, 1949.
——*The Archaeology of Palestine and the Bible*. New York, 1932.
Allison, Dale C., Jr. v. Davies, W. D.
Armstrong, A. H. and Markus, R. A. *Christian Faith and Greek Philosophy*. London, 1960.
——*Hellenic and Christian Studies*. London, 1990.
——(In honour of). *Neoplatonism and Early Christian Thought*, ed. H. J. Blumenthal and R. A. Markus. London, 1981.
——*Plotinian and Christian Studies*. London, 1979.
Augustine, *De Trinitate* ed. W. J. Mountain and Fr. Glorie (Corpus Christianorum, Series Latina, 50 and 50A). Turnhout, 1968.
Bardy, Gustave (ed. and tr. Jean Sender). *Théophile d'Antioche: Trois Livres à Autolycus* (Sources Chrétiennes). Paris, 1948.
Barnes, T. D. *Tertullian: A Historical and Literary Study*. Oxford, 1971.
Barr, James. *Biblical Faith and Natural Theology* (Gifford Lectures, 1991). Oxford, 1993.
Barth, Karl (tr. G. W. Bromiley). *The Christian Life: Church Dogmatics*, IV, 4: *Lecture Fragments*. Edinburgh, 1981.
——(tr. J. S. McNabb). *Credo*. London, 1936.
——(tr. Grover Foley). *Evangelical Theology: An Introduction*. London, 1963.
Beck, M.-D. 'Trinität in der Kunst'. *RGG* VI (1962), 1038-41.
Berthelot, M. *Collection des anciens alchimistes grecs*. Paris, 1888.
Bettenson, Henry. *The Early Christian Fathers*. Oxford, 1956; repr. 1969.
——*The Later Christian Fathers*. Oxford, 1970.
Betz, Hans Dieter. *Lukian von Samosata und das Neue Testament*. Berlin, 1961.
Bianchi, Ugo (ed.). *The Origins of Gnosticism*. Leiden, 1967.

Bigg, Charles. *The Christian Platonists of Alexandria*. Oxford, 1913; rev. edn. 1968.
Böhlig, Alexander. 'Triade und Trinität in den Schriften von Nag Hammadi', in B. Layton (ed.), *The Rediscovery of Gnosticism* (Leiden, 1980), Vol.II, 617–42.
Bornkamm, Günther. (tr. D. M. G. Stalker). *Paul*. London, 1971.
Bowden, John. *Jesus: The Unanswered Questions*. London, 1988.
—— v. Richardson, Alan.
Brock, Sebastian. *Saint Ephrem: Hymns on Paradise*. New York, 1990.
Brown, David. *The Divine Trinity*. London, 1985.
Brown, Raymond E. *The Gospel according to John I–XII* (Anchor Bible). New York, 1966.
Bruce, F. F. *1 and 2 Corinthians* (New Century Bible). London, 1971; repr. 1981.
Bultmann, Rudolf (tr. Louise P. Smith). *Faith and Understanding*, I. London, 1966.
Carrington, Philip. *The Earl Christian Church*. Vol.II: *The Second Christian Century*. Cambridge, 1957.
Chadwick, Henry. *Early Christian Thought and the Classical Tradition*. Oxford, 1966; repr. 1984.
——*The Early Church*. Harmondsworth, 1967; repr. 1971.
——*Origen: Contra Celsum*, tr. with Introduction and Notes. Cambridge, 1953; repr. with corrections 1965, 1980.
——'Philo and the Beginnings of Christian Thought', in *The Cambridge History of Late Greek and Early Medieval Philosophy*, ed. A. H. Armstrong (1967), 137–92.
——v. Oulton, J. E. L.
Clark, Mary T. 'The Neoplatonism of Marius Victorinus the Christian', in *Neoplatonism and Early Christian Thought (In honour of A. H. Armstrong)*, ed. H. J. Blumenthal and R. A. Markus (London, 1981), 153–8.
Clemen, Carl (tr. R. G. Nisbet). *Primitive Christianity and its Non-Jewish Sources*. Edinburgh, 1912.
Cousins, Ewert H. *Process Theology: Basic Writings*. New York, 1971.
Cross, F. L. and Livingstone, E. A. v. *ODCC*, Abbreviations.
Crouzel, Henry (tr. A. S. Worrall). *Origen*. Edinburgh, 1989.
Cullmann, Oscar (tr. S. C. Guthrie and C. A. M. Hall). *The Christology of the New Testament*, 2nd edn. London, 1963; repr. 1980.
Cupitt, Don. *Taking Leave of God*. London, 1980.
Daniélou, Jean. 'Christianity as a Missionary Religion', in *The Crucible of Christianity*, ed. A. J. Toynbee (London, 1969), 293–8.
——(tr. D. Attwater). *Primitive Christian Symbols*.London, 1964.
Davies, Pennar. *Y Brenin Alltud*. Llandybïe, 1974.
Davies, William David. *Jewish and Pauline Studies*. Philadelphia, 1984.
——*Paul and Rabbinic Judaism*. London, 1948; new edn., Philadelphia, 1980.
——*The Setting of the Sermon on the Mount*. Cambridge, 1964.
——and Allison, Dale C., Jr. *The Gospel according to Saint Matthew* (ICC). Vols.I and II. Edinburgh, 1988, 1991.
Dörrie, Heinrich. 'Ὑπόστασις (Hypostasis): Wort- und Bedeutungs-geschichte'. *Nachr. Göttingen* (1955), 35–92.
Dörries, Hermann, with E. Klostermann, and M. Kroeger, (eds.). *Die 50 geistlichen Homilien des Makarios* (Patristische Texte und Studien, 4). Berlin, 1964.
——*Symeon von Mesopotamia. Die Überlieferung der messalianischen 'Makarios'-Schriften* (Texte und Untersuchungen, 55, Heft 1). Leipzig, 1941.
——*Die Theologie des Makarios/Symeon* (Abh. Göttingen, III, 103). 1978.
Dulière, W. L. *De la dyade à l'unité par la triade*. Paris, 1965.
Dusen, Henry P. van. *Spirit, Son and Father*. New York, 1958.

Evans, Ernest (ed.). *Tertullian's Treatise against Praxeas*. London, 1948.
Fausset, W. Yorke (ed.). *Novatiani ... De Trinitate liber*. Cambridge, 1909.
Feenstra, R. J. and Plantinga, C., Jr. (eds.). *Trinity, Incarnation, and Atonement*. Notre Dame, Ind., 1989.
Fenton, J. C. *The Gospel of St Matthew*. Harmondsworth, 1963; repr. 1974.
Ferguson, George. *Signs and Symbols in Christian Art*. New York, 1966.
Foerster, Werner (ed. R. McL. Wilson). *Gnosis*, 2 vols. Oxford, 1974.
Fortman, Edmund J. *The Triune God*. London, 1972.
Frankfurter, David. *Elijah in Upper Egypt: The Apocalypse of Elijah and Early Egyptian Christianity*. Minneapolis, 1992.
Franks, R. S. *The Doctrine of the Trinity*. London, 1953.
Frend, William H. C. *The Early Church*. London, 1965; repr. 1971.
——*The Rise of Christianity*. London, 1984.
——(ed.) Revised Edition of J. Stevenson, *A New Eusebius*. London, 1987.
Fuller, Reginald H. *The Foundations of New Testament Christology*. London, 1965.
Gärtner, Bertil (tr. E. J. Sharpe). *The Theology of the Gospel according to Thomas*. New York, 1961.
Georgi, Dieter. *The Opponents of Paul in Second Corinthians*. Edinburgh, 1987.
Gerlitz, Peter. *Ausserchristliche Einflüsse auf die Entwicklung des christlichen Trinitätsdogmas*. Leiden, 1963.
Gerlo, A. (ed.). *Tertullian* (Corpus Christianorum, Series Lat. II). Vienna, 1954.
Gilmore, A. (ed.). *Christian Baptism*. London, 1959.
Glover, T. R. *The Conflict of Religions in the Early Roman Empire*, 10th edn. London, 1953.
Goodenough, Erwin R. *By Light, Light*. New Haven, 1935.
Goppelt, Leonhard (tr. R. A. Guelich). *Apostolic and Post-apostolic Times*. London, 1970.
——(tr. D. H. Madvig). *Typos: The Typological Interpretation of the Old Testament in the New*. Grand Rapids, Michigan, 1982.
Grant, Frederick C. *Roman Hellenism and the New Testament*. Edinburgh, 1962.
Grant, Robert M. *Gnosticism: An Anthology*. London, 1961.
——*Gods and the One God*. London, 1986.
Greenfield, Jonas C. Review of Yousef Hajjar, *La Triade d'Héliopolis-Baalbek*. *Numen* 37 (1990), 280–3.
Griffiths, D. R. 'Baptism in the Fourth Gospel and the First Epistle of John', in *Christian Baptism*, ed. A. Gilmore (London, 1959), 149–70.
Gunton, Colin E. *Becoming and Being: The Doctrine of God in Charles Hartshorne and Karl Barth*. Oxford, 1978.
Gwyn Griffiths, John. *Atlantis and Egypt, with Other Selected Essays*. Cardiff, 1991.
——'A Note on the Anarthrous Predicate in Hellenistic Greek'. *Expository Times* 62 (1951), 314–16.
Hanson, R. P. C. *The Search for the Christian Doctrine of God: The Arian Controversy, 318–381*. Edinburgh, 1988.
Harnack, Adolf von. *Porphyrius 'Gegen Christen'. 15 Bücher Zeugnisse, Fragmenta, und Referata*. Abh. Berlin, 1916 (Einzelausgabe).
Hefele, Charles J. *History of the Councils of the Church*, Vol.II. Edinburgh, 1876.
Hengel, Martin (tr. J. Bowden). *The Son of God*. London, 1976.
Hennecke, E. (ed. W. Schneemelcher; tr. and ed. R. McL. Wilson). *New Testament Apocrypha*, I. London, 1963.
Heron, Alasdair I. C. *A Century of Protestant Theology*. London, 1980.
Hick, John (ed.). *The Myth of God Incarnate*. London, 1977; 2nd edn. 1993.

Hodgson, Leonard. *The Doctrine of the Trinity*, 2nd edn. Welwyn, 1944.
Jackson, F. J. Foakes. *The History of the Christian Church*, 6th edn. Cambridge, 1914.
Jenkins, David E. *The Contradiction of Christianity*. London, 1976.
Jonas, Hans. *The Gnostic Religion*, 2nd edn. Boston, 1963.
Jüngel, Eberhard (tr. Horton Harris). *The Doctrine of the Trinity: God's Being is in Becoming* (tr. from 2nd edn. of *Gottes Sein ist in* Werden, 1966). Edinburgh, 1976.
Kee, Howard C. *Christian Origins in Sociological Perspective*. London, 1980.
Kelly, J. N. D. *Early Christian Doctrines*, 5th edn. London, 1977; repr. 1985.
King, Karen L. (ed.). *Images of the Feminine in Gnosticism*. Philadelphia, 1988.
Kinkel, Gary Steven. *Our Dear Mother the Spirit: An Investigation of Count Zinzendorf's Theology and Praxis*. New York, 1990.
Klostermann, E. v. Dörries, Hermann.
Knight, G. A. F. *A Biblical Approach to the Doctrine of the Trinity*. Edinburgh, 1953.
Koch, Hal. 'Origenes (Alex.)'. *RE* (1942), 1037ff.
Kroeger, M. v. Dörries, Hermann.
Krause, Martin. 'Ägyptisches Gedankengut in der Apokalypse des Asclepius'. *ZDMG*, Suppl. I (Wiesbaden, 1969), 48–57.
—— 'Der *Dialog des Soter* in Codex III von Nag Hammadi', in *Gnosis and Gnosticism*, ed. M. Krause (Leiden, 1977), 13–34.
——(ed.). *Gnosis and Gnosticism. Seventh Conference on Patristic Studies, Leiden, 1977*; also *Eighth Conference ...* Leiden, 1981.
—— 'Koptische Quellen aus Nag Hammadi', in *Die Gnosis*, ed. W. Foerster (Zurich, 1971), 1–170.
Kretschmar, Georg. *Studien zur frühchristlichen Trinitätstheologie*. Tübingen, 1956.
Krüger, Gustav. *Das Dogma von der Dreieinigkeit und Gottmenschheit*. Tübingen, 1905.
Küng, Hans (tr. Ed. Quinn.). *Does God Exist?* London, 1984; repr. 1991.
—— —— *Eternal Life?* London, 1984; repr. 1991.
—— —— *On Being a Christian*. London, 1978.
—— and Ed. Schillebeeckx (ed. Leonard Swidler). *Consensus in Theology?* Philadelphia, 1980.
Lampe, G. W. H. *God as Spirit* (Bampton Lectures, 1976). Oxford, 1977; repr. London, 1983.
——(ed.). *A Patristic Greek Lexicon*. Oxford, 1961.
Lash, Nicholas. *Believing Three Ways in One God: A Reading of the Apostles' Creed*. London, 1992.
Layton, Bentley. *The Gnostic Scriptures*. London, 1987.
——(ed.). *The Rediscovery of Gnosticism*. 2 vols. Leiden, 1980.
Lebrereton, Jules (tr. A. Thorold). *History of the Dogma of the Trinity*, Vol.I. London, 1939.
Leisegang, Hans. *Die Gnosis*. Leipzig, 1924.
Lietzmann, Hans (tr. B. L. Woolf). *A History of the Early Church*. I: *The Beginnings of the Christian Church*. II: *The Founding of the Church Universal*, in 1 vol. London, 1961.
Livingstone, E. A. v. *ODCC*, Abbreviations.
Lonergan, Bernard. *The Way to Nicea*. London, 1976.
Mackey, James P. *The Christian Experience of God as Trinity*. London, 1983.
Mackintosh, Hugh Ross. *Types of Modern Theology*. London, 1937; repr. 1945.
MacMullen, Ramsay. *Christianizing the Roman Empire (A.D. 100–400)*. New Haven, 1984.

Manaranche, André. *Le Monothéisme chrétien*. Paris, 1985.
Marcovich, Miroslav (ed.). *Hippolytus, Refutatio omnium haeresium*. Berlin, 1986.
——*Studies in Graeco-Roman Religions and Gnosticism*. Leiden, 1988.
Markus, R. A. and Armstrong, A. H. *Christian Faith and Greek Philosophy*. London, 1960.
Marsh, John. *The Gospel of St John*. Harmondsworth, 1968; repr. 1974.
McCool, Gerald A. *A Rahner Reader*. London, 1975.
McGrath, Alister. *Understanding the Trinity*. Eastbourne, 1987; repr. 1990.
McNeil, Brian. 'New Light on Gospel of Philip 17'. *JTS* 29 (1978), 143-6.
Meeks, Wayne A. *The First Urban Christians: The Social World of the Apostle Paul*. New Haven and London, 1983.
Moffatt, James. *The First Five Centuries of the Church*. London, 1938.
Moltmann, Jürgen (tr. J. Bowden). *History and the Triune God*. London, 1991.
——(tr. M.Kohl). *The Trinity and the Kingdom of God*. London, 1981.
Momigliano, Arnaldo (ed.). *Conflict between Paganism and Christianity in the Fourth Century*. Oxford, 1963.
——*On Pagans, Jews, and Christians*. London, 1987.
Moore, Herbert. *The Treatise of Novatian on the Trinity* (tr. with Introduction). London, 1919.
Moule, Charles F. D. *The Birth of the New Testament*, 3rd edn., revised and rewritten. London, 1981.
——*The Holy Spirit*. London, 1978.
——'The New Testament and the Doctrine of the Trinity'. *Expository Times* 88 (1976), 16-20.
——*The Origin of Christology*. Cambridge, 1977.
Nielsen, Ditlef. *Die altarabische Mondreligion und die mosaische Ueberlieferung*. Strasbourg, 1904.
——*Ras šamra Mythologie und biblische Theologie*. Leipzig, 1936.
Nineham, D. E. *The Gospel of St Mark*. Harmondsworth, 1963; repr. 1975.
Nock, Arthur Darby (ed. Zeph Stewart). *Essays on Religion and the Ancient World*. Oxford, 1972; repr. 1986.
Osborn, E. F. *The Philosophy of Clement of Alexandria*. Cambridge, 1957.
Oulton, J. E. L. and Chadwick, H. *Alexandrian Christianity*. London, 1954.
Owen, Huw Parri. *Christian Theism*. Edinburgh, 1984.
Pagels, Elaine. *The Gnostic Gospels*. Harmondsworth, 1979; repr. 1982.
Panikkar, Raimundo. *Myth, Faith, and Hermeneutics*. New York, 1979.
——*The Trinity and the Religious Experience of Man*. New York, 1973.
Pannenberg, W. (tr. L. L. Wilkins and D. A. Priebe). *Jesus – God and Man*. London, 1968.
Perkins, Pheme. 'Sophia as Goddess in the Nag Hammadi Codices', in *Images of the Feminine in Gnosticism*, ed. Karen L. King (Philadelphia, 1988), 96-112.
Peterson, Erik. *EIS THEOS*. Göttingen, 1926.
——*Der Monotheismus als politisches Problem*. Leipzig, 1935.
——*Frühkirche, Judentum und Gnosis*. Rome, Freiburg and Vienna, 1959.
Piault, Bernard. *Der dreieine Gott*. Aschaffenburg, 1956.
Pittenger, Norman. *Catholic Faith in a Process Perspective*. New York, 1981.
——*The Lure of Divine Love*. New York, 1979.
Plantinga, C., Jr. v. Feenstra, R. J.
Rahner, Karl (ed.). *Der eine Gott und der dreieine Gott*. Munich and Zurich, 1983.
——'The Triune God', in *A Rahner Reader*, ed. Gerald A. McCool (London, 1975), 142-3.

——and Vorgrimler, H. *Kleines Theologisches Wörterbuch.* Freiburg, 1932.
Rees, Brinley Roderick. *The Letters of Pelagius and his Followers.* Woodbridge, 1991.
——*Pelagius, a Reluctant Heretic.* Woodbridge, 1990.
Richardson, Alan. *Creeds in the Making.* London, 1972.
——and Bowden, John. *A New Dictionary of Christian Theology.* London, 1983; repr. 1987.
Ridder, Cornelis A. de. *Maria als Miterlöserin?* (Kirche und Confession, 5). Göttingen, 1965.
Robinson, H. Wheeler. *The Christian Experience of the Holy Spirit*, 3rd edn. Glasgow, 1930.
Sandmel, Samuel (ed.). *The New English Bible*, Oxford Study Edition. New York, 1976.
Schillebeeckx, Ed. v. Küng, Hans.
Schipperges, Heinrich. *Dreifaltigkeit* (Der Bilderkreis, 39). Freiburg, 1954.
Schneemelcher, W. v. Hennecke, E.
Scholer, David M. *Nag Hammadi Bibliography, 1948–1956.* Leiden, 1971.
Shorter, Aylward. *Towards a Theology of Inculturation.* London, 1988.
Söderblom, Nathan. *Vater, Sohn, und Geist.* Leipzig, 1909.
Spiceland, James D. v. Toon, Peter.
Spiess, Edmund. *Logos Spermatikós.* Leipzig, 1871.
Stannus, Hugh H. *A History of the Origin of the Doctrine of the Trinity in the Christian Church.* London, 1882.
Stead, Christopher G. *Divine Substance.* Oxford, 1977.
——*Substance and Illusion in the Christian Fathers* (Variorum Reprints). London, 1985.
Stevenson, J. *Creeds, Councils and Controversies.* London, 1966; repr. 1972.
——*A New Eusebius.* London, 1957.
Swidler, Leonard. v. Küng, Hans.
Theissen, Gerd (tr. J. Bowden). *The First Followers of Jesus: A Sociological Analysis of the Earliest Christianity.* London, 1978.
Thompson, John. *Modern Trinitarian Perspectives.* Oxford, USA, 1994.
Thornton, Lionel S. *The Incarnate Lord.* London, 1928.
Toon, Peter, and Spiceland, James D. (eds.). *One God in Trinity* (essays by various authors). London, 1980.
Torrance, T. F. 'The Soul and Person, in Theological Perspective', in *Religion, Reason and the Self (In honour of Hywel D. Lewis)*, ed. S. R. Sutherland and T. A. Roberts (Cardiff, 1989), 103–18.
——*Trinitarian Perspectives: Towards Doctrinal Agreement.* Edinburgh, 1994.
Toynbee, Arnold J. (ed.). *The Crucible of Christianity.* London, 1969.
Trigg, Joseph Wilson. *Origen.* London, 1985.
Vermes, Geza. *Jesus the Jew.* London, 1973; 2nd edn., 1983.
——*Jesus and the World of Judaism.* London, 1983.
——*The Religion of Jesus the Jew.* London, 1993.
Vorgrimler, H. v. Rahner, Karl.
Wainwright, Arthur W. *The Trinity in the New Testament.* London, 1962; rev. edn. 1969.
——*Holding Fast to God.* London, 1982.
Ward, Keith. *A Vision to Pursue: Beyond the Crisis in Christianity.* London, 1991; repr. 1993.
Waszink, J. H. and Winden, J. C. M. van (eds.). *Tertullianus, De idolatria.* Leiden, 1987.

Welch, Claude. *The Trinity in Contemporary Theology*. London, 1953.
White, R. E. O. 'The Baptism of Jesus' and 'Baptism in the Synoptic Gospels', in *Christian Baptism*, ed. A. Gilmore (London, 1959), 84–115.
Whittaker, John. 'Plutarch, Platonism and Christianity', in *Neoplatonism and Early Christian Thought (In honour of A. H. Armstrong)*, ed. H. J. Blumenthal and R. A. Markus (London, 1981), 50–63.
Williams, Cyril G. *Tongues of the Spirit*. Cardiff, 1981.
—— *Yr Efengyl a'r Crefyddau*. Llandysul, 1985.
Williams, Rowan. *Arius: Heresy and Tradition*. London, 1987.
Wilson, Robert McL. *Gnosis and the New Testament*. Oxford, 1968.
—— *The Gospel of Philip*. London, 1962.
—— 'The Spirit in Gnostic Literature', in *Christ and Spirit in the New Testament (In honour of C. F. D. Moule)*, ed. B. Lindars and S. S. Smalley (Cambridge, 1973), 345–55.
—— *Studies in the Gospel of Thomas*. London, 1960.
—— 'The Trimorphic Protennoia', in *Gnosis and Gnosticism*, ed. M. Krause (1971), 50–4.
Winden, J. C. M. van. v. Waszink, J. H.
Witt, R. E. 'The Importance of Isis for the Fathers'. *Studia Patristica* 8 (Berlin, 1966), 135–45.
Wolfson, H. A. *The Philosophy of the Church Fathers*. Vol.I: *Faith, Trinity, Incarnation*, 3rd edn., Cambridge, Mass., 1970.
Wood, H. G. (ed.). *Amicitiae Corolla (For J. Rendel Harris)*. London, 1933.
Woolf, B. L. v. Lietzmann, Hans.
Zaehner, R. C. *Concordant Discord* (Gifford Lectures). Oxford, 1970.
Zandee, Jan. 'Die Person der Sophia in der vierten Schrift des Codex Jung', in *The Origins of Gnosticism*, ed. U. Bianchi (Leiden, 1967), 203–14.
—— *'The Teachings of Silvanus' and Clement of Alexandria: A New Document of Alexandrian Theology*. Leiden, 1977.

APPENDIX ON CHINA'S PANTHEON

Eichhorn, Werner. *Die Religionen Chinas*. Stuttgart, 1973.
—— 'Taoism', in *The Concise Encycl. of Living Faiths*, ed. R. C. Zaehner, 2nd edn. (London, 1971; repr. 1983), 374–92.
Eliade, Mircea. *From Primitives to Zen*. London, 1967; repr. 1977.
Giles, Herbert A. *A History of Chinese Literature*. London, 1901.
Girardot, N. J. 'Chinese Mythology', in *Encycl. of Religion*, ed. M. Eliade, 3 (1987), 296–305.
Graham, A. C. *Chuang-Tsŭ, The Inner Chapters*. London, 1981; repr. 1986.
Granet, Marcel (tr. M. Freedman). *The Religion of the Chinese People*. Oxford, 1975.
Groot, J. J. M. *The Religious System of China*, 6 vols., 1892; repr. Taipei, 1972.
Hawkes, David. *Chinese: Classical, Modern, and Humane* (Inaugural Lecture). Oxford, 1961.
Hughes, E. R. and K. *Religion in China*. London, 1950.
Lau, D. C. *Confucius, The Analects*. Harmondsworth, 1979; repr. 1986.
Legge, James. *The Four Books. Confucian Analects, The Great Learning, The Doctrine of the Mean, and The Works of Mencius*. Shanghai, 1923; repr. New York, 1966.

Mathews, R. H. *Chinese-English Dictionary*, revised American edn. Cambridge, Mass., 1963.

McFarlane, Stuart. 'Chinese Pantheon', in *Dict. of Religions*, ed. J. R. Hinnells (Harmondsworth, 1984), 85-6.

Overmyer, Daniel L. 'Chinese Religion: An Overview', in *Encycl. of Religion*, ed. M. Eliade, 3 (1987), 257-89.

Soothill, W. E. *The Three Religions of China*, 2nd edn. Oxford, 1923; repr. Westport, Conn., 1973.

Thompson, Laurence G. *Chinese Religion*, 3rd edn. Belmont, California, 1979.

Watson, Burton. *Basic Writings of Mo Tzu, Hsün Tzu, and Han Fei Tzu*. New York, 1967.

Weber, Max. *The Religion of China*. Glencoe, Ill., 1951.

Williams, Cyril G. *Crefyddau'r Dwyrain* (The Religions of the East). Cardiff, 1968.

Yang, C. K. *Religion in Chinese Society*. Berkeley, 1961.

Notes to the illustrations

Frontispiece *One of the Triads of Mycerinus*
Fully discussed in ch.1, section 4; cf. ch.14, section 4. Cairo Museum, 121. Diospolis Parva was the 7th Upper Egyptian nome. Date *c.* 2480 BC, Mycerinus being a King of Dynasty IV.

Fig. 1. (A, B, C) *A possible prehistoric triad* (p. 12)
Fully discussed in ch.1, section 1. After E. J. Baumgartel, *Cultures of Prehistoric Egypt*, Vol.II (London, 1960), Pl.13.

Fig. 2. (A, B). *Osirian triads* (p. 47)
Ch.2, section 3 and passim. A. Courtesy of the Louvre, Paris. Height 9 cm. Material, gold and lapis-lazuli. The inscription names King Osorkon II, Dyn. XXII, *c.* 860 BC. The form of Horus is that of the Elder Horus or Haroeris, a tall and mature figure with the head of a falcon. B. After Morenz, *Gott und Mensch im alten Ägypten* (2nd edn., 1984), Pl.65. Group of statuary in black granite from Saqqara. Height 68 cm. Cairo Museum. Dyn. XXX, *c.* 370 BC.

Fig. 3. *Pompeii: Sarapis with Isis and Harpocrates* (p. 48)
Ch.2, section 3; ch.14, section 5. After V. Tran tam Tinh, *Essai sur le culte d'Isis à Pompéi* (Paris, 1964), Pl.IX, 1(= Cat. no. 136, pp. 172-3). A relief from a rural villa in the Pompeiian plain, probably brought there from Pompeii itself at the time of the eruption of Vesuvius in AD 79.
Isis is shown on the left holding aloft a sistrum in her right hand and a branch of laurel in her left hand. Between her and Sarapis the child Harpocrates is shown, standing on an altar and with a finger held to his mouth in the conventional style. Sarapis is shown bearded and holding a sceptre in his left hand. Both he and Isis wear a lotus flower on the head.
Tran tam Tinh (p.8) remarks that there were temples of Isis or of Sarapis (or Serapis) at Alexandria, Memphis, Delos, Rhegium Julium, Beneventum, Rome, Ostia and Sabratha; the Serapeum of the neighbouring Puteoli should be added, as well as the Iseum of Pompeii itself, the two phases of which he fully deals with. He also surveys the Isiac centres in Greek and Roman areas. Tschudin, *Isis in Rom* (1962), 16 ff., gives a brief survey too; but the full number of these centres is much larger; see the works of Françoise Dunand, M. Malaise, J. Leclant and Fabio Mora.

Fig. 4. *Amarna: Triad of God, King, and Queen* (p. 58)
Ch.3, section 1. After Siegfried Morenz (ed. Elke Blumenthal and Christian Onasch), *Gott und Mensch im alten Ägypten* (2nd edn., Leipzig, 1984), Pl.26. Cf. Hans Bonnet, *Bilderatlas . . .Ägyptische Religion* (1924), nos.23 and 102, the latter showing the house-altar from Amarna which featured this relief. The Aten's rays,

which end in helping hands, are depicted as reaching both Akhenaten and Nefertiti, who are also shown fondling and giving presents to their three children. The limestone relief, now in the Cairo Museum, is 43·5 cm. high. Dyn. XVIII, *c.* 1350 BC.

Fig. 5. *Ptah–Sokar–Osiris: three gods merged into one composite deity* (p. 84)
Ch.4, sections 2 and 4; ch.13, section 6; ch.14, section 4. Photograph by Roger P. Davies. A painted wooden figure of Ptah–Sokar–Osiris in the Wellcome Museum at the University of Wales, Swansea, (W 2001 C), published by permission of the Hon. Curator, Dr Kate Bosse-Griffiths and her successor Dr. David Gill. It probably derives from the early Ptolemaic period (*c.* 200 BC perhaps). Height 78 cm.; length of base 37·5 cm. It is mummiform in the manner of Osiris, but the headdress comprises high plumes, sun-disc, and ram's horns. A solid rectangular base contains a wooden falcon facing the statue; and there is a hidden cavity at the back of the head. The hieroglyphic inscription in front refers to *Osiris, foremost of the West*; the longer inscription on the back pillar begins with the name of *Sokar–Osiris*, where a careless scribe has omitted the initial element *Ptah–* which occurs in numerous other cases. Three gods are thus merged into one composite deity, whose primary cult-centre was Memphis. While there is ostensibly a parity of status between the three, the iconography is mainly Osirian.
See Kate Bosse-Griffiths, 'Problems with Ptah–Sokar–Osiris Figures' (abstract), in *4th International Congress of Egyptology*, ed. Sylvie Schoske (Munich, 1985), 26. See also Maarten J. Raven, 'Papyrus-Sheaths and Ptah–Sokar–Osiris Statues', *OMRO* 59-60 (1978-9), 251-96.

Fig. 6. (A, B). *The principal Theban triad* (p. 87)
Ch.4, section 3; cf. ch.4, section 4. A. is after Bonnet, *Bilderatlas*, no. 99. A High Priest of Amûn is shown bearing figures of the Theban triad of Amûn, Mut, and Khons. Dyn. XX, *c.* 1150 BC. B. is after a drawing by Joh. Strecker in Roeder, *Die ägyptische Götterwelt* (Zurich, 1959), Abb.48, p.257; the drawing is based on various sources. This group of deities is specially related to Thebes, and is to be distinguished from the Theban State Triad of Amûn, Rê, and Ptah, discussed in ch.4, section 4.

Fig. 7. *The crowning of Philometor* (p. 109)
Ch.4, Appendix, end, s.v. Unspecified. After Lehnert and Landrock (Cairo), 'The Crowning of Philometor', from the temple of Edfu. Ptolemy VI Philometor was the son of Ptolemy V and Cleopatra I, and succeeded to the throne in 180 BC. Here the King is being fitted with the Double Crown, which includes the Red Crown of Lower Egypt, worn by Wadjet on the left, and the White Crown of Upper Egypt, worn by Nekhbet on the right. Cf. Bonnet, *RÄRG*, 398, Abb.101. Pharaonic dogma, which persisted into the Ptolemaic era, regarded the King himself as divine.

Fig. 8. *Shiva-Trimūrti* (p. 131)
Ch.6, section 2, with n.86. After A. L. Basham, *The Wonder that was India* (3rd revised edn. London, 1967; repr. 1988), Pl.XLIII, facing p.184. Photograph by the Department of Archaeology, Government of India. Dated to the eighth–ninth century AD. A doctrine of classical Hinduism concerned the three forms of a Supreme Spirit manifested in Brahma, Vishnu, and Shiva (*Trimūrti*). In this rock masterpiece, 'perhaps the best known of all Ancient Indian sculptures' (Basham, p.372), the doctrine is focused on the god Shiva. But there are some anticipations

of the doctrine in the much earlier *Rig-Veda*. Of the three-headed Shiva, Basham says that 'the serene god is perhaps the highest plastic expression of the Hindu concept of divinity'.

Fig. 9. *Triads of Celtic mother-goddesses* (p. 179)

Ch.10, section 2. A. After Sheppard Frere, *Britannia* (London, 1967), Pl.29 b. with p.320. Height 2 ft 7 inches. Cf. Anne Ross in *Y Gwareiddiad Celtaidd*, ed. Geraint Bowen (1987), Pl.IX with p.109; also Anne Ross, *Pagan Celtic Britain* (1974), 268ff. The goddesses are bearing loaves and cakes or fruits. B. After Sheppard Frere, op. cit., Pl.30 a with p.320. On this relief, from Ancaster, Lincs. (height 16·5 inches), the goddesses are seated on a couch. Their rather stern countenances (not seen of course in the headless central figure) need not be judged to be hostile. Cf. Anne Ross, *Pagan Celtic Britain*, 269, Fig.133.

Fig. 10. *Abraham encounters Three Visitors* (p. 195)

Ch.11, section 2 (on Genesis 18: 11–16). After Heinrich Schipperges, *Dreifaltigkeit* (Freiburg, 1954), 4 with Pl.3. Part of the bronze portal of the Cathedral, Monreale (near Palermo), west side, 1385. The words ascribed to Abraham are TRES VIDI UNUM ADORAVI (I saw three, I worshipped One.) Clearly a Trinitarian interpretation of the episode is given.

Fig. 11. *The Trinity in the Baptism of Jesus* (p. 235)

Ch.13, section 3. After Schipperges, op. cit., 6 with Pl.9. Part of a bronze baptism basin (*c*. 1220), Hildesheim, Dom. The Father on high blesses his Son: HIC EST FILIUS MEUS DILECTUS. Cf. Matt. 3: 17: *Hic est Filius ille meus, dilectus ille* ... The Holy Spirit rests as a Dove on the Son's head. The Son bows to the ascending waters while John humbly touches his head and awaiting angels are ready to serve him.

Fig. 12. *The Trinity, with the Madonna as Holy Spirit* (p. 237)

Ch.13, section 3. After Schipperges, op. cit., 10 with Pl.18. An English miniature in the British Museum, AD 1012–20. The central Father-figure turns to the figure of the Son as though in converse with him. On the left is a female figure crowned with a Dove (= the Holy Spirit) which rests on the Madonna holding the Child. Below are the downtrodden and scorned forms of Satan, Arius and Judas. The principal group is Trinitarian, but with a conflation of the Holy Spirit and the Madonna.

Fig. 13. *The Trinity as God with three visages* (p. 238)

Ch.13, section 3. After Schipperges, op. cit., 9–10 with Pl.17. An icon from Siebenbürgen in Romania. Date, probably medieval. The artistic form aims to emphasize the unity or oneness of God in spite of his triplicity. His head is set against the Star of David. Beneath his left hand God holds a globe, showing his sovereignty over the world. His right hand has two fingers depressed, the others thus pointing to the Trinity – a point which had escaped me until my wife mentioned it to me. A cross surmounts his crown, and is also shown three times on his robe as well as six times in embellishments to the throne. Above the throne are two cherubim facing each other and topped with eagle heads. No symbol of the Holy Spirit seems to emerge, the three faces being identical. There are parallels in Indian art, as with Shiva-Trimūrti (Fig.8), and in Greek art, as with Hecate.

NOTES TO THE ILLUSTRATIONS 353

Fig. 14. *Rome: Sarapis with Isis and Harpocrates* (p. 301)
Ch.14, section 5. After Carlo Pietrangeli, *Musei Capitolini: I Monumenti dei Culti Orientali* (Rome, 1951), 30f., no.15 with Pl.IX. The relief is 90 cm high and 31 cm. thick; breadth 1·26 m. Date, second century AD. The work probably of an Alexandrian artist, it was discovered in 1941 in the Via della Conciliazone. In the centre is an enthroned Sarapis with the child Harpocrates to his left and Isis to his right. Sarapis leans on a sceptre with his left hand, and with his right hand caresses the leonine triple head of Cerberus, watchdog of Hades. To his right the figure of Isis bears attributes of Demeter in the calathus on her head and the torch in her right hand, while her dress shows the 'Isis-knot'. But the figure to the far left of Sarapis is likely to be Isis–Aphrodite; she holds a sceptre and a sistrum. See also Theodor Kraus, 'Alexandrinische Triaden der römischen Kaiserzeit', *MDAIK* 19 (1963), 101 with Pl.XVII. In such contexts Sarapis seems to be regarded as the father of Harpocrates.

Fig. 15. *Delos: The temple and statue of Isis* (p. 303)
Ch.14, section 5 (ad fin.). A. Photograph by K. Bosse Griffiths. B. After a postcard by E. Diakakês & Son, Athens. The statue is much larger than life in size, but the temple is a small one and is enclosed within Sarapieion C. It was built possibly about 150 BC. by the Athenians; it has a graceful Doric façade while the remainder is less imposing. The abundant inscriptions relating to the Egyptian cults make it clear that the most popular divine triad was that of Sarapis, Isis and Anubis, although Osiris (probably equated with Sarapis) and Harpocrates also occur. See F. Dunand, *Le Culte d'Isis*, II (1973), 109; cf. R. E. Witt, *Isis in the Graeco-Roman World* (1971), 95ff. with Pl.14.

Index

Numbers in italics refer to pages with illustrations.

Abraham and the three visitors 194–6, *195*, 203, 245, 281
Abû-Hôr East (Ajûala) 92
Abu Simbel temple 83, 90, 92
Abusir el Meleq 92
Abydos 21, 50, 92–3
Accho 93
Adam 292, 293
Aditi 139
Adonai 240
Aether 156
Agathe Tyche 94, 98
Aglibol 123
Agni 117, 132–4, 137, 138, 140
Ahura 151
Ahura Mazdâ 151, 203, 204
Akent (Qudshu) 85
Akhenaten 56, 57, *58*, 59–61, 62, 63, 64–5, 70, 71–3
Akori 163, 258, 263
Alalakh, tablets from 121
Aleppo 121
Alexandria 93–4, 199, 211, 213, 215–16, 217, 226, 227, 247, 254, 256, 266, 282, 291, 302, 304
Allanzu 122
Amaethon 175
Amarna 56–79, 94, 233
Amaunet 86, 88
El-Amrah, vase *12*, 14, 15
Amen-Kamutef 59
Amen-Rê 57, 88, 90, 92, 96, 98, 102, 104, 105, 107
Amen-Rê-Atum 91, 110, 255
Amen-Rê-Harakhty 91, 110, 255
Amen-Rê-Mont 91, 110, 255
Amenophis II 24
Amenophis III 88
Amenophis IV 69
Amesha Spentas (Bounteous Immortals) 151, 203
Amon 90
Amratian culture 14
amulet (Abraxas gem), Egyptian, in British Museum 163, 230, 260, 263
Amûn 49, 57, 80, 83, 86–9, *87*, 93, 97, 101, 103, 104, 105, 106, 108, 252, 253, 255, 261, 289
An 117, 118, 120
Anat 97; Anath 83, 85–6, 122
Anath-bethel 99
Ancaster 178, *179*
Anebo, priest 242
angels 203–4, 242, 244
Antioch 217, 227, 267
Anu 228
Anubis 34, 36, 93, 97, 106, 210, 264, 304
Anukis 57, 81–2, 86, 92, 99, 105, 107
Apedemak 105
aphoristic triads 182–3
Aphrodite 200
Apis 91, 104, 249, 250, 256, 302, 304
Apollo 100, 156, 157, 181, 249, 259
Apopis 34, 45, 159
Apuleius 246, 299–300, 305
Arensnuphis 98, 105, 106
Ares 157, 169
Arius 216, 248
Armaiti 151
Armant (Hermonthis) 86, 95
Arsai 122
Arsinöe 94, 98
Artemis 157, 158, 265
Arthur 176–7
Aryaman 139, 140
Asbet 33
Asclepius 100, 157
Ashertu (Asherah) 122
Ashim-bethel 99
El-Ashmunein 101
Ashtar, *see* Ishtar
Ashur 121
Assyria 121
Astarte 83, 85–6, 93, 97
astral triads 118–19, 123
Asvins 141, 143, 144, 145, 146
Aswân 95
Atargatis 123, 289

INDEX

Aten 57, *58*, 59–69, 71–3, 289, 296
Athanasius 215–17
Athena 52, 94, 170, 251
Athens 156, 157
Athribis 95
Atum 11, 59, 287; as one of *baw* of the West 44, 45; as the father 32, 289; in Heliopolis 29, 30–1; in local triads 91, 96, 101, 104, 110, 255; as Rê 50, 51, 56; Shu and Tefnut as children of 63, 64, 65, 252, 254, 289
Augustine 209, 267, 280, 291, 296
Australian tribes 135

Baal 122
Baalshamin 123
Baba 120
Babylon 228–9, 284
Bahnasa (Oxyrhynchus) 95
Baït 163, 258, 260
Bak (Quban) 83
Banba 178
Banebdedet 104
Barbelo 232
Basilides 248
Bastet 21, 88, 96
Bathwick 178
Bavay, vase 181
baw 45–50, 80, 290; of Buto 45, 96; of the Easterners 45, 83; of Heliopolis 45, 101; of Hermopolis 45, 101; of Hieraconpolis 45; of the Westerners 44–5, 110
being 247; and becoming, 298
Beit el-Wali 96
Bel 123, 228
Book of the Dead 34, 44–5, 50, 51–2, 70, 256
Brahma 129, 130
Brigits 178
Bubastis (Tell Basta) 96
Buddhism 136, 285, 315
Busiris 50, 96
Buto 29, 45, 50, 96, 263

Canopus 162–3
Carrawburgh 182
Carvoran 263
Cautes 153, 286
Cautopates 153, 286
Celsus 211, 240, 242, 250
Celtic triads 183, 280, 290
Cerberus 158, 159, 265
Ceres 171
Cernunnos 182
Chalcis 97
Chaos 156
Children of Don 175
children in triads 57, 157
Chimaera 265
China 314–16

Christianity 56, 70, 204, 207–22, 290–307; Alexandrian Christians 248–51; missionary motive 236, 239–48; sources for 153, 223–79 *passim*; three faces 138; *see also* Holy Spirit; Trinity
Cirencester 178, *179*
city deities 29, 80, 117, 119–21, 157
Clement of Alexandria 1, 211–13, 224, 231, 234, 247, 248–50, 267, 282
Coffin Texts 29, 30, 31, 34, 35, 45, 52, 63, 65, 67, 254, 287
conceptual triads 50–2
Coptic texts 261–2
cosmological deities, Mesopotamian 117–18
Coventina 182
Cretan religion 246
Cúchulainn 174, 176
cults 236, 239–48
Curiatii 174–5
Cynopolis 21–2

Dâbôd 97
Dante 160
Deed 152
Deir el-Bahari 24
Deir el-Medina 86, 97, 107
Delos 97–8, *303*, 304
Demeter 94, 156, 157, 171, 200, 227, 231, 299
Demiurge 259, 267
Dendera 23, 80, 83, 98
Dendûr 98
Depth 231
Derr (Ed-Derr) 98
Dikaiosune (Justice) 94
Dionysus 94, 171, 259, 302
Diospolis Parva 21–2
divine triads 3, 226–31
Djoser, King 22, 25, 59
Donar 183, 185, 183
dove, *see* Holy Spirit
Duamutef 45, 46
dyad 19–21, 30, 46, 57, 81, 86, 89, 157, 227, 306

Ea 117, 118, 228, 285
Early Doctrinal Name, Triad of the 61–9
East (of Heaven) 99
Ebionites 231, 267
Edfu, temple 19, 63, 99
Efeidd 175
Egypt 11–43, 198, 200, 217, 239, 242, 290, 306; calendar 136; early religious texts 29–36; and Graeco-Egyptian systems 251–69, 284–7, 289, 292; *great invisible spirit* 232; influence of 226–7, 230, 248–51; literary sources 44–55; origin of the world 197; prehistoric triad, on vase 11–16, *12*; statuary 26–9; temples 225
El 122

INDEX 357

Elephanta Island *131*
Elephantine 99; dyad and triad 81-3; Jewish settlement 198
Eleusis 225, 239, 299
Elkunirsha 122
Elohîm 193ff, 281
Enki 117, 118, 120-1
Enlil 117-18, 120-1
Enneads 4, 17, 89, 251, 252, 80, 117, 164, 210; *see also* Heliopolis, Ennead of
Epidaurus 100
Erebus 156
Eridu (city) 120
Erinyes 156
Ériu 178
Esna 100
Esus 180
Etruscan Triads 169-73
Euhemeria 100
Eusebius 244
Eve 232, 292, 293

falcon deities 49; *see also* Horus
family triads 11, 21, 25, 26, 30-2, 35, 57, 80, 81, 95, 157, 229, 233, 249, 255, 284, 292-5, 305
Fates 162
Fayûm 45, 100, 231
females 210; in Celtic triads 177-8, *179*; in Christianity 293-5; in Egypt 83, 85-6, 284; in Etruscan triads 170; and Gnosticism 231-6; in Greece 156, 231; as Holy Spirit 231, 232, 234, 252, 293; Roman 166; in Ugarit 122
fertility 15, 25, 122, 169, 177-8, 181, 302
Florence, Church of Orsanmichele 160
Fótla 178
Freyr 185, 186
Fricco 185, 186
Frö 186
Furies 162

Gamla Uppsala 185-6
Gandharva 140
Gaul (Gauls) 180-1, 183, 184
Geb 15, 32, 35, 46, 117, 252
Gebel el-Silsila 66, 68, 97, 107
German tribes 137, 183-5, 280
Geryon 159, 164, 258, 265
Gibil 228
Gilfaethwy 175
Gîza 26, 28
Gnosticism 218, 231-3, 248, 281, 295
God, King and Queen triads 57-9
goddesses, as triads 33, 83, 85-6, 177-8, 183; *see also* females
Gofannon 175
Graces 156
Great Hymn to the Aten 56, 60
great invisible spirit 232

Greece 1, 2, 3, 70, 137, 156-65, 194, 209, 210, 211, 217, 282-4, 287, 288, 290, 295-6, 299, 302, 307; females 156, 231; Graeco-Egyptian systems 251-69; influence in Etruria 170, 171; sources 223-6, 239, 245-6, 247, 248-9, 255, 265, 268-9, 280-1
Gudea of Lagash 120, 121
Gwenhwyfar 176-7
Gwydion 175, 180

Hadad (Adad) 122, 123
Hadad-Jupiter 289
Hades 259
Hapy 45, 46, 64, 65, 96
Harakhty 35, 93, 99
Haroëris 94, 102, 107
Harpies 156
Harpocrates 46, *48*, 49, 93, 94, 95, 98, 104, 105, 106, 107, 210, 268, *301*, 304
Harprê 86, 95, 102
Harsiesis 102, 104, 256
Harsomtus 98, 99
Harsomtus-Harsiesis 102
Hathor: on amulet 163, 258, 230; as one of *baw* of the West 44; Iehi as child of 80; with King or Queen 57, 59; in local triads 23, 88, 97, 98, 99, 101, 102, 105, 106, 110; in Mycerinus triad 11, 21-3, 25, 26, 289; on Narmer palette 15-16, 20, 23-5, 59; seven Hathors 19; as soul of the West 34
Hathor Lady of the West 97
Hathor (Mistress) of Dendera 23, 83
Hatmehit 104
Hebat 121, 122
Hebrews 143, 193-202, 203-4, 213, 231, 250, 252, 281-2
Hecate 158, 159, 161, 265
Heka 82, 100
Heliopolis 30, 45, 89-90, 100-1, 123, 289; Ennead of 11, 17, 18, 19, 29-30, 32, 63, 64, 252
Heliopolis-Baalbek 122-3, 289, 306
Helius 163, 259, 261, 302
Helius-Osiris-Sarapis 163
Helius Sarapis 259, 289
Hera 157, 170
Heracleopolis 86, 101
Heracles 94, 161
Hercules 184, 185
Hermes 161, 164, 181, 185, 194, 257, 264, 265
Hermes-Thoth 210, 285
Hermes Trismegistos 159, 164, 264, 265, 284
Hermopolis 21, 45, 81, 86, 88; Ogdoad of 11, 17, 260; Hermopolis Magna 101, 264
Hesperides 156
Hieraconpolis 29, 45, 50

INDEX

Hittites 121
Holy Spirit 162, 204, 207–9, 223, 233, 239, 243, 252, 282, 290, 291, 294, 297, 306; and Clement of Alexandria 211–12; and dove 160, 234, *235*, 236; as female 231, 232, 234, 252, 293; and fire 228; as Madonna 236, *237*; in Origen 213, 214–15; Rabbinic 202–3
Horatius 175
Hor-Hekenu 96
Horus: in Amarna doctrine 66, 71; as Anubis and Thoth 264; as one of *baw* 45; birth of 33–4; companion of King 32; in dual group 20; eye of 33, 34, 51; falcon 49; as fighting god 34; four sons of 19, 46, 49; Greek marriage oaths 231; Horus-centres 29; in local triads 29, 50, 83, 91, 94, 96, 97, 99, 104, 105, 106, 108; and mother (Hathor) 23–4, 25, 59; in Osirian Triads 46, *47*, 49, 210, 227, 249, 265, 284, 299; *pillar of his mother* 35; prehistoric group 15, 16; as the present 52; son of Isis 217; sun- disc 49–50; three Horuses 29, 49–50, 290; title of *Ka Mut-ef* 252
Horus-falcons, triple 83
Horus-Harpocrates 100
Horus-Khenty-khety-Osiris 95
Horus-N 68
Horus-Sopd 31
Horus of Bak 83, 92, 96
Horus of Behdet 59, 99
Horus of Buhen 83, 92
Horus of Edfu 29, 83
Horus of Miam 83, 92
Hurrians 122
Hydra 159
Hygieia 100, 157
hypostasis 2–3

Iah 88
Iaru 33
Iehy 80, 83, 98
Iemsety 45, 46, 96
Iesdes 34
Ignatius of Antioch 217, 267
Iguvium 166, 167, 169
Ihnasya (Heracleopolis) 101
Imhotep 82, 106
Inanna 119, 121
India 129–55, 166, 175, 183, 226, 228, 265–6, 290; Three Social Classes 141–6
Indra 136, 137, 138, 141, 143, 145–6, 175
Indra-Donar-Taranis 183
Intelligence 247
Iou 166
Iran 13, 151–5
Iraq 13
Ireland 174, 175–6, 178, 180, 181, 182, 189
Irenaeus 229–30, 233, 244
Ishtar (Ashtar) 118, 119, 121, 123, 200

Isis: baptismal rites of 153; cult of and Christianity 246; Delos, temple *303*; dyad with Osiris (Sarapis) 227, 304; in Ennead 252; in Greek marriage oaths 231; in Greek papyrus 269; with King or Queen 32, 33, 57, 59; in local triads 50, 92–102 *passim*, 104, 105, 106; and monotheism 230; as *Mother of the God* 217; as mother of the universe 300; and Origen 250, 251, 268; in Osirian triads 46, *47*, *48*, 49, 50, 57, 249, 284, 299; Roman period 225–6, *301*, 302, 304–5; and Sophia 199, 200, 232, 286; and the Suebi 185; Tertullian on 210, 268
Isis-Hathor 102
Isis Lactans 104
Isis-Pharia 304
Isis Sononaei 107
Isis-Thermuthis 104
Israel 143, 193, 199, 234, 281–2, 286, 306
Istustaya 121
Iunyt 86, 95

Judaism and Jews 197, 198, 202–4, 213, 239, 245, 247, 281–2, 288, 306
judging deities 34, 151–2
Julian 240, 243–4
Juno 157, 170
Juno Curitis 170
Jupiter 166, 169, 180, 186
Jupiter Dolichenus 246
Jupiter-Hadad 122
Jupiter Heliopolitanus 122, 123
Jupiter Optimus Maximus 157, 170
Justin Martyr 153, 196, 241, 244, 282

Kalabsha (Talmis) 101, 262
Ka-mutef (Ka-mwt.f) 16, 252, 253, 285
Ka-nofer, tomb 26
Karnak 29, 57, 60, 88, 101–2, 256–7; chapel of Sesostris I 59; temple of Opet 49, 102, 256
Khemanefer 100
Khentamenthes 36
Khenu 27
Khepri 50, 51, 56, 83
Khnum 21, 57, 73, 81–2, 92, 99, 100, 105
Khons 34, 46, 49, 80, 86–9, *87*, 99, 101, 102, 103, 107, 108, 257
Khshathra 151
Khwrer, the calf 35, 83, 99
King, in triads 31–2, 33, 35, 56, 57–9, 60–1, 72–3, 110
Kôm Ombo (Nubyt) 45, 81, 102
Konosso 103
Korê 94, 157, 200, 227, 231
Kulitta 121

Leiden Hymn to Amûn 89–91, 253, 260, 261
Leto 157

Liber 171
Libera 171
Life 230, 247
Llew Llaw Gyffes 180
local connections of deities 50, 80-91;
   topographical list 91-113
Logos 197, 200, 202, 207, 211, 216, 217,
   218, 223, 224, 230, 231, 232, 242, 243,
   247, 264, 267, 268, 285, 286, 294
Lucian the satirist 240-1
Lug or Lugos 180
Luna 184
Luxor 24, 89, 103, 257

Maat 56, 71, 72, 73, 88, 97, 198, 200
Macarius 294
Macha 178
Madonna 236, *237*
Maenads 156
Maiden Castle, bronze bull 181
Malakbel 123
male triads 83, 166-9, 178, 180, 255
Man 231
man and wife, Egypt 20-1
Mandulis 92, 101, 106
Mannus 183, 185
Marduk 121, 159, 228, 285
Mars 166, 169, 170, 180, 183, 184, 185
Mart 166
Mater Matuta 146, 166
Math 175
Matrae 177
Matralia 177
Matres 177-8, 290
Matronae 177, 290
Memphis 80, 81, 82, 89-91, 103-4, 197,
   255, 268, 289, 302, 304
Mendes 104
Menerva 170
Menhit 82, 100
Mercury 122-3, 180, 181, 185, 289
Meret 105
Mersuankh 28
Mertitefes, Queen 27
Meryrê, tomb 64, 72, 73
Mesopotamia 20, 104, 227, 290, 294, 295,
   306
Miam (Aniba), temple of Horus 83, 92
Min 15, 85, 86, 97, 106, 252
Min-Amûn 252
Mind 218, 224, 230, 231, 247
Minerva 157, 170
missionary motive 236, 239-48, 244-8
Mit Rahina 104
Mithra 151, 152, 286
Mithraism 152-3
Mithras 153, 262
Mitra 139, 140, 143, 145, 146, 151
Mitra-Varuna 183
Mitras 258

Miysis 96
Modron 178
Mohenjo-Daro 129, 130
Moirae 121, 210
monotheism 56, 162, 239-40, 244, 245, 263,
   267
Mons Claudianus 257
Mont 86, 95, 102, 103, 105, 108, 110
Mont-Rê 95
Morning Star 35, 83, 99
mother-goddess 15, 177-8, *179*, 183, 233,
   286, 290
mounds or villages 32-3
Mummu 285
Musawwarat es-Sufra 105
Mut 49, 57, 80, 86-9, *87*, 101, 103, 107,
   108
Mycerinus 11, 15, 21-6, 57, 289
mystery cults/religions 227, 239

Nabu 123
Nag Hammâdi Codex 3, 224, 230, 232
Naqa 105
Narmer palette 15, 19-20, 23-5, 59
Naucratis 251
Naunet 86, 88
Nebo 228
Nebseny, text of 44-5
Nedjem-yeb 21
Nefer-Hor 264
Nefertari, Queen 57, 92
Nefertem 80, 81, 82, 96, 103, 57
Nefertiti 57, *58*, 59, 60-1
Nehmet-away 264
Neïth 52, 80, 100, 103, 251
Nekhbet of El-Kâb 20, 21, 24
Nemesius, bishop of Emesa 241, 242
Neoplatonism 161-2, 219, 223, 243, 255,
   260, 267, 282, 286, 288
Neper 15
Nephthys 32, 33, 46, *47*, 49, 50, 51, 99,
   102, 210, 252
Nerthus 185
Nesmin, papyri of 268
Nestorius 217
New Testament 162, 204, 207-8, 216, 227,
   228, 229, 239, 242, 245, 253, 266, 286,
   290
Nilus 94
Ninatta 121
Nippur 117, 120
Nitocris 106
Nodens-Teutates 183
Noise 176
Nome 105
Northern European triads 183-6
Nous 218, 224, 231, 282
Nubia 83, 92
Nudimmud 120
Numa 139

numbers 4–5, 16–19, 135–7; two 5, 19–21, 162, 163; three 4–5, 16–19, 135–7; four 4, 18–19; seven 18, 19, 135, 159, 162; nine 18, 19, 29; fourteen 162; *and see* dyad; Enneads
Numenius of Apamea 224, 229, 251, 266
Nun 86, 88, 100
Nut 31, 32, 46, 100, 107, 117, 252

Odin 185, 186
Ogdoad 17, 89, *and see* Hermopolis, Ogdoad of
Ohrmazd 152
Old Testament 2, 193–4, 202, 213, 215, 228, 229, 239, 242, 245, 247, 248, 281
Olympians 164
One 163, 218, 223–4, 243, 247, 260, 283
One God 2, 163, 246, 267, 287, 289
one sex triads 83–6, 255
Opet (and temple) 49, 102, 106
Origen 211, 213–15, 224, 239–40, 244, 247, 248–9, 250–1, 266, 267, 268
Orion 31, 32, 33, 194
Osiris: crook 15; death and funerary associations 27, 28, 33, 34, 35, 44, 46, 250, 268, 300; dyad, with Isis 227, 250, 251, 252; feast of 248; fertility 15, 153; Geb, his father 32; and Greece 163, 231, 285; as Horus of Horuses 29; with Isis and Nephthys 33, 46, 49, 289; in local and Theban triads 49, 50, 80, 88, 92, 95, 96, 97, 99, 101, 102, 105; mounds and villages, in triad associated with 32–3; as Nubian deity 83; Osirian Triads 34, 46–50, *47*, 92, 110, 210, 214, 249, 255, 256, 284, 289, 290, 299, 300; Osiris-King 31, 32; as the past 52; in Roman systems 210–11, 268; in tetrad 47, 91; *see also* Ptah-Sokar-Osiris
Osiris-Apis 104, 302
Osiris-Hemag 104
Osiris Hydreios 95
Osiris-Onnophris 106
Osiris-Sethos 92
Oxyrhynchus 95, 268–9

Palmyra 123
Papaya 121
Papyrus of Ani 52
Paris, manuscript 160
Patrick, St 189
Pen-meru, tomb 26, 27
Pepy I 23, 29
performative triads *109*, 110
perichôrêsis 291ff.
Persephone 171, 231, 299
Philae 50, 105–6
Philo of Alexandria 197, 199, 202–3, 211, 212–13, 214, 217–18, 232, 247, 248, 256, 259, 262, 267, 282, 283, 286

Philometor *109*
Pidrai 122
Plato 153, 162, 211–12, 218, 229, 250, 255, 283
Plotinus 218–19, 223–6, 241, 283
Plutarch 46, 52, 153, 199, 210, 211, 225, 246, 248, 299, 300, 302
Pluto 157
Pnepheros 100
Pneuma ('Spirit') 200, 202–3, 208, 229, 232, 252, 282
Pn-mrw 26–7
polytheism 56, 162, 239, 240, 242, 246
Pompeii *48*, 153
Porphyry 225, 240, 241–3, 247
Poseidon 194
Prê 104, 256
Premarres 107
priestly and prophetic triads 59–61
Proclus 161–2
Proserpina 158
Psosnaus 100
Psyche 200
Ptah 80, 82, 88, 89, 90, 91, 92, 93, 96, 98, 101, 102, 103, 104, 106, 108, 197, 253, 255, 256, 268, 289
Ptah-Sokar-Apis, temple of 104
Ptah-Sokar-Osiris 80, 83, *84*, 91, 92, 93, 103, 255, 268, 289
Ptah-Sakhmet-Nefertem 57
Pyramid Texts 17, 19, 23, 29, 30, 31, 34, 35, 50, 80, 132, 252

Qadesh 106
El-Qala, 106
Qebehsenuef 45, 46
Qudshu 83, 85–6, 97, 106
Queen, in triads 57–9, 60–1, 72–3
Quirinus 166, 167–8, 169
Qumrân 199, 204

Ramesses II 57, 83, 88, 89, 90, 92, 95, 96, 98, 101, 108
Rashnu 152
Rat-tawy 86, 95, 102
Rê, sun-god 50–1, 56; in Amarna triadic doctrine 61–73 *passim*; as one of *baw* 45; and death 34, 35, 71; and festivals 72, 73; as the future 52; judging deity 34; and King 31, 32; in local and Theban triads 89, 90, 91, 100, 101, 102, 104, 108, 253, 255, 256, 257, 289; Maat as daughter 71, 72, 198; nine children 19
Rê-Harakhty 51, 57, 61–9 *passim*, 71, 72, 73, 83, 90, 92, 96, 98
Rê-Harakhty-Atum-Osiris 91, 255
Rê-Harakhty-Osiris 91, 110, 255
Rê-wer, tomb 26, 28
Reims 181
Renenwetet 15

INDEX

Resheph 85, 86, 97
Ribhus, three 140, 144
Rig-Veda Samhita 129, 130, 132-4, 136, 137, 139, 140, 142, 144, 145, 146
Romans 143, 144, 146, 166-9, 174-5, 183, 184, 185, 210, 241, 245, 256, 289, 302, 304-5; cults 239
Rome 106, 164, 258, *301*; Capitol, Etruscan temple 170; Capitoline Triad 166-9; rites of Osiris 210-11; temple of Isis 225-6
Romulus 139, 143, 169
Rosmerta 181, 290
rûach as spirit 200-2, 281-2
Rudra 130
Rudras 138

Sabaoth 240
Sabellius and Sabellianism 216, 290-1
Saccas, Ammonius 224
Saïs 80, 106-7, 251
Sakhmet 57, 80, 81, 82, 88, 101, 103, 106
Saoshyant 152
Sarapis 46, *48*, 93, 94, 95, 97, 100, 104, 163, 210, 227, 230, 249, 251, 257, 258, 262, 268, *301*, 302, 304-6
Sarasvatīs 140
Satis 57, 81-3, 86, 92, 99, 107
Savitar 140
seasons 50
Sebiumeker 105
Seden-maat 27
Sedment, statue from 28
Sehel 107
Selene 158, 265
Sesebi 107
Sesostris I 29, 59, 81, 82, 99
Seth 20, 29, 31, 32, 33, 34, 52, 93, 159, 252, 292, 293
Sethos I 57, 92-3, 107
Shamash 118, 119, 123
Shamrock 189
Sharruma 122
Shepenwepet II 106
Shiva 129, 130, 132
Shiva-Trimūrti *131*
Shu 30-1, 45, 61, 62, 63-9, 71, 73, 96, 103, 105, 117, 252, 287
Shu-Arensnuphis 105
Sia 45, 101
Siebenbürgen, Romania, icon 236, *238*
Silsila, Gebel es-, *see* Gebel es-Silsila
Simios 123, 289-90
Sin 123
Sirens 156
Slavs 182
Sobek 34, 44-5, 73, 80, 81, 97, 102, 105, 107, 110
Sobek-Shedty-Horus 100
Sokar 103, 104, 268, 289
Soknopaiou Nesos 107

Sol 184
Soma 138, 140
Sophia 156, 199, 200, 202, 231, 232, 233, 234, 247; and Isis 286
Sothis 31, 32, 105
Soul 218, 247
Soxis 100
Space 152
Spain 180
Spenta Mainyu 203
Spirit 200-2, 231, 234, 252, 281-2
Sraosha 152
Stela of 'Kia' 67
Stoicism 199, 202, 282, 285
Subordinationism 2, 215, 291, 300
Suen 118
Sufism 201
Sumer, *see* Mesopotamia
Sun-cult, Egypt 50-1, 56, 59, 61-4, 70; *see also* Aten; Rê
Sūrya 117, 132, 138
Sweden 185-6
Switzerland 180
Syria 5, 85, 86, 97, 122-3, 227, 294, 295

Tallai 122
Tanis 108, 29
Taranis 180, 183
Tatenen 102
Tefnut 45, 63, 65, 103, 105, 117, 252, 287; = Tefenet 30-1
Tefnut-Bastet 96
temples 81
Tenenet 86, 95
Tertullian 1, 153, 163-4, 209-11, 227, 229, 244, 258, 265, 267, 268, 282, 284, 305
Teshub 122
Tetrads 34, 46, 89, 90, 91, 152
Teutates 180
Thebes 21, 49, 80, 81, 82, 86-9, 89-91, 103, 108, 110, 253, 255, 256, 268, 289
Thor 183, 185, 186
Thoth 32, 33, 34, 45, 88, 101, 102, 107, 257, 264
Thoth-Rê of Pnubs 105
Thoueris 97, 107
Thought 152
three brothers, Celtic 174-7
three divine judges 151-2
three faces or heads 4, 290; Celtic 181, 182; in Christianity 159-61, 182; in Greece 158-9, 161; Indian 137-8; in Roman Gaul 180-1; Slav 182
Three-headed Ellén 181
Trefoil 189
Time 152
time (past, present, future) 51-2
Tinia 170
Tîwaz 183, 185
Tongres, bronze statuette 181

Tricephaloi 180–2
Triglav 182
Trimūrti 228
Trinitas 1–2
Trinity (Trinitarian doctrine) 1–2, 5–6, 11, 56, 140, 152, 161, 162, 182, 196, 207–22, 223, 290–306 *passim*; iconography 138, 234, 236; Italian painting 160
triplets 175, 176, 290
triple-named deities 91, 268, 289
Triptolemus 227, 231, 299
Tutu 100
Tvashtar 140
Twelve Gods 164, 166, 210
Typhon 159, 299
Týr 183, 185
Týr-Odin 183

Ugarites 122
Umbrian triad 166–8
Uni 170
Upper Anio (Vallepietra), church of Santissima Trinità 159–60
Uppsala, temple 185, 186
Uruk (city) 117
Uṣás 166
Utu 119, 120

Vāja 140
Valentinus 1, 199, 232, 248
Varuna 139, 140, 143, 145, 146, 151
Vasus 138

Vāta 138
Vāyu 117, 132, 145
Venus 122, 123, 289
Vibhvan 140
Victorinus, Marius 219
Virgin Mary 60, 217, 233, 236, 293–4, 295
Vishnu 129, 130, 132, 134, 138
Viśvarūpa 137
Vofiono 166, 167, 168
Vulcanus 184

Wadjet 20, 24, 263
Wales 175, 176–7, 178, 180, 182, 183
Wenw 105
Wepwawet 20
Weret-hekaw 106
West 110
Wisdom 2, 152, 198–200, 201, 202, 267, 286, 294
Wodan 185, 186
Word 152, 196–7, 200, 202
World Spirit 212

Yahweh (Yahu) 99, 193–4, 196, 204
Yarhibol 123

Zervanism 152
Zeus 156, 157, 162, 163, 170, 194, 249, 259, 264, 288
Zeus Helius 257
Zeus Sarapis Helius 258, 306
Zoroastrianism 151, 152, 203
Zurvân 152